D0933596

HISTORY
Choice and
Commitment

HISTORY
Choice and
Commitment

FELIX GILBERT

The Belknap Press of
Harvard University Press
Cambridge, Massachusetts
and London, England
1977

Copyright © 1977 by the President and Fellows of Harvard College
All rights reserved
Printed in the United States of America
Library of Congress Cataloging in Publication Data
Gilbert, Felix, 1905–
    History: choice and commitment.

    Bibliography: p.
    Includes index.
      1.   Italy—Politics and government—Addresses, essays,
lectures.   2.   Italy—Historiography—Addresses, essays,
lectures.   3.   Machiavelli, Niccolò, 1469–1527—Addresses,
essays, lectures.   4.   Historians—Germany—Addresses,
essays, lectures.   I.   Title.
DG470.G46   320.9'45   76-27352
ISBN 0-674-39656-1

PREFATORY NOTE

The idea for this book originated in discussions among Mary Dunn, Richard Dunn, Doris Goldstein, and Arno Mayer. As friends, former colleagues, and students of Felix Gilbert, it was our intention to gather together a selection of his major articles, book reviews, and addresses, many of which are known only to specialists in widely separated fields. We set out to design a volume that would not only present the unusual range and diversity of Felix Gilbert's historical scholarship but also reflect important developments in historical studies during the last forty years.

To achieve this dual objective we have included, in translation from the German, a chapter from Professor Gilbert's seminal study of Johann Gustav Droysen's philosophy of history, and his article on the decisive impact of the upheavals of 1848 on the historical vision and method of Lorenz von Stein. Moreover, Professor Gilbert has written, for inclusion in this volume, an assessment of the work and career of Friedrich Meinecke, his principal teacher. Lastly, we also decided to print an unpublished address on the development of the historical profession, one of the author's enduring interests.

The choice and arrangement of these essays were made in consultation with Felix Gilbert, who has also written the short source notes for each selection. Franklin Ford, a close friend since he served with Felix Gilbert in the Office of Strategic

Services, enthusiastically agreed to write the general introduction, which comes to terms with the overall contribution and significance of these essays.

Except for minor stylistic changes, all the materials in this volume are printed in the version in which they were originally published or spoken. Of course, the scholarly apparatus has been standardized.

The undersigned prepared this volume for publication and in this work had the assistance of Doris Goldstein. He wishes to thank Robert Kimber for translating the pieces on Droysen and von Stein. He would also like to express his gratitude to Betty Horton of the Institute for Advanced Study, Princeton, New Jersey, who assumed full responsibility for most of the difficult typing.

Arno J. Mayer

Contents

Contents

HISTORY
Choice and
Commitment

INTRODUCTION
Franklin L. Ford

The author of the essays to follow has been a teacher, though not always in the classroom, for several decades. In itself that fact imposes no misgivings upon a writer of introductory comments; for we often write about our teachers, and sometimes our students write about us. What does cause trepidation is the knowledge that all those who know him have learned many different things from Felix Gilbert. To his innumerable "pupils" I offer my apologies, for remarks with which some will surely not fully agree and for the omission of points which others will just as surely think ought to have been included.

A word should perhaps be said at once about the value of a collection of essays, chapters, and reviews, whoever may have written them. The returns are far from guaranteed, for they depend not only upon the quality of the pieces as such but also upon their relationship to the major works of the scholar involved. More than one historian has written short scholarly pieces whose substance can be found even better expressed in his books. This is not, I think, true of Felix Gilbert. He has, of course, published a number of significant books and has edited several collections of chapters or documents, as the bibliography at the end of this volume makes clear. At the same time, he has characteristically presented some of his most important findings and some of his most trenchant reflections in closely defined essays that together stand as a permanent contribution

1

Franklin L. Ford

in their own right. Not a few of these pieces have appeared in journals or printed collections outside the ordinary ken of many professional historians and of others not primarily concerned with Renaissance studies. For that reason, it seems appropriate to make available a selection of Gilbert's writings in a convenient form, one which takes account of the remarkable range of his inquiries.

The essay, in modern use, has been familiar since the time of Montaigne—one of Gilbert's favorite writers, by the way. It is not, however, a required vehicle for conveying historical ideas. Some short papers, while worthy enough, can scarcely be called essays in the full meaning of the term. Twenty to thirty pages in print *may* turn out to be a chapter pulled from a longer exposition and marked by the exposure of disconnected wires dangling from both ends. All the more reason, then, to be explicit about what it is that makes the papers presented here genuine examples of the essay as an integrated genre. Every one of them, I submit, brings forward fresh information or original interpretive suggestions, or both. In addition, and this goes to the crucial requirement, each of them embodies the aim of relating the specifics of the topic to a more general historical question. The insights are born of masterful research, wide reading, and mature reflection. Intuition, which also has a part to play, serves here as it serves best, giving clues to research, direction to reading, and challenges to reflection. Felix Gilbert's role as essayist provides further justification for the present volume, in recognition of the gifts he has shared so generously.

The opening section, comprising discussions of Johann Gustav Droysen, Otto Hintze, and Friedrich Meinecke, might appear at first glance to place their author firmly within the "Prussian school" of German historical writing. Before rushing to any such conclusion, however, the reader would do well to reflect on a central point of the three chapters. It is that the Prussian School has often been too narrowly defined in treatments both German and non-German, its membership lumped together as though there were no difference between a Treitschke in the nineteenth century and a Hintze in the twentieth, or as though the nationalism of a Droysen and that of a

2

Meinecke were cut from the same bolt of flag cloth. With that warning in mind, one may safely identify elements in Gilbert's thought which do reveal the influence of Prussian historians, both those he has studied as subjects and those he encountered as professors. In particular, his sensitive treatment of the complicated interplay between power and ideas, and of the latter's role in shaping approaches to the former, seems to me an understandable outgrowth of thinking about the German national experience during the more than two centuries since the accession of Frederick the Great.

Felix Gilbert does not underestimate the complexity of the Prussian legacy, its intellectual, ethical, and literary elements (Kant, Humboldt, Novalis, and Kleist were all Prussians), as well as its historically conditioned emphasis on public administration and on the role of an efficient bureaucracy. Thus, while he does not deny neither does he exaggerate the military preoccupation which to some students of Prussia has seemed the dominant characteristic of its thunderous role in modern history. In his doctoral thesis on Droysen, for example, Gilbert is at pains to point out the peculiar dilemma which faced national liberals well before 1848. It was first clearly acknowledged in 1831 by a Württemberger, Paul Pfizer, when he observed that much as he and his fellow-reformers might yearn for the "constitutionalization" of autocratic Prussia, they had to recognize that every step in that direction would strengthen Prussia's sense of separate identity, a paradoxical but very real obstacle to its absorption into a future German nation. As things turned out, of course, Bismarck solved the problem by imposing unification through power, without the embarrassment of any significant reform in the dynastic stronghold of the Hohenzollerns; and at least until 1918 the difficulty of absorbing Prussia took a form very different from that envisaged by Pfizer, Droysen, and other thinkers of the *Vormärzzeit*. Still, the point remained, becoming especially important during the years of the Weimar Republic: Prussia should not be thought of as nothing more than the fortified home of one simple tradition. In another connection, when discussing the works of Hintze, Gilbert identifies the shift from the Prussian School's first generation and its preoccupation with external considerations such as diplomacy and military preparedness to the increased interest after 1871 in the administrative and especially the economic concerns of an Empire now in being.

This is not, however, to say that Gilbert's essays are dominated by Prussian values. He was born in Baden; and though his education centered in Berlin, he seems to me always to have retained much of the southwestern German's perspective, the angle of vision that made Franz Schnabel, a liberal, Catholic Badenser, the most effective antidote in twentieth-century German historiography to the ferocity of Treitschke, the Protestant northerner, in the nineteenth. In any event, Gilbert's background and life experience alike have pushed him toward a cosmopolitan view of history. Thus, he registers surprise and implied disappointment at the way in which his teacher, Meinecke, treated as "progress" the emergence of German nationalism as a departure from eighteenth-century *Weltbürgertum* (literally "world citizenship").

The son of an English doctor transplanted to Germany, the product of mixed Jewish and Christian elements in the patriciate of Berlin, he is also a descendant of French Calvinists, through his great-grandmother, née Jeanrenaud and married to the composer, Felix Mendelssohn Bartholdy, whose first name came down through the succeeding generations of the Mendelssohn family. The Prussian school helped to form the Berlin student in the 1920s, but more by its rigorous methodology and its fascination with the moral and practical problems of power than by its particular concern for the German national epic. To be even more explicit, one can say that while Felix Gilbert, like his friend and contemporary at the University of Berlin Hajo Holborn, revered the historical discipline to which they had there been introduced, both of them saw in the Prussia of those Weimar years a stronghold not of reaction but, at least potentially, of social democracy under a liberal constitution. They were not alone in cherishing that hope.

These remarks suggest an explanation of the relative weight assigned by Gilbert to German subject matter in his own historical writings. There is no suggestion here of conscious avoidance. His dissertation on Droysen, the critical appreciations of Hintze and Meinecke—enriched as they are by careful references to Ranke, Schmoller, Lamprecht, Sombart, Troeltsch, Weber, and Dilthey—show full command of a wide swath of

German intellectual history. Though decidely not doctrinaire, Gilbert has felt the influence of many theories set forth in his first language. His edition of Hitler's strategic conference minutes is of obvious value to any student of the Third Reich. As a political analyst for the OSS during the Second World War, he concentrated on Germany. And as a classroom teacher, he has always paid close attention to his native country's past in European history.

On balance, however, it is clear that Gilbert's interest in Italian Renaissance studies, an interest which existed even before he wrote the thesis on Droysen, has supplied the most consistent force behind his scholarly efforts over the past half-century. Conceivably, the visible torment of masters such as Hintze and Meinecke, struggling in the 1920s to come to terms with the collapse of the proud German Empire, left the young student not repelled but less than captivated by the once-heroic saga of the Reich and its rise to world power. There were, of course, defeats and tragedies in the annals of the Renaissance too; but they were far enough away to be studied dispassionately. There were things to be learned from them, as there were from the history of classical antiquity; but they were more nearly timeless than the German historical lessons clamoring to influence one's vote in the next elections. Finally, of course, it should not be forgotten that Felix Gilbert has lived since the 1930s in Italy, England, and for the most years of all, the United States, and that he has sought to know all those countries more deeply by delving into their histories.

Whether or not this turn from modern German subject matter to the chronicle of older times, in other lands, was related to a further element in his developing stance vis-à-vis history, that element does become prominent early in his career, as early as his treatment of Droysen the politician and historian. I am referring, and shall return a bit later, to an undercurrent of pessimism, a sense of flux in human affairs and of impermanence in mankind's achievements. It helps to explain his sympathy for Droysen, to whom the defeat of the Prussian constitutional movement in 1848 "signified the collapse of an entire historical-political world of ideas." Translated into historiographical terms, this pessimism, or at least undazzled realism, appears in the recognition that Droysen's world of ideas belonged "to a period that lies locked away behind us" (*die abgeschlossen hinter uns liegt*). The same awareness of the transient quality of history and of its insights has led Gilbert, in a review of the English translation of Meinecke's *Historism,* to observe that "with the few exceptions of those historical works which are literary masterpieces, works of historical scholarship do not in general gain with age."

Two things more, however, need to be said about the attitude just noted, lest it be confused with defeatism. First, Gilbert's awareness that no historical interpretation can be final is matched by an energizing conviction that it can always be improved upon, thanks to continuing research and experience over time. Although no simplistic notion of uninterrupted progress informs his work, the belief in an uneven increase in self-understanding, helped by a commitment to history for its own intrinsic interest, does emerge from his long and cheerful involvement with the discipline.

The second point goes to the matter of history as endeavor. Just as a sober realism about the impermanence of intellectual solutions can live with, and even support, a certain view of progress, so too for Gilbert even a departed world of ideas remains a worthwhile object of study. No sooner has Droysen's *Gedankenwelt,* for example, passed behind us than it re-emerges as a challenge to historical analysis, a test of historical empathy. Meinecke and Hintze in post-1918 Germany did not, could not, understand all that had happened before, was happening in the Weimar years, or would happen in the future. Nevertheless, their responses as contemporary observers possessed of powerful minds and moved by honest, if limited, impulses deserve the attention of every student of our century.

As already noted, Felix Gilbert's interest in the Italian Renaissance began early. It had to yield for some years to his thesis research and to his work as a junior editor of the diplomatic archives published as *Die Grosse Politik;* but when from 1931 to 1933 he spent a good deal of time in Italy, the old love reasserted its claims. Here a personal observation seems justified, in defense of that sentimental metaphor. Gilbert, as a friend, is dependably warm, humorous, and enthusiastic. As a scholar, however, he displays a strong feeling for form, including decorum in professional manners. Although far less remote than Otto Hintze, described by our author himself as a "tall, erect figure who fended off anyone whose words or behavior raised claims of familiarity," and about whom Meinecke is quoted as saying that he "was too proud to make his work easily accessible to the world," Gilbert, as all his acquaintances know, withdraws on occasion into a kind of diffident formality.

The exception to this distinction between personal and professional styles is apparent, however, to whoever spends any time with him in Italy. The land and its people put him at ease. He does not believe that the Italians can do no wrong—in fact he seems prepared to have them do quite a bit of it—but he finds them easy to forgive. This is no expression of the patronizing view too many northern Europeans bring with them when they cross the Alps, chuckling and shaking their heads at the ebullience of the Mediterranean peoples, with the Spanish set apart, uneasily, as an obvious exception. Quite the contrary, in Gilbert's case the affection seems to have begun with a recognition of the subtle, realistic intelligence of a culture which at its best reminds us of that hard-won capacity for facing facts, including tragic facts, we find in Thucydides's portrayal of Greeks in the age of Pericles.

At the same time, one can appreciate Felix's reaction, as much amused as bemused, to the discovery that the two ladies, the sisters Bandini, at whose *pensione* he used to stay while working in Florence, had decided that he should never lack mail to read with his breakfast—and so were holding back some of the letters delivered on particularly "good days," for rationing out to him later, on slimmer mornings. I think also of repeated dinners with him, out of doors on warm evenings in Rome's Piazza Navona, with the façades, the fountains, and the statues floodlit against the soft, black sky. A more contented man would be hard to imagine.

The Italian studies presented below are only a selection, but even so they constitute all of Parts II and III and claim further space in the remainder of the volume. Gilbert's contribution to the study of Machiavelli is a subject in pursuit of which the non-specialist could easily go astray. It is therefore not my intention to offer any judgment upon the absolute value of his close textual analyses of dating and order of composition, as applied to

The Prince, The Discourses, and *The Florentine History,* and other matters addressed in a host of reviews or articles not included here. Having observed the difficulty with which the cognoscenti seek agreement on some of these points, the student of later centuries and more northern lands may be forgiven if he avoids immersion in technical arguments, limiting himself instead to a few reactions which any reader interested in European history might conceivably share.

Seen from that point of view, Gilbert's work on Machiavelli is particularly striking for the author's insistence upon an unflinchingly historical approach. Not only does he balance the elements of adoption and rejection in the great Florentine's attitude toward humanistic scholarship, setting him in the context of contemporary canons of subject matter and style, he also refuses to let Machiavelli become a disembodied voice in some timeless debate among political philosophers. Instead, he treats him as very much a Florentine of the late fifteenth and early sixteenth centuries, a man who had his political ups and downs, who learned, like Thucydides before him and Guicciardini in his own day, to exalt the perverse power of Fortune, and who composed his major works over time, with discernible changes of emphasis and even with some shifts in purpose. Partly as an aside, though certainly not a minor one, Gilbert explores the emergence of the *official* historian—Navagero and his successors in Venice, Machiavelli and his in Florence—suggesting rather than asserting the significance of this Renaissance legacy to the later German world of Ranke. Finally, the essay on "Machiavellism" reviews the procession of changing portrayals of the Florentine secretary and the protean influence of his ideas across the modern centuries.

Part III proceeds, in one sense, quite effortlessly from the focus on Machiavelli to considerations of Venice in the Florentine thought of his and Guicciardini's time, a time of great troubles for both cities, and to a look into the garden of the Rucellai family in Florence, where met and argued the patrician critics of the post-Lorenzine Medici. The piece on the Orti Oricellari, as these gardens were called, is considerably older than those surrounding it; but its recent publication in a new format insures its strong, continuing influence on students of the period.

Before turning from Part III to the ensuing essays, we should at least note in passing a theme which assumes considerable prominence in Gilbert's recent work on Venice. This is the role of religion, as important to the future Cardinal Contarini as to his Camaldolese friends in the patriciate, at the highest spiritual level. It is precisely the tension between Contarini's sincere Christianity and his deep sense of public responsibility that makes him an absorbing figure for the historian of ideas. The frightened revivalism of the Venetian republic facing the League of Cambrai in 1509 and after, like Savonarola's puritanical regime in Florence only a few years earlier, seems less congenial to Gilbert's own feeling for the intellectual aspects of the Catholic Reformation still to come. This populist theme, however, receives its share of attention, alongside the aristocratic. The author seldom makes religious thought his central concern; but it is never out of sight in his treatment of topics ranging from the impact of humanistic scholarship, with its implicit regard for pagan antiquity, to the ethical implications of raison d'état.

Part IV's title, "Diplomacy: Old and New," rightly suggests a shifting of gears, a sharpening of topical focus accompanied by an extension of chronological range. This section also raises another issue which has held for its author a continuing fascination, that of *Zeitgeschichte,* the writing of contemporary history by scholars both past and present. While willing to concede that the analysis of the most recent past presents special difficulties, both of documentation and of the interpreter's perspective, Gilbert argues that the historian can and must see his own "present" as open-ended, as already the continuation of what has gone before. Others, in the future, are sure to rewrite our estimates of the events of our own time; but we are not for that reason relieved of the obligation to be more than passive chroniclers and to make all the sense we can of the history we actually live through, not least by relating it to what we know of the larger past.

The three chapters on diplomacy, Venetian in the dangerous mid-1520s, European and American in the eighteenth century, Fascist Italian on the eve of the Second World War, illustrate the value of depth in time, at some inevitable cost to breadth of theme. Any appearance of narrowness, of overconcentration on foreign affairs disappears, however, if there is clear recognition of what this section represents: not a self-conscious tour de force, but a demonstration, no less clear for having been unplanned, of the value of close attention paid to several different periods. The focus is on diplomacy, in theory and in practice; but the value of comparison seems fully applicable to politics, to economic problems, to social structure, or to any of a number of other challenges the historian may choose to accept.

Specific insights to be found in these essays are rewarding, and occasionally surprising. Thus, as we might expect, Gilbert analyzes the Venetian dilemma in the period between the capture of Milan by the French in 1524 and their defeat by Charles V's Spaniards at Pavia the following year, using his own extensive research to test the accounts and interpretations by sixteenth-century historians: Guicciardini, Contarini, Paruta, Morosini. What might not have been expected, but what seems to me to give the essay its special added quality, is the concluding paragraph, summing up the transition from the reality of Venetian weakness and indecision to the clutching for an assertion of ancient republican wisdom. Here is the myth as defense mechanism, explained by the author both with understanding and with full awareness of the significance of that Venetian myth for later generations of Europeans, not only in Europe but also beyond the "ocean sea."

Much of the chapter on the new diplomacy in the eighteenth century necessarily deals with ideas about relations among states expressed by philosophers and publicists who had in fact never been involved in the conduct of such affairs. However, the tension between ideology and practical demands created when the French Revolution brought new men to power is described in terms which derive added interest from their bearing on Albert Sagnac's celebrated assertion that an iron continuity linked the Old Regime, the Revolution, and the Napoleonic Empire. Comments on the American experience, aside from the fact that the essay adumbrated Gilbert's subsequent book, *To the Farewell Address,* are perhaps most arresting for what they have to say about this country's continuing affinity for critiques of the old diplomacy inherited from our colonial and earliest national experience. At its best, this tendency fed the potent rhetoric of a Woodrow Wilson. At its worst, it has on occasion left America looking "out of touch" with the realities of power, sometimes its own power and, increasingly in recent years, the power of other forces.

It is this being out of touch, worrisome in America's case, which Gilbert sees as literally disastrous in that of Ciano's Foreign Office under the government of Benito Mussolini. There is a certain wry amusement to be found in comparing the difficulties of Italy in the late 1930's, trying to steer a course at once heroic and safe between Nazi Germany and the ever-dangerous naval threat of Britain, with the mounting anguish of the Venetians in the 1520s, caught between King Francis I and Emperor Charles V. The main point, however, is that Count Ciano, proud of his good looks and illustrious parentage, confident of his ability to speak for the "young Fascists," intent on snubbing the career diplomats in the Palazzo Chigi, had neither a realistic sense of possibilities nor a coherent idea of what an Italian foreign policy should or, more important, could be. He showed no ability to discern the motives of other governments, nor did he bother to ask himself about the steps such governments might take under varying sets of circumstances. Grudging admirers of Bismarck used to concede that he often understood the interests of friends and opponents alike better than they did themselves. Poor, swaggering Ciano, it would seem, did not understand those even of Italy.

The question of contemporary history arises again in the concluding group of essays. There is, to take an example drawn from an earlier age, the effort to explain, in connection with Lorenz von Stein's work, why the French Revolution of 1848 triggered an uncommonly arresting set of immediate interpretations, in addition to Stein's: those of Marx, of Tocqueville, of Blanc, of Lamartine, to cite only the most famous. Gilbert's argument is subtle, bears reading in full, and should not be summarized in an introduction. Also, the general problems of *Zeitgeschichte* have already been touched upon. It is enough to say here that they are further explored in Part V. This section, however, raises other issues as well.

In the essay on Politian, our author displays his deep love of literature, in this case of Renaissance Italian literature, com-

11

bined with a keen appreciation for the philological achievements of Poliziano and, finally, a sure knowledge of the Medicean court which the latter understandably idealized. The introduction of Hofmannsthal, in relation to the Florentine poet and scholar, is further proof of Gilbert's continuing sensitivity to modern Germanic subject matter and to belles lettres in general.

His treatment of Italian national consciousness in the sixteenth and seventeenth centuries, with special reference to historians from Guicciardini to Muratori, is not only one of the most recent of his essays included in the present volume but also, in my opinion, among his very best, in its mature subtlety. With one hand he delineates the tension between secular Italian and papal univeralist appeals. With the other he takes his reader into the political and social workings of Spanish rule, from Naples to Milan, and the deep effects the stratification it engendered had upon the possibility of any shared allegiance. Yet the historians are not forgotten, and at the end it is their voices that one hears expressing the dilemmas of their time.

Quite another concern, the quest for a wholeness of view, dominates Gilbert's critique of the biography of Aby Warburg by E. H. Gombrich. There is no quarrel with Gombrich's estimate of Warburg as historian of art. Instead, there is an assertion of the further need to recognize the subject's achievement in upsetting certain nineteen-century views of Renaissance civilization as a whole. It was Warburg, for instance, who attacked head-on the temporarily popular thesis that continuity with the Middle Ages had outweighed the revival of interest in pagan classics. Throughout the review, Gilbert presses his demand for a broadened conception of the history of culture, drawing upon themes he has himself developed with care, over a long career as scholar, and themes he has left primarily to others.

The volume concludes, fittingly I think, with a lecture delivered by the author on "The History of the Professor of History." Here he is able to combine an appreciation of earlier German studies devoted to the professionalization of the field with his own observation of many careers. The result is a partly, though never explicitly, personal account of how the realm of moralists and amateurs, which became in due course a calling, a *Beruf* in Weber's formulation, now imposes its expectations on us all. In the course of the discussion, Gilbert pauses to reflect on an aspect of nineteenth-century thinking about history which he has obviously adopted as a part of his own:

> [It] is the view that history is indivisible and that everything that happened in the past belonged to the domain of the professor of history. History became an independent and autonomous field of study because it was recognized that special methods and procedures were necessary to study the past, but also because these methods and procedures were regarded as applicable to any aspect and period of the past. Before the nineteenth century history was chiefly an auxiliary science, and as an auxiliary to other fields of knowledge, historical study and research will always remain alive—now, perhaps, as an aid to political science, sociology, and area studies, rather than, as in the past, to moral philosophy, theology, or law. But if historians want their discipline to be more than an auxiliary science and to remain an autonomous and independent field of study, we should keep in mind that isolating our subjects is only one part of our work; the other is to seek for relationships, comparisons, and analogies . . .
>
> Our willingness to see the past as a whole, our willingness to take a stand, constitute our card of identity.

Save for a few remarks about Felix Gilbert's stance vis-à-vis Germany and about his discernible feelings toward things Italian, my introduction has not been a very personal one. This is not, as I hope the above references have made clear, because he challenges Otto Hintze in the capacity for communicating aloofness. Instead, concentration on the essays themselves has been born of a conviction that they deserve nothing less than level treatment, eye to eye. There is also, of course, the recognition alluded to at the outset, namely, that everyone who knows Gilbert will reserve his or her own right to characterization.

A few concluding suggestions on this score, however, may not be out of place. In particular, I think that a volume of published writings calls for some appreciation of the less formal but no less direct influence of their author viewed simply as a teacher. That he has been, in his sixteen years on the faculty at Bryn Mawr and in his frequent visits as lecturer or guest professor at other colleges and universities. Somewhat less obviously, he has also been that as a professor at the Institute for Advanced

Study, where yearly "classes" of younger scholars have profited from his learning, his advice, and his example. Least obviously, he has touched many of us as a friend and correspondent. If not in the sense applicable to the humanists of the Renaissance, history has always had for him a pedagogical side, the more welcome because his attention to it has been so natural.

The seriousness he brings to all matters historical is not forbidding, but it is demanding. Gilbert's comments on the work of a colleague are dependably critical, in the best sense, which is to say both searching and constructive. I remember an experience of more than thirty years ago, when he read the draft of a report I had been assigned to write for the OSS on the political implications of the July 20th bomb attempt against Hitler. Gilbert went over the pristine copy with a sharp eye and a busy pencil, leaving it, so far as I could see, pretty much in shreds. After we had discussed it, he wound up cheerfully by saying: "Very interesting, really quite good." My amazement at this turn in the conversation must have been obvious, for he added, with just a trace of embarrassment at having to explain: "If something is not potentially all right, it is not worth hard criticism."

The range of interests, the grasp of European history in many of its most important aspects and over all five of the modern centuries, the awareness of the classical tradition behind it are partly to be explained by the kind of scholarly education Gilbert received in Germany. Equally important, however, must have been the mixed background alluded to earlier and, above all, a career which has led to a close tie with Italy, a controlled yet affectionate regard for England, and a familiarity with America that has grown steadily for forty years. But in addition to the training and the rich experiences of a busy life there has been something else, a continuity of attitude, a realistic toughness about events and their interpretation combined with an unflagging interest in what does, or did, happen, and why. Perhaps all the energy illustrated by the pages to follow could not have survived interludes of discouragement over man and his affairs without the constant stimulation of a creative curiosity.

PART I.
Teachers of History at the University of Berlin

1. Johann Gustav Droysen

Johann Gustav Droysen was Prussian. Looking back on his childhood, he recalled with pride that Generals Blücher and Scharnhorst had once visited his father's study and that as a small boy he had ridden horseback in front of Blücher's saddle.[1] Belief in Prussia's historical mission is the essence of the first historical and political statement we have from him. In an essay on the revival of Bach's *St. Matthew Passion,* he notes the close tie between Prussia and Protestantism and remarks that it is this very tie that makes Prussia "a veritable hub and matrix of history."[2]

Three years passed before Droysen published another political statement. For his Aeschylus translation, which appeared in 1832, he wrote a historical introduction that contains a number of political allusions to the present and makes clear that Droysen belonged to that large group who were calling

---

This is an English translation of the first chapter of my dissertation on *Johann Gustav Droysen und die Preussisch-Deutsche Frage,* Beiheft 20 der Historischen Zeitschrift (Munich and Berlin, R. Oldenbourg, 1931). Since its appearance the literature on Droysen has remarkably increased. See "Droysen" by Theodor Schieder in *Neue Deutsche Biographie* (Berlin, Duncker and Humblot, 1953—), IV, 135-137, and Günter Birtsch, *Die Nation als sittliche Idee,* Kölner Historische Abhandlungen, X (Köln, Böhlau, 1964). However, the more recent literature does not contain the extensive treatment of Droysen's early development presented here.

for a "liberalization" of Prussia. He criticized Prussia's absolutistic system of government and the lack of independence in her foreign policy,[3] and at the same time he extolled the advantages of a free constitutional life.[4] It is not clear from these statements whether Droysen regarded the "liberalization" of Prussia as concomitant with a more solid national unification of Germany. But his private correspondence of this period—particularly two letters written in the summer of 1831—indicates that he did indeed see such a connection between liberal and national demands.

In a letter of May 28[5] he developed plans for publishing a "journal dealing with historical and political subjects," and mentioned that he had already written several articles for it. "The first presents Prussia as *le juste milieu* of Europe, as the middle between the extremes, the point across which the compass needle of Europe wavers, the place too, unfortunately, where the contemptible indifference of our official gazettes holds sway, that attitude of neither too much nor too little that leaves nothing in the end, not even a principle. The second essay deals with the vital principle of Prussian politics, Prussia's need to march forward." He hoped to avoid censorship by "speaking about the most daring principles—for example, the people constitute a part of the state; freedom of the press is not reprehensible, and so forth—as if they were generally accepted facts."

As we discover in another letter dated July 31,[6] Droysen's plan did fail after all because of interference from the censors. In this same letter Droysen mentioned another literary project, the publication of an exchange of letters in which state and religion, art and learning in contemporary Germany would be discussed as "general topics that are, or should be, of immediate concern to everyone." "Let us begin with the assumption that we in Germany still have our history before us; we must therefore still explore these topics for ourselves. Let us describe precisely and bluntly what has been accomplished in each of these four areas, what mistakes have been made, what reforms are necessary." His aim was to overcome the "lifeless fragmentation" evident in each of these areas. This publication was also to contain a recently completed study on peerage, that is, on the merits of a monocameral or a bicameral system. For the highest legislative authority, that representing the people, he recommended establishing only one house. The people are a community to which every human being belongs because he is an individual, and community understood in this sense does not permit of any distinctions in rank. But in terms of his property —of what he has—each individual belongs to still another community, a community defined by differences in place and rank. These communities must also be represented, and he assigned this task to the provincial diets.

> This, you see, is how I justify the high value I place on the role I think our hitherto ridiculous provincial diets will have in the future . . . Of course, they are unfortunate institutions as long as the differences between the provinces are not resolved in a higher unity, but within the context of an empire, the provincial diets are a valuable guarantee that personal freedom, local interests, and distinctions by birth and circumstance not be damaged or, indeed, threatened in their very existence. Germany's particularism cannot be allowed to be an eternal misfortune. It must lead to a higher, more perfect form, or we will be the dupes of our own aspirations. Let us hope the future will justify this apologia for local division. I, for one, claim that only by virtue of their constitutions will Braunschweig, Kassel, and so forth earn the right to become members of the Prussian empire sometime in the future. History, I think, requires this of us. Needless to say, the road will be long and arduous, perhaps bloody and ignominious. But hope is stronger than fear and faith brighter than the night in which we dream and sometimes despair.

This is the material we have to draw on in reconstructing Droysen's political thinking at the conclusion of his studies early in the 1830s. In terms of the Prusso-German question, the focal point of this study, the two letters from the summer of 1831 are the most important documents we have. For they are not only Droysen's first detailed political statements but also the only ones for a number of years. The fact that these letters were written in the summer of 1831 is not accidental. They bear witness to the brief wave of political interest that the July Revolution sent sweeping over Germany. The radical tone of the letters is typical of the mood of these years. Just as Hegel and Hölderlin's generation has seen the French Revolution of 1789 as a "glorious dawn"[7] that signaled a new era, so this young generation, too, thought it was witnessing in the July Revolution the beginning of a new age.

If we examine Droysen's political statements, we find that they contain both liberal and national demands in the form of conclusions drawn from history. We also find that concern peculiar to German national strivings in these years: a concern for both a German national state and a general political renewal.[8] Even this first glance at Droysen's political thinking shows the central importance of his conviction that Germany's future was linked to and dependent on Prussian policy. But the expression "Prussian empire" that he used to describe this German national state of the future is ambiguous and raises a number of questions. Did he mean that the future national state would be an expanded Prussia and that the pursuit of a national policy would involve absorbing the other German states? Or did he merely mean to suggest that Germany's future evolution was now solely in Prussia's hands and no longer in Austria's? We cannot answer the questions on the basis of Droysen's statements alone. Only when we relate his views to the political thinking of his time do they take on a clearer form. There is no material relating to the development of Droysen's political veiws before the summer of 1831, so we can only surmise what influences led to his national and liberal position.

Droysen was seventeen when he went to Berlin to begin his university studies. He spent all his student years in Berlin, but the university was not the only channel through which he encountered the intellectual currents that dominated the Prussian capital. He belonged to the circle around the Mendelssohn family,[9] whose home was a focal point of intellectual and artistic life in Berlin. Liberal political sentiments predominated there.[10] In this circle, Droysen made the acquaintance of Varnhagen von Ense and Eduard Gans, both convinced liberals who exerted an important influence on the forming of political opinion in Berlin. He also met Börne and Heine, the "fathers of Young Germany."[11] Droysen was taken into this circle partly because of his artistic interests and gifts. During his Berlin years he seems to have been primarily concerned with aesthetic problems, so much so that Erich Rothacker has even spoken of this time in Berlin as Droysen's "aesthetic period."[12] It may well be that this preoccupation with art became a major source of his German national feelings, that the idea of the German national state became an urgent necessity for him precisely because of his deep involvement with Germany's culture.

But the basic element in his political thinking was a Prussian patriotism that he had imbibed in his own home and that drew renewed strength from the ethos of the reform period and recollections of the Wars of Liberation.[13] Droysen's stay in Berlin, the heart of the Prussian state, where the spirit of those years still lived on in both individuals and institutions, must have reinforced the patriotic feelings he brought with him from home and directed any considerations of Germany's future into definite channels. Schleiermacher, Eichhorn, and Reimer were still living and working in Berlin while Droysen was a student. With these men the idea of Prussian leadership in Germany had taken root and flourished during the years under Napoleonic subjugation.[14] Though we have no evidence of contact between Droysen and this circle, the possibility of influence from this group cannot be excluded. Of all the writings that contain their ideas, the brochure *Preussens Recht gegen den sächsischen Hof,* in which the great classicist Barthold Niebuhr first articulated the Prussian view of history,[15] must have been known to the young philologist and have impressed him deeply. Niebuhr's ideas on Prussia's German calling combined German national feelings with loyalty to the Prussian state in a way that surely had an impact on a political sensibility based on the same two sources.

Clearly these were basic elements in Droysen's political thinking. The form it took in 1831, however, reflected the intellectual climate of that year. The political questions Droysen dealt with in his letter of July 31—peerage, reform, *juste milieu*—were the same ones that dominated most political discussions in Berlin then;[16] his literary projects, too, were just as closely linked to the intellectual currents of the times.

It cannot be mere coincidence that Droysen described the magazine he planned to publish as a "journal dealing with historical and political subjects," giving it almost the same name that Leopold von Ranke chose as a title for his famous *Historisch-politische Zeitschrift.* It is even possible that Droysen's plan and Ranke's journal both have the same origin.[17] The idea for Ranke's journal came from Friedrich Perthes, who suggested it in November 1830 in a letter to Count Bernstorff, then Prussian foreign minister. In December 1831, Perthes described his plan in detail to Varnhagen von Ense. Perthes hoped, by means of historical studies based on official records, to raise the general level of political sophistication and at the same time to provide justification for the policies of the Prussian government. But Perthes also wanted the journal to emphasize Prussia's German calling and to urge on Prussia a more decisive policy toward German unification. It is likely that Droysen heard of Perthes's ideas either through Varnhagen himself or through Varnhagen's close friend, Eduard Gans; when Droysen saw time slip by without anyone acting on Perthes's proposal, he may well have decided to carry it out himself. It is an appealing idea to think that Ranke and Droysen both responded to the same suggestion, each in his own way. Ranke focused on explaining and comprehending the current political situation by means of historical studies.[18] Droysen, however—if I am correctly interpreting the remarks he made about his proposal—was most interested in the future, in the political goal. These differing reactions to the same stimulus seem to suggest contrasting political ideas. But this difference in approach was also the result of a difference in temperament that is reflected in Droysen's and Ranke's conflicting views on the forces determining the movements of history, a difference that continued throughout their lives.

Perthes's suggestion may have had some influence on Droysen's view of the role Prussian policy should play in the future. But Droysen could not learn anything specific from Perthes, who stated only that Prussia should initiate a popular policy, whereupon Prussia and Germany would begin to grow together, thus creating the basis for Prussian hegemony. A more concrete discussion of the problem began at this time, however. The first edition of Paul A. Pfizer's *Briefwechsel zweier Deutschen,* which appeared in 1831, made a convincing case for Prussian hegemony in the German national state of the future. Although it may have been generally accepted that the first essential step in this direction was to transform Prussia into a constitutional state, Pfizer was the first to recognize that such a transformation entailed a difficult problem: it would strengthen

Prussia as a separate political entity, and thus aggravate the division between Prussia and Germany and complicate the founding of a national state.[19]

Pfizer's book had an obvious influence on Droysen's other literary project: the publication of a political correspondence. This influence extended beyond adopting an exchange of letters as a literary form. The content of Droysen's proposed work was to be an analysis of the intellectual situation in contemporary Germany. Here he seems to be singling out for detailed study a theme that Pfizer only touched on in Letter 13 of his work, which dealt with "literature, church, state, and life in present-day Germany," and suggested that the artificiality and unproductivity prevailing in these areas resulted from the lack of a "genuine focal point for life"[20] in Germany.

Pfizer's influence is also evident in the special significance Droysen attributed to the role of the provincial diets in the Prussian constitution.[21] If we consider that the letter in which Droysen used the phrase "Prussian empire" was written with Pfizer's book in mind,[22] then we can probably conclude that Droysen, in using that phrase, was accepting Pfizer's main thesis, namely, that Austria should be excluded from any role in Germany's future and that one should envisage the future German state having only one major power—Prussia—within the confederation. Droysen hoped to solve the problem of joining Prussia to the other German states by granting the Prussian provinces equal status with the German states and by allowing them, within the framework of the empire, an independent development guaranteed by the provincial diets. He did not think it necessary to maintain Prussia as a separate political entity in the future national state. In emphasizing the importance of the provincial diets, Droysen enlarged on an idea which Pfizer had hinted at in the first edition of his book and which he would later justify in detail in subsequent editions. What we can say of Pfizer we can also say of Droysen: he advocated national hegemony for the Hohenzollerns but not a hegemony of the Prussian state.[23]

But a problem lies hidden in the apparent agreement between these two men. Pfizer's call for the dissolution of the Prussian state originated in his fear that the North German element would dominate in the new German state, and it had the concrete purpose of lowering South German resistance to Prussian hegemony. At the same time, it expressed a very real awareness of Prussian autonomy and of the obstacles Prussia could put in the way of founding a German national state. Droysen, who was a Prussian, could not have shared these feelings with the South German Pfizer. Why, then, did he make the same demand on the Prussian state, and why could he accept without reservation the sacrifice of Prussia as an individual political entity in the interests of German nationality?

The formation of a German national state as we have just sketched it implied for Droysen the realization of a political structure richer than any Germany had previously had. In his view, conditions in Germany were ripe for such a structure, and history was leading Germany inevitably toward it.[24] This was the conclusion he reached in his study of peerage. In that study, Droysen took as his point of departure the general historical premise that "the new era will, through the agency of the state, raise the individual into freedom" and this process would be the "suum cuique of history."[25] He claimed, in effect, that his political demands were dictated by the course of history, that this was their justification. His political thinking in general and his view of the Prusso-German problem were rooted in his concept of history and of the role of the state in history.

II

Are we dealing here with historical views inspired by Pfizer's book that Droysen held for only a short time, or is Droysen expressing a well-grounded theory of history? We have ample material for answering this question: the historical introduction to the Aeschylus translation, which Droysen had begun during his student years[26] and completed in 1832, clearly reveals a definite theory of history.

The history of Greece held a particular meaning for Droysen. If filled "the wide gap between the dreamlike selflessness of the Orient and the postulates of absolute freedom and of individual rights" that arose in the West.[27] This introduction to Aeschylus is based on the same idea that informed his political statements, the idea that the realization of freedom is the essence of world history. Greek history represents the beginnings of this development. In Greece, the human intellect became aware of its power and pitted itself against "nature and fate."[28] History consists of the struggle of mind against nature; it begins at the point where the intellect emerges from the state of nature and challenges nature. But the end result of the historical process is a return to the natural condition, for the mind never tires "of casting its terrible 'Why?' in the face of all that exists. It shatters, undermines, and destroys until it has finally ground away all distinctions, reduced all being to the level of envy, selfishness, and knowledge. What remains is an atomistic universe characterized by ochlocratic uniformity. Confronted by this dullness, this dreary, distorted, Medusa-like image of freedom, intelligence is paralyzed, and the mindless masses slowly degenerate, returning to the old vegetative state of nature." Droysen saw this cycle, which he calls "an eternal law inherent in all historical processes and the inevitable result of those processes," realized in the history of every nation.

Despite this, he still regarded world history as a coherent process. A continuity between the histories of individual nations is provided by the fact that a certain intellectual principle is articulated, a certain "deed" accomplished,[29] in the history of each nation. This is the "apex"[30] of the development toward which the history of a nation rises and from which it begins its decline. A progressive development, whose essence is the realization of freedom, links all these "principles" together. The entire cultural and intellectual growth of a nation is embodied in this realization of its principle, and a people's literature and philosophy record this growth of the national mind.[31] As a consequence, they represent "a development that meshes with world history and that is, we might say, conceptually linked to it."[32] The basis for historical research on a universal level therefore derives from the conviction "that nothing essential in the flow of time is lost, that history has left no gaps at any point where it is important for us to comprehend the uninterrupted progress in the history of the mind."[33]

This theory of history is in accord with his historical and political thinking, and we can regard his political statements as projections of his theoretical views into the future. Prussia embodied a principle that would make it possible for Germany to realize in the empire a new and higher form of political existence and thereby advance one step further in the evolution of the human mind. With this, it is evident that our inquiry into the origins of Droysen's political thinking must branch out and focus on the decisive factors in his intellectual development.

Droysen had just completed his studies at the University of Berlin when he wrote this interpretation of Athenian history. He had studied classical philology with August Böckh. At the time, classical philology was more than an isolated field of study. It was a major educational force[34] and represented a specific philosophical position. It certainly would have been capable of forming young Droysen's view of the world, but this was not the case. A glance at the field during that period will show that classical philology was not decisive in shaping his theory of history. On the contrary, his historical ideas were a reaction against it. But an understanding of Droysen's relationship to classical philology will cast into sharper relief the forces that did in fact determine his thinking.

The "conceptual structure of classical studies"[35] derived from views developed during the period of German classical literature. German classicism had found in ancient Greece the rules and models it felt were binding for all humanity. F. A. Wolf, who is considered the founder of this new discipline of classical studies,[36] defined the goal toward which the various fields included under classical studies strive as "a knowledge of humanity in the ancient world. This knowledge is the result of observing, by means of studying ancient remnants, and organically developed national culture."[37] This culture seemed significant to Wolf because only in ancient Greece do we find "what we have sought almost everywhere else in vain," namely, "nations and states that possessed in their very nature most of the qualities essential to forming a character in which humanity is fully developed."[38]

For this founder of classical studies, ancient Greece possessed normative value, and for classical scholars of the nineteenth century, "transforming an aesthetic and absolute evaluation of the ancient world into a historical and relative one" was a major preoccupation.[39] Böckh and Niebuhr together with Wolf led the way in broadening classical studies to include disciplines dealing with every aspect of the ancient world, not, as had been the case before, only with ancient languages and literature. Yet Böckh and Niebuhr also opposed the exaggerated idealization of the Greeks and Romans[40] and the idea that the ancients provided standards valid for all time.[41] They remained in agreement with German classicism, however, in seeing the ancient world, particularly Greece, as a whole in whose various manifestations a unifying idea was present.[42]

Coexistent with this idea of a unified classical culture was the notion that the history of the ancient world represented a complete and terminated chapter in cultural evolution[43] and that the idea underlying that evolution was fully realized. It was Böckh's intention to substantiate this view of antiquity in his book *Hellen,* a project he worked on throughout his lifetime.[44] The same view inspired Otfried Müller's plan for a history of Greece, which he expected to be the crowning achievement of his career. His *Geschichten hellenischer Stämme und Städte* contained only preliminary studies for this work.[45]

The Greek ideal of humanity (*Humanitätsidee*) represented the essence of the ancient world for Böckh.[46] Conscious as he was that this ideal was valid only for the ancient world and comprehensible only within that context,[47] he still found normative value in the fact that ancient Greece provides the first and only case in history in which a cultural idea achieved its full bloom.[48]

The normative character that classical studies had in Böckh's time becomes clear to us when we see how the ancient and modern worlds are compared with each other in historical studies.[49] When such comparisons are made—and they are made most often in discussions of political life—the institutions of the ancients appear as models to be emulated. Normative studies of this kind tend, of course, more to betray the political ideals of their authors than to describe actual conditions in the ancient world.[50] Niebuhr's *Römische Geschichte,* for example, use the constitutional experiments of the French Revolution[51] as a foil for his ideal constitution, which develops organically and keeps the estates in a natural equilibrium.[52] Otfried Müller compares "the sublime freedom of the Spartan or Hellene," whose greatest desire was to be "a living member of the whole," with "what we call freedom in modern times." This modern version of freedom, Müller says, consists "of contributing as little as possible to the commonweal or, in other words, of dissolving the state as much as possible."[53] Böckh states explicitly: "The ancient world shows us what true political freedom is and what the basic principles of that freedom are."[54] When he compares the advantages of the Athenian free state with the arbitrary government of the modern absolutistic one[55] and when he praises the Greeks' devotion to freedom, he is clearly expressing his own political preferences.[56]

Although classical studies may have influenced Droysen's thinking at certain points, the differences between his views and those of the classical philologists are much more striking than the similarities. In regarding the ancient world as a closed unit and history as divided into ancient civilization and modern civilization, the classical scholars' theory of history is at odds with Droysen's dynamic view of historical processes. For Droysen, the history of the Greeks stands at the beginning of a historical continuum that reaches into the present. But Droysen's rejection of a philological view in favor of a historical view of the ancient world signals more than the adoption of a different mode of research. It reflects, too, the vision of a new era. The perfect human individual was no longer the ideal in relation to which all historical phenomena were measured. The individual no longer stood alone; he was part and parcel of a community that patterned and set limits to his evolution.

Droysen thought his view represented an advance beyond the vision of classical scholars. In his inaugural lecture,[57] which was of a programmatic nature, he claimed that the ancient world can no longer provide a model for the present because the value of each era depends upon its own development. The term "philology" represents no more than a "chimera" at this point because it is no longer possible to regard the history and languages of the classical nations, "as a closed chapter, as an isolated evolutionary process." Today's scholarship has to regard "the multifariousness of past circumstances and efforts as just so many transitional phases in historical developments that finally, after innumerable permutations, are drawn together in the web of the present." Every scholarly effort to understand the classical world should focus on its historical significance.

Clearly Droysen's appreciation of the ancient world as a phenomenon of purely historical significance was not the product of an empirical preoccupation with it. Rather, the application of a philosophical concept—the concept of development—made him "the first real historian of the Greeks that Germany had ever seen."[58] This brings us to the other major school of thought that reigned at the University of Berlin during Droysen's studies there and that exercised an influence on him: the philosophy of Hegel.

III

As early as his third semester Droysen began to attend Hegel's lectures. In the course of his studies he went to nearly every major lecture series Hegel delivered.[59] But, as he later wrote, he was never a member of the Hegelian school,[60] nor had he ever written in the "language of that school."[61] He never accepted the philosophical foundations of the Hegelian system,[62] according to which the entire world of phenomena, both nature and historical life, becomes a reflection of the spirit, as proved by the dialectic—that is, nature and history become involved in a logical process. Droysen does, of course, make some use of Hegel's dialectic in historical writings,[63] but it by no means represents the only logical framework within which he places the events of history. Nor is there in Droysen's thinking any trace of that metaphysically derived premise in Hegel's theory of history that reduces every historical occurrence to its intellectual content and that finally regards historical reality as no more than appearance. Only the historical and political aspects of Hegel's system influenced Droysen,[64] providing him with concepts and intuitions with which to give order to the life of the social world.

The theoretical view of history reflected in Droysen's survey of Athenian history is dominated by the spiritualistic premise of Hegel's philosophy of history. Still other elements in Droysen's thinking must also be regarded as based on Hegel's system. For example, Droysen, like Hegel, sees history as the evolution of the world spirit, and for Droysen, too, the essence of history is a process by which the principle of freedom gradually takes shape, progressing step by step, passing from one nation to another and achieving ever higher forms. Droysen's remarks on peerage may serve as another example of the influence Hegel exerted over his historical and political thinking. Not only does Droysen use concepts drawn from Hegel's philosophy of law here[65]— opposition of society and state; artisans, peasants, and noblemen as categories of estate organization—but also, and more important, he sees the institutions of countries like England and France as expressions of specific principles at work in those countries. Indeed, his view of England as "the country where freedom means nothing more than personal freedom" bears a close resemblance to ideas on the "English principle of the positive"[66] that Hegel later developed in his essay on the English Reform Bill.

Droysen's view of history is clearly dependent on Hegel's philosophy of history, but to what extent can Droysen's statements on predicting the future on the basis of the past and defining political goals as necessary consequences of historical developments be traced to Hegel's influence?

For Hegel, historical development had come to an end. The major premise of his philosophy of history is the conviction that "with the Christian-Germanic era the historical process had, in essence and for all practical purposes, reached completion."[67] Thus the entire intellectual content of history could be surveyed by a philosophical observer. Hegel concludes that the modern principle of the state was embodied in the Protestant and monarchistic Prussia of the Restoration, the state that would usher in an age of new and realistic political thinking.[68]

Droysen's image of the future is, then, in large part influenced by Hegel's ideas on the modern era. His concept of the new state as a vehicle for all cultural and intellectual values; his conviction that this new state will arise in Protestant Prussia, that Prussia will be the world historical nation of the modern age, are crucial elements in Droysen's political thought. But where Hegel saw the new state already taking shape in contemporary Prussia, Droysen places the realization of the new principle in the future and connects its emergence with the creation of a German national state. Thus the law of necessity that dominated in the retrospective constructions of Hegel's philosophy of history is expanded by Droysen into the future. His liberal and national convictions—which were formed under the impact of other intellectual currents and had no place in the framework of the Hegelian system—and, above all, his optimism as a member of a new generation just embarking on its life's work led him to modify Hegel's ideas and to apply the Hegelian theory of history to the future. This shift in thinking is common to the entire Hegelian left,[69] and it explains the critical tone

Droysen used in this period when he referred to Hegel in his letters. Hegel believed this was "a time for thought," not "a time for action."[70] Droysen, oriented as he was toward the future, saw in Hegel a "philosopher of the Restoration"[71] whose usefulness had come to an end with the July Revolution.[72]

From the foregoing analysis we can see how closely Droysen's thinking about the national state is linked to and meshed with supranational speculations. For him, the German national state could be justified only as an ultimate goal in the evolution of all mankind. Compared to the lively and passionate feelings that surround his statements about Germany's future, this ideology seems pale indeed, no more than a lifeless shell he will soon put aside. But we must not forget that these universalistic notions formed the point of departure for his interpretations of Pfizer's remarks on the provincial diets and shaped his ideas on the "dissolution" of Prussia, ideas he would hold into the Revolution of 1848. Only after a long intellectual development and considerable political experience would he assign to the rights of the individual state and the right of national self-determination an importance distinct from these universalistic ideas.

IV

Other writers have often pointed out, of course, that one of Droysen's major ideas is in conflict with these universalistic elements. They claim that in his history of Alexander the Great, specifically in his description of Macedonian relations with Greece, Droysen was alluding to the goal of Prussian hegemony in Germany and that in demonstrating the necessity of the alliance between Macedonian military power and the Greek states, Droysen was attempting to justify the role of the Prussian administration and military apparatus for Germany.[73]

If this claim is correct, Droysen's history of Alexander the Great contains the germs of *Realpolitik* and power politics. This claim will have to be examined in order to arrive at a complete picture of Droysen's political convictions in the early 1830s. But the Alexander study is important for another reason as well: it reveals the significance of the religious and Christian element in Droysen's thinking.

Droysen regarded his history of Alexander as a preliminary

31

study, an introduction to a history of Hellenism,[74] for which he first made plans as a student.[75] His study of Alexander therefore belongs to the first of the three great historiographical conceptions "on which his scholarly reputation rests"[76] Up to that time, the Hellenistic period had had little attraction for historians and philologists. They had regarded it as the time of Greece's subjugation and the decline of Greek culture—a time of decadence, insignificant in the framework of a history of the ancient world.[77] Droysen was the first scholar with a different evaluation of this era. He saw it as a necessary stage in historical development which brought Greek life into the Orient and thereby created a unified culture that formed the basis for the Christian world religion and the Roman world empire.[78] He established the view of Hellenism that has served as a basis for research ever since.[79] To understand how he came to his new evaluation of the Hellenistic period and why he chose as the focus of his life's work a field that his contemporaries considered unfruitful and unrewarding is a problem crucial to Droysen's political thought.

Johann Gustav Droysen is one of those great figures in German intellectual history raised in Protestant parsonages. The Protestant faith of his parents' home left a deep impression on his character. Throughout his life his religious faith provided a firm base for his thoughts and actions. We have no evidence of inner crises that might have threatened his intellectual being. His thinking seems to have developed and matured gradually in an organic manner. On the other hand, we have no indication of what his reactions were when he arrived as a student in Berlin. The idea of the perfect nature of the ancient world conveyed by a philology dominated by the notions of German classicism was accompanied by a freedom of spirit that was bound to clash with the strict faith of his home. If his life ever was shaken by a crisis, it must have been then.[80] Perhaps we can suggest that his concept of Hellenism is a product of his struggle to reconcile the values of the classical world with those of Christianity, to tie them together in a unity which would show them to be dependent on each other.[81]

We can fully understand the nature of Droysen's historical thinking only if we take his religious faith into account.[82] Both the immediacy of his historical vision and his feeling for historical detail are explained by his conviction that the historical world in all its aspects was created by God and must therefore be affirmed. This conviction infuses his historical writing with warmth and vividness.[83] His belief that God directed the course of history permitted him to surrender to the "restless dynamic of history that destroys in order to build and builds in order to destroy."[84]

But this raises the question of the relationship between the religious element of his historical thought and the influence of Hegel's philosophy of history. Droysen's Christian faith is sufficient explanation for the fact that although he assimilated Hegel's political theory and philosophy of history, he never, as we have seen, accepted Hegel's system in its entirety. Even here there was a conflict between a philosophy that considered its main task to be "proving"[85] what was real and a religious conviction that regarded historical events as given facts. The divergence of these elements that constituted his historical thought inevitably led to revision and reevaluation; actually Hegel's influence on him did not extend beyond the first half of the 1830s. Thereafter he developed new perspectives on the philosophy of history, solved the problems that troubled him in this field, and finally formulated his solutions in his methodological study entitled *Historik*.

But this was a slow and gradual development accompanying his historical research. We should keep in mind that in the early 1830s, when Droysen was at the start of his historical career, the religious element in his thinking could have made him all the more receptive to Hegel's influence. If, as we assumed, Droysen's conception of Hellenism resulted from his effort to do justice to both Christianity and antiquity, Hegel's philosophy provided him with the means for solving this problem. In Hegel's philosophy of history, despite the emphasis on progress and the increasing value of successive epochs, every era possessed its own individual meaning and was a necessary link in the chain of historical development. We also must recognize that Droysen's conception of Hellenism expresses the "old idea of a Christian plan for salvation" in a new guise.[86] This could be another point of contact with Hegel; for Hegel's philosophy is also a secularized form of this same idea, and it, too, originated from a similar basis, the religious conflict in Hegel's youth.[87]

For a believing Protestant like Droysen, who always regarded history as a "theodicy," a philosophy of history that presumed to demonstrate necessity and meaning in the historical process could appear to be the appropriate framework for historical research. It is important to note that regardless of how strong a determining element Droysen's Protestantism had always been in his thinking—one totally unrelated to Hegelianism—it by no means precludes the influence of Hegel's theories of history and politics or necessarily stands in conflict with them.

Droysen's *Alexander*[88] still belongs entirely to the period of Hegel's domination: its decisive points of view are dervied from Hegel's philosophy of history. Hegel was the first to see the great importance of the cultural development connected with the era of Alexander, and it was Hegel who rescued Alexander from those "Philistine historians"[89] who misused him for moralistic purposes. For Hegel, Alexander was "the embodiment of youth" who stood at the end of Greek history—just as Achilles had stood at its beginning—and completed that history by avenging the Greeks against Asia.[90] "On the one hand he avenged the Greeks for what they had suffered from Asians, but on the other he also repaid Asia a thousandfold for the cultural impulses it had brought to Greece. He spread the mature and sublime culture of Greece to the East and transformed occupied Asia into a Hellenistic country."[91] Droysen, too, saw this accomplishment as Alexander's great contribution to history,[92] and the presentation of this accomplishment was the purpose of his book on Alexander, which, as he expressly said in his introduction, was not meant to be a monograph or a biography but a "history" of Alexander, a history of his accomplishment "written in the awareness that his personality was only the agent that made the accomplishment possible." For this reason Droysen, too, judges Alexander not in terms of morals but solely in terms of historical significance. "Great men have the right to be measured by their own standards, and there is a profounder meaning in what we might be tempted to call their errors than there is in the moral code they have the courage to violate. Embodying the ideas of their time and of their nation, they act out of an obscure passion that elevates them—just as their field of activity separates them from the humdrum world of other men—into the lonely realms of historical greatness, where only the admiring gaze is able to perceive them."[93]

Droysen's conception of a personality that is representative of its entire era and expresses itself only in its actions goes back, of course, to Hegel's idea of the hero in world history whose goals coincide with the will of the world spirit.[94] With Droysen this idea takes the form of recognizing in Alexander's character and life a special instrument of Providence.[95] Consequently, for him just as for Hegel, success is the criterion of a genuine "world historical calling" as well as a justification for the hero's deeds.[96] Still another consequence of this theory is evident in Droysen. He has "no pity for the heroism of the defeated."[97] Demosthenes had previously been regarded as a heroic pioneer in the fight for Greek freedom. Droysen portrays him here as a shortsighted, obstinate demagogue, "as pathetic a figure" as history has ever produced.[98]

Droysen's book on Alexander sees the permeation of Asia with Hellenistic culture as a necessary stage in the process of world history and portrays Alexander as the hero commissioned by the world spirit to carry out this task. Hegel did not like the modern philological and critical school of historiography.[99] It robbed him of the solid footing he needed for his construction of history, and it therefore comes as no surprise that Droysen's book, which took Hegel's ideas on Alexander the Great as its point of departure, does not represent an advance in critical historiography. We could best describe it as a vivid rewriting of the sources, incorporating and emphasizing perspectives of universal history.[100] Droysen himself wrote in his preface that with this book he said farewell to the "happy years of youth." The book is a work of youth in the sense that the imaginative force with which Droysen portrays Alexander and Alexander's great historical task far overrides any critical considerations. But it is also a youthful work in the sense that in reading it we feel the spell of gifted and enthusiastic youth.

But now we must return to the question that prompted our close examination of Droysen's *Alexander:* has the book a direct relationship to Droysen's political views?

Certain passages in *Alexander* are obviously colored by Droysen's views of contemporary political developments. The contempt he had for German particularism sharpened his judgment of the defects of the policies of the Greek states in Alexander's time[101] and led him to reevaluate predominant contemporary interpretations of them. He believed that universal conscription was beneficial for Prussia and this view clearly influenced his favorable description of the Macedonian military constitution.[102] It is likely, too, that the negative picture he paints of the reactionary party at the Macedonian court alludes to a similar group in Prussia.[103] But neither of these points indicates whether the leadership the Macedonian military monarchy assumed over the Greek states was symbolic of the role Droysen assigned to Prussia in the future German national state or whether the figure of Alexander was meant to proclaim the necessity of Prussian hegemony over Germany. Just as Droysen felt that German history in his time had not yet achieved its goal, he also felt that the national mission of Greek history had not been accomplished before Alexander. The "national task"[104] of Greek history, however, was the Hellenization of Asia. He never suggests that the Macedonian hegemony over Greece had any purpose other than the conquest of Asia[105] or that any special value lay in the alliance between the Macedonian military monarch and the Greek spirit or that he saw in that alliance any more than a tool that the hero Alexander used to fulfill his role in world history. The portrait of this hero in world history is the focal point of Droysen's book, and behind this figure stands quite another experience of Droysen's time. As he himself wrote, Napoleon had reawakened "a sense for historical greatness."[106] The unquestionable link which Droysen established between these figures should teach us not to find in such allusions analogies between present and past but to recognize in them that participation in the life of the present from which concern with the past always draws its greatest strength.

Thus, our examination of Droysen's *Alexander* does not add new elements to our understanding of his political thinking.[107] It is a misapprehension—one that arose in a later time, that of *Realpolitik*—to believe that the military and bureaucratic Prussia of the time represented all that Droysen meant when he used the word Prussia. Schleiermacher wrote to Friedrich von Raumer in 1807: "I am, of course, committed to an idea of Prussia that few would recognize in the concrete reality of that state."[108] Droysen's political thinking also revolved around an idea of Prussia that was not identical with the concrete reality of Prussia in his time. But for him—and here he differs from Schleiermacher and Schleiermacher's generation—the realization of this idea involved not only an ethical imperative but primarily a historical necessity. In Droysen's concept of history the question of how to realize political goals—for us the most important question—plays only a secondary role. He thought that if the goal were only clearly envisaged, then history would create, as it always had in the past, the proper means for achieving that goal. In this view of history, the reality of historical forces lies in their intellectual content and ethical power. Because Droysen saw the relationship of Prussia to Germany from this perspective, he conceived of it as a confrontation not of existing states but of ideas. As a result, the "dissolution" of Prussia in a future German state did not strike him as a sacrifice but as the realization of the Prussian idea. Prussia and Germany would become one, and in history, to be dissolved in a higher unity meant destiny and fulfillment.

2. Otto Hintze

Those acquainted with the work of Otto Hintze are unanimous in regarding him as one of the most important, if not the most important, German historical scholar of the period of William II and the Weimar Republic. Yet the number of those to whom his writings are known is small; and his influence on historical scholarship, although profound and decisive in individual cases, has been limited. Hintze's fame has certainly not reached far beyond the German frontiers.

This neglect of one of the most important historians of the twentieth century can be explained. The foremost reason has been the inaccessibility of Hintze's writings. He published only one book of a narrative nature—*Die Hohenzollern und ihr Werk*—and even this book, although intended for the educated public, has a rather austere character. For the most part his studies were published as introductions to source publications or as articles in learned journals. A first, posthumous, incomplete collection of his essays appeared in Germany during the Second World War, and a revised and enlarged edition was published only recently.

Hintze was little concerned with the reception of his writ-

Originally published in *The Historical Essays of Otto Hintze,* ed. Felix Gilbert, with the assistance of Robert M. Berdahl (New York, Oxford University Press, 1975), pp. 3–30.

ings, and naturally this was a reflection of his temperament. Friedrich Meinecke, a close friend of his, wrote in his memoirs that Hintze "was too proud to make his work easily accessible to the world," and added that many considered him a "knight in armor who did not open his visor and did not permit his face to be seen." Even in advanced age Hintze remained a tall, erect figure who fended off anyone whose words or behavior raised claims of familiarity. Hintze was not the type of academic who sought to impress others by his knowledge. He was cast in the mold of a high civil servant to whom distance and reserve in public contacts had become second nature. External circumstances reinforced these inclinations: illness, particularly steadily deteriorating eyesight, forced him to give up his professorship at the University of Berlin in 1920 when he was fifty-five years old. Thus his contacts with the outside world became even more restricted. His wife Hedwig Hintze, also a historian who taught as well at the University of Berlin, was eager to keep him in contact with historians of younger generations. Yet even to those who had the opportunity of meeting him, Hintze was a remote figure.

There has been a further obstacle to the recognition of Hintze's achievement. Through his training under Droysen and Treitschke in Berlin in the 1880s, and through his concern with the history of Prussia, Hintze has frequently been stamped as a prominent member of the Prussian Historical School and accordingly disposed of as representative of a historical trend that distorted history by subjecting it to a political aim: to the justification of the Prussian rule over Germany. It is indeed true that for many years Hintze was a collaborator on one of the chief enterprises of the Prussian Historical School, the *Acta Borussica*; that the chair of Constitutional and Administrative History, to which he was appointed at the University of Berlin in 1902, placed upon him the duty of teaching Prussian history; and that he was the last officially appointed Royal Prussian Historiographer. But it is misleading to deduce from this that Hintze shared the views and interests which had inspired the founders of the Prussian Historical School. When Hintze became a collaborator on the *Acta Borussica* the work of the Prussian Historical School had veered away from its original course. Moreover, Hintze had too independent a mind to accept traditional patterns of thought. He admired Prussian institutions and took great pride in the empire which Bismarck had founded. Yet its structure was for Hintze neither final nor perfect; he insisted on the need for adjusting its constitution to new social developments. Hintze never felt any sympathy for the Weimar Republic, but nothing was farther from his mind than restoration of the Hohenzollern monarchy. And there was never any doubt about his categorical rejection of the Nazi movement. His wife emigrated and then committed suicide when the Germans invaded the Netherlands, where she had found refuge. Hintze was unable to leave Berlin, but when the Prussian Academy sent him a questionnaire about his racial descent he added in his reply the blistering remark that withdrawal from an institution which asked such questions was for him a matter of course; he cut himself off from everything that happened in Germany after 1933 and in 1940 died in Berlin in loneliness and isolation.

I

When Hintze embarked on his scholarly career German historical scholarship was at its pinnacle. It was a model for historical work in most other countries, and the Prussian Historical School, although not without critics, was an essential part of the German historical establishment. Although Hintze was in many respects a product of this school, he should not be identified with it. It is in any case erroneous to consider the Prussian Historical School as possessing a fixed, unified outlook, unchanging in its political and historical ideas, interests, and methods. The leading Prussian historians were highly individualistic, and the school itself underwent numerous major developments. The historians of the middle of the nineteenth century who founded the Prussian Historical School—Droysen, Duncker, Treitschke—regarded history as an ethical process: the nations or states that prevailed were those embodying the higher morality. For the founders of the Prussian School the establishment of Prussian rule over Germany was a demand of morality; it allowed the application of all the means suitable to the desired end. Consequently in their study of Prussia these historians of the mid-nineteenth century focused on foreign policy, wars, and power politics.

But after Bismarck had united Germany by "blood and iron," an epoch of a different character followed, that of "the internal organization of political and economic life which was accompanied by party struggles and conflicts of interest."[1] Accordingly, the concern of the younger generation of historians of the Prussian School shifted from foreign policy and power politics to internal developments, to the administrative and economic history of the Hohenzollern state. Whereas, the source publications which the older generation of Prussian historians had initiated—the *Urkunden und Aktenstücke zur Geschichte des Grossen Kurfürsten,* and the *Politische Correspondenz Friedrichs des Grossen*—were intended to throw light on the developments of the foreign policy of Brandenburg-Prussia, the *Acta Borussica,* begun in 1887, were to deal with internal administration of the Prussian state. The *Acta Borussica* owed their origin to a scholar of a younger generation, to the economist Gustav Schmoller; one of the first whom Schmoller invited to collaborate in this work was Hintze, then twenty-seven years old. When Hintze began working in Prussian history the study of administrative and economic issues had become an integral part of the problems with which the Prussian Historical School was concerned.

The shift in the direction of interest which took place in the Prussian Historical School was closely related to wider questions about the nature and aims of historical scholarship—questions that became a central point of discussion during the last decade of the nineteenth century. The triumphant emergence of historical scholarship during the nineteenth century and the pre-eminence of German historical scholarship were due to the theoretical and methodological principles which underlay the work of Leopold von Ranke, who had just died at age ninety-one, when Hintze began to work in the *Acta Borussica.*

The foundations of Ranke's historical thought were formed by his doctrine of ideas and his notion of uniqueness (individuality). Europe was for Ranke the center of history, and Europe's history was the history of the world; the intermingling and the clashes of the two racial groups that lived in Europe—the Latin and Teutonic peoples—had created a political system which consisted of a number of independent nations and states, each of them different from the other, each of them embodying an original and individual idea. The competition and the clashes among them had been the decisive factor in shaping the unique character of each of these nations and states. These assumptions suggest some of the characteristics of Ranke's historical writings and of the shape that historical scholarship took under his influence: emphasis on foreign policy as the factor determining the life of states; rejection of causality and laws in history and of the idea of progress because of the uniqueness of historical phenomena; limitation of the historian's task to description of the unique and individual so as to reveal the richness and variety of life.

Ranke's views of history reflected the romantic and idealistic trends which prevailed in the first half of the nineteenth century; they became far less compatible with the intellectual atmosphere that developed in the last quarter of the nineteenth century. The rapid and astounding advances in the natural sciences seemed to proclaim that only researches which proceeded from the observation of single cases to the formulation of valid generalizations could claim to be scientific. Areas of historical developments such as those in economics could be explained as determined by laws. And the experimental-scientific approach to psychology then arousing wide attention seemed to show the dependence of human nature on external conditions and stimuli, and to indicate the possibility of shaping and changing human nature by means of changes in surroundings. It was natural to ask whether in the face of these discoveries and developments the Rankean assumptions could be maintained, and whether it was not necessary to adjust work in history to the advances in other fields of knowledge.

In almost all European countries voices were heard that demanded a re-examination of the assumptions of historical scholarship and a reorientation of historical work. From England there came John Bury's emphatic statement that "history is a science"; Henri Berr in France began to advocate *histoire de synthèse*; and the New History of James Harvey Robinson and Charles Beard in the United States is a later offshoot of the same trend. The immediate impact of the historical revisionists in France, England, and other European countries was not great, although gradually and slowly they had some influence on transforming the subject matter and methods of historical scholarship.

In Germany it was different, and the dispute over methods which took place at the end of the nineteenth century and the outcome of the dispute proved to be nearly fatal for the development of German historical scholarship. The struggle was conducted with a passionate vehemence that frequently degenerated into personal abuse. It is called the *Lamprecht Streit,* because Karl Lamprecht, who had done important work in medieval economic history, was the chief protagonist in the struggle for a change in historical outlook and methods. He opened the fight in 1896 with an essay which bore the characteristic title "Old and New Trends in German Historical Scholarship," and the polemic which this treatise triggered and in which most of the better-known German historians became involved continued for several years. Lamprecht's attack on the German historical establishment ended in complete failure; and his few pupils became outsiders in the German historical profession. If German historians had always been inclined to concentrate on foreign affairs and political history, this attitude was now rigidified into a doctrine: The primary subject of history was political history. Although it was not immediately noticeable, from this time on German historical scholarship ceased to be the stimulating and leading influence it had been throughout the nineteenth century.

The categorical, contemptuous rebuff to demands for a new direction in historical scholarship may be ascribed to the fact that Lamprecht had presented these demands in the form of a pointed attack on Ranke. Lamprecht asked that Ranke's political history be replaced by a history of culture. He called Ranke's doctrine of ideas mystical; he suggested that the historian should aim at arriving at generalizations rather than merely at describing the unique, at analyzing the general intellectual atmosphere of a time rather than the thoughts or actions of individuals. And Lamprecht believed that psychology offered the possibility of revealing the evolution of the human mind, so that the study of the collective psychology in the various periods of the past would make possible discovery of a strictly logical and causal connection in the historical process. What was more, he suggested that Hegel was right, as against Ranke, in assuming the existence of a logical progress in history.

Had Lamprecht's demand for a new direction in history been

presented in a less polemical and aggressive form, it might have aroused less attention but might also have been more effective. Against the attempt to disparage the work of the revered master of their profession, the German historians closed ranks.

For an appreciation of Hintze's thought and work the issues of the *Lamprecht Streit* are important because they allow a glance at Hintze's historical views and position when his apprentice years were over and he was beginning his work as a university teacher (1895). Meinecke has told us how in debates among youthful colleagues Hintze always insisted: "There are laws in history"; and his work in the *Acta Borussica,* with its emphasis on economic issues, must have made him aware of the limitations in Ranke's historical concepts. Hintze's intervention in the Lamprecht struggle—according to Meinecke "the best that was said about Lamprecht"—was remarkably moderate. Hintze recognized the feasibility of going beyond Ranke and the desirability of broadening the ranges of history. "To use a geographic metaphor, we want to know not only the range and summits but also the base of the mountains, not merely the heights and depths of the surface but the entire continental mass." Hintze asserts that there is a natural tendency toward a regular pattern in the development of a nation. Nevertheless, in history general factors interact with individual factors, so that the forces which work and conflict in the historical process acquire an individual character. The unique is a basic inexplicable element in history and there is valid truth in the views which Ranke had so brilliantly set forth.

Hintze's attitude in the Lamprecht struggle reveals the problem—one might almost say dilemma—that remained crucial to his views on the theoretical questions in history. In fundamental respects Hintze adhered to the Rankean tradition. He was a political historian who placed great emphasis on foreign policy as a determining force; he regarded European history and the development of a European state system as the central event in the historical process; he upheld the role of the unique and individual as an important, unexplainable factor in history; and he did not deny that ideas influenced the course of history. But Hintze believed also in the existence of physical and psychological needs and necessities which evoked identical human reactions and whose fulfillment required a basically identical institutional structure. The action of the individual took place within a structural pattern that had its own laws. Analysis of the interaction between the necessarily evolving general pattern and the influence of individual factors and actions on shaping its particular character became the task of the historian. This task was not—or not primarily—attainment of new insights in the richness and variety of life, but improvement of the possibilities for correct action in the present by analyzing the various factors and forces that had given the present its particular character and were working in it.

II

Although this problem—the relation of individual factors and forces to general patterns of behavior and action—is at the core of all of Hintze's historical studies and theoretical reflections, its pursuit takes different forms in the course of his life. Three periods can be clearly distinguished in his intellectual production.

The first is identical with that of his active participation in the work of the *Acta Borussica* from 1888 to 1910; naturally, the research and the scholarly activities of this period were concerned with the history of Brandenburg and Prussia, and the main scholarly achievements of these years were the book-length introductions to the documentary volumes he edited for the *Acta Borussica:* on the Prussian silk industry (1892) and on the Prussian bureaucratic structure at the time of the accession of Frederick the Great (1901). In connection with the second work, Hintze also published briefer studies on the administration of Brandenburg and Prussia in the time of the Elector Joachim II and that of the first king.[2]

Although clearly an immense amount of labor, care, and thought had gone into the explanation of a rather ill-defined and rudimentary administrative structure, Hintze's studies on these subjects remained somewhat static. They appeared to be the detailed presentation of a table of organization rather than a demonstration of the effects of bureaucratic action on social life. Yet, by describing in detail what government did and could do, and by indicating to what extent its actions were dependent on and limited by communications, the structure of agriculture and trade, and the availability of human resources, Hintze revealed the limits of monarchical power. In contrast to the traditional view of the "Great Hohenzollern" as creators of a new society and a new state, Hintze showed that the power which the monarchs exerted was limited by institutions created and shaped by the needs inherent in every society. The bureaucracy was the instrument of the rulers, but an instrument that followed its own rules. Only in relation to the impact that a ruler exerted on the functioning of the existing institutions was it possible to judge whether and to what extent the individual Hohenzollern prince was an innovator or reformer. However, Hintze was less interested in evaluating the achievements of the individual Hohenzollern than in readjusting the relation between change and continuity. "Below the upheavals in the court circles the basic political and social institutions preserve their coherence and advance in slow transformation; in this historical continuity becomes visible."[3] Hintze provided a demonstration of his views on the decisive importance of institutional continuity in his study "Prussian Reform Movements before 1806." The study was revolutionary in that it broke with the accepted historical picture in which all light was focused on the work of the Prussian reformers and no judgement harsh enough could be found for the actions and ideas of the statesmen of the preceding period. Admittedly, Hintze's study was influenced by Tocqueville, who had demonstrated that the French Revolution continued and completed the work of the *Ancien régime;* but such a thesis had never been put forward in Prussian history. Hintze's essay has exerted great influence on all later work in this field.

Next to the issue of the relation between individual initiative and institutional continuity there was another problem Hintze probed thoroughly during this first period of his scholarly career: the question of the interconnection existing among all social activities and their subordination to one central political purpose. In his introduction to the volume on administration in the *Acta Borussica,* Hintze wrote that "the cultural and welfare programs of the state yield to the requirements of power politics." Hintze did pioneering work in the economic—particularly industrial—activities in eighteenth-century Prussia, and was clearly deeply interested in these aspects of history. But it is doubtful whether he would have worked along these lines if the economic policy of the government had not been a crucial factor in making possible the maintenance of a large army and the rise of Prussia to a Great Power.

As we mentioned before, there was no doubt in Hintze's mind as to the validity of Ranke's thesis of the primacy of foreign policy, but Hintze modified and broadened it. If Ranke had meant that considerations of foreign policy must take precedence over all other political considerations and that other political interests and aims should be tackled only when and after the external security of the state was guaranteed, Hintze extended the thesis by maintaining that the government ought to aim at orienting all activities in the state—most of all, economic activities, but also education—toward strengthening the state against outside powers; concretely, the purpose toward which all governmental activities were to be directed was the maintenance of a strong military posture.

The first studies in which Hintze went beyond the Prussian sphere were devoted to an examination of the general validity and applicability of this thesis. In the essay "Military Organization and the Organization of the State" he emphasized the role which the "pushing and pressing" of states against each other had in forcing each state to seek an appropriate military organization and consequently in shaping the state's internal structure. In the essay "The Formation of States and Constitutional Development" Hintze tried to demonstrate the existence of a relation between the size of a state, its available means of organization, the character of its religion, the extent of its political integration, and its constitutional form. Hintze asserted that it should be possible to establish a typology of constitutional forms of which constitutions existing in the present or in the past were individually modified embodiments; and he suggested also that the particular form which the constitutional life of a state took was a modification of a general pattern underlying all constitutional development.

With these studies Hintze went far beyond his original interest in Prussian history and entered the broader field of general European history; the problems he raised in these articles occupied him throughout his life and became the center of his attention in the second period of his activity—after he had left the *Acta Borussica*.

This might be the place to comment on the influence of Hintze's work in Prussian history on the development of his theoretical ideas. It was very fruitful because it made him aware of the impact that administration had on the general course of politics, not only in Prussia but also in all of European history. But Hintze's point of departure—Prussian history—also played a role in causing what might be regarded as limitations and weaknesses in his approach.

Prussia was for him a model, particularly a model of the absolutist state, which he regarded as a pre-formation of the modern state. Hintze therefore never asked whether the strict regimentation in eighteenth-century Prussia, particularly the organization of economic life according to the will and aim of the absolutist monarch, had its reason in the fact that the nations and states of central and eastern Europe were underdeveloped in comparison to the economically more advanced societies of western Europe. Hintze's understanding of French and English history, although far-reaching and penetrating, had its blind spots. He subordinated economics to politics; in the relation between the state and its economic forces he viewed the government as the active partner which provided impetus and direction.

Hintze did not want to admit that the world of economic life had its own particular driving force and its own gravity. He was not fully aware of the complexity of the relations between the state and economic forces. This was not a serious drawback, insofar as early modern European history was concerned; and his studies of this period are his masterpieces. It is also not surprising that after the First World War he followed developments in Russia and Italy with an interest in which comprehension and criticism were finely balanced.[4] But of the development of democratic governments in the nineteenth century he had less understanding; and although all his writings show that economic developments were for him an essential part of history, we look in vain in his writings for an investigation of the rise of an industrial enterprise or a study of the development of labor. Such phenomena interested him only insofar as they came within the compass of political or governmental action. He looked upon social life from the viewpoint of government; he was above all a political historian. And in his writings up to

1920, traces may be found of a mystical belief in the state as a higher entity with a life of its own.

Hintze's notions appear highly idiosyncratic in our time, when social historians give concentrated attention to conditions and attitudes existing and developing beneath and outside the political sphere. But because there is some danger that modern social studies may come to consist of collections of factual material without meaningful results or conclusions, Hintze's approach—although perhaps overestimating what political action and governmental direction can achieve—has the merit of suggesting that studies of isolated phenomena must be complemented by investigations that show political and social life as an interconnected whole. Even if Hintze's views are no longer fully acceptable, they have value as a corrective.

III

The second period of Hintze's scholarly work begins around 1910 with his withdrawal from active participation in the *Acta Borussica,* and extended over the next ten years. The enormous amount of archival research which collaboration in the *Acta Borussica* had required had put a severe strain on his eyes from which they never fully recovered. But new, widened historical concerns rather than physical necessity provided the spur for a change in the direction of his work.

Hintze had become primarily interested in pursuing the course on which he had embarked in his essays "Military Organization and the Organization of the State" and "The Formation of States": the investigation of problems related to administration and constitutional affairs within the framework of general European history. Indeed, in 1908 and 1910 he published two articles—"The Origins of the Modern Ministerial System" and "The Commissary and His Significance in General Administrative History"—which may be regarded as single chapters in a history of European administration. These essays are superb pieces in raising questions that had never been asked before, in assembling and controlling an almost unending mass of source material, and in focusing this material on the solution of a specific problem.

According to Hintze these are studies of a comparative nature. But they are comparative history only in a limited sense.

The essays deal with developments in different European countries which have a common root, and Hintze demonstrates the presence of such common root by examining the situation existing before the formation of different national entities in Europe. Comparisons serve to show the existence of a common element behind the institutional variations which developed in the course of time. Comparisons are illustrations; they do not form the point of departure for raising questions or indicating problems that need investigation. Hintze assumed that the situation which led to the development of an administrative structure was identical in almost all Latin-Teutonic peoples. From the same beginnings they all developed a centralized bureaucracy, and each government was composed of ministers in charge of departments with separate functions. The means, however, by which these institutional developments came about and the extent of power which bureaucracy and ministers possessed depended on circumstances in which external factors—particularly issues of security and actions of individuals—played their role. Thus, although fundamental needs were identical, led to similar patterns of development, and produced institutions resembling each other, the bureaucratic structure and the ministerial system of each European country had its peculiar aspects and features and each was a unique formation. The difference between the English system of government and those of the Continental countries was among the most striking examples of a deviation from a common pattern.

In these articles Hintze demonstrated also that changes in the methods of government are not purely nor even primarily the result of necessary technical changes or improvements, but are produced by shifts in the distribution of power within the state and by the need for adjustment to new external threats and new social forces. In this way administrative history becomes not only a mirror but also an integral part of European history, as well as a means by which the various stages of its development can be more sharply delineated. These two studies are administrative history in a new key; and it must be added that few, if any, works of similar scope and importance have been done in this field since then.

Hintze's intention of concentrating his future efforts on a "constitutional and administrative history of the modern European states" was clearly stated in his response to the address with which he had been welcomed to membership in the Prussian Academy in 1914. One might find this same intention of occupying himself with a broader area in the fact that in 1909, in four small volumes, he brought out a collection of his studies and essays mostly concerned with Prussian history, so that, taken together, they could be considered as a summary and *finis* of his works and views on Prussian history.

Although in the life of a writer or scholar different periods of activity may be distinguished, they can never be sharply separated; either because of previously entered commitments, or because of the intellectual investment he has made, he will keep up his contacts with his previous interests. In the decade following his departure from the *Acta Borussica,* Hintze continued to publish a considerable number of articles on Prussian history. Two of them deserve particular attention because they reveal his theoretical views and attitudes on the problem of Prussia. In the article "Preussens Entwicklung zum Rechtsstaat," Hintze criticizes the general view that an independent judicial power or political guarantees were sufficient to establish the rule of law in a political body; he considered the establishment of a code of administrative procedures as crucial. Clearly this study is not only an assertion of the importance of administrative issues for history and politics but also a defense of Prussia, which, though it might have lacked some of the usual features providing safety against authoritarianism, possessed a thoroughly organized and strictly regulated administrative structure.

The other article—"The Hohenzollern and the Nobility"—is of a more critical nature. Hintze assails the view that Prussian tradition demanded the maintenance of a dominating influence of the East Elbian nobility. Although he does not deny that during a certain period the cooperation of monarch and nobility was crucial in establishing Prussia as a Great Power, he emphasizes the tensions and conflicts which originally characterized the relations between the Hohenzollern and the nobility, and he maintains that with the rise of a new industrial society the monopoly of power by the nobility could no longer be justified.

Some of Hintze's articles on Prussian subjects during these years may have been results of research undertaken in the course of his work in the *Acta Borussica*; others may have been by-products of the book *Die Hohenzollern und ihr Werk,* on which he worked in these years and which appeared in 1915. The article "The Hohenzollern and the Nobility" in particular was a short résumé of the basic views which he had explained in the larger work, which might be regarded as the last but also the best history of Prussia written by a member of the Prussian Historical School. Yet one might question, whether, during this period, when his interests had gone beyond the borders of Prussia, Hintze would have undertaken the task of writing a comprehensive history of Prussia had it not been his duty as Royal Prussian Historiographer to celebrate the five-hundredth anniversary of Hohenzollern rule in Brandenburg-Prussia.

Yet there was a compelling reason why it was difficult, if not impossible, for Hintze to lay aside the problems of Prussian and German history: the increasingly critical period into which German politics had entered after 1905—internally, the steady growth of the Social Democratic Party, and externally, the formation of the Entente Cordiale and the Triple Entente. Hintze's basic political attitude was not different from that of most professors at Prussian universities. They considered themselves influential civil servants who expected from the government ample support in all that concerned the conditions of their work. But they also felt it their duty to render loyal service to the monarch. They gave advice to the government; if they recommended reforms their intention was to make only the necessary adjustments to changed circumstances in order to maintain the existing system. To the outside world Prussian professors or academicians were defenders of the status quo, not its critics.

It was almost a matter of course that Hintze would write frequently on the political issues of his time and that he would take his stand on the side of the government. It must be admitted that he used his historical expertise to become a committed and persuasive advocate of the main tenets of the government in domestic and foreign policy. Hintze rejected parliamentarism in favor of the existing half-constitutional, half-authoritarian régime, and advocated the building of a navy that would permit Germany to enter upon *Weltpolitik* and become a world power.

For the Hintze of this period Prussia's importance reached beyond a particular period of history. It was not only the model of an absolutist state; its structure enjoyed features that every healthy modern state ought to possess.

Maintenance of the privileged position which the nobility possessed in eighteenth-century Prussia was no longer justifiable. In the same manner that the Hohenzollern monarchs had fought and tamed the nobility and taught them to become valuable servants of the kings of Prussia, monarchy and civil service now had the function and the duty to grant bourgeoisie and workers the position due to them and to establish the right balance among the various groups of society. Monarchy and civil service stood above parties and classes, and could and should act as arbiters among them. As Hintze explained in the article "Das Monarchische Prinzip und die konstitutionelle Verfassung" (1911), the guiding and directing position of monarch and civil service had been brought about because in Prussia "in the age of absolutism the state has almost entirely absorbed society with its economic interests".[5] The reasons for the maintenance of a strong authoritarian system in Prussia-Germany were historical, which meant that the reasons for the rise of parliamentarism were historical also; thus parliamentarism should not be assumed to be a progressive step above monarchical constitutionalism. In Hintze's view it was a complex concatenation of events which resulted in the establishment of a parliamentary republic in France; under other circumstances France could have become a constitutional monarchy like Prussia. In any case, "the monarchical principle has become so intertwined with the entire political structure in Prussia and Germany that, without the complete transformation that only a revolution could bring about, it cannot be replaced by the principle of parliamentary government."[6]

As always with Hintze, however, the explanation of an individual phenomenon was complemented by a general one; and the genetic explanation was supplemented by a functional one. The existence of a competitive European state system in which the various powers "push and press" against each other required—at least on the European continent—a political organization in which military needs are of primary inportance. The constitutional monarchy in Prussia-Germany epitomized this requirement: "The most essential reason for our monarchical constitutional system of government is the fact that we are surrounded by the greatest military powers of the Continent and that an enormous military-political pressure from the outside weighs upon our long frontiers which nature has given no protection,"[7] wrote Hintze in his essay "Machtpolitik und Regierungsverfassung" (1913).

These notions are a direct—and almost crude—application of the idea of the primacy of foreign policy. The same idea in a somewhat modified form made Hintze a protagonist of German *Weltpolitik*. If in previous centuries the "pushing and pressing" that controlled the formation of states and their internal life had been limited to Europe, rivalries and tensions now began to extend over the entire globe; any state that remained content with what it had in Europe would sink to the level of a second-rank power; if a state wanted to remain a Great Power it would have to take part in this race for overseas possessions.

In the essay "Imperialismus und Welt-Politik" (1907), Hintze distinguished twentieth-century imperialism from the imperialism of earlier times which aimed at establishment of one empire comprising the entire known world. The new imperialism of the twentieth century, according to Hintze, is a historical necessity, a step forward in the process of history. "The movement of imperialism appears to introduce a new epoch in the political balance of power. The old European system of states is to be replaced by a new world-system of states; the powers begin to arrange themselves on this new broadened base and to delimit among each other their spheres of interest."[8]

Hintze realized that overseas expansion required the creation of a strong German navy, and that a particular purpose of naval construction would be to check British power. To Hintze, Great Britain was the great obstacle to the establishment of a world-state system and a global balance of power; Great Britain sought to maintain an empire of the old style—one that exerted domination or at least control over the entire world. Thus, Britain's traditional policy was in opposition to what Hintze regarded as the desirable feature of world politics: "Not *one* world empire is the aim of modern imperialism, but a number of world empires, coexisting or equally independent, and in a balance of power similar to that which existed in the old European system of states."[9] When the First World War began, Hintze conceived of it chiefly as a struggle "to destroy the pre-

55

dominance of England." "The requisite of a true balance of power in the world-state system at which we aim is England's abandoning her claim to domination of the seas."[10] In Hintze's mind Germany pursued in the First World War the just aim of preventing England from establishing its rule over the world.

In all Hintze's political discussions the factors of national security and military strength played a prominent role; one is even tempted to say that his misjudgements reflect the influence which military considerations exerted in his historical and political thought; Prussian military thinking inclined to focus on land warfare and tended to underestimate or overlook the problems that arose when their plans extended beyond the Continent. Despite shrill and repellent notes, however, his political views should not be judged particularly nationalistic or militaristic; in their main political content they are those of the professional and social group to which he belonged. It might even be said that, in contrast to the emotional chauvinism that many of his colleagues displayed, Hintze always argued coolly and rationally, and he never disparaged the historical achievements of other nations, nor did he deny their right to exist. It is important, however, to be aware that in this period of his scholarly and academic activity when Hintze began to work in a wider scholarly field, he still remained firmly tied to the problems, the traditions, and also the prejudices of the world in which he lived, that of imperial Germany; the continued existence of this bond indicates the extent of the reorientation which the collapse of this world made necessary for him.

IV

In Hintze's case the shock of defeat and revolution in Germany in 1918–1919 was aggravated by its impact on his scholarly concerns and tenets. Prussia, although it continued to exist, had lost all the features that had made it in Hintze's eyes a unique formation and in many respects a model. The outcome of the war demonstrated that the authoritarianism of a constitutional monarchy did not guarantee superior military order or strength. Nor did a constitutional monarchy, in contrast to what Hintze had believed and written, appear to be more than a transitional stage on the road to parliamentary democracy. In foreign affairs Germany's career as a world power had been terminated before it had really begun, and the influence and strength that non-European powers like the United States and Japan had acquired undermined Hintze's thesis that the European state system would be succeeded by a world-state system in which, in a widened theater, the same European powers that in the past had been the driving forces in world history would continue to have the dominating role.

The questions which the course of political events necessarily raised for Hintze's historical thinking were intensified by events in his personal life. He was pursued by illness, his eyesight further deteriorated, and he gave up his professorship at the University of Berlin, making use of his right to early retirement. These circumstances determined the form and character which his scholarly work took in the last period of his life, after his retirement from the university in 1920.

Hintze's weak eyesight made it impossible for him to undertake archival research, and he had to be economical in his reading. There was little chance of his completing the large work on European administrative and constitutional history which he had projected before the war; instead he expressed his ideas in a number of lengthy essays. One can observe that most of the material on which these essays were based—whether sources or monographic literature—had been published before or during the First World War; it was then that he had studied this material. Even the essay "Calvinism and Raison d'Etat in Early Seventeenth-Century Brandenburg" of 1931, which uses archival material, is written on the basis of excerpts made in earlier years in the context of his work in the *Acta Borussica*. He returned to these notes because he had developed a special interest in the influence of Calvinism, as a result of an intensive study of the writings of Max Weber in the 1920s, and he wanted to investigate Weber's thesis in a concrete case. This procedure—examination of the historical validity of modern theories on the basis of material collected in former years—is characteristic of Hintze's working methods in this last period.

His reading focused on important contemporary works of sociological and historical theory. His reviews of the works of Sombart, Troeltsch, and Franz Oppenheimer were full-length essays. But he wrote also extended criticisms of Max Scheler and Hans Kelsen, and the various reviews in which he discussed

Max Weber's writings and studies on Weber show the importance he attributed to him. It is evident that in this last period of Hintze's scholarly activity Max Weber was the dominant intellectual figure with whose thought he felt he ought to come to terms. Theoretical interests, as we have noticed, had always been strong in Hintze, and the physical difficulties under which he labored in later years made work along such lines particularly appropriate. His main interest became the problems of historical conceptualization and the relation between history and sociology. Nevertheless, his writings were never purely theoretical; they were saturated with facts. Only by means of facts was it possible to demonstrate the contribution that a clear conceptual system could make toward a better understanding of the past or to test the correctness and applicability of theories—whether those of others or Hintze's own. It was a fortunate coincidence that for such purposes extended research in source materials was hardly needed. Hintze re-examined—it might be more appropriate to say, he rethought—the developments that had been the object of his research in previous years in the light of recent historical and sociological theories. The essays in which he expressed his views were published in scholarly periodicals like the *Historische Zeitschrift* or among the reports of the Prussian Academy; and although they reached only a restricted audience, they made a great impression on those who read them and were appreciated as important attempts to invigorate the study of history.

Hintze's essays of this period may be divided into two groups: one is formed by studies of primarily theoretical content; the other consists of studies in which Hintze applies these theoretical insights to a reconstruction of important stages in the historical process. To the second group belong the articles "Calvinism and Raison d'Etat," "Wesen und Verbreitung des Feudalismus," "Typologie der ständischen Verfassungen des Abendlandes," and the extended essay "The Preconditions of Representative Government in the Context of World History," which might be regarded as a summary and conclusion of the preceding studies on feudalism and on the system of Estates.

In many respects these studies continue the work which Hintze had done or planned in earlier years. Although they are concerned with the history of constitutional forms, Hintze placed them in close connection with the development of an administrative apparatus and, as in the studies "The Commissary" and "The Origins of the Modern Ministerial System," he demonstrated that the constitutional developments of the various European nations, as much as they might vary in details, originate from a common root and follow a similar pattern. But these articles show also significant modifications and changes in Hintze's views. He now considered the most striking feature in European constitutional history to be the development of representative government, which found its most recent and modern form of expression in parliamentarism. Although on various occasions Hintze suggested that parliamentarism might not be the last and final step in constitutional development, he now accepted the notion that it represented a later and higher stage than the constitutional monarchy or other forms of government; explanation of the development toward parliamentarism became his central concern.

An interesting illustration of a modification in Hintze's views is the fact that he now took a different, much more positive view toward British political developments in the eighteenth century. A more important indication is the change in his conception of the state, which he conceived no longer as an institution with a life of its own existing independently and above social groups; it had become a mere apparatus, changing in its functions and purposes according to external circumstances and alterations in the distribution of power. This re-evaluation of the role of the state was prerequisite for the most important scholarly contribution made by these essays: the description of the Estates system as a form of government, as a "state" that provided the link between feudalism and representative government.

These essays show also how Hintze modified and refined his notion of the comparative method. He continued to examine and to explain why, out of common roots and similar patterns of development, institutional organizations of an individually distinctive character arose. But if, despite differences in particular aspects, the system of representative government was common to all European states, it was also a particularly European phenomenon. In order to prove and to explain this thesis, Hintze went beyond the frontiers of Europe and compared the development of European civilization with that of other civilizations. In his opinion the distinctive feature of European civilization was the separation between secular and spiritual power which stood in the way of the rise of an all-powerful despotism extending over the entire civilization. In contrast to the unified political organization characteristic of most other civilizations, this separation of ecclesiastical and political power in Europe allowed and promoted the formation of a number of different states—of a European state system. Since Europe was a relatively small geographical area, the various European states "pushed and pressed" against each other, and this led to a "consolidation and rationalization of state operations";[11] that explains the particular role of European civilization in the history of the world.

Hintze uses here the comparative method "to give a greater precision to the pecularity of a phenomenon."[12] At another place—in his discussion of the sociological views of Franz Oppenheimer—he expresses the same idea although in a somewhat different context: "You can compare in order to find something general that underlies the things that are compared, and you can compare in order to grasp more clearly the singularity (*Individualität*) of the thing that is compared, and to distinguish it from the others. The sociologist does the former; the historian, the latter."[13] It should be added that in Hintze's eyes the problem of the relation between history and sociology was more complex than this brilliant, if somewhat pat, formulation would suggest; he returns to this problem again and again in his essays of a theoretical character.

Hintze's theoretical essays are important in a twofold way: as disclosing the basis of his insights on the course of European constitutional history, and as contributing to the discussion of problems with which the historical thinking of our time is still concerned.

If these essays are read together they seem to contain a strange contradiction. Hintze admires Sombart for conceiving of capitalism as a "historical entity of singular nature" (*Historisches Individuum*); and yet has great reservations about the manner in which Troeltsch places the notion of "individuality" in the center of historicist thought.[14] What this apparent contradiction shows is that Hintze is still trying to reconcile the Rankean historiographical tradition with the less idealistic attitude which characterizes the scholarship of the twentieth century. The chief difficulty seems to him the emphasis that traditional history places on historic totalities possessing an original and unique character; they are regarded to be "individualities" and, as such considered to have a value of their own. Because of this connection between individuality and value the historian is inclined to be satisfied with an aestheticizing description of the appearance of the original and unique in history. For Hintze, who is interested in social groups or institutions rather than in persons, the uniqueness of a historical entity, its "individuality," is constituted by the fact of its being different from something else. Briefly, Hintze tries to divest Rankean ideas of their transcendental connotations.

The same tendency may be found in Hintze's observations on the role of ideas in history or in his criticisms of the use of notions of evolution by historians. Hintze came to eschew the belief that ideas are a superstructure over material conditions (this is an instance of an allusion to Marxist theories in Hintze's work: he sometimes refers to particular aspects of Marxist thought but never discusses them systematically). To Hintze ideas were important. Yet he does not accept the Rankean theory that ideas have a life of their own and possess the force to determine the character of an age and the course of its events. For Hintze ideas become a historically effective force only if they are in combination with concrete interests, with a drive for greater power or material advantage.

Hintze's objections to the use of evolution by the historian are of a similar kind; he fears that this notion can seduce the historian into assuming that historical institutions grow according to an innate tendency and that their evolution is metaphysically determined, beyond human control. For Hintze the determinants of historical development are human needs and desires that stimulate human action; these the historian must describe, explain, and understand. Movement in history can lead upward and downward; progress cannot be excluded, but it cannot be taken for granted. In all the essays of his last period Hintze's conception of history is strictly pragmatist. He fights on two fronts: against defenders of Rankean idealism he might take a strictly pragmatist line; against positivists he might defend the value of Rankean notions. His aim is to transform the traditional Rankean concepts in order to make them compatible with a pragmatist view of history. The historian, he believes, can attain this end by extended use of a comparative method and a stricter system of historical conceptualization.

If the uniqueness of a historical event or force, its "individuality," is not to be grasped intuitively but has to be demonstrated pragmatically, unavoidably comparison then becomes the appropriate method for the establishment of the particular nature of a historical entity. But comparison between two or among several phenomena requires some general element common to all of them—that is, a system of concepts into which the various phenomena of historical life can be fitted. In his search for a firmer conceptual base of historical work Hintze was decisively influenced by Max Weber's "ideal types" (*Idealtypen*),[15] but he did not consider them entirely satisfactory for the purposes of the historian. It was not enough to form a wide-meshed system of logical concepts into which the material of history could be organized. Historical events and entities were peculiar modifications of, and deviations from, a general pattern that itself was formed by history and historically conditioned. The concepts which the historian needed must partake of both the general and the particular, because if "they were only concrete and individual they would never lead to insights of wider significance, and it they were only abstract and general they would never have applicability to particular situations or circumstances." "From the material which the experience of political observation and historical study places at our disposal we select according to our judgment—and that means not without a certain arbitrariness—characteristic features, reduce them to their essential forms, and combine then in a creative mental act to a lively totality"; by means of such constructs "we can orient ourselves amid the disturbing abundance of phenomena and possess a criterion for scientific judgement."[16] The "ideal types" that historians could usefully employ were "visual abstractions."[17]

Hintze indicates in these sentences that the formation of such concepts presupposes a certain amount of "historical intuition"; despite his pragmatic and even rational approach, he had no reservations about trusting historical intuition. We might see a weakness in this reliance on intuition. It was deeply rooted in an approach to historical theory that began with Droysen and had been elaborated by Wilhelm Dilthey. Clearly this is an issue on which further work is required, but it is clear also that Hintze touches upon a point which is crucial for the distinction between sociology and history when he demands for historical works concepts which lie between the abstract and the concrete and are nourished by the material of history. Hintze could refer to the two articles of this period which we discussed before as proof of the fruitfulness of historical intuition in creating concepts that serve to illuminate the entire process of European history.

V

What is the contribution of Hintze's work to the present-day discussion on the nature and function of history? To a large extent Hintze's views are the result of personal experiences. He experienced the collapse of the Bismarckian Reich whose foundation must have been the great event of his boyhood, experienced, too, the victory of the Western democracies, the emergence of the United States and Japan. Clearly these events are reflected in the revisions and modifications that his views on the nature of the state, on the development of representative government, and on the importance of Europe underwent in the 1920s. He could gauge the importance of these events with a cool objectivity, free from traditional prejudices, because he was now no longer a participant but merely an observer of the political and academic scene.

But the 1920s, the years after the First World War, represent also the beginning of an important new chapter in historiography, and Hintze's work and views have to be seen in relation to this development. The struggle of political versus social and cultural history which had been a crucial event in the early years of Hintze's scholarly career was now renewed; but in the changed circumstances of the postwar situation, the result was different. Social and cultural historians began to dominate the scene. Even in Germany, where the political historians had triumphed and reigned more completely than in any other country, the intellectual atmosphere changed, although the period of greater intellectual openness was brief and succumbed soon to the suffocating pressure of the Nazi regime. There can be no doubt that the altered intellectual climate provided an added stimulus to Hintze's thinking and writing in his later years. Among the recognized historians in Germany he was one of the very few who had manifested constantly an interest in a beneficent relation between history and the social sciences. Because in Germany the change to new forms of history and new methods represented a radical departure, the interest in historical theory and in finding a firm theoretical foundation for the new approach was particularly strong.

Thus, Hintze's writings belong to the debate on the relation between history and the social sciences that started in the 1920s and has been going on since then. What does his work contribute to these discussions? There is no doubt that his ideas on these questions are still stimulating and deserve our attention. Despite his interest in sociology and related fields, the importance of history remained for him indisputable; he placed great value on the study of the past. Not only the content of our thinking but also the forms of social life and the character of our institutions are patterned by events of the past; the shape that they have or take cannot be deduced from scientific investigations establishing generalizations about human behavior, about the functional character of organizations and institutions, about psychological structure, and about the order of economic values. All these phenomena are subject to the impact of external forces, to the accidents of history; and they continue to exist and work in history in a modified form which they have received in these clashes with historical accidents. The past cannot be removed from the world in which man lives; it has entered into man's thought, into the institutions which surround him or which he creates, and into the manner in which he looks upon the world.

The historical dimension forms an integral part of human life and action. But recognition of the existence and different entities determined in their formation by the vagaries of past events did not induce Hintze to conclude that the historian ought to focus primarily or exclusively on the particular and individual factors and forces of historical phenomena; his attention ought to be directed to the interaction between the patterns of general development and the modifications they undergo through the accidents of history. The historian must find a middle way between history as application of general laws and history as demonstration of the individuality and variety of life. This involves more, however, than acquaintance with the work in the field of social sciences which of course Hintze regarded as quite as necessary for the historian as is knowledge of history for the social scientist. It meant that the generalizing approach ought to be built into the work of the historian. Hintze suggested the creation of a conceptual framework which would bridge the gap between the abstractness of generalization and the concreteness of aesthetic description. This idea still seems valid and deserves further exploration. By means of strict concern with his conceptual apparatus the historian might be able to erect a framework which overcomes the division of history into work that analyzes long-range trends and work that focuses on factual description of events—and which again makes universal history possible.

It is true, of course, that historians will be judged according to their discoveries about the past as set down in their writings, rather than according to their theories. And in fact, as we have indicated, Hintze has written some of the most important and illuminating historical essays of the twentieth century. But their relation to his theory is significant. Historians frequently shy away from theory and leave it to philosophers who are remote from the practice of historical work; or they consider theory as a place for giving vent to private confessions of personal philosophy. It is one of the most impressive features of Hintze's work that it shows that when theory and practice go hand in hand they support and fructify each other.

3. Friedrich Meinecke

With the publication of an English translation of Friedrich Meinecke's *Historism* in 1972,[1] the three works that established his reputation as a master historian—*Cosmopolitanism and the National State*,[2] *Idea of Reason of State in Modern History*,[3] and *Historism*—became available to the English-speaking world. This may be justification enough to inquire about the importance of Meinecke's historical writings for us today. Such an investigation has additional significance, however, because of a change in the evaluation of Meinecke's work which has taken place in his own country, in Germany.[4] In the first three decades of the twentieth century, until the rise of National Socialism, Meinecke was Germany's leading historian; after the Second World War he was almost the only surviving representative of Germany's great academic past and one of the very few whose work and voice helped to join present and future with the

---

This essay is published here for the first time. Some sections appeared on pp. vii-xiii of my introduction to the English translation of *Cosmopolitanism and the National State* (copyright 1970 Princeton University Press, reprinted by permission) and other sections on pp. 61–64 of my review of the English translation of Meinecke's *Historism*, published in *History and Theory*, 13 (copyright 1974 Wesleyan University Press, reprinted by permission). Although there have been many treatments of Meinecke's political notions and his ideas on the theory and philosophy of history, a study focusing on his chief historical books seems to me to be lacking.

better traditions of German scholarship. But when the universities came to life again after the Second World War, the younger generation of historians—whatever their personal attitude toward Meinecke was—almost contemptuously turned away from the history of ideas, of which Meinecke had been the most brilliant practitioner, because they felt that approach to history avoided the hard political issues which historians ought to confront. One is tempted to say that they turned with an almost exaggerated enthusiasm in the opposite direction—toward social history and analysis of the relationships between economics and politics. Because of the skeptical and negative attitude of many German historians toward Meinecke's work, I include in this discussion of Meinecke's significance for historiography the question of the extent to which his work is an expression and a reflection of the political weaknesses and deficiencies of German academic society, or even beyond that, of the German bourgeoisie.

I

There was always a close connection between the books that Meinecke wrote and the political situation that existed at the time of their composition. This is particularly evident in his first major work, *Cosmopolitanism and the National State,* for which he was immediately recognized as Germany's leading historian.

Meinecke composed this book in the middle of his life.[5] Born in 1862, he was forty-five years old when it was published. Until the publication of *Cosmopolitanism and the National State* his career had been the usual one of a German academic. Like many other German professors in the nineteenth century, he came from a family of Prussian civil servants and Protestant ministers. Meinecke was perhaps closer to the spirit of the first half of the nineteenth century than many of his contemporaries because he grew up in a small, isolated town of the Mark Brandenburg. In his advanced age he still remembered the sounding of the post horn when the daily mail coach passed the house of his parents. The atmosphere of his father's house was closer to an earlier time in its way of thinking and living as well. It was permeated by a pietistic and conservative spirit. At the beginning Meinecke's scholarly career proceeded along entirely traditional lines. His first publications were concerned with themes of Prussian history and his first large work was a biography of General Hermann von Boyen, one of the reform-minded military heroes in Prussia's fight against Napoleon. After a long period of waiting for academic advancement, in which Meinecke earned his living as an archivist, the publication of the Boyen biography led to his appointment as professor of modern history in Strasbourg in 1901. Five years later, unwillingly but feeling unappreciated by the officials in charge of Strasbourg University, he accepted a chair at the University in Freiburg. Two years later *Cosmopolitanism and the National State* was published.

With the appearance of this book the external circumstances of Meinecke's life and, to a certain extent, the nature of his historical concerns changed. After he had declined various offers of professorships, he accepted in 1914 the most prestigious chair of history in Germany, that at the University of Berlin. Moreover, Meinecke became a figure in political life. In the last years of the Empire he became an advocate of reform, particularly of an electoral reform in Prussia which would have broken the hold of the Junkers over German policy. All these developments originated from the publication of *Cosmopolitanism and the National State* insofar as with the publication of this work Meinecke had emerged as a person of a well-defined intellectual profile.

At first, today's reader may not get the impression that the political assumptions and concepts of this book are different from those notions we consider typical of the political ideas of the first decade of the twentieth century. The main theme of the book is intended to show that when the ideas of nationality and nationalism began to take hold in Germany they were imbedded in a universalistic framework; it is almost shocking to discover that Meinecke regarded the development from universalism and cosmopolitanism to nationalism as clear, unquestioned progress. The process which he describes and on which he comments with approval is that of the gradual renunciation of all commitments to cosmopolitan values until at the end the sovereign national state is recognized as the supreme value and final goal of history. According to Meinecke this is a process which possesses "necessity, greatness, and ethical dignity." This glorification of nationalism and of the national state—dangerous and even repulsive as it might appear to us—was in

accord with the political climate of the years before the First
World War. These were the convictions and values of the time,
and Meinecke shared them to the fullest. He went far in accepting the consequences of this worship of the national state.
Because he regarded the state as an independent entity, he
believed that a state had to fight against others to maintain itself. "Struggle, care, and conflict are the destiny of the genuine
national state, not peace and calm." Even the Wilhelminian feeling of German superiority is noticeable in this book. But, of
course, there are few products of this time that are not infected
by the Jingoistic climate of the period.

It is more remarkable that conventional political attitudes can
also be observed in Meinecke's remarks on German domestic
and constitutional issues. Meinecke's admiration for Bismarck
seems unbounded: Bismarck's methods were the only ones
suited to achieve German unification. Bismarck might not have
solved all the problems of German politics, but what he had
done was perfect. Meinecke accepts the need for a strong and
independent executive. When he writes approvingly of the parliamentary character of the Bismarckian constitution, he means
to acknowledge his belief in the necessity of a parliament, but
he does not intend for the government to be dependent on this
parliament.

These were views which might be found among most of the
high-ranking members of the German civil service, and they do
not differ from those which other German political historians
expressed. Nevertheless—although it might not be evident at
first sight—Meinecke's book goes beyond the conventional assumptions of these groups. It is a work on German unification,
on German political history; as such it should center around the
actions of the policymakers and explain them on the basis of
documentary sources preserved in the archives. Meinecke's
book, however, analyzes the thought of philosophers like
Hegel and Fichte, of literary figures like Novalis and Friedrich
Schlegel, of scholars like Ranke, Droysen, and Niebuhr, and of
political thinkers like Adam Muller, Haller, and Stahl. When
Meinecke discusses statesmen like Stein or Humboldt or even
Bismarck, he is more concerned with their thought than with
their actions. Accordingly, the sources for this work are primarily printed books or pamphlets, personal letters, lectures,
and only to a very small extent documents from archives. This is

a book on the influence of ideas on the course of politics and also on the influence of politics on the development of ideas.

With this approach Meinecke challenged the traditional notions of political history because this concept implied that a political history that was limited to an investigation of the day-to-day business of statesmen remains superficial. The springs of political action must be traced back to the world of ideas which formed the intellectual atmosphere of a time, and out of which the individual shaped his own particular view of the world. There was nothing novel in assigning to ideas a role in history. The two thinkers who exercised the greatest influence on historical thought in Germany in the nineteenth century—Hegel, the philosopher, and Ranke, the historian—had both stressed the importance of ideas in history. But for both of them ideas floated above the events of history; they served to designate the particular character of a period and to distinguish it from others. Meinecke, however, as he said in a letter written during the composition of *Cosmopolitanism and the National State,* employed a "psychological empathizing method." He did not concern himself with ideas as abstracts indicating the common qualities of a variety of phenomena. For him man was the medium through which ideas worked in history; they established a common basis for thought and action among men but they also gave each individual the opportunity for developing a distinctive personality. The interplay between common ideas and the different shapes which they assume in individual minds, the evolution which ideas undergo in consequence of this interplay, the manner in which they pattern the course of action and the manner in which they are transformed as a result of their application to reality—these seemed to Meinecke questions which the historian must study if he wants to achieve a full understanding of the events of the political world.

These views not only represent an enlargement of the concept of political history; they also imply a new approach to the history of ideas. Meinecke's effort to place political history in a broader context had to be complemented by demolishing the compartmentalization which kept the history of ideas isolated from the rest of history. As long as it was regarded as a separate pursuit the history of ideas was fragmented into different histories, each describing the development in different areas of man's intellectual activities—the history of philosophy, the history of historical scholarship, or the history of economic thought. Or else it meant dealing with the history of single concepts such as immortality, progress, or sovereignty. In this approach the history of an idea has its inner logic. It is the gradual unfolding of all its immanent qualities. In Meinecke's view, however, ideas and actions were interdependent. The emergence and the evolution of ideas had to be presented within the framework of all that which surrounded them. Meinecke developed, therefore, a new method of intellectual history.

He abandoned the traditional procedure of presenting a man's ideas in the form of a closed system into which everything, whatever he had said or written, was fitted, in which earlier statements were used to explain statements in later works, and from which those ideas which did not fit were eliminated as immature or not seriously meant. In analyzing a man's thought Meinecke would adopt a genetic method, that is, he would follow an individual's intellectual development from step to step, from one written work to the next.

A particularly brilliant example of Meinecke's method in *Cosmopolitanism and the National State* is the long chapter on "Fichte and the Idea of the German National State." In carefully outlining Fichte's intellectual development, he revealed the philosophical assumptions behind Fichte's famous addresses to the German nation. Meinecke demonstrated that the glorification of the German nation, which earlier interpreters had taken as an expression of pure nationalism and as an appeal for a fight against Napoleon, had an educational aim and was the outline of an ideal nation which did not exist in reality. In this interpretation the addresses fitted the idealistic, ethical concerns of Fichte's philosophy. This approach also involved new emphasis in analyzing literary sources or documents. In elucidating the intellectual development of an individual the key concepts and fundamental assumptions of writings were more important than content. Changes in subject matter might be forced by external circumstances; shifts in key concepts reflect the inner development of an individual. They also allow the perception and definition of the intellectual relationship which exists among various individuals. In this manner Meinecke showed the wide ramifications and the importance of Christian-Germanic romanticism for political thought in the first half of the nineteenth century—one of the discoveries of *Cosmopolitanism and the National State.*

It would be wrong to claim that the genetic method in intellectual history was Meinecke's invention. To find the connecting thread in European intellectual history had been the lifework of the Berlin philosopher, Wilhelm Dilthey. As a student Meinecke had found little stimulus in Dilthey's lectures, but he began to read him again when he took up the studies which led to the composition of *Cosmopolitanism and the National State* and he was then deeply impressed. Dilthey's *Jugendgeschichte Hegels (History of Hegel's Youth)* and his *Leben Schleiermachers (Life of Scheiermacher)* were and remain penetrating studies of the intellectual development of important thinkers and they opened new perspectives. But Dilthey used the genetic method for purely biographical purposes. Meinecke applied this method to a group of thinkers; in his hands it served to establish a connection between the political and the intellectual world and to show the features which on the one hand tied together and on the other divided one generation from the next. In *Cosmopolitanism and the National State* Meinecke used the genetic method of intellectual history in such a way that it could be made applicable to broad historical themes.

The application of a new historical method was not the only reason this work impressed its readers as something novel. We must return once again to the issue we have discussed before: the political attitude this work reflects. We have seen that it was permeated with a German nationalistic spirit, characteristic of the period before the First World War and particularly characteristic of the work of political historians of this time. But by demonstrating that the guiding principles of the political world originated in the world of thought—in literature, in philosophy, in scholarship—Meinecke reduced the supremacy of politics and by this implied a sharp criticism of Wilhelminian Germany. He suggested that the exclusiveness of the ruling group in Prussia-Germany represented a weakness because it cut political life off from its creative source, namely, the world of ideas, and the men who generated them. German politics was in danger of becoming sterile and rigid. It could be—it ought to be—revived by granting influence to those classes, forces, and ideas which were growing up outside the narrow Prussian ruling group. These views were not in contradiction to Meinecke's admiration for Bismarck and his work because, although he considered Bismarck's solution of German unification as the only solution attainable in the political circumstance of the nineteenth century, he emphasized that Bismarck's work was unfinished and needed to be completed. Nor were these demands incompatible with Meinecke's belief in the greatness of the Prussian tradition. Like his contemporary and friend Otto Hintze, the prominent scholar of Prussian institutional history, Meinecke believed that the Prussian reforms in the Napoleonic era consisted of two parts: one was the modernization of the bureaucracy so that Prussia would have the necessary strength and elasticity to maintain its position among the European powers; the other was a "program for the future" which would realize the principle of the participation of the citizens in political life. While the first part of the reform had been successfully carried out, the program for the future had never been taken in hand.

It might be questioned whether Meinecke would have recognized the importance of this issue if his own move, first to Strasbourg, then to Freiburg, had not given him an opportunity to look upon the Prussian state from the outside; in the relaxed liberal atmosphere of southwest Germany the virtues of Prussia's disciplined and hierarchically organized society may have lost some of their glamor. But whatever the motives of Meinecke's adoption of a progressive outlook were, *Cosmopolitanism and the National State* was viewed as a historical justification of the demands for political reforms—and that was part of its impact. In this book Meinecke proffers a political message; and although it does not aim at revolution, it certainly aims at reform.

II

After Meinecke became a professor in Berlin in 1914, his influence on a new generation of historians and on the development of German historical scholarship became stronger and broader. He also came into contact with the policymaking group in Imperial Germany. In Chancellor Bethmann Hollweg and other high civil servants he had an interested audience for his views, which he expressed both in person and in written memos.[6] Meinecke regarded the role of adviser to government officials as not only suitable for himself but also the appropriate political stance for the German academic in general. So the German defeat and the end of the imperial regime changed not only his political goals but also the circumstances under which he could hope to make himself heard. Under the impact of the parliamentarization of the Reich, a few weeks before the military collapse, he noted in his diary: "Our small circle has only the ideas, but not the needed forces. Ideas and forces, will and wisdom have separated from each other."[7]

Whether in this changed situation a professor would be able to continue to act as adviser to the policymakers was to him a matter of deep concern. He set down the result of his reflections on this problem in an article on "The Political Attitudes of German Academicians," which he published in 1922.[8] According to Meinecke the political ideas of German academicians were something unique. The authoritarian structure of the Germans kept the professors—themselves civil servants—away from the practical conduct of politics; they were "outsiders." "For this reason, however, they could express in their political ideas a spirit of purity and strength of principle, of idealism and independence from interests and their conflicts." A good part of Meinecke's article was devoted to an outline of the political attitudes of German academicians during the nineteenth century—from an idealistic beginning, in which national goals were set, to a second liberal-constitutional stage, and finally to a phase in which economic and social reforms were considered. Meinecke reflected on these historical precedents as background for a discussion of whether professors, viewing political struggles from a distance and serving as impartial advisers and arbiters, still had a place in a democratized Germany, in which government policy was no longer in the hands of civil servants who believed themselves to be above group interests and acting for the whole of society. Meinecke's conclusion was that, although the means and methods of politics had changed, the academicians still had a political role to play, very similar to that which they had played before 1918: their task was "to weaken the impact of the destructive class struggle and to surmount it through social reforms and the creation of ethical, humane and national values embodying these reforms."

Although, in their origin and their meaning, Meinecke's ideas were very different from Karl Mannheim's notion of a "free floating intelligentsia," both shared the assumption that the academician was able to hold views transcending group interests and embracing the interest of the whole of society. Even after the establishment of a parliamentary democracy in Germany, which placed government in the hands of parties that represented the parts comprising society, Meinecke held to the belief that the state had a life of its own, distinctive from and superior to the interests of the classes and groups that existed within it.[9]

For an understanding of Meinecke's second great historical work, his *Idea of Reason of State in Modern History,* it is essential to realize that he remained convinced that the state was an all-embracing organic whole. The conception of *Idea of Reason of State,* which appeared in 1924, went back to the years just before the First World War. Meinecke intended to show how the conduct of politics became refined by the gradually increasing consciousness of the differences in the interests of the various European states, each of which had its own distinctive needs and individual character. Originally Meinecke believed that such a study could be closely connected with a study of the evolution of the modern historical outlook because he regarded recognition of the individuality of the various European nations as one of the great achievements of modern historism. This original plan was decisively modified by the First World War and its aftermath. Power politics, the conduct of foreign policy, had become the crucial factor through which a nation revealed its individuality and, in Meinecke's view, overshadowed all other aspects of the art of politics. Meinecke became perturbed and fascinated by the problem of to what extent power politics could be justified in its disregard for, or transcendence of, the rules of law and the prescripts of ethics and morality. This issue became the center of Meinecke's book. It developed into a historical study of the relation of morality and politics in European history. This shift in Meinecke's plan reflects the impact of the war and postwar events. In the unwillingness to compromise with the aggressiveness of Germany, in the war-guilt clause of the Treaty of Versailles, in the exclusion of Germany from the League of Nations, moral attitudes had shown themselves to be powerful political forces. But it would appear that Meinecke, though his war aims for Germany had been moderate, was disturbed because at certain moments he himself had expressed expansionist demands which, soon afterwards, he realized had transgressed justifiable limits.

Thus in Meinecke's *Reason of State* three interconnected but also distinctive issues are combined. One was the question of the interrelationship between morality and power politics; Meinecke deals chiefly with political thinkers who wrote about this problem, beginning with Machiavelli who, according to Meinecke, placed it in the center of modern political thought. Then, in some sections, Meinecke studied problems that were part of his original plan; he examined the genesis and development of the doctrine of the interests of the states. The search for a practically useful, generally valid formulation of the concept of reason of state resulted in the opposite: new insights into the differentiated nature of the interests of each individual state. Finally, chiefly in the last chapters of the book, Meinecke was concerned with the question whether and to what extent Imperial Germany, in its intense pursuit of power, was rightfully accused of a ruthless disregard of moral considerations. This last section is probably the weakest of the book since the discussion wavers between acceptance of the accusation and defense against it. In later years Meinecke stated that he ought to have been sharper in condemnation of the excesses of German nationalism.

The book has other weaknesses too. Probably its most serious deficiency is that Meinecke went so far in identifying power politics with foreign policy that he entirely overlooked issues in the area of domestic politics. A violent struggle for power among groups and classes of society had been the rule until these conflicts were pacified by the establishment of a generally recognized legal order. English political thinkers, for instance John Locke, are neglected; C. J. Friedrich recognized correctly the existence of this gap in Meinecke's work and tried to fill it with his study on *Constitutional Reason of State*. It must also be said that Meinecke's book is more concerned with the treatment of the problem of the relationship between morality and politics in the writings of philosophers, historians, and political publicists than with the role it played in the practical conduct of foreign policy; nor did he try to evaluate the influence which the theories he analyzed exerted on statesmen or on a wider public. Finally, because of the shifts in Meinecke's interest while he was working on this book, it is not a unified story. He waited until the last moment to decide whether some chapters should be included or left out. The work is a collection of essays around a problem rather than a tightly knit whole.

However, considered in this manner—as a rather irregular formation, "grown rather than made," as Meinecke himself said,[10] it becomes clear that it is a work of great distinction; some of its chapters are outstanding achievements of twentieth century historical scholarship. The first chapter on Machiavelli, with its analysis of the basic categories with which Machiavelli tried to organize the confusing materials of politics and history, has formed the point of departure for discussions which are still going on. The chapter on the beginnings of the doctrine of the interests of the states, with its explanation of the turbulent career of Prince Henri de Rohan suggests the variety of contradictory motifs—passion and rationalism, patriotism, religion and ambition—which give to the politics of the early seventeenth century its instability and sudden reversals. The hundred pages on Frederick the Great, although they may not do full justice to the king as ruler, establish the relation of the king to the intellectual movements of his time more clearly and more convincingly than had ever been done before and shed new light on both the king and the thinking of the Enlightenment. Perhaps it is unfair to say that the book does not represent a connected whole because behind the writers and thinkers whose ideas are analyzed in detail in the various chapters there emerges a picture of the developing and changing European intellectual movements since early modern times.

III

Just as the political events of the First World War and of the years immediately after provided a key to the understanding of Meinecke's interests and intentions in *Idea of Reason of State,* the book itself serves to explain Meinecke's political attitude in the following decades. He became a supporter of the Weimer republic and democracy—not sentimentally but rationally, a "Vernunftrepublikaner," as he himself described his attitude. He reasoned that, in order to avoid a dissolution of the German national state and a renewed fragmentation of Germany, it was necessary to rally around the one national center that still existed, the republican government, and to strengthen it. He feared that the adventurous policies which the adherents of the old regime—and old and young nationalists—advocated would lead to external pressure and internal tensions which would end with the destruction of the unity of the Reich. The need to preserve the German national state made him a defender of the cautious and conciliatory policy of the Weimar Republic.

The attempt to maintain—externally and internally—the status quo proved at the end to be futile; it might even have contributed to the overthrow of the Weimar Republic by the National Socialists. For this catastrophe could have been avoided only by radical social reforms which would have loosened the hold of the old ruling group on the bureaucratic apparatus and would have given wider social and economic groups an interest in maintaining the democratic order. Meinecke's history of ideas has been attacked for having been instrumental in turning attention away from the crucial social problems of the time. This view is rather misleading. Per se, a historical method is neither virtuous nor evil, and Meinecke could have developed his history of ideas in different directions; indeed it might have helped to clarify social problems. The reasons why Meinecke, in his studies on the history of ideas, did not take this course, but focused instead on issues connected with power politics and high culture, go far beyond preference for a particular historical method or approach. Meinecke was and remained a member of the German academic class and still more of the German bourgeoisie, which inclined to "internalize" questions of political freedom. In Germany, political absolutism and a relatively late industrial development had obscured the importance of freedom for the vital functioning of society, and limited it to the sphere of the individual.[11]

From 1918 on, Meinecke published a number of essays dealing with questions of historical theory.[12] Meinecke had a sharply logical, but not an abstract-philosophical mind, and the attempts which have been made on the basis of these theoretical essays to construct a generally valid theory of history seem to me unfortunate. These essays contain so many metaphysical and religious presuppositions that they can hardly claim wide acceptance; rather, they are interesting and enlightening for an understanding of Meinecke's own historical works. An essay on which Meinecke himself set great store was entitled "Causalities and Values." The realm of necessity in history is formed by physical conditions and material needs; a good part of human action is determined by these factors and therefore belongs to this realm. But in human nature there is also a belief in values. The struggle to maintain values under the pressure of causal necessities is the permanent task of man, changing in its forms and problems with the change of times, and it is this struggle which really forms the substance of history. This philosophy has some bearing on Meinecke's *Reason of State* because it explains why Meinecke, in this book, is less concerned with the question whether the amorality of power politics destroys the entire fabric of social life than with the conscience of those who conduct such a policy. But certainly this philosophy sheds light on a much discussed issue: Meinecke's attitude toward the Nazi regime.

Some of Meinecke's admirers liked to emphasize that he was a hero of the resistance, which prompted an almost unavoidable reaction on the part of others, who pointed out that his belief in the state, his nationalism, and the tepidity of his democratic convictions was compatible with National Socialist notions. Indeed, in the early years of the Nazi regime, Meinecke was impressed by the dynamism with which the National Socialists seemed to recreate a strong national state. The stress which he himself had always laid on power politics as an indication of the vitality of a state raised doubts in his mind as to whether, instead of the cautious and gradual course which the republic had pursued and he had defended, a more active and even aggressive foreign policy would have been more appropriate. But his positive evaluation of these aspects of Nazi policy diminished when this policy led to war; when defeat threatened, Meinecke was in close contact with people active in the resistance.

It would not be fair, however, to suggest that only the approach of defeat made Meinecke an opponent of the Nazi regime. As the author of *Idea of Reason of State,* Meinecke must have wondered whether the brutality and the contempt for law which this regime showed would not destroy the bonds that held society together. Meinecke's particular concern was the Nazi policy of controlling and directing cultural life. In this they touched upon those possessions in which the autonomy of the individual resided—freedom of conscience and independent criteria of values, and these were sacred to Meinecke. These were possessions which he was not willing to surrender. Meinecke did not allow political interference to enter into his relations with old friends and former students. Any appearance in the public area was for him impossible under this regime. He was retired from his professorship when the National Socialists came to power, and could live withdrawn from the outside world. In this way, without directly turning against the German national state, he tried to maintain what he considered the other great value of human existence, his individuality.

In this situation he wrote and published the last of his three great works: *Historism: The Rise of a New Historical Outlook.* It has been said that, at the time of its publication, a book with an emphatically nonpolitical content demonstrated distance and disapproval of the Nazi regime. There is some truth in this. In any case, Meinecke's last great work is different from its predecessors in that it is pure "Geistesgeschichte."[13] In *Historism,* intellectual history is not combined with political history or political aims. Whereas in *Cosmopolitanism and the National State,* and still more in *Idea of Reason of State,* intellectual and political developments are tightly interwoven, the rare allusions to political and social events in *Historism* are only intended to elucidate particular aspects in the thought of an individual writer.[14]

There are three closely connected but also clearly distinguishable issues in this book. First of all—and I quote here from the foreword which Sir Isaiah Berlin contributed to the translation—Meinecke "described the gradual waning of an older European outlook dominated by the notions of a timeless unaltering Natural Law," and the slow emergence of the notion of "individuality," in the formation of which emotional and irrational factors and forces play a significant part. This change from a belief in universal laws and generally valid norms to enthusiastic appreciation of the spontaneous and original was for Meinecke an intellectual revolution, "one of the greatest intellectual revolutions that has ever taken place in Western thought"; it seemed to him no less important than the political revolution which went on in France at the same time. This use of the word "revolution" is an interesting indication that since the 1920s, under the influence of fascism and nazism, the view had spread from the socialist to the bourgeois camp that any change of significance had to be a "revolution." In any case the term provided Meinecke with the opportunity to claim that, next to and in opposition to the French Revolution, there existed a German movement that brought about an equally important change. One of the aspects—and for Meinecke probably the most important aspect of this "revolution"—was the genesis of a true historical outlook which made possible the great developments of historical scholarship in the nineteenth century.

Analysis of the features which characterize the new historical outlook is the second issue of the book. It is not a history of historiography but a work on the emergence of that kind of thinking from which the development of nineteenth-century historical scholarship arose. It is significant that the book deals with Ranke only at the end in a kind of appendix. The concepts which Meinecke regards as crucial in breaking up the mold into which thinking had been pressed by the assumption of a causal mechanistic natural law system were the ideas of "individuality," which ascribed uniqueness not only to the character of persons but also to entities, and the idea of "evolution." These notions were closely connected with other concepts like genius, originality, and enthusiasm.

Defense of the value of history is the third issue with which Meinecke is concerned in *Historism.* The intellectual revolution of the late eighteenth and early nineteenth century, Meinecke wrote in one of his essays, "has opened up for us the marvelous world of new historical understanding in respect to everything that wears a human look." But it has also "gradually undermined all the firm ground of definite and absolute ideals on which humanity had up till now reckoned to have a solid foothold." Meinecke felt he must refute the assertion that historism, in undermining belief in the absolutism of moral values, has led to skepticism, immorality, and brutality. His answer was almost implied in the term "marvelous" with which he characterized the "world of new historical understanding" that historism opened up. The richness and variety of the past which a true historical approach discloses should not produce moral indifference and disrespect, but ought to awaken and strengthen understanding, appreciation, and even reverence for human endeavors in all their various forms and for the ethical energy shown at all times.

In Meinecke's treatment of this last problem—his defense of historism—an entirely subjective element prevails. This definition of the function of history is founded on a religious belief which might be described as pantheism. It is the same belief Goethe held and expressed in his poetry and writings. This is the reason why more than one-quarter of Meinecke's book is devoted to an analysis of Goethe's attitude toward history. In itself this is an interesting section because Goethe's views of history have never been isolated from the general body of his work and subjected to such a comprehensive and subtle scrutiny. Yet this long section on Goethe undoubtedly demonstrates that *Historism* is a late work, a work of high age. Meinecke deeply enjoyed the opportunity of reading again Goethe's works and of studying them systematically; and he followed this inclination beyond what the problem of his book required and what was appropriate to its structure. For it cannot be denied that, although the notions of "individuality" and "evolution" were important, even fundamental, to Goethe's view of life and nature, he was not very concerned with their application to an understanding of the past. His attitude toward history remained ambiguous. History aroused in him—and Meinecke is too good a scholar not to recognize this—"displeasure" (Missvergnügen).

Meinecke's second thesis—that the discovery of the notions of "individuality" and "evolution" was a decisive feature in constituting the modern historical outlook—has roots other than those of Goethe's famous enthusiasm about "individuum est ineffabile." Meinecke's emphasis on the notion of individuality can be traced back to suggestions in the teachings of Droysen and Dilthey, and was decisively influenced by Rickert's attempt to effect a clean separation of natural sciences and cultural sciences. Otto Hintze, the only figure among the German historians of the first decades of the twentieth century equal to Meinecke in intellectual stature, wrote in a review of Troeltsch's *Der Historismus und seine Probleme* (1922) that indeed the historian must be concerned with the uniqueness and "individuality" of historical phenomena, but he ought not to assume that the fact that a phenomenon is unique, or "individual," means that it embodies a value. Hintze also warned of the use of the concept of evolution, because in its application to history it contained a metaphysical element; it implied that historical entities were organic wholes growing like plants and following their own innate tendencies outside and beyond human control. Hintze found in the concepts of individuality and evolution as they were used by German historians a metaphysical element which he regarded as a fatal flaw. Hintze was a pragmatist concerned with causal connections and he regarded "explaining" how things had come about as quite as important as "understanding" what they were. It is well known that Troeltsch wrote his book on the problems of historism under the influence of Meinecke; thus Hintze's criticism of Troeltsch was also directed at Meinecke, who then had begun to work on his book on the origin of historism. Meinecke and Hintze had been close friends although they differed in their intellectual outlook. In the early times of their friendship Hintze's insistence that there are laws in history had met Meinecke's sharp opposition. It is not astounding therefore that Meinecke in his *Historism* did not heed the admonitions which Hintze's review of Troeltsch had contained. The review remains relevant, however, because it implies that, insofar as Meinecke's *Historism* was intended to analyze the basic features of the modern historical outlook, the author looked upon the issue from a peculiar, somewhat narrow angle.

Meinecke gave scant attention to the problem of structure, to questions of causal explanations and pragmatic aims in the study of history. They appear to him issues of a lower order; the emphasis is placed on the richness of values which become revealed in a study of the past which focuses on an understanding of historical phenomena in their "individuality." In this sense the history of ideas in which these values are reflected—Geistesgeschichte—is not one of the aspects of history but its central area. One need not deny importance to the notions of uniqueness and evolution in order to see that each of these notions must be neatly defined and divested of their metaphysical element in order to be compatible with modern attitudes toward history. The metaphysical aspect which they have in Meinecke's work places them in close connection with his religious pantheism and undermines the value of *Historism* as an analysis of the constituent elements of the modern historical outlook.

But these criticisms of Meinecke's theoretical views do not imply criticism of *Historism* as a work of historical analysis. At the end of the eighteenth century when the notions of individuality and evolution first were "discovered" and conceived as keys to open the doors to a better understanding of the world, they undoubtedly had a metaphysical aspect. More recent studies have only confirmed Meinecke's thesis that the roots of an intellectual development which broke with rationalist universalism and acknowledged the significance of the psychological, the irrational, and the emotional factors are to be found in the eighteenth century; there was not only contrast but also continuity between the Enlightenment and the Romantic age. We would hesitate to claim that the revolt against rationalism was a purely German movement and that it could be called a German revolution. Meinecke devoted lengthy chapters to Voltaire and Montesquieu, the British Enlightenment historiography and the English pre-Romantics before, in the second part of the book, presenting the ideas of the chief protagonists of this intellectual revolution—Möser, Herder, Goethe. Although he assigns to German thinkers the decisive role, the rise of the new historical outlook he saw as a European process. Meinecke does not conceive of intellectual history as a part of social history. The book presents the general intellectual development in the form of an analysis of the thought of the most prominent writers and thinkers of the period. Within this compass it is superb. As in his first great work, Meinecke applies in this, his third and last great work, the genetic method—but with a consummate mastery which, as Berlin writes in the foreword, uses "an infinity of tiny strokes" but achieves a portrait in which the main lines clearly emerge. In its manner of presenting the ideas and the development of great intellectual figures *Historism* can still serve as a model for the historian of today.

That Meinecke has a secure place in the history of historiography as one of the earliest and most accomplished practitioners of the history of ideas is not the only, and, in my opinion, not even the most important reason why his writings deserve attention today. Meinecke once explained that he did not write "narrative history" but "history around problems" (Problemgeschichte).[15] Whatever subject Meinecke dealt with in his great works—German political developments in the first half of the nineteenth century, changing attitudes in the handling of foreign policy, the evolution of a new historical outlook—the subject matter was important to him for partly personal, but chiefly political reasons. His attitude toward domestic reform in the Empire, toward Germany's war guilt and his own participation in this guilt, toward a defense of historical scholarship against the accusation that it had contributed to intellectual and moral decline: these concerns of the day were driving forces in his study of the past. In all his works there was a convergence of interest in special aspects and persons of former times with political issues and concerns of his own time and questions of his own personal responsibility. This configuration gives historical study vitality and is what Meinecke meant when he spoke about the need for writing history "around problems."

He had become aware of the need for such an approach when, as a young scholar, he had observed the contrast between technical virtuosity and intellectual emptiness which dominated German historical scholarship after the disappearance of the great masters of the nineteenth century. The validity of his attitude, however, reaches far beyond his particular situation. Whenever a new historical approach has gained general recognition, it soon becomes rigidified; new approaches open up the possibility of studying an endless number of previously neglected issues, but their study no longer requires creative effort, only an application of the new methods. Meinecke had a sovereign contempt for those who considered historical work as identical with working through masses of archival materials, manuscripts, and papers according to taught and accepted methods—the "Stoffhuber," as he called them. But his rejection of those whom he considered to be doing chiefly mechanical work was balanced by his interest in those whom, he supposed or hoped, would be able to inject into their studies something of their personality, their "individuality."

Perhaps it is true that Meinecke did not go to the end of the road which he had entered; he did not pursue the study of intellectual trends to an analysis of the social forces which they represented. Nor did he systematize the insights in the historical process which he had gained. Yet these weaknesses were also a strength. For Meinecke, results or conclusions were only a part—and not the most important part—of the work of the historian. Meinecke's interest was the particular form which ideas assumed in the mind of an individual. It was the richness and variety of the individual that he was primarily concerned with. Meinecke was, as we have said, Germany's most influential historian. He was also a great teacher because he urged his students to find their own way, the way most appropriate to their personality. But it is an error to assume, as has frequently been done, that Meinecke founded a school of historians of ideas. Actually his students have worked in the most varied areas of history: political, social, institutional, intellectual. It was Meinecke's concern for their finding in history both a strict discipline and creative expression that brought students close to him and generated veneration for him, even if in their life and work they went on different roads.

PART II.
The Historian's Machiavelli

4. The Humanist Concept of the Prince and *The Prince* of Machiavelli

The attention of one who studies the development of political thought, particularly of that gravitation toward political realism which was accomplished at the beginning of the modern era and is associated with the name of Machiavelli, is constantly arrested by that passage in the fifteenth chapter of *The Prince* in which Machiavelli himself speaks of the guiding principles underlying the whole of his observations.[1]

> It now remains for us to consider what ought to be the conduct and bearing of a Prince in relation to his subjects and friends. And since I know that many have written on this subject, I fear it may be thought presumptuous in me to write of it also; the more so, because in my treatment of it I depart from the views that others have taken. But since it is my object to write

Originally published in *Journal of Modern History,* 11 (1939), 449–483, reprinted by permission of the University of Chicago. For the dispute connected with the theses of this article see Sergio Bertelli's introduction to *The Prince* in the Feltrinelli edition of Machiavelli's *Opere,* I (Milan, 1960). I myself have explained my position in Felix Gilbert, *Niccolo Machiavelli e la vita culturale del suo tempo* (Bologna, Il Mulino, 1964), pp. 244–246. I remain convinced that chapters 15–19 of *The Prince* were written as a satire on the mirror-of-princes literature, and that Machiavelli composed the treatise in stages, but this does not mean that I think the composition extended over a long stretch of time.

what shall be useful to whosoever understands it, it seems to me better to follow the real truth of things than an imaginary view of them. For many Republics and Princedoms have been imagined that were never seen or known to exist in reality. And the manner in which we live, and that in which we ought to live, are things so wide asunder that he who quits the one to betake himself to the other is more likely to destroy than to save himself.[2]

In this passage Machiavelli succinctly summarizes the methodological principles underlying the argument of *The Prince* and later of the *Discorsi,* and draws a firm and definite line of demarcation between himself and his "idealist" predecessors, who sought to adapt and subordinate political theory to a theological or metaphysical pattern. Machiavelli took his stand on observation and experiences derived from political practice; without a purely empirical foundation all insight into the true nature of politics, all comprehension of the laws behind political phenomena, seemed to him impossible. A sense of pride seems to emerge from his repudiation of the standpoint of his predecessors and from his statement and defense of the revolutionary position which he had adopted; it is as if he himself foresaw the far-reaching consequences implicit in the application of the methods of realism to the realm of political thought.

It may perhaps be legitimate to draw yet another conclusion from the passage quoted. Machiavelli's attack on the political theorists of the last hundred years[3] shows that he was perfectly well aware that with *The Prince* he was plunging into a highly controversial subject; therefore a comparison of Machiavelli's work with the literature he attacked may give us a clue to the origins of *The Prince* and the reorientation of political theory that it implied. For it is common experience that the real substance of an intellectual discussion is not at the time fully recognized by the disputants themselves. Differences of opinion that later only seem to be differences of a "technical" kind appear at first to be profound and insuperable, and the fundamental principles common to both sides in the discussion are overlooked. And even when the cleavage is really as profound as the disputants themselves suppose, concentration on the same question creates a certain connection between the opposite sides; in a new theory there is often to be traced the influence of an old one which it has combated and superseded. For this reason it may not be without interest to devote some attention to those writers whom Machiavelli subjected to such trenchant criticism in *The Prince.*

When Machiavelli wrote *The Prince,* humanism was the ruling intellectual force of the day. It has exercised its influence on political theory and produced its own political literature, which, particularly the writings of the humanists on the subject of the prince, Machiavelli must have had in mind. The political ideas of the humanist writers of the quattrocento are, however, so largely overshadowed by the systematic social philosophy of the middle ages which preceded them and the "realist" political science that immediately followed them, that they have never so far been thoroughly examined.[4] Since an investigation of the quattrocento literature on the subject of the prince may perhaps throw Machiavelli's book into sharper relief, we seem to be justified in devoting our attention to this neglected sphere and in attempting a comprehensive survey of the conception of the prince as it had developed in the humanistic literature of the quattrocento.

I

When he wrote *The Prince,* Machiavelli, as we have said, plunged into a highly controversial subject. It occupied the center of the stage in the intellectual discussions of his day. Now, the nature of princeship and princes is an ancient, ever recurring theme in political literature.[5] The main outlines of the discussion were laid down in antiquity in the various writings on kingship;[6] and in the middle ages the tradition was transformed and developed into a complete and compact literary form, that of the "mirror of princes," which survived until the nineteenth century.[7] This literary form, although the course was never quite interrupted, was of little importance during the earlier phase of the Italian humanist movement, and it was not until the second half of the fifteenth century that it re-emerged as a favorite topic of discussion. A great variety of writings appeared on the subject of the prince, which suddenly occupied the center of the intellectual stage.[8] Political interest was concentrated on it. The humanists, who, to begin with, had almost completely neglected the subject, suddenly developed an intense interest in it. The explanation lies in the political trends in

Italy, of which some description is essential to a study of the humanist literature on the prince.[9]

The defeat of the emperor in his struggle with the Pope had involved the breakdown of the universal political conceptions of the middle ages, and it was in Italy that the change in the political and intellectual atmosphere became first and most acutely perceptible. For after the elimination of Emperor and Pope there was no central power in Italy and there was no longer any firm ideological basis for Italy's political and social life. The medieval conception of a universal, organically articulated political order was no longer compatible with the complete independence which, in practice, the individual Italian states enjoyed; it was this situation, and the consequent need of an intellectual reorientation, that made humanism possible and determined the course of its development, particularly in the sphere of political thought.

This situation resulted in the political interest of the humanists being at first directed toward republicanism—the republicanism of the Italian city-state; for, where autocratic forms of government survived, the rulers theoretically derived their authority from the empire and sought to have their position legalized by it. In these cases the tie with the political system of the middle ages survived—at any rate, theoretically. But in the case of the republican cities of Italy, no tie bound them to the medieval world-state; in the political history of the Western world they represent the first appearance since antiquity of the self-sufficient autonomous state. As such they inevitably constituted both the chief interest and the chief difficulty of the political theorists of that time. The celebrated formula of Bartolus, *Civitas sibi princeps,* which made it possible to include the republican cities of Italy within the system of Roman law,[10] derived from the attempt to legalize the new state of affairs. But even more effective than this theoretical impulse in focusing interest upon the republics was the weight of political events. For the republics had led the victorious struggle against the emperor; it was they who had become the decisive political and economic factors in Italy. To think of Italy in the fourteenth century is to think of her city-republics: Florence, Siena, Venice, Pisa, Genoa.

But while political theory associated with, and deriving from, this bourgeois-capitalist development was still germinating, the political aspect of Italy began to alter. A period of stagnation and retrogression followed a period of world-wide economic expansion. Italy was thrown back upon herself, and out of the welter of Italian states there crystallized a group of great powers, which overthrew the smaller and weaker ones and reduced them to dependency. Corresponding to this alteration in the distribution of power in Italy and the concentration of it in the hands of the more powerful states, an alteration took place within the states themselves. Power tended to be concentrated in the hands of a few families or a single one. The democratic wave with which the fourteenth century began was followed by a period of reaction, and in the course of the fifteenth century autocracy became the predominant form of government in Italy. Venice alone, of the more important states, preserved the forms of a republican aristocracy. The Visconti had established autocracy so firmly in Milan that, when their line extinguished, opposition to the rule of Francesco Sforza was quickly overcome. In Florence the quattrocento saw the rise of the Medici, who preserved the appearance of a republican form of government but gradually succeeded in gathering all the essentials of power into their hands. But the most vital alteration in the world of Italian states came from the south. After a period of internal discord and dissension, order was re-established in Naples, which once more assumed an active role as one of the great powers of Italy. Thus, side by side with bourgeois-capitalist city-states that had become the prevalent pattern in northern and central Italy, a monarchical, territorial, feudal state reasserted its claim to political power; and its overlord, Alfonso of Aragon, was legitimized because of the glamour that surrounded an ancient hereditary dynasty.

Such was the political development which called forth a new interest in princes. Its consequence was that the political thought of the humanists, which started by being "republican," became "monarchical."[11] But it was plain that it was a new kind of prince that had arisen in Italy.[12] The *condottiere* who founded a dynasty and the city family that worked its way up to a ruling position in its own city were phenomena that could only have occurred in a self-sufficient world of entirely independent states. Political theory was faced with the problem of legitimizing this new kind of prince and assimilating him to the still surviving medieval concept of kingship. The new interest in princes implied the existence of new, unprecedented problems.

II

In an account of the political trends in the Italy of the quattrocento, the necessary basis for our main task, the description and analysis of the prince-literature of the humanists, is to be found. Yet, by affording this description of the political situation and by showing the connection between the political events and the reawakening of the interest in princes and princeship, we seem already to have arrived at an opinion on this subject contrary to that usually held. For Machiavelli's censorious verdict, quoted above, has been often reiterated, and it has been generally accepted that the political writings of the humanists lacked the urge of political conviction and were remote from, and alien to, reality;[13] whereas we, by drawing attention to the political developments which led the humanists to take up the question of the prince, seem, on the contrary, to demonstrate a direct connection between the literature of this genre and the political conditions under which it was written. Yet such a statement is not intended to imply more than that the original impulse sprang from reality. Beyond that, the question as to what extent the humanists were influenced by reality, and what rudiments of realism there were in their writings before Machiavelli set up the realistic principle as the basis of his political thought, can be determined only by a detailed consideration of their writings; it can be determined only by finding out whether these writings represent more than a resuscitation of known and traditional ideas or whether they deviate from the traditional mode and contain new and original thought. Our task, therefore, of examining the prince-literature of the humanists distinctly falls into two parts: first, to investigate these writings in their relation to their literary models and try to distinguish between what is new and original and what is traditional in them; after this to more closely examine the respects in which these writings deviate from tradition with special regard to their connection with the political situation of their time. Thus we shall try to find out whether they form a link in the chain that led to Machiavelli's realism.

96

There can be no doubt that these writings are, in the main, of abstract nature. As has already been hinted at, two intellectual currents met in the humanist literature on the subject of the prince. In the first place, as products of humanism these writings were based on antiquity and were chiefly intended to be a reproduction of ancient ideas. In the second place, they were part of the centuries-old stream of the mirror-of-princes literature. Unlike the problem of the "good citizen" or "the best state," antiquity provided no authoritative literary pattern for the problem of the "good prince."[14] There was scope for ancient influence to show itself in the treatment and handling of individual aspects of the problem. But the medieval "mirror of the accomplished prince" was the sole available pattern for its treatment as a whole.[15]

The medieval picture of the prince had not been static and unchanged.[16] Beginning in a limited way, by emphasizing the religious significance of the prince's function, it had enlarged its scope by adopting the concept of the prince as the governing member of a living body. Then, at the end of the thirteenth century, it had undergone a fundamental transformation, mainly as a result of the impact of the political doctrine of Aristotle, and had tried to embrace the whole field of political institutions, especially in its military and judiciary aspects. It was in this highly developed form, in which the influence of antiquity was already apparent, that it exercised an influence on later times. The best and fullest example of this development is the work of Egidio Colonna.[17]

Egidio's book had an enormous scope, which was probably the main reason for its popularity. Egidio aimed at completeness in dealing with his subject. He intended to leave no aspect of it untouched. He dealt alike with the prince as a personality and with princedom as an institution; he dealt as well with the prince's character and the ordering of his court and household as with the object of the state[18] and its administration[19] and with the art of war.[20] Yet, in spite of the handbook character of his work, Egidio's rigidly dogmatic attitude is essentially that of the middle ages. The medieval character of the book is demonstrated, in the first place, by its method. Egidio argues purely deductively from general propositions and assumptions regarding the nature of the universe. In the second place, his work is infused with the concepts of medieval Christianity. In his eyes the whole of man's worldy, social existence is coordinated with the life beyond. From this assumption he deduces the prince's place in the world. The prince is the intermediary between God and man. Most of the attributes Egidio demands of kings and kingship he deduces from this proposition. He states, for instance, that the prince's goal should not be the acquisition of power, honor, or wealth, but that he must aim rather at developing those qualities in himself that fit him to fulfil his religious functions. Egidio proceeds to build up a system of Christian princely ethics.[21] The prince, he says, must set an example to his subjects, both in the conduct of his private life and the ordering of his court and household. Thus, when Egidio describes the ordering of the prince's household, he merely draws a picture of how a model household ought to be managed according to the precepts of religion.[22] He deduces the prince's political duties from those principles of natural justice by which the prince himself was bound and which it was his duty to see applied.[23]

On comparing Egidio's treatment of the subject with that of the humanists, one is at first struck by the apparent absence of any common feature. The writings of the latter are characterized, above all, by those elements which distinguish the political thought of humanism from that of the middle ages. The religious orientation of political life has lost its former predominance. Thus, while for Egidio the good ruler's reward was an outstanding position in the hierarchy of the next world, for the humanists his reward was fame. That is but one example of how the humanists abandoned religious motives in their political theory. Further, the humanists introduced a new basis for discussion. They founded their arguments on historical example instead of abstract theoretical deduction. The historical examples that they used were, of course, taken exclusively from the ancient world, particularly the Roman world;[24] and all their political theorizing was patterned on antiquity.

Beyond these characteristically humanist features, however, a careful study of these writings on the prince will reveal a number of traits which they have in common with the medieval conception. Like the medieval authors, the humanists attempted to discover a norm and to describe the ideal prince. In both cases the qualities of this ideal prince were determined by a political conception which is fundamentally peaceful and unrealistic: the tasks of the quattrocento prince were exclusively confined—like those of his medieval predecessor—to the administration of justice and the maintenance of peace. In accordance with this basic principle, the just and mild king, surrounded by wise councilors and keeping within the confines of the law, remained the ideal of the quattrocento.

Even apart from this common basic attitude, however, it is possible to trace the direct influence of Egidio in the quattrocento literature on the prince and especially in the works of the two writers who dealt most fully with the subject: Platina's (1421–81) *De vero principe*[25] and Francesco Patrizi's (1412–94) *De regno.*[26] These authors, like Egidio, dealt both with the personal side of princeship and with princeship as an institution, and thus a certain resemblance between their works and his was created. Egidio had set up a kind of standard of completeness to which any subsequent treatise on the subject was expected to conform. Nevertheless, Patrizi's and Platina's books both exhibit certain characteristic deviations. Patrizi expanded the boundaries of his subject by a section devoted to the prince's education, in which he classified the art of warfare as a necessary part of the prince's training. With Platina the problems of state administration are considered in relation to ethics, to a certain extent as practical examples of the application of virtues. This shows that more importance was attached to the personal than to the institutional side of the problem. The shorter writings, such as those of Majo,[27] Poggio,[28] Pontano,[29] and Beroaldus,[30] are confined to dealing with the personality of the prince and consist of no more than catalogues of virtues.

Thus, besides the introduction of a new method of approach and the omission of the religious motivation, the emphasis on the catalogue of virtues is the main feature by which these humanist writings are distinguished from their medieval predecessors. It is not hard to explain why the humanists focused on and developed the subject of princely virtues as formulated in the medieval mirror of princes. The explanation lies in the influence of the classical world. By confining themselves to the composition of catalogues of virtues, the writers could pattern themselves closely on ancient models and adopt the schemes provided by Aristotle in the *Nicomachean ethics* or by Cicero in *De officiis.* Under this influence the humanist catalogue of virtues took on a new aspect and came to differ from those of the middle ages. Purely worldly virtues took their places beside the religious ones and even superseded them in the degree of interest they aroused;[31] moreover, those worldly virtues were considered purely from the point of view of their effect, their advantages and disadvantages being exactly weighed.

This is particularly true of the virtue of *liberalitas,* which was now regarded as a means of consolidating the position of the ruler. The question whether a prince should strive to make himself feared or loved was discussed as a serious, practical problem; and though it was invariably answered in the traditional idealist manner, opportunities for realistic observations were necessarily provided in the course of the discussion.[32] With Pontano (1426–1503) this literary form ceased to be merely an enumeration of individual virtues and emerged as a compact and comprehensive psychological sketch.[33] The specific contribution of the humanist writers to the development of the mirror-of-princes literature can thus be characterized as an amplification and a more searching discussion of the problems raised in the earlier catalogues of virtues. Starting from this approach, they succeeded in presenting a new problem: Was it permissible, they asked, to apply to the specific case of the prince the ethical norm postulated quite generally for every human being? Must not the prince practice virtues differing essentially from those of his subjects or of the ordinary citizen?[34]

At this point we have found a connecting link between the humanists and Machiavelli—this despite the fact that at first sight an abyss seems to separate the idealist conception of the prince from the realistic conception of power-politics which dominated Machiavelli's writings. The quattrocento, by concentrating attention on the ethical problems of princeship and thus on the personal characteristics of the prince, started a tendency which reached its culmination in Machiavelli's proposition that the vital, the determining, factor in politics was the prince's personality. And one can say that the famous chapters[35] of *The Prince,* in which Machiavelli investigates the qualities that make the successful prince and in which he falls most foul of conventional morality, were but a consequence of pushing to its logical conclusion the argument that first appeared in the writings of the humanists: whether the virtues and characteristics of the prince ought not to be different from those of the private citizen.

III

While indicating that there is some connection between the humanists and Machiavelli, we have already broached the important question whether the humanist writings were touched by the politics of their time and can be considered as having presaged the realism of Machiavelli. This question cannot be answered in the affirmative simply on the strength of this one point—that the humanists were already aware of the problem as to the difference between prince and private citizen—since this problem did not present itself to them in the light of its true importance but rather as a by-product, an unexpected result reached almost automatically in the course of the inquiry. On the contrary, in general we have seen that the humanist writings invariably started by accepting the traditional identity between the ideal prince and the ideal human being; and, because of this fact, their contents and form were, to a large extent, predetermined by the medieval tradition of the mirror of princes. And even those elements which they added—the more comprehensive catalogue of virtues and the stronger emphasis on the personality of the prince—were endorsed by a literary authority, that of antiquity.

Yet these innovations, though facilitated by a literary authority, cannot be said to have originated there. With regard to the enlargement of the catalogue of virtues, the manner in which it was transformed and the choice of the secular virtues selected for particular emphasis clearly reveal the influence of contemporary reality. One result of this influence is that the external signs of princely power and display now receive particular attention. Egidio had considered the possession of power and worldly honors as of no significance. He even regarded with a certain amount of distrust all bodily games and exercises which provided opportunities of princely display.[36] But in the writings of the quattrocento, hunts, tourneys, and games counted as the essential constituents of the princely life and were described in great detail. They belonged to *magnificentia,* which now made its appearance as one of the most characteristic virtues of the prince.[37] And in company with *magnificentia* there was introduced the pregnant idea of *majestas,* a heading which included everything that contributed to making an outward impression of princely power. How completely Majo (d. 1493) identified this conception with the very idea of the prince is shown by the fact that he entitled his book *"De majestate."*

Pontano attached no less importance to the new conception of *majestas.*[38] A great part of his work[39]—and he himself regarded it as a particularly important and original part—is devoted to the question of princely deportment.[40] Pontano maintains that the prince's gestures, his way of speaking, the sound of his voice, and even his dress and table manners—the whole of his life, in fact—must be subject to exact rules which are stated in minute detail;[41] Pontano's view amounts to the claim that the respect accorded to the prince is determined by his outer bearing and deportment. He must rise above his subjects by the strict observance of an elaborate ceremonial. This is a superficial answer to the question concerning the essence of princely power, but it is an attitude that wholly corresponds to the excessive regard for form which characterizes the Renaissance and is reflected in the ceremonial prescriptions of the lists of court precedence which originated in Italy at that time.[42]

But it is the declining interest in the institutional aspect of the problem and the concentration of the writers' attention on the personality of the prince which most clearly reveals the influence of political reality. For this change in emphasis was wholly appropriate to the ruthless character of quattrocento princeship with its dependence on the personal qualities of the ruler. The purely personal approach to the subject is apparent in Majo's book,[43] more perhaps than in any other. At the same time it is a good illustration of a work intimately associated with a specific political situation. It is distinguished from the remaining prince-literature by the fact that its primary purpose was to prove that a contemporary ruler, Ferrante of Naples, was to be regarded as an embodiment of the ideal prince. Majo planned the book with that object in view. He starts each chapter with a brief description of a special virtue; he then goes on to demonstrate with the aid of quotations from ancient authors how necessary that virtue is for a ruling prince, and ends the chapter by quoting some deed or incident from the life of Ferrante as an illustration of that particular virtue having been realized in practice. There is, of course, a large dose of humanist flattery in this method of treatment. This is made abundantly plain when Majo's idealized portrait is compared with the character of the real Ferrante, which was certainly not ideal. But Majo's work does not consist entirely of empty eulogy. He makes a serious attempt to survey and appreciate with some completeness the historical events of Ferrante's reign. The attempt, of course, led him into making some remarkably false judgments and ascribing some remarkably unreal motives to Ferrante.[44] Nevertheless, Majo had a certain feeling for the historical significance of individual events. For example, in his section on "Justice" he deals very thoroughly with the overthrow of the powers of feudalism in Naples and the establishment of a strong, central government and quite rightly emphasizes it as the most important event of Ferrante's reign.[45] Majo regards every historical event as being purely and simply the consequence of the prince's personality. History had ceased to be conceived of as being controlled by the intervention of God or supernatural powers; the only decisive factor was now the personality of the prince. Majo's attitude illustrates a conception of history generally accepted at the time. It shows that the tendency of the quattrocento princeship literature to accentuate the personal aspects of the problem was rooted in the historical individualism of the age.

In spite, however, of these traits by which contemporary politics have left their stamp on the humanist writings, in the main, as we said, the idealistic conception remained unchanged; and, although there are instances where practical problems crept in and are clearly recognizable,[46] there is no manifestation of a thoroughgoing realism, no appreciation of the power-factor and the egoistic purposes which dominate the political life. That is the more strange since a definite trend of realism did exist in the quattrocento, and since writers, having practical aims in view, knew and used the vocabulary of unqualified realism.

An example of this in the prince-literature is Diomede Carafa (1406–87), *De regis et boni principis officio*.[47] That Carafa's interests were entirely concentrated on practical questions is shown by the very chapter headings of his book: "De tuendo imperio, de jure dicendo et justitia servanda, de re familiari et vectiga-libus administrandis, de subditorum civitatisque commodis pre-servandis." Certainly, Carafa, like his contemporaries, was fond of quoting maxims from ancient authors[48] and apophthegms from traditional controversies;[49] but he is basically concerned only with the practical lessons to be drawn from these general-izations,[50] and the conclusions at which he arrives are often sur-prisingly similar to Machiavelli's. The best illustration of this is the sentence in which he announces that the guiding principle of politics is self-interest: "Kings and peoples of the whole world, deliberating concerning the government of their affairs, pursue their own advantages and are wont to put their interests before the ties of relationship and friendship."[51] But Carafa's work derives its exceptional character simply from the fact that it does not belong to the scheme of humanist prince-literature: it was a political memorandum,[52] written by the leading Nea-politan minister for the use of a Neapolitan princess who had just been married to the Duke of Ferrara; it was not in-tended for publication.[53] As soon as an author had literary am-bitions, he felt it necessary to set an ideal standard and write of an imaginary political world.

Thus, the humanist prince-writings only reflect contem-porary reality to the extent of embodying the historical individ-ualism of their age; they do not go so far as to adopt a thorough-going realism. Yet even their inability to go beyond a purely lit-erary and idealistic attitude to politics has a factual cause and should be explained in terms of the author's general intellectual background.

Political consciousness in general, no less than the specific historical individualism embodied in the works we are dis-cussing, was decisively influenced by the fact that Italy of the quattrocento was politically isolated from the rest of Europe. It was an epoch of mutually balancing powers striving after an equilibrium. The Italian political situation in the quattrocento consisted of a number of known and calculable forces, and suc-cess was in the hands of him who knew how to calculate and give due weight to each. All the factors of the political situation were within the perspective of the intelligent observer. This ceased to be the case after the French invasion of 1494, which put an end to Italy's isolation and brought her once more within the orbit of the inexorable dynamics of world-historical events. History, in other words, once more appeared as the manifestation of an incomprehensible and uncontrollable power.

Underlying the political rationalism of Machiavelli and the cinquecento was a passionate concern to discover the hidden laws of history's involutions. The principle of political realism was born on men's striving to learn the laws of politics by penetrating to their very essence. By the application of those laws, once they had been discovered, Machiavelli's prince would have it within his power to be the master of politics. Thus, all trace of the idealized human personality as such vanished from Machiavelli's portrait of the prince, and its place was taken by the superpersonal conception of reasons of state.[54] Prior to the upheaval of the French invasion an optimistic faith in man's power to have the whole of politics within his purview, and understand it, could still be preserved. In concentrating attention on the personal factor in politics, the quattrocento writers prepared the way for a "realistic" psychological approach to politics, such as exists now; but, inasmuch as the limits of man's control over history had not yet been discovered, there was, as yet, no need to abandon the ideal standard of the middle ages, and it was still possible to regard the setting-up of the notion of an ideal human being, with all the pedagogic appeal that such a notion possessed, as a serious contribution to political thought.

IV

In so far as we have shown the humanist contribution to prince-literature in relief against the background of that literature as a whole, our survey can be called complete. Yet there is one element present in the intellectual interest in the prince which our analysis has not touched upon: the need, in the quattrocento, for a new justification and legitimization of princeship. This was a point of great and immediate importance: the princes were, for the most part, usurpers; the existence of neighboring republics showed that autocracy was, by no means, a necessity; monarchy having been shorn of its religious significance, the notion that it was ordained by God had lost its once unassailable power. In the light of these three points, what necessary justification was there for monarchy? On what authority could princes prove their right to hold sway over other mortals?

It is hardly surprising that this subject was not dealt with in the works we have analyzed, since, in choosing the prince as their subject, these authors had implicitly allied themselves with the monarchical idea.[55] The problem was seriously discussed only when it occurred under more general headings in the philosophical literature of the time. Thus, it is there that we must seek to learn the contemporary attitude toward the problem of the justification of the prince. Until we have done this, one fact of our subject—a survey of the position of the prince in the consciousness of the time—will have been neglected.

Whenever the problem had been raised in history, the solution was sought along one or the other of two contrary intellectual lines. One was the "democratizing" conception,[56] which regarded the prince as the holder of an office with definitely circumscribed functions. The other, the "absolutist" conception, sought the solution of the problem along the lines of the personal elevation of the prince, who was regarded as directly inspired by God and thus as the unrestricted arbiter of the state.[57] The thinkers of the quattrocento, no less than the others, adopted one or the other of these lines. In consequence we may confine our survey to those quattrocento writers who developed one or the other of these lines in an original way.

The first to deal thoroughly and at length with the democratic conception of monarchy was Leon Battista Alberti (1407–72).[58] His treatise, *De iciarchia*,[59] is written in the form of a dialogue between some young Florentines and Alberti in his old age. The younger men, when asked what they would best like to be in the world, reply without hesitation that the height of their desire would be to be princes. Further questioning elicits the information that princeship appears desirable to them because it involves the right to give orders and to do what one likes one's self. Alberti answers them by describing what he considered princeship to involve. Like everybody else who has ever drawn a picture of a democratic prince,[60] he compares the relation of the prince to his people to that of a father to his family.[61] The prince, he says, is not outside or above his people, but the latter are a community of which the prince is an indispensable member.[62] Alberti then goes on to define in detail the prince's functions in the commonwealth. In his eyes the prince is a state functionary. He deduces the necessity of functionaries in general from the consideration that there must be somebody whose business it is to see that the laws are applied.[63] The prince is the supreme magistrate;[64] it is his responsibility to preserve the foundations of the social life of the community, to keep the state peaceful within and free and inviolate among the neighbors.[65] With the prince's functions circumscribed in this way, there was no question of his possessing unlimited power. The most he could ask of any of his subjects was what a patriotic "good citizen" would regard it his duty to do in any case. Hence, the prince's function consisted less in giving orders than in admonishing and exhorting.[66]

Thus the conception of the prince assumed a specifically bourgeois character in Alberti's thesis, and, if we consider that the humanists in their catalogue of virtues took over the civil virtues of the Stoics practically unaltered[67] and that whole passages in Platina's *De principe vero* are practically interchangeable with parts of his treatise *De cive,*[68] it will be seen that Alberti's views represent only the conscious culmination of a train of reasoning which was quite widespread. Apart from Alberti's fundamental ideas, it is interesting to note the importance he attached to the influence of personal insight and wisdom in political life. One is involuntarily reminded of Plato's famous saying that philosophers should be kings and kings philosophers.

This is a sign of the influence of Plato, which showed sporadic traces in the first half of the fifteenth century and became predominant only in the second half of the century. The development which the "democratic" theory of princedom underwent toward the end of the century bears witness to this fact. For under the influence of Platonism the democratic theory was driven to its logical extreme, though in a form so refined and spiritualized as to be deprived of all practical political content. This is manifested in Ficino's (1433–99) commentaries on Plato's *Politikos.*[69] According to Ficino, Plato wishes to describe the world-monarch in the *Politikos.* If Plato did not entitle his book "monarchos" but called it "politikos," that is, *vir civilis,* he meant to imply that the world-monarch must make his appearance in a mild and human form, as a citizen among other citizens.[70]

Ficino himself recognizes the remoteness of all this from reality; so he logically makes a radical distinction between the ideal and the real world. But, philosopher and Platonist as he is, he attaches value to the ideal world alone. The true ruler was not he who possessed the position and outward trappings of power, but he who surpassed all others in intellect and uprightness, even though he occupied no public position at all.[71] One criticism of the institution of monarchy had constantly recurred since ancient times. Although it might be the best form of government when a good king is on the throne, it was objected that there had never been a really good king and never could be one. In Ficino the argument is pushed to absurd extremes. It is not he who has the outward power who is king, but only he who is legitimized by his own inner deportment, even if outwardly no trace of his kingly situation is perceptible.

The democratic theory was very closely bound up with the whole intellectual trend of humanism. Its contrast, the absolutist theory, was much harder to reconcile with the intellectual tendencies of the day—and there were much greater difficulties in providing it with a convincing moral justification—still it corresponded to a more primitive attitude of mind, and this lent it an obstinate vitality. The situation is well illustrated in Alberti's *De iciarchia,* in which the point is made that, though the sophisticated would accept the more enlightened conception of the prince, the people would never understand it and would cling to the idea of the prince's natural right to unlimited power.[72] Absolutism can only really be justified by religion. This is why Platonism exercised a decisive influence on the absolutist as well as the democratic line of thought, for it replaced the obsolete medieval theological conception of rulership by a new religious conception appropriate to the age.

Before we can make clear what use the absolutists made of Platonism, we must consider the wider question: What aspects of the Platonic political doctrines bore fruit in the intellectual soil of the quattrocento as a whole?[73] The most important influence of these doctrines was that they directed attention to the laws and constitution of the state.[74] Entirely new vistas were opened up when men had their attention drawn to constitutional problems; the state ceased to be regarded as something permanent and unchanging and came to be looked at as pliable raw material, susceptible of being molded at will.[75] The ancients had attributed divine honors to the founder of the state, and the humanists had copied them. But now he had to share his honors with a new figure, that of the lawgiver; and not only he who put a new code into force was regarded as such, but also he who merely worked out a new code in theory. Political philosophers, such as Plato himself, were considered as important to politics as practical statesmen like Solon and Lycurgus.[76] A divine revelation resided in wisdom, and wisdom empowered the wise to rule[77] and freed them from all limiting or binding restraints. This theory admirably suited the entirely undynastic character of the rulers of Italy at that time but became remarkably debased in practice.

The Platonic postulate that the prince must be philosopher receded into the background. The idea which became uppermost in men's minds was that the possession of power itself presupposed divine inspiration, and that he who founded a state was absolved from all restraints and could give the state the shape that it pleased him to give.[78] Thus it came about that an idea which ripened only in the age of absolutism was preconceived in the quattrocento. A saying of Lorenzo the Magnificent, "Rappresentano il tutto i signor veri,"[79] reminds one of the saying of Louis XIV, "L'état c'est moi." In the absolutist theory of the quattrocento the prince for the first time assumed the role which later became the basic theme of Machiavelli's *The Prince:* the prince not as a dependent member of a given moral order but as the creative political man.[80]

Thus a variety of ideas developed in the course of this discussion—ideas that pointed toward the future but that, on the other hand, are connected with the very traits which we have characterized as peculiar to the humanist prince-literature and which lent to that literature a substratum of philosophy.

V

The humanist prince-literature both influenced the later mirror-of-princes writings and contributed to the classical political theories of the Renaissance which developed in the cinquecento. That is to say, it lived on in the two literary trends from which it was chiefly composed. Yet it is not these trends that we wish to follow now. It was some passages from Machiavelli's *The Prince* that afforded a starting point for this study by suggesting that there was some connection between Machiavelli's *The Prince* and the humanist prince-literature. Has this proved to be the case? At various points we have found definite links between Machiavelli and the humanists: when they raised the problem as to the difference between prince and private citizen, when they envisaged the prince as a creative political force—these are tendencies which clear the way for Machiavelli and which he took up. Thus it can be said that, although in the decisive factor of political realism, this literature did not, in any sense, pave the way for Machiavelli, Machiavelli nevertheless incorporated in his book certain intellectual trends that had already been developed by the humanists.

Yet it is not these general trends alone that associate Machiavelli with the humanist prince-literature. Machiavelli was aware that he dealt, though from a new point of view, with matters that had been treated before; we now maintain that he was consciously refuting his predecessors and that this intention has left its mark on the structure of the *The Prince*. That, then, is the thesis we hope this study will enable us to prove. First, there is reason to believe that Machiavelli endeavored to adapt the form of his book to the conventional literary form of this genre. There are especially two facts which render this supposition probable. In the first place, like the works of Machiavelli's predecessors, all the earliest manuscripts of *The Prince* have Latin chapter headings.[81] Secondly, however, the dedication of *The Prince* to Lorenzo Medici is an imitation of Isocrates' *Address to Nicocles;*[82] and, as already stated, it is this address that was considered as the best-known ancient example of a mirror of princes. Since for that reason the humanists frequently referred to this speech, it is clear that Machiavelli followed an established tradition when he adopted Isocrates as his model.

But the connection is a far more specific one. We have already drawn attention to the fact that certain sections of *The Prince* relate to the discussion raised by the humanist catalogue of virtues,[83] and it is my contention that Machiavelli deliberately undertook these chapters as a refutation.

I refer to chapters 15–19 of *The Prince*. They constitute a coherent section, distinct from the remainder of the work; for in chapter 15 Machiavelli states that he is about to examine the qualities necessary for a prince, and, after enumerating them one by one, he writes in chapter 19, "Having now spoken of the chief of the qualities above referred to, the rest I shall dispose of briefly with these general remarks," and indicates that, having discussed the more important qualities in detail, he will deal summarily with the remainder. This summary forms the substance of the nineteenth-chapter. Thus, the subject taken up in chapter 15 is concluded with the termination of chapter 19.

The contention that these chapters form a whole is further supported by the opening sentence of chapter 15: "It now remains for us to consider what ought to be the conduct and bearing of a prince in relation to his subjects and friends," in which Machiavelli himself indicates that he is commencing a new theme with this chapter. This sentence indicates, moreover, that the chapters were written with the deliberate intention of providing an up-to-date rendering of the subject matter contained in the humanist catalogues of virtue, for it was the habit of the humanists to deal with general questions, such as that of a prince's relations with his subjects and friends by introducing them into the conventional literary framework of the princely qualities, which, in its turn, was presented as a catalogue of virtues. And this is precisely what Machiavelli sets out to do, only from a new and realistic point of view. It is this chapter, moreover, which contains Machiavelli's criticism of his predecessors' approach to politics quoted at the beginning of this essay—the passage, that is to say, in which he expressly states that he is about to treat of matters that have often been dealt with before.

A passage in chapter 16 affords further support to this theory. When Machiavelli starts discussing whether a prince should strive to be loved or feared, he characterizes the question as a *disputà* and thus shows that he was well aware of previous discussions of the subject. His chapter headings make the link we are trying to establish even plainer. The headings of chapters 16, 17, 18, and 19, respectively, are: "De liberalitate et parsimonia"; "De crudelitate et pietate; et an sit melius amari quam timeri, vel e contra"; "Quomodo fides a principibus sit deservanda"; "De contemptu et odio fugiendo." Practically the same chapter headings might have been used by the humanists in their catalogues of virtues; and, although the latter discuss the subject in far greater detail, Machiavelli has emphasized precisely those qualities which, in the works of the humanists, it appears important for the prince to possess.[84]

There appears to be no doubt that Machiavelli did not merely refute the idealist interpretation of politics in general but that he wrote with the conscious aim of discrediting the idealized conception of the prince as contained in the catalogues of the virtues.[85] The "realistic" thesis of chapter 15 was intended to replace that false conception. It is possibly another instance of the fact, often to be observed, that in proclaiming certain aspects of his thesis Machiavelli was motivated by a spirit of contradiction—perhaps even by a certain exuberant pleasure in paradox. Such an idea is thoroughly consistent with the view of those of Machiavelli's contemporaries whose opinions we have reason to value and who stress this trait as a characteristic feature of his work.[86] They were fully aware of the polemical character of Machiavelli's writings, concealed for us by the originality of his principles and the positive value of his contribution to political thought.

Let us now inquire whether our conclusion that chapters 15–19 form a compact, independent whole, written by Machiavelli for the express purpose of adding a sequel and a refutation to the humanist's catalogues of virtues, tallies with what we know of the composition of *The Prince*.

The most recent comprehensive discussion of the composition of *The Prince* is to be found in Friedrich Meinecke's introduction to a German translation of *The Prince*.[87] Meinecke bases his conclusions on Machiavelli's letter to Vettori of December 10, 1513, the only document in which Machiavelli himself refers to his own work. He writes:

> I have composed a treatise *De principatibus* in which I enter as deeply as I can into the science of the subject, with reasonings on the nature of principality, its several species, and how they are acquired, how maintained, how lost . . . [Philippo] will be able to inform you about it, and about the discussions I have had with him on the subject, although I am still amplifying and pruning the work.

Meinecke claims that Machiavelli's remarks in this letter must apply not to the whole of *The Prince* but only to the first eleven chapters of it, and he also states that there are certain signs that chapter 11 was originally intended to be the final chapter. He therefore infers that the work originated in sections and that the chapters following chapter 11 did not form part of Machiavelli's original conception but represented a subsequent addition. In the second part of *The Prince,* which he states begins with chapter 12, Meinecke also distinguishes various subsections. Thus, chapters 12–14 belong together, because they deal with military affairs; and chapters 15–18 seem to him "a small special treatise on the relations of politics to the ethical values and feelings of the prince's subjects."

All this fits admirably into our own thesis. Meinecke mentions in support of his theory that Machiavelli changed the title of the work from *De principatibus* to *Il principe,* thereby indicating that a change of emphasis had occurred in the course of writing it and that a new theme had forced its way into the foreground. We may perhaps add that *De principe* was the title used by the humanists and that the alteration of title thus confirms our theory of a close connection between the train of thought of the second half of *The Prince* and the humanist's writings on the subject.

So far, our views correspond exactly with those of Meinecke. But in other respects the acceptance of our thesis involves parting from him. Although, as we mentioned above, Meinecke distinguishes various subsections in the second half of *The Prince,* beginning with chapter 12, he believes that the second half of the book was conceived as a whole. This view is not, however, compatible with the thesis we are advocating, for it is an essential implication[88] of our thesis that chapters 15–19 did not originate as an elaboration of a trend of thought suggested by the general scheme of *The Prince* but rather in response to an external literary stimulus. It follows that chapter 15 begins an entirely new section and that no link whatever bridges the gap between it and the three preceding chapters. We must rather assume that the second part of *The Prince,* commencing with chapter 12, consists of several distinct complexes of ideas loosely grouped together.

We therefore suggest the following sequence in the composition of *The Prince.*[89] Having completed working out his original idea in the first eleven chapters, Machiavelli proceeded to revise and amplify his work. In the course of this revision he added a more detailed account of his favorite subject, the art of war. He then felt impelled to examine his work from the point of view of the problems dealt with in the writings of his humanist predecessors, and was thus induced to write a polemical reply to the traditional catalogues of virtues. In the remaining chapters he discussed at length certain additional problems raised in the literature of his time.

The structure of *The Prince* has always been examined in the hope of finding a solution to the much debated question whether the Italian nationalism of the last chapter formed an integral part of Machiavelli's political outlook or whether it was merely a decorative conclusion—a rhetorical, humanist ornament. If we are right in our theory that from chapter 15 onward Machiavelli was inspired by opposition to the humanists who preceded him and that, consequently, the second part of *The Prince* is very loosely composed and forms no connected unity, I believe we have to accept, as a further result, that also the last chapter, which is not prepared for by any hint in the preceding sections of the book, stands by itself, mainly intended as a concluding rhetorical flourish. This conclusion must not be interpreted as a denial of national feeling in Machiavelli, but it does show that nationalism had no definite and prescribed place in his system. It indicates that nationalism and realism, the appearance of which revolutionized political consciousness and political thought, were only gradually conceived as interdependent forces.

5. The Composition and Structure of Machiavelli's *Discorsi*

A review of L. J. Walker's translation and edition of Machiavelli's *Discorsi*[1] is a puzzling and disturbing task; it is extremely difficult to arrive at a definite and unequivocal evaluation of the work. The first reaction this edition evokes is that of gratitude; it is truly astonishing that there has been no scholarly edition of the *Discorsi,* explaining and commenting upon the many historical and classical allusions of the text, until the appearance of these two volumes. Mr. Walker's work goes far to explain the reasons for this delay; it shows the almost Herculean task involved in providing an edition that fulfills scholarly demands. The entire 390 pages of Mr. Walker's second volume are devoted to explanatory notes, to chronological tables, to discussion of the sources of the *Discorsi,* and to indices. Although a number of objections against details of the scholarly apparatus

Originally published in *Journal of the History of Ideas,* 14 (1953), pp. 136–156. About the discussion provoked by this article see Sergio Bertelli's introduction to the *Discorsi* in the Feltrinelli edition of Machiavelli's *Opere,* I (Milan, 1960) and also the very recent survey of Machiavelli literature by John H. Geerken, "Machiavelli Studies Since 1969," *Journal of the History of Ideas,* 37 (April–June 1976), 351–368. The one part of this article which I no longer maintain is the thesis that Machiavelli became interested in humanistic literature only after his dismissal from office; we know now—through the researches of Bertelli, Fredi Chiappelli, Mario Martelli, and Gian Roberto Sarolli—that such concerns go back to his early years, although they certainly increased in his later years.

can be raised, there can be no doubt that now, for the first time, we have a scholarly commentary on the text of the *Discorsi;* all further discussion of Machiavelli's work will be based on Mr. Walker's edition.

Unfortunately, Mr. Walker has not limited himself to a purely editorial task; he would have given more if he had given less. As frequently happens, in pursuing his editorial function Mr. Walker arrived at a special and definite interpretation of the *Discorsi* and of the issues connected with them. He has presented his views in a long introduction; they penetrate into the scholarly apparatus and even invade the text, parts of which bear not only the titles given by Machiavelli but also headlines derived from Mr. Walker's views of the *Discorsi.* This is regrettable, because Mr. Walker's conception of the *Discorsi* is open to grave doubts. Since Mr. Walker's edition will and should be frequently used, his views may gain greater authority than they deserve. I shall not enter upon a comprehensive critical discussion of Mr. Walker's interpretation of the *Discorsi,* because previous reviews have proceeded along this line.[2] I shall take up one single issue, on which Mr. Walker has expressed very definite opinions, namely the question of "the composition and structure of the *Discorsi*"; in investigating this problem, the merits and the limits of Mr. Walker's edition will emerge clearly.[3] Thus the following study may serve as an example of the equivocal importance of Mr. Walker's edition; it will illustrate that Mr. Walker's work is of the greatest assistance to the study of the *Discorsi,* while his theories about the *Discorsi* should not be accepted without thorough re-examination.

I

Those who try to envisage the Machiavelli who emerges from the scholarly researches of recent years may sometimes wonder what our virtuous and law-abiding republican has to do with the conjurer of hellish powers, from whom former centuries learnt that

> Might first made kings, and laws were then most sure
> When, like the Draco's, they were writ in blood.[4]

Certainly, Machiavelli's teachings are so rich that in them each succeeding century can find answers for the political issues which are its main concern, and the myth of Machiavelli can grow and vary without losing contact with the personality which inspired it. It is probably fair to say, however, that in the case of Machiavelli the change in evaluation which critical historical scholarship has brought about has meant a particularly radical break with the picture which previous centuries had created. This development is reflected in the fact that, while to former centuries Machiavelli had been chiefly the author of *The Prince,* students of our century have given their chief attention to the *Discorsi* as containing the essence of Machiavelli's political teachings.[5] Nevertheless, the traditional emphasis on *The Prince* still exerts influence on recent scholarship to the extent that, despite the assumption of the decisive significance of the *Discorsi,* they have not been considered in isolation, but have been studied chiefly in their relation to *The Prince.*

This seems to me at least a possible explanation for the strange lack of interest among students in investigating the formal questions connected with the *Discorsi.* We have no detailed structural analysis of the *Discorsi;* we do not even have attempts to clarify some of the preliminary questions that could be solved on the basis of a careful reading of the text and that might help to define the problems involved in an examination of the structure.[6] Scholars have been vague concerning such preliminary questions as the time of the composition of the *Discorsi* and the problem of the formal unity of the work, though mere analysis of the text permits quite precise conclusions.

The standard works on Machiavelli refer to the time of composition of the *Discorsi* as falling between 1513 and 1519.[7] The year 1513 is set as the beginning date because Machiavelli states in *The Prince,* composed in 1513,[8] that he has discussed republics in another place;[9] it has always been understood that this sentence is an allusion to the *Discorsi.* The year 1519 is taken as the date for completion because in the *Discorsi* Cosimo Rucellai, to whom the work was dedicated, and the Emperor Maximilian are mentioned as being alive, and both died in 1519.[10]

The *Discorsi* contain a great number of chronological references;[11] on the basis of these references it is possible to give more precision and meaning to the inference that the composition of the *Discorsi* extended over six years. Of course, many of the chronological references are so vague that for the purposes of exact dating they are of no value.[12] But two statements point to a definite date. In book II, chap. 10, Machiavelli writes that "if treasures guaranteed victory . . . , a few days ago the combined forces of the Pope and the Florentines would have had no difficulty in overcoming Francesco Maria, the nephew of Julius the Second, in the war of Urbino."[13] This refers to a definite event, the conquest of Urbino in 1517. Another reference to a definite time can be found in book III, chap. 27. "Fifteen years ago Pistoia was divided, as it is still, into the Panciatichi and the Cancellieri, but in those days they were armed, whereas today they have given this up."[14] Since Machiavelli refers here to the civil strife which had taken place in Pistoia in the winter of 1501–02, and about which he had reported in his "relation on the events in Pistoia," this sentence must have been written late in 1516 or in 1517. Other chronological indications also point to the special significance of the year 1517 for the composition of the *Discorsi*. A number of events which took place after 1513 are mentioned, allusions to events which happened as late as 1515, 1516, and 1517 are scattered over all parts of the work,[15] but there is no reference to any event that took place after 1517.[16] Thus a consideration of the chronological references leads to the conclusion that of the six years during which the *Discorsi* are supposed to have been written, the year 1517 was particularly important.

If we ask what the significance of this year for the composition of the *Discorsi* might be, a possible answer would be that at this time Machiavelli produced the version of the *Discorsi* we possess today. For an examination of the text of the *Discorsi* suggests that their present structure developed very gradually. Undoubtedly the *Discorsi* were intended to appear as a consciously and systematically organized whole. Statements about the principles of organization can be found in prefaces and introductory chapters.[17] The place of single chapters is explained by references to the overall organization.[18] There are frequent references from one chapter to other chapters, not only from later chapters to earlier ones but also—what is a more significant indication of a conscious composition—from earlier chapters to later ones.[19]

On the other hand, the clearly stated principles of organization do not seem really to have permeated the text of the work. There are chapters which deal with problems that have nothing or very little to do with the topic of the book within which they are placed.[20] Sometimes the same problems are treated in quite different parts of the work, so that the impression of repetitiveness is created.[21] Scholars have debated whether the issues that Machiavelli proclaims form the principles of organization of his work were really the problems in which he was interested, or whether the collecting and grouping of the material was actually determined by different concerns.[22] The possibility of doubts on this point supports the view that the formal structure was not clear in Machiavelli's mind when he began his work. The present organization seems to be more an afterthought, a framework which was imposed from the outside to give his work a unified and presentable pattern.

This examination of the most manifest chronological and structural data of the *Discorsi* cannot be regarded as having provided definite proof that in the year 1517 Machiavelli transformed the material which he had previously collected into the work that has come down to us. But this preliminary analysis has certainly revealed some rather rough seams in the structure of the *Discorsi,* and suggests that an investigation of the composition of the *Discorsi* might have significant results for an understanding of the work.

II

What means do we have to gain further insight into the process of the genesis of the *Discorsi* and to advance the analysis of the composition of the *Discorsi* beyond the stage we have reached? The original manuscript of the *Discorsi* no longer exists.[23] Thus we have only one lead for establishing the method of their composition: the *Discorsi* are commentaries on the first decade of Livy's *History of Rome;* through clarifying the relation of the chapters of the *Discorsi* to Livy we might be able to reconstruct Machiavelli's procedure. Such a confrontation will be of a very technical character, but as the reader will see, the results will permit some fundamental observations on the position of the *Discorsi* in Machiavelli's work and on the development of his ideas and the influences which formed them.

The idea of using the relation to Livy as the key for an under-standing of the composition of the *Discorsi* is not a new one, but an analysis along these lines has never been fully carried through.[24] The reason is that such an investigation encounters an obstacle which seems to make clear-cut results impossible. Though almost half the chapters of the *Discorsi* comment on only one chapter or story from Livy,[25] there are a large number of chapters which quote several Livy passages, and which there-fore seem to prevent the establishment of a definite scheme of relationship. But this difficulty is actually less serious than it ap-pears. For a careful consideration of the *Discorsi* chapters with several Livy references shows that it is generally possible to es-tablish one particular Livy passage as the main reference among several (see the following table).

CHAPTER IN *Discorsi*	LIVY REFERENCES IN		
	BOOK I	BOOK II	BOOK III
1	general[a]	general	general
2	no[b]	general	I, 56–59
3	II, 27–33	general	II, 4, 5
4	same[c]	V, 33–34	I, 42, 46, 48
5	IX, 26	same, no[d]	I, 49–58
6	no	general	no
7	II, 34–35	V, 30	same (as chap. 5)
8	VI, 15	V, 33, 34	II, 41; VI, 11, 14–20
9	I, 7, 14	VII, 29–31	same, no
10	no	same	VII, 12
11	I, 19–21	same	IV, 48
12	V, 22	same, no	IX, 1
13	same	VIII, 4	II, 39
14	X, 40	same	II, 64
15	X, 38–39	same	IV, 31
16	II, 1–5	VIII, 7–II	no
17	same	same, no	no
18	same, no	II, 20, general	IV, 37–39
19	I, 4–31	VII, 38	II, 58–60
20	same	VII, 38–41	V, 27
21	same	IX, 20	same, no
22	I, 24–30	VIII, 11	VII, 4–10, 33; VIII, 7–10
23	same	VIII, 13, 21	V, 23
24	same	same, no	VIII, 26
25	II, 1–2	II, 44, 45	III, 26, 27, 29
26	same, no	same	IV, 9–10

continued

CHAPTER IN *Discorsi*	LIVY REFERENCES IN		
	BOOK I	BOOK II	BOOK III
27	same, no	same, no	same
28	II, 2 and 7	V, 35–36	IV, 13–15
29	same	V, 37–38, 48–55	V, 28
30	same, no	same	VI, 6
31	V, 8–11	VIII, 24	VI, 7
32	II, 9	VIII, 22–23, 25–26	VI, 21
33	II, 18	IX, 35–36	VI, 28–30, 41
34	same		VII, 5
35	III, 32–54		VII, 6
36	II, 46		VII, 10
37	II, 41		VII, 11
38	III, 6		VII, 32
39	III, 9		VII, 34
40	III, 31–39		IX, 2, 3
41	same		IX, 4
42	same		IX, 8, 9
43	same and III, 41–42		X, 10
44	same and III, 44–53		X, 16
45	same and III, 54–59		X, 28–29
46	III, 65		IX, 33, 34
47	IV, 6		IX, 38
48	IV, 7		X, 3, 4
49	IV, 8		VIII, 18; IX, 46
50	IV, 26		
51	IV, 59, 60		
52	same		
53	V, 24, 25		
54	same		
55	V, 25		
56	V, 32		
57	VI, 4		
58	VI, 14–20		
59	same, no		
60	VII, 32		

[a] Chapters of a quite general character; they cannot be considered as comments on the Livy passages they mention.

[b] Chapters without Livy reference.

[c] Chapters which comment on the same Livy passage as the previous chapter.

[d] Chapters which continue the line of thought of the previous chapter without referring to Livy.

In a number of chapters containing allusions to several Livy passages, the decisive importance of one particular quotation is evident.[26] Then there are Livy stories on which Machiavelli comments in a consecutive series of chapters;[27] in considering the same story from different angles, additional material from Livy is sometimes adduced but the subordination of this additional material to the Livy passage that started the whole discussion remains obvious. A few chapters summarize an entire development of Roman history; in such cases the Livy passage which describes the beginning of that development is the main reference.[28] In one case all uncertainty about the relative importance of various Livy references in the same chapter is solved by statements in a later chapter.[29] In only three[30] cases doubts remain as to the main reference.[31]

A first survey of the relationship between the individual chapters of the *Discorsi* and Livy reveals one striking fact: in extremely few cases has the same Livy story served as main reference in different *Discorsi* chapters—that is, duplications are extremely rare,[32] so rare that their paucity cannot be accidental. This fact proves that we are on the right track in pursuing an investigation along this line. Evidently Machiavelli intended each chapter, or sequence of chapters, of the *Discorsi* to be a commentary on a different chapter or story from Livy, and it seems a worthwhile attempt to find out whether, from a closer and detailed analysis of this relation, a scheme will evolve which will permit the reconstruction of the process which Machiavelli followed in composing the *Discorsi*.

No pattern with regard to Machiavelli's use of Livy can be discerned in the first eighteen chapters of the first book of the *Discorsi*, but from the nineteenth chapter on a sequence can clearly be observed. Till the end of the book, or at least till chapter 56,[33] Machiavelli comments on successive chapters of Livy's first five books. There are only two exceptions: chapters 25 to 37 are tied to passages from Livy's second book, but chapters 31 and 35 are commentaries on passages from later books of Livy. One of these chapters, however, is evidently a later insert.[34] Thus these chapters are a striking example of exceptions confirming the rule; they reinforce the view that the section was conceived as a commentary on successive Livy chapters.

Another sequence of a similar character can be found in the second part of the third book of the *Discorsi*. From chapter 30 on, Machiavelli comments on successive chapters from books VI, VII, IX, and X of Livy.[35] Two aspects of Machiavelli's procedure in this part of the *Discorsi* deserve attention. The one is the fact that in this section he is commenting on books of Livy's with which he had not been concerned in the series of successive comments of the first book. The other is the conclusion which must be drawn if the two series of successive comments in the first and third book of the *Discorsi* are taken together: that in their successive coverage of Livy's first decade these two sections contain no discussion of Livy's eighth book and very few comments on his fifth book. It is striking that comments on chapters from these two books form the bulk of the Livy material on which the second book of Machiavelli's *Discorsi* is based.

Thus we find an underlying pattern in those sections of the *Discorsi* we have analyzed. These sections originated as a series of successive commentaries on Livy's first decade; when this material was transformed into a literary work, the series was broken in the middle, and the second part arranged into two books. The comments on Livy's fifth and eighth book, which deal chiefly with military and foreign affairs, were lifted out and assembled in a special, second book, while the remainder of the material forms the third book.

Let us now look at those parts of the *Discorsi* which do not fit this pattern: first there are single chapters like the last chapters of all three books and the first three chapters of the second book, which stand outside the series of successive comments; then there are two large sections, namely the first halves of the first and third book of the *Discorsi,* which likewise do not permit the establishment of a pattern, but intermingle references to different books of Livy's first decade. It is obvious why the Livy references which are used in the last chapters of all three books and in the first chapters of the second book break up the pattern of successive comments. These chapters have a concluding or introductory character and Machiavelli picked out Livy passages which were suited for such purposes.

The fact that neither the first eighteen chapters of the first book nor more than half of the third book fit the pattern of successive comments raises a much more serious problem. Do we really have the right to consider successive comments on Livy's first decade as the basis of Machiavelli's *Discorsi* if a large part of the work is outside such a scheme? But if we examine closely one of these unrelated parts—namely, chapters 1 to 29 of the third book of the *Discorsi*—it emerges that this part has unique and irregular features through which it stands out from the rest of the book and which point to a composition of this part at a rather late stage.

First of all, there are external indications of the special character of these chapters. In this part, duplications[36] and chapters with doubtful main references[37] are particularly frequent; as a matter of fact almost all[38] such irregularities can be found in chapters or sections which do not belong to the original order of successive comments on Livy. These sections are closely knit; Machiavelli states frequently in the closing sentences of one chapter the topic of the next. Such a device, which clearly indicates a planned and conscious composition, is used here almost regularly, much more often than in any other part of the *Discorsi*.[39] But also the contents of these chapters suggest that this section stands somewhat separate from the rest of the third book of the *Discorsi* and forms a unit in itself. The connection of these first twenty-nine chapters with the leitmotif of the third book of the *Discorsi,* namely "the example of Rome's great men," is closer than in the rest of the book.[40] The organization in the first part of the book seems to be more systematic; in the rest of the book, the chapters have more the character of a commentary and take up topics of very different scope and importance.

Machiavelli's procedure in composing the *Discorsi* has now become clear. The composition developed in two stages. The first stage was that of giving a series of successive comments on Livy's first decade. Thus, in contrast to what has been frequently assumed, Machiavelli's original intent was not the presentation of a systematic treatise on politics. This feature emerged only in the second stage of his work, in which he rearranged his material. By dividing the material into three different groups, by adding some new material, and by providing introductions and conclusions, three books were created which were to discuss different aspects of the same general political problem, so that the whole work would appear to form an interconnected and unified whole.

These observations are not meant to convey the impression that when Machiavelli rearranged his material and brought it into the form we possess he proceeded mechanically, just placing completed chapters into a new order and writing introductions and conclusions. It seems much more likely that he reworked the whole manuscript, adding suitable material from other parts of Livy. He might have elaborated single ideas into complete new chapters, so that now some Livy passages are dealt with in a series of chapters, discussing the same story from different angles. He might have condensed comments on different passages that were related in content into one greater and more comprehensive chapter.[41] A precise and detailed reconstruction of the manner in which Machiavelli proceeded seems hardly possible, however, on the basis of the material we have. But even without the details of the process out of which the present version of the *Discorsi* developed, the main fact our analysis has brought out, one with important implications for the understanding of Machiavelli's doctrine, is that the basis of the *Discorsi* was a commentary on successive chapters and books of Livy's first decade.

III

Before we discuss the wider implications of the results of our analysis, it might be appropriate to give some attention to the one part of the *Discorsi* which we have not so far examined at any length: the first eighteen chapters of the first book of the *Discorsi*.

This section of the *Discorsi* needs to be treated separately and in some detail, because its investigation opens up a somewhat different problem; the analysis of the first eighteen chapters of the *Discorsi* has its bearing upon the question regarding the time when the *Discorsi* were composed. It has been mentioned that the manner in which these chapters are tied to Livy does not reveal any clear order or pattern. The references to Livy are taken from books that are widely separated in the text and are used without any regard to chronological sequence or to their place in Livy. In addition, the relation between the Livy reference and the contents of the chapter is frequently very loose, so that the connection with Livy seems to derive from a wish to adjust the chapters to the general pattern of the book rather than from inner necessity. Moreover, this section contains a number of chapters without any reference to Livy, and it is remarkable that here Machiavelli's "Romanism" is somewhat subdued and that, apart from Rome, Sparta and Venice serve as patterns of republican life. Above all, this part stands out because of its systematic approach; it contains detailed discussions about the various types of republics, the reproduction of Polybios' theory of the constitutional cycle, the thesis of the increase of political vitality through civil strife and the usefulness of religion for the maintenance of political order, and finally the pessimistic reflection on reintroducing a free government in a corrupt society. Briefly, Machiavelli presents here his basic ideas about the nature of republican institutions.

It would seem entirely natural that Machiavelli wanted to place considerations of a general character at the beginning of his work, and this purpose would satisfactorily explain the peculiar features of the section. But the question may be raised whether the discussion of the fundamental problems of a republic in these chapters has still other roots. Machiavelli uses a number of other historians here, and examples are taken from other peoples and times quite as much as from the Roman period. Machiavelli himself seems to have felt that the discussions of this part are rather outside the stated scope of his work, because he makes a strangely apologetic remark about his slowness in arriving at the discussion of Livy's tale of Rome's beginnings.[42]

In all these respects Machiavelli's approach in these first chapters of the *Discorsi* is very similar to that in *The Prince*. There are even passages which have a close interconnection. The nineteenth chapter of *The Prince* and the tenth chapter of the first book of the *Discorsi*—both concerned with the Roman emperors—seem like two parts of a rather comprehensive reflection on the same subject.[43] The great state founders, Moses, Lycurgus, Solon, who have been characterized as the real heroes of *The Prince*,[44] make their appearance in these chapters.[45] Most important, the statements about different kinds of principalities given in *The Prince* and the statements about different kinds of republics given in the *Discorsi* complement each other, so that taken together they provide a classification of all forms of government.

We have said that in *The Prince* Machiavelli mentions having written a treatise on republics,[46] and that this sentence has always been regarded as referring to the *Discorsi.* But are the *Discorsi* correctly described as a work on republics? The name which Machiavelli's contemporaries gave to the work was *Discorsi su Tito Livio.*[47] Certainly, since Machiavelli presents his ideas in the form of comments on the history of the Roman republic, the issues of republican life and of the successful functioning of a republican constitution are in the foreground of his interest. However, one should not overlook the fact that frequently his reflections are relevant to both monarchical and republican institutions, that many chapters deal with political problems of the most general character which have no special relation to republican government, and that a large part of the work is devoted to discussions of warfare.[48] It seems legitimate to ask whether, without a systematic treatment of the problems of republican government in the first eighteen chapters of the *Discorsi,* there would be much justification for entitling the *Discorsi* a book on republics. Because the treatment in these chapters is rather different from the rest of the book, and because the approach is rather similar to that of *The Prince,* it seems possible to suggest that Machiavelli had been working on a treatise on republics when he was composing *The Prince,* and that he used this manuscript when he gave the *Discorsi* their final version and realized the necessity of providing them with a fuller introduction.

It is hardly in accord with the rules of sound scholarship to suggest the existence of a treatise of which no mention is made and for which no manuscript is preserved, if such a thesis is not forced upon us by otherwise inexplicable contradictions in our source material. There are weighty reasons, however, for doubting that the above mentioned statement in *The Prince* refers to the existing version of the *Discorsi,* and one must therefore find a different explanation for that sentence. The question of the date of the *Discorsi* makes a new interpretation of the allusion to the work on republics in *The Prince* necessary.

We have distinguished two different stages in the composition of the *Discorsi.* The later, the second stage, which was a rearrangement of previously gathered material, resulted in the version which we have today, and the analysis which we have previously made of the chronological references in the *Discorsi* permits the conclusion that this work of rearrangement and revision took place in the year 1517.

But when did the first stage of Machiavelli's work on the *Discorsi,* the writing of a serial commentary on Livy's first decade, take place? We have inferred the existence of such a first stage from an analysis of the relation of the *Discorsi* to Livy's *History of Rome,* that is, from internal evidence. We also have statements by contemporaries on the origin of the *Discorsi,* and this external evidence fully confirms the results of our analysis. In general, the accounts of Machiavelli's contemporaries emphasize the novelty of Machiavelli's attempt to transform the teachings of history into definite rules;[49] one of them, Nerli, even gives a somewhat more detailed report about the origin of the work. He narrates that a number of literati, among them Machiavelli, came together in the Rucellai gardens: "There they trained themselves, through the reading of classical works, and the lessons of history, and on the basis of these conversations, and upon the demand of his friends, Machiavelli composed his famous book the *Discorsi on Livy.*"[50] Since others also mention the meetings in the Rucellai gardens in connection with the *Discorsi,*[51] and since Nerli himself participated in these meetings, the authenticity of this report cannot be doubted.

An important aspect of Nerli's statement is that it makes it possible to establish the time when Machiavelli was concerned with the first stage of the work, the serial commentary on Livy. For Machiavelli's participation in the meetings of the Rucellai gardens cannot have taken place before 1515; this conclusion must be drawn from out knowledge of Machiavelli's life as well as from the information we possess about the Rucellai circle.

After the Medici had returned, Machiavelli was in disgrace and spent most of his time in his villa outside Florence in a self-imposed exile, cut off from friends and from Florentine society. Only gradually did his appearances in Florence become more frequent and extended, and his letters mention the names of new friends acquired through the meetings in the Rucellai gardens not before 1519.[52] When Machiavelli attended the meetings in the Rucellai gardens, the guiding spirit was Cosimo Rucellai, to whom Machiavelli expressed his attachment and obligation in the *Discorsi* as well as in the *Art of War.* Cosimo was born in 1495 and can have entered upon the role of host and intellectual leader of the Rucellai gardens meeting only after the death of his grandfather Bernardo, that is, after 1514.[53] Moreover, the many references to the flowering of the Rucellai gardens as a center of intellectual activity under Cosimo Rucellai all point to the years 1515 to 1517. It is evident, therefore, that in *The Prince,* which Machiavelli wrote in 1513, he cannot have referred to a work which owed its origin to readings and lectures in the Rucellai gardens held after 1515.[54] Thus some explanation like the one we have provided is needed for the passage in *The Prince* alluding to a work on republics.

But it should be obvious that although our explanation of the special character of these first eighteen chapters may appear probable it cannot be regarded as more than a hypothesis. Because this part of our study is speculative, it must be emphatically stated that this theory about an early treatise on republics by Machiavelli is independent of the other results of our study which have a quite definite character, showing that in the framework of discussions held in the Rucellai gardens after 1515 Machiavelli wrote a series of comments on Livy's *Roman History,* and that soon afterwards, in 1517, he transformed these notes into the book of the *Discorsi sopra la prima deca di Tito Livio* which we possess today.

Perhaps a glance at the political development during these years of Machiavelli's occupation with the *Discorsi* may help to explain why he was interested in giving, in his final product, a special slant toward the problems of republican politics. Whoever discusses Machiavelli's creative processes must go back to Machiavelli's own description in the famous letter to Vettori[55] when Machiavelli was composing *The Prince.* He writes that during the day he is sunk in vulgarity and involved in trifles, but in the evening, he puts on regal and courtly garments and enters into the ancient courts of ancient men, where, being lovingly received, he speaks with them and asks the reasons for their actions and receives courteous answers. In this letter, Machiavelli makes clear that he was studying the ancients in order to clarify his thoughts about the problems of government, and that the advancement of Giuliano Medici to captain general of the church—with all the speculation aroused by it—gave him the idea of summing up the results of his studies in a small book, useful to a new "prince." Thus in *The Prince* Machiavelli makes use of more comprehensive studies for a clearly delimited, particular purpose.[56] Three years later, Giuliano Medici was dead and Lorenzo Medici had become duke of Urbino; the Medici family had no obvious candidate for the rulership over Florence. The Medici themselves played with the idea—or at least pretended to—of restoring freedom to Florence. The Florentines were deeply excited about this prospect; the following years saw a great number of writings, one of them by Machiavelli, discussing the way in which a republican constitution could be reintroduced and the form which the republic should take. The question of the advantages of republican institutions had again become a practical concern in Florence.[57] Though the *Discorsi* are more general and theoretical than *The Prince,* Machiavelli must have been aware that if, in giving his comments on Livy a more literary and systematic form, he placed special emphasis on the problems of republican government, he was again transforming his theoretical knowledge into practical usefulness. He was too good a student of the ancients not to know about the power of καιρόσ.

IV

It remains to investigate the implications of our study for the understanding of Machiavelli's political science and intellectual evolution. They are rather far-reaching, and lead into the center of the questions with which students of Machiavelli have been concerned. The following, therefore, will be only a sketch indicating briefly to what extent these questions may appear in a new and different light.

The crucial issue on which our investigation has bearing is that of Machiavelli's "new method," the question of what he conceived to be the "new way as yet untrodden by anyone else," on which he had decided to enter.[58] The results of our investigation bring this problem into new and sharp relief. For while in the past *The Prince* and the *Discorsi* have been considered as having been composed at the same time and therefore as using the same methodological approach, our analysis eliminates the possibility of a simultaneous conception of *The Prince* and the *Discorsi.* Even though not more than two or three years separate the composition of the two works, Machiavelli could not have placed such emphasis on the novel character of the method applied in the *Discorsi* if he had already used the same approach in *The Prince;* he must have believed that with the *Discorsi* he had undertaken something which he had not done before.

In order to avoid misunderstandings, it must be said immediately that the extent to which the methods of the *Discorsi* differ from those applied by Machiavelli in his previous works and especially in *The Prince* is limited. From the time he began to write on politics, Machiavelli's thoughts moved around the same fundamental questions; the necessity of transforming politics into a science, the significance of history for political practice, the importance of the ancients.[59] Changes in method are limited, therefore, to variations in the combination of these elements and to changes in the relative weight given to each of them. Within this framework, however, there seems to be some justification for Machiavelli's claim of having entered with the *Discorsi* a "path as yet untrodden by anyone else," for taken by themselves the methods of *The Prince* and of the *Discorsi* are somewhat divergent.

This difference emerges chiefly in Machiavelli's attitude toward history. The historical material which Machiavelli uses in *The Prince* comes chiefly from modern times and the contemporary scene; in the *Discorsi,* most of the illustrations are taken from ancient history, and Machiavelli sometimes even makes an apologetic remark when he refers to contemporary events in proof of a thesis.[60] Even though the greater emphasis placed in the *Discorsi* on ancient history comes to a large extent from the purpose of this work, the lower evaluation of contemporary history remains significant. For it is accompanied by a change in attitude toward the importance of history for the construction of a political system. In *The Prince,* though Machiavelli's realism leads to new results, history is used in the same way it had been used in the previous political literature; history serves as example, it illustrates a general statement. In the *Discorsi,* history provides the material from which a general conclusion is drawn; the theoretical statement arises from an analysis of the empirical facts of history. While the "political laws" of *The Prince* are deductions, the *Discorsi* represent an attempt at carrying through an inductive method.[61] Machiavelli's contemporaries agree fully with his own view that, with the *Discorsi,* he had entered a "path untrodden by anyone else." Their accounts all stress the novelty of his undertaking; in particular they characterize his new method as an attempt to "gain from history definite rules which everyone could easily comprehend."[62] These attempts seemed to them the sensational feature of the *Discorsi*. We would now hardly regard the abstract and even meaningless norms to which the richness of empirical observations and realistic insights is condensed as the most significant aspect of the *Discorsi*. Yet it frequently happens that contemporaries misjudge the true significance of an intellectual achievement. Instead of realizing that its impact derives from a fundamental incompatibility with the traditional system of thought, they concentrate their attention on those somewhat more superficial results which are slight additions to the prevailing intellectual system and which build on it without bursting the framework. Thus Machiavelli's contemporary readers, like Machiavelli himself, saw in the *Discorsi* chiefly an attempt to achieve for the field of politics what humanist scholars were trying to do in other areas of learning, that is, an attempt to rediscover the laws the ancients had known and followed in the various fields of human activity.

In the introduction of the *Discorsi,* Machiavelli remarks that "the civil law is nothing but a collection of decisions, made by jurists of old, which the jurists of today have tabulated in orderly fashion for our instruction; nor, again, is medicine anything but a record of experiments performed by doctors of old, upon which the doctors of our day base their prescriptions," Following these examples Machiavelli wanted to deduce from the experiences of ancient history the laws of political behavior. Our analysis that before the *Discorsi* took their present form they were strictly a series of comments on Livy, gives still greater emphasis to the point that, in the *Discorsi,* Machiavelli followed a method which he believed to be the recognized scholarly procedure of his time. The *Discorsi* were conceived in the form of a traditional literary genre and in line with what Machiavelli considered to be the modern scholarly tendency of elaborating general rules from ancient authors.[63] In other words, with the *Discorsi* Machiavelli adjusted his new political concepts to the method and normative approach of humanism, the dominating intellectual trend of his time.

In pointing out this aspect of the *Discorsi,* we touch upon the other significant issue on which our study has bearing; it sheds new light on Machiavelli's intellectual evolution and on his relation to the intellectual trends of his time, in particular humanism. Unquestionably Machiavelli's later works, the *Art of War* and the *Florentine History,* have a strongly humanist flavor. There is an obvious difference between *The Prince,* which was written in direct opposition to the usual contemporary treatments of this subject,[64] and the later two works which fit the prevailing humanist pattern. *The Art of War* is mainly a modernization of an ancient author in the classicizing form of a dialogue. In the *Florentine History* Machiavelli uses a method, namely the reduction of historical events to typical situations, which is pointedly humanistic. Our investigation would suggest that these two works were only further stages in a development toward adoption of humanist concepts which had begun with the *Discorsi.* This view would also be supported by observations on changes in Machiavelli's style which, it has been said, from the *Discorsi* on begins increasingly to show rhetorical and Latinizing features.[65] The methodical differences between *The Prince* and the *Discorsi* can be considered, therefore, as a first sign of Machiavelli's inclination to accept orthodox humanism, and the contrast between the political realism of *The Prince* and the political idealism of the *Discorsi* would appear to be the result of an intellectual development rather than an expression of a tension in Machiavelli's mind.

It is easy to explain biographically Machiavelli's increasing interest in the humanist approach. When Machiavelli composed the *Discorsi,* he had become a member of that humanistically inclined group which assembled in the Rucellai gardens; he was in closer touch with the prominent intellectuals of his time than he had ever been before.[66] But there is also an inner logic in this development: for there are few if any who, after having once stared unblinkingly into the face of what man is, have been able to hold to that vision and have not escaped into dreaming of what he ought to be.[67]

6. Machiavelli's *Istorie Fiorentine:* An Essay in Interpretation

The *Istorie Fiorentine* is unique among Machiavelli's writings; of his larger works, its place in the development of European historical thought—and in Machiavelli's own intellectual development—has not yet been clearly established.

Diverse judgments have been made on the character and value of the *Istorie Fiorentine.*[1] For some it is an amplification and exemplification of the rules and laws Machiavelli had expounded in *The Prince* and the *Discorsi:*[2] it is proof that Machiavelli was no historian, only a political scientist.[3] For some it is a landmark in the development of modern historiography;[4] for others it is a chain of episodes.[5] For some it is a sign that after Machiavelli's system had been formed it underwent no further change;[6] for others the *Istorie Fiorentine* represents a new and final stage in the evolution of Machiavelli's thought: less utopian and more concrete and realistic but also more pessimistic than his previous writings.[7]

Originally published in *Studies on Machiavelli,* ed. Myron P. Gilmore (Florence, Sansoni, 1972), pp. 75-99, reprinted by permission of Villa I Tatti, the Harvard University Center for Italian Renaissance Studies. With one exception (see "Discussione," *Rivista Storica Italiana,* 86 [1974], 720-722), this article has not been attacked, and in John H. Geerken's survey (see the note on p. 115), its thesis is accepted.

I

It is the fate of almost all of Machiavelli's political writings that they have aroused discussion and dispute. Nevertheless, the case of the *Istorie Fiorentine* is peculiar because the judgments about this work vary so fundamentally that they cannot even be narrowed down to issues on which a dispute could focus. The main problem, I submit, is to establish Machiavelli's aims in writing the *Istorie Fiorentine*. The difficulty is that the *Istorie Fiorentine* was a commissioned work. It is shaped, therefore, by the requirements involved in this commission and it is necessary to find out whether Machiavelli in writing the *Istorie Fiorentine* had any purposes beyond the requirements of his commission, and if so, what they might have been.

On November 8, 1520, the officials of the Studio Fiorentino "conduxerunt Niccholaum de Machiavellis civem florentinum ad serviendum dicto eorum officio, et inter alia ad componendum annalia et cronacas florent. et alia faciendum."[8] What were the implications of this commission and in what ways did it determine the nature of the work Machiavelli was expected to do? Italian princely rulers had appointed public historiographers ever since the early fifteenth century.[9] But such a position did not exist in republican city-states. The first such was that of Andrea Navagero, whom in 1516 the Venetian government salaried to compose a history of Venice.[10] Machiavelli's appointment to a similar position followed four years later.

Navagero was in Rome when his appointment was decided upon. He was one of the prominent intellectual figures at the court of the first Medici Pope and it is tempting to assume the existence of a connection between the Venetian and the Florentine appointments. The old traditional rivalry between the two sister republics might have induced the Florentines to follow the Venetian example lest their reputation suffer in comparison to that of Venice because of lack of historical glorification; Machiavelli's numerous friends in Rome might have considered this an opportunity to get employment for the unfortunate former secretary. These conjectures cannot be proved. Nevertheless, the Venetian measure throws some light on the intentions of Machiavelli's Florentine employers.

In the past it has not been recognized that the creation of the position of a public historiographer was a novelty. Navagero is supposed to have succeeded Sabellico[11] and Machiavelli himself referred to Bruni and Poggio as his predecessors.[12] But neither Sabellico nor Bruni nor Poggio composed their Venetian or Florentine histories for a salary; Sabellico wrote his work in order to gain the favor of the Venetian government and indeed in recognition of his efforts the Venetians appointed him lecturer in rhetorics—a position which he held up to the end of his life.[13] Bruni and Poggio were Florentine chancellors and wrote their histories as a voluntary homage to the city republic which had placed them into this high office.[14]

The allusions to Sabellico in Navagero's appointment and to Bruni and Poggio in Machiavelli's *proemio* are significant, however, for our understanding of the ideas connected with the creation of the position of a public historiographer. Sabellico, Bruni, and Poggio were humanists; they intended to pattern the narration of the events which were the subject of their story according to the rules found in the classical historians, to create what they considered to be "true histories." Such a true history was political history. It was meant to present significant events in an impressive form so that the readers' political pride and moral courage would be strengthened; they intended to perpetuate "those things worthy of honor, excluding those that were not considered worthy."[15] Thus, they were less interested in completeness of facts and in details than in style and form. Facts were taken from the best-known available chronicles or similar sources. The task was to select the important ones and to present them in beautiful style. Histories were divided into books, beginning with a lengthy general consideration, and historians were expected to embellish their story with speeches in which actions or events were placed in a wider philosophical and moral context. Courage revealed itself particularly in military affairs which were regarded as a crucial part of political history, and battles were described in elaborate detail. This was history of a particular kind—rhetorical history—concerned with the "inculcation of moral and spiritual values" and "the elegant inspiration of the reader to right conduct."[16] Navagero was a humanist and as such could be expected to hold the same concept of history as these other humanists; the decree of his appointment made it abundantly clear that a work of this kind was expected from him: his history was to take care that the memory of "preclari et memorandi facti" were preserved for posterity, and this ought to be done in a history "autentice, elegante et floride," "ornate de elegantia et eloquentia," so that "le cose narrate recevono augumento e se fanno piu illustri."[17]

Unquestionably a work of similar character was expected from Machiavelli and there is proof that this was his own view of his task. When his appointment was hanging fire he composed a *Vita di Castruccio Castracani* which he asked his friends to read and to criticize as a "modello" for a larger history.[18] Machiavelli's *Castruccio* was a typical piece of rhetorical history. There is the elegant story of the birth of Castruccio; there is the compression of Castruccio's military and political career into a few memorable actions; and there is the indispensable ingredient of any humanist history, Castruccio's eloquent speech on his deathbed. Machiavelli's friends took this work as an experiment in rhetorical history; their criticism focused on style and form of presentation.

Machiavelli knew what he was expected to do when he received his commission from the Studio. One should be cautious therefore to draw from his adoption of a humanist pattern of history conclusions about changes or developments in his attitude toward humanism. One should also be careful in using the *Istorie Fiorentine* as a basis for an analysis of Machiavelli's views on the nature of historical work. He was not expected to do original research, nor was he to establish new historical facts. He was required to present the extant historical narratives in a stylistically more elevated form. He was to concentrate on significant and memorable events; his procedure of jumping from one elaborately described event to another chronologically distant one and neglecting to treat the intervening years with care corresponded to the pattern he followed.[19] We find the attempt to heighten attractiveness of the work by elegantly and eloquently told stories and one has the feeling that this requirement suited Machiavelli's literary talents extremely well: Machiavelli appears to have found great pleasure in telling the story of Rosmunda;[20] and the foundation of the monastery of Annalena,[21] and the misfortunes of the Count Poppi[22] seem to take more space than they deserve in a history of Florence. In its form the work follows strictly the prescriptions of humanist history: the narration is embellished with speeches, the history is divided into books, and each book has introductory chapters containing general reflections.

It is entirely evident that Machiavelli was eager to demonstrate that he was fulfilling his side of the contract which he had entered. However, just when one becomes fully aware of Machiavelli's efforts to fit his *Istorie Fiorentine* into a prescribed pattern, one also becomes conscious of a startling and striking difference between the humanists' histories of city-states and Machiavelli's *Istorie Firoentine.* The histories of a city-states usually were composed to keep the memory of the great deeds and achievements of the past alive and to strengthen patriotism among the citizens. But Machiavelli's *Istorie Fiorentine,* with its report of passionate factional struggles and increasing military incompetence, can hardly be considered as an appeal to the Florentines to live up to the greatness of their past,[23] and the account is not rich in examples of virtue. Machiavelli who was used to focusing on "quello che si fa" and not on "quello che si doverrebbe fare"[24] might have found it difficult to idealize the Florentine past. Still, the grim and gloomy picture which Machiavelli presents in the *Istorie Fiorentine* points to a serious dilemma. In agreement with humanist historians Machiavelli was not concerned with historical research or the discovery of new facts, but he agreed with them that history ought to be of political use and to teach something. He says explicitly: "E se ogni esemplo di republica muove, quelli che si leggono della propria muovono molto più e molto più sono utili."[25] What then did Machiavelli want to teach with his *Istorie Fiorentine?* Did he consider the *Istorie Fiorentine* purely as another vehicle to present the rules which he had propounded in *The Prince* and the *Discorsi?* Or does he add with the *Istorie Fiorentine* a new facet to the body of his political thought? That is the issue which we want to pursue and that is the issue on which a discussion of the *Istorie Fiorentine* ought to focus.

II

If insight into the various stages of the development of a work and into the process of its composition is possible, it ought to be one of the surest means of clarifying the intentions of an author. But before we attempt such an analysis it might be well to establish what external facts we know about the progress of this work.[26] In March 1520 Machiavelli visited Cardinal Giulio Medici who, after the death of Lorenzo de' Medici, had come to Florence to take over the rule of the city; it seems likely that the idea of entrusting Machiavelli with the writing of a Florentine history originated on this occasion.[27] One month later, in April 1520, we hear in a letter to Machiavelli from his friend Battista Palla about "una provisione per scrivere o altro."[28] In the summer months Machiavelli went to Lucca and wrote his *Vita di Castruccio Castracani* in preparation for the commission to write a history. The commission was finally given to him on 8 November 1520—for two years—on the basis of a draft Machiavelli himself had prepared; it was subsequently renewed for further years.[29]

Machiavelli then set down to work and the manuscript of the present text of *Istorie Fiorentine* must have been finished by the end of 1524.[30] The work was interrupted by his mission to the Franciscans in Carpi for two weeks in May 1521. Guicciardini and Machiavelli—in letters which were exchanged between Modena, where Guicciardini was governor, and Carpi—joke about the manner in which the experiences of this important mission might further Machiavelli's work on the history. "Maxime nelle comparationi, perché dove io habbia a ragionare del silentio, io potrò dire: gli stavano più cheti che i frati quando mangiono."[31] In the summer of 1521 Machiavelli must have spent some time on reading proofs of his *Arte della Guerra*.[32] From 1523 on diversions seem to have been manifold and Machiavelli's zeal sometimes seems to have flagged.[33] In the summer of 1524 Machiavelli was working on the last books of the present version.[34]

In May 1525 Machiavelli traveled to Rome to present Pope Clement VII with the *Istorie Fiorentine* and the Pope expressed his appreciation by giving him 120 ducats out of his private purse.[35] Moreover, Machiavelli achieved a further purpose from this visit. An increase in his salary was promised to him,[36] and when the official decree had been issued he immediately resumed writing: "Et mi sfogo accusando i principi, che hanno fatto tutti ogni cosa per condurci qui."[37] It is probable that the political business into which he was drawn in the last years of his life[38] did not leave him much time for continuing his historical work.[39] But for the interpretation of the *Istorie Fiorentine* it is important to keep in mind that what we have and call Machiavelli's *Istorie Fiorentine* is not a completed work; it was expected to be carried up to the time when he was writing.

Thus, the process of the composition of the *Istorie Fiorentine,* even in its present incomplete form, extended over at least four years. However, although a few autograph manuscripts showing stylistic deviations from the final text have been available,[40] it has seemed impossible until now to make any significant statements about the stages of the work's composition.[41] This has recently been changed by a find which Dottoressa Eugenia Levi has made in the Biblioteca Nazionale.[42] She discovered a fragment which contains the beginning of book VI of the *Istorie Fiorentine* and shows that the first introductory chapter was composed after what is now the second chapter had been written. The combination of this discovery with previously available manuscript material indicates that the introductory chapters of books II-VI[43] were later additions made when Machiavelli had arrived at the beginning of book VI. The introductory chapters of the following books, VII and VIII, however, were composed in the order we find in the final version.[44]

The conclusions which can be drawn from the discovery of these manuscript fragments are fully confirmed and reinforced by a closer examination of the various introductory chapters. Those of the last two books, VII and VIII, differ considerably from those of books II-VI. Only in the introductions to the last two books did Machiavelli make the statement that it was his custom to begin each new book with general reflections. Also the relationship between the introductory chapters and the contents of the books which they introduce varies between books II-VI and books VII and VIII. The introduction to book VII which describes the rise of Cosimo Medici discusses the method by which private citizens can rise to power in a republic: "O per vie publiche o per modi privati." Book VIII is devoted to the Pazzi conspiracy and its introductory chapter stresses that conspiracies, whether they succeed or fail, are always disastrous. Briefly, the introductory chapters of the last two books are closely connected with the historical account which follows. This cannot be said, however, about the introductory chapters of books II-VI. These chapters are connected with only the first few chapters of the books which they begin or are of an entirely general character, but they have no close relationship to the entire content of the books which they introduce.[45] A still more striking distinction is formed by the fact that the introductions of books VII and VIII lack a feature which dominates the preceding introductions, namely, a comparison between ancient and modern institutions. All the introductions to books II-VI emphasize the difference between the perfection of the ancient world and the meanness of the modern world. The general theme of all these introductions is struck in the first sentence of the introduction to book II: the "grandi e maravigliosi ordini delle republiche e principati antichi . . . in questi nostri tempi sono spenti."[46]

In all the introductory chapters from book II to book VI the attention of the reader is directed to the corruption which has taken place since the end of the ancient world. We find this same theme in Machiavelli's description of the Medici rule in the quattrocento and in the first book of the *Istorie Fiorentine* which gives a survey of the course of foreign affairs from the end of the Roman Empire to 1434. But in the first book and in the sections on the Medici rule the themes of decline and corruption are woven into the narration rather than explicitly stated. However, the importance of this idea of corruption for these parts of the work can easily be demonstrated.

Machiavelli's treatment of the Medici is a debated issue. Remarks which Machiavelli made in a letter to Guicciardini[47] and which he is reported to have made to Giannotti[48] show that he found it difficult to combine his aversion to the Medici rule with his obligations to Giulio Medici, the Cardinal and Pope, who had granted him his commision. Machiavelli was aware that he had to disguise his anti-Medicean feelings; nevertheless, in my opinion, an attentive reader can discover these feelings behind the praise and glorification.[49]

Giannotti has Machiavelli saying that Machiavelli's true feelings about the Medici might be deduced from the speeches which he attributed to the enemies of the Medici. There are indeed a number of speeches that contain strong accusations against the Medici: Niccolò da Uzzano's warning against exiling Cosimo,[50] or the speeches of Florentine exiles to the Duke of Milan and the Doge.[51] The severest condemnation of the Medici regime, however, is contained in a speech which is not made by an enemy of the Medici but by Piero Medici himself who criticized his own supporters for their arrogant and rapacious behavior.[52] "Non vi basta essere in tanta città principi e avere voi pochi quegli onori, dignità e utili de' quali già molti cittadini si solveono onorare; non vi basta avere intra voi divisi e' beni de' nimici vostri: non vi basta potere tutti gli altri affliggere con i publici carichi e voi liberi da quelli avere tutte le publiche utilità; che voi con ogni qualità di ingiuria ciascheduno affliggete. Voi spogliate de' suoi beni il vicino, voi vendete la giustizia, voi fuggite i giudicii civili, voi oppressate gli uomini pacifici e gli insolenti esaltate. Né credo che sia in tutta Italia tanti esempli di violenza e di avarizia quanti sono in questa città."

But Giannotti's emphasis on speeches as revealing Machiavelli's true views on the Medicean tyranny is somewhat misleading; Machiavelli's entire account of this period is meant to demonstrate the abasement of Florentine political life under the Medici. Cosimo's rise was due to his wealth by means of which he had corrupted the citizens and gathered a group of followers. Instead of using "modi publici," as appropriate in a republic, he had used "modi privati."[53] Since, for Machiavelli, a flowering of military virtues is incompatible with a cultivation of arts and letters, Machiavelli's stress on the Medicean patronage of artists and scholars suggested that, in Florence, there was no longer a place for heroic virtues.[54] In a previous part of the *Istorie Fiorentine,* Machiavelli had indicated that the decline of Florence had set in when the merchant class took over power after it had defeated the nobility. "Il che fu cagione che Firenze non solamente di armi, ma di ogni generosità si spogliasse.[55]

The same view determines Machiavelli's delineation of the contrast between Rinaldo degli Albizzi and the Medici. Rinaldo, usually considered one of the less attractive figures of Florentine history, becomes in Machiavelli's *Istorie Fiorentine* a hero of almost Roman stature.[56] Although in the war against Lucca he had done his duty, he had been slandered so that, like Coriolanus, he returned in disgust to Florence and asked the magistrates "per lo avvenire essere più pronto a difendere i suoi cittadini, acciò che quelli fussero ancora più pronti a operare bene per la patria."[57] When Cosimo's return was under discussion, Rinaldo, like an honest man, placed his trust in the word of others who then betrayed him. When he had to leave Florence Machiavelli has him making a speech in which Rinaldo becomes a second Cato or a second Brutus." De' giuochi della fortuna io ne ho assai buona experienza; e come io ho poco confidato nelle prosperità, così le avversità meno mi offendono; e so che quando le piacerà la mi si potrà mostrare più lieta; ma quando mai non le piaccia io stimerò sempre poco vivere in una città dove possino meno le leggi che gli uomini . . . sempre agli uomini savi e buoni fu meno grave udire i mali della patria loro che vedergli; e cosa più gloriosa reputano essere uno onorevole ribello, che uno stiavo cittadino."[58] In Machiavelli's *Istorie Fiorentine* Rinaldo degli Albizzi is the great symbol that Florence had no use for military heroes and republican virtue; the Medici ruled in a corrupt Florence.

The notion of corruption is quite overtly the dominant theme in the first book of the *Istorie Fiorentine*. This first book is rather uneven. As has been frequently remarked, Machiavelli made extensive use of Biondo in this first book. Many chapters read like an accumulation of notes, but there are others which present a brilliant condensation of long, complicated developments. The subject matter, also, is revealing. The primary purpose is to provide an account of Italian foreign affairs from the end of the Roman Empire to the rise of the Medici in 1434. But ancient historians—and humanists imitating them—were accustomed to beginning their work with a survey describing the situation existing at the start of their story,[59] and Machiavelli followed this pattern by discussing at some length in this first book the formation and growth of those four powers—Papacy, Naples, Milan, and Venice[60]—which, next to Florence, determined the course of Italian politics in the quattrocento. But this first book has another striking feature: it has a large number of allusions, more than any of the other books, to events and developments of the sixteenth century. Machiavelli mentioned the policy of the Borgia Pope, his success in destroying the power of the small feudal lords in the church state[61] as well as his failure to establish the Borgias as a ruling dynasty in Italy.[62] He referred to the rule of Charles V in Naples, which had just been established in 1516,[63] and discussed such recent events as the League of Cambrai[64] and its aftermath and the siege of

Rhodes.[65] The first book therefore could stand as a description of the situation which existed in Italy at the beginning of the sixteenth century quite as well as a description of the fifteenth century.

This is relevant in understanding the role which the notions of decline and corruption played in the first book of the *Istorie Fiorentine*. The initial story of a decline is that of the Roman Empire from the beginning of the invasion of the Germanic tribes to the reign of Theodoric. Before Theodoric began his reign Italy found itself in the most miserable state it had ever experienced.[66] The existing forms of policitical and social life were undermined and overthrown and, according to Machiavelli, the most tragic aspect of the situation was that schisms had developed in the Christian religion. The people "sendo la maggiore parte di loro incerti a quale Iddio dovessero ricorrere, mancando di ogni aiuto e d'ogni speranze, miseramente morivano."[67] However, Theodoric's reign represented only a short respite. The empire was soon entirely extinguished,[68] but because a low point had been reached the wheel was now turning upward again and Machiavelli focused on those political bodies which arose out of the extinction of the Roman Empire: the Papacy and "quegli altri principati che di poi la Italia infino alla venuta di Carlo VIII governorono,"[69] Machiavelli's story now becomes that of the four great powers: Papacy, Naples, Milan, and Venice. It is significant that Machiavelli gives particular attention to those two powers which in his own time were not yet under foreign rule: the Papacy[70] and Venice. They progressed to great power and influence, but their rise was followed by decline. It is striking and certainly intentional that Machiavelli used the same formulation when he described the low state into which these two formerly powerful and flourishing political bodies had fallen in his own time: "stanno a discrezione d'altri" and "a discrezione d'altri, come tutti gli altri principi Italiani, vivono."[71] The last chapters of this book then, depicted the helplessness and dependence which became the fate all over Italy and stressed the role which the abandonment of "proprie armi" and reliance on the *condottiere* system[72] had in extinguishing Italy's power.

Thus, the first book is close to the later books which describe the rule of the Medici in Florence, not only in time but also in contents. These are the parts in which the reader receives a graphic impression of the process of corruption and decline, and the first book and the books on the Medici regime complement each other because the first book shows that what happened in Florence happened all over Italy: the developments in Florence were only the particular aspects of a general Italian process.

The close relationship between the first book and the books describing the rule of the Medici raises some interesting questions about the place of the first book in the structure of the entire work and about its form of composition. Undoubtedly the organization of the *Istorie Fiorentine* is rather artificial. First a separation of foreign and domestic affairs—with foreign affairs in the first and domestic affairs in the three following books—then, from the fifth book on, an interconnected treatment of foreign and domestic affairs—all this results in a form of presentation which, because of its complexity, has not been carried through by Machiavelli in any systematic manner. It is almost unavoidable to ask whether Machiavelli had a detailed outline of the entire work in mind when he began to write the *Istorie Fiorentine* or whether the organization suggested itself to him only when he re-examined the work and composed introductory chapters which served to group the *Istorie Fiorentine* around a unified theme.

The first book has one unique feature; it lacks an introductory chapter. The obvious reason is that the first book is preceded by a *proemio* which takes the place of an introductory chapter. It would seem that the *proemio* was written at the same time as the bulk of the other introductory chapters. It contains a similar confrontation of ancient and modern institutions as in the introductory chapters to books II-VI; at the end it gives a very precise description of the content of the first four books. It is most unlikely that any writer can give such an exact statement of the divisions in his manuscript without having a detailed draft of the entire work in front of him. The question therefore is whether the first book might not belong to a later stage in the composition of the work, namely to the time when Machiavelli interrupted his account and composed the introductory chapters and the *proemio.*

Some facts give strong support to such a suggestion. Whoever reads the fifth chapter of book V, with its report on Alfonso's conquest of Naples, can hardly assume that the issue of Alfonso's claims on Naples and the relation of Queen Giovanna to the Anjous had been previously treated in the 38th chapter of the first book. On the other hand, in chapter 39 of the first book Machiavelli refers to book IV[73] and such a reference requires knowledge of what this later book contains. Nor can this reference have been a later insert because if Machiavelli had reexamined the first book at a later time he certainly would have changed the passage which refers to Rhodes as "unico ostaculo alla potenzia de' Maumettisti"[74] and which became erroneous with the fall of Rhodes in December 1522.

The statement about Rhodes is significant for still another reason; it seems to be an allusion to the attack to which Rhodes became exposed in 1522, after Suleiman had abandoned the idea to follow up his conquest of Belgrade—this "outer wall of Christendom"—with a second expedition against Hungary.[75] The outcome of the siege of Rhodes remained uncertain for quite a while; until November it seemed that the Knights of Rhodes might weather the storm as they had in 1480. The late summer of 1522 therefore appears to be the most likely date for Machiavelli's statement. But since Machiavelli was then working on the *Istorie Fiorentine* for almost two years, it is impossible that he had not advanced beyond the seventeenth chapter of the first book. This would seem to indicate that the first book belongs to a later stage in the composition of the *Istorie Fiorentine*.

In the fall of 1522 Machiavelli had some reasons for giving his work a somewhat more finished form; because in 1520 his commission had been given to him for two years, a renewal was due.[76] Moreover, the originator of the commission, Cardinal Giulio Medici—unhappy in Rome because of the loss of influence which he had suffered under Pope Adrian VI—returned to Florence in October 1522.[77] Machiavelli could expect that some interest might be shown in what he had written so far. In this context it is interesting that in all the early manuscripts of the *Istorie Fiorentine* the first five books have dedications to Cardinal Giulio Medici; the easiest explanation[78] would be that a first clean copy of the work was made after Machiavelli had written the first five books and while Giulio was still Cardinal and not yet Pope.

III

Whatever the exact facts about the composition of the *Istorie Fiorentine* might be they are less relevant than the insights into the intentions of the author which these facts can help to uncover. The facts that stand out are that in writing on the past Machiavelli had his eyes very much on his own time and he regarded the preceding centuries as a steady process of decline. This seems to reveal a thoroughly pessimistic view of history and might be regarded as a justification of those[79] who regard the Machiavelli of the *Istorie Fiorentine* as a somewhat changed man, resigned and with less confidence in the possibilities of action than the author of *The Prince* and the *Discorsi* had been. I consider this to be a misinterpretation. But in order to demonstrate that this is a misconception we must look beyond the form and content of the *Istorie Fiorentine* to its basic historical assumptions.

As we have seen, the notions of decline and corruption are central in Machiavelli's historical thought. The concept of corruption embodies a moral opprobrium. On the other hand it also contains an element beyond praise or reproach, an element of inevitability; it is not granted "alle mondane cose il fermarsi."[80] They move in a cycle, they decline and they rise: "Cosi sempre da il bene si scende al male, e da il male si sale al bene."[81] In the Renaissance the cyclical theory of history was widely accepted as defining the nature of historical movement.[82] And it certainly determined Machiavelli's historical approach: it held a prominent place in the *Discorsi*,[83] and as we have seen, it underlies his ideas about the end of the Roman Empire and the rise of new political formations on the Italian peninsula.

The cyclical theory was fundamental to Machiavelli's thought because the usefulness of history was predicated upon it. Rules could be drawn from history only if human nature was unchanged and the same situation repeated itself. And that, of course, is what the cyclical theory implies because it assumed a return to what had existed before: that history repeated itself.

This was the basic conceptual structure into which Machiavelli fitted the material of the past. But Machiavelli nourished some particular historical notions which, although they were not incompatible with this general structure, loosened its hold. For Machiavelli there were only two historical periods of relevance. There was the ancient world, particularly Roman history, and there was the experience of modern times, which Machiavelli limited mainly to events within the memory of his own lifetime. Occupation with the past, historical work, consisted in confrontation of "cose antique" and "cose moderne."[84] This confrontation had a practical purpose as well. Because the ancient world represented the high point of a historical cycle, consideration of the ancient world would produce those rules of political behavior which brought political success. Machiavelli's historical interest centered on these rules and was particularly concerned with their deduction and formulation.

These notions permeate all of Machiavelli's political and historical writings: *The Prince* and the *Discorsi* as well as the *Arte della Guerra* and the *Istorie Fiorentine.* Nevertheless, in some of his works Machiavelli places greater emphasis on confrontation between ancient and modern, in others on the cyclical development. In *The Prince* and the *Discorsi* Machiavelli wants to solve concrete political problems and he looks upon history primarily or almost exclusively in order to deduce the rules which show how to attack these problems and which will give guidance to individuals for the actions which they ought to take. The cyclical theory remains somewhat in the background , although it is essential in indicating that problems and men remain the same.

In the *Istorie Fiorentine* Machiavelli encountered a somewhat different problem. As the introductory chapters of books II-VI show, the confrontation of the excellence of ancient historical arrangements with the defects of modern institutions continued to remain Machiavelli's concern. The confrontation could no longer serve as a central theme, however, because in the *Istorie Fiorentine* he had to concern himself with the development from the ancient to the modern world—how the one declined into the other. It was difficult to deduce from a story of decline rules of successful behavior. Nonetheless the cyclical theory could also serve to make such a story instructive. Machiavelli's attention shifted from establishing rules to an interest in recurrent patterns and regularities and in demonstrating the repetitiveness of history. One of the many statements of this sort is that after every tumult some old laws are abolished and some new ones decreed,[85] or that the Popes always call foreign barbarians into Italy.[86] Machiavelli extended his views of the immutability of human nature to countries, institutions, and families. It is not difficult to discover in his characterization of Niccolò Soderini as "nel risolversi dubbio e lento"[87] an allusion to Piero Soderini whom Machiavelli had banned into "limbo tra' bambini".[88] One even suspects that Machiavelli inserted a kind of self-portrait in the *Istorie Fiorentine* when he reported at somewhat astounding length on the execution of Girolamo Machiavelli for his opposition to tyranny.[89] The emphasis in the *Istorie Fiorentine* on the repetitiveness of history raises the question of what Machiavelli thought about the situation of sixteenth-century Italy. Does he point to any analogies which might serve to define the historical stage in which Italy found itself in his own time?

We have mentioned that the *Istorie Fiorentine* is not a complete work. Even before Machiavelli had received from the Pope a raise in his salary which obligated him to continue the work, he had stated in his dedication to Clement VII that he intended to "seguitare l'impresa mia" and that the events which happened after the death of Lorenzo Magnifico "sendo più alte e maggiori" deserve to be described "con più alto e maggiore spirito."[90] Evidently, Machiavelli believed that the following decades, to which he had frequently alluded in his story as demonstrating the impotence of Italy, not only were a continuation of his study of decline but also would demonstrate the complete ruin of Italy. The cyclical theory of history, however, held that if a low point is reached the rise will begin again. It would seem possible to suggest therefore that Machiavelli intended to represent the situation in which Italy found itself in the early sixteenth century as carrying with it the possibilities of a new ascent. In proof of this Machiavelli might have referred to an analogy of the past. In the fifth chapter of the first book of the *Istorie Fiorentine* Machiavelli had characterized the period preceding the rule of Theodoric as Italy's most miserable time[91] and he had emphasized that the sufferings of the poeple had become particularly unbearable because of the split of the Christian church. No reader in Machiavelli's time could have missed drawing a parallel between that period and his own time and

Machiavelli's Istorie Fiorentine

finding some hope in Machiavelli's account describing the growth of new political life out of this low point of Italian fortunes.

It is dangerous, of course, to suggest statements which an author might have made in something that he hasn't written. Nevertheless, if one takes into account the drift of the *Istorie Fiorentine* toward an evaluation of the present and the increasing stress on the need for "armi proprie," it is not far-fetched to infer that Machiavelli wanted to end the *Istorie Fiorentine* as he had ended his other political writings: that Florentine and Italian history were joined in the same grim fate, that the desperate situation in Italy could be remedied if the Italians themselves took up arms—"Se voi el tempio riaprissi a Marte."[92] Such a conclusion would have shown not only the unity of Machiavelli's thought from *The Prince* to the *Istorie Fiorentine* but also unity of thought and action. For when Machiavelli appeared in Rome in 1525 he presented to the Pope not only the manuscript of the *Istorie Fiorentine.* He submitted to him also a political plan to arm the people of the Romagna; it was his old project of the *armi proprie* adjusted to the situation of the Papacy.[93] Although in the end his suggestion was rejected, Machiavelli had come close again to Italian policy makers and he observed and discussed passionately any political move which might influence the possibility of Italy's liberation from the "barbarians." When a situation which offered some changes had arisen he wrote to Francesco Guicciardini in words which are reminiscent of the last chapter of *The Prince* and might have formed the conclusion of the *Istorie Fiorentine:* "Voi sapete quante occasioni si sono perdute: non perdete questa . . . Liberate diuturna cura Italiam."[94] What Machiavelli did or wrote in the twenties does not suggest a resigned Machiavelli: it would seem strange if the *Istorie Fiorentine* had been inspired by a pessimistic mood. This is so improbable that it seems justified to propose an interpretation of the *Istorie Fiorentine* which places this work next to Machiavelli's other great writings and suggests that the *Istorie Fiorentine* contained the same political message as his other works.

Italy expects its *redentore.*[95] This idea has a relevance for Machiavelli's thinking beyond its first formulation in the last

151

chapter of *The Prince*. The widening corruption, the accelerating decline which Machiavelli depicted in the *Istorie Fiorentine* precipitated a situation in which the alternative is annihilation or redemption. Machiavelli's thought contains an apocalyptic element. From a strictly logical point of view an apocalytpic notion is incompatible with a cyclical theory of history. But if the stages of a cyclical process are separated, the assumption of inevitabel decline to a level of complete disintegration can certainly create apocalytpic fears. Stress on this element in Machiavelli's historical outlook is important because it distinguishes his historical work from that of his contemporaries.

In the Renaissance writers began to conceive of history as a man-made process.[96] Certainly they did not mean to exclude other factors, nor did all writers agree on the nature of human qualities which determined the course of history. Humanists might explain action as caused by those virtues and vices which had been codified in the ethical theories of ancient philosophers. Writers of a more practical political bent might consider social groups with common interests or the ambitions of individuals as the moving factors and arrive at penetrating individual characterizations. Insofar as historical events could be explained, the explanation had to be found in human psychology.

Machiavelli's story, too, is a description of human behavior and human action. Nevertheless, to him the course of history is not a man-made process. It moves in its own predestined direction which is beyond human control. Man's role consists in the strength with which he can promote this process or with which he can retard it by resisting. The virtue required for such a role is not something that can be learned; it is a gift from above. The heroes of Machiavelli's *Istorie Fiorentine* exist in a strangely isolated world. They are inspired without being committed to the values of a higher order. They cannot change the process of history, and they organize and use the human material which surrounds them rather than being united with other human beings in work and in the hope of achievements. Machiavelli's world of history is not very different from the Christian world of history, even if it is a world without God. As there are in Christian history a few saints inspired by divine grace who testify that the great mass of humanity might not be entirely lost, so in Machiavelli's secularized history there are a few heroes endowed with *virtù* who demonstrate that man can become an actor in the historical process. But ordinary human beings live oppressed and in darkness, anxiously waiting for redemption, just as the ancestors of Christ in Michelangelo's Sistine Chapel are waiting for the coming of Christ. Michelangelo and Machiavelli have been frequently named together and there is reason for this. Separated in age by only a few years, they were both able to remember the splendor of the age of Lorenzo Magnifico and to have noticed its reliance on human reason and its pride in human dignity. But both were young enough to be deeply shaken when this confidence was upset by the apocalyptic preachings of Savonarola and when his prophesy of the collapse of the existing world came true with the French invasion. Neither earlier nor later generations can have had this experience of a revolutionary change with an impact not only on external conditions but also on intellectual values. The tension between confidence in the power of a rational intelligence and belief in the unlimited possibilities of an inspired will remained a constant factor in Machiavelli's thought and has played its part in making the *Istorie Fiorentine* a work of a puzzling character. For with its emphasis on the role of personalities and its presentation of history as an inevitable process, it seems very close to the two most important modern ideas about the moving forces in history. But actually neither Machiavelli's view of the divinely inspired hero nor his concept of a predetermined unbreakable cycle has bearing on modern ideas of the role which the individual or collective forces play in history. No clear path connects Machiavelli's *Istorie Fiorentine* with the developments of modern historiography. As in his political thought, so in his historical thinking, Machiavelli stands for himself.[97]

7. Machiavellism

Machiavellism has historically come to mean that effectiveness alone counts in politics; political actions should not be restricted by considerations of morality, of good or evil.

In this sense Machiavellism existed before Machiavelli, and is as old as politics itself. The view that the struggle for political power should be excepted from the usual norms of ethical behavior was widely recognized in the ancient world. It was stated in the dialogue between the Athenians and the Melians in the fifth book of Thucydides' *History of the Peloponnesian War* and was given a simple poetic formulation in Euripides' *Phoenician Maidens* (lines 524–525): "If wrong may e'er be right, for a throne's sake were wrong most right:—Be God in all else feared." In these quotations the drive for power appears as almost instinctive, something that cannot be kept in check. Roman writers were more conscious of the problems involved in the transgression of moral laws. Cicero (*De officiis*, book III, chap. 2) and Tacitus *Annals*, book XIV, chap. 44) said that they

Originally published in *Dictionary of the History of Ideas*, ed. Philip P. Wiener (New York, Scribner, 1973), III, 116–126. Because the history of Machiavellism is usually presented in books, some of them devoted only to a single country, or dealing with a particular problem like J. G. A. Pocock, *The Machiavellian Moment* (Princeton, Princeton University Press, 1974), a brief treatment surveying the entire development may be welcome. For literature on the problem of Machiavellism see the note on p. 490.

believed violation of moral law was permissible only if the *utilitas rei publicae* (public welfare) required it. With this they introduced an idea that would become of great importance in the history of Machiavellism.

Despite recognition of the problem in the ancient world there are good reasons why discussions on the general validity of moral norms in politics are connected with the name of Niccolò Machiavelli. The ancient world and the Renaissance were separated by the Christian middle ages in which justice and peace were regarded as the only legitimate purposes of government. Admittedly, even in the middle ages rulers had not always acted according to the prescriptions of the Christian religion. Canonists and legalists, aware of this fact, had tried to determine the situations and conditions under which the *ratio publicae utilitatis* or the *ratio status* (reason of state)—to use some of their terms—allowed violations of the common law or the moral code. It has been argued therefore that the doctrine of "reason of state" which exerted great influence in the political thought and life of the sixteenth and seventeenth centuries was actually a medieval doctrine. Such a thesis disregards the medieval legal doctrine that violation of law and ethical rules was permitted only in order to protect the community instituted by God and the law of nature as necessary for achieving the social and political ends of man on earth. A lower law could be disregarded for a higher, divine law. In contrast to the doctrine of "reason of state" which was developed in the centuries after Machiavelli, in medieval legal doctrine the government or the ruler remained subordinated to a higher—divine or natural—law.

With the Renaissance the gap between underlying assumptions and the practical conduct of politics widened. Doubts about the general validity of the accepted moral code became a powerful ferment in modern political thought and in this development Machiavelli's writings have been crucial.

However, many of the notions associated with the term Machiavellism were not explicitly stated by Machiavelli but only implied in his political writings. Of these Machiavelli's *Istorie Fiorentine* was significant because it contained an attack against the worldly power of the Papacy which weakened the hold of the preachings of the church. However, the doctrines of Machiavellism were chiefly developed from *The Prince* and the *Discorsi*. Machiavelli's treatment of virtues and vices in chaps. 15–19 of *The Prince* was meant to shock and it had this effect. One can see this from the frequency and passion with which its theses were discussed and rejected. There are many vehement refutations of Machiavelli's suggestion that a prince ought not to scorn murder if this serves his purposes, or that in order to be popular and secure in power a prince need not be virtuous, only appear so. It is evident from the frequency with which writers debated the issue that they were puzzled and bothered by Machiavelli's view that princes could be expected to keep promises, commitments, and alliances only as long as these agreements corresponded to their interests.

Of course, the most novel and startling feature in *The Prince* and the *Discorsi* was the open recognition of the role of force in politics. "You must know, then, that there are two methods of fighting, the one by law, the other by force: the first method is that of men; the second of beasts; but as the first method is often insufficient one must have recourse to the second" (*The Prince,* chap. 18). The *Discorsi* possessed other features of a startling and upsetting character; they presented a defense of freedom and republicanism. Since republican government was a rarity in these centuries of the rise of monarchical absolutism, Machiavelli's defense of republicanism reinforced the impression that he advocated doctrines which undermined the fundamental tenets of the existing political, social, and moral order.

In 1559 Machiavelli's writings were placed on the Index. Insofar as this measure had any meaning it was limited to Italy and Spain. Manuscripts of Machiavelli's writings, particularly of *The Prince,* circulated widely in France and England, and Machiavelli's works continued to be printed and translated. However, Catholic writers shied away from open acknowledgment of their acquaintance with Machiavelli. Allusions to his theories and writings were made in a somewhat cryptic manner. This secretiveness had its bearing upon the image of Machiavelli and Machiavellism. It was easy to assign to him views and ideas which were only loosely connected with the theories of the great Florentine.

I

From the middle of the sixteenth century until the French Revolution Machiavellism represented a powerful current in intellectual life. In the 1580s Machiavellism was so much acknowledged as a recognizable, distinct attitude that the term Machiavellist appeared in print (1581 in France in Nicolas Froumenteau's *Finances;* 1589 in England in a treatise by Thomas Nash).

Although Machiavelli's exclusive concern had been politics, the mystery which the condemnation of his writings wrapped around him fostered the belief that his teachings were applicable to any kind of human activity. The common denominator of all Machiavellist attitudes was doubt that successful action was compatible with living according to a strictly moral code. Despite agreement on this basic assumption, and despite the fact that the development of Machiavellian attitudes toward life and a Machiavellian outlook on politics went hand in hand, a historical presentation of the unfolding of Machiavellism might most conveniently separate the story of Machiavelli as teacher of human behavior from that of Machiavelli as political counselor. In the area of Machiavellian politics it might be advisable to make a distinction between Machiavelli's views on the management of the internal affairs of a society and Machiavelli's notions about the conduct of foreign policy.

The sixteenth-century view of Machiavelli's prescriptions for human behavior can be summarized in the simple formula that he was considered to be a teacher of evil. His message was that being evil was more useful and efficient than being good. One might deceive, lie, commit crimes, even murder, if this helped to achieve success. As an advocate of such evil doctrines Machiavelli moved close to the Devil.

An identification of Machiavelli with Satan was made early in the sixteenth century by Reginald Pole in his *Apologia Reginaldi Poli ad Carolum V* (1539), and the acceptance of this view is reflected in the widespread belief that "Old Nick," the name given to the Devil, was an abbreviation of Machiavelli's first name. (Actually the name Old Nick for the Devil is older than the sixteenth century.) The French held the same view about those who regarded Machiavelli as their *Évangile* (Gospel): "To better betray affect an air of benevolence,/ Lie, beguile, disguise the truth,/ Cover the wolf with a pretence of holiness,/ Seem devout and be nothing but a hypocrite."

Machiavellian doctrines were the instruments by means of which the Devil exerted his influence in the world. Huguenots saw the satanic character of Machiavelli's advice in the actions of their enemies; they considered the Guises as faithful pupils of Machiavelli. The first systematic attack against Machiavelli—Innocent Gentillet's *Discours sur les moyens de bien gouverner . . . contre Nicolas Machiavel Florentin* (1576)—was composed by a Huguenot and dedicated to the Duc d'Alençon who was in sharp opposition to his mother, Catherine de'Medici. She was said to have Machiavelli's works at her bedside, and the massacre of Saint Bartholomew was viewed as a plot inspired by a study of Machiavelli.

There were particular reasons for the rise of an ardent anti-Machiavellism among Protestants and in northern Europe. Machiavelli was an Italian, and as such, his ideas were assumed to guide the behavior of two kinds of people who were regarded with distrust and hatred north of the Alps: Italians and Jesuits. The activities and resources of Italian merchants and bankers had given them influence and power at the courts and among the ruling groups of most European countries. Their reputation as leaders in art and scholarship made them much sought after for prominent positions in chancelleries and universities. Papal legates played a determining role in the ecclesiastical affairs of Catholic countries; they were mostly Italians and often brought Italians with them in their suites, and among them, Jesuits. The dominant position of these Italian foreigners naturally aroused the enmity of the natives. Italians were held responsible for misgovernment and corruption, for diverting the rulers from their traditional honest ways of government. It was this anti-Italianism which also fed anti-Machiavellism.

In France, from 1559 to 1574, during fifteen politically crucial years, the Queen Mother, Catherine of Medici, exerted decisive political influence. She showed a great preference for Italians and things Italian, and opposition to her policy was reinforced by strong anti-Italian feelings. Catherine's policy was wavering and tortuous and although this might have been due to weakness rather than to calculation, the impression which she gave was that of deceitfulness and unreliability. Her policy confirmed the equation of Machiavellism and Italianism. François Hotman, the most powerful voice among French anti-Catholic polemicists, identified in a quite crude way Italy, Catherine de'Medici, canon law, and Machiavelli. In England the religious content of the political struggles made the Papacy, and the Jesuits as the Papacy's most effective defenders, the chief target of attack, and Machiavellism and Jesuitism were frequently seen as identical. Even English Catholics regarded the Jesuits as ambitious Italian foreigners who wanted to rule the church and—to quote from an English Catholic pamphlet of 1601—whose "holy exercise" was "but a meere Machivilean device of pollicie."

Because Machiavelli's doctrines were seen as embodied in personalities with particular characteristics, the author of these doctrines also acquired personal features and became a recognizable individual. As such Machiavelli entered literature and became the prototype of a character that in different forms has appeared in drama and in novels. The imaginative creation of a Machiavelli figure has significance in the history of literature, but the existence of such a concrete image of Machiavelli has also reinforced interest in political Machiavellism and its impact.

Machiavelli's entry on the literary scene took place in the Tudor and Stuart period. In Christopher Marlowe's *Jew of Malta* (ca. 1589) Machiavelli himself comes on the stage as Prologue. His words enunciate in a simplified manner basic features of Machiavelli's political ideas: "Might first made kings, and laws were then most sure,/when like the Dracos they were writ in blood." These notions, however, were only applications of a more general philosophy; Marlowe's Machiavelli is a man who disregards moral bonds in every sphere of life: "I count religion but a childish toy/and hold there is no sin but ignorance." Marlowe's contemporaries and successors quickly recognized the dramatic possibilities inherent in the Machiavellian figure.

The literature on this topic is extended and it might be enough here to indicate Shakespeare's use of the Machiavellian prototype. The figure in Shakespeare's oeuvre that is clearly conceived as a personification of Machiavellian doctrines is Richard III. Shakespeare acknowledged the Machiavellian aspects of his concept of this king openly in the words which in *Henry VI* (part III, act III, scene ii, lines 182–195) he put into the mouth of the young Duke of Gloucester:

> Why, I can smile, and murder whiles I smile;
> And cry content to that which grieves my heart;
> And wet my cheeks with artificial tears,
> And frame my face to all occasions.
> I'll drown more sailors than the mermaid shall;
> I'll slay more gazers than the basilisk;
> I'll play the orator as well as Nestor;
> Deceive more slily than Ulysses could;
> And, like a Sinon, take another Troy:
> I can add colours to the cameleon;
> Change shapes with Proteus for advantages;
> And set the murderous Machiavel to school.
> Can I do this, and cannot get a crown?
> Tut, were it further off, I'll pluck it down!

Richard III is an amoral human being rather than a purposeful politician. Nevertheless, his Machiavellian activities have politics as their center. Shakespeare has created another Machiavellian figure, however, whose evilness is purely personal and has nothing to do with politics: Iago in *Othello.* Iago lies, deceives, intrigues, conspires to reach his own personal ends. By his devilish acts he forces others who stand morally far above him into his nets and destroys them. In Othello's words Iago is a "demi-devil" who has "ensnar'd my soul and body."

Iago demonstrates that the name of Machiavellism could be affixed to any kind of evilness as long as it was evilness on a grand scale. The Machiavellian looked only after his own interests and desires and was willing to lie and to deceive, to use crooked means, in order to obtain them. He concealed his true intentions and masked them behind words of piety or good will. He liked to work in the dark and without others knowing it he maneuvered them into doing his bidding.

Because in its broadest sense Machiavellism is assumed to be synonymous with amorality and evilness in general, every class and profession can have Machiavellians. Since Machiavelli made his appearance on the Elizabethan stage literature has been full of figures who are Machiavellists or have some Machiavellian flavor. Certainly figures from the ruling group—court favorites, diplomats, ministers—are most easily presented as Machiavellists. Marinelli in G. E. Lessing's *Emilia Galotti* (1772) is probably the best-known figure of a Machiavellian courtier in dramatic literature. But persons with Machiavellian behavior are to be found also in novels or plays that describe the life of the middle classes or of the bourgeoisie. A favorite figure in eighteenth-century literature is the intriguing evil kin who tries to ruin the naive honest hero. There is in Henry Fielding's *Tom Jones* (1749) Master Blifil "whose affections are solily placed on one single person [himself] whose interest and indulgence alone they consider on every occasion." There is Joseph Surface in Sheridan's *School for Scandal* (1777) who has the "policy" not to deviate "from the direct road of wrong." Admittedly all these figures are variations on the theme of hypocrisy.

But the eighteenth-century notion of Machiavellism patterned the qualities and actions which writers assigned to the hypocrites of their creation. The eighteenth century was a moralist century, however, and usually the honest hero triumphed over his sly antagonist; in this respect the Machiavellism of eighteenth-century writers is somewhat defective. There is one thoroughly Machiavellian eighteenth-century novel, however—Choderlos de Laclos' *Liaisons dangereuses* (1782)—which depicts a world in which goodness and morality unavoidably succumb to the powers of vice, deceit, and egoism. The struggle for domination between men and women which forms the content of this novel is conducted with strategies, ruses, moves, and countermoves like the conflicts of politics and war. It should be added that Julien Sorel in Stendhal's *Le Rouge et le Noir* (1831) is in this tradition. Stendhal actually mentions the Machiavellism of his hero and uses quotations from Machiavelli for chapter headings. Nevertheless, Julien Sorel is an exception in the nineteenth century; pronouncedly Machiavellian characters are becoming rare.

Heroes in the novels by George Meredith (*The Egoist,* 1879) or Henryk Sienkiewicz (*Without Dogma,* 1891) are egoists out of weakness, out of fear of life, not out of strength. In the nineteenth century the belief which gave to Machiavellism its attraction and fascination—namely, that behind evil there was a demonic strength which made evil an equal rival to good—disappeared. The maintenance of evil was not in the plan of providence but right measures would progressively remove it. Goethe's *Faust* (pub. 1808) might be taken as a sign of the change which took place with the nineteenth century. For actually in Goethe's *Faust* God is the Machiavellian. He robs the Devil of Faust's soul by a trick; as a force "which wills evil and yet does good" (I, line 1335) the Devil is an instrument of the divine will. In Hegelian terms nothing is entirely negative because even what might appear so is only *List der Vernunft* (the cunning of reason). Such a unifying and reconciling conception of the process of world history is incompatible with Machiavellism which, at least as a doctrine bearing on all aspects of human behavior, draws its power from the belief in the ineradicability of evil.

Machiavelli's ideas could form a point of departure for all those who transformed Machiavelli into a devil incarnate recommending evil-doing in all spheres of life. But actually the connection between Machiavelli's views and such recommendations for a general code of human behavior is tenuous. Machiavelli's writings aimed at political action; therefore, only interpretations of his thought concerned with questions of political conduct should be closely linked to his views. In political Machiavellism we find the outgrowth of Machiavelli's own ideas, although he might not always have liked the conclusions which were drawn or approved of the extreme simplifications of his views.

Machiavelli's *The Prince* was addressed to a man who wanted to found a new state in divided Italy. The slow rise of absolutism in the sixteenth and seventeenth centuries made this advice appropriate and timely for the handling of internal affairs all over Europe. The absolute monarch tried to cut off all outside interference in the affairs of the territory which he was ruling and to make his power independent of the approval of those he was ruling; this involved subordination of the church, reduction of the power of the estates, disregard of old rights, and infringement of privileges. Because Machiavelli had allowed and recommended violations of legal commitments in the interest of self-preservation and aggrandizement, it was easy to see his spirit behind the actions of the absolute rulers or their ministers.

In France and England the cry "Machiavellist" was raised

against all those who tried to enlarge royal power. In France the writers of the *Fronde* claimed that Mazarin, in his attempt to destroy the old French liberties, followed *Maximes Italiennes et Machiavélistes* which he had brought into France from the other side of the Alps (Claude Joly, 1652). In England the opposition to the financial and religious policy of Charles I saw in this Stuart king a disciple of Machiavelli "who counseled his Prince to keepe his subjects low, by taxes and impositions and to foment divisions among them, that he might awe them at his pleasures" (from a pamphlet of 1648).

One issue in particular drew Machiavelli's name into the political discussions of this period, that of religion and the church. Machiavelli was believed to have been an atheist to whom religion was primarily a useful instrument in the hands of the rulers. When in France a group of politicians suggested the possibility of ending the civil war by tolerating two churches in one state these men (*politiques*) were immediately called Machiavellists, that is, men who subordinated religion to worldly political interests. When in England dissension developed among the various religious groups about the part of religion and the church in the ordering of society, each group accused the other of Machiavellism; in particular the Presbyterians were accused of "Jesuitical and Machiavellian policy." The same critism—that of pursuing politics under the name of religion—was used against Cromwell after he had become lord protector; to his opponents Cromwell was also a Machiavellian.

The tone changed somewhat when in the eighteenth century the struggle about the extension of royal power had ended and at least on the continent monarchical absolutism had won out. The critics of the existing regimes—the *philosophes*—were no opponents of monarchy or even absolutism; what they demanded was that the ruler follow the rules of reason and morality, that he carry out his functions in the interest of all. Their fight was directed against despotic arbitrariness which imprisoned people in order to gratify personal wishes and desires, which burdened the subjects with taxes in order to waste money on luxurious buildings, which sacrificed the lives of peoples in wars for prestige and fame, and which maintained the irrational rule of the church in order to keep people quiet and obedient. Machiavelli was a chief target of the *philosophes* because he preached an amoralistic selfishness which promoted despotic arbitrariness.

Voltaire characterized as the great principles of Machiavellism "ruin anyone who might someday ruin you; assassinate your neighbor who might become strong enough to kill you." And Diderot defined Machiavellism briefly as *l'art de tyranniser.* This moralistic view colored also the views which eighteenth-century statesmen held about Machiavelli. Although Bolingbroke, well acquainted with the political literature of the past, had great respect for Machiavelli's understanding of political techniques, his Patriot King (*Idea of a Patriot King, 1749*), faced like Machiavelli's prince by the task of restoring political life in a corrupted society, contained a sharp rejection of Machiavelli because, according to Bolingbroke, he lacked true patriotism which was concerned with the well-being of everyone. The most famous eighteenth-century condemnation of Machiavelli, of course, is the *Anti-Machiavel* (1740) of Frederick the Great in which every one of Machiavelli's maxims is refuted.

Since, in Catholic countries during the sixteenth and seventeenth centuries, Machiavelli was an author whom one was not supposed to know and therefore not to quote exactly, the qualities which in the eyes of the people of these centuries distinguished a man as a Machiavellist, must be deduced primarily from the image which anti-Machiavellists had formed. However, because the defenders of the old rights and privileges saw in Machiavelli an inspirer of the new absolutist policy, their opponents, the advocates of royal power, became anxious to know whether these bitter attacks against Machiavelli meant that the Florentine offered a reasonable justification of absolutist policy, and they took a careful look at his writings. Therefore in the seventeenth century there were not only anti-Machiavellists but also men who defended Machiavelli as a political thinker of insight and understanding.

In Venice, where the long struggle with the Papacy over the boundaries between political and ecclesiastical jurisdiction reached its critical highpoint in the first years of the seventeenth century, Machiavelli was said to enjoy great popularity, and in the writings defending the position of the Venetian government, particularly in those of Paolo Sarpi, echoes of Machiavelli's theories can be found. The firs openly positive evaluations of Machiavelli's theories, however, were composed in France and came from the surroundings of the great royal ministers who led the fight against the restricting and inhibiting influence of the French nobility: Richelieu and Mazarin. Gabriel Naudé in his *Considérations politiques sur les coups d'état* (1639) started with the traditional thesis that the *bonum commune* justified actions neglecting legal forms. But he then argued that such justification of violence ought to be extended to sudden *coups d'état* like the assassination of the Duc de Guise; politicians condemned Machiavelli in theory but acted according to him in practice. In Louis Machon's *Apologie pour Machiavelle* (1641) a vehement anti-clericalism was combined with an exaltation of monarchical absolutism resulting in an appreciation of Machiavelli's theories. The climate of the decade in which the German emperor found it necessary to order the murder of his General Wallenstein was certainly conducive to a better understanding of Machiavelli.

The tendency to recognize Machiavelli as an important political thinker received impetus and confirmation from a group of writers whose views on Machiavelli were diametrically opposed to the interpretation given by the anti-Machiavellists. These political writers did not regard Machiavelli as an advocate of despotism or power politics; if Machiavellism is understood as an intellectual attitude which permits amoral actions for political ends, it is questionable whether the views of these admirers of Machiavelli form part of the history of Machiavellism. The thinkers of this group saw in Machiavelli primarily an advocate of republican freedom. *The Prince* was meant as a warning. The book showed what would happen if people became negligent in protecting their liberty. The idea that *The Prince* was meant to put people on guard against the rise of tyrants had been suggested already in the sixteenth century; it can be found, for instance, in Alberico Gentili's *De legationibus* (1585) and it has had adherents ever since, even in the twentieth century, although all the documents bearing on the composition of *The Prince* show that there is no substance behind it. For the history of Machiavelli's reputation, however, the suggestion was important because it directed attention away from *The Prince* to the *Discorsi* as containing Machiavelli's authentic message. Thus

Machiavelli began to take on a Janus face. The inspirer of despotism was also the defender of freedom.

The discovery of the republican Machiavelli in the seventeenth century was chiefly the work of a group of English political writers. In England alone a relative free discussion of political ideas was possible and a radical trend of ideas, generated in the period of the Commonwealth, lived on under the Restoration. The chief representatives of this opposition have been called "classical republicans." They were steeped in the admiration of classical political wisdom and wanted to reorganize English political life according to classical principles. They were attracted by Machiavelli's writings because he was one of the few if not the only republican political theorist in modern times. Moreover, they considered him to be the most important transmitter of classical teachings to the modern world. There were also some more particular reasons for their interest in Machiavelli. His insistence on the necessity of going back to the beginnings, "the principles," was compatible with their plan for rebuilding society on new foundations. And Machiavelli had given some praise to the notion of mixed government which they believed would secure England from another civil war between extremes. Thus James Harrington, the author of the *Commonwealth of Oceana* (1656), called Machiavelli the "prince of polititians" and for Henry Neville, the author of the *Plato Redivivus,* Machiavelli was the "divine Machiavel."

Although the particular emphasis which these writers placed on Machiavelli's ideas was conditioned by the political situation in England, their views indicate that below the surface of criticism and condemnation there were students of politics who recognized that one could learn from Machiavelli because his views were based on acute and realistic observations of political life. This attitude can be traced back to Bacon who in his *De augmentis scientiarum* (*Advancement of Learning* [1623], book VII, chap. 2) confessed that "We are much beholden to Machiavelli and other writers of that class who openly and unfeignedly declare or describe what men do, and not what they ought to do."

This aspect of Machiavelli's writings could not fail to impress the great political thinkers of the eighteenth century. To Hume Machiavelli was a "great genius"; Montesquieu frequently referred approvingly to Machiavelli's views. These eighteenth-century thinkers were repulsed by his amoralism but they suggested that the stress on the political effectiveness of amoral actions was the work of later writers. They separated Machiavelli from Machiavellism and emphasized that Machiavelli himself had loved liberty. Diderot, who in the *Encyclopédie* characterized Machiavellism as an "odious kind of politics, which can be described briefly as the art of tyranny," also said in his article on Machiavelli that the purpose of *The Prince* was to depict the terrors of despotism: "See here the ferocious beast, to whom you abandon yourself." It was the fault of the reader that he took "a satire for a eulogy."

By the end of the eighteenth century, therefore, the image of Machiavelli had become rather complex and even contradictory. The contrast between the devilish Machiavelli whom Marlowe had brought on the stage and the sagacious Machiavelli who appears in Goethe's *Egmont* (1788) is instructive. Goethe's Machiavelli knew that people need to lie and to deceive in politics, but he knew also that such measures have little effect if they do not take into account the real feelings of the people. You cannot force religious convictions on them or treat them arrogantly from above. Goethe's Machiavelli implies that Machiavellism is necessary and appropriate only because—and as long as—rulers give no rights to their people. A new time in which the people will have power will make Machiavellian policy superfluous; *Egmont* was written in 1787, two years before the French Revolution.

When Frederick II of Prussia became involved in the struggle for Prussian aggrandizement Rousseau said that it was appropriate for a disciple of Machiavelli to begin his political career with a refutation of Machiavelli. Frederick's *Anti-Machiavel* has frequently been characterized as hypocritical, but this accusation is not quite fair. In his *Anti-Machiavel* Frederick had pointed out that Machiavelli's political experience came from a scene in which princes "are only in fact hermaphrodites of rulers and individuals; they play the part of great lords only with their servants." Frederick denied that this Italian world of small princely states could serve as a model for the conduct of politics. He thought it necessary to distinguish between petty intriguing, characteristic of small states, and the justifiable aims of a great power to expand.

In Frederick's times it had become a widely recognized theory that powerful states had a right to expand and to pursue their interests by all possible means. Machiavelli was certainly the most important influence in the development of these ideas. However, because of the evil repute in which his name was held in the sixteenth and seventeenth centuries it was regarded as inopportune to mention his name, and consequently the name of Machiavelli remained rather detached from that development of thought with which his ideas are most closely linked—the attitudes toward foreign affairs.

A point of departure for the development of new ideas on the nature of foreign policy was Machiavelli's thesis that the decisive factor in politics was power, not justice; and that the attainment of political ends permitted the use of force, violence, even crime. The ensuing discussion centered on the problem of whether there were limits to the application of force in the struggles among states, and if so, what they were. The crucial concept in this development was the notion of *ragione di stato* (reason of state), which implied that the relationship among states had its own rules, different from those determining human behavior in other spheres of life. Although some statements made by Italians of Machiavelli's time suggest that they recognized that in affairs of state actions might be necessary that are not permissible in other fields of human activities, the term *ragione di stato* neither occurs in Machiavelli's writings, nor was it used in the early sixteenth century. It came into use in the middle of that century and then soon became immensely popular. It was heard in the marketplace but also in the council room; for instance, as early as 1584, James IV of Scotland declared to his Privy Council "that he married for reasons of state, chiefly to provide his kingdom with an heir."

Originally the meaning of *ragione di stato* was not very different from that of the medieval notion of *ratio status* or *publicae utilitatis* which permitted the ruler to violate positive law if the promotion of the higher spiritual aims of the social order made such action necessary. But the idea of reason of state became strikingly transformed in the modern period. The religious struggles of the sixteenth and seventeenth centuries—or, more precisely, weariness produced by these struggles—gave rise to the view that one state could embrace adherents of different churches and that politics had its own principles independent of those of religion. Politics had its own law, that of the interest of the state. Furthermore, the rise of absolutism resulted in an identification of prince and state. The interest of the ruler became the reason of state. Nevertheless, a line was drawn between those political aims in which the interest of the prince coincided with the interests of the entire political body and those ambitions which arose from personal desires or arbitrary whims. The latter had to be repudiated as signs of tyranny.

From these assumptions there developed an extensive literature on the interests of the state and of the princes. The writers of this school tried to establish criteria for distinguishing between true and false interests and to determine those factors which constituted the true interests of the state. Because the presupposition of these thinkers was that politics was an autonomous field, speculations about the interests of the state were calculations in terms of power politics. They were concerned with those factors which constituted the strength of a state and would make aggrandizement possible: population, geographical position, financial resources, military posture, relation to neighbors. In the seventeenth and eighteenth centuries the writings on reason of state and interests of state amounted to a considerable part of the existing political literature.

The crucial influence of Machiavelli on the development of these ideas is obvious. He had proclaimed that politics ought to be conducted for purely political ends, for increasing the strength of the political body. He was instrumental, therefore, in introducing into the theory of reason of state that element which separated it from the older medieval concept in which the *ratio status* remained subordinated to nonpolitical or supra-political values. The emphasis on competition for power as the central factor in political life was thoroughly Machiavellian, although in Machiavelli's writings the word *stato* in the modern sense of embracing territory, ruler and ruled, rarely occurs. Machiavelli's prince had only to be interpreted as synonymous with the state in order to find in Machiavelli's writings a serious discussion of the problem of *ragione di stato.*

Although the writers on the interests of state did not acknowledge their debt to Machiavelli, and even concealed it by attacking him, their writings reflect their careful reading of the Florentine's works. Giovanni Botero, whose *Della Ragione di Stato* (1589) is one of the most influential early statements of the problem, accepted Machiavelli's thesis that no reliance could be placed on alliances or treaties. Traiano Boccalini (1556–1613) commented in his *Bilancia politica* on many of Machiavelli's theses and made the very Machiavellian statement that self-interest "is the true tyrant of the souls of tyrants as well as of princes who are not tyrants." Although Paolo Paruta (1540–1598) declared in his *Discorsi politici* that Machiavelli was "buried in perpetual oblivion" he agreed with him on many issues and acknowledged that the operations of a prince should be measured by quite different rules from those of a philosopher.

Two centuries later, in the eighteenth century, discussions of the European political situation, historical works, invented political testaments ascribed to famous rulers and statesmen, and pamphlets—all made use of reason of state and interests of princes in their arguments; at that time Machiavelli's name was no longer to be passed over in silence. However, the connection of his name with the ideas of this school of political thought did not help Machiavelli's reputation among the *philosophes* and the reformers. They were profoundly critical of the manner in which foreign policy was conducted in this period. They saw no sense in wars of aggrandizement and regarded the money spent on the maintenance of a large army as an obstacle to the economic well-being of the masses. These were features of the *ancien régime* that ought to be eliminated. As a master in the arts of *ragione di stato* Machiavelli became associated with the *ancien régime*.

The most characteristic representatives of the abhorred policies of the *ancien régime* were the diplomats—the "ministers" as they were called at this time. They became the particular target of the reform-minded writers of the eighteenth century who, in their descriptions of the activities of the diplomatic profession, endowed ministers with Machiavellian features. Such ministers, according to G. F. Le Trosne, cultivated "a dark art wrapping itself up in the folds and cloak of dissimulation"; because they lack frankness they become *compétiteurs en grimaces* (Mirabeau).

Machiavellists, as we mentioned before, can be found in all groups and professions. If one profession is particularly identified with this attitude it is the diplomatic profession, and in the popular view it has remained so since the eighteenth century.

In the last year of the eighteenth century a French translation of the works of Machiavelli was published with an introduction by T. Guiraudet who had first served the *ancien régime,* then the Revolution, and was finally a high official in the Foreign Office under the Directorate. With its emphasis on Machiavelli's anticlericalism and his nationalism Guiraudet alludes to aspects of Machiavelli's thought, one of which had agitated his readers in the past, and the other was to occupy students of Machiavelli in the future, although the prominent place given to these two ideas echoed the ideas of the French Revolution. But the most striking and interesting feature is the attempt of Guiraudet to reconcile those contradictory features of Machiavelli which in the course of the eighteenth century had emerged in sharp contrast:

> Machiavelli, with his enlightened love of freedom, knew that men, who have united in society, came together primarily to be happy and not simply to be free . . . They have seen that freedom was a means and not the end . . . that the primary good is the welfare of the State, the happiness and prosperity of its members, who can be hurt for a while by unlimited freedom; now to allow momentarily certain limits to be imposed on their freedom does not mean being a slave or a coward, but only proves that we are not always as free as a madman.

II

It is most doubtful that Machiavellism survived the fall of the *ancien régime.* This statement does not imply that interest in Machiavelli diminished or died; on the contrary, in the nineteenth and twentieth centuries an extended literature concerned with Machiavelli and Machiavelli's thought was produced, but the nature of interest in Machiavelli has changed.

In previous centuries Machiavelli's ideas had been regarded as the nucleus of a system which was of practical significance for every kind of political action and human behavior. With the political and social transformation brought about by the French

Revolution Machiavellism lost the environment in which its notions would strike sparks.

A secularized outlook on the world, frequently coupled with an optimistic belief in progress, could regard evil actions as a result of strange, abnormal circumstances or psychology. But that awe for the demonic power of evil that had made Machiavelli's recommendations not only abhorrent but also tempting was lost.

Likewise, after the French Revolution, tyranny and despotism seemed to belong to a discarded past. Even if the march to full democratic rule of the people was slow, even if a written constitution limiting the extent and the forms of government interference and a determination of the rights of man had become accepted features of a civilized political society, much of the advice which Machiavelli had given to his prince and on which Machiavellist writers like Naudé or Machon had enlarged became irrelevant.

Finally, the rise of nationalism stripped the Machiavellist theories on the unlimited use of force in foreign affairs of much of their explosive character. If the nation and the national state embodied the supreme ethical value and the individual could accomplish his own ethical ends only within a strong nation, then application of force to secure the life of the nation was easily justifiable and Machiavelli's views sounded much less extravagant than when they seemed to proclaim the unlimited right of the stronger over the weaker. In this changed political atmosphere people were inclined to minimize the consequences of Machiavelli's thought rather than to face them in their ruthless radicalism. Because of the appeal to liberate Italy from the barbarians in the last chapter of *The Prince,* Machiavelli was transformed into a prophet of the age of nationalism, and the amorality of his doctrines was explained as a result of the hopelessness of the Italian political situation: it was so desperate that Machiavelli was forced to prescribe poison, to use the words of the German historian Leopold von Ranke.

In the changed climate of the nineteenth century, with the development of a new and differentiated outlook on internal politics and foreign affairs, Machiavellism lost the appearance of providing a coherent system. This is reflected in the manner in which the words "Machiavellian" and "Machiavellist" are used in language and literature of the nineteenth and twentieth centuries. Whoever takes mental note of the occurrences of the term "Machiavellist" in modern times will be amused and fascinated by the widely varied and even contradictory applications of the word.

It is logical—and in accordance with the history of Machiavellism—that those features in modern political society which still bear the traces of the *ancien régime* frequently receive the label "Machiavellian." Diplomats are regularly suspected to be Machiavellians and Americans in the times of Woodrow Wilson were inclined to regard the entire European system of foreign policy, based on the assumption of sovereignty, as containing a Machiavellist element. Likewise statesmen proceeding in an authoritarian manner are usually considered as disciples of Machiavelli; in the nineteenth century both Metternich and Bismarck were called Machiavellian.

It is a small step from here to a use of the word that regards every clever political maneuver as Machiavellian. And the reading of political biographies, for instance, the biography of *Huey P. Long* (1967) by T. Harry Williams, or of issues of the *American Historical Review,* will provide many examples of this.

Cleverness, of course, arouses distrust because a clever man is suspected of keeping something back, and of not being entirely frank and open. Briefly, he behaves very much as a Machiavellian would be expected to behave. And indeed, "Machiavellian" and slyly "clever" are often used synonymously. The concept "Machiavellian" has become so vague and ambiguous that every human activity which tries to achieve its ends through exclusion of all extraneous—human or moral—considerations is called "Machiavellian"; a businessman, therefore, might have a Machiavellian strategy. The application of technical devices, because they reduce human or moral qualities to calculable factors, is frequently considered Machiavellian. In the 1960s the labels of Machiavellian or Machiavellistic could be affixed to anything that was considered to be wrong or inhuman.

If the idea of Machiavellism lost coherence and significance in the nineteenth century, the development of scholarship, and particularly of historical scholarship, maintained and perhaps intensified interest in Machiavelli; however these scholarly concerns separated Machiavelli from Machiavellism and placed Machiavelli in a very new light.

The historical literature on Machiavelli pursued two lines of research. The one was to determine his place in the development of political thought. The other was to see him as a figure of his time, of the Italian Renaissance. In the field of political thought the relation of his thought to classical or medieval political theorists became clarified, and detailed investigations established the influence of his thought on later political thinkers like Montesquieu, or even more recent ones like Gaetano Mosca or Antonio Gramsci. The study of Machiavelli as a figure of the Renaissance resulted in a better understanding of the institutional and social milieu in which he lived and to which his writings were aimed; the difference between his real aims and those ascribed to him by later generations emerged sharply. Because these scholarly efforts described Machiavelli as an Italian of the Renaissance or as a link in the development of political thought, because they "historicized" Machiavelli, they contributed to the decline of Machiavellism as a system of permanent validity and applicability.

On the other hand, the scholarly approach placed Machiavelli at the beginning of a development which has extended into modern times. Machiavelli was shown to have touched upon many questions of political techniques—control of the masses by psychology, the role of an elite—which are recognized as essential factors in every political society and, as such, have become objects of intense study in the development of political science. Moreover, because the Renaissance was believed to have begun the modern period of history, the characterization of Machiavelli as a typical representative of this period made him a forerunner of modern man. Actually it was not so much Machiavelli as his picture of Cesare Borgia which was regarded as characteristically modern—a personality which emancipated itself from the bonds of conventional morality and lived a free life according to its natural instincts. This was Nietzsche's view of Cesare Borgia which he had taken from Machiavelli's *The Prince.* Thus, even in the efforts of modern scholarship, Machiavelli has remained—although remotely and tenuously—tied to the concerns of the present day.

This is important because it has its bearing on what might be called the latest, most recent chapter in the history of Machiavellism, the relation of Machiavellism to twentieth-century totalitarianism. Fascist dictators liked to refer to Machiavelli as a master who had understood the true nature of politics; Mussolini professed that he wanted to write a dissertation on Machiavelli. But there is no sign that Hitler or Mussolini had any concrete knowledge of Machiavelli's writings or ideas. They were influenced by social Darwinist ideas of the necessary triumph of the stronger over the weaker. And in the popular mind this was a theory which Machiavelli had already advanced. They pretended to be adherents of Nietzschean philosophy, and thought of Machiavelli's Cesare Borgia as a model of the superman. In the organization of their party and their government system the concept of elite was crucial, and Machiavelli would be mentioned as one of the first political scientists raising this issue.

These were probably the contexts in which they became aware of Machiavelli. They ascribed to him basic ideas of intellectual movements of their own time which had molded their minds, and they found this convenient because they liked to place their policies and systems under the protection of the name of the great Florentine. To maintain the existence of a serious connection between Machiavelli and the ideas and policies of the modern totalitarian dictators is a misunderstanding. It must be added, however, that the history of Machiavellism is quite as much a history of misunderstandings as a history of the impact of Machiavelli's true ideas.

PART III.
Florentine and Venetian Studies

8. The Venetian Constitution in Florentine Political Thought

Two Italian cities, writes Jacob Burckhardt in his *Civilization of the Renaissance in Italy,* have been of the greatest significance for the entire history of the human race: Venice and Florence—"cities which cannot be compared to anything else in the world."[1] Although Renaissance historians now may be inclined to focus their attention less exclusively on these two cities, Florence and Venice still remain primary centers of interest and attraction. In the same passage in which Burckhardt emphasized the eminence of Venice and Florence in the complex of Renaissance civilization, he stated that "no contrast can be imagined stronger than that which is offered us by these two." Thus a comparison of Venice and Florence, an investigation of how they differed, has usually served to point up the particular features of each. But the two cities did not exist in separate worlds. Although the cities were different, Venetians and Florentines were in steady contact and there was a lively exchange of ideas between them. This essay will be concerned with the

Originally published in *Florentine Studies,* ed. Nicolai Rubinstein (London, Faber and Faber, 1968), pp. 463–500. This essay is closely related to an earlier one on Bernardo Rucellai (see Chapter 9) and two later ones on Gasparo Contarini (see Chapter 10) and The Battle of Pavia (see Chapter 12). It is placed ahead of the others because it provides a survey on the genesis of the Venetian myth, with which the other pieces are concerned.

intellectual relations between Venetians and Florentines, particularly how Florentine political thought was influenced by the image of Venice.[2] But before proceeding with the story proper, the problems inherent in this topic should be indicated.

The first difficulty is that Italian cities had no written constitutions. What we call their constitutions were a set of laws and regulations which established the functions and composition of councils and set forth the qualifications and duties of the magistrates. These laws and regulations issued over the course of centuries lay buried, for the most part, in folios in the chancelleries. Thus the most striking and prominent features of the government of a city-state might be quite generally known, but precise and detailed knowledge of how a government functioned was difficult to acquire.

The influence which constitutional forms of a city-state might have had on the constitution of another is further complicated because men were inclined to reject the entire idea that one government could be or ought to be patterned after another. Each city was thought to be a unique formation; each city had its own patron saint: Venice was the city of St. Mark; Florence of St. John the Baptist; Milan of St. Ambrose.[3] It was assumed that the patron saint held his protecting hand over the fate of the city. The institutions which had been created in earliest times when the city had acquired its patron saint were held sacred. According to a legend believed in Venice since the twelfth century, St. Mark had rested in the lagoons at the place Venice was founded; God had shown him in his dreams that this was the place he would be buried and that at this place a city would arise and grow to greatness and power under his protection. The towns and lands which Venice conquered surrendered to San Marco and were obliged to have the *laudes* of San Marco sung in the churches at all festival days. The older the institutions of a city the more purely were they believed to carry the imprint of the city's saintly protector. And this had an impact on politics far into the sixteenth century. After the death of the last Visconti, when the Milanese attempted to regain freedom, they named their newly established republic the "Ambrosian Republic" and tried to revive institutions which they believed had existed in the times of Sant' Ambrogio. The Florentines, under the influence of Savonarola, believed themselves to be charged with a special mission by God and proclaimed their city the "City of Christ." Close association of a city's existence with an individual saint formed an obstacle to the imitation of foreign political institutions.

Yet this belief in the uniqueness of one's city did not exclude all interest in political experimentation. The norm of a perfect society at which every city ought to aim always existed. In the fifteenth century the spread of a more extensive knowledge of classical political writings provided new material for attempts to transform the existing political order according to abstract principles. Nevertheless, the idea persisted that each city-state was unique. In some respects, one might even say that the revival of the ancients resulted in a secularization of previous beliefs: the figure of the patron saint was merged with that of the lawgiver, and the idealization of the classical world strengthened the view that "return to the beginnings," to the institutions which had been established when the city was founded, was the only true way of making political changes and reforms.

When the ideas and terminology of classical political theories began to permeate the thinking of the literati and the ruling groups the reputation of Venice as the model of a free republic began to rise. In this development political events played as much a part as changes in the intellectual climate. During the fourteenth century in a slow but irresistible process the smaller Italian city-states had been absorbed by the greater Italian powers; by the beginning of the fifteenth century only two republican city-states—Venice and Florence—had survived among Italy's great powers. But they were, as Burckhardt remarked, cities of contrast. To him, Florence was "the city of incessant movement," whereas Venice appeared as unchanged and unchangeable. Thus, while Florence, which underwent several revolutions and frequent changes of government, could hardly serve as a model for imitation, the Venetian government seemed to approach the realization of a perfect republic.

Thus in analyzing the relation between Venetian and Florentine political thinking, we must keep in mind that it was not a reciprocal relation; the connection is limited to the problem of the influence which the view of the excellence of Venetian institutions had on Florentine political thought. Because the traditional resistance against the adoption of foreign forms of government was strong, the question must be raised whether and when the discussion of Venice as a pattern for imitation reached beyond a small group and had an impact on political practice. Moreover, because Venice became the pattern of an ideal republic only in the fifteenth century and the emergence of this image was closely tied up with humanist thinking, it must be asked whether the view of the excellence of Venetian institutions represented chiefly the application of an ideal classical pattern to Venice, or whether it was based on an intimate knowledge of the functioning of Venetian institutions. Thus, an investigation of these questions is closely connected with the broader issue of the growth of realism in political thought.

I

The story of Venice as a political model begins in the fifteenth century, but Venice was regarded as a miracle inspiring a myth ever since it emerged as a community of significance.[4] And some aspects of this myth shaped the view which people held about Venice as a political pattern.

Venice was never a city like other cities. The "churches, monasteries and houses, all built in the sea" as Comines stated,[5] aroused the wonder and the admiration of travelers of earlier centuries as much as it does today. Venice's extraordinary situation invited even in the fifteenth century typographical descriptions—some in prose, some in verse—which are so detailed and so precise that they could almost serve as a modern guide book.[6] Visitors were astounded at the sight of canals that replaced streets, and gondolas that replaced wagons and carriages. The mosaics, the rare and precious stones in which San Marco and the other churches of Venice abounded, evoked awed comments and the envy of the citizens of other states. The ceremonies and rituals surrounding the election and the death of a doge, the arrival of ships from the Orient, the confluence of merchants from every part of the world offered spectacles which could be seen nowhere else. From the time of its foundation it appeared that a fairytale had become reality in Venice.

The myth that Venice inspired from early times had its political aspects: the one was that Venice was the city of liberty; the other, that Venice was a city of domestic peace and stability.

Liberty (*libertas*) had a double meaning. If it was used in reference to political institutions *libertas* indicated a regime that was not tyrannical. But *libertas* could also be used to characterize the position of a city-state in relation to other city-states and then it signified independence. The Venetians believed they possessed *libertas* in both these meanings. As writers frequently mentioned, Venetian independence was celebrated in two paintings, one to be seen in the Hall of the Consiglio Maggiore, the other in the Hall of the Senate. Both depicted the events of 1177 when emperor and Pope concluded their peace in Venice and when, according to Venetian writers, the Pope conferred special privileges on the doge, granting him political status equal to Pope and emperor.[7] About the freedom that reigned within Venice, writers liked to refer to the statement in St. Thomas Aquinas' *De regimine principum,* that of all the rulers in northern Italy the doge of Venice alone was not a tyrant and had only limited powers.[8] The notion of the stability of the Venetian government grew steadily and it had become accepted opinion in the fourteenth century. Petrarch's words in praise of Venice almost summarized the notions which in previous centuries had been formed about the "miracolissima Venetiae civitas": "a city rich in gold but richer in repute; strong in power but stronger in virtue; built on solid marble but more stably and solidly established on the more secure foundations of its citizens' concord, fortified and made safe by the intelligence and wisdom of its sons rather than by the sea which surrounds the city."[9]

These two themes—of Venice as an independent republic and as a model of stability and changelessness—recur almost regularly. In the fifteenth century, when political circumstances accentuated the importance of Venice, speculations about the nature of the Venetian government also became more elaborate. A crucial turn was given to these discussions by the humanists who began to identify Venice with classical models of republicanism. Members of the Venetian ruling group encouraged these efforts to present the Venetian constitution as a modern embodiment of ancient political wisdom. This was clearly in their political interests. A political myth was a precious political asset because it unified the citizens and reinforced their willingness to undergo sacrifices for their commune.[10] When the writings—the histories and laudations—of humanists like Salutati, Bruni, and Loschi extolled Florence and Milan and compared them to Athens, Sparta, and Rome, Venetian patricians became understandably anxious to find humanist writers who would do the same for Venice; they searched anxiously for a humanist who would serve as public historiographer and write the history of Venice praising the achievements of Venetian politics and the public spirit of Venetian citizens.[11] Venetian nobles and even the Venetian government were particularly interested in those humanist treatises which described the Venetian government in terms of classical political theories. The most important notion developed by humanists in the fifteenth century was that of the Venetian constitution as a realization of the classical idea of mixed government: the doge represented the monarchical element; the Senate the aristocratic element; and the Consiglio Maggiore the democratic element. This concept of the Venetian constitution exerted a great influence in the development of European republicanism far into the eighteenth century.

The notion was probably first adumbrated by Pier Paolo Vergerio in a fragment on the Venetian republic.[12] He characterized Venice as an aristocracy but he added that Venice was a particularly well-constructed aristocracy because its government had also some monarchical and democratic features. This concept was fully worked out only in the middle of the fifteenth century and this development is connected with the name of one of the best-known Venetian patricians of that time, Francesco Barbaro, and with his intellectual circle.[13] Barbaro was the patron of the Greek scholar, George of Trebizond, whom Barbaro had brought from Crete to Venice in 1417. From Rome, in December 1451, Trebizond wrote to Barbaro that "your ancestors who have founded your republic have certainly taken from Plato's *Laws* everything that makes the life of a republic long and happy. For it would be quite incredible that things could be so completely identical by accident. Plato said that no republic could live long and happy if it did not contain elements of all forms of government: of one-man rule, of aristocracy and of democracy."[14] George of Trebizond added that the Venetian constitution corresponded even in its details to Plato's ideal republic. Barbaro in his answer expressed his delight about George of Trebizond's discovery. He asked him to write an introduction to his translation of Plato's *Laws* in which he should point out the similarity between Plato's theories and Venice's political practice, and he promised that he would distribute this book among his Venetian compatriots and George of Trebizond would receive a rich compensation.[15] George of Trebizond wrote such an introduction[16] and Barbaro was pleased to hear that through the Greek scholar's efforts "as the Athenians took pride in Solon, the Spartans in Lycurgus, the Venetians could take pride in Plato as their law-giver."[17] George of Trebizond then dedicated the entire translation including the preface to Barbaro, but before he could harvest from his dedication the promised gain, Barbaro died. So he then composed another dedication, this time to the doge, and this dedication finally brought him the expected benefits. The Venetian Senate decided to give him a remuneration "which would be honourable and useful to George and to our state."[18] And in October 1460 George of Trebizond was appointed to the chair of humanities and rhetoric in the School of San Marco. The Venetians were proud to give their approval to a thesis which linked together Venice, Plato, and the idea of a constitution which combined all three forms of government.[19] In later years Venetians frequently referred to these ideas as containing the truth about their system of government and almost one hundred years after George of Trebizond, Gasparo Contarini systematized this view of Venice in his famous and influential book.

The idea of a mixed government combining monarchical, aristocratic, and democratic elements was, however, only one of the various notions classical writers employed in defining the nature of a good republic. Mixed government did not necessarily mean a combination of monarchy, aristocracy, and democracy. People ascribed to Plato the view that mixed government must contain three forms of government because he had written that a well-organized government ought to stand on the middle ground between monarchy and democracy.[20] Aristotle already observed that Plato, in the outline of his ideal republic, actually envisaged a mixture of democracy and oligarchy rather than a combination of all three forms of government.[21] In Aristotle's own discussions of mixed government this combination of oligarchy and democracy received most attention.[22] In other passages, however, Aristotle seems to suggest that aristocracy was superior to all other forms of government,[23] and the view of the excellence of aristocracy was reinforced by the authority of Cicero.[24]

Thus, not all humanist writers who praised Venice as a realization of the classical prescripts for an ideal republic saw in the Venetian government a combination of all three forms of government; some regarded Venice as a mixture of oligarchy and democracy, others as an aristocracy. For instance, Francesco Patrizi, who in his treatise on republics expressed his admiration for the immutability of the Venetian government, regarded Venice as excelling all other states in "justice, power, wealth and splendour."[25] According to Patrizi a perfect republic required a mixture of democracy and oligarchy.[26] But there were a great number of writers—probably the majority of those dealing with this subject—who characterized Venice as an aristocracy. Poggio Bracciolini, relying on Cicero's view that an aristocracy was the best form of government, advanced the thesis that Venice was the only truly aristocratic government that had ever existed. In Venice "the best citizens rule and serve the well-being of the state without regard to their personal interests."[27] Likewise, Sabellico in his treatise on the Venetian magistrates declared that Venice was that aristocracy which Plato had praised. Eternal harmony which reigned in Venice guaranteed that the city would withstand all the attacks of ruthless fortune.[28] The most extensive and detailed account of Venice as an aristocracy was given by Francesco Negri.[29] Like Poggio, Negri asserted that the only state in which an ideal government, namely, an aristocracy, had come to life was Venice.[30] And Negri justified this thesis by a long praise of Venice's great men and of its political, intellectual, and artistic achievements.

It has been mentioned that the Venetian ruling group promoted these praises of Venice because they served to strengthen the civic spirit. On the other hand most of the humanist authors composed these flattering descriptions because they wanted to gain the protection and favor of the Venetian government or of individual Venetian nobles. This purpose is evident and unconcealed in the case of Francesco Negri and it is not without significance that Negri had no qualms about calling Venice an aristocracy. Negri must have been sure that such a characterization of the Venetian government would be welcomed by the men who were in power in Venice. We can assume that whatever particular description of their constitution the Venetians believed to be most appropriate—whether they accepted the thesis that their constitution contained monarchical, aristocratic, and democratic features, that it was a mixture of oligarchy and democracy, or that it was a pure aristocracy—they all regarded the aristocratic element as the prevailing one in the structure of their society.

II

The question of the influence which the image of Venice as an ideal republic exerted on politics in fifteenth-century Florence cannot be answered in clear and simple terms. As we shall see later some circles in Florence shared the high estimate of Venice by the humanists and regarded Venice as an ideal republic. But in general the praise of Venice did not shake the conviction that Venice and Florence were very different political formations. The gap between them grew wider.

Of the various humanist writers on Venice whom we discussed, Poggio alone was a Florentine. He had his personal reasons for composing a laudation of Venice. He was deeply incensed about taxes which, unjustly in his opinion, the Florentine government asked him to pay.[31] He thought of leaving Florence and settling in Venice. Disgusted with the arbitrariness and unreliability of the Florentine democracy, he painted in radiant colors the strict observations of law and justice in an aristocracy. Thus Poggio, five hundred years before Burckhardt, regarded restlessness as characteristic of Florence, stability as characteristic of Venice. The application of the terminology of ancient political science to Venice and Florence only reinforced the feeling of the distinctiveness of these two cities.

The Florentine views about the different and alien character of Venice emerged clearly when adoption of Venetian forms of government became a question of practical politics. In the winter of 1465–66 and the summer of 1466, after the death of Cosimo Medici and before his son Piero had gathered the reins of government firmly in his hands, an attempt was made to limit the power of the Medici, perhaps even to deprive them of their power. The institutional changes which the opponents of the Medici tried to introduce are not known to us in detail.[32] The main features seem to have been to make the eligibility to government offices a permanent privilege of a restricted group. In the deliberations on this, one of the speakers stated that of the three forms of government only a system in which the people ruled guaranteed stability.[33] Florence possessed such a system; Florence was a democracy. This argument was repeated by another speaker who said that innovations were dangerous and that the changes which were now suggested would introduce an aristocracy in imitation of the Venetian republic; in the opinion of this speaker "our republic has most brilliantly flourished under a democratic form of government."[34] The speaker saw the principal difference between aristocracy and democracy, between Venice and Florence, in the manner in which offices were filled. In Venice magistrates were elected; in Florence men were assigned to offices by lot.

It is evident, however, that in rejecting imitation of the Venetian model Florentines were guided not only by rational arguments but also by emotions. The two republics were old political enemies and regarded each other with distrust and hostility. From the diatribe against the greediness of Venice which Villani inserted in his chronicle in the fourteenth century[35] to the anti-Venetian letter of Benedetto Dei, in which the author defended Cosimo Medici's alliance with Milan in the fifteenth century,[36] references to this traditional enmity between Venice and Florence are frequent.

Although feelings of being different may have been the prevailing mood in the Florentine attitude toward Venice, there were factors that worked in the opposite direction. Venice and Florence alone had been left as independent and powerful republics on the Italian political scene; republicanism created an ideological bond. This aspect of the relation was usually emphasized in the speeches with which ambassadors began their diplomatic missions: there was a close relation between those two city-states because of the "similarity in their forms of public rule and in their ways of living and conducting business."[37] Nevertheless, the feeling of a certain ideological affinity was transformed into common political action only when the interests of both cities were threatened by the same enemy.

It is true, however, that business ties formed bonds between individual members of the Venetian and Florentine ruling group. Of Florentines, the Medici and their circle had close friends in Venice; Cosimo took up residence in Venice when he and his family were driven out of Florence in 1433; and the Medici continued to maintain the contacts with members of the Venetian nobility which had been established in the times of their exile. Of Venetians, those patricians who delighted most in the new world of humanism cultivated friendships in Medicean Florence. Francesco Barbaro was a friend of the Medici family, and especially close to Lorenzo de' Medici, Cosimo's younger brother.[38] Barbaro's Florentine contacts extended to other members of the Florentine ruling group. Among the Venetian nobles who enjoyed friendship with Florentines in the second part of the fifteenth century was Bernardo Bembo; he served several terms as Venetian ambassador in Florence and belonged to the circle of Marsilio Ficino.[39] Bembo's popularity with the Florentine ruling group was so great that a special attempt was made to prevent his recall from Florence. In later years Bembo seems to have been the chief expert in the Venetian government for Florentine affairs; he was usually charged with taking care of the Florentine ambassadors who came to Venice.[40]

A slightly younger Venetian aristocrat with close connections in Florence was Pietro Delfino. Lorenzo Magnifico, with whom Delfino had come in contact through his duties as general of the Camaldulensian Order, esteemed Delfino highly, and Delfino was also a particular friend of Lorenzo's brother-in-law, Bernardo Rucellai, with whom he corresponded on intellectual problems and political events. It is from Delfino that we have one of the few direct testimonies of Florentine admiration for the Venetian constitution. In a letter addressed to a Venetian friend, Delfino stated that he had heard in Florence about Poggio's treatise in praise of Venice and that he was sending to Venice a copy of this manuscript. Delfino added that he had been able to observe that the whole of Florence shared Poggio's high opinion of the Venetian system of government.[41] When Delfino wrote "entire Florence" (*universa Florentia*) he doubtless meant the Florentine ruling group, the circle around Lorenzo Magnifico.

One can probably say that in the fifteenth century admiration for Venice was limited to members of the Florentine aristocracy who favored an oligarchic regime. But among them this attitude was almost traditional. Already Rinaldo degli Albizzi complained that Florence had not a government like that of Venice; and the same attitude can be observed in the strange abortive conspiracy which was undertaken in 1459 or early in 1460.[42] Benedetto Dei, one of the conspirators, and our only witness of this event, was an adherent and probably an agent of the Medici. He and his companions wanted to introduce a reform which, after the Venetian model, would entrust the government of Florence to a doge and to members of about two hundred Florentine families.

In the fifteenth century, admiration for Venice and the wish for changing the Florentine government in accordance with the pattern of the Venetian constitution was limited to Florentine aristocrats, and even a particular group among them; they alone had access to the knowledge needed to introduce features of the Venetian constitution into the Florentine system. One may question whether the various treatises on Venice which we have discussed were widely known. Even if they were, their authors did not offer much detailed information about Venetian political life or give a concrete or realistic picture of the functioning of Venetian institutions. The intellectual aim and ambitions of the humanists were satisfied when they had identified the Venetian government with one of the categories of classical political thought. Then they might explain that this system of government was suited to realize virtues like justice, fortitude, or charity, or they might assert that the Venetians were "new Romans."[43] In Sabellico's comparison of Roman and Venetian achievements which he inserted in his history, Venice came out best. Its constitution was better than that of the Roman republic and Venice excelled all states that had ever existed. But from these treatises the reader will not get much information about the institutions which distinguished Venice, only that Venice had a doge, a Senate, and a large council. A few arrangements of the Venetian constitution attracted attention. For instance, the combination of election and the use of lots which the Venetians employed in filling vacancies among their magistrates is frequently described in detail.[44] Likewise the ceremonies surrounding the death of a doge and the election of his successor. Special praise is given to the care with which secrecy was maintained.[45]

Some of these writings contain a list of magistrates. Such an enumeration forms the contents of one of Sabellico's treatises on Venice,[46] but although Sabellico was relatively well informed, this listing gave no clear picture of the functioning of the various magistrates nor did he study the relationships which existed among them. The most extended and best-informed discussion of the Venetian government in the fifteenth century was Paolo Morosini's letter to Gregory of Heimburg.[47] But despite many interesting details, particularly about the administration of justice and about the procedure in the various councils, Morosini did not explain how these various governmental agencies were connected with each other and how such a collection of magistrates could effect a centrally directed policy. Florentine politicians who came as ambassadors to Venice were probably better equipped than literati to acquire knowledge of Venetian institutions. It is significant that alone Dei, who was close to the Medici, put his finger on the crucial issue when he intimated that the center of the Venetian government was a council strictly limited and controlled by a finite number of patrician families.

Thus, at the end of the fifteenth century, when the French invasion and the flight of the Medici opened a new chapter in Florentine constitutional developments, all the praise which had been bestowed upon the Venetian government had not resulted in the acceptance of Venice as a model for Florence. The great majority of the citizens remained convinced that Venice and Florence were very different formations—Venice an aristocracy and Florence a democracy—and that it was best to preserve a city's ancient and original form of government. Moreover, only a few men possessed insight into the real functioning of the Venetian government; the tendency toward imitating the Venetian government can be found only in the group around the Medici. These men thought that an adoption of the Venetian constitution, perhaps with a member of the Medici family as doge and a council limited to families loyal to the Medici, might be desirable and give stability and permanency to the rule of the Medici in Florence.

III

With the overthrow of the Medici in 1494, we enter upon a period of Florentine history in which the constitutional forms of Venice became an openly discussed and important issue of Florentine politics. In 1494 the Florentines established the Great Council after the Venetian model. And the hall in which its meetings took place was constructed according to the measurements of the hall of the Venetian Consiglio Maggiore. In 1502, the highest Florentine office, the gonfalonierate of justice, became a lifetime position: Florence became headed by a doge. However, these two reforms, both undertaken in the Venetian pattern, ought to be sharply differentiated. The institutional innovation of 1502, the creation of the Gonfaloniere a vita, was, as we shall see later on, urged by the Florentine aristocrats and was in line with the interpretation that Venice was mainly an aristocracy. But the motives for the creation of the Great Council in 1494 were quite different. Through a *parlamento,* which followed the overthrow of Piero de' Medici, power had been placed in the hands of a small oligarchy, more or less the same group that had been predominant before the revolution—only without Piero de' Medici as the head. The establishment of the Great Council on December 23, 1494 aimed at broadening the government. In this respect it was an antiaristocratic movement. Thus, in 1494 the Venetian pattern served democratic purposes. And eight years later it served the opposite aim of an aristocratic reaction. How was it possible for the Venetian pattern to be used for different ends?

In order to answer this question we must investigate the motives which determined the adoption of the pattern of the Venetian Consiglio Maggiore in 1494,[48] and this in turn means an analysis of the attitude of Savonarola, who was the most powerful spokesman for the adoption of the Venetian model by Florence. Savonarola's political attitude in 1494 has aroused much discussion, for it is not easy to understand or to explain.[49] Savonarola was not a systematic thinker; he was a powerful preacher and his sermons, even after almost five hundred years when they are read but not heard, still have a compelling and moving force. When his sermons had a practical aim he was able and anxious to bolster his point by rational arguments taken from philosophy, theology, or history. But his arguments always remained subordinated to the purposes of his sermon. He could employ different, even contradictory, arguments whenever his aim had changed. Savonarola did not hesitate to use a variety of rationalizations because he was a visionary to whom ideas came by inspiration.

With increasing involvement in Florentine politics his approach to political problems became more sophisticated. But in the winter of 1494 his political approach was rather naive. For Savonarola there were two types of government: monarchies and republics.[50] The republican form was more appropriate to Italy; Savonarola seemed unaware of the distinction which the humanists had made between aristocratic and democratic republics. If the republican government in Florence did not work, this was caused by the selfishness and viciousness of individual citizens who tended toward tyranny. These were the assumptions behind Savonarola's intervention in Florentine politics in December 1494. From December 14 to 21, with exception of the 20th, he preached daily until, on December 22 and 23, the Florentine councils adopted a constitutional reform and established the Great Council. In Savonarola's sermons the foremost admonition was that of the need for a moral conversion: the citizens ought to place the common good above private interests. They ought to live virtuously and treat each other with love and charity. Savonarola's demand for moral reforms extended into the sphere of political reform because the existing government system gave dominating influence to a few ambitious citizens and prevented unity and harmony.

Savonarola drew two practical conclusions from this situation. First, he insisted on the necessity of introducing new institutions.[51] The vehemence with which he justified the need for departing from the past and for the imitation of foreign institutions indicates the strength of the resistance to deviation from the traditional concepts of Florentine politics. Savonarola's sermon of December 17, which is chiefly devoted to this issue, is a very impressive document.[52] It contains a poetic description of the meeting of two women, one representing Truth, the other Tradition. Savonarola wanted to show that tradition was inferior to truth. Second, Savonarola recommended speed in effecting institutional reforms. This suggestion arose from the tense internal situation in Florence which was threatened by outbreaks of violence. But Savonarola seems also to have feared that delay would give those who held power an opportunity to reinforce their position.[53]

In political terms one can say that Savonarola's demands were democratic. They aimed at curtailing the power of the Florentine oligarchy. But Savonarola himself hardly saw his suggestions in these political terms. To him the struggle was not one of aristocrats versus democrats, of an oligarchic regime against a more broadly based government, but of good against evil, of virtue against vice. In Savonarola's view the existing regime of a small elite was bad, not because a regime of few was inferior to a regime of many, but because the few who ruled were evil men.

Savonarola's recommendation of the Venetian model must be seen in this context. Savonarola was not interested in the question of whether Venice was an aristocracy or a democracy or a mixed government. The Venetians were no better than the Florentines. If Venice lived without internal revolutions and dissensions—and Savonarola accepted this myth of the harmonious stability of the Venetian government—then the Venetian institutions were better than those of Florence and ought to be imitated by the Florentines.[54] Savonarola singled out the Venetian Consiglio Maggiore and the Venetian method of electing officials as particularly suited for adoption by Florence. Actually, he regarded the creation of a Great Council as a necessary precondition for the crucial innovation, the introduction of an elective system: the Great Council was the instrument which served to place officeholding on an elective principle. Certainly, Savonarola regarded as crucial an enlargement of the circle of citizens directly involved in the ruling of the city. If citizens had a chance to receive honors they would live more virtuously.[55] From Savonarola's sermons one does not get the impression that he had concrete or detailed ideas about the changes which ought to be made, and one might wonder whether he had very clear ideas about the Venetian constitution. He was not aware that these measures might work a revolutionary change replacing one social group by another. He looked upon these reforms from the point of view that they would result in moral improvement.

It is reliably reported that Savonarola's recommendation for imitating Venice was encouraged and perhaps inspired by others. If Savonarola himself had no clear notions about the political consequences involved in the establishment of a Great Council, were these others equally unaware of the implications of this suggestion?

We have little information about the exact course of events which preceded the acceptance of the law of December 23 establishing the Great Council. We know that a large number of proposals were submitted to the government but only a few of them are preserved. And their authorship cannot always be established. Thus, our knowledge of the extent and character of the controversies going on in Florence is fragmentary. In the few drafts we have, the impact of Savonarola's recommendation can certainly be noticed. Emphasis is placed on the adoption of the Venetian procedure of election rather than on the creation of the Great Council. Few Florentines seem to have recognized the revolutionary impact which the establishment of the Great Council would have. Although there was agreement on the principle that membership in the Great Council should be granted only to those citizens whose ancestors—father or grandfather—had been entitled to hold office, there were disagreements about the precise form in which this principle should be carried through. Very few, however, seemed to have had any clear idea of the size the Great Council should be. An exception was Piero Capponi who, because of his courageous stand against the French, was then probably the most influential member of the Florentine ruling group. In his proposal Capponi expressed the view that the Great Council might be much larger than people seemed to think; he insisted therefore on the importance of having also a smaller council which would control the actual conduct of affairs. As pattern for such a smaller council Capponi referred to the Venetian Council of the Pregadi. This corresponds to our observation that precise knowledge of the Venetian constitution would be found chiefly among Florentine aristocrats; only an aristocrat like Capponi realized the crucial significance of the Council of the Pregadi in the Venetian aristocratic system of government.

The final outcome of these discussions and proposals, the law of December 23, reflected less the Venetian pattern than one might have expected after Savonarola's intervention. It is difficult to decide whether the departures from the Venetian model were due to lack of knowledge of Venice, recognition of the impossibility of transferring Venetian institutions to Florence, or unwillingness to follow foreign examples. In the law of December 23 the Florentine Great Council was called Council of the People and of the Commune and this name indicates that the Great Council was meant to be an outgrowth and continuation of traditional Florentine institutions rather than an innovation. Although in addition to the Great Council a smaller council was established, the functions of this Florentine Council of the Eighty were much more limited than the functions of the Venetian Council of the Pregadi.

The establishment of the Great Council and the introduction of elections for offices failed to bring internal harmony and peace to Florence. For us, this is easily understandable because the Florentine Great Council lacked the homogeneity of its Venetian pattern: it contained both aristocrats and men of the middle classes, and conflicts between them were unavoidable. The Florentines did not see their domestic difficulties in this light. Nevertheless with increasing internal tension views about the usefulness and applicability of the Venetian pattern began to take a new and more pronounced shape. In opposition to the dissatisfaction of the aristocrats who regarded the Great Council as the principal cause for their diminished authority, the middle classes defended the Great Council. It became to them the bulwark of Florentine democracy. In the sermons of the following years Savonarola emphasized this aspect of the Great Council.[56] In Savonarola's references to Florentine politics defense of the Great Council became his main theme, and his argument about the meaning and significance of this institution shifted. Savonarola now mentions the existence of three forms of government: monarchy, aristocracy, and democracy.[57] Florence, he says, is a democracy, a *vivere populare,* and the democratic nature of the Florentine government is embodied in the Great Council.[58] Savonarola continued to insist that foreign institutions, if they had shown themselves to be conducive to good life, should be studied and imitated, but he mentioned as possible patterns Lucca and Siena as well as Venice.[59] In Savonarola's defense and praise of the Great Council the notion that the Great Council was constructed after the Venetian model began to disappear. According to Savonarola Florence had become a reformed city and the centerpiece of this reform was the Great Council. But it was God who had granted Florence this remarkable institution. In Florence a perfect social order had been realized; other cities ought to look up to Florence and imitate her.[60] Other partisans of Florentine democracy gave to these arguments a somewhat different turn. Certainly, the Great Council was the "soul of Florence" and it was given to Florence by God. But it represented also the ancient and original form of Florentine political life: its *antico vivere populare*.

IV

If, after 1494, the partisans of a democratic political organization began to minimize the role the Venetian model had played in the introduction of the Great Council, the utterances of their opponents, the aristocrats, show that they saw in Venice the embodiment of their political ideal: an aristocratic government.[61] When the government asked for advice on issues like the opening of new sources of revenue, or improvements in the administration of justice, the aristocrats frequently pointed to the manner in which such affairs were handled in Venice. The main concern of the aristocrats, however, was a constitution that would restore political control to them, and their plans for such a reform were modeled after Venice.

This aristocratic attitude is exemplified by Bernardo Rucellai, one of the most vehement advocates of an antidemocratic revision of the Florentine constitution. Rucellai regarded the Venetian constitution as almost perfect. Its ideal character was one of the topics discussed in the Rucellai gardens, where prominent Florentine politicians and literary men met and debated literary and political subjects.[62] It was also Rucellai who, in consultations about public matters, most frequently adduced the example of Venice. In Venice, Rucellai explained, unity and harmony existed because the citizens placed the public good before their own interests. But the exemplary organization of the political life in Venice was the result of a long development. In the early years of its existence Venetian politics had also suffered from internal conflicts and tensions. The Venetians had changed and reformed their original institutions until the present situation had been achieved. According to Rucellai the Venetian constitution was a mixed government: the doge embodied the monarchical element; the aristocratic element was represented by the Senate. The great masses of the people, however, had no part in the government.[63] The conclusions Rucellai drew were that Florence ought not to consider the constitution of 1494 as sacrosanct and unchangeable but rather as in need of improvement, the most necessary being a strengthening of the influence of the Florentine aristocrats. This could be effected by the creation of a smaller council on the pattern of the Venetian Council of the Pregadi. This council, composed exclusively of Florentine aristocrats, would handle all the important government business.

Rucellai's views were those of most Florentine aristocrats. From 1498 on, almost regularly, rumors went around about plans to "hand over the government to three hundred prominent citizens." These plans developed from rumors into issues of practical politics when, in the first years of the sixteenth century, a crisis threatened the political existence of Florence. The financial means needed for fending off an external enemy could be provided only by the aristocrats, who made reform of the constitution in their favor a precondition for giving help. Consultations which were held recommended the introduction of a small council controlled by the aristocrats that would become a decisive factor in determining Florentine politics. But this was not the solution that was finally reached. The constitutional innovation of 1502 was the election of a Gonfaloniere a vita; the highest official, the head of the government, would now hold his position for his lifetime. Instead of getting a council of Pregadi the Florentines got a doge.

The aristocrats agreed to this measure because they believed that the creation of the Gonfaloniere a vita was only a step in making the Florentine constitution similar to that of Venice and that this first reform would soon be followed by another one which would complete the process of imitation by adding the lacking middle link, a Senate. This further step was never taken and the aristocrats ascribed responsibility for this failure to the Gonfaloniere a vita, Piero Soderini, who did not want his powers curtailed by a council dominated by aristocrats. Thus, the aristocrats became vehement opponents of Soderini and their hostility contributed to the inglorious collapse of the So-derini regime in 1512. In the short period between Soderini's flight and the return of the Medici the aristocrats were in complete control. The first step they undertook was to revise the constitution and to create that small aristocratically dominated council for which they had striven for the last fifteen years. The introduction of the law that established this council on September 7, 1512 referred to "the governments of ancient and modern republics which have had a long life and ruled in peace and harmony"; obviously the modern republic to which this sentence alluded was Venice. These well-organized republics, so the law continued, possessed a Senate and the introduction of a Senate in Florence had been frequently recommended by thoughtful citizens. Only now did people recognize the wisdom of this advice. The law was in force only a short time, but it marked the period of closest similarity between the Venetian and Florentine constitutions.

Nevertheless, even the law of September 7, 1512 gives no clear answer to the question to what extent notions about the ideal nature of the Venetian constitution were based on a detailed knowledge of the functioning of Venetian institutions. There are significant parallels between the development and functioning of the Venetian Council of the Pregadi and the Senate created by the Florentine law of 1512. In both, Pregadi and Senate, there were two kinds of members: those who received membership because they were holding high government posts and those who became members through election by the Great Council. In both cases, the function of the Senate was to elect ambassadors, to appoint administrators for dominated territories, and to handle government finances. But there were also differences; the Venetian Pregadi were elected for one year only. In Florence the senators had membership for life and fifty of them would be chosen by the three highest Florentine magistracies sitting together. The latter regulation assured aristocratic domination of this body because when the law was passed the aristocrats controlled these magistracies. The power of the Senate as the controlling factor in Florentine politics was further reinforced by the rule that the Senate would elect the Signoria and the Ten. In Venice the election of the highest officials remained in the hands of the Consiglio Maggiore. On the other hand, the financial power of the Venetian Pregadi was greater than that of the Florentine Senate. In Florence the Senate would initiate financial legislation and after approval by a two-thirds majority, the proposed financial legislation would go to the Great Council for acceptance or rejection by a simple majority. In Venice the handling of financial affairs was left entirely to the Pregadi. These variations in the handling of financial affairs are not without interest; they point up the differences between Venice and Florence. In Florence influence on taxation was left to the Great Council because the constitutional reform had to be passed by the Great Council, and some concession to the democratic forces was needed in order to make the reform acceptable. On the other hand, because of the strength of democratic elements in the Great Council, the aristocrats were anxious to make the Senate as powerful as possible in administrative affairs. Such compromises were unnecessary in Venice, because the Consiglio Maggiore was socially homogeneous and the Council of the Pregadi was mainly a smaller, more manageable committee of the larger council. The Florentines rightly regarded the Council of the Pregadi as the crucial factor in the Venetian government, but such a council transplanted to Florence fulfilled there an entirely different function. In Venice, the Council of the Pregadi represented the executive arm of the aristocratic ruling group which was fully and exclusively gathered in the Consiglio Maggiore; in Florence an aristocratic Senate was to wrest control from a democratic Great Council.

In Florence the idea of mixed government as it was realized in Venice was a weapon in the political struggle. Certainly, some Florentines, like Bernardo Rucellai, had information about details of the Venetian constitution. But for most of them concrete knowledge of the functioning of Venetian institutions was not really involved in their appeals to the Venetian example: it was the Venetian political myth which influenced Florentine political thought in the republican period between 1494 and 1512.

V

After 1512 no change in Florentine constitutional legislation was inspired by the Venetian example. But this did not mean that speculations about the exemplary character of Venetian institutions ceased. On the contrary, political theorizing and speculation were even intensified,[64] and the pattern of Venice continued to play a crucial role in political deliberations. This was natural. If the overthrow of the Medici in 1494 had opened the door to political experimentation, their return in 1512 necessarily strengthened this trend. With two breaks in political continuity, tradition lost its hold over the minds of men: they became more interested in foreign patterns and more willing to accept them.

Nevertheless, for a number of years after 1512 political speculation evolved in rather narrow channels because power was in the hands of the Medici and political behavior and action were determined by this fact. The middle classes and the bulk of the population were dissatisfied with the situation, but stunned by the slaughter of Prato and humiliated by the unheroic collapse of the Soderini regime, they remained in grumbling silence. Their dissatisfaction found its expression chiefly in rumors reviving Savonarola's prophecies of a complete change and reform. The aristocrats were busy jockeying for positions of influence with the Medici. Moreover, in 1513, the coming of the younger Lorenzo de' Medici to Florence revealed an entirely new possibility: the establishment of an absolutist ruler in Florence. Most of the aristocrats were horrified by the possibility of such a development and concentrated on proving that an absolutist regime was not feasible in Florence and suggesting stop-gap measures, such as the formation of a small advisory committee which they hoped might restrain Lorenzo.

But with the death of Lorenzo in 1519, yet another change in the political scene took place. The death of the last legitimate male descendant of Lorenzo il Magnifico unavoidably aroused discussions about the political future of Florence. Moreover, the two senior members of the Medici family, Pope Leo X and Cardinal Giulio, gave indications that they intended to liberalize the government system. We have a few of the blueprints then drawn up for a Florentine constitution. In all of them the example of Venice played an important role. Francesco Guicciardini wrote that the Venetian government "is the most beautiful and best government that any city, not only in our times but also in the classical world, ever possessed; the reason is that it embodies all three forms of government: those of one, of a few and of many."[65] The views about the value of the Venetian constitution which had been formed in the fifteenth century were now taken as generally recognized truth.

But when these ideas were applied to the elaboration of a constitutional program for Florence we find few references to details of the Venetian institutions and frequent statements that particular Venetian arrangements were not suited for Florence. Alessandro de' Pazzi referred to the Venetian council of the Ten, but he had doubts that such an institution would be appropriate for Florence.[66] Guicciardini was acquainted with the procedure followed by the Venetians in electing a doge but he rejected it for Florence because it invited bargaining and compromises. Moreover, in Guicciardini's opinion the minimum age which the Venetians had set for becoming a doge was too low.[67] For all these writers the crucial feature of a mixed government and the most important institution in Venice was a Senate; they regarded the creation of such a body to be the most needed reform in Florence. But in details they all deviated from the Venetian pattern.

Thus these projects again raised the question whether a fuller discussion of Venetian institutions did not take place in Florence, because imitation of the details of the Venetian pattern was considered unfeasible, or whether precise knowledge of the working of the Venetian constitution was lacking.

An observation by Guicciardini in his dialogue on the *Reggimento di Firenze* is suggestive in this context. Guicciardini maintained that the members of the Venetian Consiglio Maggiore were called nobles for reasons of prestige, but that in fact they were private citizens. If in Florence those who were members of the Great Council and as such entitled to hold office were called nobles, it would appear that there was no difference between the Venetian and the Florentine system: "The government of Venice is as democratic as ours and ours is no less aristocratic than is theirs."[68] This remark indicates that Guicciardini was unaware of the caste character of the Venetian nobility, which excluded shop owners and craftsmen; its heredity character impeded the ascent of new men into its ranks. Because the Venetian Consiglio Maggiore was limited to a hereditary ruling group there was more truth behind the characterization of

Florence as democratic and Venice as aristocratic than Guicciardini assumed. The somewhat vague character of the knowledge which Florentines possessed about Venice is underlined by the fact that whenever in Guicciardini's dialogue observations were made about Venice, the speakers sought confirmation for the correctness of their statements from Paolantonio Soderini, the one participant in the dialogue who had been Florentine ambassador in Venice.[69] Information gathered on diplomatic missions seems to have been the best source available on the Venetian government. This suggests that, even in this period, Venice interested Florentines as a realization of the idea of mixed government rather than because of concrete knowledge of Venetian institutions.

This can be seen from the writings of Machiavelli, the only Florentine political thinker who was not an admirer of Venice. The harshness of his judgments about Venice has been frequently remarked upon.[70] It is true that Machiavelli rejected Venice as an ideal pattern. But he did not deny the Venetian constitution all merit. Machiavelli recognized that among modern republics Venice stood out.[71] He praised the Venetian speed in handling emergency situations;[72] he lauded the Venetian efficiency in administering justice[73] and the continuity of government.[74] But there were features for which he had less admiration.[75] His main objection to Venice was that the Venetian constitution, although fitting for people who were willing to live in peaceful isolation,[76] was unsuited for expansion and conquest of an empire. Briefly, Venice offered Machiavelli an example for his favorite thesis on the deficiency of the military organization in the Italian city-states. The neglect of military power was particularly inexcusable in Venice because the Venetians were greedy and ambitious.[77] It was inevitable that they would suffer defeat and whenever this happened they became abject and lacked the courage which might have saved them.[78] They relied on their money, not on power.[79] It was natural that Machiavelli, as a democrat, was anxious to destroy the image of aristocratic Venice as an ideal republic. Beyond this, he does not seem to have had much further interest in Venice. His remarks on the Venetian nobility are still more misleading than those of Guicciardini.[80] But although Machiavelli repudiated Venice as a pattern for Florence, his outline of a Florentine constitution[81] contained the same basic elements as the drafts of his contemporaries. His ideal republic had three parts, Gonfalonier of Justice, Senate, and Great Council, and he thought that Senators should be elected for life. If Machiavelli, who made no use of the Venetian pattern, outlined the same fundamental structure as the admirers of Venice, it seems a justified conclusion that general notions about an ideal government rather than detailed knowledge of Venice determined the character of the political projects of this period.

VI

In 1527 another change of regime took place in Florence. Again the Medici were driven out of the city; again a discussion began on the form of government Florence ought to take; and again Venice was adduced as an example Florence ought to imitate. But the allusions to Venice in the constitutional projects then suggested were more detailed than previously and revealed a much more intimate knowledge of the working of Venetian institutions. The reason was that, between the discussions at the beginning of the twenties and the revolution of 1527, a work had been written that provided a detailed analysis of the Venetian government, Donato Giannotti's dialogue *Della Repubblica de' Veneziani*.[82] Although the manuscript was printed only in 1540, it circulated freely in Florence in 1527–28.[83] Giannotti's dialogue represents the climax of Florentine political thinking on Venice in the Renaissance period.

Giannotti wrote his dialogue while he was living for some months in Padua and Venice. He departed from Florence at the end of 1525 accompanying Giovanni Borgherini whom Giannotti made one of the main speakers of the dialogue. Giannotti returned to Florence in November or December 1526 but he left again in February 1527, this time as chancellor of Alessandro de'Pazzi who had been made Florentine ambassador at Venice. Giannotti came back to Florence in the summer of 1527 and by then the manuscript of his dialogue on the Venetian Republic was completed. Changes Giannotti made before its publication in 1540 are insignificant.[84]

When Giannotti started out for northern Italy in 1525 he was thirty-three years old and had been a lecturer on poetry, rhetoric, and Greek at the Studio in Pisa. He belonged to the circle around the philosopher Francesco Cattani da Diacceto who was the teacher and mentor of many young men of prominent Florentine families. There is every reason to assume that the purpose of Giannotti's treatise on Venice was to gain for the author standing and reputation in the world of letters. Many features of the work reveal and emphasize his familiarity with humanist ideas. He chose the dialogue form which was regarded to have been the classical vehicle for conveying knowledge. The description of the harmonious setting in which the conversation took place—a secluded room in Pietro Bembo's house in Padua—and the introductory reflections on *vita activa* and *vita contemplativa* are meant to evoke the atmosphere of a Platonic or Ciceronian dialogue. Giannotti justified the choice of his topic—the analysis of an existing government—by the example of Aristotle who treated similar subjects; as usual in humanist writings, Rome forms the ideal norm for politics. There are many admiring remarks about the leading humanists of Padua as mirrors of knowledge and behavior. Bembo appears as a great intellectual figure to whom people come from all parts of the world. Leonicus, the famous teacher of Greek philosophy in Padua, is mentioned as one of the chief sources of information about Venice. And the main speaker in the dialogue who explains the functioning of the Venetian government is that somewhat elusive but widely admired Venetian patrician and humanist, Trifone Gabriele.[85]

In the same year Giannotti began to write his work on Venice, 1526, two books appeared which might have provided stimulus for the undertaking. A contemporary and friend of Giannotti, Antonio Brucioli, who had been forced to flee from Florence in 1522 because of his involvement in a conspiracy against the Medici, published his *Dialoghi,* which discussed political themes and outlined the scheme of an ideal republic,[86] and Pietro Paolo Vergerio, then a lawyer in Venice, published a dialogue, *De republica Veneta,* in which the speakers were Bembo and Leonicus, the two great Paduan humanists whom Giannotti admiringly mentioned.[87]

But if Brucioli's and Vergerio's dialogues provided a stimulus for Giannotti, the utopian and idealizing character of their treatises must also have aroused Giannotti's opposition. For, despite the humanist appearance of this dialogue, Giannotti presented a much more concrete and realistic treatment of political problems than the humanists. Giannotti was quite aware of this difference between his approach and theirs, and he was openly critical of their methods. To Giannotti it seemed a lack of judgment to pretend that Venice was superior in all respects. The Venetian institutions might be better than those of any other city-state, but in military deeds Venice was not the equal of Rome.[88]

Giannotti found the humanist histories of Venice of little practical use. Leonicus and the Venetian patrician Marcantonio Michiel had placed documents and old chronicles at his disposal. He studied them carefully and found that they contained "interesting facts worth considering"[89] which the polished humanist histories did not mention, but which were more revealing than the published historical accounts. The sources he used seemed to show the impossibility of the story that Venice had received its definite constitutional form at the time of its foundation, and so he gave a description of the gradual development of Venetian institutions which, even if it is not our view, shows a remarkable historical sense.[90]

Giannotti was critical of all previous descriptions of the Venetian system of government, and his particular target was Sabellico's treatise on the Venetian magistrates. In Giannotti's opinion a pure listing of the existing magistrates was of little use. A state is like a natural body; in order to understand how it functions it is necessary not only to describe its various parts but also to show "how they hang together and are dependent upon each other."[91] In carrying out this plan Giannotti discovered the importance of features in the Venetian administrative system to which insufficient attention has been given previously.

Not all sections of Giannotti's work are new or original, however. Frequently he is descriptive rather than analytical. He explained that because his book was addressed to non-Venetians, he had to describe Venice's external features, its situation, its canals and streets, its means of transportation. And although Giannotti's picture of life in Venice is pleasant enough, these topics had been frequently treated before. Like others before him he was attracted by the picturesque and complicated procedure for the election of a doge. But the lengthy details of this description, though they might show the reader Giannotti's familiarity with Venetian customs, contributed little to an understanding of the functioning of Venetian institutions. Giannotti gives a rather traditional outline of the Venetian government which he says resembles a pyramid with the Consiglio Maggiore as the broad base, the Senate and the Collegium as the narrower superstructure, and the doge as the apex. Giannotti emphasized, however, that this outline must be filled out with details if it is to be true to life. And this is where the originality of Giannotti's approach is revealed.[92] Instead of describing in succession the nature and function of the various parts of this pyramid, Giannotti asked what the main tasks of government are and then he investigated the role these institutions have in fulfilling them.

This method directs attention to the importance of two features of the Venetian government. The one is the Council of the Pregadi. In contrast to the larger Consiglio Maggiore, the Pregadi is a deliberative body. In this council both general policy and particular measures are discussed and voted on. But because the important officials have to present and justify their proposals and recommendations in the Pregadi, this council serves also as a place where the capacity of individuals for political leadership can be tested and gauged. Thus the procedure in the Pregadi guarantees that only men who are equal to their tasks are selected for responsible positions. The other crucial element in the Venetian administration are the *savi,* who usually act together with the Council of the Doge. They meet every day; they discuss whatever new business has come up and decide upon the questions which have to be brought before the Pregadi; and they supervise the work of the other government agencies. They remain in office for six months, but all do not leave office at the same time; only half of them are replaced every three months so that continuity in administration is assured.

Thus, in Giannotti's hands the customary survey of Venetian institutions becomes an analysis of decision-making and leadership selection in an aristocracy. The intellectual roots of his realistic approach are not difficult to establish. When Giannotti discussed what he considered to be the principal functions of government he characterized them as the election of magistrates, the introduction of legislation, the conduct of foreign affairs and war, and the organization of the judiciary. According to Aristotle the right to decide on these matters constitutes the criterion for determining the character of a government.[93] Thus Giannotti not only referred to Aristotle in justification of his subject, but, as could be expected from a lecturer in Greek, he applied concepts from Aristotle's *Politics.*

Giannotti's knowledge of Aristotle assisted him in presenting a concrete and realistic analysis of the Venetian government, but his political realism was rooted in the Florentine political situation in which he had grown up. The regime which the Medici had established after their return in 1512 demonstrated that constitutional forms did not always indicate, and might even conceal, the locus of real power. In the decade before Giannotti's dialogue, Machiavelli had approached the study of politics with the intention of revealing the true driving forces behind the external façade, and Giannotti was a friend and admirer of Machiavelli.

But Giannotti was not a disciple who followed blindly the precepts of the master. The differences between Giannotti's and Machiavelli's views on Venice bring Giannotti's ideas into stronger relief. Machiavelli would never have chosen the Venetian government as the subject of a special treatise. Moreover, to Machiavelli, the aristocratic character of the Venetian system which Giannotti emphasized excluded the possibility that such a republic could function satisfactorily and serve as a model for others. Nor did Giannotti share Machiavelli's stress on power and on the struggle for greater power as the one and only significant factor in politics. Giannotti believed that a state could remain securely in possession of a relatively limited territory;[94] whereas Machiavelli's contempt for the mercenary system formed an integral part of his views on the role of power in politics, like views cannot be found in Giannotti's dialogue. The most significant difference between the two is that Giannotti upheld the tradition that the administration of justice is the principal task of government.

Giannotti's dialogue contains a long exposition of the Venetian judicial system.[95] He placed particular emphasis on two aspects of the Venetian administration of justice: that it provided possibilities of appeal to financially weak and politically power-

less people, and that extensive precautions were taken for securing impartiality. The lack of political interference was presented as a striking feature of the Venetian administration of
justice. Evidently Giannotti was concerned with the question of
how harmony and internal stability were to be obtained in a
society in which power was concentrated in the hands of a small
group of nobles. To Giannotti the solution seemed to be that
the main need of those who did not belong to the ruling group
was legal protection and security; since the Venetian government fulfilled this need the population was content and loyal.
Clearly the sections on the Venetian judicial administration,
which to the mind of the modern reader seem disproportion-
ately detailed, were written with the Florentine situation in
mind. Giannotti was aware of the conflicts between aristocrats
and democrats in Florence, and he explained how and why
these tensions had been overcome in the Venetian republic.
Giannotti did not propound that Venice had a mixed government; indeed, this concept is not mentioned in his dialogue.
But he was certainly aware of Aristotle's view that a good republic represented a mixture of oligarchic and democratic elements. Giannotti's discussion of the Venetian judicial system
implies that an oligarchy could function only if the democratic
elements of the social body were kept satisfied.

We have said that with his dialogue on Venice Giannotti
wanted to establish his position in the literary world. But the
political interest which permeates the book is so intense that
Giannotti must have had a political aim connected with the
Florentine political situation in the years the manuscript was
written. This was a peculiar time of Florentine history. The Medici rulers, Leo X and Clement VII, soon abandoned their plans
for liberalizing their regime after the death of the younger
Lorenzo. Clement VII sent Alessandro and Ippolito, two
fourteen-year-old boys, to Florence with the obvious intent of
making them rulers of the city. Because of the youth of these
two boys Florentine affairs were directed from Rome by the
Pope, and Florentine pride was hurt by the city's inability to decide upon its own fate. The prospect of the permanent establishment of a Medici dynasty in Florence horrified almost all
groups of the population. The masses of the population followed the Savonarolan tradition of identifying the Medici

regime with tyranny. The aristocrats resented their loss of political control; and some of the aristocratic families who were closely connected with the Medici began to turn away from them. Ippolito and Alessandro were of illegitimate birth and some of the relatives of the Medici were unwilling to accept bastards as heads of their family.

In the years of the composition of Giannotti's dialogue this opposition became more evident because the entire political scene had become fluid. It was obvious that Francis I would seek revenge for his defeat at Pavia; in the spring of 1526 the League of Cognac, which united the Pope and the French king against Charles V, was concluded. However, the campaign against the Spaniards soon ran into difficulties, and it was realized that, as a result of the war against Charles V, the position of the Pope might be weakened and opportunities might arise for the overthrow of the Medici regime in Florence. Although Venice was a partner in the League of Cognac, its government was very reluctant to take decisive action against Charles V, and many Florentines who were opposed to the Medici assembled in Venice. Giovanni Borgherini was a speaker in Giannotti's dialogue because he had been Giannotti's companion and patron on his travels to northern Italy in 1526; in the same year Borgherini became the son-in-law of Niccolò Capponi, the recognized leader of the Florentine anti-Medicean aristocrats.[96]

Another Florentine who at this time resided with his family in Venice was Lorenzo Strozzi.[97] He was in close contact with Borgherini and became a friend of Giannotti. Lorenzo Strozzi was a near relation of the Medici; his wife, a daughter of Bernardo Rucellai, was a niece of Lorenzo il Magnifico, and his brother Filippo was married to a sister of the younger Lorenzo. Lorenzo Strozzi had always opposed the Medicean tendency toward absolutism and in 1526 his hostility against Clement VII was increased by the treatment which his brother Filippo received at the hands of the Pope. Lorenzo Strozzi's animosity against the branch of the Medici family headed by Clement VII showed itself in his great intimacy with members of other branches of the Medici family. If the two bastards, Alessandro and Ippolito, had not been put forward by Clement VII, two other boys, descendants of the younger branch of the Medici family, namely Lorenzino, the son of Pierfrancesco de'Medici, and Cosimo, the son of Giovanni delle Bande Nere, would have been heads of the Medici family. These two boys were also in Venice at that time and they were solemnly welcomed as persons of high standing by the Venetian government. Alessandro de'Pazzi, the Florentine ambassador to Venice whom Giannotti served as chancellor in 1527, was another nephew of Lorenzo il Magnifico and he too was a pronounced adherent of Florentine freedom.[98] There is no proof that these Florentines, who were closely connected with each other, were actively preparing an overthrow of the regime of Clement VII. But they would not have regarded such an event as a cause for regret.

This group of Florentine aristocrats formed the circle in which Giannotti moved. These men must have discussed what ought to happen in Florence if the regime of Clement VII was overthrown, and Giannotti must have written his dialogue with these considerations in mind. All these men were aristocrats and their traditional interest was the establishment of an aristocratic republic. Because the bulk of the Florentine population was disgruntled with the Medici regime it would applaud any change of regime. But an aristocratic coup d'état could result in the creation of a stable government only if some satisfaction could be given to the democratic elements of the population. Giannotti's dialogue showed that in Venice an aristocratic regime managed to keep the masses of the population satisfied; that constituted its relevance for the Florentine political situation.

While Giannotti was still in Venice the victorious progress of the troops of Charles V resulted in the hoped for collapse of the Medici regime in Florence. Niccolò Capponi, Borgherini's father-in-law, now became Gonfalonier as leader of the aristocratic opposition against the Medici, and Giannotti, on the recommendation of Borgherini, became first secretary of the Ten, occupying the post which Machiavelli had held under Soderini.

For Capponi and his aristocratic friends the problem of the constitution which Florence ought to receive was posed anew, and Giannotti's knowledge of the Venetian institutions gave him an important influence in these deliberations. On Capponi's request he composed a paper explaining the institutional changes and innovations which he regarded as desirable and necessary.[99] It is not surprising that in Giannotti's project the example of Venice played a pivotal role, but memoranda which others composed also referred to Venice and showed that their authors were acquainted with Giannotti's dialogue.[100] All these projects envisaged a mixed government in which the Senate would hold the key position. Great emphasis was placed on a feature of the Venetian government which Giannotti had stressed: namely, that the Gonfalonier, like the doge, should act together with a small body of officials who would control and supervise the entire administration, take care of the conduct of current affairs, and give continuity to the government. Giannotti in his dialogue on Venice had indicated that Venice drew most of its political strength from the unified control and direction of policy by a small body of high officials, and this idea was now accepted as an essential feature of constitutional reform in Florence.

All these memoranda of the years 1527–1528 aimed at limitation of the power of the Great Council in favor of the patrician ruling group. But none of them was written in a situation in which the shaping of Florentine institutions was entirely in the hands of the aristocrats. Although the overthrow of the Medici regime had been planned as an aristocratic coup d'état, as such it had failed. A decisive factor in forcing the withdrawal of the Medici from Florence had been a widespread popular movement, and the democratic forces were not content to leave all power to the aristocrats. Thus the situation which developed in 1527 was very similar to that after the overthrow of the Medici in 1494. The democratic elements forced the aristocrats in power to grant a reopening of the Great Council, and the constitution which had existed before 1512 was again put in force. Thus the aristocrats began again their old struggle for a strengthening of their position in the government, and the memoranda which recommended to the Florentines an imitation of the Venetian pattern were written for this purpose. But this campaign for an aristocratic reform of the Florentine constitution was in vain. The powers of the Gonfalonier, Niccolò Capponi, were not enlarged but curtailed. And in April 1529, Capponi was deposed. In the years of the last Florentine republic the influence of the radical faction of the middle classes steadily increased until they completely ruled the city.

The victory of these radicals was probably unavoidable.

Under progressively mounting pressure from without, the appeal of those who called upon the Florentines to unite as equals was stronger than the voices of those who stressed the social differences in Florentine society.

In contrast to the defenders of the aristocratic position who composed elaborate constitutional projects placing the aristocrats firmly into the center of power, the democrats did not and could not express their views in detailed constitutional schemes. The economic, social, and intellectual eminence of the upper group in an Italian city-state prevented an elaborate rationalization of democratic thought. The democrats appealed to tradition, and their strength lay in the emotions which such an appeal aroused. Thus, with the democrats gaining the upper hand in Florence the last Florentine republic returned to its beginnings, to the traditions of medieval Florence. It emphasized the legal and economic equality among citizens; it recreated the old citizen militia; it fought as a Guelph city with the French king against the Ghibelline emperor, and Florence was again proclaimed to be the City of San Giovanni and of Christ. The heroism with which the last Florentine republic conducted its futile resistance against the return of the Medici came from the revival of the spirit of the medieval commune.

We might see behind the victory of the Medici the beginning of a new development: the city-state giving way to the territorial state. But to many contemporaries the defeat of the Florentine republic was the end. When in 1538 Giannotti prepared his dialogue *Della Repubblica de' Veneziani* for the printer, the work had lost the political aim and meaning which it had possessed when he wrote it: "Because we cannot discuss our own affairs, we discuss the affairs of others."[101] At the same time Francesco Guicciardini was writing his *History of Italy,* in which he described the events of 1494 that had led to the establishment of the Great Council.[102] All the arguments we saw at work—for and against the imitation of foreign institutions, for and against the suitability of the Venetian constitution as a model—are set forth in two brilliantly constructed invented speeches. Yet there is no indication of the value of these arguments; it is as if Guicciardini wanted to convey to the reader how little practical importance these arguments had had. But in a study of the influence of the Venetian constitution on Florentine political thought it might be best to leave the last word to a Venetian. From 1528 to 1529, the Venetian ambassador in Florence was Antonio Suriano. Giannotti was among his close friends, and there can be no doubt that Suriano had real insight into Florentine affairs. But when he came to describe the Florentine situation in his final report before the Pregadi, Suriano saw only differences between Venice and Florence; the weakness of Florentine politics seemed to him so deeply ingrained that he saw no chance of Florence ever becoming a stable republic. Florence is, said Suriano with a certain contempt, a democracy in which people who do not understand the art of government rule. "Rarely have such democratic republics had a long life."[103]

9. Bernardo Rucellai and the Orti Oricellari: A Study on the Origin of Modern Political Thought

In his Florentine history, Francesco Guicciardini, writing almost simultaneously with events in which he himself had participated, describes the clashes of personalities and the conflicts of the factions involved in the disintegration of the regime of the Confaloniere Piero Soderini. The reader of Guicciardini's narrative see Bernardo Rucellai, a leading representative of the Florentine aristocracy, emerge as one of the leading figures in the struggle against Soderini; and Guicciardini follows with special attention the activities of Rucellai in these crucial years.[1] The historian mentions at one point that Rucellai, who had absented himself from Florence and gone into voluntary exile, sent the Florentine government a letter of justification, in order to fend off an accusation of treason. In this letter Guicciardini says Rucellai explained his political attitude in the times of Lorenzo il Magnifico, Piero de' Medici, and Savonarola and tried to show

Originally published in *Journal of the Warburg and Courtauld Institutes,* 12 (1949), 101–131. The thesis of this essay—to show that Machiavelli's thought came out of the Florentine intellectual and political milieu of the early sixteenth century—has since been studied extensively by Rudolf von Albertini, *Das Florentinische Staatsbewusstsein im Ubergang von der Republik zum Prinzipat* (Bern, Francke, 1955) and J. G. A. Pocock, *The Machiavellian Moment* (Princeton, Princeton University Press, 1975)—to name only the two most important and comprehensive studies.

his aim had always been the maintenance of peace and freedom in Florence.[2] This letter is still in existence in the Florentine archive a striking tribute both to the historical exactitude of Guicciardini and to the efficiency of the Florentine Chancellery.[3] The main point in the document is correctly stated by Guicciardini.[4] In addition, however, to asserting his consistent adherence to the republican ideal, Rucellai emphasizes that on various occasions during his travels in France and Italy he has tried to get in touch with the Florentine government in order to warn it against certain hostile conspiracies being hatched abroad. Hence, the letter provides a rather comprehensive itinerary of Rucellai's travels and is an important source for any attempt to retrace the story of his life.[5]

Rucellai's career is worth investigating. Neither his political activities not his efforts as a writer and humanist deserved to be so completely forgotten as they have in fact been. He was not, to be sure, one of the chief political protagonists in the time of Florence's greatness, on a par with the Medici, Strozzi, and Soderini. He has not left an indelible imprint on political thought like that of Machiavelli, nor fitted the events of his age into an unforgettable picture as did Guicciardini in his historical works. Yet he was active in politics and letters, and his contemporaries evidently placed him near the first rank. Not only Guicciardini but all other contemporary historians mentioned his name frequently and reported his doings in detail.[6] It would, in fact, appear that his contemporaries expected Rucellai to play a more decisive role in the political life of Florence than actually proved to be the case. Yet, quite aside from his political success or failure, he deserves a significant place in history for his intellectual activities and his relation to humanism. Rucellai's book on the classical antiquities of Rome is one of the first topographical studies[7] on this subject. His history, *De Bello Italico,* represents the first attempt to evaluate the significance of Charles VIII's invasion of Italy, and was praised by Erasmus as the work of a new Sallust,[8] as well as highly appreciated by the Florentine political writers.[9] The book, it may be noted in passing, still receives occasional mention, if only because it introduced the term "balance of power" into political literature.[10] Finally, Rucellai's claim to fame is most solidly based on the fact that he was the owner of the Rucellai gardens, the "Orti Oricellari," and presided over the celebrated meetings which took place there. These gatherings had a decisive influence on the development of the Italian language and literature; though they are today most widely known for having provided the select audience to which Machiavelli expounded the ideas of his *Discorsi*.[11]

It should be added that a study of Rucellai's life not only will restore to his proper place a secondary, but nevertheless significant, figure of the Renaissance but also may contribute directly to our insight into the development of Florentine political thought. Recent research has emphasized two previously neglected aspects of this field.[12] One is that the political thought of the Renaissance was characterized by a structure in terms of schools: Machiavelli and Guicciardini, although certainly the most profound and most brilliant representatives of Renaissance political science, were not isolated phenomena, for they proceeded from political and historical concepts which were the common property of a whole group of Florentine writers. The other point of recent emphasis is the great significance for the development of political thought of the two decades between the fall of the Medici in 1494 and their restoration in 1512. Hence, the years of Savonarola and Soderini, when a bitter fight was raging over the form of the Florentine constitution and when this domestic issue became involved in the broader problems of Italian foreign policy, are now regarded as having been crucial for the formation of a new outlook.

It is in terms of just these points of recent scholarly interest that the career of Bernardo Rucellai assumes considerable importance.

The purpose of the present essay is to examine the significance of Rucellai, his circle, and his times for the rise of modern political theory. It will be appropriate, in order to appreciate the background of his thinking and the milieu in which his group lived, to reconstruct the man's own activities during the crucial period we have set out to examine. Thereafter, we can turn to the personnel and subject matter of the meetings in the Rucellai gardens. And finally, we shall make an effort to characterize their contribution to the evolution of political thought at a portentous juncture in its development.

I

Among the buildings of Florence, one of the most famous is
the palace which Leon Battista Alberti built for Bernardo Rucellai's father, Giovanni, in the Via della Vigna Nuova, and in
which Bernardo lived during most of his life.

For our present purpose, the focus of interest is the shield of
the Rucellai, cut by Bernardo Rosellino[13] and mounted in the
center of the court. On its ornate crest is a ship, the mast of
which is formed by a nude woman who holds in her raised left
hand the mainyard and in her right the lower part of the
swelling sail. It has been suggested that the explanation of this
crest offers an insight into both the attitude and the position of
the Rucellai family in fifteenth-century Florence. The scene represented on the crest was carefully thought out by the elder
Rucellai and had a definite meaning. We know that Giovanni
was deeply puzzled by the fundamental problem which runs as a
leitmotif through the thinking of Italian humanism from Petrarch to Bruno, namely, the relation of *virtu* to *fortuna:* Is man,
even if he applies all his powers of reason and foresight, able
successfully to counteract the accidents of fate?[14] In his per-
plexity, Giovanni Rucellai turned for advice to Marsilio Ficino,
the ruling philosopher of his time. According to this same
theory, the crest reflects the views which Ficino had expressed in
his answer to Giovanni Rucellai and which Giovanni Rucellai
had made his own. The female figure in the middle of the boat
is Fortuna, who symbolizes the power of the storm. No one can
successfully resist this powerful and inclement goddess, but the
man who, like the sailor in the boat, recognizes her strength and
adjusts himself to the wind will be able to use her to bring his
ship safely into port. Thus, by prudent adjustment to Fortuna,
virtue may hold head against the adversities of chance.

Yet behind this general philosophical explanation of the
crest, another meaning may be hidden, a meaning which alludes
to the particular position of the Rucellai in the Florence of the
Medici. The Fortuna, to which the Rucellai are willing to adapt
themselves, may represent the Medici. By following the course
of the Medici, they hope to secure success and happiness. This
particular key to the crest was suggested by a contemporary
print which shows an interesting transformation of the design:

in the middle of the boat stands a young man, in whom one interpretation sees Bernardo Rucellai, while at the helm is a young woman, who would then represent Nannina de' Medici, Lorenzo il Magnifico's sister and Bernardo's wife.

Thus, by family tradition, the relation to the Medici became a fundamental issue in Bernardo Rucellai's entire life,[15] and the sphere within which he moved during his first forty years was clearly defined by this relationship. He was on intimate personal terms with the Medici. He shared Lorenzo's philosophical and intellectual inclinations. He was one of those Florentine aristocrats on whom Lorenzo chiefly relied for the execution of his political aims.

The closeness of Rucellai's personal ties to the Medici family is clearly reflected in his correspondence.[16] The letters he exchanged with the elder generation, Piero de' Medici and Piero's wife, Lucrezia Tornabuoni, do no perhaps go beyond paying the respects due to parents-in-law, whose approval he asks for family events as the engagements of his children. But his letters to his contemporaries Giuliano and Lorenzo de' Medici show him not only as a brother-in-law but also as a personal friend, who had grown up with them and had shared their youthful adventures and interests. This tone of personal intimacy is discernible even in his later official correspondence with Lorenzo il Magnifico: for instance, in a report from Rome concerning an audience with the Pope, he writes[17] that the conversation had lasted so long that if His Holiness had not assisted him in changing from one knee to the other, he would have become so stiff that he would never have been able to continue his trip to Naples. On this same mission, Rucellai was charged not only with diplomatic affairs but also with Medici family business. He was entrusted with negotiations which led to the marriage of the Magnifico's eldest son, Piero, to Alfonsina Orsini; and, after the successful outcome of these negotiations, he acted as his nephew's proxy at the wedding.[18]

Family ties were in this instance reinforced by an identity of intellectual and aesthetic interests. The Rucellai were outstanding patrons of art, perhaps the only Florentine family of the fifteenth century that can be regarded as equaling the Medici in this respect. "For fifty years," writes Bernardo's father, Giovanni Rucellai, in his memoirs, "I have done nothing but earn money and spend it; in so doing I have learned that I enjoy spending money more than earning it." The list of artists, whose works decorated the Rucellai palace in the Via della Vigna Nuova, includes nearly every leading name of the second half of the quattrocento: Castagno, Desiderio da Settignano, Filippo Lippi, Majano, Pollaiuolo, Uccello, and Verrocchio. Among the public works donated by the Rucellai is Alberti's façade of Santa Maria Novella, one of Florence's greatest glories.[19]

Bernardo was an active participant in all the humanistic and philosophical activities which took place in Lorenzo il Magnifico's Florence. He is mentioned as a member of various intellectual discussion groups.[20] Humanists like Bartolommeo della Fonte turned to him for support.[21] He and Lorenzo were both members of the committee charged with the reorganization of the University of Pisa.[22] The friendly relations his father had cultivated with Marsilio Ficino he maintained and made even closer; Giovanni Corsi, Ficino's biographer, calls Bernardo one of the disciples nearest to the master.[23] After Ficino's death, his role as intellectual oracle and guide to the leading Florentine citizens fell to the Neapolitan humanist and statesman Giovanni Pontano, and Rucellai shared wholeheartedly this admiration for Pontano.[24]

The combination of relationship and common intellectual interests made Bernardo Rucellai Lorenzo's trusted lieutenant in the management of Florentine affairs. When Lorenzo was absent from Florence, Rucellai acted as his representative, relayed to him the views of leading Florentine citizens regarding current political problems, and advised Lorenzo as to the best means of assuring himself of their support.[25] Lorenzo's reliance on Rucellai is also reflected in the latter's diplomatic activities.[26] He was Lorenzo's companion at the Cremona meeting in 1483, when the Medici tried to unite the Italian rulers for common action against Venice. In addition, Lorenzo entrusted him with two particularly crucial diplomatic missions: he was ambassador in Milan from 1482 to 1485, and from 1486 to 1487 ambassador in Naples. In Milan, he had to maintain, in critical circumstances, the friendship with the Sforzas, which had, ever since the rise of the Medici, constituted a cornerstone of their power. The embassy to Naples was important because it aimed at the establishment of better relations between Naples and the Pope after the War of the Barons, relations which formed the basis of Lorenzo's foreign policy in his later years when he was seeking to secure peace within Italy.

Rucellai's position in the Florence of Lorenzo il Magnifico is well summarized in a letter from Lorenzo's eldest son to his father. Piero reports a dinner which he gave when Ermolao Barbaro, the famous Venetian diplomat and humanist, was visiting Florence. He writes that he invited the leading humanists of Florence and, in addition, Bernardo Rucellai "in order to have the company of a leading citizen but at the same time not to step outside the circle of family and scholars."[27]

Was Bernardo Rucellai content with the role he played in Lorenzo il Magnifico's Florence, with being recognized as an influential member of the Florentine ruling group, but without being able to make any final decision in state policy? There is reason to believe that in Lorenzo's later years the relations between him and his brother-in-law became somewhat strained, that Rucellai criticized Medici's high-handed ways with his fellow citizens and that only their ancient friendship restrained Lorenzo from taking action.[28] Rucellai's letter to the Signoria, in which he alludes to his own advocacy of freedom in the times of Lorenzo, seems to confirm this story.[29] Perhaps even the passage in Piero's letter to his father just quoted is an indication of this rift; at least it has a strangely apologetic quality as if the invitation to Bernardo Rucellai needed some special justification. Rucellai's behavior after Lorenzo's death seems to supply final proof that only with some reluctance had he remained in the shadow of his great brother-in-law. From Lorenzo's death in 1492 until the election of Soderini as Gonfaloniere in 1502, his name was mentioned again and again as one of the chief protagonists in the events which shook Florence to its foundation: the formation of an opposition to Piero de' Medici's absolutism, the struggle for Florentine independence against Charles VIII, the opposition against Savonarola's reforms, and the struggle for a reorganization of the Florentine constitution after all these upheavals. Rucellai emerges as a new man, personally active in politics and burning with ambition to exert a controlling influence in Florence.

Rucellai by no means follows a straight or clear line during those years. Immediately upon Lorenzo's death he supported

Piero but advised him to exercise great restraint in the use of his power and to concede greater influence to the Florentine aristocrats. When Piero disregarded this advice, Bernardo turned against him and became one of his bitterest opponents. The break became final when, without Piero's permission, he gave his daughter in marriage to a member of the Strozzi family, old adversaries of the Medici; here was unmistakable proof that he had deserted the faction supporting Piero. He allied himself with Lorenzo di Pierfrancesco de' Medici, a member of the younger, rival branch of the family; he conspired to replace Piero by Lorenzo di Pierfrancesco and, as a result, Bernardo's sons were banned from Florence, even though Piero dared not take direct measures against Bernardo himself.[30]

There can be no doubt that Bernardo had felt encouraged to such open opposition by the visible weakening of Piero's power resulting from the latter's mismanagement of foreign affairs. When the invasion of Charles VIII brought about Piero's downfall, Rucellai, now Piero's declared enemy, belonged to the group that tried to assume power. He became a member of the Committee of Twenty which received authority to reorganize the government and to make appointments for all public positions.[31] The new government entrusted him with its most crucial diplomatic tasks: he was sent to Milan to persuade Lodovico il Moro to exert his influence with the French king against any plan to restore Piero de' Medici in Florence, and later he was dispatched to Naples and Rome in order to obtain from Charles VIII himself the return of the Florentine fortresses of Livorno, Pietrasanta, Sarzana, and Pisa, previously surrendered to the French as pledges of loyalty.[32]

After Rucellai's return from this mission, less is heard about his political activities. He took his regular share in government affairs to be sure. In addition, in 1497 he was a member of the reconciliation commission which tried in vain to ease the mounting tension between the adherents and enemies of Savonarola, and after Savonarola's fall, he is reported to have exerted his influence to save the life of Savonarola's aristocratic adherents, Ridolfi and Paolantonio Soderini.[33] But none of these tasks was of really crucial importance, and when, in 1498, a prominent position was at last within his reach, it being his turn to serve as Gonfaloniere di Giustizia, he declined, pleading illness.[34] The explanation for Rucellai's disappearance from the foreground of Florentine politics after 1495 is not that he had lost interest in politics, but simply that he was, almost inevitably, an opponent of the popular regime Savonarola had introduced. The groups that now held power did not regard him as reliable, and he, on his part, wanted to have as little as possible to do with them.

The policy of withdrawing from government activities in those years was not peculiar to Rucellai; most Florentine aristocrats adopted the same course.[35] Boycott of the government was the weapon by which they hoped to achieve their own restoration to power, and these efforts bore fruit. Because of inexpert handling, the political situation in Florence deteriorated, unrest increased, and the return of Piero de' Medici through a coup d' état, supported by foreign powers, loomed as an imminent possibility. In view of this critical situation, the aristocrats finally succeeded in carrying through a constitutional reform designed to diminish the democratic influence by transforming the highest Florentine office, that of the Gonfaloniere, into a lifelong position, modeled on that of the Venetian doge.[36] Bernardo Rucellai had been one of the most active advocates of the change, but when Piero Soderini was chosen Gonfaloniere a vita, Rucellai became his bitter enemy and withdrew once more from all participation in the government, making himself ineligible for office by remaining in arrears on his tax payments.[37]

How can this attitude be explained? It has been taken as proof that personal ambition was the driving force in Rucellai's political activities and that his opposition to Soderini was determined by the disappointment of someone else's having achieved the position to which he himself had aspired. Certainly, the element of personal ambition cannot entirely be excluded; Rucellai's rudeness in omitting, after Soderini's election, the congratulatory visit to which a new Gonfaloniere was accustomed, seems to have been inspired by personal pique. Yet a closer examination of Rucellai's political attitude since Lorenzo il Magnifico's death reveals that, dominating his rather complicated political moves and tergiversations, there was a fundamental political conviction to which he rigidly adhered. Rucellai's political aim was the establishment of a restricted government, over which the aristocrats would have full control.

He was an enemy of the absolutist role of one man, but he was an equally decided opponent of any popular form of government. To Rucellai the stability of an aristocratic government had seemed compatible with a somewhat privileged position for the Medici and might even have best been guaranteed by having a Medici as *primus inter pares.* But because of Piero's tendency to transform this position into real domination he turned against Piero. The overthrow of Piero seemed to revive the hope of realizing his ideal of an aristocratic regime, and he threw himself wholeheartedly into politics. On his return from Naples in 1495, however, he found that the government had slipped out of the control of the aristocrats and that under Savonarola's influence a popular regime has been established: now again he was thrown into opposition and when the opportunity arose he worked for a constitutional change which would restrict the democratic influence and would return the aristocrats to power. In his book on the classical antiquities of Rome, written a few years later, Rucellai states quite explicitly that he considers popular rule fatal for Florence and that, when after his return from Naples he found a popular regime established, he concentrated all his energies on purging the city from the weight of this dross.[38]

The establishment of a lifetime Gonfaloniere appeared to him a step in the right direction, but only if accompanied by the abolition of the Great Council; and this second part of the reform program seemed to Rucellai even more important than the first. He was deeply disappointed when only one aspect of the reform program, namely the creation of a lifetime Gonfaloniere, was accepted, while the Great Council remained in existence. In his opinion, rephrased in modern terms, Soderini had betrayed his class in accepting the election under these circumstances.

The views Rucellai held were by no means unique. Most of the Florentine aristocrats regarded the establishment of a lifetime Gonfaloniere as a half measure and considered necessary a further restriction of the popular influences. But Rucellai differed from his fellow aristocrats concerning the means by which these further reforms could be achieved. The majority of the aristocrats, with the two Salviati brothers at their head, believed that they should now accept the newly established system, should participate in the government, and should thus try to effect the necessary improvement by boring from within. Rucellai, and a very small group around him, believed that the only policy was to refrain from cooperation in the administration; in other words, the same means which had brought about the first success should be further applied in order to remove the democratic element from the government altogether.[39] Up to this time, Rucellai had been a rather typical representative of the Florentine aristocracy, and the story of his life has been bound up with the political fortunes of this group. Henceforth he was to follow a rather lonely course.

The remaining twelve years of Rucellai's life fall into two parts. The first few years he ramained in Florence refraining from all contact with the government; most of the second part was spent in voluntary exile, traveling through France and Italy. During the years in Florence his main concern was ostensibly literary studies; "no longer concerned with the actions of the Princes or in fear of the power of Kings, he retires to his flowering garden and lives alone for posterity," as a contemporary wrote of him.[40] He surrounded himself with literary men. He composed his book on the Roman antiquities[41] and he may have begun to work on his history of the French invasion, the plan of which he had conceived on his mission to Naples in 1495.[42]

The abandonment of the *vita activa* for the *vita comtemplativa* was, however, not so complete as Rucellai pretended it to be. We have seen that his withdrawal from active participation in the government had originally been intended as a form of political pressure, and Rucellai did not cease mixing in politics during these years of seeming retirement. His fundamental opposition to the existing government system in its entirety necessarily led him toward conspiratorial activities. Most important of all, he re-established contact with the exiled Medici, a step made possible for him by the fact that Piero, with whom reconciliation would have been out of the question, had died.[43] The central event in Florentine politics in this period was the formation of a powerful group opposing Soderini's regime through the reconciliation of the Medici with the Strozzi, their old enemies, a reconciliation symbolized by the marriage of Piero de' Medici's daughter to Filippo Strozzi.[44] The very fact that Filippo

Strozzi dared to undertake this legally forbidden marriage to a member of the exiled Medici family represented a serious blow to Soderini's prestige. The marriage negotiations had started when Alfonsina Orsini, Piero's widow, had visited Florence to settle some financial affairs. Bernardo Rucellai, who thirty years before had acted as Piero's proxy at Alfonsina's wedding in Naples, was frequently seen in her company; and it was generally assumed that he had had his hand in preparing the alliance.

Shortly afterwards Rucellai left Florence. His decision was probably connected with his part in these marriage negotiations, for he may well have felt that this time he had gone so far that Soderini might take positive action against him.

Rucellai's travels provide a characteristic picture of the interests and the horizon of a wealthy Florentine of this period. In May 1506 we find him with one of his sons, Giovanni, in Avignon, where they spent the whole summer. The Rucellai stayed at the house of one of the Strozzi, who had a branch of their banking house in France. They lived the life of tourists, visiting the house where Petrarch was said to have written his sonnets and admiring the portrait which was supposed to represent Petrarch's Laura.[45] Marseilles was Rucellai's next stopping place, his chief companion there being a Genoese noble who, like himself, had left his city because of dissatisfaction with its democratically inclined government. Both Rucellai and his Genoese friend devoted themselves to studies and literary activities.[46] We have a long Latin description of Marseilles which Rucellai composed at this time, and we learn that he was at work on his history of the invasion of Charles VIII.

News from home forced Rucellai to cut short his stay in Marseilles.[47] He was informed that it was being said of him in Florence that he had secretly gone to the Emperor Maximilian in Germany, just at a time when the emperor was believed to be preparing an invasion of Italy and the attitude of Florence toward such plans was being hotly disputed. Some of the aristocrats favored an understanding with Maximilian, but Soderini preferred to maintain the traditional pro-French foreign policy. Rucellai's presence at Maximilian's court would thus have amounted to open revolt against Soderini and might have led to reprisals against his family or property. Under these circumstances, Rucellai found it safer to return to Italy. First he went to Milan, where he enjoyed the hospitality of Trivulzio, a friend who dated from Bernardo's mission to Milan in Lorenzo il Magnifico's time. Rucellai believed his staying with Trivulzio would be to his credit with the Soderini government; for the Condottiere, whose name and career is interwoven with all the splendor and all the crimes of Lodovico il Moro's rule, had, in his old age, become one of the chief partisans of the French king and had for a time ruled in Milan as French governor.

From Milan, after a short time spent in Bologna, Rucellai went to Venice, the last of his travel stations.[48] The most noteworthy person with whom Rucellai became acquainted there was Erasmus, although it cannot have been a very interesting meeting because Erasmus spoke no Italian and Rucellai refused obstinately to speak Latin.[49] By this time Rucellai had completed his history of the French invasion.[50]

Rucellai was back in Florence in 1511[51] to find the political scene fundamentally changed. Soderini's persistence in maintaining the alliance with France was ruining him. The opposing bloc of emperor, Spaniards, and Pope was in the ascendance, and supporting the Medici in order to oust the Gonfaloniere.

The question was rather when than whether the Medici would return. With a strong pro-Medici faction coming increasingly into the open, even in Florence, Rucellai could again feel safe at home, but he was now an old man and his energy appears to have been flagging. Rucellai was, to be sure, still mentioned as being involved in various attempts to overthrow Soderini in favor of the Medici. His political activities along this line were so well known that in April 1512, at the high point of the political crisis, when the troops of Pope and emperor were before Florence to demand a restoration of the Medici, Soderini, in a last desperate gamble, arrested the Rucellai together with other pro-Medici aristocrats. It was too late. The Sack of Prato reversed the situation. The people turned against Soderini and the Gonfaloniere was forced to throw himself upon the mercy of those whom he had imprisoned a few days before.[52] But it is indicative of Rucellai's declining vigor that in the reports of all these events his name never occurs alone. He is always mentioned together with his sons. They are now the main representatives of the Rucellai and seem to determine the family attitude. As their later careers were to show, they were less hesitant to give unequivocal support to the Medici than their father had been.[53]

From the return of the Medici until Bernardo's death, the relations between him and the restored rulers remained outwardly excellent. Bernardo was paid the respect due to the senior member of the family and a last survivor of the former period of greatness. He was a member of all the councils and committees which had to effect the necessary constitutional changes.[54] The Rucellai, on their part, spared no pains to show that they viewed the return of the Medici as their victory.

When the news of Giovanni de' Medici's election to the Papacy reached Florence, the Rucellai palace in the Via della Vigna Nuova was one of the chief places of celebration. Money was thrown from the windows to the crowds in the streets, food was distributed, and red and white wine flowed from morning until night out of large casks placed in front of the palace.[55]

Yet there are indications that this cordiality, at least as far as Bernardo Rucellai himself was concerned, was façade. He is said to have been dissatisfied at the Medici's disregard for traditional political institutions and their decision to rule by an emergency committee forced upon the city by a coup d' état. Much as he had wished for the return of the Medici, their victory was now too complete. Still clinging to his old ideal of government by the aristocrats, as he had done in the times of Piero de' Medici, he revolted against the clearly emerging inclination of the members of the new Medici generation to arrogate to themselves full power over Florence. Thus he refused to go to Rome when he was chosen a member of the embassy to congratulate Leo X on his election. His official excuse was age and illness but the general opinion was that he was using once again his old technique of boycott to express his dissatisfaction with the government methods which the Medici were using.[56]

Two years after the return of the Medici, one year after Leo X's election, Rucellai died in his sixty-seventh year. It is reported that he wanted to have the manuscript of his *History of the French Invasion* buried with him. Whether or not this story is true, it sheds an interesting light on his contemporaries' feeling that, regardless of whatever success or failure his political actions had brought him, his fame would depend on what he had achieved in the world of letters.[57]

II

Certainly not the least of Rucellai's claims to a leading position in the intellectual life of Florence stemmed from the meetings held in his large garden along the Via della Scala. He himself had bought the tract of land where the meetings took place. Situated between Florence's second and third wall, the garden was shut off from the outside world by the high ramparts and only the bifurcated hill, on whose saddle Fiesole is built and from whose slopes the summer homes of the wealthy Florentines glistened in the sun, looked down into it.[58] The garden was praised as particularly cool and shady. Rucellai himself had supervised its arrangement and had imported a number of rare plants, with an eye to having represented all the species mentioned in classical literature. Along the paths were mounted the busts of famous men of the classical world—emperors, statesmen, poets, and thinkers. A summer house and marble benches, placed under the larger trees, invited quiet reading, serious conversation, or discussions in larger groups.

To what extent does our investigation of Bernardo Rucellai's career make a new contribution to the history of these meetings? First of all, a new and somewhat surprising light is shed on the question of when the meetings started. It has been generally assumed that the meetings of the Orti Oricellari must be placed in the second decade of the sixteenth century.[59] Yet in delineating Rucellai's life, we have found that in the period between the election of Soderini and his own departure from Florence, he retired from political activity, devoting himself to studies and surrounding himself in his garden with literary men. This would mean that the meetings of the Rucellai gardens started and achieved their first importance from 1502 to 1506, about ten years earlier than they are usually placed.

Justification of this assumption can be found in the testimony of the philosopher Pietro Crinito. He related in his book *De Honesta Disciplina*[60] that he participated in the meetings of the Rucellai gardens and at various places refers to discussions which took place there. Crinito's book was published in 1504, and because he died in 1505, his references place the existence of such meetings in the first years of the sixteenth century beyond dispute.

A careful reading of the other contemporary material per-
taining to the Orti Oricellari reveals that his conclusion is not
only compatible with these other sources, but, if once admitted
as a possibility, is actually their natural interpretation and re-
solves most of the difficulties and contradictions which have
plagued students of the Orti Oricellari. It seems desirable to
undertake this detailed re-examination of the sources for two
reasons: first, it will remove definitely and completely all
reasons for the traditional thesis that the meetings began only in
the second decade of the century; and second, such an investigation will make it possible to establish precisely who were
the participants of these meetings in their various stages.[61]

We have two types of sources for the meetings in the Rucellai
gardens; thay are discussed by sixteenth-century Florentine historians, and they are occasionally mentioned in the writings of
literary men who were participants in the meetings.

The historians who provide information about the meetings
are Nardi[62] and Nerli.[63] Since, however, history was in this
period exclusively political in scope and purpose, these writers
display an interest in little beyond the political significance of
the Orti Oricellari. They discuss them in connection with the
conspiracy against Cardinal Giulio de' Medici in 1522, that is to
say, with events *after* the return of the Medici. Nardi reports
that the chief conspirators, Luigi Alamanni,[64] Zanobi Buondelmonte,[65] Antonio Brucioli,[66] and Francesco and Jacopo da
Diacceto[67] had met repeatedly in the Orti Oricellari, as guests
of Cosimo Rucellai, Bernardo's grandson. Machiavelli's dedication of his *Discorsi* to Cosimo Rucellai and Buondelmonte indicates that he also belonged to this group. But at the same time,
Nardi makes clear that men of quite different interests, the philosopher Francesco da Diacceto for example,[68] frequented the
Orti Oricellari "because this spot was a general meeting-place
and refuge for people with intellectual interests, whether foreigners or Florentines, because of the magnanimity, liberality
and hospitality of Bernardo Rucellai, his sons and his
grandsons."[69]

Nerli's story[70] agrees with that of Nardi, a confirmation
which has special value because Nerli reports that he was himself a participant in the meetings in the Orti Oricellari during
these years. He adds a further name, that of Battista della

Palla[71] to the list of those who were members of both the 1522 conspiracy and the Rucellai garden meetings; and he underlines the influence of the reading of history and of Machiavelli's teaching on the minds of these young men. Yet it has been overlooked that Nerli also mentions the Orti Oricellari at an earlier point in his history,[72] and that this passage confirms our thesis of earlier meetings. He reports that when Bernardo Rucellai, after his clash with Soderini, had withdrawn from politics in 1502, his garden had become a well-known meeting place for Florentine citizens and in particular for a group of young men who began to direct contemptuous criticism against the Gonfaloniere. Nerli's belief that the meetings in the Rucellai gardens had attained major importance in the times of Soderini emerges also from the fact that when he describes Soderini's overthrow, he reports that the young men trained in the "school of the Rucellai gardens" had a leading part in it.[73]

Turning now to men of letters who were participants in the meetings of the Rucellai gardens and who refer to them occasionally in their literary works, we must mention Brucioli and Gelli[74] as having the most valuable accounts. The two moral philosophers, Brucioli and Gelli, were too young to have frequented the Orti Oricellari before the second decade of the sixteenth century. They confirm Nerli's and Nardi's statements of the presence of Luigi Alamanni and Zanobi Buondelmonte at these later meetings and, being chiefly interested in intellectual developments, they add to the list of participants a few names from the field of scholarship and literature—Trissino, the philologist Lascaris, and the poet Francesco Guidetti.[75] Neither Brucioli nor Gelli[76] can serve as direct witness of gatherings in the first decade of the century, but at one point in his work Gelli makes a remark which suggests that he knew about the existence of such meetings in the earlier years. He writes[77] that "in the times of his childhood Bernardo Rucellai, Francesco da Diacceto, Giovanni Canacci,[78] Giovanni Corsi,[79] Piero Martelli,[80] Francesco Vettori[81] had frequent meetings and discussions in the Rucellai gardens."

Two points are significant in this remark. First, it contains a list of names which is, except for Diacceto, entirely different from that given by Nardi, Nerli, and Brucioli in their reports on meetings in the second decade of the century. The other point is that Gelli, who was born in 1498, would hardly have spoken of himself as a child[82] in referring to events after 1510. When combined with the fact that Bernardo Rucellai was absent from Florence from 1506 to 1510, Gelli's reference points clearly to the conclusion that there must have been an important "first period" of the meetings in the Rucellai gardens during the first five or six years of the sixteenth century.

The results of our investigation thus far may be summarized in a few lines. There were two stages to the meetings in the Rucellai gardens. To date, scholarly attention has been chiefly centered on the meetings in the second[83] decade of the sixteenth century. In these Luigi Alamanni, Zanobi Buondelmonte, Antonio Brucioli, Niccolò Machiavelli, and the three Diacceto participated, and Cosimo Rucellai, Bernardo's grandson, was the host and the central figure. But we have demonstrated that the gatherings had started much earlier and had flourished particularly in the first five or six years after 1500. With one exception, that of the philosopher Francesco da Diacceto, no important name appears in the lists of *both* sets of participants, those of the first stage and those of the second. In the former the guiding spirits were Bernardo Rucellai and his sons. The participants were a mixture of older men who, like Bernardo himself, Giovanni Canacci, and the somewhat younger Crinito, had played a role in Lorenzo il Magnifico's time, and youths, comtemporaries of his sons: Giovanni Corsi, Piero Martelli, Francesco Vettori. A few names can still be added as likely guests at the meetings in this first stage. Fontius' correspondence with Rucellai[84] and Giovanni Corsi's references—in the forewords to this biography of Ficino and his edition of Pontano's *De Prudentia*—to the intimate relationship between Bernardo Rucellai and Bindaccio Ricasoli and Cosimo Pazzi strongly suggest that Fontius,[85] Pazzi,[86] and Ricasoli[87] were also regular frequenters of the Rucellai gardens in their early stage.

We must now ask whether these conclusions provide any new insight into the significance of the meetings in the Rucellai gardens. The second stage of the meetings has been extensively and repeatedly studied.[88] The famous discussions held there on the relative advantages of the vernacular as compared to Latin had a great influence on the development of the Italian language. A number of works, which form landmarks in the history of Italian literature, can be shown to owe much to the stimulating effect of these meetings. It was in the Orti Oricellari that the first modern Italian tragedy, Giovanni Rucellai's *Rosmunda,* is said to have been staged. The cultivation of a republican spirit and of Roman traditions had a deep impact on the political development of Florence and on political thought in general. Now, did the earlier gatherings in the Rucellai gardens display the same character, or were they fundamentally different? What were in fact the chief interests and concerns of these first meetings just after 1500?

The only writer who gives us a direct report of the discussions in their early period is Pietro Crinito in his *De Honesta Disciplina.* According to his account, then, as later, literary and political interests existed side by side. He records, for example, such topics as the character of individual Latin poets and the relative value of the classical comedy writers.[89] Besides these primarily literary questions, the frequenters of the Rucellai gardens were interested in problems which would not be termed historical and philological in nature: whether human beings were sacrificed by the ancients[90] and whether the character of Cato or Fabius deserves greater admiration.[91] Yet Crinito also indicates the great role political problems played in these discussions: the political institutions of the ancients, the form of the best state, and the foundations of the strength of Venice.[92]

For further information about the discussions we may avail ourselves of the circumstance that during the first years of the sixteenth century several participants of these meetings were composing larger literary works. Francesco da Diacceto was then revising his *De Pulchro,* of which the first draft had been finished in 1499, and of which the final version was not completed before 1514.[93] Giovanni Corsi was at work on two books, already referred to, his biography of Ficino, the dedication of which is dated April 18, 1506, and his edition of Pontano's *De Prudentia.*[94] Bernardo Rucellai himself was then completing his work on the classical monuments of Rome and was planning his historical study on the invasion of Charles VIII. Finally, Pietro Crinito's *De Honesta Disciplina* was written during these years. It seems likely that these men discussed their literary enterprises in the Rucellai gardens and that their works reflect the discussions and interests of these gatherings.[95]

There does not seem to have been any startling new departure reflected in their handling of philosophical and literary problems. The frequent emphasis on beauty and love indicates that they were all thinking in terms of Ficino's neo-Platonism, where these concepts were posited as the great creative forces, which offer man the opportunity to raise himself above the transitory and to take a place in the eternal.[96] The interest in the literary problems of the ancient world seems to have been chiefly of a scholarly and antiquarian nature.[97] In both these aspects, in the cultivation of an esoteric philosophy and in the encyclopaedic, somewhat unselective interest in the classical world, the concerns of the Rucellai garden meetings seem to have continued the tradition of the circle around Lorenzo il Magnifico and reflect the stage which the humanist endeavors had reached in the second part of the fifteenth century.

What is very striking, however, is the great role which politics played in the discussions of the Rucellai gardens. As we know, the meetings were initiated when Rucellai, in disgust with the political developments in Florence, withdrew from active participation in political life. Yet we have also seen that the purpose of this boycott of the government was to effect its reorganization. It was only natural, therefore, that Rucellai and the group around him should continue to show an interest in politics while remaining in opposition to the existing government. In all the works of those who assembled in the Rucellai gardens, we find strong expressions of dissatisfaction with the situation which had developed in Florence. "It is a miserable time," says Francesco da Diacceto, "Florence, once flourishing, is sick; the most valuable citizens, and particularly the aristocracy, are persecuted by envy and exposed to insults and injury."[98] Giovanni Corsi too complains of the masses' unjust oppression of the aristocracy.[99] In contrast to the unhappy present, all these writers look longingly toward the past and with one voice praise the times of Lorenzo il Magnifico.

First of all, it was Lorenzo's patronage of art and letters which evoked their enthusiasm. Crinito contrasts the present time, in which simultaneously "with the freedom of Italy" art and letters have perished, with the age of Lorenzo, a man of highest wisdom and magnanimity, who accorded men of letters the honors due them.[100] Similarly to Giovanni Corsi the Florence of the Medici presents itself as a reborn Athenian age; and among the Medici it is Lorenzo with whom the Periclean apogee has been reached. Yet with Corsi, this praise is not limited to Lorenzo's support of art and literature. It extends to the order of society. Instead of discipline and knowledge, which ruled in Lorenzo's time, there is now licentiousness and ignorance; instead of generosity, greed; instead of moderation and self-restraint, ambition and extravagance; no longer is action taken in accordance with the traditional constitution and laws, everything is arbitrary.[101] In Rucellai's history, Lorenzo appears as the master mind, whose wise policy maintained peace within Italy and successfully defended it against foreign encroachments.

This high praise for the rule of the Magnifico was by no means a matter of course. On the contrary, it must be viewed as a rather astonishing evaluation. Certainly in Lorenzo's own time the humanist writers and poets, who had depended for their livelihood on the ruler's favors, had flattered him profusely in the dedications of their works.[102] But the basic views of his Florentine contemporaries were quite different; they ranged from unimpassioned appraisals of his policy to expressions of angry dissatisfaction with his despotic rule.[103] Even those Florentine aristocrats who formed Lorenzo's inner circle, who had received special advantages in reward for their support, and who were fully aware of his consummate political skill, never lost the feeling that they were living under a tyrant. This is clearly reflected in the penetrating, but somewhat equivocal characterization of Lorenzo which Guicciardini, the member of such a family, gives in his Florentine history.[104] A few years before the Rucellai garden meetings all these criticisms of Lorenzo had been summed up by Savonarola in a masterful picture. In his powerful sermons he discussed the characteristics of tyranny and enlivened his descriptions by giving his tyrant the features of Lorenzo il Magnifico. There Lorenzo appears contemptuous of law and tradition, arbitrary and suspicious, dishonest in his use of public funds, cynical in his corruption of the masses by celebrations and callous in fomenting wars to maintain himself in power.[105] The fact that Ficino, whom Corsi in his biography depicts as a shining representative of Lorenzo's Golden Age,[106] died an admirer of Savonarola is an indication of the lengths to which the group around Rucellai was willing to go in retouching the truth for the sake of Lorenzo il Magnifico's memory.

That such a change in the evaluation of Lorenzo was taking place in the first years of the sixteenth century was quite clear to contemporaries. Several times during these years, we find in the diary of the Florentine Piero Parenti remarks such as the following: "The disorder existing in Florence has made people praise the times of Lorenzo de' Medici and many have demanded that a return be made to the constitution of that time. They disseminate among the masses praise of the good old days and criticize the present."[107] The unanimity with which the members of the Rucellai group sang the praises of Lorenzo il Magnifico's rule suggests that they were making a conscious effort to reverse the previously held opinions and to start a process of idealization of Lorenzo.

Why it was important for them to show Lorenzo il Magnifico in a new light will become clear once we have investigated the other aspects of the political discussions. What Crinito said was that the chief topics were the political institutions of the ancients, the form of the best state, and the foundations of the power of Venice. That these were really crucial issues is revealed by statements which Rucellai makes in the foreword to his book on the classical monuments of Rome.[108] He says that when he attempted to persuade the Florentines to abandon the broad popular form of government which Savonarola had introduced, he supported his arguments by examples taken from experiences of the ancient world and from Venetian history. When he saw that his efforts were in vain, so he tells us, he decided to return to his studies and to investigate the nature of Roman society so that even if his own contemporaries had neglected his advice, he would at least earn the gratitude of future generations and of other nations. The study of the topography of Rome was intended to be the beginning of a series of studies, which would provide a safe guide to those who realized the need of definite knowledge of the functioning of ancient institutions for any attempt to use the ancient pattern in political reforms of the present.

Rucellai's words not only confirm Crinito's account but also indicate the inner connection existing between the various political topics mentioned by Crinito. Here we must probably not take too seriously Bernardo's assertion that he had retired to compose history for the use of posterity. The central theme of the political discussions of the Orti Oricellari was evidently the reform of the Florentine institutions in terms of the best possible constitution for Florence. Yet these discussions were not of a predominantly abstract character. They did not aim at discovering the perfect state on the basis of abstract philosophical considerations. They sought to determine what would be peculiarly suitable for Florence and to do so on the basis of the experience of political organizations which had proved their efficiency in practice. The contemporary experience of Venice, the historical experience of Rome, were to provide the material which the framers of a new Florentine constitution should use. From the emphasis on Venice and from what we know in general about Rucellai's political program, it can be deduced that is was an aristocratic regime with a monarchical head which seemed to him the secret of the success of both Rome and Venice, and which he tried to justify as the best solution for Florence as well.

This sheds light on the previously mentioned question as to how the transformation of Lorenzo il Magnifico's age and system of government into an ideal age fitted this whole approach. Experience was regarded as the true guide to politics, and aside from what could be learned from the contemporary scene, it was history which contained experience. The instances of success in history had to be studied in order to improve and reform the present. But the same logic demanded that, if there had been a period in which stability had been achieved, the organization which had then existed must, in its essential elements, have been identical with that existing in other tranquil periods. In Lorenzo's period there had been stability and peace, the great needs of the present. So the secret of his system of government must have been that he had attempted a mixed system of monarchy and aristocracy, which had been the secret of success in other times in Rome and Venice. One might discern that the idealization of Lorenzo's time had also more personal motives: personal justification of one's own participation in his rule, avoidance of the Medici's popularity being used to justify an antiaristocratic tyranny.[109] Unconsciously or, more probably quite consciously, the idealization of Lorenzo il Magnifico was posited as a necessary element in this historico-political attempt to justify aristocratic rule.

It was the necessary concomitant of this attitude that history was a decisive concern of this group. In the realization of the importance of history for politics, Rucellai's group was in agreement with the entire trend of subsequent political thought, an essential feature of which was that it was "politics based on history" (*politica storica*).[110] As Rucellai's correspondence shows,[111] the question of how history should be written was a central theme of his intellectual discussions with his friends. Rucellai's work on the French invasion, which he undoubtedly regarded as his chief literary effort, clearly reflects the attention he had given to the question of historical method. He not only emphasizes the necessity of discovering the truth but indicates that he follows conscious principles of selection, eliminating everything that has no direct bearing on the main subject. This does not make Rucellai's *De Bello Italico* a great historical work; but it is definitely a work of modern political history, in which history is neither romanticized nor used for the purpose of teaching morality, but from which the reader is supposed to learn in the political mistakes there revealed the true basis of practical politics. It is chiefly psychological history in so far as the events are explained as the result of decisions motivated by the main actors' personal desires and ambitions.

This emphasis on history belongs quite logically to the political approach cultivated in the Rucellai gardens. The study of history, the interest in the concrete functioning of political institutions, the idealization of Lorenzo il Magnifico's system of government, all were intimately connected. They were, in fact, only different aspects of the same effort to find an objective and rational basis for politics applicable specifically to the contemporary Florentine situation.

III

Having established—somewhat circumstantially and sketchily, to be sure—what the men who, in the first years of the sixteenth century, assembled around Bernardo Rucellai in his garden along the Via della Scala were discussing, we should now be able to assign to these meetings their place in the Renaissance intellectual development and to evaluate their historical significance. From what has been said, it should be clear that, if they have special historical importance, it must lie in the impact these meetings had on political and historical thinking. With regard to other problems which formed topics of discussion, notably philosophy and literature, the meetings remained within the framework evolved in the preceding period of Lorenzo il Magnifico. But on politics and history they evidently placed a much greater emphasis and in these fields they went beyond the quattrocento's approach.

It is interesting to observe the extent to which their treatment of political and historical problems resembled that of Machiavelli and his contemporaries in the decades that followed. In this respect, the discussions in the Orti Oricellari during the second decade of the sixteenth century seem to have been a direct continuation of those which had preceded them just after 1500. The interest the earlier meetings took in the concrete functioning of the institutions of other countries and particularly of Rome as a yardstick for the policies and institutions of their own time is repeated in the later stage as shown by Machiavelli's *Discorsi.* In this respect it is interesting that Bernardo Rucellai is also reported to have written a commentary and explanation of Livy.[112] The works of the great historians of the following decades, of Francesco Vettori and Francesco Guicciardin, are in the line of succession from Rucellai's historical efforts, at least in so far as the broad Italian framework, the use of history as a practical guide to politics, and the emphasis on the psychology of the participating statesmen are concerned.[113] Thus the early discussions in the Rucellai gardens seem to have laid out the program which the great masters of political realism. Machiavelli, Guicciardini, Vettori, Giannotti, were to carry out in the following decades.

This emphasis on the elements common to the meetings of the Rucellai gardens in their earlier and in their later stage is not intended to obscure important points of difference. The political conclusions the group around Machiavelli drew from Roman history and especially from Livy were exactly opposite to the views cherished by Bernardo Rucellai and his circle. While Rucellai and his generation sought to justify a limited aristocratic regime with a Medici as its head, Machiavelli and his friends used classical history as a justification of broad democratic government and their enthusiasm for the republican virtues of Rome was sharply pointed against the Medici.

This contrast, however, does not preclude the existence of an intellectual continuity in the Orti Oricellari meetings with regard to the approach to political problems. The unifying bond is the historico-political method, and one might even say that Machiavelli proves the strength of this tradition in that he evidently did not expect his democratic views to be accepted unless he could demonstrate, as he tries to do in the *Discorsi,* that this same method, when correctly applied, leads to conclusions exactly the reverse of those which the elder generation believed could be derived by its use.

There are other differences. Machiavelli and the great political and historical writers of his generation shook off the shackles of Latin and wrote in Italian. This not only indicates that they felt themselves nearer to and more urgently concerned with the contemporary scene but it also gave them the opportunity to express their views more forcefully and directly than the older generation had been able to do. It must be added, of course, that Machiavelli's achievement is only partly based on the method developed in the Rucellai gardens, namely on seeing the ancient political world in concrete and realistic terms and in re-examining the contemporary problems in the light of this new insight. Machiavelli's political vision gains greater depth because of his unique sense of power element. It has a new dimension because of the heroic disillusionism with which he regards the struggle between man and fate.

The fact remains that basic elements in the new realistic approach to political problems were adumbrated in discussions of the Rucellai gardens in the first years of the sixteenth century, a decade before it was fully developed in the writings of Machiavelli, Guicciardini, and their school.

Having traced this development to a time somewhat earlier than that at which it is usually placed, we have now to ask whether even the political discussions in the Rucellai gardens were the true starting point of this approach and represented a new departure, and, if so, what was the peculiar intellectual constellation out of which this development emerged.

There is something novel in the simple fact that politics had such a large place in the early meetings at the Orti Oricellari, quite aside from the manner in which political problems were dealt with. Discussion groups composed of prominent Florentine citizens and humanists were, to be sure, nothing new in themselves. Since the end of the fourteenth century, when such meetings took place in the Augustinian monastery of Santo Spirito around Luigi Marsigli and Coluccio Salutati, circles of this kind had been in existence;[114] and a culmination had been reached with Ficino's Platonic Academy in the second part of the fifteenth century. But the topics of discussion in these older groups were chiefly of a philosophical or literary nature; as far as we know, political themes of practical import were not discussed. The Florentine citizen-statesmen who participated in these meetings took an interest in the concerns of the humanists and perhaps made them their own, but they did not expect these discussions to provide answers to the problems arising out of their own political activities. It is characteristic that, with regard to Lorenzo il Magnifico, a certain dualism in his intellectual outlook has often been pointed out: Lorenzo the Statesman and Lorenzo the Humanist were separate personalities.[115] This does not mean that Florentine humanism was entirely lacking in political interests. The way in which the humanists dealt with political problems, however, could not give Florentine politicians the feeling that the approach had real significance for their political activities.

Throughout the fifteenth century, the politics of humanism could justly be called "rhetorics";[116] taken too literally this characterization is not without danger for it could easily be taken to mean that humanist views were entirely valueless in this respect and could safely be left aside in studying fifteenth-century political issues. This would go much too far. Frequently the subjects of humanist political writings—the advantages of a citizen army, the differences between monarchy and republican government, the duties of citizenship—reflect the political interests of their time, and can enlighten us as to the chief concerns as well as the shifts which occurred in them. The weakness of these humanist writings, however, lies in the fact that they were at best a somewhat blurred mirror and never more than that: they remained "merely an expression of aspirations and desires and never passed from the stage of nostalgia to that of deliberate planning."[117] Contemporary problems were only the peg on which to hang the description of some ideal situation which had existed in the ancient world. There was no attempt to investigate how the ideal might be brought to earth.

This equivocal attitude of the humanists is also reflected in the role they played in practical politics. A great number of them made their living in public positions. They were employed as secretaries or chancellors; formulation of political documents was entrusted to them, because such documents might have greater propagandist effect if presented in Ciceronian Latin; as official historians they were useful in elevating their city or country to a pedestal of dignity by draping the events of the past or of their own time in classical dress. Yet, they hardly ever took part at a policymaking level. Neither Bruni Aretino nor Poggio nor Decembrio nor Scala belonged to the ruling group. There remained a wide gap between the humanists and the ruling classes of their time. To this extent, their political discussions inevitably remained rhetorical. This is the background against which emerges the unique character of the Rucellai meetings in the first years of the sixteenth century. The distinguishing feature was a combination of subject matter and personnel. Not only were the topics with which the humanists had been concerned discussed; but, more than that, those problems which were chiefly the concern of the Florentine aristocrats were also taken up, and these aristocrats now became interested in what humanism could offer with regard to the exigencies of the political situation. Their hope of getting practical political guidance from such discussions was something new.

But why, just at the beginning of the sixteenth century, did the politicians feel the need for a broader, more systematic justification of their political attitude? This question leads us to a consideration of what were the new factors in the political situation, under which the meetings in the Rucellai gardens took place. The obvious answer is that a new historical period had opened with the French invasion of 1494. Yet it is perhaps possible to define more precisely why this event impelled the Florentine ruling group to a re-examination of its political position.

That Charles VIII's Italian campaign was a decisive turning point in history has become so axiomatic that the date has sometimes been used as marking the beginning of modern European history. But it is not always realized that in ascribing to the French invasion of 1494 such decisive significance, historians have only accepted the historical scheme which was outlined in the Renaissance period itself by the great Florentine political and historical writers Guicciardini, Machiavelli, and Vettori, and which probably was first formulated in Rucellai's *De Bello Italico*. What gave these writers the intellectual power to see the events, to which they themselves were still quite near, in such broad perspective? One has to acknowledge that this realization of the full implications was by no means obvious, certainly it was not unanimous. Although Charles VIII's campaign had displayed from the outset some extraordinary features, many considered it just another one of the foreign invasions which Italy was accustomed to suffer;[118] and after Charles VIII's quick retreat, it appeared to many all the more as a rather ephemeral interlude.

It was no accident that those who were immediately awake to the full portent of the French influx were Florentines. For in Florence, the invasion was accompanied by a domestic revolution, a revolution in which the previous basis of political existence disappeared. The establishment of the Gran Consiglio, in which Savonarola's reform culminated, had considerably broadened the base of the government. Middle class groups, which in the aristocratically ruled Florence of the fifteenth century had had no influence, now gained the right to participate in the government. The aristocrats were set on re-establishing the situation that had existed before Savonarola's reforms, in other words, on once again excluding from political control those groups that had recently gained access to it. Lacking the power to bring about the reactionary change by force and realizing the danger of calling in outside forces which after the event might disregard the aristocrats and establish a one-man rule,[119] they were obliged to adapt themselves to the situation that existed and had to work for their aims within the existing democratic framework. They had to convince the groups participating in the government that a restored aristocratic regime was the best form of government, and they had to provide a theoretical justification for it. This change in the situation had a crucial impact on the evolution of the Florentine political party system; one might perhaps go so far as to say that it led to the evolution of political parties in the modern sense.

We are accustomed to speak of political parties in fifteenth-century Florence, adopting the terminology used by the humanist historians, in accordance with classical patterns; but in reality, what have been characterized as party struggles, the clashes between the Albizzi and Medici, for example, were nothing more than fights between rival factions within the same narrow class of wealthy merchants, competing against each other for exclusive possession of the state machine and the economic advantages which resulted from such possession.[120] Family relationship and business co-operation were the bonds that held groups together and differentiated one group from another. When the Medici established their rule, the most prominent families of the opposing groups were sent into exile. The less prominent and less active families of the former opposition were permitted to stay in Florence and were gradually tied to the Medici by grants of financial advantages and by marriage arrangements so that eventually the entire ruling group was interrelated.[121] The result was a somewhat loose but none the less recognizable one-party state. This background explains why Florentine historians paid such close attention to the arrangement of marriages between members of the ruling group and to the dissolution of business associations, and also why the rulers of Florence—Lorenzo, Piero, and even Soderini—regarded the conclusion of a marriage without their permission as a hostile act. At the same time it explains why Savonarola's democratic constitution represented an entirely new development in Florentine politics. After 1494 the traditional means were no longer applicable. The middle class groups, which had now acquired the right to government participation, could no longer be amalgamated by the aristocracy through the traditional means of business ties and intermarriage. In order for these wider groups to be moved in some desired direction they had to be successfully persuaded; an ideological justification became necessary, especially in questions of constitutional reform; the contrasts became ideologically justified, that is, factions solidified into parties.

It is this practical need to find a generally valid intellectual justification for their constitutional recommendations that is the driving force behind the emergence of modern political thought in this era. The writings of the new realistic school sought to create a system of politics, but behind the general laws they claimed to have discovered, the line of special pleading is always noticeable. Whether it is Guicciardini or Machiavelli, Vettori or Giannotti, in outlining the motivating forces of politics and history, they aim at justifying either the democratic or aristocratic attitude. Through the attempt to raise the specific party point of view to the level of general validity, they became the founders of political science.

As we have seen, the contemporaries of these writers regarded the new political science as a revival of the political wisdom of the ancient world. It was to the representatives of humanism that Rucellai and his group turned when, in the first years of the sixteenth century, they needed a political ideology to regain the power which had slipped from their hands. It was the amalgamation of classical concepts with modern political practice out of which the thinking of modern political realism emerged. It is perhaps justified, therefore, to suggest that the problem we have been investigating may throw some light on the significance of humanism in general.

Few movements have undergone so thorough changes in their historical evaluation as has humanism. Since the time of Jacob Burckhardt, when humanism appeared as a central element and motivating force of the whole period, its prestige has steadily declined. With the greater interest in social and economic developments and a clearer realization of the significance of these forces, humanism was reduced to a secondary status, a simple manifestation of a new secular culture.[122] The impact of humanism even on the intellectual sphere—on scholarship and science—now seems of questionable significance. Perhaps humanism is still maintained in a parental role to classical philology, but on the development of philosophy and science it appears to have had a rather small part in comparison with the less startling but more broadly based influence of the mediaeval philosophical tradition and methods rooted in institutions which continued from the middle ages to modern times.[123]

The development we have studied, however, suggests that the evaluation of Italian humanism should not remain quite so negative, that it should be based less on what humanism achieved in the time of its emergence and its greatest extension than on the role it played at the end of the fifteenth and the beginning of the sixteenth century, the time of its decline.[124] Then the Italian secular culture had reached the stage in which it was to work out its own system of values and concepts; and this system has remained one of the main constituent elements in our modern civilization. But for the special character which this system took, it was of decisive importance that when it was being evolved its constructors were surrounded by materials and concepts which humanism had prepared and that they integrated these and and made them their own. Thus the historical significance of humanism lies not in what it means as an independent doctrine and method but in what was the outcome of the absorption of many of its materials and concepts into the new intellectual system of the High Renaissance.

The political thought of humanism we have said was rhetorics; forces and developments quite outside its intellectual scope were necessary to awaken the need for a new, systematic, and rational approach to politics. But the school of modern political realism would not have received the form it has assumed without using for its structure the stones which humanism had provided. The happenings of the Rucellai gardens are important in this respect. To one whose father had found expression for his new secular feeling of man's responsibility for his own successes and failures in the symbol of the ancient goddess who smiled on those who helped themselves, it was a matter of course that the combining of his own experience with a deeper understanding of ancient politics would indicate the course along which he could steer his ship into port through the rising storms of his time.

10. Religion and Politics in the Thought of Gasparo Contarini

Stepping from the gates of his palace in Venice,[1] Gasparo Contarini was immediately drawn into the teeming life of the city in whose triumphant history his ancestors had played a leading part since earliest times. But from the rear of his palace Contarini could see across the lagoons the Camaldolese monastery of San Michele with the white dome of its recently built church and, beyond San Michele, the dark cypresses of Murano. These islands were the refuge of those who rejected the value of worldly activity and believed that man's only concern ought to be the salvation of his soul.

These were the two worlds in which Contarini lived. On the one hand, he had a political career which led him to high positions in the Venetian government. And his political interests found literary expression in his famous treatise on the institutions of the Venetian republic.[2] On the other hand, he was an intellectual who wrote extensively on philosophical, moral, and theological issues. And the religious bent of his intellectual con-

Originally published in *Action and Conviction in Early Modern Europe,* ed. Theodore K. Rabb and Jerrold E. Seigel (Princeton, Princeton University Press, © 1969), pp. 90–116, reprinted by permission. To the literature referred to in this article ought now to be added the excellent bibliographical survey by J. B. Ross, "The Emergence of Gasparo Contarini," *Church History,* 41 (1972), 22–45.

cerns brought him, at the end of his life, from Venice to Rome where he became a member of the College of Cardinals and a guiding spirit in the last great attempt to bring the Lutherans back into the fold of the church.

Much has been written about Gasparo Contarini.[3] His treatise on Venice has had a great influence on the development of constitutional thinking, and its importance for later political thought has been frequently analyzed.[4] Contarini's theological position and his activities as a church reformer have been of crucial interest to students of the Reformation period.[5] But those who have written on Contarini's views about Venetian politics seem only vaguely aware that he was also a religious thinker, whereas those who have investigated Contarini's role in the confessional struggle have given little or no attention to his earlier career as a Venetian statesman.[6] This partitioning of Contarini's life seems contradictory to what we know about human nature.[7] Thus we are justified in looking for the intellectual bond which explains the road Contarini traveled from Venetian statesman to reforming Cardinal.

I

Gasparo Contarini was the eldest son of his parents, and as such he was expected to take an active part in business and politics; but his remarkable intellectual gifts—that, at least, is the report of his biographers[8]—became evident at such an early age that he was permitted to devote himself to a life of study. In 1502 Gasparo's father died, and Gasparo, then a student at the university in Padua, went back to Venice. As soon as he had put in order the affairs of his family and set up his brothers in their careers, however, he returned to Padua. This episode is revealing because it shows that, despite his scholarly incliations, Contarini was very much aware of the obligations involved in being a member of his family and a Venetian patrician. Contarini's years of study in Padua ended in 1509, when the war of the League of Cambrai forced a closing of the university. Contarini returned to Venice with a high reputation as a philosopher, even though he had not yet published anything. That he had made a great impression among the intellectuals of Padua is indicated by the fact that the university's most brilliant and audacious teacher, Pomponazzi, dedicated a treatise to him.[9]

The war that forced Contarini's return to Venice brought about a serious crisis in his native city.[10] In a few weeks Venice lost her possessions on the *terra ferma,* and, although the situation soon improved, the war continued and Venice could begin to feel safe only in 1515. Venetian nobles were deprived of remunerative administrative positions on the *terra ferma.* The Venetian government was in desperate financial straits and had to take recourse to the imposition of new taxes and to forced loans; payments from the Monte ceased. For those able to pay, admission to the Great Council was eased. The Venetians who had prided themselves on their role as protagonists of Christianity against the Turks turned to the Sultan for help; and, in order to separate the Pope from the anti-Venetian alliance, they conceded their claims to be free from papal interference in ecclesiastical affairs.

This reversal of Venetian fortunes made an immense impression. To the Neapolitan Tristano Caracciolo, the unexpected collapse of the Venetian empire, of "this miracle of wisdom and strength," was a striking example of "God's providence" and demonstrated "that we ought never to cease to fear God."[11] To the Venetians themselves, their fall from the heights of power meant the destruction of a historical image which had grown slowly throughout the centuries: the image of Venice as a perfect political society, of the God-willed expansion of the Venetian empire, of the excellence of Venetian institutions that guaranteed internal stability and safety from external enemies.[12] The impact of this blow was the greater because in the previous decades Venetians had begun to question whether Venice was not defecting from its old, true traditions. Warnings had been uttered against overindulgence in luxury and pleasure; and laws had been issued to stem the spread of corruption in government. To many Venetians this time of troubles appeared as divine punishment for the sin of surrender to worldly concerns.

When Contarini returned to Venice in 1509, he came in close contact with a group of young Venetian nobles who had felt repelled by the materialistic atmosphere of Venetian political and social life and had withdrawn to Murano and San Michele to contemplate in isolation the salvation of their souls. Like Contarini, they came from Venice's oldest and most distinguished patrician families: Giustiniani, Quirini, Canale. Paolo

Canale had just begun to achieve literary fame when he suddenly decided to become a Camaldolese monk on San Michele;
his early death strongly reinforced the belief his friends had in
the vanity of worldly ambitions and aims. Tomaso Giustiniani,
the strongest personality in this circle, had traveled in 1507 to
the Holy Land where he intended to remain as an eremite for
the rest of his life. Before leaving Venice he gave his villa on
Murano to Quirini and other friends, stipulating that they remain unmarried. However, Giustiniani found conditions in Pal-
estine unsuited to his plans to withdraw from the world, and,
when Contarini came to Venice in 1509, Giustiniani was back
in Murano. Shortly afterward, in December 1510, Giustiniani
discovered in the mountain wilderness above Arezzo a Camaldolese monastery; here were the surroundings which he believed would permit him to lead the life of an eremite undistur-
bed by the troubles of the world. Nine months later Vincenzo
Quirini followed Giustiniani to Camaldoli. Quirini's decision
provoked tremendous excitement, because shortly before he
had been entrusted with important diplomatic tasks by the
Venetian government and he seemed to stand at the beginning
of a brilliant political career. Even as monks Giustiniani and
Quirini kept in contact with their Venetian friends, and it is
from Contarini's correspondence with Father Paolo and Father
Pietro, as Giustiniani and Quirini were now called, that we can
gain insight into Contarini's aims, intellectual interests, and
spiritual struggles.[13]

Contarini never intended to follow the example of Giustiniani and Quirini and become a monk.[14] In the first letter Contarini wrote to Giustiniani in Camaldoli, he stated: "I shall not
say, lest I deceive you, that I am coming to keep you company.
Such good thoughts are not in me."[15] There was no doubt in
Contarini's mind that he was unsuited for life in a monastery, or
as an eremite. He might sometimes regret that he would never
achieve that peaceful and quiet life which his friends enjoyed;
but he had no illusions that, in this respect, he was different
from them.[16]

Contarini had ambivalent feelings toward those who withdrew from the world and concentrated exclusively on their own
salvation. Contarini revealed these feelings when, after a few
months in the hermitage, Quirini fell ill and had to go to

Florence. For a while it seemed possible that Quirini might not return to Camaldoli, especially since his family found itself in financial difficulties. Contarini urged his friend to regard this illness as a sign from God and as an opportunity to reconsider his decision. The fulfillment of one's duties to one's family and one's city, Contarini wrote to Quirini, were also sacred obligations. Giustiniani then reproached Contarini vehemently for attempting to divert Quirini from his religious calling, and Quirini did return to Camaldoli.[17] Yet Contarini stuck to his views: when, in 1514, Quirini hesitated to accept the Cardinal's hat offered him by Pope Leo X, Contarini, in order to persuade Quirini to submit to the Pope's wishes, used arguments very similar to those he had used a few years before. Quirini, he said, ought to examine whether it would not be egoism and self-love if he placed the concern for the salvation of his soul above service to others and work for the well-being of all Christianity.[18] In Contarini's view, man was a social being and withdrawal from the world was unnatural.[19]

This does not mean that Contarini condemned those who, like Giustiniani and Quirini, broke with the world. On the contrary, he admired them greatly; such men were higher human beings who were attempting to raise themselves above human limitations. However, this course was possible and permissible only for a select few.[20] It was not the appropriate road for the great majority of people. There was value, too, in remaining in the world and in the fulfillment of man's duty toward his neighbor. Contarini was not willing to say that one way of life was of intrinsically greater value than another: "Although the contemplative life is nobler than the active life, nevertheless the active life in which man helps others in their spiritual struggles has greater merits."[21]

The difference between Contarini and his Camaldolese friends should not be reduced, however, to the simple formula of the contrast between *vita activa* and *vita contemplativa*, between action and thought. The passage just quoted indicates that Contarini regarded the assistance which man could lend to others in their striving for spiritual perfection as the chief justification for remaining in the world. There is no reason to doubt that from his earliest years Contarini was a person of deep religiosity. But the crisis which the war of the League of Cambrai brought about in Venice, together with the intimacy which developed between him and the group around Giustiniani and Quirini, certainly served to place religious problems into the center of his thought. In discussions with Giustiniani and Quirini he arrived at the decision to devote himself, after the termination of his philosophical studies, to the study of theology for the rest of his life.[22] Thus Contarini and his Camaldolese friends were agreed that concern for the salvation of one's soul ought to be man's supreme interest. But Contarini did not share the convictions of his friends that there was only one sure way to obtain salvation, namely, withdrawal from the world. Contarini believed it could be attained also by remaining within the world.[23]

In theological terms, the problem which faced Contarini was that of man's justification before God. The great issue which in later years was to be a stumbling block to Contarini's efforts to reconcile the Lutherans with the church emerged early as a central theme in his religious thinking.

When, in 1511, Giustiniani wrote Contarini from Camaldoli that, despite "having left the world for the love of Christ and leading an ascetic life," he did not feel confident of his salvation, Contarini was deeply disturbed about what his own fate might be.[24] But he could also report to Giustiniani that during Easter week, through the counsel of a wise priest, his worries and troubles had been lifted. He had realized that man could never expiate his sins by his own efforts. God had shown through the sacrifice of his son that he was willing to proceed with charity toward man. What could be expected from man was only to meet God's forbearance with faith, hope, and charity. "Now I shall sleep securely, although in the midst of the city, although I have not paid off the debt I had contracted, since I have such a Payer of my debt. Truly, I shall sleep and wake as securely as if I had spent all the time of my life in the hermitage, with the intention of never letting this support go. . . Vivamus ergo laeti, ut ex hoc timore liberati, in laetitia serviamus illi omnibus diebus nostris."[25]

Yet this was not a problem that could be solved once and for all. A year later fears and anxieties again arose in Contarini's mind, this time even more intensely. He had completed his philosophical studies, and the time had come to turn to theology.

But, he wrote, "I have begun to hate studying and what once was my delight, the reading of the Holy Bible, now fills me with ennui."[26] In this spiritual crisis, as in the one of the preceding year, Contarini arrived at the solution that man with his own forces is unable to work his salvation, that he must trust God's love that is proved by Christ's death. This trust in God's abundant love had now reinforced his conviction that man has the right to live in the world and for the world. God could never demand from man more than what is appropriate to the nature which God had given him. Contarini thought that he had deceived himself when formerly he had believed himself to be one of the elect who, by virtue of their intellectual gifts and the earnestness of their efforts, might be granted security and peace.[27] He was not, as he had formerly supposed, a man superior to others; on the contrary, he was one of the lowliest creatures. Nature had not fitted him to live the life of a religious, so he would spend his life in the world according to the status in which he had been placed by God. And because God had given him this place, this way of life would not separate him from God. He would keep up the hope that one day God might help him to arrive at a deeper understanding of divine wisdom and a fuller realization of his peace. But this was only a remote hope. Contarini was aware that his life would be full of uncertainties: sometimes he might believe he could rise to heaven; sometimes he might feel himself to be as low as brute animals. Life in the world is a constant struggle. Contarini used the same image which others, concerned with the renewal of true Christianity, employed when they taught that man, whatever he did and wherever he was, could serve God. The life of a Christian is like that of a knight.[28]

Contarini's letters to Giustiniani and Quirini were written on an abstract and theoretical level. Contarini himself said that in these letters he did not want to discuss at length the "particular causes" that had shaped his views.[29] Nevertheless, Contarini did mention activities and used arguments which permit some insight into the more practical considerations and social pressures that influenced his thinking. Clearly, the duties a man owes to his family weighed heavily in Contarini's mind; and he was aware that abandoning a political career might be taken as a sign of despairing of the future of Venice.[30] Moreover, the correspondence testifies to the extent to which Contarini felt himself to be a member of a scholarly community. Besides the circle around Giustiniani and Quirini, he had many friends in intellectual life, particularly among the professors and humanists of Padua.[31]

Giustiniani and Quirini, although highly educated and sophisticated men fully cognizant of the intellectual trends of their time, regarded intellectual activities as basically futile. After Giustiniani had arrived in Camaldoli, he wrote his Venetian friends a long and detailed report about his voyage into the wilderness.[32] With evident satisfaction, Giustiniani mentioned that he had met a priest whose sermons had made little impact as long as he had occupied himself with modern theological writings and interpretations but whose preaching had become effective as soon as he had gone to the true sources, the Bible and the church fathers. Giustiniani's views emerge still more clearly in a letter which he wrote after the death of Marcantonio della Torre, a scholar and a common friend of his and Contarini's. The scholarly works to which della Torre had devoted his life—"dialectical arguments, philosophical disputes, mathematics and medicine, Greek, Latin, and Tuscan"—would be of no use in heaven, where "without rational arguments one will know all truth."[33]

Contarini did not share Giustiniani's contempt for humanism and philosophy. Like many of his contemporaries, Contarini believed that a simple man could have insights which to the ordinary secular mind might appear foolish but which in reality were an expression of divine wisdom.[34] Contarini had reservations about the unlimited enthusiasm of many of his contemporaries for the classics. He was sure that a full understanding of the Bible and the church fathers required acquaintance with the languages in which these works had been written. Knowledge of Hebrew, Greek, and Latin helped to foster a true Christian spirit. And the establishment of correct texts was a worthwhile and necessary undertaking.[35] But, whereas in the rest of Europe interest in classical studies came about simultaneously with interest in church reform, in Italy humanist studies had flowered long before religious reform became urgent. Thus, like Giustiniani and Quirini, Contarini regarded the passionate fascination of Italians with all aspects of the pagan world with distrust. The titillating eroticism of the classical poets seemed to him morally dangerous. Nevertheless—and here he deviated from Giustiniani and Quirini—his views about the value of pagan authors were ambiguous. Contarini's interest in ancient thought and classical studies was more pronounced than his correspondence with Giustiniani and Quirini suggests. Even these letters, however, give us some glimpse into his involvement in humanistic studies. They testify to his intimacy with Trifone Gabriele, the friend of Bembo and the translator of Horace; and they show Contarini's interest in the progress of the work of his friend Egnazio, who wrote about the outstanding men of Venetian history in the pattern of Valerius Maximus.[36] In one letter Contarini described the great impression which Francesco da Diacceto, the Florentine neo-Platonist philosopher, had made on him.[37] Contarini mentioned that immediately upon its publication he studied the Greek Plato edition which Aldus was publishing and frequently in these letters he expressed his immense admiration for Plato.[38] Contarini was convinced of the value of philosophical studies, and he justified this position against the opposition of Giustiniani and Quirini. He admitted that the pagan philosophers could not have known the highest truth; still, he argued, the knowledge that can be obtained by means of man's "natural light" is of value. For the "natural light" is "a great gift of God."[39] Philosophy has its function even if it does not lead to absolute wisdom.

Against the persuasions of Father Paolo and Father Piero, Gasparo maintained his right to remain in the world, to be a Contarini, a Venetian patrician, a humanist, and a philosopher—that emerges from an analysis of Contarini's correspondence with his Camaldolese friends. Yet the fundamental religious problem in which he became involved through his friendship with Giustiniani and Quirini left a sharp imprint on his mind; from then on, life assumed a new aspect for him. He had become deeply convinced that all secular activities had to be placed in a Christian framework and that social life had to be ordered in such a way that man would be ready to receive what only God could give—the salvation of man's soul.

II

After arriving at some settlement of his spiritual crisis, Contarini felt free to devote himself to politics and literary work. In 1515 Contarini was for the first time a candidate for public office; in February 1518 he was elected to his first government position, beginning a brilliant career in the service of the Venetian republic. It was also in 1515 that Contarini embarked upon a period of intense literary productivity. His book against Pomponazzi's treatise *De immortalitate animae* and a work entitled *De officio episcopi* were completed in 1516 and 1517. A second book against Pomponazzi followed in 1518. Then, between 1522 and 1526, during his diplomatic mission to Charles V, Contarini composed his chief philosophical study, the *Compendium primae philosophiae,* as well as the main sections of his treatise *De magistratibus et republica Venetorum.* The *Compendium* was corrected and revised in 1526–27, and the book on Venice was completed only after 1531.[40] Nevertheless, in their basic features, all his more important and extended works were written or conceived and drafted in the decade between 1516 and 1526.

Because these works originated close to each other, it is not astonishing that their ideas are interrelated.[41] Contarini frequently referred from one to the other; indeed, they represent the application of the same general system of thought to different aspects of life and nature. Moreover, one can also observe that the ideas at which he had arrived in the course of his exchange with Giustiniani and Quirini were basic elements of his philosophical writings.

Contarini was not a thinker of great originality. He explained his methods in his chief philosophical work, the *Compendium primae philosophiae.* He presented what he had learned about a particular problem from the study of other authors and then added the results of his own reflections.[42] Contarini was a slow and careful reader. But he had a prodigious memory, so that he was able to reproduce the statements of other authors almost word for word. He was eclectic, too, and referred in his writings to a large number of philosophical authors: Aristotle, St. Augustine, St. Thomas, Plato, Plotinus, Themistius, Duns Scotus, Averroes, Avicenna, Dionysius Areopagita. The indiscriminate manner in which he cited the most diverse authors provides no secure basis for establishing the particular philosophical school to which he belonged. It is evident, however, that Contarini's philosophical point of departure was Aristotelian, as was appropriate for one who had studied in Padua. But Contarini was also a careful student of Plato and neo-Platonism, and he was inclined to tie the phenomena described by Aristotle into an interconnected structure emanating from a spiritual center. On purely theological issues this approach was comparable with the views of St. Thomas, whose authority Contarini regarded as supreme. But in its more general aspects Contarini's philosophical thought was similar in many respects to that of Avicenna, with whom he agreed on particular problems, like the role of imagination or the influence of celestial bodies. Hence, there is reason for characterizing him as an Avicennist Aristotelian.[43]

Contarini's first and, in his own lifetime, most widely circulated work was his polemical treatise against Pomponazzi's *De immortalitate animae*.[44] Contarini differed from Pomponazzi on two basic points: the relation of faith to reason and the connection between the spiritual and the material world.

Pomponazzi's treatise had raised fundamental questions about the relation between faith and reason because, in Pomponazzi's opinion, it was impossible to provide valid proof of the immortality of the soul on the basis of rational argument. However, the immortality of the soul as a doctrine of the church had to be accepted by faith. Contarini argued against this separation of faith and reason. On the one hand, such separation seemed to him conducive to overestimating the power of reason. Man might be inclined to believe that "the natural light must suffice him in everything" and that what could not be explained by reason did not exist. "We believe that this is a very dangerous philosophy which might instill in man's mind the pestilential and harmful poison of unbelief and impiety."[45] On the other hand, Pomponazzi's thesis about the relation of faith to reason seemed to Contarini to devalue reason. Reason is a gift of God. Thus, the "natural light" of reason cannot be contrary to the supranatural light; it is only less perfect.[46] In his *Compendium primae philosophiae* Contarini gave these ideas about the value of reason a still more positive form. Reason provides the criterion through which man can avoid the traps of speculative fantasies; in purifying man's mind from depraved emotions, reason prepares him for entering the realm of the divine, because—and here Contarini quoted Plato—"the impure cannot touch the pure."[47] Nevertheless, "human intellect by its nature cannot go beyond certain limits in providing knowledge."[48] Reason leads to God but cannot reveal anything about the divine world. Reason can show that man's soul is immortal, but it cannot show what happens to the soul after man's death.

In Contarini's views about the character and the role of reason his differences with Pomponazzi about the connection between the spiritual and material world are implicit. Pomponazzi maintained that the functioning of man's intellect is dependent on sensory perceptions which man, as part of the material world, receives from it. Thus, the end of man's bodily existence implies the end of his spiritual life, at least according to rational considerations. For Contarini, the relation is the reverse. The spiritual world is independent of the material world, and the phenomena of the material world assume shape and distinctive character only when and insofar as they are permeated by the spiritual world. The spiritual world gives form to matter.[49] In the context of the problem of the immortality of the soul, this means that every human represents a convergence of spiritual and material factors and that the spiritual factors do not necessarily disappear when the body dies.

Again, these ideas are developed at greater length and more systematically in Contarini's *Compendium primae philosophiae*. There he stated that "nothing among the things of this world is of simple substance but everything consists of two parts, one form, one matter. Form gives to everything its aim and its particular nature."[50] Contarini saw the universe as a great hierarchy, and the *Compendium* gives an outline of Contarini's views on the order of the universe. The source of all spiritual forces is God, the pure spirit; below him are those beings that have a primarily spiritual nature, like the angels; next come the celestial bodies and then the human beings, which exist at the place where spiritual forces and material factors are in balance; and finally, below man come those bodies which are weighted toward matter: animals, plants, metals, the elements. Clearly, this is a strictly graduated hierarchical structure.[51]

The feeling that an ordered world meant a hierarchically organized world was extremely strong in Contarini and permeated his entire thinking. In discussing in his book *De officio episcopi* the support which ought to be given to the poor, he emphasized that poor members of the nobility ought to be assisted before all others.[52] Nevertheless, because every being and every thing receives its particular existence from the imprint of an ideal form on matter, not only is each being placed in relation to higher and lower things but also each has its own particular function: to divest itself as far as possible of matter and to realize its own ideal form, to reach perfection.[53] Full perfection is not obtainable for beings and things of this world because, as long as they exist in the world, they remain bound to matter. But striving toward perfection is possible for everyone because the world is God's creation and an outflow of his spirit. "All nature, in so far as it possesses the quality of being, is good and can never abandon the appetite for good."[54] Evil is not a force by itself but something negative—inability to overcome matter.

This entire system comes sharply into focus in Contarini's attitude toward the problem of the relation between *vita activa* and *vita contemplativa.* "Nobody can doubt or fail to comprehend that the contemplative life must be preferred to practical and active work."[55] Contemplation seeks a vision of the divine world. Yet the achievement of a direct contact with God is not a question of knowledge: a simple good man can come nearer to God than a learned man. In any case, closeness to God is possible only for a select few, and even they can never arrive at complete knowledge of God. "For such secrets, words and concepts fail and they must be venerated in holy silence."[56] Because man remains bound to matter, a full entering into the spiritual world is not possible for him.

Contarini formulated this view most strongly in a small treatise which was directly devoted to the question whether "the speculative sciences are nobler and more perfect than the moral virtues."[57] Abstractly Contarini felt that science stands above moral virtue because action must be directed and intellect gives the direction. But, if man cannot have both, then he should choose moral virtue. "Moral virtue and active life are appropriate to man. The contemplative life is beyond man."[58]

This view of the relation between contemplative and active life is entirely consonant with the concept of a graduated hierarchy which dominated Contarini's ideas about the universe. "Before man can obtain full perfection he must reach an imperfect one."[59] It is not possible to leave the level of existence into which things have been placed and to leap into a higher or different level. Thus, Contarini rejected the possibility of arriving at truth through magic and astronomy, because those who practice these arts believe or pretend that they have direct contact with purely spiritual beings, like demons, to which man, by his nature, simply cannot have any access.[60]

Nevertheless, Contarini's emphasis on the value of the *vita activa* was not merely the result of theoretical considerations; it had an undertone of emotion and was the result of personal experience. For Contarini, pure thinking, pure contemplation, was something cold and dead. For instance, he mentioned that a statue by Praxiteles may be perfectly beautiful but remains unsatisfactory because it lacks the warmth of life.[61] Or, he said that friends have served him as "living books," that he has learned more from them than from the study of what has been written or printed.[62] It was possible for Contarini to consider his personal inclination toward the *vita activa* as philosophically justifiable and justified because love has a central place in his theoretical system and love must express itself in actions toward fellow men. Because God forms the source from which the spiritual forces flow out to imprint their form on the material world, all that exists has an innate tendency toward the good. This means that "the foremost and primary motive power of man's rational will is love because good and love are connected. Good is the object of love."[63] But, for anyone who is inspired by love for the good, it would be contradictory to look down upon others and to reserve the good for himself. On the contrary, he would want to impart good to all who are receptive, for, by the good and through the love which he imparts, he will awaken a response and arouse a desire for perfection and for the good in those who are lacking in love. Theoretical speculations and moral philosophy were inextricably tied together in Contarini's philosophical system.

Thus, for Contarini, the treatment of problems of the social order was combined with philosophical discussion, and, vice versa, philosophical discussion issued frequently into consideration of social and political problems. This point is clearly illustrated by Contarini's early work *De officio episcopi*.[64] Only its last part provides what a book with such a title can be expected to contain. There Contarini inveighed against the luxury of the princes of the church, the frequent absences of bishops from their diocese, the use of churches for business negotiations or political discussions, the superstitious veneration of *reliquiae* and the exaggerated adornment of chapels; he urged a bishop to have a simple but dignified household, to study Christian and not profane authors, to preach, to take a personal interest in the moral well-being of the people of his diocese, and to use his income for the support of the poor. Thus, like many of his most distinguished contemporaries, Contarini demanded a reform of the church, and his ideas are close to those which his friends Giustiniani and Quirini formulated in the *Libellus ad Leonem X*,[65] which has been called "the most comprehensive and most radical of all reform programs since the conciliar period."[66] It seems likely that Contarini knew this work of his Camaldolese friends. He certainly discussed its ideas with them.

Contarini's outline of the functions of a bishop is preceded by a discussion of the personal qualities which a bishop ought to possess. And this part, in turn, is preceded by a section which places the entire problem in a philosophical context. Contarini began by emphasizing that, although perfection cannot be reached by man, the striving for perfection is implied in man's rational nature. On certain levels of human existence this struggle for perfection can be conducted with man's natural faculties. On a higher level this striving requires divine assistance. The goal to which man aims with his innate forces is less worthy than that for which he struggles with God's help. Yet the striving for perfection on the lower level represents the necessary preparation for the striving for perfection on the higher level. The application of these theoretical statements to the concrete issue with which Contarini was concerned is that man lives in two societies: in a political organization and in a Christian world, the latter being ranked above the former. These societies must be organized in such a way that they are directed toward perfection, that they permit an approach to the realization of the ideal by which they were formed. According to Contarini, it is inherent in the concept of society that it has both rulers and those who are ruled. A society must be organized in such a way that it places the right ruler in control. And the ruler himself must possess qualities that make him fit to rule. He must have an image of the idea toward which the life of society ought to be directed, and his own conduct must provide an example of a life directed toward this perfection.[67] Thus, in accordance with his idea of establishing the ruler not only as the organizer of society but also as a pattern for the moral conduct of its members, Contarini embarked on a long discussion of the qualities demanded of a bishop. It was in accordance, also, with his view of a graduated hierarchy, in which the Christian society stands on the base of the political society, that he discussed first the virtues required of a member of political society and then the particular Christian virtues a bishop needs. "Someone might object that so far we seem to describe a citizen rather than a bishop. Our answer is that a bishop should not lack in the moral and social virtues although they do not belong to him alone but also to others. They are the foundations; without them those which are peculiar to a bishop and properly his would necessarily collapse."[68]

This somewhat more extended discussion of *De officio episcopi* seems appropriate because this book discloses some fundamental ideas of Contarini's thinking. Despite the evidently eclectic character of his philosophy, it was permeated by one assumption that was very much his own and that represented a result of his exchange of ideas with Giustiniani and Quirini. This assumption was that behind every existence and every status there is an idea which is an outgrowth of the divine spirit and which man, by his own innate goodness, is drawn to realize. Thus, every activity, if it is moving in the direction of perfection, is hallowed. Furthermore, Contarini saw a close connection between political organization and the church. The political society may stand lower than the Christian community in the universal hierarchy; nevertheless, the right political organization is the necessary basis on which to prepare for the development of the life of the church. This interconnection is strikingly formulated in a sentence of *De officio episcopi* dealing with heresy: "It removes not only the foundations of faith but it also undermines the foundation of any government."[69]

III

We can now turn to Contarini's *De magistratibus et republica Venetorum.*[70] It should be clear that Contarini's interest in politics was inseparable from his philosophical and religious concerns; the problems of social organization formed an integral and essential part of his philosophical system. Politics was, for him, a subordinate branch of philosophy and, as such, had a moral purpose: to teach how man's virtues could be developed in society and through society. Contarini's book on Venice was intended to demonstrate the importance of a right social order for man's striving toward a higher life. This basic theme is clearly stated in the first book of the work. Man, Contarini explained, is a social being and must live together with others for material reasons. But, because men need each others' help and assistance, their living together serves also to develop their innate inclination toward the good. Thus, from the outset the purpose of social life is not only to secure man's material existence but to lead him to a good and blissful life.

This view of the nature and aim of political organization gives to Venice its particular importance. People admire Venice because of its wealth and the splendor of its houses, because of its situation, which provides security from external enemies, because of the extension of its empire, because of its commercial importance, which brings into the city peoples and goods from all corners of the world. Contarini was enough of a Venetian patriot to admit that these facets of Venetian life were marvelous. Nevertheless, he stated, these were not the things for which Venice ought to be admired: "There is one more thing in this city which far exceeds all those things we have spoken of. That is not only my opinion but also the opinion of all those who do not believe that a city is walls and houses only, but think that a city is primarily constituted by the assemblage and the order of the people who live in it and deserves the name of a republic only if its aim and organization enables man to lead a blissful life."[71] "No state has existed which possesses institutions and laws equally apt to lead to a good and blissful life."[72] The Venetian constitution is better suited to approach a realization of the moral purpose of political society than any other. That is why, Contarini believed, Venice needed to be studied and to become better known.

Contarini was proud of the excellence of the Venetian institutions; with the knowledge with which his position as a Venetian noble and his experiences as a Venetian politician had equipped him, he was able to describe with precision and in detail the political procedures in Venice which for many decades had aroused astonishment and admiration in the minds of foreigners. Although some reports of the manner in which a doge was elected or the Venetian councils deliberated had been provided in previous writings,[73] Contarini's account of these transactions was far superior to anything written previously. This disclosure of the arcana of Venetian politics constituted the chief attraction of Contarini's book in subsequent centuries. However, Contarini was not only better informed than previous writers; his basic approach was different. In earlier discussions of the Venetian form of government, the thesis that Venice was an ideal state had been mainly a label that justified the attention given to this subject. In Contarini's mind, on the other hand, the idea of what a republic was or ought to be was primary, and a description of the working of Venetian politics seemed to him a worthy undertaking because—and insofar as—it approached this idea.

Contarini's attempt to place Venetian politics *sub specie* of a permanent, divinely inspired idea determined the distinctive character of this work and goes far to explain its weaknesses and its strength. His treatise is an idealization because it emphasizes only those aspects of Venetian political life that help to explain how governments can lead people to perfection. War and power politics are almost entirely omitted. Venice undertook military action only when it was attacked, and even then its citizens avoided bearing arms.[74] These aspects of politics must be minimized because nothing can be gained for the moral purposes of society by involvement in war. The need to eliminate force in relations between states was Contarini's deepest conviction. In all his diplomatic missions he pursued constantly and tenaciously the aim of the establishment of peace among the Christian powers. And it was his good fortune that in the times of his political service this aim coincided with the interests of the Venetian government.[75]

But the internal organization of Venice, also, was presented by Contarini as having come about from wise deliberation and general agreement rather than from clashes and conflicts among the groups of society. For instance, annals and histories of Venice available to Contarini[76] offered enough material to show clearly that the Great Council was the product of conflicts arising from efforts to limit the power of the dukes and to secure control for a wealthy aristocracy. For Contarini, however, the Great Council owed its origin to prudent discussions and harmonious agreements among the citizens about the best government. This was the manner in which Contarini thought that men ought to proceed in forming a political organization. His treatise was intended to show how men ought to act in politics rather than how they did act. Like so many political treatises of his time, it was a normative treatment. Yet this approach constituted its strength. Because, in Contarini's view, social life was meant to serve man's development toward the spiritual world, his point of departure was a concern for the welfare of all human beings living together in a community rather than the efficiency of that community's institutions. His view extended beyond the discussion of government machinery and of prescriptions for the behavior of rulers to embrace the entire body of society. For instance, he included in his discussion of Venice the organization of the fraternities and guilds of the craftsmen and artisans, who, from a political point of view, were ruled and not rulers; mention of them was usually omitted from writings on politics. In focusing on those elements related to a philosophical concept of society, he presented Venice as an idea rather than a concrete reality. Probably it was just this aspect of the treatise which obtained for it a significant place in the political thought of the following centuries.

Although a close connection existed between Contarini's treatise on Venice and his philosophical and religious thought, one still may ask whether there was a particular occasion that stimulated him to take up this object.

At the end of the fifteenth century Bernardo Giustiniani, an old Venetian noble who had had a distinguished political career, composed a life of San Marco.[77] At the beginning of this work Giustiniani explained that he was led to the undertaking because the saint seemed to have become almost forgotten; many, to Giustiniani's horror, did not seem to know any longer where he was buried and what Venice owed to its patron saint.[78] Giustiniani was deeply concerned that the new intellectual interests and activities of the time were corroding the old beliefs, customs, and traditions which had made Venice great. Giustiniani's concern was the more striking because he had been a prominent patron of humanists.

265

The defeat Venice suffered in its war against the League of Cambrai intensified the doubts of those who feared that the Venetians, seduced by new philosophies and greater material prosperity, had deviated from the ideals of their ancestors and lost their old virtues. In these years Egnazio, a Venetian scholar, began to write a book in which he compared the great figures of Venetian history with those of the ancient world and tried to demonstrate that the heroes of Venetian history had cultivated the same simple virtues that the great men of the ancient world had possessed. It is interesting that Egnazio referred to Bernardo Giustiniani as an example everyone should hold before himself "like an oracle."[79] Clearly, Egnazio's book was intended to be an appeal to return to the old virtues and customs of Venetian life. Egnazio was a close friend of Contarini's;[80] Contarini's treatise on Venice also belongs within this context—hope that Venice could be saved by returning to its traditions. Like the church, which needed renewal through a return to the spirit of its beginnings, Venice too needed reform by means of a return to the ideas expressed in the myth of its past.

But was there still another and more particular stimulus for the composition of this work on Venice? There is an incident in Contarini's life which raises an intriguing question. He began to write his treatise on the Venetian government during his diplomatic mission to Charles V. In the beginning of his work Contarini mentioned that information about Venice ought to be particularly welcome to foreigners who had no opportunity of knowing about the excellent and almost perfect political order Venice had achieved.[81] Certainly, Contarini must have met on this mission many foreigners who, Contarini might have thought, were in need of information about Venice. Yet among them there was one whose lack of knowledge he might have particularly regretted. In Bruges, on August 18, 1521, he invited for dinner "a very learned English gentleman named Master Thomas More."[82] This characterization suggests that Contarini was well aware of the intellectual importance of his English guest. E. H. Harbison has described More as "a deeply devoted Christian and a scholar in all his instincts, but one who was called early to a busy and exhausting career as a lawyer and public official. The strong streak of Christian piety in him almost led him to become a Carthusian monk."[83] It would not be wrong to describe Contarini in almost the same way. One cannot help wondering whether Contarini's meeting with a man of such similar sympathies might not have stimulated the Venetian to the writing of a work which could show that, in order to find a place that can lead its citizens to a good and happy life, one need not travel as far as Utopia.

The biographies of Contarini written soon after his death[84] have somewhat the character of hagiography. They show him dying like a martyr, crushed by the burdens of his religious duties. And these writings have played their role in creating the view that only in the last period of his existence, in the years of his cardinalate, had Contarini arrived at the appropriate setting for his life. His previous political activities seemed of subordinate interest, a side issue rather than a central factor in his life. But there are some other contemporary portraits of Contarini composed when he had just been made a Cardinal.[85] They appear to give the picture of a very different person, a man involved in every worthwhile concern of his time: a philosopher, a scholar, a political thinker, a successful diplomat, and a devoted servant of his republic, highly respected and admired because of the selflessness with which he strove in all these activities for the realization of the common good. These characterizations suggest, more correctly than the later biographies, that Contarini possessed a view of life which saw fulfillment "in the midst of the city." If Contarini is seen in this way, the famous scene of May 21, 1534 in the Venetian Great Council[86] gains full poignancy: the message was brought of Contarini's appointment to the cardinalate; most members applauded, old Alvise Mocenigo fiercely shouted, "These priests have robbed us of the best gentleman this city has," and Contarini himself, stunned and uncomprehending, could say only, "Why Cardinal? I am a councillor of the government of Venice."

11. Venice in the Crisis of the League of Cambrai

The battle of Agnadello was lost; three weeks later the Venetians were forced to abandon Padua. The only foothold Venice was able to keep on the *terra ferma* was Treviso. With the loss of most of its possessions in northern Italy the Venetian empire was confined to the sea.

For the Venetians the grim summer of 1509 invited reflections about the mutability of fortune. Indeed, in the pages of the diary Girolamo Priuli kept, the report on the events of this summer is interspersed with meditations on the causes of this sudden fall from greatness and power. That this reversal was God's will was clear to Priuli as well as to all his contemporaries. The question Priuli pondered was why God had found it necessary to mete out this cruel punishment to Venice.[1]

In his search for an answer Priuli discovered one reason after another why Venice had aroused God's ire. First of all, there was the immoderate pride and arrogance of the Venetian ruling group, of the *padri et senatori et nobelli veneti*. In their contempt and disregard for all those who did not belong to this group they neglected their foremost duty, the dispensation of justice. They were dilatory in granting people a hearing and in pro-

---

Originally published in *Renaissance Venice,* ed. John Hale (London, Faber and Faber, 1973), pp. 274–292. This is the first, preliminary outline of a subject I intend to treat in broader compass.

269

nouncing judgment; consequently, court proceedings became protracted and as expenses increased many found it impossible to gain justice and maintain their rights. As administrators on the *terra ferma* the Venetian nobles had lived in pomp and splendor. Because many of them could ill afford this life of luxury, which they believed their exalted position required, they accepted bribes. When complaints about their behavior reached Venice, their families and friends defended them; and the support of influential patricians was exchanged for promises to vote for them. In consequence, these accusations were disregarded, however justified they might have been, and it is easily understood why, in despair, the population of the *terra ferma* revolted against Venetian rule when the opportunity arose.

In other aspects of public life, too, the Venetian patricians had offended God by disregarding their sworn duties. Despite vows to keep government business secret, everyone knew almost immediately what had been said and decided in meetings of the Council of Ten or the Senate. Despite an oath to elect officials without disclosing their choice, electors signalled how they would vote to the candidate they preferred; those who refrained from such bargainning were kept out of office.

In Priuli's view maladministration was only a particular aspect of a more general process: moral corruption was widespread. Many of the nunneries in the city were actually brothels. Because of the influence of those who frequented them—not only youths and foreigners but also older patricians in high positions—and because of the social status of the nuns, who frequently came from noble families, all the measures adopted to eradicate this evil remained ineffective.

Another sign of moral turpitude was the openness with which homosexuality was practiced in Venice. Young men made themselves look like women: they wore jewels; they perfumed themselves; and their clothes exposed most of their naked bodies. Parents did not dare to discipline their sons, and let them go their own ways. Again, the reason was that high officials, members of the Senate, were practitioners of this vice. Even the Venetian noblewomen, who in olden times had been distinguished by chastity and simplicity, were now eager for all kinds of amusement and tried to appear and behave as seductive as possible. Again, there was no strict enforcement of the laws against luxury; a week after they were issued they were forgotten.

Priuli was convinced not only that these vices had provoked divine retribution but also that the moral corruption of the Venetian ruling group was the direct cause of political mistakes that had created the difficult, almost desperate, situation in which Venice found herself in 1509. The Pope had become hostile because the greed of the Venetian patricians in reserving ecclesiastical benefices for themselves had violated papal rights. Because the Venetian nobles had become accustomed to a soft life they had neglected to take appropriate measures for defense. "The doge and the Venetian senators wanted both to remain quietly and comfortably at home and to sleep in their own beds but they also wanted to be victorious. To have these two things together is difficult, almost impossible."[2] One could scarcely expect mercenaries and foreign soldiers to fight courageously and tenaciously if they were not commanded by men whose existence depended on the outcome of the battle. "If the Venetian rulers wish to keep their Italian possessions they will have to learn the military art."

For Priuli morals and politics were closely connected. Venice's fame and greatness were due to its overseas enterprises and these had required a hard and strenuous life. The expansion over the *terra ferma* had been a mistake—the result of a search for a life in less arduous and more pleasant surroundings.

Priuli's outcry against the Venetian ruling group must be an expression of views widely held at the time; at least very similar complaints and criticisms can be found in the diary of Marino Sanuto four years later. The war was still going on with all the ups and downs and sudden changes of fortune characteristic of military events of that period. Padua, whose loss Priuli had regarded as sealing the fate of Venice, had been reconquered in July of 1509 and Venice had regained some of its possessions on the *terra ferma*. The Venetians even succeeded in separating Julius II from the anti-Venetian coalition by surrendering to him the disputed territories and control over ecclesiastical appointments in their domain. The French and German armies in northern Italy remained formidable, however, and after fighting and maneuvering with alternating success, the French and Germans advanced far into the *terra ferma* by the end of the summer of 1510. In the campaign of the following year the French and the Germans continued their advance and approached the lagoons. The Pope and Venice realized the need for allies and in October they concluded a Holy League with Spain and England against France. The magnificent procession with which this event was celebrated showed the relief the Venetians felt: "Cessa i sospir, cessa li to pianto, che felice ti farò più ch'a inanti," was inscribed on the statue of St. Mark.[3]

The campaign of the summer of 1512 was full of sudden, dramatic changes. First the powers of the Holy League advanced, but then the French won the battle of Ravenna and northern and central Italy seemed to be at their feet. However, the losses with which the victory had been bought were high, and the French withdrew. At the end of May the Venetians were again in possession of most of the *terra ferma*. But in Julius II's view the French remained a dangerous threat and he believed he could be secure only if he broke up the French alliance with the German emperor. Consequently the Pope tried to pressure the Venetians to cede Verona, Vicenza, and Brescia to Maximilian. The Venetians were unwilling to give up these towns and the result was a sudden reversal of alliances. On November 23, 1513 an alliance between Venice and France was signed. The event was greeted with the same enthusiasm with which the conclusion of the Holy League had been welcomed a year before. The new alliance seemed to establish a balance of forces which would quickly lead to peace, especially since by then Julius II was dead. Even when, against expectations, Julius' successor Leo X continued the war, the Venetians were confident that the French and Venetian military forces would quickly gain the upper hand in northern Italy. But in May 1513, at Novara, the Swiss inflicted a heavy defeat on the French. Padua came under siege; for the rest the entire *terra ferma* was lost again to the advancing Germans. The villages along the Brenta were looted. Mestre was burned. After four years of war the situation in the summer of 1513 was as desperate as it had been in the summer of 1509.

To Sanuto, who observed from the bell-tower of St. Mark's the burning and looting of the enemy, the entire area along the Brenta appeared "red like blood."[4] His reaction was very much like that of Priuli four years earlier.[5] He ventilated his desperation in bitter criticisms of the Venetian ruling group. He accused them of negligence in taking defensive measures and arranging for provisions. The patricians were so wed to their soft life that even in the present emergency they convoked the Great Council only to transact routine business. Instead, they ought to call the people together in Piazza San Marco, arm them, and send them out against the enemy. So advised Sanuto.

Priuli and Sanuto indicated that they not only spoke for themselves but also reproduced the opinions they had heard expressed by their compatriots. Their diaries show that doubts about the political course, which difficulties and defeats inevitably raise, were widened to questions about the efficiency and equity of the Venetian system of government and about the contrast between the reality of the situation and the values from which the Venetian system of government was traditionally believed to draw its strength. The political issues were extended into social and moral areas. Undoubtedly, the war of the League of Cambrai brought about a deep crisis which invited reexamination of Venetian society in all its aspects. How probing was this self-examination? Did it lead to changes in the Venetian political and social system? Did the crisis which the League of Cambrai precipitated represent a turning point in Venetian history? The following examination does not fully answer these questions, but perhaps it will direct attention to the importance of the problems.

I

The view that moral corruption was the decisive reason for the decline of Venetian power was not only one expressed by private citizens but also an officially held and recognized thesis. In the rare speeches the doge Loredan (doge 1501-1521) made in the Great Council, he stressed regularly that immorality was the basic reason for the difficulties in which Venice found itself.[6] He argued that the power Venice had achieved had made its citizens so proud and overbearing that God was forced to humiliate them, although it was to be hoped that he would not abandon them forever. In the desperate days of October 1513 Loredan discussed Venetian moral failings at greater length than ever before. Venice had been unjust and unfair in its treatment of foreigners. Loredan criticized the pomp with which the Venetian officials on the *terra ferma* conducted their lives. But the doge's chief target was the Venetians' indulgence in luxury. He mentioned that the large hall on the ground floor of their palaces, which in earlier times had served for the transaction of business and in which weapons had been kept hanging on the wall, was now transformed into a festival dining room. Loredan confessed his own responsibility and guilt for this; he had been among those who had abandoned the traditional custom.[7]

In accordance with the view that the political crisis was the result of divine punishment, measures to regain God's good graces formed a considerable part of Venetian war legislation. At crucial moments in the war or during diplomatic negotiations the patriarch was asked by the doge to arrange that in all churches prayers were said "so that God would assist this republic against its enemies."[8] On the occasion of feast days or victories the government ordered the distribution of alms to the indigent or money to poor monks in order to implore "the favor and the assistance of all-powerful God"; those who received these gifts were expected to pray to God "for our state."[9] The timber of an old galley was ordered to be used for the building of a church and a monastery in honor of St. Joseph "so that, by means of his merits and his intervention, God might be inclined to pity and mercifulness toward our state."[10] When success came it was acknowledged to be God's work who, "without any merits on the part of the Venetians" had shown "in a miraculous way His power and His mercy."[11] The day of Santa Marina, on which Padua was reconquered, was decreed a feast day. On that day it was strictly forbidden to work or trade and the doge led the procession to the Church of Santa Marina and attended a mass at St. Mark's.[12] Certainly, such governmental measures were customary at critical moments in all Renaissance states. Nevertheless, the manner in which the councils gave direct commands to the patriarch and intervened in ecclesiastical affairs reveals an assumption of the existence of a complete integration of all civic activity—political, religious, social, and economic.

The view that political salvation depended on calling a halt to moral decline found expression in legislation regulating the conduct of social life. Of course, this again must be considered customary, but it is characteristic that just in the critical summer after the battle of Agnadello, on June 29, 1509, the government decided to give a more stringent form to a law of 1486 directed against immorality in the nunneries.[13] Anyone who had sexual relations with nuns in the monasteries or lured them away from the nunneries was banned from Venice for life; should such a violator be found on Venetian territory he would be put into prison and anyone denouncing him would receive 500 ducats. Moreover, laywomen were forbidden to use nunneries as their residence and servants had to wear clerical habits; no longer were they allowed to enter the nunnery in secular dress.

Laws regulating morals required a magistracy assuring their observance, and all such legislation, particularly the laws against luxury, were accompanied by attempts to establish such an office.[14] After officals had been elected for this purpose from time to time a special office of three *savi* for enforcing the sumptuary laws was established in 1476, but it was short lived. Closed in 1503, its functions were transferred to other magistrates, who were expected to deal with these problems in addition to their regular duties. But the defeat of Agnadello revived the notion of the need for a special magistracy to enforce strict observance of the laws against luxury. In 1510 the Senate decided to elect from the procurators of St. Mark two members who would "curb, correct, and punish" transgressors of the sumptuary laws. However, in these difficult years the procurators found themselves overburdened with business and unable to give these problems the necessary attention. On March 13, 1512 the Senate decided that, in the serious situation in which the city found itself, it was urgent to "placate the anger of Our Lord" and to establish a permanent magistracy consisting of three *provveditori* with the function of preventing "immoderate and excessive expenditure." The *provveditori sopra le pompe* issued a decree covering all aspects of luxury.[15] Some of the articles of the decree repeated previous legislation and others were to become obsolete through subsequent laws, but the decree of 1512 might be regarded as a basic code providing a survey of Venetian sumptuary law. As such, this code deserves attention because it throws light on the habits of the Venetian upper class.

The decree aimed at restricting luxury in three different categories: dress, housing, and festivities. The regulations concerning the manner in which men and women should dress were mainly inspired by regard for morality. Women's clothes were to be simple, each dress made out of one kind of material. Transparent materials and lace could not be used for gowns. Men were forbidden attire that would increase physical attractiveness. Shirts were to cover the entire upper part of the body and close neatly around the neck. There were detailed rules about the jewelry women might wear. The value of golden necklaces or pearls woven into ladies' hair was not to surpass 100 ducats and the use of golden or silver threads or golden belts was prohibited. All this illustrates that status was largely determined by ostentation and that the open display of wealth was customary in the upper class and distinguished it from the rest of Venetian society.

The same basic motive—stricter morals and greater economy —can be seen in the regulations on housing and festivities. A maximum of 150 ducats was placed on expenses for decorating a single room with wood panelling, goldleaf, or paintings. In addition, the list of objects the householder was forbidden to buy was long: gold boxes, gilded mirrors, cushions of silk decorated with pearls, curtains of brocade or damask, silk hangings, gold or silver vessels; if, after the issue of this decree, anyone acquired any of these objects they would be confiscated and the owner fined.

Under the decree of 1512 marriage celebrations were sharply regulated; what the law still permitted gives us some idea of the immense luxury in vogue on such occasions in times when conspicuous waste provoked no criticism. According to the decree, the family of the bride was still expected to give six small parties for not more than twenty people and two big parties for fifty people in the interval between the engagement and the wedding. The bridegroom was permitted to give two parties, one for eighty and the other for fifty people. In decorating the house and the tables expensive novelties could not be introduced and torches or candles for lighting the rooms were to be used with economy. Delicacies—pheasants or expensive sweets—could not be served, but the prohibitions did not include marzipan. Responsible for observance of these decrees

276

and susceptible to punishment in case of transgression were not only heads of houses but also cooks.

Modesty of expenditure was one aim of the sumptuary legislation; the other was to discourage lasciviousness. New dances popular with the young were condemned, particularly the "most shameless dance of the cap and other French dances full of lecherous and sinful gestures."[16] Balls were to be confined to the palaces of those who gave them; no dancing outside in the streets; masks were forbidden.

These regulations were dictated by a variety of reasons. One was political. If the wealthy patricians in power continued their luxurious manner of life while the majority of the population suffered from the war and had to make sacrifices, dissatisfaction and unrest were unavoidable and the will to resist would be weakened. In a decree of February 14, 1511, the Senate stated that some "do not cease to make many superfluous and extraordinary expenses by which they throw away great sums of money. This arouses general dissatisfaction and causes damage. Such people demonstrate that they have no real love for their fatherland; in addition many of these lavish spenders haven't paid their taxes which are raised for no other purpose but for preservation of the state and every person's life."[17] The last sentence of this decree indicates another cause for the increased attention given to sumptuary laws during the war of the League of Cambrai. Money spent on luxuries could not be taxed and the reason for the restrictions placed on the acquisition of gold or jewels was that the wealthy people invested their capital in such objects to avoid being taxed or forced to give their money to the Venetian state bank, the Monte, whose shares were steadily declining in value. There are also indications that these measures were intended to prevent Venetian gold reaching foreign, hostile countries, although the particular emphasis which was given to a ban on foreign fashions and materials may have been simply an outlet of xenophobic emotionalism which always arises in wartime.

Nevertheless, religion was the decisive motive in the legislation against luxury. This was regularly emphasized in the introductions providing justifications for these decrees. Here it was stated that these laws were made to "avoid offending the divine majesty,"[18] or that, by spending money for the gratification of their desires, people act "with little reverence for God and show little fear of Him."[19] To return to God's good graces was the primary reason for reintroducing and reforming the sumptuary laws at the time of the war of Cambrai.

These laws were designed to restore the way of life that had existed in the early times of the Venetian Republic. They were necessary because "we must with all possible zeal and care imitate our ancestors."[20] For the Venetians, as for all of that time, perfection existed at the beginning; then corruption set in and decline ensued. The true aim was "to return to the beginnings" and to restore life as it had been then: simple, modest, in accord with God's law. The simple life had created the strength which had made possible the rise of Venice. To revive this way of life was the precondition for Venice's salvation. It appears that measures toward restoring religious faith and moral discipline required complementation in political and social life.

II

It is easier to appeal for religious and moral renewal than to undertake political reform and institutional change. Did the criticisms Priuli and Sanuto expressed in their diaries have any political consequences? To what extent did the crisis of the war of the League of Cambrai represent a turning point in Venetian political and institutional history?

A study of the Venetian archives from the years 1509 to 1517 gives the impression that a small group of men was desperately struggling with an endless number of unexpected and diverse tasks.

There was the problem of the refugees from the *terra ferma*. In 1509 the peasants from the area around Padua streamed into the city fleeing from the burning and looting of hostile mercenaries. Homeless, they wandered with their animals through the streets. The government housed them in monasteries—in San Giorgio Maggiore, San Niccolò, and Sant' Andrea—which stood emtpy because the monks were disinclined to share the hardships of the war with the Venetian citizens and had abandoned them "with scant charity."[21] The return of the peasants to their homes after improvement of the military situation posed new problems. They needed seed to sow their land. Decrees were issued which stated that the landowners must provide seed and described how they were to be compensated.[22] But the refugee problem continued to plague the government. In 1510 refugees from Vicenza arrived and were eventually housed in the Fondaco dei Tedeschi.[23] The crowding of the city created serious problems of security and health. Laws against theft, robberies, and violence had to be tightened; carrying of arms was prohibited.

The councils were continuously occupied with intervention in economic affairs necessitated by the impact of the war on trade. In general the interruption of shipping, particularly to and from northern Europe, resulted in intensive smuggling against which measures had to be taken.[24] The loss of control over the *terra ferma* aroused the fear of famine. Warehouses were built to store grain.[25] Actually the fear of starvation was exaggerated, although at certain times food for the refugees seems to have been minimal or lacking.[26] Because the enemy troops had driven away the cattle there was a serious shortage of meat and measures were taken to bring cattle into Venice by ship.[27] As a result of the war the ordinary course of business was disrupted and emergency situations requiring extraordinary measures arose.[28] At the beginning of the war the government was engaged in winding up the affairs of the Agostini bank which had failed in 1508. In May 1509 there was a run on the Pisani bank; the government intervened and gave assistance in order to avoid a failure which might shake confidence in the financial strength of the Venetian republic. In November 1513 when a run started on the bank of Girolamo Priuli, government officials went to the Priuli office and guaranteed full payment to the creditors; with this act they dispersed the crowd demanding payment. (The Priuli bank was not saved but an ordinary liquidation had been assured.) Government intervention in business affairs was not unusual but became more pressing and more frequent in wartime.

A wearisome, unending concern of the officials and the councils was the situation on the *terra ferma*. Because it was sometimes in Venetian control and sometimes in that of the enemy, administrators left on the approach of the enemy and returned with his retreat. Changes in personnel were common because in the interval of enemy occupation some officials were elected to new positions; others became ill or died; and for others the term of office had ended. Careful supervision of the affairs of the *terra ferma* was particularly important because the regular administrative functions were now coupled with additional tasks.[29] It was necessary to punish traitors and to reward those who had remained loyal. Compensation had to be determined for those who had suffered losses because of their adherence to the Venetian cause. This was a difficult job because these proceedings offered many opportunities for deception and fraud. Yet, because of the closeness of the enemy, the establishment of a stable situation on the *terra ferma* was urgently needed.

In order to be sure of administrators who would handle affairs on the *terra ferma* effectively, the Collegio and Council of Ten made many appointments disregarding the electoral rights of the Senate and the Great Council. This created friction; indeed, after the emergency was over, the Senate and Great Council annulled the appointments made by the Collegio and successfully reclaimed the right to elect.[30]

The war on the *terra ferma* also involved the Venetian government in military administration. The government had to take measures to protect the citizens of the towns on the *terra ferma* against vandalism and robbery by the soldiery. Among the Venetian troops there was a militia composed of men from the villages and towns of the *terra ferma.* If they deserted, the government decreed, their noses and ears were to be cut off.[31] But the inhabitants of villages that had been loyal to Venice were freed from taxes or received special privileges.[32] Jobs had to be provided for individuals who had lost a limb fighting for Venice and could no longer do military service or continue their regular activity; and provision had to be made for widows.[33] There was no general law covering the various aspects of the ravages of war; each case was determined separately and then presented to the Senate for approval.

The burden of this extraordinary work had to be carried by men whose duties were heavy in peacetime: they were administrators of a city with 100,000 inhabitants and policymakers of a world power. For these responsibilities the number of men in direct authority, as in all states of this time, was small: the Collegio with the *savi,* the Council of Ten, and the Quarantia. The ruling group was well aware of the need to distribute these charges among a greater number. Different methods were used to ease the pressure. Special committee for the execution and supervision of particular tasks were established, although the *savi* set the guidelines for the work of these committees and then selected and defended them in the councils. For the time of the emergency the number of the *savi* was increased—a necessary arrangement because some of the *savi* served as commissioners with the military forces and for long periods were absent from Venice.

Nevertheless, the strain on those who filled the high offices was immense, because in addition to the variety of tasks mentioned they were continuously harassed by what was their most important and most arduous task: providing money for the conduct of the war. Campaigns lasted from early spring to October and each year arrangements had to be made with *condottieri* for the army which Venice could field. In 1509, after Padua had been reconquered, expenses for the troops to defend it amounted to 50,000 ducats.[34]

Venetian state finances grew precarious during the war because, as with all wars, the usual sources of income declined or dried up altogether. The revenues of the Venetian government consisted, like the finances of the other Italian city-states, of indirect and direct taxes. The indirect taxes comprised a great variety of imposts: tolls, customs on imports, sales taxes on grain, many foodstuffs, and on clothes, duties on financial transactions, rents for shops and offices in buildings belonging to the government, particularly on the Rialto, and so forth. Some of these taxes were raised directly by government officials, others were farmed out. It is obvious that the decline in economic activity, particularly in trade, decreased and in some cases almost extinguished the revenues from these taxes or duties. For instance, the rents on shops had to be lowered continuously and promises of special privileges, such as exemption from taxes for a number of years, were made in order to find occupants. The shrinking of indirect taxes had its impact on direct taxes as well, because the revenue from some of the duties was reserved for the payment of interest on the consolidated public debt, the Monte from which the government drew money for current expenses.

There were three kinds of direct taxes in Venice. One was tax on landed property on the *terra ferma;* in normal times it produced a good solid revenue but during the war of the League of Cambrai this tax became almost negligible. Secondly there was the *decima,* a property and income tax which was raised from time to time. And thirdly there were the forced loans to which the government took recourse in times of urgent financial need; for the money the citizen loaned to the government he received shares in the Monte which bore interest. Steadily rising government expenses increased the capital of the Monte derived from forced loans, and even before the war interest payments were in arrears. The original Monte, the Monte Vecchio, became complemented by another Monte, the Monte Nuovo to which other sources of revenue for interest payments were assigned. But when in wartime the indirect taxes failed to produce enough revenue both Monti went bankrupt and a new Monte, the Monte Novissimo, was established in the fall of 1509. But these bankruptcies reduced the citizens' capacity to pay the *decima* and made them much averse to lending money to the government.

The Venetians had to chart their course in a situation of decreasing economic opportunities, declining revenues, mounting expenses, and rapid need for ready money. They did what, almost up to the present, governments have always done in such situations: they tried to reduce expenses wherever possible, they tried to discover new sources of revenue, and they raised taxes.

One of the economy measures adopted in previous times was to stop paying official salaries, and with the exception of some lower offices and of administrators on the reconquered *terra ferma,* this policy was maintained throughout the war. Loopholes in the taxation system were filled; an attempt was made to bring up to date estimates of taxable property which frequently had become obsolete.[35] Supervision of accounting methods was tightened.[36] Special committees were appointed to examine possiblities for greater economy in the administration and in the conduct of the war. For instance, in their eagerness to eliminate waste the *savi* investigated the rumor that the painters entrusted with the decoration of the hall of the Great Council had recived 750 ducats for two paintings which they had not even begun, whereas other good masters were willing to execute these paintings for 250 ducats. In the end the painters in charge provided a satisfactory explanation and consequently Titian could continue his work.[37]

In the search for additional revenue the obvious method was to eliminate exceptions. In 1509 foreigners were required to pay in taxes 50 per cent of the rent they were paying for houses.[38] And employees in the Fondaco dei Tedeschi were taxed.[39] Goods which the government had confiscated as security for unpaid taxes were sold. And payments which the Jews had to make for being allowed to live Venice were increased.

Yet all these measures were makeshift. The government had to place its reliance primarily on the *decima* and forced loans. The *decima* was raised with increasing frequency and the demand for forced loans, which was addressed particularly to wealthy citizens, became more immediate and urgent. In speeches to the Senate the doge appealed for loans and then spoke to each member individually.[40] Those who had no cash for taxes for forced loans were asked to deliver household objects made of sivler or gold. The government tried to obtain quick and prompt payment of taxes by announcing that those who paid at the earliest set term could use for payment of subsequent taxes part of the assignments on the Monte Novissimo which they would receive. Although such promises might have helped to meet a particularly urgent need, the final result was to decrease the amount of revenue from further taxes. As the war dragged on the financial situation became increasingly difficult.

Under this pressure the government took a step that was felt to jeopardize a basic tradition of Venetian political life: the government began to sell offices.[41] The process started in 1510 with a category of minor officials employed in the magistracies as scribes, notaries, accountants, and assistants; they were allowed to buy the positions they held either for a limited term or for life and in the latter case they could hand them over to their descendants subject to the payment of a certain percentage of the proceeds from their offices. In the same year nobles who loaned the government a specified sum of money were admitted to the Senate, but without voting privileges. In 1514 young noblemen who were eighteen years old or over but had not yet reached the required age of twenty-five were admitted to the Great Council in recognition of a loan. And nobles could be elected to the Collegio as *savi agli ordini* for the sum of 200 ducats even if they were still below the required age. A decree in 1515 made entry to Quarantia possible to men below the age limit in return for 100 ducats. Even admission among the procurators of St. Mark was tied to a financial offering.[42]

The most shocking measure of this kind was adopted late in 1515. It was established that the names of those who made loans to the state together with the amount, as well as the names of those who had refused to make loans, should be published before the Great Council proceeded to elections. Evidently those who had made loans would be elected and those who had lent the highest amount had the best chance. The functioning of this new decree can be easily studied in Sanuto;[43] for instance, on December 30, 1515, he reported that Zuan Emo had promised 900 ducats, Niccolò Malipiero 200 ducats, Christofal Canal 800, Sebastian Badoer 1,000, Sebastian Malipiero 300, Andrea Balbi 200, and Girolamo Bragadin 720. The outcome of the election was that both Zuan Emo and Sebastian Badoer—that is, the two who had given the highest amounts—were elected: the one *governador de l'intrade,* the other to the Council for Cyprus; and Andrea Balbi became judge of petitions. Among the candidates for these offices those whose names Sanuto did not list as having offered a loan received only a small number of votes. It should be noted, however, that some precautions were taken against granting electoral office to the highest bidder; to the four candidates among which the Great Council had to choose, the Senate assumed the right to add a fifth candidate, and the prestige the candidate supported by the Senate enjoyed could sometimes outweigh purely monetary considerations. There is no doubt that the result of this system of coupling elections with payments resulted in a considerable augmentation of government funds. In the following year, 1516, the list of offices to which this system was applied was extended even to offices such as governors on the *terra ferma* or *avogadori di comun.*

By waiving age requirements for membership in councils and by allowing financial considerations to influence elections the Venetian government was driven far off its traditional course. But these arrangements were emergency measures and they were abolished as soon as the crisis was over. In the war years there is no discernible trend toward changing or reforming existing institutions. From time to time appeals were issued for suggestions of new methods for raising taxes; in March 1515, proposals were made for a thorough reorganization of the tax system.[44] This suggestion was justified as a return to the past; as it was said, it is always "appropriate to follow the steps of our ancestors." The Venetians of earlier times intended to impose only one tax equal to all, although "because of the revolution of the times, that changes financial resources," new estimates should henceforward be made every five years. It was suggested that Venice ought to return to the imposition of a uniform tax. But such a fundamental change was rejected as inappropriate for the present. Clearly there was disinclination to make any systematic change.

The war increased the daily business of the ruling group to the limits, and the high-ranking officials were entirely satisfied with taking those measures which helped to get Venice through the extreme crises that rapidly followed one upon the other. The ruling group had neither the time nor the possibility to make institutional or constitutional innovations.

The dangers which threatened the state forced the small group of high officals to take quick action and to assume great responsibility. They worked closely together with the Senate; but with both councils—particularly with the Great Council—there was friction because the councils felt that their functions had been abrogated and their rights slighted. In addition it can be observed that high officials acted high-handedly and ruled somewhat recklessly over the population, even over other nobles. Consequently within the Venetian nobility a split developed between those in the highest offices who had a strong base in the Senate and the majority of the nobility sitting in the Great Council. Echoes of this split come to us from the diaries of Priuli and Sanuto with their criticism of the ruling officials, and the existence of this split might be deduced from the complaints about low attendance in the sessions of the councils.[45] Evidently the feeling had spread that it was not worthwhile attending the Great Council because nothing of much importance was done there. It might be added that the advantages—resulting from the financial emergency—which wealthy nobles had in obtaining office widened the distance between the effective ruling group of the nobility and the bulk of the patricians.

Because of the powerful hold this ruling group had over the whole range of Venetian life, the question with which we are concerned must focus on an examination of the extent to which its attitude and structure was changed by the war.

III

Among the eventful times through which Venice passed in the years of the war of the League of Cambrai, the summer of 1513 was the most dramatic. The high hopes with which the campaign began in spring, engendered by the conclusion of the French alliance, were dashed to the ground by the French defeat at Novara, which, among its consequences, brought the enemy again to the gates of Padua and Treviso.

On July 10 Doge Loredan appeared in the Great Council to speak to the Venetian patricians about what they should do in this critical situation.[46] As in some of his other speeches, he began by attributing the dangers and defeats to the sins and arrogance of the Venetian patricians. He admonished his audience to pay taxes and grant loans because, should defeat be the outcome, gold and silver would profit them nothing. Loredan insisted that those who had failed to pay their tax debts should be dismissed from their offices and excluded from the councils. Then he ended with an appeal—the core of his speech—to the patricians to go themselves out to the field, to the defense of Padua and Treviso.

In connection with this last demand a proposal was made by members of the Quarantia that those who did military service could be elected to any office in spite of tax debts, but after their return from the war they could take office only if they paid their taxes. This proposal aroused resentment and was quickly revised: by paying half of one's tax debts one could hold office. Even this revised proposal was not enthusiastically received, but nobody dared to oppose it. At this moment Marino Sanuto, who had never before spoken in the Great Council, arose and delivered a speech which he noted in his diary,[47] evidently convinced that this was his finest hour. The gist of the speech was that the poor nobles who scraped together some money to equip themselves for military service and to go to the defense of Padua and Treviso were unfairly treated if, having been honored for their service by election to an office, they were prevented from enjoying the fruits of this honor should they be unable to pay their tax debts. Sanuto therefore suggested that payment of tax debts be suspended for six months after a noble returned from the war. His proposal was accepted by an overwhelming majority: 1,019 to 159.

The interest of this story goes beyond the particular situation Sanuto described, for it illustrates the attitude of the Venetian ruling group toward participation in politics. This attitude is characterized by contradictory features: patriotism coupled with concern for personal interest and gain.

We cannot doubt that, as Priuli wrote in his diary, the great mass of the people "loved the republic and were devoted to it"; the people were convinced that "the freedom of Italy depended on the defense of Venice."[48] They felt that they had upheld Christianity against the Turks and that, even if their present enemies were Christians, they were again fighting to defend civilization against the barbarians. The only people to whom the Venetians could compare themselves were the Romans.

Gestures in imitation of ancient Roman courage were not lacking. Paolo Nani, who had inherited the magnificent palace of Doge Agostino Barbarigo outside Padua, ordered the building to be burned so that it could not serve as a stronghold for the enemy. Modeling himself after the Roman example was Andrea Gritti; when he and Giorgio Corner were sent out as commissioners to the army they refused to take any salary.[49] Gritti was almost continuously employed in difficult military enterprises. He spent some time as prisoner in France and when he first returned from there in 1513 he was looked to as the obvious candidate to be placed in charge of the defense of Padua. A decree was proposed which said that a person elected to this position who refused to take it would be fined 500 ducats. Gritti opposed this law saying that it was intended to make it impossible for him to decline should he be elected. He added that he had suffered much in the service of the state and was exhausted. But when the decree was adopted and, as he had foreseen, he was elected, he went to the Signoria "saying that he had never refused to make efforts for this distinguished state as it was the duty of every good patrician."[50] All this seems to be in accord with what Hieronimo Borgia, a contemporary historian and secretary to Bartolomeo d'Alviano, the chief Venetian general during the war, said: "Not even the Romans behaved toward Hannibal with greater courage than the Venetians."[51]

But there is also a different aspect which suggests an unrefrained concern with personal comfort and prosperity even in wartime. The appeal to the Venetian nobles to go as military leaders of small groups of citizens to the defense of Padua and Treviso had mixed reception.[52] There were complaints that the sons of some of the influential nobles, among them the sons of the doge, had not volunteered. There seemed to have been many cases in which nobles had declared their willingness to go but did not appear when they were called upon. The long lists of volunteers Sanuto published[53] deserve more careful study than they have received. The names of members of the upper ruling group are rather few and, not altogether unnaturally, military duties seem to have been undertaken primarily by the younger sons of these families. The possibility of being elected to office, even if in debt for taxes, and the establishment of monthly salaries showed the need to provide some stimuli to take on military duties; apparently the appeal was chiefly aimed at the poorer nobles. Great astonishment was aroused when Bernardo Boldù appeared in Padua with seven men whom he maintained at his own expense and did not ask for any compensation. It is characteristic that when in the summer of 1509 the first appeal to the nobility for military service was made the doge emphasized that "those nobles and citizens who will go into these cities can be sure that they will be as secure as if they were in Venice."[54] Their presence would chiefly serve to guarantee and protect the citizens of Padua from molestation by the soldiery.

The financial situation of Venice also throws a rather dubious light on the patriotism of the patricians. Tax morality in Venice—as in most other city-states—was low and the war did not better it. In the urgent need for money the deadlines for payment of tax debts were frequently prolonged because it was deemed more convenient to get cash payments than to confiscate goods or take other measures. A much used procedure for forcing the payment of taxes was to publish in the Great Council the names of those who were delinquent in paying their tax debts and to announce that they would be excluded from the councils and from holding office if they did not pay within a certain time. But there was great hesitation to apply this decree, and when it was finally done it emerged that some of the most prominent and wealthiest members of the ruling group—names that appear in crucial measures during these war years—were on this list:[55] in 1511, Gabriele Emo, Paolo Capello, Girolamo Quirini, and even Andrea Gritti; in 1512, Luca Zen, Antonio Grimani, Giorgio Corner, Antonio Tron, and again Paolo Capello, and in the same year Domenico Trevisan, Bernardo Bembo, Piero Badoer, Domenico Malipiero—all men who played a prominent role in Venetian politics in these decades.

Similarly the demand for loans gave occasion to subterfuges. It happened frequently that, when the doge made his appeal in the Senate for forced loans, people pledged large sums but did not appear with the money when it was requested. Again it had to be decreed that their names would be published in the Great Council and that they would be excluded from office; it is perfectly clear, however, that such a decree was used primarily as a threat; there was no great willingness to proceed against wealthy and influential patricians.

There are signs that people were aware of the contrast between reality and the façade of public virtue. Priuli, on the occasion of the recalling of Grimani from his exile in 1509, noticed that in its present ruined state Venice no longer maintained the principles of strict and equal justice and had lost its pride in maintaining its own laws and order.[56] Members of the ruling group felt themselves entitled to special privileges. At the wedding of a niece of the doge and at another wedding of a member of the Grimani family, permission was given to transgress the limits of the laws against luxury;[57] some weddings—for instance, a Contarini wedding—remained within the demands of the laws, but many others evidently did not care to observe the rules. As Sanuto noticed with displeasure in 1513, in spite of the war, amusements and dances were held in great numbers.[58]

Undoubtedly, there were men among the ruling group who were most earnestly concerned with the restoration of what they considered to have been the simple and strict life of earlier times. Some indication of this tension is the contempt shown by older members of the Senate toward those who had bought their entry into the council: some newcomers felt so uncom-

fortable and excluded that they asked to have their money returned because they wanted to abandon their seats.[59] But attempts to reject those who had paid their way in soon ceased.
One cannot suppress the feeling that for many members of the
wealthy upper group the main reason for making a show of
heroism was to maintain the morale of the Venetian population,
of the citizens as well as of the poorer members of the nobility.

It is obvious that this general characterization of the attitude
of a group does not do justice to the motives and expectations
that influenced individuals in participating in decisions or accepting them. There is little reason to doubt that in the days of
greatest danger belief in a connection between defeat and sin-
fulness was widespread, almost general, in Venice, and that
even if politics played an important part in the official emphasis
on renewed piety, in the legislation against luxury, and in the
establishment of a strict supervision of morality, such measures
also corresponded to what many considered a moral duty. Only
few, if any, embarked upon such measures for purely pragmatic
or opportunistic reasons. We can find in the Venetian life of
these years every nuance between worldliness and religiosity.
Precisely in these years a group of young patricians withdrew
from public life to Murano and the two leaders of this group,
Giustiniani and Quirini—both at the beginning of great political careers—became eremites in the mountain wilderness of
the Apennines; the cruelties of the war, as they wrote to their
Venetian friends whom they tried to persuade to join them,
were a sign of the futility of life on this earth.[60] A third member,
Gasparo Contarini, although he did not renounce the world,
conducted his life in such a manner that when as a mature man
he was a appointed cardinal, his election was regarded as a sign
that the church was embarking on the path of true reform.
Although it seems that for most members of the Venetian
ruling group the experiences of the war did not change their
outlook on life, for some it did, and gradually this had its influence on religious thought in Venice.

Likewise, it might be said that, although the adoption of a
Roman heroic attitude was facade rather than reality, it was not
without further significance. The government become concerned with rebuilding the School of St. Mark's, the Venetian
center of humanistic studies, as soon as opportunity arose, and
it furthered those who found in the Roman past lessons for the

Venetian present.[61] It encouraged writings about the war of the League of Cambrai, appointed an official historiographer in 1516, and thereby helped to give a firm form to the Venetian tradition. Again, the years of the war started a development which contributed to giving Venetian society that aspect of awesome discipline for which it became famous in the later sixteenth century.

Nevertheless, I would like to suggest that the developments that began at the time of the war of the League of Cambrai gained importance only because of the impact the war had on the structure of the Venetian ruling group.

Venice had always been a city with sharply separated strata of population. There were the citizens, and above the citizens, the nobility. It seems evident, however, that during the war of the League of Cambrai two groups developed within the nobility: a relatively small upper group drawn from the Senate, among which the high offices circulated, and the rest of the nobles partly from the Senate but chiefly from the Great Council. The weight, the closeness, and the exclusiveness of this upper group was strengthened by the war, and the reasons were partly bureaucratic. The tasks of the war required close cooperation among officials as well as a certain amount of continuity, obtained by creating special committees, or by extending terms of office, so that even those whose term of office had officially ended continued to play an active role in the conduct of affairs. Another reason for the rigidification of this upper group was financial need (with the accompanying sale of offices) which united the wealthy members of the nobility with them.

Of course the struggle of the young against the old, of the poor nobles against the rich, of the old families against the new has been a constant feature in Venetian history.[62] Nevertheless, it might be suggested that the formation of a firm bloc consisting of the traditional ruling families and the newer familes of great wealth, distinctly separate from the rest of the nobility, achieved its completion and perfection in the time of the war of the League of Cambrai. The institutions of Venice were not changed by the war but in these critical years the final step was made in establishing as rulers of Venice a small, closely united group, which kept in its hands all decisions about the life of the inhabitants and the policy of the Republic.

PART IV.
Diplomacy:
Old and New

12. Venetian Diplomacy Before Pavia: From Reality to Myth

In discussing the policy Charles V ought to follow in Italy after his victory at Pavia, the emperor's great chancellor, Gattinara, spoke with special scorn of the rulers of Venice; he emphasized that they should make a great display of support for Charles V in order to make amends for their "faults."[1] This condemnation stands in strange contrast to the tributes usually paid to the wisdom of Venetian diplomacy. Gattinara, however, had good reason for his contempt of Venetian policy: in the period before the Battle of Pavia it had pursued a disastrous course. At the beginning of the campaign between Spain and France that decided the fate of Italy, the Venetians had been the allies of the Emperor Charles V. The Venetians then broke this treaty and made an alliance with King Francis I of France; three months later Francis I was defeated and a prisoner of Charles V. The Venetians had, at a critical moment, broken an imperial alliance and sided with the French, who then lost the struggle.

Venetian foreign policy in the years 1524–1525 certainly was "faulty." And the question might be raised whether the praises which have been sung to the wisdom of Venetian diplomacy in the seventeenth and eighteenth centuries should also be be-

Originally published in *The Diversity of History*, ed. J. H. Elliott and H. G. Koenigsberger (London, Routledge and Kegan Paul, 1970), pp. 79–116.

stowed on the Venetian conduct of foreign affairs in the Renaissance.[2]

Sources on which judgments on the Renaissance period of Venetian diplomacy can be based are scanty. But some papers preserved in the Biblioteca Correr contain the texts of speeches given in 1524 when the Pregadi debated whether Venice should change from the Spanish to the French side.[3] With the help of this material, it is possible to throw some light on this particular episode in the history of Venetian diplomacy. It was an episode which—probably because of the obvious mistake the Venetians committed—has aroused the attention of many historians of the sixteenth century: Guicciardini, Morosini, Contarini, Paruta. All have treated in some detail the developments of Venetian foreign policy in the years 1523–1525. Thus a new analysis of Venetian diplomacy before Pavia is of interest not only to provide a factual basis for judgments on the quality of Venetian diplomacy in the Renaissance period but also to gain a clearer view of the methods of Italian sixteenth-century historians and their concept of historical truth.

I

The decision of the Venetians to switch from the Spanish to the French side in 1524 was not the first breach of a treaty by the Venetians in this period. In Blois on March 23, 1513 Venice concluded an alliance with the French king, Louis XII, in which the contracting parties promised each other assistance in the war which would bring Milan back under French rule and would restore to Venice its lost territories on the *terra ferma*. This treaty settled the boundaries between Milan and Venice and established that "sunt atque erunt perpetuis temporibus Amici et Confoederati."[4] It was reconfirmed and renewed on October 8, 1517. "Ut omnes intelligant praefatos Serenissimum et Christianissimum regem et illustrissimum ducem et dominium Venetiarum arctissimo vinculo conjunctos esse."[5] Changed circumstances, however, required some modifications. Francis I had succeeded Louis XII as king of France and he was in possession of Milan, so that the treaty now specified the number of troops which either of the contracting parties ought to provide for the defense of the existing situation.

This was the treaty Venice broke when six years later, on July

29, 1523, it concluded an agreement with Emperor Charles V, King Henry VIII of England, Archduke Ferdinand, and Francesco Sforza, who, in consequence of Spanish victories over the French, had been reestablished as Duke of Milan.[6] Two clauses of this treaty were significant. Venice obtained from the emperor and the archduke recognition of all its territorial possessions, but agreed to pay to the emperor 200,000 gold ducats in eight annual installments of 25,000 ducats. Moreover, Venice and Charles V were to provide an equal number of troops to the defense of Milan; if Naples were attacked by a Christian ruler, Venice would send fifteen galleys to support the Neapolitans.

The conclusion of this treaty had been urged on Venice by Pope Adrian VI. The Pope was no partner to the treaty, but concluded on August 3, 1523 a special agreement with Charles V for reciprocal defense.[7] A clause of this agreement stated that the treaty would remain in force one year beyond the death of either of the partners; payment for the troops which the signatories had agreed to provide would have to be renegotiated every three months. These arrangements are of importance for events in the autumn of 1524. Adrian VI died on September 14, 1523, one month after the conclusion of his agreement with Charles V. In the autumn of 1524, one year after Adrian's death, the strange situation had come about that the church-state, whose ruler had urged the Venetians to ally themselves with Charles V, was no longer tied by an alliance treaty to Spain because Adrian's alliance with Charles V was no longer binding on Adrian's successor, Clement VII.[8] The Venetians, however, remained allies of Charles V. Thus, when after the fall of Milan to the French in October 1524 Clement VII urged the Venetians to break with Spain and to join him in an alliance with the king of France, the Venetians were legally less free than the Pope. This represented an additional problem for the Venetian policymakers when they began to deliberate about abandoning Charles V and allying themselves with Francis I in 1524.

II

The following description of the negotiations of 1524, which resulted in the conclusion of an alliance with France, will be better understood if it is preceded by a discussion of the negotiations of the previous year, which led to the Venetian change from the French to the Spanish side.

Information about the negotiations in 1523 is much less extensive[9] than that about the events in the following year. The statements in Marino Sanuto's diary show that the conclusion of the treaty with Charles V was bitterly fought in the Senate. The Senate encompassed a pro-Spanish and a pro-French party. Most vocal in recommending the alliance with Spain were Gabriele Moro and Domenico Trevisan, but also pro-Spanish were Alvise Mocenigo, Marcantonio Venier, and Giorgio Corner, to whom the actual conduct of the negotiations was entrusted.[10] Continuation of the alliance with the French king was recommended by Marin Morosini—who, according to Sanuto, spoke like an advocate of the French king[11]—Gasparo Malipiero, and Paolo Capello.[12] The most important figure among the advocates of the French alliance was Andrea Gritti. He was elected doge in the midst of these negotiations, and Guicciardini maintained that the elevation of Gritti damaged the pro-French cause because, after his election, "he never wished by words or acts to show his preference for any side."[13] This statement cannot be regarded as entirely true, because Sanuto noted that, even as doge, Gritti bestowed signs of approval on those who spoke for continuing the alliance with France.[14] Gritti, however, was considered authoritarian, and his election might have strengthened opposition to the French alliance because it implied a challenge to the influence of the doge.

The struggle between the adherents of Spain and the adherents of France was not fought out in one great debate. The discussions extended throughout the nine months the negotiations were being conducted. Even when the negotiators had finally agreed on a treaty and presented a text in the Pregadi, the adversaries of the alliance with Charles V continued the struggle by insisting on a firm stand on details, demanding changes in formulations and in the amount of the payment to be made by Venice. The final vote at the end of a long day was 152 to 39 with 19 abstentions: "Those who held to France were like dead."[15]

The groupings and animosities which had developed in the course of these discussions about the usefulness of changing from the French to the Spanish side played their role when, fifteen months later, in October 1524, the issue reappeared in reverse, as a proposition to change from the Spanish to the French side.

The fundamental reason for a reconsideration of the Venetian course in foreign policy was the change in military fortunes which had occurred in the interval. In 1523 Spain had defeated the French and had the upper hand in northern Italy. But an advance into Provence in the spring of 1524 failed and Francis I was able to use the disorganization in the enemy's camp for a renewed invasion of Italy. On October 24 Milan was in French hands.

Most immediately and most critically affected by the reappearance of the French in Italy was Pope Clement VII.[16] The independence of the Papacy was menaced if, as seemed possible, the French king should become master of the whole of Italy. The integrity of the church-state was endangered because it could be expected that the French king would want to annex Parma and Piacenza to the Dukedom of Milan and would support the claims of the Duke of Ferrara on territories of the church-state. Pope Clement VII was, however, particularly disturbed because an overthrow of the Medici rule in Florence was an obvious possibility. The Medici rule was precarious because of the lack of an adult Medici heir. Clement VII thought that immediate negotiations and an understanding with the king of France might reduce the dangers threatening the church-state and the Medici rule in Florence. Even before the French had entered Milan the Venetian ambassador in Rome, Marco Foscari, reported[17] a conversation in which the Pope indicated that he was inclined toward an agreement with the French king and hoped that the Venetians would act together with him; he wished to remain in close touch with Venice and asked the Venetians for advice on how to proceed.

This report arrived in Venice on October 25; the Council of Ten and the Collegio drafted a reply to be sent to Foscari, and the Pregadi were assembled to give their approval to this instruction.[18] The main issue of this meeting, of course, was whether Venice should agree to negotiations with France—an issue which was regarded to be of such importance that the discussion in the Pregadi was treated as "materia secretissima."[19]

The instruction submitted to the Pregadi for approval expressed pleasure at the willingness of the Pope to act in accord with Venice and stressed Venetian confidence in the wisdom of the Pope. The Venetians emphasized that the situation had become more critical than it had been when the Pope had talked to Foscari, because since then Milan had fallen into French hands and this conquest had proved the great power of the French king. "Et se a sua Beat.ne paresse, chel tempo necessiti de pratticar accordo con il Re Christianissimo, Nui siamo ben contenti: et ne par esser cusi stretti, et coniuncti insieme con sua San.ta che non si po far cosa, salvo a commun beneficio." This was the key sentence of the instruction and it generated a vehement debate which set the tone for all further discussions of this issue.[20]

Girolamo Pesaro and Domenico Venier emphasized that the issue was of such importance that it needed lengthy and careful consideration. They moved that the debate be postponed till the next day. In 1523 Girolamo Pesaro had been an adherent of the alliance with Spain. It seems likely, therefore, that he wanted to prevent a panicky rush to a treaty with France. In this meeting, however—as also in all the following meetings—the main advocate of loyal adherence to the alliance with Charles V was Zaccaria Bembo, a *savio* of the *terra ferma.* Instead of the sentence that expressed approval if the Pope regarded an agreement with the French king necessary, Bembo suggested an innocuous phrase that merely emphasized that Venice and the Pope ought to act in accord and that assured the Pope Venice would not conclude an agreement with Francis I without him. The speech in which Bembo justified this altering of the wording of the instruction makes it clear that he intended to prevent Venice from changing sides. Bembo argued along a number of different lines. It was against Venetian tradition to break a commitment. The military situation of the army of Charles V and his allies could not be considered desperate; by abandoning Milan, the adversaries of France had been able to save their troops and consolidate their position in Pavia, Lodi, Alessandria, and Cremona. And if a battle should occur the outcome was uncertain. Without the help of Venice, the French king could not establish himself securely in Milan. There was no need for Venice therefore to humiliate itself, to abandon the

Spanish alliance, and to implore the friendship of the French king.

Bembo's speech seems to have made a great impression; the alteration of the instruction which he suggested was not accepted,[21] but in the vote the opposition showed such strength that it was necessary to hold another meeting on the same issue the next day.

For this meeting a new instruction had been drafted and in the end the Pregadi accepted this revised version of the instruction.[22] The formulations of the new instruction were somewhat more favorable to the Spanish side than the draft votes on the previous day: now the Venetian government expressed no opinion about the desirability of an alliance with France, but limited itself to saying that the Pope ought to decide soon what ought to be done, because delay might be dangerous. This draft carried the signatures of many of those who one year earlier had advocated the alliance with Charles V—namely, in addition to that of Zaccaria Bembo, those of Alvise Mocenigo and Girolamo Pesaro. The advocates of the French alliance moved unsuccessfully for an addition which contained an explicit statement that if the Pope decided on an alliance with Francis I Venice would join him. The proposed amendment was signed by old adherents of France like Paolo Capello, but also had the names of two influential patricians, Luca Tron and Leonardo Mocenigo, who in 1523 had favored Charles V.[23] Their transition from the Spanish to the French side probably was a crucial factor in swinging the Ten and the Collegio over to the French side. However, the number of those who changed sides was limited. Although the instruction in its final form permitted negotiations with France, the opposition was strong enough to prevent any expression that would have been taken as a positive affirmation of the desirability of such an alliance.

Venetian reticence displeased the Pope. He expressed to Foscari his astonishment[24] that the Venetians had given no clear answer to his request for an explanation of their views. His eagerness for an agreement with Francis I steadily increased. He explained to the Venetian ambassador that Charles V could not reinforce his troops because of lack of money; the position of the French seemed to him overwhelmingly strong. For this reason, in the Pope's opinion, a quick decision was needed.

This report arrived in Venice on October 28; it made evident that the Venetians could no longer delay a definite explanation of their attitude toward a treaty with France. And so, on October 29, the Pregadi decided to instruct Foscari[25] that the Venetians were satisfied if the Pope negotiated with the French king in a manner that seemed appropriate. Foscari was given power to conclude, together with His Holiness, "bona, et syncera Pace cum il Re Christianissimo"; the Venetian wish was for restoration of the status quo that had existed before the outbreak of the war between Venice and France. Furthermore, because the Pope had said that he wanted to negotiate and conclude "intelligentia secreta fra lei, il Christian[mo] Re, et la Signoria nostra," Venice was ready to make such a treaty after the conclusion of peace. In vain did Zaccaria Bembo attempt to achieve a postponement of this decision. Considering the cautiousness with which the Venetians moved and their great hesitation in changing sides, it is surprising to hear that Foscari—even before he had received this instruction—told the Pope that he could be sure of Venice's full agreement to an alliance with France, "a rather unheard-of thing that an ambassador presumes so much without having received from the Senate instructions which might have been to the contrary."[26]

The negotiations which now began were much more complicated than the Pope or even the Venetians expected when they entered upon them. Because Clement VII regarded the situation of the Spaniards to be desperate, he believed that Charles V would welcome an end to the war; the Pope envisaged the negotiations with Francis I as a prologue to the establishment of peace between Charles V and Francis I, with the Pope himself as mediator.[27] The Venetians hoped the same.[28] But when the Pope's confidant, Matteo Giberti, visited the Spanish and the French camps in northern Italy, he discovered that neither the Spaniards nor the French were inclined toward an ending of hostilities.[29] The consequence was that if a treaty with the French king were concluded by Venice and the Pope it would imply a complete break and probably war with Charles V.

Under these circumstances many seem to have felt that the decision taken at the end of October might have been overhasty and that a reconsideration of Venice's position in the conflict between Charles V and Francis I was desirable. Simultaneously, however, the Venetians were made aware of the urgency to come to a decision. Characteristic was the scene which took place on November 19. There appeared in the Collegio first the French ambassador emphasizing that the French king was anxious to be "buon amico" with Venice; the doge assured him of the great esteem in which the French king was held in Venice. Immediately afterward the ambassadors of Charles V and Francesco Sforza appeared and demanded orders for the Venetian troops to join the imperial forces in accord with the alliance existing between Charles V and Venice; the Doge assured them of Venice's friendly feelings.[30] The Pope was also put under pressure and in an even more direct way: the French threatened with an invasion of Naples. But while pressures mounted the decision which had to be taken became more difficult; the panicky reaction produced by the French conquest of Milan was now followed by quieter considerations and the military situation appeared less certain and more balanced.

These problems came out into the open in crucial meetings of the Pregadi in the middle of November. Their occasion was a report from Rome in which the Venetian ambassador wrote about a conversation with the Pope and requested an immediate answer. The Pope had told Foscari that he had come to the conclusion that if Pavia could withstand the French attack he would spin out negotiations with the French king and try to establish general peace. However, if the French succeeded in conquering Pavia then he would make an agreement with the king of France and ask Charles V to cede to France those parts of the Dukedom of Milan which the Spaniards were still holding. If Charles V refused it would be necessary to take up arms against him. The Pope was anxious to hear what the Venetian government thought about these ideas.[31]

The debate in the Pregadi on the answer which ought to be given to the Pope lasted over two days and the speakers on both sides tried carefully to marshal all the arguments that could be made in favor of their cause. Because of the decisive importance of this debate, it deserves a somewhat extended description.[32]

On the first day, November 15, the Collegio presented the draft of an instruction to Foscari. Controversy focused on one passage of this draft; it said that if the French should take Pavia the Venetian government would approve of His Holiness's making peace and coming to an agreement with the French king for himself and for Venice as it had been stated in the instruction of October 29. The opposition suggested that this passage should be replaced by a formula which, if Pavia should fall, encouraged the Pope to continue negotiations with the French king, but stipulated that no treaty should be concluded without special orders from the Venetian government.[33] A proponent of this amendment and the chief opposition speaker was a *savio* of the Consiglio, Alvise Mocenigo.[34] He reiterated[35] the reasons brought up in previous deliberations on this issue—namely, that it was against Venetian tradition to break a treaty and that the military position of the Spaniards was strong (it would not be desperate even if Pavia were lost). Mocenigo also added a new argument. The Pope's real intention was to get Ferrara. Alberto Pio da Carpi, the French ambassador at the papal court, considered the Duke of Ferrara his oldest and most deadly enemy. Carpi had set his heart on a joint enterprise of the French and the Pope against Ferrara and he had promised the Pope the possession of Ferrara if he would come over to the French side.[36]

Mocenigo's speech must have been very effective. Although the change in the draft which he had suggested was not adopted, the instruction as it had been drafted also found no majority.

Thus, the deliberations had to be resumed the next morning. By then new reports had arrived. The Venetian ambassador in Vienna wrote that Archduke Ferdinand intended to invade Italy with military forces. Foscari reported from Rome that the Pope did not intend to press the negotiations with France if Pavia was held by the Spaniards. But if Pavia should fall he would immediately conclude a treaty with Francis I. The majority of the *savi* (Domenico Trevisan, Leonardo Mocenigo, Paolo Capello, Luca Tron, Andrea Trevisan, Niccolò Bernardo of the *savi di Consiglio;* Antonio Contarini, Domenico Venier, Giovanni Francesco Badoer of the *savi della terra ferma*) now submitted to the Pregadi the draft of an instruction similar to the one presented on the previous day; it was somewhat toned down, however, and emphasized the importance of the news about the possible coming of Archduke Ferdinand. Alvise Mocenigo and Zaccaria Bembo offered a different version, which stressed that even if Pavia should fall the Spaniards would remain strong and would receive reinforcements: briefly, one should then reconsider the entire situation.

Mocenigo again rose to speak in order to justify the version he had drafted.[37] He enlarged on a statement he had made the day before—namely, that the interests of the Pope were very different from those of Venice. The Pope might be strengthened by getting Ferrara, but in the case of a conflict with the Habsburgs Venice would be immediately exposed to great dangers, not only because of the possibility of an attack on the *terra firma* by the Austrian Archduke but also because Venetian trade would suffer, since Venetian galleys would not be able to enter Spanish ports. Moreover, if foreigners had to exert control in Italy the rule of Charles V was much preferable to that of the French king. The French ruled as tyrants (*tirannicamente*) because by nature they were arrogant and overweening.[38] Charles V, however, permitted Italians to rule themselves.[39]

Zaccaria Bembo, who supported Mocenigo, placed moral considerations in the foreground. It was against all traditions of Venetian policy to break faith: "Our wise ancestors had at no time, in no calamity, at no opportunity, wanted to break faith with any prince, Christian or infidel, except when their state was placed in obvious danger."[40] At first sight, it might appear most expedient to be the friend of the emperor in his time of prosperity and to abandon him when fortune favored the French king—briefly, to always be on the side of the victor. "But such behavior is so ruthless and unnatural that it can give no secure and solid basis."[41] To this moral appeal Bembo also added political arguments. The king of France had no reason to love Venice, which the year before had defected to Charles V. Thus, after a treaty with France Venice would be isolated, and if the emperor wanted to revenge himself on Venice he could probably come to an understanding with the French at the expense of Venice; briefly, Bembo envisaged the possibility of another League of Cambrai. Changing sides from the Spanish to the French was a radical step,[42] and Bembo felt it was neither unusual nor beyond reason to demand information from Rome about the contents of the treaty before giving Foscari permission to sign it.

With this last point, Bembo referred to remarks of Luca Tron, an advocate of the French alliance. Tron had said that if Venice withdrew from the position of October 29—when it had given Foscari power to sign the treaty the Pope might negotiate—the Pope's confidence in the Venetian government would be destroyed. Venice would find all doors to negotiation with the French king closed; it would be left without allies. Other advocates of the French alliance, too, were perturbed by the possibility of friction with the Pope if the instruction of October 29 were withdrawn. Chiefly, however, emphasis was placed on the military strength of the French. It was also said that Mocenigo was wrong: French rule over Milan was less a threat to Venice than was rule by the Habsburgs.

A position somewhat in the middle was taken by Girolamo da Pesaro, one of the *savi del Consiglio* who had signed neither of the two drafts. Pesaro stated that he was generally in accord with Mocenigo and Bembo, but he agreed with Tron that it was highly important not to shake the confidence of the Pope. In his opinion, the instruction given to Foscari on October 29 should not be withdrawn. However, the Pope ought to be told politely that French military superiority was not as great as it appeared; the Spanish troops were receiving reinforcements, so that even if Pavia fell the Spanish situation was not hopeless. So there was no desperate hurry for an agreement with France, and the Pope and Venice did not have to bow to the wishes of the French king.

The middle position of Girolamo da Pesaro carried the day, and he was asked to draft the instruction to Foscari. His instruction was in many respects very similar to that which Mocenigo and Bembo had drafted; it emphasized that even the conquest of Pavia would not make the French king all-powerful in Italy and that the possible appearance of Archduke Ferdinand in Italy deserved serious consideration. Nevertheless, the instruction left the final decision to the Pope[43] and did not withdraw the instruction of October 29, which had given power to the Pope to conclude an agreement with Francis I in the name of Venice. The Venetian government indicated, however, that they were anxious to get more information before a final decision was made. The Venetians warned against undue haste in coming to an agreement with Francis I. Clearly, this was a compromise intended to be acceptable to the diverging opinions of the members of the Collegio and the Pregadi.

The Pope disregarded the Venetian advice to go slow in the negotiations with France. His emissary, Giberti, had reported to him that he felt sure the French king had decided on a campaign to conquer Naples.[44] The Pope believed he had to do everything possible to avoid such an enterprise, which he considered fatal for the independence of the Papacy. Thus he decided on a last great attempt to establish peace between Charles V and Francis I. But since Clement VII was convinced of the superiority of the French, he felt that he had to make far-reaching concessions to the French king if he wanted to persuade him to keep away from Naples and to make peace. His proposal was to guarantee Charles V the possession of Naples, but Charles V would have to cede Milan to Francis I; if Charles V refused, the Pope was willing to go over to the French side.[45] In order to facilitate cession of Milan, the Pope was willing to make Francesco Sforza, the Duke of Milan, a cardinal.

When Foscari's report about these plans of Clement VII arrived in Venice the Venetians themselves had received a strong reminder of the urgency of the situation. On November 23 the ambassadors of Charles V and of the Sforza Duke of Milan appeared before the Collegio and presented a note[46] in which they demanded that Venice fulfill its alliance obligations and command its troops to join those of Spain and Milan; the ambassadors emphasized that such action was without great risk because Spanish and Milanese troops were superior in strength to those of Francis I.[47] Thus, when on Saturday, November 26, the Pregadi met to consider what answer to give the Pope, they were aware that time was running out.[48] The instruction presented to the Pregadi bestowed high praise upon the Pope for his proposal to establish peace in Italy by guaranteeing Naples to Charles V and Milan to Francis I.[49] But this instruction was accompanied by a further instruction which said that even if Charles V would not agree the Venetian government was willing to make a treaty with the French king, as the Pope desired. It was this second instruction which once again started a debate on the course Venice ought to follow. Girolamo Pesaro and Zaccaria Bembo expressed misgivings about this second instruction. They tried to prevent the Venetian government from taking any irrevocable step; both warned against unnecessary haste. Zaccaria Bembo urged them to honor the often-proved wisdom of using "the benefit of time," and Pesaro supported him by referring to the proverb that "Who rushes ahead in affairs of state will soon repent."[50] Pesaro suggested that it might be possible to wait for Charles V's reaction to the Papal proposals. In any case both wanted a postponement of the decision until Monday, so that everyone would have time to consider the matter carefully and dispassionately.

Their views were opposed by Luca Tron, who put up a powerful defense of the instruction as it had been presented to the Pregadi. In Tron's opinion, nothing could happen that would change the situation; hesitation and delay would only arouse the resentment of the Pope. The suggestion of Clement VII to guarantee Charles V's rule in Naples and to give the French king a secure position in the north was excellent; if carried out, there would always be a counterweight against any attempt of the French king to make himself ruler of Italy and against any attempt of Charles V to become monarch of the world.[51] Luca Tron's views carried the day; the Pregadi accepted the draft in the form in which it had been proposed.

Clement VII now had the Venetians where he wanted them. He could act for them even if Pavia did not fall. He did not allow the Venetians to forget that they had bound themselves. When he heard about the requests of the Spanish ambassador for support by Venetian troops and about the Venetian delaying answer, he showed a lively annoyance; in a letter of explanation and apology, the Venetian government assured him that never under any circumstances would they separate themselves from His Holiness.[52] This instruction to Foscari also stated that in case the negotiations with the Spanish did not lead to an understanding which might establish general peace the Venetians were anxious that the Pope should go ahead with the secret agreement between the Pope, France, and Venice.[53]

The secret treaty by which Venice moved from the Spanish to the French side was signed on December 12.[54] Before it was concluded, the matter came up once again in the Pregadi[55] in an almost indirect way: the issue was what ought to be said to the commander of the Spanish troops in reply to his renewed request for support from Venice.[56] The answer was negative,

although the rejection was put in diplomatic form. It emphasized the significance of the peace efforts of the Pope; of
course, since these efforts involved the cession of Milan to
France, the answer implied that Venice did not intend to fulfill
its obligations to Charles V regarding the defense of Milan. The
debate was short but lively. The Spanish cause was defended by
a new but powerful voice, that of Gabriele Moro.[57] He stated
that Venice ought to tell the viceroy that it was willing to come
to his assistance and to defend Milan for Charles V. Moro's
abortive intervention was memorable because it contained a vehement outbreak of indignation against the leaders of Venetian
policy. Four men, Moro maintained, dominated the Collegio
and did not allow others to express themselves freely.[58] They
were responsible for having brought Venice between "hammer
and anvil." Even the doge had tried to exert influence in favor
of the French cause. But he, Gabriele Moro, was a man who was
born in a free city, and so he said freely what he thought.[59]

Thus, the last debate about Venice's change of sides in the
conflict between Spain and France brought into the open that
the issue had aroused deep passions[60] and that the opponents of
the French alliance believed that Venice had been maneuvered
into a fateful decision by a small, powerful group.

III

What do these negotiations reveal about the broader issue
with which we are concerned, about the nature, the strengths,
and the weaknesses of Venetian diplomacy in the Renaissance
period?

In the conduct of foreign affairs before the Battle of Pavia the
Venetians did not show that they possessed any particular foresight or wisdom. In allying themselves with the French, who became the losers, they miscalculated the strength of the antagonists fighting for hegemony. This was a mistake, however,
which almost all Italian rulers were prone to commit. Ever since
1494, when Charles VIII had made his triumphal march from
the north of Italy to the south, the Italians overestimated
French power.

The Venetians committed a tactical mistake as well. By giving
the Pope the power to negotiate with the French king on their
behalf, the Venetians could not escape signing an agreement

with the French at a time when such an alliance suited the Pope (because of the threatened French invasion of Naples), but when Venetian interests were no more endangered than before. If the Venetians had used the "benefitio del tempo" as some of the *savi* wanted, they would have been in an excellent bargaining position a few months later when the military strength of the Spaniards was increasing and the French king might have valued more highly Venetian support.

The crucial and the most questionable factor in the Venetian attitude was the desire to maintain close cooperation with the Pope. Certainly, there were advantages in leaving the diplomatic initiative to Clement VII. With the Pope in Rome as chief negotiator, the Spanish could be kept in the dark longer about Venetian intentions. The mounting Turkish threat also made the Venetians eager to secure the good will of the Pope, the head of Christianity. But there seems to have been an almost irrational element in the Venetian eagerness for cooperation with the Pope. They appear to have been haunted by the memories of the League of Cambrai. Actually the Venetians had nothing to fear of the Pope, not only because Clement VII was no Julius II, but also because an alliance of Spain and France could not be arranged. In 1509 a coalition between the Spanish, German, and French rulers at the expense of Venice had been possible; in 1524 it was not. Charles V, with his aspirations to world monarchy, could not permit a strengthening of his main enemy, the French king. Fundamentally the Venetians lacked awareness that, with the combination of German and Spanish powers in the hands of one family, the Habsburgs, a new situation had arisen in which the events of the previous decades could not serve as precedents.

Obviously becoming aware of the need for changes in basic assumptions is difficult. But because of the awe in which the wisdom of Venetian statesmen is held the point should be made that the Venetians made no better judgments than other rulers in the Renaissance period. As the speeches in the Pregadi show, their calculations were based on the same factors relied on by other Italian governments.[61] In measuring the strength of a power, its financial resources and its military assets were the prime consideration. But the size, the maintenance, and the efficiency of an army was believed to depend entirely on the availability of funds for the pay of the troops. The Venetians believed the saying that "Money is the nerve of war." They also shared the *communis opinio* of the importance of psychological factors. The actions of a ruler were viewed as determined by such factors as pride, eagerness to revenge a defeat, or hostility toward an individual. Like other governments, the Venetians were much concerned with maintaining their reputation. They were convinced that they had an outstanding record in carrying out commitments and in keeping treaties and they wanted to keep this record clean. Such protestations uttered by men who were contemporaries of Cesare Borgia and Niccolò Machiavelli may sound rather hollow and hypocritical. But every diplomatic negotiation of this period attests to the high value placed on acting within correct legal limits in the conduct of foreign policy. The Florentine attitude is almost identical with that of the Venetians; they too were proud of the loyalty with which they observed the treaties they had concluded. Legal considerations were a serious matter in diplomacy. For this reason the remark one of the Venetian patricians made in these discussions—that treaties should be broken only when the state is placed in obvious danger—deserves attention. It probably expressed more correctly than Machiavelli did the accepted opinion about the extent and limits of the observation of legal obligations in foreign policy.

If the intellectual framework in which the Venetians thought about foreign policy was the customary one, their psychological attitude was also not unique or distinguished by cool and unbiased objectivity. Many of the speeches made in the course of the debates on the treaty with France were emotional and passionate. The entire discussion had somewhat the character of a replay of the fight which had taken place one year earlier when the alliance with Charles V was concluded. The advocates of Charles V in 1523—Gabriele Moro, Alvise Mocenigo, Girolamo Pesaro—now opposed the French alliance,[62] whereas the friends of France in 1523—Paolo Capello, Andrea Trevisan—spoke for renewal of ties with France. Those who in 1523 had advocated adherence to the French alliance were anxious to show that they had been right and were not willing to let anything stand in the way of a successful conclusion of the negotiations. The outburst of Gabriele Moro against the four men who had determined the course of events probably was a reflection of this feeling that the pro-French group believed that its hour had come and was ruthless in pointing out that it must be listened to because it had been right. A striking parallel is the pro-French and pro-Habsburg division in the Florentine ruling group, when party rivalry and personal enmities also influenced the evaluation of the situation. Again, one is forced to conclude that the Venetian ruling group was neither more unified nor less emotional than that of other city-states of the Renaissance.[63]

Nevertheless, this detailed analysis of a particular diplomatic episode does reveal some features peculiar to the Venetian system of government, features which may help to explain the reputation for secrecy, finesse, and astuteness Venetian diplomats gained over the centuries. In the princely states of the Renaissance decisions on foreign policy were made by the ruler, perhaps together with a few counselors. In Medicean Florence foreign policy was the preserve of the head of the Medici family, who might act after deliberation with a few influential friends of the Medici regime.[64] Even in the Republican period of Florence, between 1494 and 1512, the Office of the Ten handled foreign affairs, perhaps after consultation, in a *pratica,* with a few members of the aristocratic ruling group; a large *pratica* in which a greater number of citizens participated was rare and hardly ever concerned with issues of foreign policy.[65]

In Venice reports from those sent on missions abroad were discussed by the Ten and the Collegio, and these officials then drafted a reply. In decisions of importance the Pregadi were assembled, although those members who might be involved in a conflict of interest were not permitted to participate in the deliberations. This meant that in the negotiations on the treaty with France—in which the Pope was prominently involved—the Papalisti, that is, those who were related to the Pope or to cardinals, were excluded. The relevant documents were presented to the Pregadi. Then the proponents of the draft defended it and its opponents explained their position and made their proposals for textual revision. Only *savi del Consiglio* and *savi della terra ferma* spoke in the debates on the French alliance.[66] At the end there was a vote to decide whether the draft should be approved, amended, or resubmitted in new form the next day.

The most startling consequence of this procedure is that the number of those who knew about the secrets of state and foreign policy was quite large. There were leaks, of course, as is shown by the many laws threatening severe punishment for those who violated the rules of secrecy. Yet it is astounding that the system worked, and there is reason therefore for the frequent statements in which contemporaries expressed their admiration for the Venetian ability to keep government affairs secret.

It is also remarkable to what extent the discussions in the Pregadi were concerned not only with broad questions about what course to take in foreign policy but also with finding the most appropriate language in the formulation of an instruction or treaty. This aspect of the discussions might help to explain the reputation Venetian diplomats enjoyed. In the times of the Renaissance and in the following centuries as well, the men who understood the technical details in the conduct of diplomacy were the secretaries, the members of the chancellery, the slowly growing number of professional civil servants. Frequently they played an important role as advisers in diplomatic negotiations or as agents preparing the ground for a diplomatic action. But they did not have enough status to head diplomatic missions of importance. Prestigious diplomatic tasks were entrusted to great nobles or, in the case of city-states, to members of the wealthy ruling group. They could learn their diplomatic tasks only slowly through experience; as the Florentine legislation on ambassadors shows, the preparation of the youth of the ruling group for diplomatic service was regarded as a constant problem never satisfactorily solved.[67] In Venice, however, presence at the discussions of the Pregadi must have served as ideal training for diplomatic duties. Even if the concepts of Venetian diplomacy were similar to those of other states and the Venetian statesmen no paragons of impartiality and far-sightedness, their experience in the Pregadi must have taught them to move in the diplomatic world with a finesse and subtlety which made them stand out.

IV

The political importance of the Venetian move from the Spanish side to the French side in 1524 is limited. It must be the contrast between the much-vaunted reputation of Venetian diplomacy and its actual performance in this diplomatic episode that has attracted the attention of historians; for the conduct of Venetian diplomacy at the time of Pavia has been described by historians of the sixteenth century with great care. Their treatment has been so detailed that in a recent study of Venetian historiography the episode has been used as a criterion for defining the differences among the Venetian historians of the sixteenth century.[68] On the basis of our reconstruction of the actual course of events, further examination of the manner in which these historians of the sixteenth century approached their task should be possible.

The first contemporary historian who dealt with these diplomatic events was not a Venetian, but a Florentine: Francesco Guicciardini in his *History of Italy*. Guicciardini was less interested in the decision of 1524 than in the events of the previous year when Venice had abandoned the French alliance and joined Charles V.[69] As we have seen, discussions in the Pregadi on this issue extended over a long period of time and were concerned with the formulation of instructions to be given to the negotiators. Like almost all the other sixteenth-century historians, Guicciardini attributed critical importance to one great debate between two speakers representing opposite points of view. The speaker in favor of the French alliance was Andrea Gritti; the speaker for Charles V was Giorgio Corner. Although a clash between Gritti and Corner in one great debate is most unlikely, because if it had happened Sanuto would have mentioned it, Guicciardini's choice of Gritti and Corner as advocates of the two opposing points of view is justifiable. Gritti was well known as "Francese" and Giorgio Corner was one of the three Venetian statesmen selected to negotiate the treaty with the ambassador of Charles V. Moreover, Gritti and Corner were the two most outstanding Venetian statesmen at this time; when the doge Grimani died in the summer of 1523 and Gritti was elected his successor, Corner was his chief rival. The speeches of Gritti and Corner are beautiful examples of Guicciardini's technique in the composition and use of speeches. Guicciardini wanted to show clearly the dilemma Venice faced. One argument was that Venice ought to try to establish a balance of forces by permitting France to rule in Milan and Charles V in Naples; consequently, Venice ought to support France. The counterargument was that if France were settled in Milan,

Venice would have a restless and ambitious prince as neighbor. From the Venetian point of view, it would be preferable to have Francesco Sforza, a weak and self-indulgent prince, as ruler in Milan. This could be done only with the help of Charles V, and thus spoke for an alliance with him. Historical events of the recent past were cited as proof for all these statements. The Italian campaigns of Louis XII, the origin of the League of Cambrai, the unreliability of the Swiss mercenaries—all were referred to in order to justify the speakers' theories.

The speakers also tried to gauge the changes of the military situation. By having the two speakers present a divergent estimate of the military strength of the Spaniards and the French, Guicciardini indicated the uncertainty which permeates all such calculations. In Gritti's opinion, the French king was strong enough to appear suddenly in Italy, and clearly this remark was meant to foreshadow what happened one year later. Many remarks in these speeches—the need for a balance of power between Francis I and Charles V, the emphasis on the crucial position of Milan, the fear of an "impero di tutta Italia" under Charles V—evoke the entire complex of problems which would dominate Italian politics in the next five years. By reminding the reader of the experiences of the recent past, and by suggesting to him some of the events that were to happen, Guicciardini succeeds in placing the present as a transitional moment between past and future. But although these speeches have their function in the structure of Guicciardini's entire history, they do not go beyond what would be appropriate to the situation Guicciardini described in this chapter. Certainly, Gritti and Corner in Guicciardini's presentation saw farther and said more than the speakers in the Pregadi did. But Guicciardini never allowed them to see or say anything that they could not have said or seen. He remained in the time and in the situation which he analyzed. However, because Guicciardini's presentation implied that prudent men who had mastered trials in the past and were aware of the dangers of the future could not find a secure road, he prepared the reader for the fateful course which events would take in the coming years, and he expressed the grand theme of his work: the impotence of men before fate.

Guicciardini's attention is directed toward an explanation of the political changes in the first decades of the sixteenth century, and in his presentation of the dilemma of Venetian diplomacy he stressed those aspects which have bearing on the entire political scene. After Guicciardini, those historians who wrote on the diplomatic maneuvers before the Battle of Pavia were Venetians. They were officially appointed to write the history of their republic and were concerned with the political lessons which might be drawn from these events for the conduct of Venetian policy; if Guicciardini treated this episode as an example of the human predicament, the Venetian writers tried to use these events to decide whether moral principles or political pragmatism ought to guide statesmen. Certainly their interest in these aspects of the events was influenced by the time in which they wrote. Their works were composed later than Guicciardini's, in the second half of the sixteenth century, in the time of the Counter Reformation.

Andrea Navagero, Venice's first official historian, died in 1529 without having started on the work he was commissioned to do.[70] His successor, Pietro Bembo, brought the official history only up to the year 1523 when he died in 1547. There was an intermission of thirteen years before the appointment of the next official historiographer, Daniele Barbaro, but he composed only a discussion of the situation at the time of the League of Cambrai when he died. However, the next three holders of this position—Alvise Contarini (appointed 1577), Paolo Paruta (appointed 1580), and Andrea Morosini (appointed 1598)—discussed the events before the Battle of Pavia.

Alvise Contarini died a few years after his appointment and his history, which begins where Bembo stopped and ends in 1570, remained in rather rough form and has never been printed.[71] The manuscript gives attention, however, to the dilemma of Venetian diplomacy in the years of the struggle between France and Spain. Contarini clearly follows Guicciardini in the presentation of this episode. Like Guicciardini in the *History of Italy,* he focuses on the decision of 1523, and his main antagonists are Gritti and Corner. But Contarini places the decision facing Venice in a different framework than had Guicciardini. The disagreement of the speakers is about means; their aim is the same: to keep Venice neutral and thereby to secure peace for Italy. Interestingly enough, Contarini finds it necessary to stress that the Venetians were not egoists. In pursuing neutrality and peace they had in mind not only the interests of their commerce and material advantages but also the freedom of Italy. The observation of neutrality and peace is the morally superior course.[72]

Contarini's successor as official historiographer, Paola Paruta,[73] is not concerned with issues of morality or religion. His only interest is to draw from the past rules for the conduct of politics applicable to the present. The aim of using history for setting down his views about the right principles for Venetian politics is so dominating that Paruta shows a sovereign disregard for factual accuracy and a tendency to make the facts fit his intellectual aims. In Paruta's story[74] the two antagonists in a discussion on the treaty with France are Giorgio Corner and Domenico Trevisan. One might say that Paruta refrained from assigning Gritti a role in this debate because he knew that in 1524 Gritti was doge and as such could not be the leading spokesman of a group in the Pregadi; Domenico Trevisan, who replaced Gritti in Paruta's story, was indeed an adherent of the French alliance. But it might be questioned whether Paruta would have selected him if in the meantime Domenico Trevisan had not risen in reputation as the father of a doge.[75] Paruta's arbitrariness is evident in his selection of Giorgio Corner as the other speaker. It is true that Corner was one of the most prominent Venetian statesmen of this period and had played an important role in 1523; but in 1524 he was sick and unable to appear in the Pregadi.[76] Moreover, as a relative of the two cardinals from the Corner family he would have been excluded from most of the discussion as a Papalista.

Paruta's tendentious arbitrariness is also reflected in the manner in which he used this episode to strengthen and justify the antipapal course Venice pursued in his time. Paruta throws the entire responsibility for the events of 1524 on Pope Clement VII. He makes the Pope the driving force in the negotiations with France. In order to show the Pope's zeal, Paruta places Giberti's mission to Francis I before the fall of Milan; he lets the Pope make the demand that the Venetians should give Foscari full power to sign the treaty the Pope had negotiated, and according to Paruta the treaty was concluded by the Pope when the Pregadi assembled "per venir all'ultima terminazione del negotio."[77]

Paruta's purpose in presenting this episode, particularly the speeches put into the mouths of Trevisan and Corner, is political instruction. The speeches contain few references to the actual situation in 1524; emphasis on the uncertainty of the military situation is the most concrete issue the speakers discuss. Paruta uses the speeches to set forth his views on the appropriate approach to the management of foreign affairs. The first requirement is to approach decisions in cool objectivity without passion or bias. The intellectual framework for such rational consideration is based on the concepts of "interest," "reason of state," and "balance of power." Each state or prince always pursues his own interest. He does not subordinate political interests to a higher moral law. Politics has its own law: the reason of state. Venice's dominating interest is preventing control of Italy from falling into the hands of one of the great powers. In particular, this means maintaining a balance of power between Spain and France. This is best achieved by supporting whoever is weaker at a given moment against the stronger.[78] Venice should never follow a fixed course. Its foreign policy ought to be flexible, moving from one side to the other. Loyalty to commitments has no value. In foreign policy reason of state is the highest principle.

Morosini, Paruta's successor as Venetian historiographer, took almost the opposite line. In his description of the debates which led to the decision in 1524 moral considerations are presented as decisive. The advocate of the French alliance said that the highest duty was to preserve the fatherland. Destruction threatened from iron and blood, force and rape. An adjustment to circumstances through an alliance with France was necessary.[79] His opponent emphasized that in the past the Venetians' loyalty to agreements was their highest pride.[80] One ought to explore every means before violating a treaty. The debate between the two speakers centered on the question whether preservation of the life of the state and its inhabitants or obedience to moral law is the higher duty, and the author's sympathy is clearly on the side of morality. But Morosini adds to his moral appeal some practical considerations relevant to the situation: he directs attention to the great manpower reserves of the Habsburg rulers. Moreover, he notes, Venice is not as free as the Pope, who has no alliance with France and whose position makes it easy for him to change from one side to the other. These were arguments which had actually been made in 1524. The speeches treat the issue as a problem of moral philosophy. But these theoretical discussions are embedded in a story of remarkable factual accuracy. There is no doubt that Morosini studied the records of the Pregadi before writing his story.[81] Like Paruta, he selected Domenico Trevisan as advocate of the French alliance. But Alvise Mocenigo, who in Morosini's story maintains the opposite point of view, was indeed, as we have seen, a vehement protagonist of loyalty to Spain. Morosini is also aware of the role and the attitude of Zaccaria Bembo, who, as Morosini says,[82] "magna dicendi vi atque impetu animi contradicente" delayed the sending of an instruction which would have permitted Foscari to sign the treaty. But Morosini explained correctly that the next day such an instruction was sent and he acknowledged the crucial role of Girolamo Pesaro in effecting a compromise. It is striking, however, that in Morosini's presentation the story of 1524 has no ending. He never states that the outcome of the discussion was a change of sides and the conclusion of a treaty with France.

The analysis of the manner in which this episode was described in the writings of sixteenth-century historians should be of help for our understanding of the developments of historiography and of Venetian political thought. Guicciardini's superiority as a writer of history clearly stands out. The speeches he composed form a necessary link in the explanation of events. They provide a survey of all the ingredients that go into the making of a decision. In contrast, the contents of the speeches written by Venetian historians later in the sixteenth century are extraneous to the occasion at which they were supposed to be given. They are less rhetorical, less purely decorative than the abstract and moralizing reflections in speeches by humanist historians of the fifteenth century; the speeches of the Venetian historians of the sixteenth century at least remained in a political context. Paruta set forth principles of successful political conduct; Morosini discussed problems of the relation between morals and politics. But these speeches are not closely integrated with the historical narrative; they are inserts and appear somewhat like an alien element.[83] The historical narrative runs along independent of the speeches, and it depended on the author whether the narrative was shaped for political purposes or presented with concern for factual accuracy.

In explanation of the discrepancies between Guicciardini and the later Venetian historians, it might simply be said that Guicciardini was a greater historian; this is certainly a valid explanation, but only a partial one. The problems of morals and politics and the origin of the doctrine of reason of state, which emancipated politics from subordination to the general laws of morality, were issues which the religious conflicts of the second part of the sixteenth century had raised. They were regarded as new problems causing deep concern, and historical writers were expected to take them up. Finally, it ought to be added that Paruta and Morosini were official historiographers and, as the decrees of their appointments say, their histories were expected to be of use in the conduct of government; they must have considered that abstracting rules from the presentation of the past was an inherent part of the task of an official historiographer.

As official historiographers these Venetian writers were also custodians and transmitters of the Venetian myth[84]—another important aspect of the analysis of this episode. These writers maintained that Venetian statesmen had never acted without unusual wisdom, responsibility, and foresight. That certainly is the reason Morosini did not report the outcome of the debate he described. Venetian statesmen did not commit acts of disloyalty or serious diplomatic mistakes. If in Venice the art of history had advanced in realism beyond the *quattrocento,* when humanist rhetorics smothered the facts, historical truth was now limited by a myth which had become an integral part of Venetian political life.[85] Whereas in the fifteenth and the early part of the sixteenth century the political role Venice played was not very different from that of any other Italian government, at the end of the sixteenth century Venice was in a unique position: it was the only Italian state not under the control of a great foreign power. But as great powers were now dominating the political scene, the Venetian role in foreign policy became reduced to that of an observer rather than that of a principal. Indeed, it was as outside observers that the Venetian diplomats really became what the Venetian historians claimed that they had always been: masters of penetrating and objective observations.

It was the Venetians' weakness that fostered and fortified the Venetian myth. In an age of competition among great powers, Venetian independence was due to toleration by others rather than innate strength. It was natural for the Venetians—and perhaps necessary for their self-confidence—to refuse to recognize such a humiliating situation and to explain the preservation of Venice's independence as the work of age-old political wisdom by which Venice had always excelled all other states. Thus, the Venetian myth became an integral part of the Venetian reason of state.

13. The "New Diplomacy" of the Eighteenth Century

Ever since Woodrow Wilson, in the course of his attempts to lay a new and secure basis for peace after the First World War, proclaimed the necessity for "open convenants of peace, openly arrived at," the methods of diplomacy have been regarded as having had a part in the outbreak of the war, and demands for a "new diplomacy" have been raised. Although the concept has come into frequent use only in this century, it was early realized that its history could be traced back into the nineteenth century. Its exact provenance[1] has never been fully established, however. This essay will show that the term can be found even earlier than is generally assumed, namely as early as 1793.[2] As in all such disputes about the origin of a term, it would be ridiculous to maintain that this was definitely the first time this concept made its appearance, but there is justification for placing the concept in the second half of the eighteenth century. Prior to that period the rules and methods of diplomacy were not yet fixed. Diplomacy was so young a science that the demand for a "new diplomacy" could scarcely have had meaning. On the other hand, the spirit of criticism against the institutions of the

Originally published in *World Politics,* 4 (copyright 1951 Princeton University Press, reprinted by permission), 1–38. This is an enlarged version of the third chapter, "Novus Ordo Seculorum," of my book *To the Farewell Address* (Princeton, Princeton University Press, 1961), pp. 44–75.

ancien régime which developed in the eighteenth century extended also to the customary methods of handling foreign affairs. Thus, in the second half of the eighteenth century, there existed a whole body of reformist thinking out of which the concept of a "new diplomacy" could naturally develop. In providing an analysis of this body of thought, I hope to place the discussion of the origin of the term "new diplomacy" on solid ground and thereby to direct attention to features of eighteenth-century thought of which neither the ideological content nor the practical importance have been fully appreciated.

I

The center of interest of eighteenth-century political reformers—be they literary men, economists, scientists, or pure philosophers—was domestic policy.[3] It is only natural, therefore, that this aspect of their political ideas has been examined more intensively than their views on foreign policy.[4] Yet this is probably not the only reason for the special interest in the domestic aspects of their political theories; our view inclines toward this side because we look back on their ideas from the vantage point of a later century. Aware of the immense changes in the political, economic, and intellectual spheres which have swept over Europe since the French Revolution, we naturally evaluate the importance of eighteenth-century political theorists—Rousseau and Condorcet, the physiocrats and Adam Smith, Diderot and D'Alembert—mainly from the point of view of the contribution they made to the social and political developments of the nineteenth century. To us, the historical importance of the reformers and radicals of the eighteenth century lies in the support they gave to the emancipation of the forces which shaped the future of the modern world and we are mainly interested in those aspects of their theories which can be directly connected with the trends of our own time.

The *philosophes* of the eighteenth century did not regard themselves as prophets to whose eyes a new promised land appeared only in vague outline. They saw themselves at the end of a development, resolving the contrasts and conflicts of the past in a great synthesis and taking the final steps for accomplishment of a permanent order.[5] Though each new generation of society feels itself placed at the final stage of world historical

324

development, it should be recognized that the confidence of the *philosophes* in the near approach of the golden age had its foundation in a peculiar constellation of historical factors.

At the beginning of the century the Peace of Utrecht had ended a long period of conflicts and wars and established the basis of a new political system.[6] The stipulations of the treaty extended over the non-European world, and, thereby, the treaty had shown to what extent the great European powers, though they remained of central importance, drew their strength from the resources of the entire world. This is reflected in Turgot's statement that the trend of the time was to make "the boundaries of the political world become identical with those of the physical world."[7]

This feeling that one civilization now encompassed the whole world was reinforced by the astounding growth of economic interdependence. In the centers of European civilization people could rely on having a regular supply of goods from all over the world: sugar from the West Indies, tea and china from the Far East, coffee and chocolate from the Americas and Africa. The barriers that existed seemed artificial and ephemeral in comparison with the finely meshed net by which the merchants tied the individuals of the different nations together like "threads of silk." As Sedaine says in his famous comedy, the merchants—whether they are English, Dutch, Russian or Chinese—do not serve a single nation; they serve everyone and are citizens of the whole world.[8] Through the religious wars, the common religious basis of political society had been undermined and the idea of a Christian civilization within which the single political units lived had been destroyed; the impossibility of eliminating the sectarian differences had resulted in a fading of religious emphasis per se, and the vacuum which was left was now filled by the idea that commerce bound the nations together and created not only a community of interests but also a distribution of labor among them—a new comprehensive principle placing the isolated sovereign nations in a higher political unit. In the eighteenth century, writers were likely to say that the various nations belonged to "one society"; it was stated that all states together formed "a family of nations," and the whole globe a "general and unbreakable confederation."[9]

A decisive factor strengthening the belief that history had

reached a new and final stage was the increased importance of the class to which the economic progress was due, namely the bourgeoisie—a greater importance because of increase in numbers, in wealth, and in significance for the entire social structure. The members of the bourgeoisie became conscious of being the main prop of social life and of being entitled to an elimination of all obstacles to their development. Thus happened what always occurs when a new and rising class wants to break the restraints which keep it in a subordinate and sheltered position: its members identified their cause with the cause of the human race in general and believed that they were fighting for freedom against all tyranny rather than for their special interests against feudal privileges and suppression. The victory which seemed to be almost in their grasp appeared to them to be a victory of humanity, the final solution of all historical conflicts.[10]

In analyzing the utopian ideas of eighteenth-century *philosophes,* our main concern will be with French writers. This is entirely natural. France was not only the most powerful nation of Europe in the eighteenth century but also the central theater in which the issues of the century were fought out. The contrast between nobility and bourgeoisie, between the forces of the old order and of the new, were there revealed in sharper relief than in the economically less advanced countries of central and eastern Europe, on the one hand, or in England, on the other, where, as a result of the civil wars and revolutions of the previous century, the commercial classes were securing a steadily increasing influence on policy decisions. Moreover, though the wars of Louis XIV had brought France to the zenith of power in Europe, they had eventually threatened to carry her beyond that zenith. The French people had entered the century exhausted and dispirited. The traditional policy of territorial expansion on the continent and the drive for European hegemony had lost much of their glamour. An attempt in an entirely different direction, taking the economic interests of France as guide and aiming at the enlargement of the French colonial empire and the promotion of overseas trade, was the natural reaction. French foreign policy wavered between the two poles of a territorial-continental and commercial-maritime foreign policy.[11]

Thus, in France, political problems were posed with particular sharpness because the issues cut immediately and deeply into the fabric of the existing political structure. Moreover, inasmuch as France was the hub in the wheel of European policy, a radical change in the French political system was expected to be of the greatest importance for all of Europe and to bring about a new era in the world.[12] The chief interest of the *philosophes* was the presentation of a new program of interior policy, first to be adopted in France, then to spread over other parts of Europe.

We have said that the ideas of the *philosophes* on foreign policy have been relatively neglected as compared with the attention which their views on problems of domestic policy have received because only the latter had obviously far-reaching effects. One should perhaps add that the one-sidedness of the modern interest in the ideas of the *philosophes* was fostered by the *philosophes* themselves in that they subordinated foreign affairs to domestic issues. In analyzing their ideas on foreign policy, it is important to realize that they thought of diplomacy mainly in terms of its functional relationship to domestic policy. The great role foreign affairs played in the political life of their time was considered one of the most fundamental evils of the existing political system. D'Argenson has most succinctly formulated the basic attitude of the *philosophes* with regard to the relationship between domestic and foreign affairs. "Flatterers assure the princes that the interior is there only to serve foreign policy. Duty tells them the opposite . . . The true purpose of the science called politics is to perfect the interior of a state as much as possible."[13]

The *philosophes* directed a quite systematic attack against the view that regarded foreign policy as the center and culmination of political activities. They assailed the entire concept of man underlying this philosophy of power politics. The high evaluation of military virtues is a "dangerous prejudice, a carry-over from barbarism, a remnant of the former chaos."[14] "True fame consists not in the glory which the stupidity of the people connects with military conquests and which the still more stupid historians love to praise to the point of boring the reader."[15] If the right name were to be given to conquests "which for so long have been praised as heroism," they would be called crimes.[16]

327

Beyond assailing the scale of values in which heroic military virtues occupied a pre-eminent place, the *philosophes* also tried to close every avenue of escape for those who attempted to justify the existing methods of diplomacy by maintaining that they served best to achieve the opposite aim, namely, peace. All the ideas on which such claims were based were subjected to biting criticism. The main target of the *philosophes* in this respect was the assumption that the only possibility and guarantee of peace lay in the maintenance of a balance of power among the states. There is hardly a *philosophe* and reformer who did not inveigh against the idea of balance of power, "this favorite idea of newspapers and coffee-house politicians."[17] This idea, "reducing the whole science of politics to knowledge of a single word, pleases both the ignorance and the laziness of the ministers, of ambassadors and their clerks."[18] In contrast to the ostensible aim of promoting peace, balance of power had, it was said, always done harm to the system of lasting peace and was opposed to it. The reason was that "the system of balance of power is a system of resistance, consequently of disturbance, of shocks and of explosions."[19]

With the overthrow of this central concept of eighteenth-century diplomacy, other concerns of traditional diplomacy were also re-evaluated and revealed as futile and dangerous. According to the *philosophes,* the conclusion of treaties and alliances, the most significant activity of eighteenth-century diplomacy, did not promote friendly relations among states; treaties were nothing but "temporary armistices"[20] and alliances "preparations for treason."[21] Even when they were called defensive alliances, they were "in reality always of an offensive nature."[22] Diplomatic activity, thus being identical with double-dealing and pursuing different purposes from those it openly avowed, needed to wrap itself in secrecy and had become an "obscure art which hides itself in the folds of deceit, which fears to let itself be seen and believes it can exist only in the darkness of mystery."[23] Secrecy, therefore, was not—as the diplomats pretended—necessary for the efficient fulfillment of their functions; it only proved that they were conspirators planning crimes. Diderot in a brief satirical piece entitled "Political Principles of Rulers" summarized the views of the *philosophes* on the diplomacy of their time. "Make alliances only in order to sow hatred. Incite wars among my neighbors and try to keep it going. Have no ambassadors in other countries, but spies . . . To be neutral means to profit from the difficulties of others in order to improve one's own situation."[24]

Though different writers made different aspects of diplomacy—secrecy or formality of etiquette—the chief subjects of their criticism, they were all in agreement that diplomacy could not be reformed by redressing any single abuse. The evil inherent in diplomacy could be removed only by a complete reform of the political system. The criminal manner in which foreign affairs were conducted was regarded as one of the most characteristic manifestations and a chief consequence of the basic misconstruction of political life; it was proof that, in contrast to other fields of study, "the science which is called politics" had not yet been reduced "to definite and fixed principles" and had not become a servant of "the rule of reason."[25] Foreign affairs showed most clearly and most strikingly the evil of a world not yet ruled by reason. "The blind passions of the princes"[26] were the cause of wars, conquests, and all the miseries accompanying them. A favorite story[27] of the eighteenth century illustrating the arbitrariness which dominated foreign policy was the story of the palace window: Louvois, fearing disgrace because Louis XIV had expressed displeasure with his arrangements concerning the construction of the windows of the Trianon, instigated the king to a renewal of the war against the Habsburgs in order to divert his attention from architectural matters. As long as foreign policy continued to be determined by passions, by whims and arbitrary proclivities, diplomacy could be nothing else but "the art of intrigue."[28]

According to the *philosophes,* instead of the whims and moods of an individual, the interests of the state ought to become the guiding factor. They are steady and lasting, composed of definable and calculable elements such as geographical situation, size of population, economic interests. By following them, men will be able to keep events on a calculable, well-charted course.[29] In pursuing its "true interest," each state will become—to use another favorite expression of the eighteenth century—"master of its own fortune."[30] Of course, the doctrine of the reason of state that not personal decisions but supra-individual factors determine the policy of a state—has a long history, but it received

a special turn in the eighteenth century because the true interest of a state was regarded as definable and calculable; it was believed that it could be grasped by reason. Moreover, if the
interests of the states were correctly gauged, it would emerge
that they were not opposed to one another, but compatible and
complementary.[31] War and conflict would then be at an end.

If one wants to reduce this whole complex of eighteenth-
century ideas on diplomacy to a simple formula, it can be summarized as the establishment of a rule of reason.[32] It is the same
solution which the *philosophes* had for the problems of domestic
policy; in view of the pre-eminence they gave to domestic over
foreign affairs, they considered the introduction of a new and
peaceful era in foreign policy as dependent on a reorganization
of domestic policy. There was no need to be particularly concerned about the problems of foreign policy; they were only a
partial aspect of the wider problem of placing domestic affairs
on a rational basis.[33] Yet how could this be effected? As much
as the eighteenth-century reformers agreed on the basic concepts we sketched above, they differed in their views on the
realization of their ideas; this complex of reformist ideas comprised at least two separate elements, one predominantly conservative, the other radical democratic.

A most important trend of thought in the system of
eighteenth-century ideas was physiocracy—with which a great
number of thinkers were connected, some in a more, others in a
less orthodox way. The physiocratic school cannot be clearly
and definitely distinguished from other contemporary trends of
thought. Although today it is mainly seen as propounding a new
and important economic doctrine, in the eighteenth century the
significance of physiocratic theories seemed to reach far beyond
the economic sphere and to range over the entire structure of
social and political life. The physiocrats called their political
theory "economic policy" not because they were concerned
solely with economic questions, but because, to them, economics and politics were identical. They believed that all political
problems would be solved if the right economic principles were
followed, the right economic measures adopted. The contrast
to "economic policy" was the "old policy," "the false policy," or
"power politics"—all these terms were alternately used.[34] "The
essence of power politics consists of divergence of interests,

that of economic policy of unity of interests—the one leads to war, frustrations, destruction, the other to social integration, co-operation, and free and peaceful sharing of the fruits of work.[35]

The physiocrats elaborated this contrast between "the old policy" and "the economic policy," between an "artificial" and a "natural" political situation, with great gusto and especially emphasized that as a result of the artificiality of the "old policy" dealings had to be shrouded in secrecy and mystery.[36] The diplomats had to be actors—"competitors in grimaces"[37]—and each nation was barricaded behind its own frontiers, intent on making commercial treaties to its own advantage and to the disadvantage of its neighbor. In contrast, the new world in which the "economic policy" was to be realized would have an unrestricted exchange of goods. From mutual interdependence would emerge the realization that increase in one nation's wealth means increased wealth for all other nations, and that the interests of all nations are identical; consequently, there would be no advantage in enlarging one's own territory and combating one's neighbor. A single measure, namely, the establishment of free trade, would bring about this miraculous change; it was up to the rulers of the states to take this one decisive measure. The physiocrats were favorites of many princes, and their faith in the power of reason was so strong that they believed in the probability of persuading the rulers of the states to make this change. They were no opponents of despotism; on the contrary, they were confident that the new order could be introduced quite easily with and even by means of the prince's absolute power.[38]

In their support of absolute monarchy the physiocrats were by no means representative of all eighteenth-century thought. To many *philosophes,* despotism was an integral part of the old order, which had to be overcome. To this way of thinking the decisive step in establishing the new order was a change in political leadership; the people themselves had to take over control of political life. Accordingly, the conduct of foreign affairs in a reformed world assumed a rather different aspect.

Condorcet, for instance, who gave this question extended consideration, was concerned with creating a mechanism through which the people could make themselves felt in foreign affairs.[39] He demanded that no convention between nations be valid without approval of the legislative body; moreover, as a further safeguard, political treaties should be ratified by the single districts of a state. In case of an enemy attack, war might be declared, but only by the legislature, and a declaration of war would have to be followed immediately by new elections, which would give the people opportunity to express their views on the war. Evidently Condorcet had no doubt that the people would always be peace-loving, and he was concerned with removing all obstacles to the people's directly expressing their will. Thus diplomats appeared to him mainly as intermediaries who might prevent the people from making their voice heard; he had no use for diplomats in general or for diplomatic arrangements establishing automatic obligations by which the freedom of action of a nation would be bound. "Alliance treaties seem to me so dangerous and so little useful that I think it is better to abolish them entirely in time of peace. They are only means by which the rulers of states precipitate the people into wars from which they benefit either by covering up their mistakes or by carrying out their plots against freedom, and for which the emergency serves as a pretext."[40]

Condorcet was probably the most logical and most influential representative of a strictly democratic approach to the questions of diplomacy in the eighteenth century. Another representative of the democratic point of view, Rousseau, must also be considered because although he too feels the necessity of giving the people control over foreign affairs, he adds a new element to this way of thinking. Like other eighteenth-century thinkers, he considered the prevailing customs and methods of diplomacy as anarchical and obsolete, but in contrast to them he saw necessity in the existing diplomatic forms; diplomatic manners reflected the historical development which the relations among nations had reached. The time when states lived in isolation had passed. They were now interconnected by common historical experiences and heritage, by tradition and interest; they had come to be dependent upon each other in many regards, yet because their relations were not yet brought into a fixed and permanent form, the fact of their coexistence expressed itself in the unsatisfactory form of shocks and countershocks, of tensions and conflicts. A flexible balance of power was the best possible solution to this situation. The anarchic struggle of man against man had ended only through the social contract. Unlike individuals, states still lived in a state of nature, though the increasing interdependence of the states indicated that this period was coming to a close. Governments would soon realize the necessity of ending the state of nature among nations through the conclusion of a pact which, in Rousseau's opinion, would take the form of a federation of nations and would thus assure peace. The tempo of this process would depend on the progress of republicanism, because governments controlled by the people would be more willing to subordinate themselves to a world federation.[41]

It is almost superfluous to discuss the kind of diplomacy the *philosophes* envisaged for the era when the rule of reason had been established; their views on the diplomacy of the future are implied in their attacks against existing diplomacy. The future diplomacy would be the reverse of the diplomacy of the past.[42] Relations among nations should follow moral laws. There should be no difference between the "moral principles" which rule the relations among individuals and "moral principles" which rule the relations among states.[43] Diplomacy should be "frank and open."[44] Formal treaties would be unnecessary; political alliances should be avoided particularly.[45] Commercial conventions should refrain from all detailed regulations establishing individual advantages and privileges; they should limit themselves to general arrangements stating the fundamental rules and customs of trade and navigation.[46] In such a world the connection among the different states would rest in the hands not of governments but of individuals trading with each other. If the *philosophes* failed to give a very detailed description of the diplomatic systems which would exist in the world of the future, there is a special reason—quite aside from the fact that the outlines of the utopia which radical reformers imagine usually remain rather vague and general. As we have seen, foreign policy and diplomacy were regarded as typical phenomena of the ancien régime; they owed their importance to the fact that the rulers followed false ideals and egoistic passions instead of reason. The logical consequence was that in a reformed world, based on reason, foreign policy and diplomacy would become unnecessary,[47] and the new world would be a world without diplomats.

II

The eighteenth century was less aware of the distance between reality and idea than is the present age and, therefore, less doubtful about the possibilities of realizing a utopia. To the *philosophes,* the logical and ethical correctness of an idea guaranteed that it could be carried out in practice. In further support of their concept of diplomacy, the *philosophes* liked to point out that in many respects this concept had guided the policy of two eminently successful states. Venice and the Netherlands—states entirely different from the usual pattern of early modern absolutism—were objects of fascinated curiosity and interest throughout the eighteenth century.[48] The *philosophes* directed particular attention to the fact that these repulics owed their success to the policy of avoiding political alliances and following exclusively commercial interests, trusting to the bonds which trade would establish between them and their neighbors.

One of the great literary successes of the eighteenth century was a book presumed to be the political testament of the Dutch statesman Jan de Witt. There the successes of Holland's foreign policy were characterized as the fruit of the observance of those principles recommended by the *philosophes.* Holland had avoided "all wars and alliances founded upon conquest and glory" and had "not meddled with the parting of princes." In placing commercial interets above all others she had attracted the friendship of all political powers. "He that loves himself aright is a friend to all the world."[49]

There were several attempts by statesmen influenced by the *philosophes* to conduct foreign affairs in accord with such principles.[50] D'Argenson made a rather futile and clumsy attempt to harmonize the traditional hegemonial policy of France with a policy of selflessness and renunciation of conquest.[51] Turgot fought against Vergennes, though vainly, for abandonment of all efforts to avenge the French defeat in the Seven Years' War and for concentration on domestic affairs instead of wasting France's strength in enterprises of foreign policy.[52] Leopold of Tuscany, one of the most loyal disciples of the physiocrats, abjured all power policy, dissolved the army, made Leghorn, Tuscany's main harbor, a free port, and declared his country neutral.[53] Although Catherine II's Armed Neutrality was mainly determined by anti-English considerations and aimed to free Russia from the pressure of English maritime domination, it could be regarded as an attempt to humanize war and was claimed by the *philosophes* to be inspired by their ideas.

It is evident, however, that the real test could only come when a country had broken all ties with the past. It is in the American and French revolutions that the most significant attempts were made to put the ideas of eighteenth-century *philosophes* into practice. Thus the history of eighteenth-century attempts to reform diplomacy and to introduce new principles into the conduct of foreign affairs has a second aspect; beyond the analysis of the ideas themselves we have to consider the attempts to realize them in America and France.

III

In the sequence of events which led to the foundation of an independent United States, an irrevocable step was taken when, on June 7, 1776, the Continental Congress entered upon the consideration of R. H. Lee's resolution "that these United Colonies are, and of right ought to be, free and independent States, that they are absolved from all allegiance to the British crown, and that all political connection between them and the state of Great Britain is, and ought to be, totally dissolved; that it is expedient forthwith to take the most effectual measures for forming foreign Alliances; that a plan of confederation be prepared and transmitted to the respective Colonies for their consideration and approbation."[54]

A pivot of this motion was the urgent need for foreign assistance.[55] The ban on all export and import trade put into force in the fall of 1775 did more damage to the colonists than to the British.[56] Rising prices, the impossibility of disposing of the tobacco and indigo harvests on which the economic life of the southern colonies depended, and the needs of the army—all combined to make a failure of the economic blockade by which Congress had hoped to force the British government to change its policy. Thus on April 6, Congress reversed its stand and ordered the opening of American ports to the ships of all nations except Great Britain. Because of British supremacy on the seas and the lack of an American navy, the success of this measure depended on the willingness of foreign powers not only to receive American trade but also to protect it. Political observers were aware, however, that no foreign power could risk assisting the American rebels without a definite guarantee that some stable regime would be created on the North American continent and that return to British rule would be made impossible. "Confederation" and "independence" were the necessary prerequisites for securing "foreign alliances."[57]

But what did the Americans understand by the term "foreign alliances"? This question is of central importance in determining the relationship of the American revolutionaries to enlightenment ideas on foreign policy. The question can be answered only by examining the general diplomatic terminology of the time and the views of such key figures as Benjamin Franklin and John Adams with regard to these issues. With this understanding of the contemporary meaning of the term, it is then possible to explain the meaning of the two important documents in which the colonists first formulated their ideas about the role of the United States in the state system: the draft treaty of an alliance with France and the accompanying instructions given to the commissioners entrusted with these negotiations.

The meaning of the term "foreign alliances" as it is used by the colonists at this time is by no means unequivocal. John Adams, who had been so active in promoting the cause of independence that he had earned for himself the title of "Atlas of Independence," reviewed a few years later the events of the summer and declared that in the debates of the fall of 1776 on the application to foreign powers he had laid it down as a first principle that "we should calculate all our measures and foreign negotiations in such a manner, as to avoid a too great dependence upon any power of Europe—to avoid all obligations and temptations to take any part in future European wars: that the business of America with Europe was commerce, not politics or war."[58] Since, in 1776, Adams had been a zealous supporter of Lee's resolution, this would suggest that at that time the word "alliance" was understood rather differently than we understand it today, when it is regarded as denoting the establishment of cooperation among the contracting parties in the political sphere. An examination of the manner in which the term was used in the eighteenth century in general and by the colonists in particular shows that indeed this is the case. The term did not necessarily have the meaning of creating a political bond.

It can probably be said that our identification of alliance with political or even political-military commitments derives from the fact that in the modern world diplomatic instruments which contain political or political-military arrangements are sharply separated from those concerned with regulations of trade, tariffs, and so forth. Yet this separation of political treaties from commercial treaties began only in the eighteenth century. The Peace of Utrecht, ending the hostilities of the War of Spanish Succession between England and France, for the first time dealt with political and commercial arrangements in separate documents. Even this example was followed only slowly. Political, commercial, or economic settlements still were frequently dealt with in the same document. Thus there are many nuances in the seventeenth and eighteenth centuries between the most opposite types of the "traité d'alliance offensive et défensive," clearly designating a political-military bond, and the "traité de commerce," exclusively concerned with trade. Such terms[59] as "traité d'alliance et de commerce," "traité de paix, de navigation et de commerce," "traité de navigation et commerce," "traité de marine," suggest the variety of content which could be contained in a single diplomatic document.

There is a similar lack of distinctness in diplomatic terminology in the use of such expressions as "commercial connections" and "political connections," so frequently applied by the colonists to their relations with outside powers. When, in the fall of 1775, the great debate on the opening of the ports took place, the view was expressed that with the separation of the American colonies from Britain's imperial system, the possibility of trading with the colonies would be enough attraction to the French to undertake the protection of the trade with America.[60] When Franklin wrote about the possibility of exchanging "commerce for friendship," however, he seems to have felt that a somewhat more substantial inducement in the form of some monopoly must be offered to France.[61] The French agent even reported from Philadelphia that Franklin and other members of the Continental Congress had mentioned to him the possibility of offering France "un commerce exclusif" for a limited period,[62] and Silas Deane when he arrived in France felt empowered to suggest a tobacco monopoly for a definite term. [63]

The expression "political connections," too, had varied shadings. The bond which before the War of Independence had joined the colonies with Britain was sometimes characterized as a mere exchange of military protection for commercial advantages and called an "alliance."[64] It was considered a possible dangerous consequence of the conclusion of an alliance with an outside power that "an expedient of this kind" would lead the colonists into "having their allies at last for their masters"[65]; it would produce the exchange of domination by one power for domination by another. To avoid this danger, it was suggested that the alliance be restricted to "external assistance,"[66] in other words, a distinction between cooperation on land and cooperation at sea was envisaged. While the French navy should be allowed to play a part on the sea, no assistance by a French army should be accepted.

Aside from showing the vagueness of diplomatic terminology in the eighteenth century, these remarks also indicate how little the thinking of the colonists had crystallized around any definite conception of what a foreign alliance implied when Lee proposed his resolution on June 7, 1776. Only when as a result of this resolution the members of Congress began to deliberate on the treaty to be proposed to France and on the instructions to the American agents did their ideas begin to take a definite and—it may immediately be said—a most interesting shape, showing the influence of eighteenth-century radical thought on the beginnings of American foreign policy.

The sequence of events is clearly established. On June 11, 1776, in consequence of Lee's resolution, a committee was appointed to prepare the model of a treaty to be proposed to the French court.[67] This committee handed in its report on July 18 and the report was discussed in the Continental Congress on August 22, 27, and 29. Then it was referred back to the committee for amendment and for preparation of instructions to the American agents. On September 17, the final report of the committee was made to Congress and the latter's agreement to the prepared instructions was given on September 24. Two days later, Franklin, Deane, and Jefferson were appointed commissioners to France.[68]

The story behind these factual events is much more difficult to disentangle because there are no accounts of the discussions in Congress. It must be reconstructed from a few documents—the model treaty and the instructions—and from brief references in the letters and memoirs of the main actors.

There can be no doubt that John Adams played a most decisive role in these discussions. He was a member of the committee entrusted with the preparation of the model treaty, and the task of drafting this document fell mainly on him. Thus it is of importance to understand the attitude with which he approached this task.[69] Adams had been one of the earliest protagonists of independence and as such had early realized the necessity of foreign alliances. In March 1776, evidently influenced by Thomas Paine's *Common Sense,* he had set down on paper his ideas as to the "connection we may safely form with France" and arrived at the following formula: "1. No political connection. Submit to none of her authority, receive no governors or officers from her. 2. No military connection. Receive no troops from her. 3. Only a commercial connection; that is make a treaty to receive her ships into our ports; let her engage to receive our ships into her ports; furnish us with arms, cannon, saltpetre, powder, duck, steel."[70] How fundamental these ideas were for him can be deduced from the fact that they also appear in letters which he wrote in the spring of 1776. He urges the necessity of sending ambassadors to foreign ports "to form with them, at least with some of them, commercial treaties of friendship and alliance,"[71] and when the dangers to American freedom of an alliance with a foreign power was pointed out to him, he stressed that in recommending foreign alliances he was thinking only of a contractual safeguard of America's trade relations. "I am not for soliciting any political connection or military assistance or indeed naval from France. I wish for nothing but commerce, a mere marine treaty with them."[72]

The model treaty can be regarded as Adams's work, and an analysis of this document shows that it was intended to realize the ideas which he had previously developed—namely, that alliance did not imply a political bond and that America's contacts with outside powers should be limited to trade relations. In his autobiography, Adams wrote that when he started to work on the draft of this model treaty, Franklin put into his hand "a printed volume of treaties" in which he had made some pencil marks beside certain articles. Adams found "some of these judiciously selected, and I took them, with others which I found necessary, into the draught."[73] In comparing the model treaty with earlier documents it emerges that Adams relied heavily on two particular treaties: the treaty between James II and Louis XIV of November 16, 1686, concerning the neutrality of the American colonies in case of a conflict between England and France, and the commercial treaty between England and France of 1713. Most of the stipulations of the model treaty concerned with the regulation of trade, navigation, and fishing—which is to say, the greater part of the model treaty—are taken from these treaties.[74] In other words, the agreements which regulated the commercial relations between England and France were used as patterns, with the United States being substituted for England. It seems likely, however, that the commercial treaty between England and France of 1713 was chosen not only because it was an obvious model but also because its commercial regulations were of a most liberal nature; its progressive character probably was a chief attraction to the Americans, whose entire draft is dominated by this spirit. The liberal principles of the American draft emerge particularly from the articles dealing with trade in wartime.[75] The model treaty contained a precisely circumscribed list of contraband goods which was extremely limited, even foodstuffs and naval stores being excluded from it. It provided that neutrals should have the right to trade with belligerents and asked for the acceptance of the principle that free ships make free goods. Moreover, France was to be offered either reciprocity or the most-favored-nation treatment[76]—certainly because the colonists wanted to point out the great advantages that would accrue to France from supporting the colonies, but also in all probability because these concepts corresponded to the colonists' aim of a general liberalization of trade.

It was not possible, however, to limit the model treaty exclusively to questions of trade and navigation; a number of political questions had to be taken up.[77] Thus French protection was to replace the former English protection of American ships against the attacks of the Barbary states. Moreover, a number of articles were concerned with the problems which had arisen from the war against the British and had forced the colonists into "their application to foreign powers." It was stipulated that American ships should be protected and convoyed by their allies and that France should give up any claim to territories of the North American continent, while the Americans would not oppose a French conquest of the West Indies.

But would the fact that both France and the United States were moving in a sharply anti-English direction not make it desirable that they agree on common action for war and peace and that their cooperation be given a definite form, one that we would now call a political alliance? There can be no doubt that the purpose of the approach to France was involvement of France in the war against England; hence some statement about the reciprocal obligations of the two powers fighting against the same enemy was necessary. However, the manner in which the colonists dealt with this question in article 8 was both surprising and striking, as it revealed their disinclination to be forced into any political bond with an outside power even under the pressure of war. Article 8 states that in case the alliance with the United States should involve France in war with England, the United States would not assist England in such a war. The promise which was offered in this article—that America would not use the opportunity of an Anglo-French war for coming to an understanding with England—was little more than a matter of course; its striking aspect is how little was offered. Clearly the colonists planned to avoid political and military cooperation with France even if France should enter the war against England.

A number of the members of the Continental Congress seem to have felt that such love of principle defeated its own purpose and that a somewhat more realistic approach was necessary to obtain French participation in the war. The clash of minds to which this article led is reflected in the instructions accompanying the model treaty. The article evoked a large number of comments.[78] It was admitted at the outset that this "article will probably be attended with some Difficulty." The group that felt most urgently the necessity of French participation in the war suggested a more direct inducement.[79]

If the Court of France cannot be prevailed on to engage in the War with Great Britain for any consideration already proposed in this Treaty, you are hereby authorized to agree as a further inducement, that these United States will wage the war in union with France—not make peace with Great Britain until the latter France shall gain the possession of those Islands in the West Indies formerly called Nieutral, and which by the Treaty of Paris were ceded to G. Britain: provided France shall make the conquest of these Islands an early object of the War and prosecute the same with sufficient force.

The proponents of this statement were defeated, as is shown by the fact that this suggestion was omitted from the final form of the instructions. But the commissioners were empowered to make one additional offer, namely, that the United States was willing to guarantee that she would never return to the allegiance of Great Britain and that she would grant to no other power priveleges in trade which she had not granted to the French king. Furthermore, in case France should become involved in the present war, neither France nor the United States would conclude peace without notifying the other power six months ahead.[80]

From these various suggestions on the form the relations between the United States and France should take, it emerges that the majority of the Congress—in contrast to those who believed that the war against England made it necessary for the United States to have recourse to all the customary methods of power politics—was not willing to pay the price of concluding a political alliance despite the urgent need of maneuvering France into the war. Instead, they clung to the principle that future relations with outside powers should be limited to commercial questions. This attitude has generally been explained as an early manifestation of American isolationism. Though inclinations toward isolationism doubtless played a part in this decision, interpreting these negotiations as the exclusive result of an isolationist outlook reflects too much the point of view of a later period. The colonists, in attempting to eliminate power politics and to place relations with other nations on a purely commercial basis, acted entirely in accord with radical eighteenth-century thought as shown in our analysis of the ideas of the *philosophes* on diplomacy. In modern terms, it was no less an internationalist than an isolationist attitude which prompted their action.[81]

The strong influence of eighteenth-century ideas concerning the reform of diplomacy on the formation of American foreign policy is also reflected in other parts of the model treaty and sections of the instructions, particularly in the suggestions regarding the basic principles of future commercial relations between France and the United States. As already noted, the very liberal treaties between England and France of 1686 and 1713 had been the models for the paragraphs on trade and navigation in the draft treaty. But the first two articles of the draft treaty went beyond its models; there it was suggested that the French should treat the inhabitants of the United States with regard to duties and imports like natives of France and vice versa; moreover, they "shall enjoy all the other Rights, Liberties, Priviledges, Immunities and Exemptions in Trade, Navigation and Commerce, in passing from one port (Part) thereof to another, and in going to and from the same, from and to any Part of the World, which the said natives or Companies enjoy."[82] The "instructions" added that, only if "His Most Christian Majesty shall not consent to these articles," the commissioners should try to get the French agreement to the most-favored-nation clause.[83] The fundamental concepts behind these treaty proposals are evident and, as far as the practical policy of the period is concerned, striking[84]: in drafting the model treaty the colonists were thinking not only of France but also of other powers. They were in effect creating a general pattern for future commercial treaties. Whereas usually commercial conventions were causes of friction and instruments of power politics reinforcing political alliances and blocks by commercial preferences, the Americans wanted to establish a commercial system of freedom and equality which would eliminate all cause for tension and political conflicts.

Ten years later, after John Adams had gained diplomatic experience in Paris, The Hague, and London and had acquired the arrogance of a nearsighted realism which is the professional vice of diplomats of all times, he abandoned all "hope for a 'reformation,' a kind of protestantism in the commercial system of the world."[85] He writes that "the philosophical visions of perpetual peace, and the religious reveries of a near approach of the millennium, in which all nations are to turn the weapons of war into implements of husbandry will, in a few years, be dissi-

Diplomacy: Old and New

pated."[86] His countrymen should abandon "delusive dreams of peace."[87] "We have hitherto been the bubbles of our own philosophical and equitable liberty—I hope we shall be the dupes no longer than we must."[88]

As contemptuous as these sentences are toward those who believe in the perfectibility of the world, they are valuable testimony to the influence which the ideas of a reform of the diplomatic system had at the time of the beginnings of an independent American policy.[89] It must be added that if Adams soon sloughed off the garb of an idealist, this development was not shared by many of those who had cooperated with him on the model treaty in 1776. The ideas out of which the model treaty had sprung did not vanish when the negotiations with France resulted in an alliance different in character from the one originally envisaged by the colonists and more in keeping with traditional diplomatic institutions. As soon as independence had been achieved and the need for foreign assistance in the struggle against Britain had disappeared, the French alliance lost its attraction[90] and complete neutrality and independence from all powers became the aim. The view that "the true interest of the States requires that they should be as little as possible entangled in the politics and controversies of European nations"[91] re-emerged as the fundamental principle of American foreign policy. An example of America's wish to avoid the European political scene is Jefferson's suggestion that America not aim at the establishment of diplomatic missions at the various European courts but be content with consular representation.[92]

It was not only the negative aspect of the eighteenth-century approach to foreign affairs that remained a factor in American foreign policy. Americans also clung to the positive aspects of the *philosophes'* thought in continuing their attempts to remove the causes of political conflicts by "bringing together all nations for a free communication of happiness."[93] They renewed their attempts to transform the world of traditional power politics into a new and peaceful world by a "total emancipation of commerce." This goal motivated their suggestions concerning the form of future commercial treaties as well as their attempts to humanize war and limit its impact on commerce.[94] These efforts to place foreign affairs on a new base where power politics would become unnecessary were not simply a product of the

344

enthusiasm of a new nation, inexperienced in foreign policy and taking its first steps in this field. Rather, they were the expression and reflection of currents of thought prevailing in all reformist political programs of the eighteenth century, and they remained guiding principles of American foreign policy even after it had become clear that their realization was a complicated process requiring more than the determination of a single nation to enter upon this new road.

The persistence with which Americans continued their attempts at introducing new principles and methods in foreign affairs shows that the failure of their first efforts along these lines in 1776 was not considered a refutation of the whole system of thought that eighteenth-century radicalism had evolved on diplomacy and foreign affairs. Since belief in the validity of these ideas was not shaken, it was only natural that the attempt to put them into practice should be renewed when another nation broke away from the traditions of the ancien régime. When in May 1790 the French National Assembly for the first time discussed problems of foreign policy, radicals like Robespierre, Rewbell, and Volney were the chief advocates of a new departure in foreign affairs in accord with the ideas of the *philosophes*. Their speeches and proposals sound like a brief summation of the ideas of the reformers on diplomacy. They explained that the main purpose of traditional methods of handling foreign affairs was war and that for this reason secrecy played an important role in diplomacy. "Secrecy only furthers injustice; it only produces mistakes. All our evils must be attributed to such shady procedures, to the clandestine operations of the ministers."[95] Thus, they recommended keeping away from all alliances and involvements in the European system of power politics. "Alliance treaties lead only to the right of levying new taxes and of ruining the treasury. . . . A great nation should have no other allies but providence, its power and justice."[96] Although the radicals who expressed these ideas represented only a small minority in the assembly, their arguments directed the whole debate toward the question whether France should have political connections or whether "France should isolate herself from the political system of Europe."[97] Even if the majority did not believe that the time had come for a complete break with traditional power politics, they did not want to deny the importance of these ideas for the future. Mirabeau probably summed up the *communis opinio* when he said that "undoubtedly the time will come when we shall have only friends and no allies, when there will be universal freedom of trade and when Europe will form one great family." But at present, when the other powers still clung to the old power politics, it would be inadvisable "to trust to chance the influence which other powers exert on us and which we can exert on other powers."[98]

But the radicals who had formed a small minority in 1790 were in power two years later and could then attempt to put their ideas into practice. Dumouriez, the new foreign minister, had outlined his views in a memorandum to the Jacobins: "A great nation, a free and just nation is the natural ally of all nations and does not need to conclude particular alliances which tie her to the fate, the interests and passions of this or that nation."[99] As foreign minister, he enunciated the same principles to the American minister, to whom he explained that "his system of politics was extremely simple, that a Power so great as France stood in no Need of Alliances and therefore he was against all Treaties other than those of Commerce."[100] Dumouriez tried to emphasize his break with secret diplomacy and his intention of carrying out a program of open diplomacy by communicating to the Committee of Foreign Affairs the entire diplomatic correspondence and by informing even the ministers of the foreign powers of the contents of the instructions which he sent out.[101]

Yet the pursuit of these principles clashed with the exigencies of the political situation in which France found herself when the radicals came to power. France was at war. A strengthening of the French position by rallying around France as many allies as possible seemed necessary for reasons of practical policy. Talleyrand found an ingenious way to reconcile the principle of refraining from all alliances with the necessity of getting the support of other nations.[102] A distinction was drawn between the bonds which could be established among free nations and those by which France could tie herself to a government of the ancien régime. With free nations, Talleyrand explained, France could conclude "solemn treaties of friendship in which the interests of a common defense are established and determined in an unchangeable manner, and through which new resources of trade and industry will be open to the needs and enterprises of the entire human race."[103] The contractual relation with those countries not yet freed from the chains of the ancien régime had to take a very different form. The bond between them and France ought not to be "a permanent treaty of alliance and friendship, but a temporary convention concerning political and commercial interests as they arise from circumstances."[104] By this formula the way was opened for a return to traditional power politics without directly betraying the principles that inspired the revolution.

Under the Directorate France returned to the usual methods of diplomacy.[105] Yet before this happened there was a brief return to a foreign policy of pure idealistic principles. In 1792, when Talleyrand had first made his ingenious justification for gaining allies among the states of the *ancien régime,* it had not been followed by immediate success; the objective situation had not been changed. France had remained isolated, involved in war with Holland, England, and Spain. Under these circumstances, for a short time at least, the French found it possible and even useful again to appear as protagonists of a new world order and to hoist the banner of a revolutionary foreign policy. These principles were explained in a series of articles in the Moniteur written by G. J. A. Ducher, an official of the French foreign office.[106] After the war, he wrote, France would be able to stand by herself. "She will need no guarantees, her natural strength will place her above the need for any ally whatsoever." She would take no part "in the intrigues of all the European cabinets"; "by preserving an absolute neutrality in the wars among the monarchs, she will exist in a different hemisphere," "free, peaceful, the friend of all peoples, not being tied by any of those treacherous treaties that are contradictory in themselves and which, through their formulations of clauses about defensive and aggressive assistance and about commerce, arbitrarily open the door to those who seek pretexts for conflicts and wars."[107] Yet Ducher's program also had a positive aspect, as it was expected to usher in a new and better world order. There would be no "other diplomacy than the diplomacy of commerce which forms the natural bond among people, the most solid foundation of their prosperity and the most powerful means of maintaining or recovering their political freedom."[108]

These commercial agreements should be of a general nature, should abolish all preferences, and should give to each nation equality and independence.[109] In introducing these new principles into the conduct of foreign affairs, France would become, as Ducher writes, the protagonist of a "new diplomacy."[110]

IV

Eighteenth-century attempts to put into practice the program of a "new diplomacy" are related to the isolated positions in which the United States and France found themselves in the society of states. The United States was in revolt against the subordinate place which the non-European world held in the international system; France had broken away from the economic and social order in which the bourgeoisie was dominated by a small ruling group. In both cases, the adoption of a "new diplomacy," partly at least, served the function of gaining the support of elements dissatisfied with the existing order and of overcoming the isolation in which the outsiders found themselves.

At the beginning of our analysis, we referred to the revival of the concept of a "new diplomacy" in twentieth-century politics. It occurred in two forms; for it should not be overlooked that Wilson's Fourteen Points were only the answer to the "new diplomacy" which the new communist leaders of Russia were proclaiming. The parallel between the "new diplomacy" of the French Revolution and the "new diplomacy" of the Soviet leaders is obvious. In both cases the proclamation of the necessity of a new departure in foreign policy was a concomitant of the complete break with the social and economic order existing in the outside world.

But what were the reasons for Wilson's "new diplomacy"? Intellectually, a straight line leads from the enlightenment to Wilson's concept. His ideas concerning a "new diplomacy" were certainly dependent upon and influenced by eighteenth-century thinking on this subject.[111] It raises the question whether a statesman from any other country would have taken his ideas so directly and clearly from a previous century, and is a striking manifestation of the strong hold which, in general, eighteenth-century ideas have over the American mind. But it must be kept in mind that since the United States, even after formal acceptance as a member of the state system, remained an outsider because of its geographical position, the ideas with which its foreign policy started were never fully tested and readjusted in the process of political give-and-take. Did these ideas re-emerge in their pristine form because of their enduring strength or because of their having led a sheltered existence throughout the nineteenth century? The history of the concept of a "new diplomacy" points to an inherent problem in the American approach to foreign affairs: namely, that of being ahead or behind, but not in real contact with, the outside world.

14. Ciano and His Ambassadors

"In Italy, the most Fascist ministry is that of Foreign Affairs," Galeazzo Ciano said proudly to a German visitor in October 1937.[1] The Fascist penetration of the Italian Foreign Office appeared to him a remarkable achievement, the result of a slow and difficult process; it is clear, moreover, that he believed he deserved the credit for having accomplished it. "In Italy," he confided to his diary, "fifteen years were needed to conquer the Palazzo Chigi."[2] The time span mentioned is significant. Ciano himself had become foreign minister in 1936, just as the fifteenth year of the Fascist regime was dawning; and there is no doubt that he believed that his arrival at the Palazzo Chigi was the decisive event through which Italian foreign policy became fully Fascist.

Ciano's diary is full of sudden ideas without practical consequences, of fleeting thoughts which disappeared as soon as they had been put down in black and white. As a source for the history of Italian diplomacy, the diary must be used with caution.[3] But Ciano returned so frequently and insistently to the claim

---

Originally published in *The Diplomats, 1919–1939,* ed. Gordon A. Craig and Felix Gilbert (copyright 1953 Princeton University Press, reprinted by permission), pp. 512–536. A good deal of source material on Italian foreign policy was available when this essay was written, and the image of Ciano has changed little in the last twenty-five years.

that under his direction Italian foreign policy had become a malleable instrument of the regime, that this view must be accepted as a true expression of his mind, as one of his basic ideas.

I

What does Ciano actually mean by the assertion that he had imposed a Fascist pattern on Italian foreign policy? Did his arrival in the Palazzo Chigi imply a change in Italian diplomacy? Was a tradition—the tradition of professional diplomacy which worked within the rules of the game and on the foundation of historically tested experience—thrown overboard and replaced by a new Fascist diplomacy with different methods and new aims? Was there any reality behind Ciano's airy claim of having introduced a truly Fascist diplomacy?

The most obvious explanation is that Ciano believed he was the first real Fascist installed at the head of the Palazzo Chigi. A closer examination of this statement is interesting because of the light it sheds on the view Ciano held about his own role in the Fascist regime. Insofar as it testifies to the influence which diplomatic tradition and professional diplomats had exerted in the first decade of the Fascist regime, the statement contains an element of truth. Even the appointment of such a zealous Fascist as Dino Grandi had not broken the strength of this tradition. On the contrary, the professionals had tamed the young radical and made him an advocate, among the party hierarchy, for the maintenance of the traditional course. Grandi's dismissal in 1932 was the result of Mussolini's dissatisfaction with the docility with which his foreign minister had absorbed the atmosphere of professional diplomacy. According to Mussolini, Grandi "had permitted himself to become prisoner of the League of Nations, had conducted a pacific and internationalist policy, had acted the ultra-democrat and League of Nations man; he had made Italian policy deviate from the straight course of egoism and realism and compromised the aspirations of a new generation."[4]

But when, after Grandi's departure, Mussolini took over the Foreign Ministry, changes were less radical and thorough than one would have expected. For this there were various reasons. Being not only foreign minister but also head of the government, Mussolini was unable to exert close control and supervision over the Palazzo Chigi from the Palazzo Venezia. The new situation created by the rise of Nazism demanded experience and caution. Because of the widening gap between the Western Powers and Germany, and because of the Nazi pressure on Austria, Italian foreign policy was not only offered new opportunities but also faced with new dangers. There was no fundamental conflict between Mussolini and the professionals about the evaluation of this new situation. The career diplomats shared Mussolini's view that the rift among the Great Powers offered a unique chance for the realization of Italy's African aspirations, and the Palazzo Chigi took an active part in the developments that led to the Abyssinian War.[5]

In the course of the Abyssinian crisis, however, a divergence of views emerged. The professionals were concerned with making the Abyssinian enterprise an episode rather than a new departure and with preventing a development which would constitute a definite and final break with the traditional system of Italian foreign policy. They looked with skepticism upon the Fascist claim that through the conquest of the African empire, Italy had been raised to the status of a Great Power of the first rank; thereby they laid themselves open to the accusation of diplomatic pusillanimity and betrayal of the heroic spirit of the regime. A press campaign making such charges was promoted by the Ministry of Press and Propaganda over which Ciano then presided, and this served to prepare his entry into the Palazzo Chigi.[6] Thus Ciano took over as the representative of the Fascist outlook.

Even if there is some basis for the claim that before 1936 the Italian Foreign Office had not been much affected by party enthusiasm and had preserved a traditional outlook in foreign affairs, few people in Italy would have considered Galeazzo Ciano as particularly suited for the task of accomplishing the Fascization of the Palazzo Chigi, for he was far from being a typical representative of the Fascist party. Ciano's unique position in the Fascist hierarchy is sharply outlined in a story told by Grigore Gafencu.[7] The Rumanian statesman was present when an official delegation arrived for a reception with the Italian king. The Duce was marching at the head, clad in his black shirt; his glance was imperious, his gait exaggerated, the dignitaries followed in serried ranks; in front of them, but behind the

Duce, walked Count Ciano, sprightly and carefree, waving joyously whenever he saw an acquaintance.

Ciano stood out from the bulk of Fascist hierarchs. In party circles he was a most unpopular figure. The older leaders of the party—men like De Bono and Volpi who had been well known when they had joined Mussolini's movement after the First World War—considered Ciano a spoiled child of fortune, raised to prominence because he was the son of one of Mussolini's chief assistants and the Duce's son-in-law. Ciano fully reciprocated these feelings; his diary indicates that he considered these older leaders unbearably dull and loquacious fools;[8] it seems most unlikely that in his behavior he succeeded entirely in concealing the contempt he felt for them. The widely held belief that Ciano was groomed by Mussolini to become his successor must have been resented by the men of the middle generation like Grandi and Italo Balbo whose chances for succession were ruined by the arrival of this youngster. The glee with which, in his diary, Ciano sets down every unfriendly thing he hears about them reflects the feelings of rivalry and competition which existed between Ciano and these men. Even before foreigners he gave free vent to such feelings; Grandi, he said to Serrano Suñer, was not worth knowing: "He is quite uninteresting and has the intelligence of a mosquito."[9]

Born in 1903, Ciano was a schoolboy at the time of the march on Rome. While most of the others who had reached prominent positions in the 1930s could claim to have joined the Fascist party when this action involved risks or commitments, Ciano had arrived, after the battle was over, to enjoy the victory and to participate in the loot. His claims to this privilege were supported by good looks and a nimble mind, but certainly more by the influence of a father who had been a national hero of the First World War and subsequently one of Mussolini's most valued collaborators.[10] His alliance by marriage with the family of the Duce was doubtless also useful. In any event, he had no difficulty in advancing rapidly from one interesting job to another—diplomat in Argentina and China, under-secretary and minister of Press and Propaganda—until, at the age of thirty-two, he had become Italy's foreign minister and the most important political figure after the Duce. The party hierarchs must have resented the preferment of a man who came to reap the fruits of work performed by others.

It is characteristic of Ciano that he seems to have been quite unconcerned about these chinks in his Fascist armor. He was proud of his youth and gloried in being the representative of a new generation. Institutional questions, like the corporate state—central issues of Fascist belief to a man like Giuseppe Bottai[11]—did not interest Ciano. One is tempted to conclude that he regarded concern over questions of political organization and political principles as something obsolete, as a sign that those who bothered about them had not yet freed themselves from the egg-shells of the pre-Fascist period. Ciano had no doubt that he was a true representative and embodiment of Fascism, but the precise ideas he associated with this concept are difficult to discover. Perhaps one comes closest to an explanation if one says that Ciano considered Fascism chiefly as a new "style of life"; he regarded himself as a perfect Fascist specimen because only the new generation which had grown up in an atmosphere entirely unencumbered by the heritage of the past could fully "live" the new attitude. In his diary, Ciano expressed his admiration for Gabriele D'Annunzio;[12] it seems likely that in Ciano's rather immature mind Fascism had become identified with the amoral belief in living life to its fullest that one finds in the hero of a D'Annunzio novel. Certainly there is a D'Annunzian flavor to his confession to Serrano Suñer: "Life is always good and pleasant. When I am eighty I shall stroll along here swinging my cane and enjoying the lovely sun. I want to die here in Leghorn after I have seen all my enemies passing before me on their way to death."[13]

But the doubts that could be raised against Ciano from the point of view of Fascist orthodoxy cannot have given much reassurance to the professional diplomats; they had every reason to regard the advent at the Palazzo Chigi of this self-styled leader of the young Fascist generation with suspicion and displeasure.

When Ciano spoke of the Fascist outlook which Italian diplomacy acquired in the 1930s was he thinking principally of his influence on foreign policy or could he also point to changes in personnel and organization? In the years preceding Ciano's assumption of office, Fascism had made hardly any inroads in the diplomatic service. It is true that in 1928, in order to infuse diplomacy with a new spirit, a number of Fascist party members without special professional training had been taken into the diplomatic service, but the power of the professional diplomats had been strong enough to restrict sharply the number of new admissions and to keep the "men of '28," the *ventottisti* as they were called by the career diplomats, in subordinate positions.[14]

At first glance it would seem that in Ciano's time also the diplomatic bureaucracy was able to continue its successful resistance to the penetration of outsiders and to preserve its professional and career character.[15] At least during the years before the war, all the great embassies were headed by career diplomats. The key position in Berlin was held by Bernardo Attolico. He had been a member of the Italian delegation at the Paris Peace Conference and, for five years, from 1922 to 1927, had directed the Communications Section in the League of Nations Secretariat at Geneva; he had also served as ambassador in Rio de Janeiro and Moscow before he came to Berlin in 1935. When Ciano became foreign minister, Vittorio Cerruti, who had started his diplomatic career at the Italian embassy in the Vienna of Emperor Francis Joseph, was ambassador in Paris; in 1938 he was replaced by Raffaele Guariglia whose "professionalism" is perhaps best attested by the fact that he became Italian foreign minister in 1943 when, after the fall of Mussolini, General Pietro Badoglio formed his cabinet of technical experts. Also Augusto Rosso, the ambassador in Moscow, had started his service in Italian diplomacy in the prewar era. The only prominent Fascist who directed one of the great European embassies was Dino Grandi, who was in London from 1932 to 1939, but since Mussolini had moved him from Rome to London for being too much inclined to adopt the Foreign Office point of view, Grandi can hardly have been regarded as an alien and hostile element by the professionals.

Representatives abroad had no policymaking function: the policymakers were at Rome, in the Palazzo Chigi. But here too, career diplomats were in charge. Work at the Italian Foreign Office was distributed among three political divisions, that of General Affairs, of European and Mediterranean Affairs, and of Overseas Affairs. Each of these divisions was headed by a director and throughout the 1930s these positions were held by professionals: Leonardo Vitetti, Gino Buti, and Emanuele Grazzi. Thus from the point of view of personnel there seems to be little substance to Ciano's claim of having conquered the Palazzo Chigi for Fascism.

But the impression of a continued dominance of the professional tradition in Italian diplomacy is deceiving. A report by Roberto Cantalupo gives insight into the strange situation at the Palazzo Chigi soon after Ciano had taken over.[16] Cantalupo, who was Italian ambassador in Brazil, had returned to Rome after several years of absence from Italy. He found at the same desks the same faces he had known before, but something had changed in the atmosphere. Cantalupo says he felt that "the clockwork was broken." The functionaries were like shadows, moving around in the usual way but without purpose. He was told that the officials did not know what was going on because all important work was done by the Gabinetto. And so he heard for the first time of the growth of that organization which became Ciano's chief instrument for directing the course of Italian foreign policy, and which, in relatively short time, reduced the traditional apparatus to an empty shell.

In the past the Gabinetto had been nothing more than the personal secretariat of the foreign minister. Under Ciano it grew rapidly.[17] He filled it with young men who shared his general attitude toward life and looked up to him admiringly as future leader. "The officials of the Gabinetto 'spoke seldom, but all their words were tuneful sweet,' like those of the great souls banned by Dante into the Limbo, and they treated their colleagues in the other offices with an icy, smiling and contemptuous politeness, typical of a great lord who has dealings with people who don't belong to his class."[18] Among the officials of the Gabinetto, the most influential and probably the most intelligent was Ciano's contemporary and long-standing friend, Filippo Anfuso, who in the later years of Ciano's foreign ministry became head of the Gabinetto.[19] A chief function assumed by the Gabinetto—and the function about which the professional diplomats complained most bitterly—was control over the distribution of incoming information. The officials of the Gabinetto determined whether reports should be handed over to the political desks of the Palazzo Chigi or whether they would be kept in the Gabinetto for the use of the minister. Thus the Gabinetto developed into a center where all the most important information and reports of special significance were handled.

The memoirs of Italian career diplomats are filled with stories describing the confusion and errors caused by the arbitrary proceedings of the functionaries in the Gabinetto. Newly appointed ambassadors who wanted to read the relevant diplomatic correspondence before leaving for their posts were told by division heads that the most important interchanges were kept in the Gabinetto, that they had not seen them, and that complete files did not exist. A serious mistake occurred in the critical summer of 1939, when the Italian ambassador in Moscow received detailed information about the progress of the German-Russian negotiations from his German colleague in Moscow and forwarded it to Rome. Since Soviet Russia seemed only on the periphery of decisive events, the Gabinetto simply handed the reports from Moscow on to the political desks as of no particular significance. Thus, when the news of the German-Russian agreement arrived, Mussolini and Ciano were more surprised than they should have been, in view of the fact that the Palazzo Chigi was in possession of the most relevant facts.[20] This lack of coordination was characteristic of Ciano's reformed Foreign Office and was the result of a development which was of central importance for the conduct of Italian diplomacy: the decline in the importance of the regular political divisions and of the professional diplomats who staffed them.

The key importance which the Gabinetto gained in Ciano's time explains the apparent contrast between his claim to have achieved a Fascization of Italian diplomacy on the one hand and his continued irritation against his professional diplomats and his complaints about their cautiousness, timidity, and lack of true dignity in the face of foreigners on the other.[21] When Ciano spoke of a Fascization of Italian diplomacy he did not mean that he had transformed diplomacy by infiltrating new men, Fascists, into the existing diplomatic bureaucracy. What he could rightly claim was that he had restricted the sphere of action of the professional diplomats. The diplomats were not asked to give advice or make recommendations. Decisions were made from above, perhaps prepared and discussed by the young men whom Ciano had assembled in the Gabinetto. In

Ciano's time, Cantalupo remarks, "the Ministry existed only to obey."[22]

The low estimation of the role of professional diplomacy permeated the routine business of diplomacy. There was a kind of silent war between Ciano and his young men on the one side and the professional diplomats on the other. Ciano wanted to keep all the threads in his own hands, perhaps because he was afraid that the professionals might take concerted action against him. He discouraged direct contacts and exchange of information among the Italian ambassadors. Neither information about the general political situation nor news of developments with which they were specifically concerned were regularly transmitted to the Italian representatives abroad.[23] Ambassadors had to leave for new destinations without thorough briefing; when they wanted to see Ciano before their departure he had nothing to say to them and often no time to receive them.[24] This happened so frequently that it cannot have been entirely by accident, although occasionally Ciano's lack of time may have been caused by his passionate devotion to the pleasures of Roman society.

Because of the distrust with which the Gabinetto regarded the professional diplomats, its young men placed little reliance on the heads of missions for collection and evaluation of information, but tried to develop an information service of their own, sometimes with grotesque results. When, after the outbreak of the Second World War, the Italian ambassador in Athens maintained that the British had no intentions of landing in Greece, the Gabinetto refused to accept this view and turned directly to the various Italian consuls. It is reported that even Ciano's young men were startled when in reply they received from one of the consuls the following telegram: "The hairdresser of my wife told her this morning that a British landing is expected within a week."[25]

Quite in accordance with this contempt for professional diplomats, Ciano liked to work outside the regular diplomatic channels. At important embassies he had confidants, through whom he acted behind the back of the ambassador. Particularly important contacts were established and maintained through special emissaries. One of them was Anfuso; he was sent to Franco in the early months of the Spanish civil war, and, in a secret mission to Hitler in 1936, it was he who prepared the terrain for Ciano's visit of October of that year, which marked the beginning of the close cooperation between Italy and Germany.[26] Ciano cultivated the method of direct meetings with foreign statesmen; he was frequently away from Rome, traveling to Germany and to the capitals of eastern and southern Europe.

As Ciano was quite uninhibited by the traditions of the diplomatic profession, the range of his activities went far beyond what is customarily considered to be the sphere of action of a foreign minister. He himself established contact with revolutionary forces of other countries when they could be used in favor of Fascist Italy, and he extended his interference into the military sphere when the aims of his foreign policy could be promoted by direct military action.[27] Cantalupo had a typical experience of the subordinate role which the professional diplomat held in Ciano's strategy of foreign policy.[28] Ciano had appointed him in 1936 to be the first Italian ambassador in Franco Spain. Cantalupo was most anxious to hear the views of the newly appointed foreign minister on the Spanish problem, the first great political issue with which Ciano was concerned. When the civil war broke out the Western Powers were trying to bury the sanctions issue and to build golden bridges for Italy's return to Geneva. Thus, the handling of the Spanish crisis would reveal whether the Abyssinian affair was intended to become a soon forgotten episode, permitting Italy to return to its traditional system and friendships, or whether the masters of Italy would try to embark on an entirely new course. Cantalupo found the manner in which Ciano explained the Spanish issue to him most reassuring and satisfactory. Ciano indicated that Mussolini had only very hesitantly agreed to lend Franco military support. Italy had no territorial ambitions in Spain. Aside from the fact that the establishment of Bolshevism there must be prevented, Italy was not concerned with ideological issues, and had no special interest in promoting a totalitarian regime in Spain; Franco should be advised to take a reconciliatory attitude toward other parties. Thus the Spanish conflict should not widen the gap between Italy and the Western Powers and, as soon as the Spanish affair was composed, Ciano added, he hoped to make a visit to Paris.

As satisfactory as Ciano's exposition of the Spanish situation sounded to Cantalupo, he noticed some things which disquieted him. Before he left Ciano's office, Ciano explained to him the military situation in Spain. A big map was spread out on the table, with little flags indicating the position of the various military units, and soon Ciano and Anfuso began to move them around, like enthusiastic schoolboys, becoming engrossed in planning Franco's campaign. Furthermore, Cantalupo soon learned that Ciano had established at the Palazzo Chigi a special office for Spanish affairs which was concerned with the military aspects of the enterprise. Finally, when, immediately before his departure, Cantalupo saw Ciano again for a farewell visit, the foreign minister told him that the Italian Fascist party was exerting strong pressure on him to take a radical ideological line in the Spanish issue, and that he was forced to make some concession; Roberto Farinacci, the old party wheelhorse, would therefore go to Spain on a special mission as representative of the party. Ciano assured Cantalupo that he did not need to worry about this. Actually Farinacci's presence in Spain ruined any chances Cantalupo's embassy may have had. He refused to have any contact with Cantalupo; he himself soon came to be considered as the true mouthpiece of the Italian leader in Spain; and Cantalupo could make no headway with his more conciliatory recommendations. Moreover, after he returned to Rome, Farinacci began a systematic campaign against Cantalupo's "defeatism," and the ambassador was recalled after two months. Upon his return he soon realized that he had fallen into disgrace; people studiously avoided him, and the police kept checking on all his movements and contacts. When he was finally admitted to Ciano, he found a different man, cool and distant; Ciano was unwilling to permit Cantalupo to present his views to Mussolini and showed himself entirely uninterested in what Cantalupo had to report. Cantalupo's diplomatic career had ended.

It is possible that when Cantalupo was appointed ambassador to Franco the course to be followed by Italy in the Spanish civil war had not yet been definitely set. The Italian-Spanish Agreement of November 28, 1936,[29] which preceded Cantalupo's mission, guaranteed the inviolability of Spanish territorial possessions and provided for close cooperation between the two countries. The common outlook between the Fascist regime and the Spanish Nationalist government was emphasized, though the wording of the treaty was not incompatible with what Ciano had told Cantalupo about Italian policy in the Mediterranean. After the defeat of the Italians in the battle of Guadalajara, which took place while Cantalupo was in Spain, an intransigent and radical line may have seemed necessary in order to restore Italian prestige. But it is equally possible that, from the outset, Ciano had higher aims than gaining a friend for Italy in the western Mediterranean and that he was working for the establishment of a regime identified with Fascist Italy also in internal structure. If this is the case, he used Cantalupo's mission as a cover behind which he hid his true intentions and simultaneously kept open a line of retreat in case his maximum aims could not be obtained. In any case Cantalupo's mission to Franco is a striking example of the variety of instruments on which Ciano relied in the conduct of foreign policy. Among these instruments, the professional diplomat was only a very minor and not a very highly esteemed factor.

II

As has been noted, the Spanish civil war was the first great issue with which Ciano had to deal as foreign minister. In referring to this event we have touched upon the central problem of our study. To what extent did Ciano's diplomatic methods, his Fascization of diplomacy, change Italy's attitude to the outside powers and vary or deviate from the traditional course of Italian foreign policy?

Ciano indicated frequently that the traditional diplomats had failed to give foreigners the right impression of Italy's newly acquired strength. Now the diplomats were supposed to show a stern and imperious face to the outside world, they were expected to employ a *tono fascista*.[30] In his diary, Ciano notes with evident contempt occasions when foreign statesmen or diplomats showed signs of emotion when they were worried or perturbed, or became pale or had tears in their eyes. He evidently expected that Italy's representatives would show none of these weaknesses, and his diplomats were well aware of how they were supposed to behave. The reports which they sent home sound frequently more like the descriptions of military encounters than the résumés of polite diplomatic interviews.[31] It is reported that Grandi during the Abyssinian crisis delivered a conciliatory speech in England. The conciliatory passages were carefully deleted from the text which he sent to the Palazzo Chigi.[32] When Guariglia was appointed ambassador in Paris, he showed Ciano the draft of a speech which he wanted to deliver in presenting his credentials to the president of the French Republic. This draft contained the customary allusions to the common European heritage and the historical bonds between the Italian and French people, but when Ciano returned the draft these innocuous expressions of diplomatic politeness had been cut out.[33] Ciano modeled his own conduct upon the precepts he gave to his ambassadors. When a report had arrived that the Greek military attaché in Budapest had made some disparaging remarks about the military qualities of the Italian army, Ciano threatened to break off diplomatic relations between Italy and Greece, and serious consequences were avoided only because the Greek government agreed to retire the talkative officer.[34]

The same brutal disregard of custom was shown also in the use of intercepted messages.[35] The Italian government had a particularly well-functioning secret service which provided the Palazzo Chigi with complete information about the interchanges between the British ambassador in Rome and the London Foreign Office, and also with the diplomatic correspondence of many other countries. Ciano was not satisfied with using the secret information for the planning of his diplomatic moves; he was eager to impress other statesmen with Italian omniscience and he used the material as a means of increasing tension. On a famous occasion, a dossier of English reports about Germany was prepared and shown to Hitler with the desired effect of inciting him against the British; on another, Kurt von Schuschnigg of Austria was harassed with some incautious remarks which the Austrian foreign minister had uttered when he was dining at Geneva with Robert Vansittart.

The *tono fascista* of Italian diplomacy in itself did not represent a new course of action but it was important in determining and restricting the framework within which Italian policy could and would take action. Slow proceedings and cautious legal formulas were considered as contradictory to the emphasis on decisive action which was supposed to be characteristic of Fascism and to animate its diplomacy. Collective agreements and multilateral treaties were condemned;[36] preference was given to those countries where an individual had the full power of decision, where concern for parliamentary bodies was unnecessary, and where agreements could be reached in personal meetings. Ciano was much influenced by his personal impressions of foreign statesmen; he preferred to deal with those who corresponded to the "new fascist type."

The development of relations between Yugoslavia and Italy offers a characteristic example. In March 1937, an agreement was signed between these two countries who had been bitter opponents. From the Italian point of view the agreement represented an attempt to undermine the Little Entente and thereby to weaken the French influence in the Balkans; at the same time, it was meant to block the expansion of Germany which was beginning to draw Austria more and more into her orbit. Ciano was particularly proud of this agreement, in which he saw a first fruit of his own activities as foreign minister, but his "new course" was based entirely upon his estimate of the personality of Yugoslav Premier Milan Stojadinovic, whom he regarded as a man of the new type. When in 1939, the future Yugoslav dictator was thrown out of power like any weak parliamentary prime minister, Ciano took this almost as a personal affront and immediately resumed plotting with the Croatian opposition against the existence of the Yugoslav state.[37]

The contempt for the usual procedures and customs of diplomacy and the disregard of the rules which had been developed in international relations aggravated the difficulties of cooperation with those nations which placed emphasis on these rules and tried to reinforce them. Though Mussolini's Italy had never been friendly to the League of Nations, a working relationship had existed in the 1920s. The completely negative and aggressively hostile attitude toward the League which had developed in the Abyssinian crisis and was maintained and accentuated by Ciano's foreign policy rigidified the Italian position. By hardening the contrast between Italy and the West into a conflict between two opposite ways of life, it placed formidable obstacles in the way of eventual resumption of cooperation.

With increasing emphasis on the contrast between the democratic and the Fascist concept of foreign policy, Italy was naturally drawn to emphasize similarities with the other great anti-Western power, Germany. Even in the earlier years of his regime, Mussolini had expressed the idea that a new world war was inevitable, and he had pointed to the 1940s as critical years. At that time, he regarded England and Russia as the great antagonists and believed that the conflict should be used by Italy to cut out an empire of her own.[38] With Italy moving close to Germany, the idea of an inevitable new world war persisted, but the perspective changed. The war become a war between totalitarian and democratic powers; together with Germany, Italy would be one of the main protagonists, Germany destined to rule in the north, Italy in the south of Europe. One can see in Ciano's diary how, in his discussions with Mussolini, the decadence of the democracies and the inevitability of war became recurrent themes.[39] It is true that the time of this war remained vague and in a not clearly defined future; but the feeling that the world would soon assume an entirely new aspect could only strengthen the tendency toward an irresponsible freedom of action in foreign policy.

It is hard to imagine Ciano achieving prominence in any other situation. In his pride of being the representative of a new, ruthless generation, he fitted perfectly into a *fin de siècle* atmosphere where everything that served to improve Italy's position for the future decisive clash seemed justifiable, and in which, under the threat of a coming world war, he could carry out actions which, in less critical times, would have been impossible for him. Ciano was not concerned with the slow and gradual strengthening and widening of the foundations which had been laid in the past. Instead, he groped in all directions where opportunity for gain or prestige and expansion of power seemed to beckon, becoming deeply involved in the military aspects of the Spanish civil war, and after Stojadinovic's fall, promoting plans to partition Yugoslavia and to bring Croatia under Italian control. But in Spain and Yugoslavia Ciano was dealing with situations which had arisen before he took office; the enterprises into which he put his whole energy were those which he conceived and planned personally: the actions against Albania and Greece.

Although the operation against Greece was probably conceived before 1939,[40] it was executed only after the European war had started, and it need not be considered here. In any case, the military action which led to the incorporation of Albania into the Italian empire is sufficiently typical of Ciano's methods.[41] There was no pretense, as in the case of Greece, of military or strategic considerations; and despite Ciano's later pride over having acquired Albania for the Italian crown, it still seems to have been a superfluous acquisition. Absorption of Albania by a more gradual procedure would have been entirely possible although even this seems unnecessary in view of the protectorate which Italy had acquired in the 1920s. Yet, when Ciano represented the Italian government at the marriage of King Zogu in May 1938, he decided that Italian policy should be directed toward complete and outright acquisition of Albania; and he obtained Mussolini's agreement and stuck to what he called the "integral solution." Ciano kept all the threads of this coup in his own hands; in the diplomatic sphere he agreed with Stojadinovic on compensating Yugoslavia by a strip of territory in northern Albania, but abandoned the idea of such a grant after Stojadinovic's fall. He prepared an internal revolt against Zogu's regime by organizing the distribution of money to the Albanian opposition leaders, and he supervised the military preparations for the enterprise. Finally, when the military action started, on Good Friday of 1939 (a day which to many people seemed hardly fitted for an action of this kind), Ciano himself flew to Albania to watch over his private experiment in empire building.

The Albanian annexation was achieved without raising more serious repercussions than paper protests. The Italian leaders regarded this enterprise as a sign of the freedom of action which Italy had achieved in the Mediterranean area. But actually this was an illusion and shows only how little Ciano was able to conceive of Italian foreign policy as an integrated and coherent whole. Ciano once made a remark which shows how precarious the Italian position actually was. He said that one of the desirable consequences of the establishment of Italian power in the Balkan peninsula would be that it would create a balance against the growth of German influence there.[42] This was almost an admission that by conducting an expansionist policy which pointed toward the east, the south, and the west of the

Mediterranean, and threatened the status quo, Italy had thoroughly disturbed her neighbors and greatly increased the possibility of interference by outside powers in this area. By replacing a policy of clearly limited aims with a policy of unrestricted use of power within the whole of the Mediterranean area, Italy was in fact more deeply drawn into the vortex of European power politics and lost much of her freedom of action in her relations with the Great European Powers.

The advantages gained in the Mediterranean necessarily remained insecure because the fate of Italy depended on Italy's alignment in the constellation of the Great European Powers. The central issue of Italian foreign policy in the three years before the Second World War was the relation of Italy to Germany and to Britain. As we have said before, in the summer of 1936, when Ciano took over the direction of Italian foreign policy, Italy had to decide whether she wanted to reestablish the traditional cooperation with Britain disturbed by the Abyssinian war and to resume in the European state system the balancing role which she had played in former years.[43] When Ciano became foreign minister, not more than fifteen months had passed since the Stresa Conference, at which Italy had aligned herself with France and Great Britain against Germany, and the increase in power which Nazi Germany had gained in the intervening period through the reoccupation of the Rhineland gave special urgency and importance to the decision which Italy would now have to make. The Western Powers tried to terminate whatever actions they had undertaken against Italian aggression, and efforts were begun to relieve the Anglo-Italian tension. The progress of negotiations was slow, cumbersome, and interrupted, however.

A first positive result was obtained in January 1937 when the two governments published a declaration usually called the Anglo-Italian "Gentleman's Agreement," a reciprocal agreement to preserve the status quo in the Mediterranean.[44] But in the face of Italy's increasing military commitments in the Spanish civil war the value of such an assurance became questionable; and a bitter anti-British press campaign reduced relations to the previous state of tension. Even an exchange of messages between Mussolini and Chamberlain in the summer of 1937 did not revive the Anglo-Italian talks. It was only after

Eden's dismissal in February 1938 that negotiations were resumed, resulting in the conclusion of a British-Italian Accord on April 16. This treaty reaffirmed the agreement of 1937 and regulated a number of issues in the Mediterranean and Near Eastern area connected with Italy's conquest of Abyssinia, but its real point was Britain's recognition of Italy's African empire and Italy's agreement to withdraw a substantial number of volunteers from Spain.[45] Once again, however, the Accord seemed to remain a piece of paper because Italy did not carry out the latter condition.[46] Nevertheless, after Munich, Chamberlain considered himself satisfied with a token withdrawal of volunteers, and the Accord finally came into force in November 1938. This was immediately followed, however, by violent anti-French demonstrations in the Italian Chamber and in the press; and Ciano showed little interest in the British attempts to improve Franco-Italian relations.[47] Nevertheless Chamberlain and Halifax carried out a visit to Rome in January 1939 to put the seal on the normalization of Anglo-Italian relations; but, as Ciano wrote, from the Italian point of view it was a visit "on a minor scale."[48]

In contrast to the hesitant course along which Anglo-Italian negotiations proceeded, Italy's advance toward friendship with Germany seemed smooth and steady.[49] Germany had been quick in recognizing Italy's African empire; and in October 1936 Ciano visited Germany and saw Hitler. A few days later in a speech in Milan on November 1, Mussolini, in evaluating the importance of this visit, coined the famous phrase that the Berlin-Rome line represented "an Axis." Both countries, Germany and Italy, were quick in recognizing Franco and acted in concert in the London Non-Intervention Committee. Visits of Nazi hierarchs to Italy emphasized the maintainance of close contacts and Mussolini's visit to Germany in September of 1937 became an imposing demonstration of the closeness of Italian-German relations. By signing the Anti-Comintern Pact and by abandoning the League of Nations Italy increased the impression of Italo-German solidarity. On Hitler's visit to Rome in May of 1938 drafts for an alliance treaty were exchanged. These negotiations were interrupted by the Czech crisis, and, after their revival in October, were further slowed down by the attempt to include Japan in the treaty. But on May

6, 1939, after a meeting of Ciano and Ribbentrop in Milan, an announcement was made that a German-Italian alliance was concluded and on May 22 the Pact of Steel—a military alliance which did not even contain the usual escape clause restricting the obligations for assistance to the case of an enemy attack—was solemnly signed in Berlin.

During the tense years preceding the outbreak of the Second World War, many people believed that an alliance had existed between Germany and Italy ever since 1936 and that they had conducted a concerted policy in which every move was carefully planned and agreed upon. This theory assumed that the leaders of the two countries denied the existence of an alliance treaty and pretended to act independently and on their own in order to obtain greater concessions from the Western Powers; that they did not want to lose the advantages to be gained by holding out as a bait the possibility of an alignment with the West; and that by maintaining contacts with Britain and France they were better able to prevent common action against aggression or at least to delay such action till the dictatorships had acquired enough strength to resist.

The documents which have been published since the war prove irrefutably the erroneousness of this interpretation. The Italian leaders were surprised by Germany's occupation of Austria, they were left guessing about Germany's true intentions in the Czech crisis, they had no previous knowledge of Germany's move into Prague. On the other hand, Germany was not previously informed about the Italian action against Albania. Both countries—Germany and Italy—did not feel sure that the other might not be willing to make a deal with Britain. Ciano prepared his famous dossier to incite Hitler against Britain; when the British-Italian agreement came into force Joachim von Ribbentrop appeared in Rome with offers of an alliance. Behind the façade of public proclamations of German-Italian solidarity there appears lack of frankness and hidden doubts of the reliability of the partner.

Since the days when the myth of German-Italian solidarity was widely accepted, opinion has shifted and currently the view is often expressed that it would have been possible for the Western Powers to win Italy away from Germany and to prevent the conclusion of the German-Italian alliance. According to this view, Britain acted slowly and hesitantly; the Quai d'Orsay was haughty and prejudiced especially after the bitter Italian attacks against France in the winter of 1938–1939; feelers which one group in the French government put out were counteracted by another so that the Italians could not be convinced of the seriousness of the French intentions; and these mistakes of the Western Powers drove Italy into German arms.

Ciano's diary has been adduced as proof of the contention that Italy was not given a full chance to disentangle herself from the German embrace or at least to keep Germany at a respectable distance. The diary shows irritation against the Germans after the Anschluss and particularly after the coup of Prague;[50] and it makes clear that the question of the South Tyrol and that of the Brenner frontier remained sore spots in Italy despite Hitler's solemn renunciations. Italy was deeply upset by the extension of German influence into the Balkans; after the occupation of Austria as well as after Munich, Ciano toyed with the idea of supplementing the horizontal Rome-Berlin axis with a vertical Rome-Belgrade-Budapest-Warsaw axis which was to form a barrier against further German penetration into southeastern Europe.[51] Furthermore, various moves undertaken by the Italian leaders in 1938 are regarded as symptoms of Italian hesitancy. Despite the official assurances that the Anglo-Italian negotiations were not directed against Germany, Italy began to show serious interest in their progress at the very moment in February 1938 when Germany resumed an aggressive policy against Austria.[52] On Ribbentrop's visit to Rome in October 1938 Mussolini, despite an emphatically stated enthusiasm for a German-Italian alliance, mainly elaborated on the necessity of delay and of cautious procedure.[53] The quickness and willingness with which Mussolini grasped at the offer to act as mediator in the Czech crisis has been taken as a sign that he was glad to retreat from the exposed position into which Italy had advanced.[54] When Hitler had come to power in 1933, Mussolini had proposed a Four Power Pact and—it is said—this remained the true aim of his policy throughout.

Finally, the dramatic clash between Ribbentrop and Ciano in August 1939 is often regarded as decisive proof of the reluctance with which Italy had tied herself to Germany and of the divided mind of the Italian leaders.[55] If, then, we are to judge the strength of the thesis that Italy could have been detached by the Western Powers and the validity of the evidence which seems to support this, it might be well, first, to recapitulate briefly the circumstances of the Ribbentrop-Ciano meeting and the effect it had on Ciano's subsequent conduct in August 1939.

Attolico, the Italian ambassador in Berlin, had for some time been sending alarming reports to Rome, stating that the Germans had decided to take military action against Poland and were willing to risk a general war.[56] The ambassador suggested a meeting between Hitler and Mussolini at which Hitler would be forced to define his plans and at which Mussolini should, if necessary, exert a moderating influence. Ciano was displeased at being pushed into the background, and there seems to have been some suspicion in Rome that Hitler might persuade Mussolini to rash commitments, instead of Mussolini restraining Hitler. Thus, after some hesitation and delays, it was decided that Ciano should go to Germany. When he arrived in Salzburg on August 11, he seems to have considered Attolico's fears as exaggerated and to have felt reasonably sure that a common line leading to a conference of the Great Powers and to a peaceful international settlement could be worked out by Italy and Germany. After his first talk with Ribbentrop, however, Ciano's mood was grim. "We have come to blows," was his résumé of the interview and it is clear that Ribbentrop had admitted that Germany now intended to push things to the utmost. The luncheon following took place in an icy atmosphere; hardly a word was exchanged between guest and host. In further talks with Ribbentrop Ciano emphasized his conviction that Britain and France would support Poland if she were attacked and that the military outlook for the Axis powers would be doubtful. Italy in any case would not be ready to participate in such an adventure. Ciano had the courage to maintain this position even against the prophetic assuredness of the Fuehrer.

Back in Rome Ciano began his fight to keep Italy out of the war which he now considered inevitable. The Duce was deeply disturbed by the idea that Fascist Italy—like the Parliamentary Italy of 1914—should renege her word and become again a "traitor nation." One of the most violent discussions, wrote Ciano, took place on August 21: "Today I have spoken clearly, I have used up all my ammunition. When I entered the room Mussolini confirmed his decision to go along with the Germans. "You, Duce, cannot and must not do it. The loyalty with which I have served you in carrying out the policy of the Axis warrants my speaking clearly to you now. I went to Salzburg in order to adopt a common line of action. I found myself face to face with a *Diktat*. The Germans, not ourselves, have betrayed the alliance in which we were to have been partners, and not servants.'"[57]

In his efforts to persuade Mussolini Ciano had the loyal and enthusiastic support of the professional diplomats, especially Attolico who traveled back and forth between Rome and Berlin and who worked hand-in-hand with him. Ciano had at long last become the protagonist of the traditional line of Italian foreign policy. But he was handicapped now by the carelessness of his own new diplomacy. In negotiating the alliance with Germany, the initiative was left to the Germans, and drafts which they submitted formed the basis of the treaty; a decisive weakness of the Italian position was the lack of written German assurances that the alliance had been signed with the understanding that action which might lead to war should be avoided for the next few years.[58] Because he had neglected to weigh carefully the reports about the German-Russian negotiations,[59] Ciano was surprised when the news of the Nazi-Soviet Agreement arrived; the situation seemed again transformed and the fight for Italy's neutrality had to be resumed. In the end Ciano succeeded in gaining Mussolini's agreement to Italy's neutrality. A professional diplomat put the final seal on this decision. On August 26 Attolico had been instructed to transmit to the German government a long list of military material which Italy needed to enter the war and which Germany was asked to provide. When the German officials wanted to know when the delivery was expected Attolico replied on his own initiative and without instructions "immediately before the beginning of hostilities," barring all possibility of further negotiations on the topic.[60]

There can be no doubt that, from the moment when Ciano met Ribbentrop at Salzburg, he was a changed man, thoroughly upset by the recklessness with which the Germans had violated the clause of the alliance providing for reciprocal consultation, and by the lightheartedness with which they embarked on a general war. And there is no question that, from this time on, he remained suspicious of the Nazi leaders and hostile to them. But, granted all this, what bearing does it have on the argument that Italy might have been won from Germany's side if only the Western Powers had been more intelligent in their diplomacy?

The answer to this question depends on our understanding of Mussolini's own position and upon an appreciation of the relations between Mussolini and his son-in-law.

The bulk of available evidence indicates that Mussolini was irrevocably set on a pro-German course of Italian foreign policy. He too may have had moments of doubt—particularly because he must have been continuously aware of Italy's economic deficiencies—but if so, he overcame his doubts quickly under the sway of Hitler's persuasive personality or under the impact of demonstrations of German strength. Ciano's diary makes it quite clear that Mussolini's outbursts of irritation about German arbitrariness were short-lived—shorter than Ciano's; Mussolini always returned quickly to his pro-German course.[61] After Munich he scotched Ciano's plan of insisting on a common Polish-Hungarian frontier, in order to permit the formation of a vertical Axis.[62] Mussolini may have been utterly sincere when in October 1938 he justified to Ribbentrop his hesitation to conclude an alliance by citing the unprepared state of public opinion.[63] Soon after the meeting with Ribbentrop, however, the Italian claims against France were announced and a bitter press campaign was unchained; and this widened the rift between France and Italy and served to demonstrate the usefulness of German support to the Italian public.[64] In comparison with the overwhelming amount of material which shows Mussolini's steady determination to arrive at a complete identification of German and Italian policy the few indications of doubt and hesitation can have no weight.

But could not Ciano himself, if given proper encouragement by the Western Powers, have prevented the full consummation of the German-Italian rapprochement? This would, in view of Mussolini's attitude, have involved an assertion of independence on his part. Was he capable of such a gesture? There is every reason to doubt it. The tone of his diary in the years before the outbreak of the Second World War was one of unreserved admiration for the Leader of Fascism.[65] The pervading theme is that "the Duce is always right." Doubts and criticism appear only later; it is possible that some resentment had already developed in earlier years and was then suppressed. The close family relationship may have had its drawbacks; Mussolini disapproved of his son-in-law's personal conduct quite as much as Ciano of his father-in-law's.[66] But if Ciano began to have some reservations they lay almost certainly in the purely personal sphere. There is no indication that before the summer of 1939 they extended into serious doubts about the Duce's political wisdom.

Moreover, in reshaping Italian diplomacy Ciano had been a true follower of the Duce. It has been shown[67] that Mussolini took over power full of contempt for the international system established at Paris and anxious to inaugurate an active foreign policy based on force, but he had been restrained by the adverse constellation in the European state system and by the impossibility of overcoming the resistance of the diplomatic bureaucracy. Ciano was the docile pupil who carried out the intentions of his master at a time when their realization was possible. The Italian diplomacy of the last three years before the war can be called Ciano's diplomacy less because the ideas of the new course were his own than because Ciano carried them out with an uninhibited and thoughtless energy, peculiar to this figure of a second-generation Fascism.

The transformation of Italian diplomacy is an interesting example of the manner in which a revolutionary regime established complete control over a bureaucracy and reduced the professionals to powerlessness. But the reorganization to which Ciano subjected Italian diplomacy is also a decisive reason for rejecting the thesis that Italy's alliance with Germany could have been prevented, or that Ciano's views on this issue differed fundamentally from those of Mussolini. Ciano had fashioned an instrument to carry out a new course in foreign policy; it would have been a denial of what he had done if he had used the new instrument for carrying out the old, traditional foreign policy. Ciano loved to imagine himself as a free agent who could shape the world according to his will, and he liked to toy with plans and with projects. In moments of doubt and annoyance he may have played with the idea of siding with the French and English but actually he could not escape the momentum and weight of the movement to which he had turned the instrument of diplomacy. A time for reflection and choice arose only when the outbreak of the Second World War created an entirely new situation.

Ciano's conversion at Salzburg in August 1939 was, then, not the result of a long evolutionary process in which he had nurtured growing doubts about the wisdom of the Duce's policy or during which he had seriously considered the advisability of returning to the traditional bases of Italian diplomacy. The important thing about the conversion was that it was sudden and, as such, in complete accord with Ciano's characteristic approach to diplomacy. As we have seen, Ciano was little inclined to base his policy on considerations of permanent and underlying forces and interests. He approached policy in terms of personality, relying heavily upon his judgment of the leading figures of other countries. Thus, Ribbentrop's arrogant announcement of Germany's approaching military action against Poland, which revealed that the Italians had been trapped and overplayed, was a blow to Ciano's pride. He must have regarded it as quite a personal failure of his diplomacy, and turned now with vehemence against those whom he had misjudged.

III

There is irony in the fact that in September 1939, Fascist Italy with her proudly advertised first-rank-power foreign policy ended up roughly in the same position in which parliamentary Italy had found herself at the beginning of the First World War. Likewise there is irony in the fact that from the summer of 1939 on Ciano developed into a practitioner of the policy of *combinazioni*—that is, of trying to reap advantages from maintaining an undecided balancing position in the struggles of stronger powers—a policy which in earlier years Ciano had regarded as characteristic of the weakness of democratic Italy and condemned as undignified and unfitting to the reborn strength of Fascist Italy.[68]

But Ciano never learned to discern the real and concrete factors of power behind the surface of appearances and his inability to see things as they are played a role in his final fate. When he left the Palazzo Chigi in 1943 he took over the embassy at the Vatican in the hope of establishing contacts with the victorious Western Powers—strangely unaware how little qualified he must have appeared to the democracies for this task. Ciano also seems to have failed to realize that he was the last who would reap benefits from taking an active part in Mussolini's overthrow. And when he was in custody in Germany he moved heaven and earth to be returned to Italy[69] where he seems to have hoped that activity would again become possible for him; actually he gave himself into the hands of his most implacable enemies.

When the ultra-Fascists who ruled Mussolini's Republic of Salò condemned him to death in Verona, Mussolini did not interfere. He decided that "sentiment" should not prevail over "reason of state"; he was nevertheless profoundly moved by the events in Verona and, indeed, regarded them "as the most dramatic chapter in his restless life."[70] Perhaps he felt that responsibility for this wasted life belonged also to those who had raised Ciano to power without making him aware of the limits of its possibilities and its uses. The German ambassador at the Republic of Salò had great difficulty in restraining Mussolini from publishing the next day in his newspaper an encomium on the Conte Galeazzo Ciano.[71]

PART V.
The Changing Lenses of History

15. History and Philology: Politian

Did Ovid err by stating in *De Arte Amandi* that the Nile was the habitat of the crocodile whose excrement was used as a cosmetic? Was Polla Argentaria, the wife of the poet Lucan, later married to Papinius Statius? Should not the name "Strotocles" be that of "noster Cocles" in the First Book of Cicero's *De Officiis* (an emendation that has proved to be correct)?

Such topics—explanations, interpolations, emendations of the texts of ancient writers—form the subject matter of the fifty-nine chapters of Politian's *Miscellaneorum Centuria Secunda* recently discovered and now published for the first time. As the title indicates the book was intended to have one hundred chapters, but Politian died in 1494, before its completion. Politian's other *Miscellanea,* the *Centuria Prima,* had been published in 1489. The editor of the *Centuria Secunda,* Vittore Branca, points out that the later work manifests Politian's views about the scope and methods of philological investigation more fully,

Originally published in *Times Literary Supplement,* November 16, 1973, under the title "In the Interests of the Text," and reprinted in *T.L.S. Essays and Reviews from the Times Literary Supplement, 1973* (London, Oxford University Press, 1974), pp. 210–216, under the title "The Great Grammaticus." The occasion for this article was the publication of the newly discovered manuscript of Angelo Poliziano's *Miscellaneorum Centuria Secunda,* ed. Vittore Branca and Manlio Pastore Stocchi, 4 vols. (Florence, Alinari, 1972).

more clearly, and in their most mature form. The manuscript is proof that by the end of the fifteenth century a new, more advanced stage had been reached in the study and interpretation of ancient literature. It is of fundamental importance, therefore, for our understanding of the history of philology.

In contrast to those who interpreted and reconstructed classical texts on the basis of rigid grammatical rules or speculations inspired by prejudiced notions about what a text ought to contain, Politian asserted the paramount importance of two rules. The one is that in suggesting interpolations or emendations of a word that is unknown or of sentences that make no sense, the first step ought to be an examination of all the manuscripts still in existence and the most ancient ought to be subjected to the utmost scrutiny. Indeed, Politian based many of his suggestions in the *Centuria Secunda* on readings which he had found in manuscripts of the libraries of Bologna or Milan, in the Vatican, or in the two Florentine libraries that were his favorite hunting grounds, that of San Marco and that of the Medici.

Politian's other basic rule also has been generally accepted although perhaps it is not always followed: a text ought to be placed in its historical context. It should not be viewed primarily or exclusively as a part of or a link in a chain of philosophical writings or epic poetry or rhetorical textbooks or whatever the genre, but it must be seen as a document of the time in which it was written.

This means that the explanation of any document requires consideration of all the writings of comtemporary authors in whatever field they were working and also of all the remnants and monuments which might throw light on the life of the period in which the author lived. For this reason and not for reasons of scholarly vanity Politian in the *Centuria Secunda* deals with a startling variety of topics: from crocodiles and elephants to a list of the jurists who contributed to the Digest and to an investigation of ancient literary genres.

A work which marks a stage in the development of the history of philology must be presented with philological concern for exactitude. The manner in which the *Centuria Secunda* has been published represents a model of editorial techniques. It consists of four volumes: the first contains Professor Branca's magisterial introduction; the second a photographic reproduction of the manuscript; the third an exact transcript of the manuscript with all its underlinings, corrections, and cuttings; and the fourth volume provides the text in a final, critical edition with notes on sources, indexes, and so on. The fact that Mardersteig supervised the printing of the work is enough to explain why the volumes are a pleasure to look at and a delight to hold in one's hands.

Does a contribution to the history of philology—important as it might be—deserve such sumptuous presentation? The answer to the question is that the *Centuria Secunda* is significant not only for the history of philology but also because the humanist who wrote it was one of the greatest poets of the Italian Renaissance and—one might add—a poet in whose person and writings we still find magic and enchantment.

Every visitor to Florence who has looked at the Ghirlandaio frescoes of the Sassetti Chapel in Santa Trinità has seen the face of Politian, young, ugly, radiating intelligence, glancing with devotion at Lorenzo Magnifico toward whom he shepherds his pupils, Lorenzo's three sons. Politian's name is firmly tied to Lorenzo and his circle, to which he brought a very personal note. Some modern verses seem to characterize him and his poetry in an astounding way:

Vom jungen Ahnen hat es seine Farben
Und hat den Schmelz der ungelebten Dinge.

One is tempted to find explanation for the outstanding aptness of this characterization in the remarkable features which, separated by four centuries, Politian and Hofmannsthal, the writer of these lines, have in common. Both were prodigies; both were still schoolboys when they began to attract the admiration of the great literary figures of their time. And the poems of both show that subtle sense for the sound-value of words which demands their being set to music. One need not know much Latin but only have a good ear to grasp that in the epigram in which Politian summarized Ovid's complaints about his exile, he wants to describe the contrast between the sensitive nature of the poet and the grim surroundings in which he had to spend the last years of his life:

Et jacet euxinis vates romanus in oris
Romanum vatem barbara terra tegit.
Terra tegit vatem teneros qui lusit amores
Barbara quam gelidis alluit Ister aquis.

Politian's *Orfeo,* of course, was accompanied by music in its first performance in Mantua in 1480 and in the following centuries its text has formed the basis for many of the operas on this theme.

But Hofmannsthal and Politian are bound together in a more meaningful way by having an identical theme which gives their poetry its splendor and its delicacy. Their works are a poetic idealization of the society in which they lived and which they saw perish.

Ever since Lorenzo Magnifico took into his household the nineteen-year-old Politian, who had attracted the attention of the Florentine literati through his poetic translation of the *Iliad,* entrusted to him the education of his sons, and made him his secretary, Lorenzo was the young poet's idol. We have known for many years now that Botticelli's *Primavera* and *Birth of Venus* were painted for Lorenzo di Pierfrancesco de' Medici and not for Lorenzo Magnifico, and that the famous school of artists in Lorenzo's Palazzo never existed. Historical scholarship asserts that Lorenzo was not the ruler of Florence but acted within a republican political tradition so that at best he was a *primus inter pares.* Nevertheless, this does not replace in our mind Politian's image "E tu, ben nato Laur, sotto il cui velo Fiorenza lieta in pace si riposa." We still see in Lorenzo and in his brother Giuliano young princes hunting in the woods and hills of Florence, and leaders of a circle of graceful youths and beautiful women united in the cult of art, the service of love and the delight in the display of manly courage.

The manner in which Politian—in his poem on Giuliano's tournament, or in his elegies on the beauty and virtue of the reigning ladies of this circle, Albiera Albizzi and Simonetta Vespucci—presented the Florence of his time as a golden age has a colorful intensity which our knowledge of how it really was cannot pale. Undoubtedly, these colors seem to us particularly strong because of the darkness of the period which followed. There is no reason, however, to assume that when Politian extolled the life in Florence under the Medici he had a presentiment of the imminence of the end of their regime. But—perhaps because of his almost miraculous rise from abject poverty to a companion of Florence's most powerful citizen—Politian had a feeling for the inconstancy of life and for the rapid passing of time which gives his poetry its fragile delicacy. And when Lorenzo Magnifico died—although his son Piero, Politian's pupil, appeared firmly established—Politian was certainly aware that the end of an age had come.

> Nunc muta omnia,
> Nunc surda omnia.
> Quis dabit capiti meo
> Aquam, quis oculis meis
> Fontem lachrymarum dabit,
> Ut nocte fleam?
> Ut luce fleam?

In his rise Politian had been a favorite of Fortuna, but the feeling of dependence on this fickle goddess made him sensitive and vulnerable. He possessed grace and charm; he was a devoted friend and full of enthusiastic admiration for what his friends achieved; he had a brilliant, quick, and sharp intelligence; but he was very much aware of this. He had no respect for established reputations and would ruthlessly and arrogantly attack and criticize whomever he considered to be wrong or stupid. But he himself easily took offense. He was not without vanity and most of all he was spoilt. Perhaps because he was conscious of the insecure basis of his position, he was proud and concerned with his dignity.

Thus, he himself created the difficulties which removed him from the paradise of his youth. The autocratic manner in which he handled the education of the Medici sons aroused the anger of Clarice Medici, Lorenzo's wife, and she turned him out of the Medici Villa in Cafaggiolo. Lorenzo continued to stand behind him. He took care that the books which in the rush of leaving the Villa he had been forced to leave behind—his Homer, his

Demosthenes—were returned to him and he kept him on as his secretary. But even Lorenzo's patience with this difficult favorite became exhausted. When Politian at first hesitated to accompany Lorenzo to Naples, on what was considered to be a dangerous trip into enemy territory, and when, after having changed his mind, Politian expected to get from Lorenzo a personal message and personal invitation, Lorenzo cut him off.

The intimacy and the close personal contact which had existed between Lorenzo and Politian was never restored. But Politian could not live outside Florence and Lorenzo never changed his mind about Politian's outstanding gifts. After a short absence from Florence Politian was called back and received a chair for Latin and Greek rhetorics at the Florentine Studio. The poet was transformed into a scholar.

This move to a new field of activity did not diminish Politian's veneration for Lorenzo Magnifico. He remained constant to what he had said in a poem: "Sum tuus, O Medices; fateor tuque ipse fateris/Sum tuus usque." But next to Lorenzo other figures become the objects of Politian's loyal admiration: Pico della Mirandola and Ermolao Barbaro. When, during his composition of the *Centuria Secunda,* Politian received the news of the death of Ermolao Barbaro he interrupted his writing with an outcry about the loss this death meant for the *bonae artes* and he inserted in the chapter on which he was working a moving eulogy. In Politian's devotion to Pico and Barbaro the personal factor was not decisive. They had the same interests in the reconstruction of ancient texts and an identical approach to this task. Politian served no longer a person but a cause.

It has often been said of Politian that in the pursuit of his cause he was acerbic, almost cruel to his antagonists; he was especially reproached for having printed, after Calderini's death, an attack against the "pseudo-scholarship" of this old humanist. But Politian defended himself by stating that he was not inspired by "fondness for controversy" nor by "any eagerness to find faults in learned men," but by a zeal for truth." "My shots are fired against those who in order to defend their own personal, entirely imaginary interpretations obstinately resist the evidence of truth." Politian was no longer concerned with his personal advancement. He felt that his responsibility extended to future generations who ought to read the famous texts of the ancient world in unmutilated form. The community within which he worked were all those who had the same aims—whether living in the present or in the future.

Politian's *Centuria Secunda* not only indicates the emergence of a new philological method but also shows that this development was simultaneous with another development: from the diffuse efforts of the humanists in whom the wish to attract attention had been an ever-present stimulus, philology developed into a self-contained and self-conscious discipline. A few decades later this development had become obvious. Budé, Erasmus, and Scaliger were the princely rulers of a field which had become autonomous and in which only those who were also philologists and had the same criteria could judge the work of others.

In Politian and his friends we can observe the growth of the conviction that they were members of a special discipline which had its own dignity. In his *Lamia* Politian declined the role of philosopher. He could claim only to be a "grammaticus." But behind this show of modesty there was great pride. "With the ancients," Politian wrote, "this profession had such an authority that the Grammatici alone were the censors and judges of all writers so that they were also called critics." This statement ought to be read together with remarks which Politian made in a letter to Cortesi, remarks which are famous because they are an early attack against the fashion of Ciceronianism. Politian was defending himself against the accusation that he is not adopting the style of the writers of the Golden Age of Rome; he maintained that he did not want to be an imitator whose writings lack strength and vitality. "I am reproached that I don't express myself like Cicero, but why should I? I am not Cicero, I am I, and I wish to express myself."

These words reveal the inner springs of Politian's interest in philology and show that as philologist he continued on the path which he had pursued as poet. Politian's main concern was language, language as a means of expression. In order to put the many nuances and endless variety of human thoughts and emotions into words one needs a vocabulary of great richness and great flexibility. This was the motive of Politian's intense efforts to establish accurately what an ancient writer had said. This was the reason why he refused to limit Latin to the vocabulary and the sentence structure of Cicero's times but extended his study to the writers of every period of Roman history. Of his aims as well as of his success in attaining them his epigrams against Marullus, also a poet and a competitor, are indicative; they have an immensely rich and varied vocabulary which consists entirely of words used by ancient writers but is also so esoteric that few will understand the epigrams fully without using a dictionary.

Certainly, Politian shared the hope of the Renaissance humanists who through their work intended to revive the ancient world. But in Politian's case these attempts are engulfed in the pedagogical aim of enlarging the conceptual faculties and the means of expression of modern man. Politian did not shy away from the possible consequence: because of the close relationship between Latin and the *volgare* an extension of the Latin dictionary might not only serve the understanding of the past but also aid in the acquisition of a greater and more varied vocabulary and so contribute to the sophistication of the *volgare*. Even as a philologist Politian remained enough of a poet to believe in the possibilities of the *volgare* as a literary language.

Thus, the *Miscellanea* of the *Centuria Secunda* have aspects which are not clearly visible on the surface. The manuscript is not only a document belonging to the history of philology but a work in which the precision devoted to the establishment of the meaning of names and things sharpens and extends the cognitive capacities of man. The "revival of antiquity" in the Renaissance has features which are easily noticed: the use of classical concepts in philosophy; the application of a classical terminology to the developments in political and social life; or the "imitation" of classical prescripts and patterns in art. But it is more difficult to grasp and to define the role which the ancient world played in the slow and gradual transformation of man's cognitive faculties. We might get glimpses of this process in studying a specialized, detailed, and almost esoteric work like Politian's *Miscellanea* because, as always, also here "le bon Dieu est dans le détail."

16. The Historian as Guardian of National Consciousness: Italy between Guicciardini and Muratori

This essay is concerned with the period of Italian history between the Renaissance and the Enlightenment. Benedetto Croce has pronounced a judgment of remarkable harshness on this period: "The histories written about Italian life during these centuries take the form of accounts of incidents of meanness, stupidity, sorrow and horror rather poorly relieved on occasions by a laugh of derision or a smile of irony." He added: "That century and one-half has acquired and still retains in our history books the designation of the decadence of Italy. The designation deserves to be kept . . . From the middle of the Cinquecento up to about the close of the Seicento Italy was not truly alive."[1] This condemnation of a period of Italian history which produced Torquato Tasso and Giovanni Bernini, Tommaso Campanella and Galileo Galilei is startling; Croce's justification was that, while in the Renaissance a movement toward an Italian national consciousness and toward social and moral reform had begun, this movement had been halted and

Originally published in *National Consciousness, History, and Political Culture in Early-Modern Europe,* ed. Orest Ranum (Baltimore, © Johns Hopkins University Press, 1975), pp. 21–42. This study of Italy in the late sixteenth and seventeenth centuries was part of a series of lectures, given by various scholars, dealing with the principal European countries from the standpoint indicated by the title of the book.

even reversed in the late sixteenth and the seventeenth centuries, and that, in this period, common aims and ideals had disappeared from Italian life.

Croce's views on the significance of these centuries in Italian history gain their full weight if they are placed into the framework of a debate which has been going on among Italian writers and scholars for a long time. When does Italian history begin? Can one trace the line of Italian national development back to the early Middle Ages, or does the lack of any common organization before the Risorgimento indicate that only after that time did the feeling of belonging to an Italian nation become a significant factor in Italian political and social life?

The period with which we are concerned plays a crucial role in these considerations about the unity of Italian history.[2] These were the years in which, under foreign pressure, the various parts of Italy were drawn into distinct orbits and the differences among the various geographical regions of Italy were considerably increased. Moreover, in this period the church tightened its grip over Italian intellectual life and created, or at least widened, the gap between religious and secular culture which formed one of the main obstacles for Italian national unification and is a threat to Italian national coherence up to the present day. The question whether the one and one-half centuries between Renaissance and Enlightenment contributed to the growth of Italian national consciousness has bearing upon the manner in which the entire course of Italian history ought to be interpreted.

In the late sixteenth and seventeenth centuries the states on the Italian peninsula were satellites of France or of the Habsburgs; even the two buffer states in the north, Venice and Savoy, had to shape their course in accord with the great powers, whose every move they anxiously watched. The Pope, the ruler of the church-state, alone could claim to be more than a satellite and could follow an independent policy. But in the seventeenth century rule over Rome did not make the Pope a protagonist of a primarily Italian policy; Rome was not the center of Italy but of the world. The colonnades which Bernini built on the Piazza San Pietro were decorated with statues of saints of all ages and all peoples; they opened their arms to pilgrims from all over the world. The river gods who rendered homage to the power of the church on the new fountain of the Piazza Navona were the Nile and the Ganges, the Danube and the Rio de la Plata, not the Tiber or the Po or the Arno. The victories which were solemnly celebrated in Rome had been obtained in distant countries in the name of Christianity, not of a particular nation: Lepanto, St. Bartholomew, the Battle of the White Mountain.

From the late sixteenth into the seventeenth century the one Italian power of European standing, the papacy, had as the paramount concern of its policy the progress of the Counter Reformation. It cut off the roots of some of the developments toward Italian national consciousness which had begun in the Renaissance. Certainly it would be anachronistic to ascribe to the Italians of the fifteenth or sixteenth century a fully developed national feeling or even a longing for a firm political union among the inhabitants of Italy. Nor is it accurate to deny the existence of national consciousness in the Renaissance. It is true that the appeals for the "liberation of Italy," for an alliance of all Italian states, usually were made when the state which issued them was threatened by Ultramontani and in need of allies; the same state had no hesitation to ally itself with a foreign power against an Italian power if such a move promised advantages. Nevertheless, these appeals to a common interest among all Italians, even if not successful or not systematically pursued, would have made no sense if they had not reflected the feeling that those living on the Apennine Peninsula were bound together in a special relationship and were different from peoples living on the other side of the Alps. How many went a step farther and recognized the need for common political action is impossible to estimate. Some did, as is evident in the writings of Francesco Guicciardini and Machiavelli. In his great work, Guicciardini described with sadness the gradual establishment of foreign rule over Italy, which he attributed to the shortsightedness of the Italian rulers and their incapacity or their unwillingness to place the common interest over personal advantage. Machiavelli, who died a decade before Guicciardini began to write his *History of Italy,* held till the end[3] to the conviction he had expressed in the last chapter of *The Prince* that the Italian rulers should join forces to drive the foreigners out of Italy.

Machiavelli's exortation to "liberate Italy from the barbarians" ends with the famous lines from Petrarch:

Vertú contra furore
Prenderá l'arme; e fia 'l combatter corto,
Ché l'antiquo valore
Ne l'italici cor non è ancor morto.

These lines indicate the sources which fed national consciousness and national pride in the period of the Renaissance. The sources were the notion of a secular political virtue[4] and it was the idea that the Italians of then and the Romans of classical times were the same people.

The church of the Counter Reformation began to look upon pagan antiquity with distrust. For instance, in Marino's *Galeria* of 1619, Erasmus, the leader of a Christian humanism who once had warned "ne sub obtextu priscae litteraturae renascentis caput erigere conetur paganismus,"[5] was banned among the Negromanti and called "falso profeta" whose "scienza chiara" concealed a "coscienza oscura."[6] A threat to the Christian religion began to be seen in the preoccupation with the literary and artistic legacy of the classical world because it might lead to a revival of paganism. On this the Popes of the Counter Reformation agreed, though it depended on their personal inclinations whether they preferred to eliminate or to absorb all traces of classical influences.[7]

When the news of the victory of Lepanto reached the Eternal City, the Romans prepared a solemn reception for their victorious compatriot Marcantonio Colonna. He was to enter the city on a gilded chariot with a laurel wreath around his head. On command of Pope Pius V, however, these plans were abandoned. Colonna rode into the city behind the standard of Christ; practices of pagan antiquity which had been used on similar occasions in Rome throughout the period of the Renaissance were banned.

If the saintly Pius V tried to erase all pagan traditions, Sixtus V, the most powerful figure among the Popes of the Counter Reformation, tried to subject antiquity to the church and to use it for the glorification of Christianity. He was proudly conscious of the Roman heritage. He was aware that ancient Rome had been the city of the Seven Hills and he was eager that Rome reach beyond the low stretch along the Tiber, to which it had been confined in medieval and Renaissance times, and occupy its seven hills. The Pope invested, therefore, a good amount of energy and money in building the aquaduct which conducted the water from the mountains to the Roman hills; Roman princes and cardinals could now build there the villas and gardens which until the end of the nineteenth century formed the pride of Rome. But, on the monumental fountains from which the waters of the aquaduct gushed, there rode no Neptune with his triton, but instead there stood the figure of Moses, whose staff indicated the opening for the outflow of the water. The columns of Trajan and Marcus Aurelius were crowned with the statues of the apostle princes, Peter and Paul, and a cross was placed on the tops of the ancient obelisks which had been excavated and re-erected with great ingenuity and immense effort. "Drizzando gli obelischi a la croce," Tasso said in a famous poem praising the works of Sixtus V.[8]

The change in attitude toward antiquity went beyond the field of religion. Art and literature show an ironic and irreverent application of classical materials. Classical mythology was used for satirizing human follies, for celebrating passion and love. The classical world is no longer seen as providing the norms and values for the conduct of life.[9] The classical stories which Marino celebrated in his poems were those of Adonis and Endymion, Ganymede and Galatea, Narcissus and Leander; Bernini gained his reputation by fixing in marble the fleeting moment in which Daphne, shying away from Apollo's embraces, is transformed into a laurel tree. On Carracci's frescoes in the Palazzo Farnese a noisy assembly of ancient gods celebrates the indomitable power of love. We are far removed from the Renaissance when, as on Raphael's *School of Athens,* the ancients were the messengers of eternal truth, or when, as in Michelangelo's *Brutus,* the example of Roman virtue is placed as an admonition before a base present.

The unlikelihood or impossibility of imagining a seventeenth-century work with the ethos of Michelangelo's *Brutus* shows the evanescence of the other element which had nourished national consciousness and pride: secular virtue and political heroism diminished in value and importance. If Machiavelli had been the main advocate of political *virtú* in the Renaissance, the manner in which his ideas were discussed in the political literature of the late sixteenth and seventeenth centuries provides a good indication for the change which took place in political thought and in the political climate.[10] In 1559 Machiavelli's name had appeared on the *Index Librorum Prohibitorum* as one of the authors "quorum libri et scripta omnia prohibentur." Despite this prohibition his work evidently continued to be read, but it is difficult to establish precisely what influence he exerted because the political writers of the Counter Reformation[11] had to use caution and concealment when they discussed Machiavelli's ideas. When they openly mentioned his name we can be sure that they were vehemently condemning the Florentine secretary. When they embarked on a serious discussion of his ideas, they concealed their interest in the writings of this dangerous and diabolical man by referring to him somewhat mysteriously as "autor discursum," or they take up arguments and issues of *The Prince* or the *Discorsi* without mentioning Machiavelli's name. They dealt with issues which were prevalent in Machiavelli's writings: the part which Fortune and Virtue played in the rise of Rome,[12] the risks involved in pursuing a "middle course,"[13] or the need for maintaining traditional institutions in newly acquired territories.[14] The weight of Machiavelli's theories hangs heavily over the political discussions of this later period.

However, acceptance of the conceptual framework which Machiavelli had created did not mean that the later political writers were his followers or that they approved his theories. The religious climate in which they lived permeated their thinking, and they felt aversion to what they considered to be Machiavelli's amorality. Their political society differed basically from that which had existed before foreign powers, particularly Spain, had gained control. Machiavelli's chief work had been commentaries on Livy who had told the story of the foundation and rise of the Roman republic. The political writers of the Counter Reformation regarded Tacitus as the "primo principe della politica";[15] they expressed their views in comments on Tacitus,[16] who had written about Rome in the times of the emperors. They lived in a world of states ruled by princes; they looked upon politics from above, from the point of view of the

ruler, his psychology, the court, and the rivalries among courtiers. There writers assumed a hierarchical structure of government in which promotions to a higher bureaucratic rank were to
proceed from grade to grade, not by jumps. They had only contempt for the groups that were at the bottom of the social hierarchy. Ammirato wrote: "the masses are a lazy beast that is
unable to distinguish truth from falsehood,"[17] and Boccalini
calls the people "a herd of sheep."[18] In contrast to Machiavelli,
who had asserted that the people possessed a *virtú* which made
them a basic force in political life, the writers of the Counter
Reformation regarded princes and rulers alone as the dominating and controlling factors in political life. Politics became an
object of cautious calculation dependent upon the intelligence
of the prince and his advisers. It is hardly possible to find a
statement more alien to Machiavelli's views than Botero's sentence: "Greatly daring plans are dangerous because after bold
and spirited beginnings they run into difficulties and troubles
and end in misery and despair."[19]

The extent to which these writers, despite their interest in
the questions which Machiavelli had raised, were remote from
Machiavelli's deepest concerns emerges from an analysis of
what is usually regarded as their main contribution to the history of political thought: their discussion of the notions of
"reason of state"[20] and of "balance of power."[21] Clearly these
notions presupposed acceptance of a basic Machiavellian assumption—existence of a separation of morals and politics. Hes-
itatingly, and with many reservations, these writers admitted
that the observance of the rules of morality might be a hin-
drance to political success. Boccalini, for instance, first declared
that the doctrine of reason of state was in contradiction to the
laws of God and man, but he then admitted that it provided
useful rules for politics.[22] Like Machiavelli they recognized the
determining role of interest in politics but they drew very different conclusions from this insight. In Machiavelli's view, conflict among states was unavoidable because each state was
guided by its own interest and survival in these struggles for
power required a dynamic and expansionist policy. The political
writers of the later period tried to analyze precisely what the
interests of the various European powers were. They had subtle
discussions about the course of action prescribed by the inter-

ests of each state, and they then tried to gauge the reactions which the move of one power might produce among all others. The aim of such considerations was not to discover how a state might augment its power and expand; rather, these writers tried to show how counter forces could be organized and mobilized against aggression and to demonstrate the futility of any action that might disturb the existing situation. The purpose to which the notions of reason of state and balance of power were applied was the maintenance of the status quo.

There is a striking example showing how these basic notions led to conclusions widely different from those of Machiavelli; that is, the admiration which the later writers had for Venice. For Machiavelli there was only one model for the conduct of policy: the Roman republic. For Venice and its policy he had only contempt.[23] The political writers of the Counter Reformation regarded Venice as a model. In their eyes the Venetians had wisely learned to manage the balance of power and thereby maintained the status quo. The reasons why Venetian policy seemed so attractive to these advocates of a rational and cautious policy were succinctly stated by Boccalini: "The Venetians have as the ultimate purpose of their existence peace, the Roman Senate only knew war . . . For the Venetians it is enough to have territorial possessions large enough to assure Venice its freedom. They want to have power not out of ambition to command others but out of their striving not to become the subject of others."[24]

The lengthy reports which the Venetian ambassadors submitted to the Senate on their return from a diplomatic mission have always been regarded as testimonies of Venetian political sagacity; they can also be viewed as practical application of the theories developed at that time. Like the political writers of the Counter Reformation, the Venetian ambassadors considered a hierarchically structured monarchy as the model of a well-organized society. Their reports focused on a description and analysis of the character of the ruler, of the court and its influential personalities, and on the relations of the country with other powers. They started from the principle that "princes do not take any action if not for their own interest,"[25] though they are aware that princely resentments and ambitions can sometimes overcome useful interests. They described in detail the relationships which existed between the state to which they had been accredited and all other states, particularly the great powers of France and Spain and their small neighbors on the Italian peninsula. Venetian ambassadors admired rulers who, on the basis of accurate information, acted rationally and according to their interests; they were antagonistic to Italian princes who aimed at expansion and caused disturbances. They praised the grand duke of Tuscany who "studied to maintain good feelings among the princes of Italy," and they considered "continua pace et felicissima tranquillita" as the highest goal that a prince might achieve.

Two different, even rather divergent, tendencies can be observed in Italian political thought of the late sixteenth and seventeenth centuries. One group of political thinkers and writers had as its aim the discovery of the rational basis of political actions. This group concluded that the guiding principle was interest, as determined by geography, economic reasons, and prestige. Concepts like balance of power and reason of state were crucial because they provided the conceptual framework for a rational analysis of politics. In the view of these writers, the prerequisite for successful political action was a correct evaluation of the motives of others. Qualities required in a statesman were cleverness, intelligence, and foresight, and his main concern was diplomacy. These writers believed in the possibility of limiting the impact of such irrational factors as force, energy, enthusiasm, and passion. The aim of a statesman ought to be to avoid situations in which irrational factors had been let loose, because events might slide out of control. In such situations the outcome was no longer in the hands of men but of Fortune. These writers were thinking in terms of the existing situation, of its correct evaluation, and its preservation. When they looked upon the Italian scene, they regarded the existence of many independent states as a permanent feature of Italian political life, and they did not envisage changes which might result in a federation among the Italian powers or which might produce a certain amount of unification. Considerations of nationalism, even in an embryonic form, had no place in the system of these writers.

While the attention of these writers remained firmly fixed to the ground so that they could not perceive any wider community beyond the small one in which they lived, there was another group of political thinkers whose thoughts dwelt so high above reality that they too could not distinguish the existence of a national entity. In histories of Italian political thought the chapters dealing with the century of the Counter Reformation have sometimes been entitled "Gli utopisti del seicento."[26] Indeed, the depiction of a utopia became in this time a favorite form for the expression of political ideas. Certainly, the utopia was not a new form of political literature. After its emergence in the ancient world it had been revived in the Renaissance and it had served well for the expression of basic beliefs of this period. The utopias of the Renaissance taught that if life were organized according to man's natural reason the miseries and vices of the present—hunger, violence, envy—would disappear. The fundamental assumptions of the most important utopia of the seventeenth century, of Campanella's *Città del Sole,* were in direct opposition to those of the Renaissance utopias.[27] If the latter were constructed on the basis of an inquiry into the needs and desires of rational man, Campanella intended to demonstrate the possibility of a society established in obedience to the principles of religion and to explain the institutional forms needed for the attainment of this goal. For Campanella the world had two centers: the sun, which represents warmth and love, and the earth, which represents coldness and hatred. The society which he envisaged would serve to establish the reign of the sun. In such a society the world would be subjected to unified rule. Campanella's *Città del Sole* embraced the entire world. Campanella, like most of his contemporaries had been deeply shaken by the discovery of the new world which had revealed the existence of human beings who had never heard of Christ and never received the word of God. He imagined for his sun city a religion which was very similar to Christianity but not identical with that known to Europe. The sun city would possess a hierarchical structure; its head would be a priest-king, and directly below him in the hierarchy were priests and knights, the priests taking care to organize the lives of all men in such a way that the spiritual ends for which society existed would be achieved. The knights would protect society against outside enemies. Activities connected with the material needs of men were of low value; agriculture found somewhat more favor with Campanella than industry or trade.

The description of particular arrangements like the recommendation of communal property has aroused the interest of later generations in Campanella's work. In our context it may be enough to point out the prevailing idea of Campanella's work: the transformation of life into a city of God and the return to a divinely inspired and controlled social order. Campanella's work exemplifies the particular character of the political utopias of this period: despite its unorthodox character the strength of the religious element made it a product of the intellectual climate of the Counter Reformation.

The utopian tendency of Italian political thought in this period has two sources. It was stimulated by the rejection of a present in which the Italian peninsula was divided into small powerless states and subjected to foreign rule. However, the utopian political thinkers refrained from a concrete analysis of this situation because they were also inspired by the second source, the universalism of the church of the Counter Reformation which hoped to regain control of the entire world. We find in literature and art the same counter-reformatory spirit which inspired the utopianism of political thought. Tasso's *Gerusalemme Liberata* proclaims the necessity of a divinely ordered European society by giving a poetic image of its existence in the past. And Francesco Borromini's creation of space and distance that deceived the eye expresses the same longing for a flight from the restricting conditions of the present to a differently ordered world. Neither acceptance nor rejection of the present offered the possibility of finding any political relevance in the notion of a national entity.

Neglect of the national element in the political literature of Italy in the late sixteenth and seventeenth centuries is astounding because the political situation in Italy was such that national feelings and reactions might well have been natural.[28] The period which we are examining was a time of foreign rule in Italy, and close contacts with foreigners, especially when contacts are of a hostile nature, have always stimulated the growth of national consciousness. The conclusion we have reached—namely, that the political literature was dominated by issues which stood in the way of a development of national consciousness—must be supplemented by the consideration of the following question: Why did the customary reaction to foreign rule—an upsurge of national feeling—*not* take place in Italy?

It must be admitted that in the middle of the sixteenth century, when the Italian wars which had begun with the invasion of Charles VIII of France in 1494 ended with the establishment of Spanish rule in Italy, we find many expressions of regret about the "infelici tempi" into which the "misera Italia" had fallen.[29] However, in the following decades, when the Spanish rule had secured stability and tranquility, the contrast between the happy past and the miserable present began to become less sharply felt. If from time to time ideas of federation aimed at driving the foreigners out of Italy reawakened, they were sudden outbursts provoked by special circumstances rather than indications of a constantly present and steadily growing trend.[30]

Such sporadic expressions of national feeling were primarily connected with the moves of Savoy, the one power whose rulers continued to harbor expansionist aims. The duke of Savoy, the first Carlo Emmanuele, wrote propagandistic poems in which he used a nationalistic appeal against the Spanish governor of Milan:

> Havemo el sangue zentil et no vilan
> Credemo in Dio, et si semo cristiani
> Ma sopra il tutto boni Italiani.

When Carlo Emmanuele dared to challenge the Spanish power and became involved in war with Spain, writers praised him as the defender of Italian liberty and tried to spur the other Italian powers to support him. Tassoni wrote the *Filippiche* in which, in a style reminiscent of the last chapter of Machiavelli's *Prince,* he complained that Italy was ruled by princes not "of our blood nor used to Italian customs"[31] and admonished the other northern Italian states, particularly Venice and Modena, to join Savoy in the attempt to get rid of foreign domination. Fulvio Testi wrote his "Pianto d'Italia" and stanzas in honor of Carlo Emmanuele—poems for which, because of their anti-Spanish content, Testi had to pay with exile from the court of Modena.

Again, in the next decade when the extinction of the Gonzaga dynasty in Mantua drew the opposing powers of Spain and France into the Italian scene, writers of pamphlets and poems tried to encourage the duke of Savoy to pursue a policy which would liberate Italy from foreign domination.

But these writers were propagandists who followed the directions of the ruler whom they served. They tried to influence the court circles in other Italian states. Though he had appealed to nationalism in the *Filippiche,* other writings of Tassoni praised the Spanish monarch as the great protector of peace in Italy; and Testi, the author of the *Pianto d'Italia,* could express views in favor of the French king. Without denying that these poets and writers took a certain amount of patriotic pride in the Italian past, a program of Italian federation had no pre-eminent or permanent place in their political thinking.

Passages in the *Filippiche,* the most important, literarily, of these national appeals, indicate a reason why the reactions against foreign rule and manifestations of national feeling were sporadic and never widespread. The author of the *Filippiche* stated that his appeal was directed to princes and nobles but not to the Italian people; the masses, he said, were cowardly by nature and in them every true feeling of courage and honor was dead.[32] These words point to a rift in Italian society, placing the upper class group in opposition to peasants and townspeople; thus the upper classes looked upon the foreign rulers not only as enemies but also as fellow aristocrats, allies, and protectors.

The political developments in those areas directly under Spanish control, Milan in the north and Naples and Sicily in the south, show this clearly. Italy in the seventeenth century was a restless country.[33] The revolutions of 1647 in Palermo and Naples were not isolated events but open expressions of widespread discontent and misery. In the course of these outbreaks some anti-Spanish slogans appeared, but these revolts were not directed against foreign rule. The people, in what might be regarded as the traditional attitude of lower class discontent in preindustrial society, appealed to the king against his incompetent officials. In Palermo as well as in Naples the feelings of the masses were expressed in the slogan, "Long live the King, and down with the taxes and the bad government." The revolutions in Palermo and Naples[34] represented conflicts among social groups, in which peasants and the urban masses, sometimes also the urban middle classes, stood against the nobility. In these regions agriculture barely provided a minimal subsistence for peasants with small holdings; when bad harvests brought misery and starvation, they moved into the mountains and became brigands or migrated to the towns and swelled the number of the poor. The middle classes of the towns shared the discontent of the lower classes because administrative centralization encroached upon their rights to self-government. The wars in which Spain was involved since the beginning of the revolt of the Netherlands aggravated these tensions because of the increasing amount of taxes imposed by the Spanish government on Naples and Sicily. Frequently urban and rural localities could procure these taxes only by taking loans from merchants, financiers, and rich landlords. The small wealthy group that provided these loans was compensated in various ways by the Spanish rulers. Members of this group received extension of their jurisdiction over the peasants on their estates. They were entrusted with the levying of taxes, and they were raised in social status. At the beginning of the seventeenth century the Neapolitan titled nobility numbered 133 families; it had more than tripled by the end of the century. The upper social group, composed of old, landowning noble families as well as newly nobilitated men of affairs, supported the Spanish regime against the discontented peasants and the urban poor and middle classes in the revolutions of 1647. The members of this upper group allied themselves with the Spanish officers because they wanted to preserve the privileges and advantages which the Spanish rulers had granted them. Social and economic contrasts within the populace of southern Italy prevented any real national movement against foreign rulers and their rule.

Though different in detail, the developments in the Spanish possessions in northern Italy followed the same general pattern. In the Duchy of Milan[35] both absentee rulership and control by Spain were novel phenomena. Tension between the governor, who was the representative of the Spanish king and a member of the high Spanish nobility, and the indigenous administrators and the Senate, composed of the Milanese patriciate and members of the landowning nobility, was unavoidable. This struggle had national undertones. A particularly vehement conflict developed over the appointment of the president of the Senate. The governor wanted this post filled by a Spaniard, but the Senate claimed the position for one of its members. The Senate won a significant victory, which assured that from this time on under the regime of Philip II an equilibrium would be maintained between the governor and the Senate, between the decision-making power of Spain and the administrative and executive functions of the native patriciate. But at the beginning of the seventeenth century this equilibrium was broken. The economic situation deteriorated, and these difficulties were compounded by Spanish demands for higher taxes and by the stationing of troops in the pivotal area of northern Italy. The members of the ruling group in the Duchy of Milan felt economically threatened; they were eager to keep the available benefices to themselves. Non-nobles were excluded from holding offices. Only those whose ancestors had been nobles one hundred years ago were recognized as members of the nobility. In order to reinforce the separation of the nobility from the rest of the population, nobles were not allowed to engage in commercial activities. Accordingly, they invested their money in landed estates. The rest of the population resented the exclusiveness of the Senate nobles, who began to rely on the Spanish government for protection of their rights and claims. As in Naples, an alliance between the Spanish king and the upper group in the Milanese Duchy was forged, and a national front against Spanish rule never gained much impetus.

The widening of the gap between the ruling group and the rest of the population was not limited to the Italian possessions of the Spanish crown; the same process can be observed in all the states of the Italian peninsula. In all of them a hierarchically organized society was created in imitation of the dominant power of Spain; a wealthy upper group began to acquire landed estates and to form a nobility just below—and allied with—the princely ruler.

The most important of these territorial states was the Medici Grand Duchy of Tuscany.[36] Its size, situation, and economic strength enabled the Grand Duke to maintain close contacts with France, which limited his dependence on Spain. Nevertheless, when the first Grand Duke Cosimo was buried, the funeral was organized on the pattern of that of Charles V. The solemn processions at religious festivals, at weddings, and at burials were arranged strictly according to rank. The bankers and merchants who had created the wealth and the greatness of Florence, even though they did not abandon commercial activities, became courtiers and finally marquisses and counts. While many features of the traditional system of government were maintained, the executive functions were carried out by a bureaucracy which no longer resided in the old seat of government, the Palazzo della Signoria, but in the extended structure of the Uffizi which Giorgio Vasari built next to it. This bureaucracy worked as the willing instrument of the Grand Duke, who resided in the Palazzo Pitti, distant from and above the Florentine populace. The Florentines of the Renaissance claimed that their government was based on the ideas of liberty and equality. Even if one takes such notions with a grain of salt, it is evident that social ideas and ideals had almost been reversed.

The one republic which still existed in Italy, Venice, was no exception to the general process.[37] From the fifteenth century on, the circle of the policymaking group in Venice had steadily narrowed. The Great Council had receded into the background vis-à-vis the numberically smaller Senate. The Senate had become an obedient instrument of the Collegio, and during the sixteenth century the Office of the Ten had taken the crucial political decisions into their hands. Its grasp of governmental functions had been so ruthless that it had aroused opposition, and in 1582 its powers were reduced. But this was a temporary setback. The Ten soon reasserted their authority. The fight with the Papacy which led to the Interdict and in which Fra Paolo Sarpi was one of the intellectual leaders was part of this development. It was not, as Protestants then and later were inclined to believe, a fight for freedom against authoritarianism. It was a jurisdictional struggle. The Venetian government refused all restrictions in its control over any of the inhabitants of the city; nor would it allow the Pope to interfere in its conduct of foreign policy. As Sarpi argued,[38] if Venice wanted to exert, as it had in the past, "il fondamento principale d'ogni imperio e dominio," namely, "la vera religione e pietà," it had to keep the right to determine where churches and monasteries were to be built "per poter ricerverle e sostentarle" and had to be able to punish criminal ecclesiastics. The sovereignty of the state, and that meant particularly the unrestricted power of a small ruling group, was the issue.

If in the various Italian states power became concentrated in the hands of a small upper group dependent on and allied with princely rulers, the focal point of attention of all those who determined Italian politics was the individual state. The preservation of territorial independence and maintenance of the status quo became their guiding principle: they were not inclined to see far beyond the social body in which they lived. If political thinkers and writers regarded "peace and tranquility" to be the highest political values, they might have overlooked or disregarded the basic importance of the element of power to which Machiavelli had directed attention. But they remained close to—and reflected—the concrete needs and aims of the rulers of their time.

In the emergence of a hierarchically structured society and of an aristocratic upper group monopolizing the positions of power, the Spanish conflicts and the religious climate of the time both played their part. But these trends were reinforced by a third factor to which we have already alluded, namely, to the economic difficulties which beset Italy at this time.[39] In the evolution of the economic situation, two different stages can be distinguished. Throughout the sixteenth and the beginning of the seventeenth century, Italian economic decline was relative rather than absolute. First English and then Dutch ships appeared in the Mediterranean and took over portions of the trade with the east which previously had been an Italian monopoly. Moreover, Italian manufactured goods, especially textiles, now encountered serious competition in the European market, particularly since, because of the maintenance of traditional guild regulations, the prices of their goods remained high. Nevertheless, the Italian economic decline was slow and gradual; and the wealth that Italians had accumulaed assured that Italian bankers would remain the financiers of Europe. In the 1620s, however, *pari passu* with general European trends, economic decline accelerated and economic stagnation set in. As happens in such situations, the prices for industrial goods began to fall more sharply than those for agricultural goods. Foodstuffs remained in demand inside and outside Italy, and consequently, whenever possible, a shift from manufacture to agriculture took place. If the Spanish government had favored the feudal nobility in Naples and Sicily for political reasons, this social group now acquired a strengthened economic basis as well. In southern Italy an almost medieval feudalism not only survived but became the dominant force of social life. The existence of a variety of independent states had created sharp divisions, but added to this was an even deeper-reaching division: the contrast between south and north, if not well defined at that time, at least became so great that it has remained a problem for Italian national thought and national consciousness until the present.

Antonio Gramsci noted that the role the middle class played in other countries was taken over by the intellectuals in Italian political development. This observation was primarily aimed at developments in later centuries. However, the ground for what happened later was laid in the period with which we deal.

The crucial fact to which we have frequently directed attention was that Italy was the center of the Counter Reformation and remained tied to the Roman Catholic Church. In countries that broke with the Pope, church and state were brought together in a close relationship in which the same person—the prince—was the head of both church and state. However, a complex and often tense situation fraught with the possibility of friction arose in Roman Catholic countries where a papal lordship, extending its claims and interests over the entire world, encountered a prince, primarily or exclusively concerned with a strictly limited territory and everyday problems. In the jurisdictional conflict between Venice and Papacy, which placed Venice from 1605 to 1607 under the Interdict, this tension came into the open. But in the other Italian states, the princely rulers were equally concerned with preventing the Papacy and the church from encroaching on what they considered the secular spheres of their government. The decades after the Council of Trent were full of disputes between the church and the Italian rulers. For example, the Farneses insisted on the right to tax the clergy; and the Senate in Milan denied Carlo Borromeo the right to call laymen before ecclesiastical tribunals.

The struggle of the princes against the far-reaching claims of the Papacy presupposed preservation of a certain amount of intellectual freedom. The rulers would not go so far as to protect heretics or those with views which clashed directly with the teaching of the church; yet the princes had a strong interest in furthering intellectual activities free from church interference. They would be particularly pleased if the artists or scholars whom they protected would glorify their deeds or those of their ancestors. But beyond that, princely patronage of art and literature, of scholarship and science, had the advantage of providing defense by the secular government against papal dogmatism. Princely patronage demanded a reorganization of intellectual activities. Italian rulers could no longer rely on the universities in which the traditional spirit of the Middle Ages was still dominant and which had become stagnant in Italy. The new centers of intellectual exchange were the academies established all over Italy, some of them on the initiative of a ruler or prince, some of them by the scholars or scientists themselves.[40] In addition to the most well known, such as the academies of the Lincei in Rome or the Cimento or the Crusca in Florence, there were the Otiosi, the Intronati, the Erranti, and the Dogliosi. The ironical flavor in these names indicates that these academies included not only professionals but also dilettantes. The nobility and the wealthier men of the bourgeoisie formed an audience for scholarly writings and scientific discoveries. Achievements in these fields became known all over Italy, and princes and towns competed for the services of distinguished literati who moved from one town to another or from one court to another.

Precondition for the creation of a wider audience was the use of the vernacular language, thereby giving an impetus to the movement for the use of the Italian language which Bembo had initiated in the first half of the sixteenth century. But dangers were perceived in the use of the vernacular for literary and scholarly purposes. It might lead to carelessness in the use of language and to its disintegration into a variety of dialects. This issue gave importance to the Crusca and its great enterprise, the Dictionary of the Italian Language. The academicians of the Crusca tried to establish a code for good linguistic usage. As Florentines they were convinced that the language in which the great Florentine writers of the Trecento had written ought to be the model—though their concept of the "buon secolo" soon became extended to the entire Renaissance. They were strict: they were not willing to recognize Tasso's vocabulary as a model because he introduced innovations that went beyond Ariosto. The decision against Tasso did not stick, however, and the academicians of the Crusca reluctantly gave Tasso a solemn reception when he visited Florence.

This was the intellectual world in which Galileo moved, from Pisa to Padua, to Venice, to Florence, and to Rome, and to which, in spite of his unique scientific genius, he remained bound in a variety of ways. His *Dialogo sopra i due Massimi Sistemi del Mondo* was addressed to the groups assembled in the academies—to the "discreto lettore," the interested laymen; accordingly it was written in Italian.[41] In the Foreword, Galileo stated that he wanted "foreign nations to realize that Italians understood this matter as much as the Transalpine (*oltramontana*) mind could imagine."[42] These words express pride in the cultural achievements and cultural mission of Italy; they testify to the strength of the feeling that, though a political organization encompassing the entire Italian peninsula did not exist, there was, below or above the external forms of a political and social bond, a bond comprised of culture, language, and literature. The contribution this period made to the development of Italian national consciousness lies in the firm establishment of the view that an outstanding and singular Italian culture existed.

This view drew its justification and strength from the achievements of the Renaissance. The basic assumption of the Crusca—that the language of the Renaissance was to serve as the model of the Italian language—is a demonstration of the paradigmatic importance which the Renaissance had gained in the Italian mind. Previously the classical world had been regarded as the only existing golden age. Now the Renaissance took its place next to the golden age of a remote past. The ancient world unavoidably became somewhat diminished in value. We have mentioned that in the period of the Counter Reformation the veneration of the classical world was regarded as a danger for Christianity; the recognition of the normative nature of the Renaissance had the same effect of weakening the hold of the classical world over the minds of men. Because the attainments of the Renaissance had proved that a new cultural highpoint could be reached even in the postclassical world, it also became evident that one needed not only to look backward toward a golden age of the past but also to look forward to a golden age in the future. All this involved a change in the conceptual scheme which had been placed on the past. Italy began to emerge from its subordination to the greatness of Rome. In the work of the historians this new image of Italy, which implied a recognition of a past national history, began to take shape.

If this essay had dealt exclusively with the development of historiography it might have been entitled "From Guicciardini to Muratori." Insofar as the development of historiography is concerned, the period with which we are dealing is an interregnum. This interregnum began after the composition of the greatest historical work of the Renaissance, Guicciardini's *History of Italy,* which was also the last such work in which Italy was presented as an independent entity in European politics. And it ended with the publication of the great documentaries which embraced the whole of Italy.

The names Guicciardini and Muratori also suggest something of the changes in concepts and methods that took place during this period. Until the emergence of modern critical history in the nineteenth century, and perhaps even up to the present, there have always been two different types of historical works: histories written by participants, by statesmen-historians, and learned histories composed by professors or professional literati. Guicciardini was a statesman-historian, one of the greatest; it is indicative of Italian political decadence that no other Italian statesmen-historians emerged in the later centuries. Muratori is the outstanding example of a learned historian who absorbed and perfected that which took place since the sixteenth century.

No Italian writer or scholar played a significant part in the development which brought about new critical methods to the writing of history and to the awareness of the distinctiveness and the differences among historical periods. The major advances in historical criticism and understanding of the sixteenth century were primarily the work of French scholars;[43] their work was largely the result of applying legal and philological methods of research to wider historical problems. In Italy legal history contributed little toward the formation of a new historical outlook. In countries with a strong central power, research in legal history helped promote national feeling, while in Italy legal studies had the opposite effect—that of deepening divisions by reinforcing the claims of the various rulers against each other. Philology and archaeology, however, greatly influenced the Italian view of the past. Classical scholarship revealed the particular conditions of life in ancient Rome, showed the connection between religion and institutions, and stressed the distance which separated the classical world from later times. The Romans became different people rather than patterns for all times.

The most impressive and most striking testimony of an attitude which divided ancient Rome from Italy was the medieval history of Italy which Sigonius published under the title *De regno Italiae*. Sigonius distinguished two forms of government in Italy: the *imperium* and the *regnum*.[44] The *imperium,* which of course is the Roman Empire, had been exhaustively studied and was well known; but the *regnum*, which originally had been introduced by foreign people—the Langobards, the Franks, and the Germans—was almost unknown and needed to be investigated. In Sigonius the interest of the philologist was combined with that of a legal historian. Clearly, the legal historian's concern with institutional continuity aroused his interest in the chronicles and documents of medieval Italy and resulted in his description of the gradual development of Italy as an individual and autonomous social body. Sigonius's story ended with the liberation of the Italian towns from foreign rule in the thirteenth century, that is, with the beginning of the Renaissance.

Sigonius's treatment of Italian history is based on presuppositions which deserve to be spelled out. The highpoint to which his description leads is the Renaissance, but he considers the Renaissance as the outcome of a long development of which the liberation from the subjection to foreign powers and the emergence of a society of free republics formed an integral part. The Renaissance therefore is not the sudden, miraculous rebirth of a golden age long past. The process which brought it forward and from which it emerged at a felicitous moment began long ago in earlier times and will continue into the future. The Renaissance was not a mirror of Rome but an Italian creation, and Italy lived before and after the Renaissance. What Sigonius shows is the connection between the pride in the cultural achievements of the Renaissance, which permeated the thinking of the intellectuals, the *literati,* and the growth of national consciousness.

As a sequel to Sigonius's history, Muratori (who opens the period of Italian intellectual history which led to the Risorgimento) initiated his own work. For Muratori, Sigonius with his *De Regno Italiae* was the first to lay "the ground on which later generations could build."[45] It was in the spirit of Sigonius that Muratori in his Preface to the *Rerum Italicarum Scriptores* wrote those moving sentences in which awareness of a sad Italian past is combined with hopes for the future: "It is a sign of arrogance and of insolence, even of ingratitude, to limit oneself to a knowledge of Italy when she was victorious and triumphant, and to turn away from her, when she is defeated and subjected to foreign nations. Italy remains our mother whether victorious or defeated, and it is the duty of her sons to acknowledge the obligation which they owe her, in good and in evil times."[46]

It is certainly true that scholars of other countries also delved into the dark ages in search of the roots of their national past. But the efforts that were made in Italy gained their importance from the fact that the notion of a national culture and of a national past was maintained in a period when outside forces—Spain, the church, a shift to the Atlantic—impinged upon the social, economic, and intellectual foundations of Italian life. This might explain why the guardians of national consciousness in this period were a small group of scholars and literati. This might also help to explain the political leadership which intellectuals have held more recently after the Italian national state was formed.

17. From Political to Social History: Lorenz von Stein and the Revolution of 1848

The influence and seminal power that Lorenz von Stein's thought has had on various scholarly disciplines can hardly be overestimated. He is clearly one of the most interesting figures the German scholarly world produced in the nineteenth century, yet few scholars seem aware of their debt to him.[1] Neither Stein's life nor work have been thoroughly studied.[2] There are reasons for this neglect. Stein's place in scholarship is difficult to define; he is both historian and sociologist, both legal scholar and economist. It is equally difficult to say whether he belongs to the idealistic, metaphysical half of the nineteenth

This is an English translation of an article in *Mitteilungen des Österreichischen Instituts für Geschichtsforschung,* 50 (1936), 369–387. Occasion of the article was the discovery in Johann Gustav Droysen's papers of two letters from Lorenz von Stein to Droysen written in Paris in the summer of 1848. The letters were published as an appendix to the article. The English translation omits the appendix, as well as an introduction and a final section referring to the contents of the letters. An important point of this article, of course, is that in considering the not yet satisfactorily solved problem of the relations between Karl Marx and Stein one must take into account not only the intellectual development of Marx but also the important change in Stein's thinking between 1840 and 1850. For a recent treatment of the work of Lorenz von Stein see Dirk Blasius, "Lorenz von Stein," *Deutsche Historiker,* ed. H. U. Wehler (Göttingen, Vandenhoeck and Ruprecht, 1971), I, 25–38 (with bibliography).

411

century or to its positivistic, realistic half. His involvement in the most diverse disciplines and intellectual movements makes it hard to single out from the variety of subjects he treated and methods he applied the underlying unifying bond and to define precisely what his contribution is. Even a recent study that makes a first attempt to provide a "biography of Stein's intellectual development" fails to achieve a sharp picture.[3] This author, too, succumbs to the temptation—strong in Stein's case—of organizing Stein's life according to predominant intellectual influences. The result is that Stein's life is divided into three different periods that do not come together into a coherent development.[4] The author fails to see that Stein's work did in fact focus on one central task: the creation of a German social science. All his intellectual efforts start with this objective, and all of them are directed toward its realization. If we view his life from this perspective, we can easily recognize a clear intent and structure in his intellectual development, and we will also see that the revolutionary year 1848 was the turning point in Stein's life. All other periods and episodes are secondary to it in importance, for the events of that year prompted Stein "to present his revised books on socialism and communism in contemporary France as a history of the social movement and thus to turn from a philosophically oriented history of ideas to sociology."[5]

I

Anyone who studies developments in France in 1848 will be struck by the fact that the classic historical works on the events of that year were by contemporaries who wrote during the February Revolution or immediately after it. Of German writings, the most important are—along with Stein's masterpiece—the essays that Marx wrote as a young man. These studies are of lasting value not only as documents in the development of Marx's thinking but also as historical interpretations.[6] But the memoirs of the French statesmen active in this period also go beyond the mere reporting of facts and move into interpretation.[7] This tendency is equally apparent whether the work in question was conceived of as a memoir, as in Alexis de Tocqueville's case,[8] or, as with Louis Blanc and Alphonse de Lamartine, as a history.[9] Why is it that historical treatments followed so closely on the events themselves here and that contemporary writings that would ordinarily be valuable only as source material or would soon be forgotten have become classic historical interpretations?

A unique constellation, it seems to me, dictated the interpretation of the February Revolution, a constellation in which intellectual receptivity and emotional shock came together as they do only on rare occasions. If the Revolution of 1789 struck like a natural catastrophe that its observers could only begin to contemplate and understand after its force was expended, then the Revolution of 1848 was more like a laboratory experiment for which all the necessary measuring instruments were carefully prepared and which its observers perceived with sharpened intellectual awareness. Men had become historically minded. Analogies derived from revolutions of the past offered solid points of comparison for understanding present and future revolutions. The conflicts from which a new revolutionary explosion could arise and the forms such a revolutionary movement could take were common knowledge. The possibility of a new revolution was even a topic of everyday conversation.

But the crucial point here is that the possession of highly perfected intellectual tools for understanding a revolutionary process did not mean that anyone was prepared for the event itself. The belief in progress that predominated among the bourgeoisie of the nineteenth century, especially in the France of the Citizen King, was too strong to admit this possibility. The "halcyon days" of the Restoration had created a sense of security that made the collapse of this bourgeois world seem unimaginable. Consequently, when the Revolution of 1848 broke out, it struck with an elemental force that no one could escape and that no amount of intellectual preparation could lessen.[10]

Tocqueville's attempt to comprehend the events of the year 1848 remains the classic statement of the feelings inspired by the collapse of this optimistic, idealistic world view.

> The Constitutional Monarchy had succeeded the Ancien Régime; the Republic, the Monarchy; the Empire, the Republic; the Restoration, the Empire; and then came the Monarchy of July. After each of these successive changes it was said that the French Revolution having accomplished what was presump-

tuously called its work, was finished; this had been said and it had been believed. Alas! I myself had hoped it under the Restoration, and again after the fall of the Government of the Restoration; and here is the French Revolution beginning over again . . . I do not know when this long voyage will be ended; I am weary of seeing the shore in each successive mirage, and I often ask myself whether the *terra ferma* we are seeking does really exist, and whether we are not doomed to rove upon the seas for ever![11]

This statement can help us understand how the February Revolution could immediately be codified in finished historical writings. A powerful emotional experience created an equally strong inner need to explain and comprehend what had just occurred, a need that allowed already formed capabilities of historical analysis to come into play.

If these assumptions can be said to apply in general, they also apply in particular to Stein.[12] The Historical School had been a major influence in the formation of this thinking. It had equipped him with all the tools of contemporary historical methodology and had produced in him an almost overly acute awareness of historical development and change. By the 1840s, he had become recognized in German academic circles as the major authority on French affairs. In his books on French socialism and communism, he had attempted an analysis of the political situation in France and had discussed the possibility of revolution there. His conclusions had been, however, that reform rather than revolution would reconcile the conflicting forces that were creating political instability[13] and that France would in fact move ahead on this evolutionary path.[14] The upheaval in France clearly must have affected him more deeply than it did other students of politics, for it touched the very heart of his research and forced him to a drastic revision of his previous views. It is hardly surprising that the result was a reassessment of all his assumptions and a change in his thinking.

Stein's intellectual reorientation was nearly completed by the late summer of 1848. At that time Stein wrote a supplementary volume to his book *Sozialismus und Kommunismus,* the second edition of which had appeared shortly before the February Revolution broke out. This supplement contains Stein's analysis of recent developments in France and presents in embryonic form all the essential new ideas that would make Stein's *Geschichte der sozialen Bewegung,* published in 1851, differ so radically from his *Sozialismus und Kommunismus* of the prerevolutionary period.[15] Viewed in terms of its concepts and methodology, this supplementary volume can hardly be called a supplement at all. It is instead a preliminary study to the *Geschichte der sozialen Bewegung.*

The first major departure from *Sozialismus und Kommunismus* is Stein's rejection of the "principle of pure democracy." He claims now that this principle he had always praised before only provides a useful tool for criticizing the existing order and therefore has an important function as a negating force. But its significance is limited to that function alone because whenever it is elevated to a ruling principle, it demonstrates its lack of positive content and its inability to govern.[16] While in the second edition of *Sozialismus und Kommunismus* Stein had shown only a slight tendency to distinguish between government and administration, he now places great emphasis on this division. The fact that Stein gives particular attention to the importance of administration goes against the generally accepted view of the time, which was concerned only with theoretical principles and the form they took in the constitution.[17] Stein's insight into the inadequacy of purely formal democracy and into the role of administration led him to see developments in France moving toward a different end than he had previously anticipated for them. The new goal is "social democracy," and Stein expects that it will be able to resolve the conflicts of the present.[18] He expects that the weaknesses inherent in purely formal democracy can be overcome by providing substantial underpinnings. An administration focusing on social betterment will win the support of the lower classes benefiting from such an administrative policy and will thereby give the state a solid basis of power.

But this view, which assumes a close connection between the state and one social class, presupposes another important conceptual distinction: contrast between state and society. This contrast will be found fully worked out only in Stein's *Geschichte der sozialen Bewegung.* Before 1848 Stein had seen state and monarchy as identical and had ascribed to the state a mediating role in the struggle between the classes; it was the state that would finally resolve the conflicts of the society.[19] But in the *Geschichte der sozialen Bewegung* the state has lost this autonomous function and, consequently, its independent status. Now the state itself is the object of class struggle, and the class that emerges dominant in this struggle will assume control of the state. Stein now sees the essence of history as a "constant battle" between state and society.[20] After it had become clear that the volcano of revolution had not subsided but had erupted once more, the most pressing question for political thinkers was whether it would ever subside again and whether it would be possible to find means of quieting it permanently. The experience of the year 1848 and the questions it had raised caused the politician Tocqueville to doubt the value of setting any goals for domestic politics. The same experience and the same questions led Stein to formulate his theory of "constant battle" between state and society.

If we can conclude on the basis of the foregoing that the work Stein wrote in the fall of 1848 already revealed the ideas that would later set the *Geschichte der sozialen Bewegung* apart from the earlier editions of *Sozialismus und Kommunismus,* then we may also conclude that this shift in Stein's thought was not initiated or influenced by other writers and that it was not a product of autonomous intellectual development.[21] It was the experience of the revolution, the direct impact of reality, that prompted this reorientation of his thought. This brings us to the crucial point in Stein's experience of the Revolution of 1848. The Revolution had consequences for him that go beyond the intellectual reassessment we have just sketched here. What is unique about Stein is that he was able to objectify the personal experience of seeing reality impinge on his thought, forcing him to conclude that his ideas could not stand the test of reality. He was obliged to revise his views of the relationship between idea and reality, and the result of this crucial transformation in his thinking was that the entire world of history and society appeared in a new light to him. This transformation led him away from the history of ideas toward social history, eventually bringing him to the new discipline of social science. But if we are to understand this change in Stein and grasp its full import, we shall have to examine more closely the relationship of idea and reality in Stein's thinking and briefly survey his entire intellectual development.

II

The importance that the relationship between idea and reality assumed for Stein shows him to be a true son of the nineteenth century. What characterizes the nineteenth century and sets it apart from any previous one is, as Friedrich Gundolf put is so succinctly, "that in the nineteenth century reality is restored to its rightful place, that the pursuit of reality replaces the pursuit of the 'thing in itself.'"[22] But the example of Stein also demonstrates that the "discovery" of reality was a logical outgrowth of the search for ideas and that the world of thought underwent an experience like that of young Saul, who set out to search for his father's donkey and found a kingdom instead.

Stein began as a Hegelian. This meant that he was not satisfied with simply establishing facts but had to penetrate into the "essence" of historical processes as well. It also meant that historical processes were spiritualized and that the only thing that was "essential" about them was their intellectual content. But for Stein and for Hegelians of his generation, the study of history was also invested with an active element that looked ahead to the future: they believed that comprehension of the logic that had controlled events in the past would make it possible to determine the course of history in the future.[23] It was this view that created unlimited faith in the power of thought and in the supremacy of "ideas" over reality. The ability "to control and shape human life," they thought, derived solely from an intellectual understanding of history. "The principle that human intelligence can control things by comprehending them has long been propounded and believed. There has always been a certain mythical quality to this belief, and it seems to me that this sublime idea is beginning to be realized."[24]

The other crucial experience in Stein's intellectual development was his contact with France and French thought. This contact opened his eyes to the world of facts and lent his research a somewhat more empirical character. As a result, some ambiguity entered into the spiritualized image of history he had taken over from Hegel. The following passage from the second edition of Stein's *Sozialismus und Kommunismus* clearly illustrates his vacillation between these two modes of thought so central to his intellectual growth.[25]

> Deeds and sufferings, competing and conflicting systems and ideas are of relevance to me only to the extent that they express and serve the ruling idea of past happenings. Does the mere fact of having existed earn anyone or anything a place in history? Yet we know intuitively—well before we are able to understand completely why this is so—that no reconstruction of the intellectual content of an era truly reflects that era in the fullness of its life. With every step forward that it takes, thought becomes more concentrated in itself, and as it hurries ahead, increasing knowledge, gained step by painstaking step, makes all previous knowledge, which was gained by similar effort, appear less significant. The higher thought reaches, the more it loses touch with the richness of life. It finally achieves its goal, but at the moment when the circle is closed, further progress becomes impossible, and everything gained up to that point becomes lifeless. Therefore it is essential to find a bridge that will lead us out of this realm of ideas back into the living world.

We cannot say that conscious doubts about the idealistic view of history are actually present here. The most we can claim is that a vague sense of dissatisfaction shows through these lines, and this impression is confirmed as we read ahead and see by what means Stein thinks he will be able to build this bridge across to the "living world." He suggests combining a study of theories with a consideration of the lives of their creators.[26] By infusing the abstract with the element of personality, Stein thought he would be able to impart to his work the "factor of life" it lacked. But this solution remained purely aesthetic and formal and shows conclusively that the entire intellectual problem posed by these opposite elements had still not been clearly defined in his mind.

In drawing a sharp line between Stein's positions before and after the Revolution, we can turn to Stein himself as our authority. In his preface to the *Geschichte der sozialen Bewegung* Stein speaks with some disdain of his earlier works on France and says that they were written from an "unclear position."[27] He remains convinced that the subject itself is a worthy one; he is dissatisfied only with his approach to it. The socialist and communist movements were not important because of their intellectual content, he feels now, but as symptoms of a social situation that later erupted in the Revolution of 1848.[28] The shift in Stein's thinking that took place here is one of great consequence. The essence of a historical event no longer inheres solely in its intellectual content. Stein distinguishes sharply between the world of ideas and the world of historical facts, and the sphere in which truth lives is separated from the world of historical phenomena.[29] It also follows from these premises that historical life can no longer be dependent upon or determined by laws that reign in the world of ideas, and the philosopher's claim to knowledge about the laws of politics is therefore invalid. "Political order among human beings," Stein writes, "cannot be achieved by concepts alone."[30]

With this insight came a complete shift in Stein's view of the relationship between idea and reality. Not only was the old dominance of idea over reality broken for him now, he also began to think that ideas may well obscure our view of actual circumstances and prevent an understanding of them. The "theoretical nature of a revolution," Stein realized, can differ fundamentally from its real nature.[31] There was another world behind the world of theories and ideas, a world of reality, a world of facts. This insight awakened what it would be no exaggeration to call a new passion in him. Historical scholarship was now faced with a task that it had hardly begun to appreciate up to now. It was obliged to reach beyond the world of theory and idea and deal with "concrete facts."[32] But this does not mean that Stein limits the province of historical research to the mere gathering of facts. On the contrary, he feels he now knows what forces actually govern this newly discovered "world of reality." He has come to the conclusion that "the true history of a society as well as the true history of freedom and of political order consists primarily in the development and distribution of wealth among the lower classes."[33] He sees economic forces as the crucial factor; they determine the course of history in the real world.[34] The methodology and structure of Stein's *Geschichte der sozialen Bewegung* present a practical application of these new principles. A consideration of developments in France from this new point of view leads Stein to assert now "that the actual motivating force in a revolution is not the idea of equality but the unequal distribution of property. Social classes, not philosophical truths, make revolutions."[35] Stein's studies in sociophilosophical and intellectual history evolved into the "history of a social movement," and that is the outward manifestation of the inner change his thought had undergone.

III

The general principles contained in the quotations above are highly significant in themselves, quite apart from what they reveal about Stein's development. They are underlying principles for an economic concept of history as well as the beginnings of a theory of ideology. As we saw, impressions of the Revolution had prompted Stein to develop these principles. It is true, of course, that he never again articulated them as clearly and sharply as he did in his *Geschichte der sozialen Bewegung,* and I have cited from this work only the most vivid and unequivocal formulations. We could readily find there any number of more cautions and tentative statements of the same principles. Then, too, the book is by no means consistent in its application of these principles. It displays instead a methodological uncertainty and vacillation that give rise to doubts about its reliability as a scholarly work. Indeed, we might even say that the historical value of Stein's *Geschichte der sozialen Bewegung* does not lie in the close analysis and comprehension of economic and political processes but rather in the originality and fruitfulness of the problem it raises.[36] The generally accepted explanation for the inconsistency in this work is that Stein's thinking contained unreconciled idealistic and realistic elements from the beginning of his career that he was never able to bring together, even though he struggled to do so and saw such a reconciliation as one of his major tasks.[37]

Our view of the importance the year 1848 had in Stein's development would seem to call for another explanation. Despite the fact that Stein was working with contemporary subject matter, his view of history had been a totally idealistic one. The experience of the Revolution smashed this view, and the ever impressionable Stein found himself assuming a radical position completely opposed to his original one. But as the calming effects of reaction began to make themselves felt, the pendulum in Stein swung back, and he did not pursue his radical thinking to its logical conclusion. He tried to reconcile his new insights with the idealistic aspects of his thought. In this context, it is inevitable that his *Geschichte der sozialen Bewegung* be characterized by a kind of double vision and that it show most clearly of all his works the traces of both tendencies. Moreover in his *Geschichte der sozialen Bewegung* he was still writing a historical work, one subject to the principle of selection on the basis of evaluation. For in historiography, the question Stein had asked in the idealistic phase of his career was still a valid one: whether "the mere fact of having existed earns anyone or anything a place in history."[38]

This does not mean, however, that the events of 1848 made only a passing impression on Stein and that his new insights and ideas were soon absorbed by and made to conform to the idealistic elements in his thought. It is certainly true that the idealistic aspect regained some ground in Stein's thinking in the course of the 1850s, and gave his version of "social science" a particular quality. But the influence the Revolution of 1848 had on him was not obliterated. On the contrary, it left a lasting imprint: the year 1848 led him away from the historical subjects and approaches of his early years and caused him to focus on the new field of social science he helped create.

18. From Art History to the History of Civilization: Aby Warburg

After Aby Warburg's death in 1929, Fritz Saxl and Gertrud Bing, his closest collaborators and in later years directors of the Warburg Institute in London, planned to bring out a many-volume edition of Warburg's published writings and of his drafts and notes so that the scholarly world would be made fully aware of his intellectual stature. Two volumes of this edition appeared in 1932, but continuation of the project became impossible when the rise of the Nazis put an end to the activities of the Warburg Institute in Hamburg. In London, where the Warburg Institute found a new home, both—first Saxl, then Bing—began to work on a biography of Aby Warburg which was to replace publication of his collected works but which might help toward an understanding and appreciation of his ideas. In both cases death interrupted the completion of such a biography.

E. H. Gombrich, with the work under review, carried out the task left to him by his predecessors as directors of the Warburg

Originally published in *Journal of Modern History,* 44 (1972), pp. 381-391, reprinted by permission of University of Chicago. My interest in Aby Warburg and his work began in my student years, and the occasion for this consideration of Warburg's intellectual position was the publication of E. H. Gombrich, *Aby Warburg: An Intellectual Biography* (London, Warburg Institute, 1970).

Institute. In 1936, as a young man in his twenties, Gombrich had come to the Warburg Institute to assist Saxl and Bing in their work on Warburg's papers; his assignment was to study and organize the great mass of notes left by Warburg. My impression is that the character of the material through which Gombrich first became acquainted with the working of Aby Warburg's mind has patterned his entire approach to the biography which he has now published. The bulk of the work consists in presenting and explaining Warburg's notes. Information about the external circumstances of Warburg's life within which his ideas developed seems a later addition rather than a fundamental basis of the work. Gombrich's extensive use of Warburg's notes—frequently only different formulations of the same thought—initiates the reader into all the nuances and shadings of Warburg's thinking. But under the mass of detail the clear lines of Warburg's intellectual development tend to get lost. Furthermore, in consequence of this approach those scholars and writers whom Warburg mentions in his notes appear as the crucial influences in his development. A fuller and also fairer appreciation of Warburg's originality and achievement would have resulted from a more comprehensive description of the general scholarly and intellectual milieu of his time. I will therefore try to outline the various stages of Warburg's intellectual development and make some suggestions about the relation between his ideas and the intellectual situation in Germany.

I

When in the early 1880s, in his last school years, Aby Warburg decided to study art history, this meant—if he did not want to go into classical archaeology—the art of the Renaissance. The image of the Renaissance was still the one that Jakob Burckhardt had created, but his beautifully clear outline was becoming blurred and frayed. Gobineau's simplifying dramatization of Renaissance life and Nietzsche's identification of Renaissance figures with his superman made the Renaissance the birthplace of a new anti-Christian, "free" morality. Scholars like Henry Thode questioned Burckhardt's view of the revival of antiquity as a crucial factor in the genesis of the Renaissance civilization and emphasized the Christian roots of the Renaissance. According to Thode, Saint Francis had fostered an awareness of world and nature from which the realism of Renaissance art had evolved. There were reasons why at the time of Warburg's beginnings Thode's theory, which seems to us an obvious misinterpretation, appealed to many scholars. It pleased medievalists by rejecting Burckhardt's view of a sharp contrast between the Middle Ages and the Renaissance and by finding the roots of the Renaissance in medieval religiosity. The view of the Renaissance as a basically religious movement also permitted the construction of a bridge from the Renaissance to the Reformation; the German nationalism of the nineteenth century was flattered by the suggestion that German Protestantism was the channel through which the discoveries and values of the Renaissance became a possession of modern man.

The fundamental question on which the validity of the theories of both Burckhardt and his critics depended was: What did the encounter with the classical world mean to the men of the fifteenth and sixteenth centuries? Although, at least at this time, Aby Warburg must be counted as a follower of Burckhardt and would not accept a thesis which replaced inspiration by antiquity with inspiration by religion, he was aware of the need for a clear definition of the magic words: "the revival of antiquity." The first serious scholarly task which he undertook was to determine precisely what the classical world meant in the work of an individual artist of the Renaissance. This was the problem of his dissertation on Botticelli's *Birth of Venus* and *Primavera,* which, after study in Bonn and Florence, he completed at Strasbourg. In this study Warburg presented two ideas which were the seedbed from which his further thinking about the Renaissance developed. He demonstrated that the subjects that were presented on Botticelli's paintings were taken from ancient works of literature; in all probability Botticelli carried out the program laid out for him by a humanist scholar. The classical influence of Renaissance art was not purely or even chiefly a question of style but arose from an encounter with the ancient world as a whole, as it had then been discovered and was conceived by the humanists. An art historian, therefore, must be a historian of the entire civilization (*Kulturgeschichte*) of the period in which the works which he studied had been created. Regarding the problem of the imitation of the classical style by Renaissance artists, Warburg advanced what at first seems a strange thesis because it appears to touch upon the fringes rather than to go to the heart of the matter. He maintained that Botticelli—and the painters of the quattrocento—learned from ancient sculpture how to depict movement. Windblown hair or floating drapes copied from ancient sarcophagi leave the impression that figures which possess these accessories are in motion; they serve to endow such figures with an element of dynamic energy, to indicate the existence of spiritual forces behind appearances. These moving figures placed into realistic surroundings appeared to be messengers of an ideal world. This somewhat eccentric theory had implications which placed Warburg in contrast to most scholars of the time and to a certain extent also to Burckhardt. Warburg asserted that the novel feature in Renaissance art was not "the discovery of world and man," that is, realism which acquaintance with the ancient world had generated. According to Warburg the examples of classical art did not promote a realistic approach. On the contrary, they helped the Renaissance artists to overcome realism and to make the beings whom they depicted embodiments of an ideal world; this development reached its acme with the great masters of the high Renaissance in the early sixteenth century.

These two notions—the need for placing art in relation to its intellectual surroundings and the significance of classical art for introducing an idealizing element into realistic art—were points of departure, not final solutions, for Warburg.

A consequence of Warburg's emphasis on the intellectual bonds between artists, humanists, and the patrons of humanists and artists was that he began to undertake intensive research in Florentine family archives. He began to view the civilization of the quattrocento as a reflection of the mentality of the Florentine upper class, and that meant of a merchant patriciate. This led him to solve a problem that had baffled him and many art historians of his time: explaining why the Florentines of the quattrocento had a particular liking and admiration for the art of the Netherlandish painters. The social structure of the towns in Flanders, Warburg recognized, was very similar to that of Florence, and this identity in economic and social concerns created a common intellectual outlook. On the basis of this insight he explored in various studies the connections between the art of the Netherlands and the art of the Florentine quattrocento. A particularly brilliant result of these studies was his demonstration that Hugo van der Goes's awkward and angular shepherds reappear in Domenico Ghirlandaio's classicizing *Adoration*.

With Warburg's increased interest in and understanding of the realistic aspects of Renaissance art the proposition of his dissertation began to appear oversimplified. He had painted the development in black and white. Realistic art was bad and idealizing art good. Realistic art remained stuck in barbarian delight for materialistic pomp; idealizing art grew out of a rational outlook which aimed at showing order behind the phenomena of the world. Realistic art belonged to the dark Middle Ages; idealizing art formed part of the modern world. But Warburg's studies—those in the Florentine family archives as well as those on the relation between Netherlandish and Florentine art—raised doubts about the appropriateness and validity of such formulas. If realistic art belonged to the civilization of the commercial towns of Flanders and Italy then identification of realism with the Middle Ages could hardly be maintained, because developments that were regarded as characteristic of the Renaissance would then have to be assigned to the Middle Ages. Moreover, in the course of a more intensive occupation with the realistic art of the quattrocento Warburg had arrived at a more positive evaluation of realism and of its role in Renaissance art. He had become aware that throughout the entire Renaissance realistic and idealizing elements existed side by side, and that a fruitful tension between realism and idealization was a formative element in the art of the high Renaissance.

He developed this view in an essay on *Francesco Sassetti's Last Will and Testament;* Gombrich rightly considers this essay to be one of the most characteristic products of Warburg's methods and ideas and has summarized its content in a careful analysis. Based on a great variety of sources which reach from business papers and family letters to humanist treatises, emblems and linguistic usage, Warburg found in the life as well as in the art of the Florentine Renaissance two elements coexisting: a passionate pagan energy and willing Christian acceptance of the rule of superhuman forces. To Warburg the secret of the greatness of the period of Lorenzo Magnifico, of its achievements in politics and art, was a balance between these two attitudes which, as he demonstrated, were symbolized as well as harmonized in the decorative scheme of the tomb of Francesco Sassetti. It will be noticed that Warburg continued to regard movement expressing dynamic energy as the crucial contribution of the classical world to the development of Renaissance art. But he no longer assumed that the effects of this influence must under all circumstances be healthy.

His definite views about the nature of the classical influence on art were embodied in a rule which is known as the *Pathosformel*. As Gombrich explains, the meaning of *Pathos* and *pathetisch* (pathetic) in German is different from that of the identical-sounding words in English. In German the term indicates possessing grandeur rather than suffering and arousing pity; it even can have the meaning of theatrical and stilted. According to Warburg the artists of the Renaissance learned from models of the classical world, like the statues of Laocöon or Nike or of the children of Niobe, how to express movement, emotion, and energy—briefly, pathos. As long as the use of the classical patterns for the expression of pathos remained subordinated to the purpose of the work of art (that is, remained under control), this revival of the forms of classical art was beneficial. But when the use of these patterns becomes an end in itself and serves to exhibit only the virtuosity of the artist, then the imitation of classical art can become destructive. Warburg did not like the Baroque; he considered the exaggerated use of pathos patterns in the Baroque as its crucial weakness.

With the introduction of the *Pathosformel* Warburg established a criterion for determining the influence of the classical world which had bearing not only on the Renaissance but on the development of art in general. Wherever the ideal patterns which the ancients had found for the artistic presentation of basic human attitudes were used, an encounter with the ancient world must have taken place. In the Renaissance the classical influence emerged sharply and clearly, but even if in earlier and later times it was repressed or seemed almost extinguished, the recurrence of these *Pathosformels* showed that classical influence continued to survive, from ancient times on, as a powerful force in European civilization. The search for the role of antiquity in

Renaissance art issued in analyzing the nature of the constituent elements in European civilization.

Warburg refrained from theoretical exposition of his views. They have to be deduced from his art-historical studies. The ideas which we have just described form the conceptual framework of Warburg's studies of the frescoes in the Palazzo Schifanoia in Ferrara which resulted in his most original work in the field of art history, the essay entitled *Italienische Kunst und internationale Astrologie.* In this paper Warburg showed that the three-tiered frescoes of the Palazzo Schifanoia represented a spherical system. The discovery which made Warburg's thesis fully convincing was that the figures of the middle tier, whose attire and pose had resisted all former attempts at explanation, were time demons of ancient Egypt transformed into Olympic gods. The demonstration of this connection implied an elaboration of the *Pathosformel.* Symbols and images are the means by which man communicates to others his emotions, his fears and hopes; to each basic human attitude a particular symbol or image is attached which, according to times and circumstances, will be changed and transformed although keeping some traces of its identity throughout all its metamorphoses. The forms which the images and symbols took in the classical world had a particular importance and significance. They were brought into a system and given a definable meaning so that the classical appearance of these images represented an attempt to subordinate the chaotic world of fears and emotions to reason. Approximation to the classical patterns was expression of an enlightened, rational outlook on the world. Remoteness from the classical images meant surrender to fears, to superstition, to magic; an inability to rise above the world of the unconscious. To what extent the modern psychological theories of this time were known to Warburg is not clear; he seems to have been interested in Jung's writings but to have disliked Freud. He certainly did not believe that removal of repressions or superstitions would smooth the way to cultural achievement. He believed in a disciplined mind, strictly controlled by reason. In his opinion the distance which reason places between an immediate impression and its intellectual fixation was necessary for cultural creativity.

But Warburg's conviction of the value of reason did not

imply confidence in the victory of reason over irrational forces. The fact that the introduction of the principle of reason and order into the world of symbols and images was the work of a short and unique period of history showed how fragile the rule of reason was in human life and made him aware of the wide areas dominated by the opposing irrational forces. With his remarkable flair for revealing connections and combinations he began to discover all over the world, even in modern times, magical thinking, superstitious practices, reliance on demonic help against irrational fear. Warburg began to occupy himself with studies on astrological prophesies in the Reformation period, and they nourished his pessimism about the human capacity to withstand irrational forces. The outbreak of the First World War filled him with dark forebodings, and his pessimism was increased when the defeat of Germany confirmed them. In the fall of 1918 Warburg suffered a mental collapse which made confinement to a hospital necessary. He returned to Hamburg only in 1924.

II

By then the Warburg Library had become connected with Hamburg University. Warburg's ideas were no longer those of an individual private scholar but had become rooted in German academic life. Still, before the First World War, in 1910, Warburg had gained as librarian and collaborator Fritz Saxl, who was then engaged in collecting and publishing ancient astrological manuscripts. Warburg was just completing his study of the frescoes in the Palazzo Schifanoia, and common interest in astrology forged bonds between Warburg and Saxl. Saxl reinforced Warburg's inclination to add to his library all possible material that might document the appearance and evolution of symbols and images: folklore and art, astrology and science, poetry and cartoons, scholarly studies and pamphlets. And Saxl played his part in arranging the distinctive organization of the Warburg Library, in which books referring to and dealing with the same kinds of symbols and images were grouped together, in an order which showed the development and metamorphoses of these symbols and images.

Helped by American money, which during the German inflation "went a long way," Saxl continued to build up the library in the years of Warburg's illness. On Saxl's initiative the library was placed at the disposal of the professors teaching at the newly established University of Hamburg. And the library became a meeting place for those interested in intellectual history. Saxl arranged for a series of lectures and publications which began with Ernst Cassirer's *Begriffsform im mythischen Denken* and Erwin Panofsky's *Idea* and included works as different as Richard Reitzenstein's *Studien zum antiken Synkretismus,* Percy Ernst Schramm's *Kaiser, Rom und Renovatio,* Eduard Norden's *Die Geburt des Kindes,* Saxl and Panofsky's *Dürers Melencolia.*

In a remarkable essay written after Saxl's death, Gertrud Bing explained the great role the Warburg Library played in German academic life in the 1920s as due to the tide of German scholarship beginning to favor work along the lines of Warburg and Saxl. Indeed, the influence of the Warburg Libary can be understood only in the general context of German scholarly development. This relationship is interesting not only because of the light it sheds on German intellectual history but also because it helps to define more precisely Warburg's originality and his particular intellectual achievement. This is not the place to provide the extended analysis which this issue deserves. But since Gombrich has scarcely gone into these aspects of Warburg's work some tentative remarks and suggestions about the connection of Warburg's thought with the scholarly trends of his time seem appropriate.

It might be well to state again, briefly, the basic notions which from the outset formed Warburg's approach to art history and history in general. Although Warburg was primarily an art historian he rejected, almost from the beginning, the view that art history ought to be chiefly concerned with the history of styles. He regarded art history as an aspect of the history of civilization (*Kulturgeschichte*). It ought to be added that for Warburg it was almost a matter of course that the aspects of civilization in which a scholar interested himself were phenomena of high culture (the arts, literature, scholarship, and science). The stress on the character and achievements of high culture had the almost unavoidable consequence that not the material or political forces of a period but its mental structure appeared to Warburg as the crucial fact determining the character of a period. Necessarily Warburg was interested in the psychological presuppositions for the creation of a work of art as well as in those that made an understanding of cultural creations by a social upper group possible. He used concepts from the area of psychology like energy and empathy and concerned himself with the meaning of symbols and images and their history. He also relied on psychology in his views on the development or "progress" of civilization, which were based on the assumption that not only reason determined action and values; in the mental structure of an individual or a period reason, emotion, and volition were variables which could widely differ in strength.

All these notions are closely connected with interests and investigations that were in the foreground of scholarly discussions in Germany at the end of the nineteenth century. A footnote in the preface of Warburg's first printed work, his dissertation on Botticelli, makes this obvious; he referred to the Festschrift for Eduard Zeller, a book that had been published a few years earlier. One of the essays in this book might almost be regarded as a Warburgian article before Warburg. Hermann Usener, who had been one of Warburg's teachers at the University of Bonn, examined the survival of pagan religious customs in Christian festivals and rituals. The particular article to which Warburg referred in his footnote was concerned with symbols. The author, F. T. Vischer, discussed two related but distinct aspects of this notion. He analyzed the relation between myth, symbol, and religion, and asserted that symbols develop out of myth and that all religious concepts contain a symbolical element. The author also investigated the psychological problem of how men come to agree on attributing to symbols a definite meaning, and, in this, man's crucial faculty is empathy (*Einfühlung*), which Vischer considered basic for the establishment of communication with other human beings. Psychology was also treated in two other articles of this volume. An essay chiefly devoted to an analysis of Comte's thought emphasized that his recognition of the differences in man's consciousness of reality provided a criterion for establishing separate and distinctive periods of history. The longest and weightiest article of this volume was contributed by Wilhelm Dilthey and dealt with the problem of poetic imagination. Reprinted in the sixth volume of Dilthey's collected works, it has remained fundamental for the understanding of Dilthey's notions on aesthetics and psychology.

The relation of Dilthey's ideas to those of Warburg deserves to be looked into; it is rather puzzling. Dilthey is not mentioned in Gombrich's book, and this must mean that if in Warburg's papers there are any references to Dilthey, they are rare. We have no means to judge whether this was accidental or reflects a lack of personal sympathy. Dilthey, the son of a court preacher, the Prussian Geheimrat, and influential member of the Berlin academic establishment, was certainly very different from Warburg, the son of a Jewish banker, private scholar, and proud member of a free city. However, there were so many intellectual and personal links between the two that Warburg must have known about Dilthey's work, or at least about his ideas. Usener was Dilthey's brother-in-law; Heinrich von Stein, whose writings on aesthetics, according to Gombrich, helped Warburg to clarify his own ideas, was Dilthey's disciple; and the book by Stein that Warburg admired originated at Dilthey's suggestion. After the completion of his dissertation Warburg went to Berlin to study psychology with Julius Ebbinghaus, formerly a close friend of Dilthey. Ebbinghaus became just then involved in a vehement dispute with Dilthey on the methods of psychology. This dispute was a cause célèbre in the German academic world. It seems almost impossible to imagine that Warburg overlooked Dilthey's famous essay on "Auffassung und Analyse des Menschen im 15. und 16. Jahrhundert," which appeared in the year of Warburg's arrival in Berlin.

Resemblances between Dilthey's and Warburg's concepts unquestionably exist. Dilthey considered as the distinguishing feature of poetic imagination the energy with which a poet absorbs external impressions and experiences; his psychological theories are built on the importance of empathy (*Einfühlung*) which to him formed a precondition for understanding the outside world. In Warburg's thought energy and empathy, as we have mentioned, are basic concepts, and he uses them in almost the same way as Dilthey. Moreover, Warburg's views about the factors which constitute the distinctions among the various periods of history are basically similar to those of Dilthey, who saw these differences determined not only by development or progress of thought, but even more by the varying role of emotion, intelligence, and volition in the mental structure of a period.

Nevertheless, this is meant to raise the question whether Dilthey directly influenced Warburg rather than to assert the existence of such an influence. The widespread scholarly interest in problems and issues on which Warburg began to work is obvious, however. And it should also be noticed that his own efforts form part of the general trend toward a broadening of the framework of history which would make not only particular fields of life but also the entire civilization the subject of investigation. This was the time when Karl Lamprecht laid down his program for a history of civilization which, according to him, progressed in stages, demonstrating a steadily increasing psychological sensitivity, and when Henri Berr advocated his *histoire de synthèse* and organized the series *Evolution de l'humanité*. But the reaction of the great majority of the historians who had grown up in the traditions of political history was vehement. They strongly resisted the attempt to supersede political history by a history of civilization and to apply to history theories and methods of the natural sciences. All over Europe the political historians won this battle. In France, Henri Berr continued his work but in an isolated position. In Germany, the advocates of a history of civilization, particularly Lamprecht as the most vocal and therefore most dangerous defender of this point of view, were "outlawed." As a result of this fight historical scholarship became rigidified, narrowly limited to diplomatic and political history. Aby Warburg as an art historian and private scholar was not directly involved in this struggle and could continue to follow his course. But for the influence which his ideas gained after the First World War this development is important. The German defeat and the collapse of the empire resulted in a reexamination of the ideas and values which had prevailed in the Second Reich, and this critical attitude extended to political history as the "official conception of history" in the empire. The demand for a broadened conception in history, which had been raised in the nineties but had been silenced by the leaders of the historical profession, regained in appeal. In the early postwar years Max Weber's historical sociology began to permeate historical work. Dilthey was rediscovered and his widely dispersed writings were collected and published. The appeal which the

Warburg library began to exert belongs in this same context; this was the tide of German scholarship of which Miss Bing wrote.

III

To understand the relationship of Warburg to the scholarly trends of the time is also to recognize the particular and original contribution which Warburg made. Of course, he approached the problem of the history of civilization from the viewpoint of art history. By placing a work of art in the context of the civilization of its time, it was not enough to show that the artist shared the general values and beliefs of his period; Warburg required a precise documentation of the relation of the artist and of his works to the literary, philosophical, religious, or social trends of his time. To Warburg empiric investigation of the connection between a work of art and its intellectual milieu appeared possible because he abandoned any preconceived idea of history as progressing in causally connected stages, and he did not claim that each of these stages was a reflection and expression of one dominating value or principle. Warburg's view that in the various periods of history emotion, reason, and volition varied in strength and weight, and that a continuous struggle between rational and irrational elements went on in man and society, eliminated the assumption that history represented a steadily accumulating process moving according to an inherent logic. In this Warburg deviated from others who, like him, tried to direct the work of the historian toward a history of civilization. Dilthey still suggested that the modern world combined the attitudes of the past, that is, the emotional religious attitude of The Middle Ages, the intellectual logical appeal of the Greeks, and the Roman will power. Lamprecht believed that progress in history was represented by increase in psychological perceptivity from one age to another. For Warburg the psychological structure of an individual or a period was so complex and precariously balanced that it could not easily swing from one direction to another. Any formula subordinating a historical period to one idea or one value falsified reality by limiting the potentialities of life open to society.

The history of civilization, therefore, must be free not only from the bonds of metaphysical systems but also from presuppositions about schemes of historical process or about causal explanations. The work to which Warburg directed himself in the five years between his return to Hamburg in 1924 and his death in 1929 was to have the title *Mnemosyne;* it was intended to be a picture atlas which would show that throughout the centuries of history the same or very similar gestures or formulas were used in the visual presentation of basic human passions.

This work remained a fragment. Its plan, however, shows clearly how far Warburg had moved away from all notions of progress and development. Although he intended to show the various forms in which, throughout the course of history, the chief human emotions were expressed in visual representation, he was not concerned with the sequence in which these images appeared and became transformed. But by placing them together according to visual resemblances without regard to chronology, he aimed at establishing the original basic form which lay behind the variety of images in which the emotion was expressed. Yet, although it would appear that Warburg's main aim was a typology of the forms of expression for basic emotional attitudes, he placed a particular emphasis on the form which was given to them in the ancient world and at least partly revived in the Renaissance. This twofold character of Warburg's concerns is reflected in the name of the Warburg Institute. Its main purpose is the scholarly investigation of civilization (Kulturwissenschaftliche Bibliothek), but its subtitle announces a special research theme. "The History of the Classical Tradition" (*Nachleben der Antike*). There is no doubt that Warburg's unwillingness to find evolution, progress, or development in history is in contrast to the normative character which he ascribed to the classical world. This contradiction in Warburg's thought deserves some discussion because it touches upon the area in which his influence has been most fruitful: the study of the Renaissance.

There seems to me no doubt that the reason for this contradiction lies in Warburg's personal psychology, that it is related to his family background and the social situation into which he was born.

The Warburgs were the only family of private bankers who, while they indisputably belonged to the German financial leadership group, were Jewish: the Bleichroeders, the Mendelssohns, the Oppenheims—to name the few banking families of equal stature—had become Christians and were ennobled. Aby Warburg's father was deeply upset when his son refused to observe Jewish rituals. His intention to marry the daughter of a Christian Hamburg patrician led to vehement opposition on the part of both families, and it took years until their resistance was overcome. Warburg served with pride in the German army as an officer's candidate. Clearly, he was inclined to identify with the social upper group of the empire, and the desperation and depression which the German defeat in the First World War produced in him confirms this notion. Even without attempting any scientific psychological analysis, some conclusions about the relationship of Warburg's social situation to his thought seem obvious. One concerns the importance he assigned to the permanency of cultural traditions. The alienation from the Jewish world of his family and the identification with the social world of the empire refined his feelings for the survival of residues from earlier times. It increased his perceptivity for the continuation of beliefs of an older culture in a later one. His family background may also have directed his attention to the cultural role of a merchant class, and the part which the merchant bankers played in the Florentine civilization of the quattrocento helped to strengthen his conviction that he had a right to belong to the ruling group of the empire. But there are still other areas where personal experience seems to have patterned his scholarly attitude. Consciously or unconsciously the conviction that he gave up something valuable for something still better must have helped him to rationalize his abandonment of a familiy tradition in favor of identification with the dominant political system. Consequently he was not inclined to probe deeply the weaknesses and defects of the German social structure. It seems characteristic that, as far as one can judge from Gombrich's book, Warburg had no interest in social questions and no contact with movements of social reform. His attention was fixed on the phenomena of high culture and on the social groups connected with them. His own life showed him to set a disciplined rational decision above patterns formed on the basis of tradition or emotions.

It is difficult not to recognize the link which existed between his personal life and the new insights about the Renaissance which emerged in his work. He considered any interpretation that forced the image of this time into the framework of a general philosophy of history to be misleading. What distinguished the Renaissance was that it could serve as a pattern for the conditions and possibilities of cultural achievement. This implied that for Warburg the Renaissance was not only an aesthetic but also a social phenomenon which arose from interaction among the social and political leaders, the intellectuals and artists. It was one of the historical periods in which rational examination and criticism had entered the world of traditionally accepted beliefs and attitudes. It was the work of an elite, a high culture which left many social groups untouched and did not fully overcome or supplant intellectual attitudes and trends of former times, although it had originated by rejecting some of them, changing and transforming others.

In Warburg's eyes the achievements of the Renaissance were the result of the meeting of a great variety of forces and ideas supporting each other, fighting each other, or amalgamating with each other. Probably the view which Warburg had presented in his essay on the tomb of Francesco Sassetti remained valid for him: that the precarious balance arising out of sharp tensions was characteristic of the artistic and literary achievements of the Renaissance. What factors and forces constituted these tensions and how they combined depended to a large extent on the individuality of the artist. The question whether the Renaissance belonged to modern history or to the Middle Ages is quite secondary to any attempt to understand the period, and to consider any particular idea or intellectual trend as representative of the period in its totality is only misleading. If the Renaissance period has any exemplary value it lies in the material which it provides for analysis of the origin and the conditions of cultural achievement.

One does not need to accept Warburg's image of the Renaissance. Probably his most important influence on Renaissance scholarship has been the spur which he gave to the careful and detailed investigation of interrelationships. Of course, it might be said that it was inevitable in the course of events that scholars would turn to research in the economic and social developments of the Renaissance. But the manner in which Warburg saw the complexity of interrelationships between the various fields of Renaissance life—economic, social, intellectual, religious, political—and insisted on their detailed and concrete investigation was new and proved to be extremely fruitful. There is a sentence which Warburg regarded as containing the essence of true historical scholarship and which might be regarded as the stamp distinguishing those who followed in his wake: "Le bon Dieu est dans le détail."

19. Reflections on the History of the Professor of History

"In saying that I come before you today with no little trepidation, I am not uttering a mere conventional profession of diffidence"—these were the words with which, in 1903, J. B. Bury opened his inaugural lecture as Regius Professor of Modern History in Cambridge University. The lecture is entitled, "The

Previously unpublished address to the Luncheon Conference of the Modern European History Section, American Historical Association, at Philadelphia, December 29, 1963. Bury's Inaugural Lecture, which represents the point of departure of this address, has been printed in his *Selected Essays* (Cambridge, Eng., Cambridge University Press, 1930), pp. 3–22. For a comprehensive survey of the questions with which this address is concerned see Josef Engel, "Die Deutschen Universitäten und die Geschichtswissenschaft," *Historische Zeitschrift,* 189 (1959), 223–378. A fundamental treatment of the developments before the nineteenth century will be found in Emil Clemens Scherer, *Geschichte und Kirchengeschichte an den deutschen Universitaeten. Ihre Anfaenge im Zeitalter des Humanismus und ihre Ausbildung zu selbständigen Disziplinen* (Freiburg, Herder & Co., 1927). My contribution to *History* by John Higham with Leonard Krieger and Felix Gilbet (Englewood Cliffs, Prentice-Hall, Inc., 1965) extended these investigations beyond Germany to France, Italy, and England. I have also dealt with some aspects of these historiographical developments in my book *To the Farewell Address* (Princeton, Princeton University Press, 1961), and in my report "Cultural History and Its Problems" in *Rapports du XIe Congrès International des Sciences Historiques* (Stockholm, 1960), pp. 40–58. The thesis of this address is based on these materials and publications.

Science of History"; the diffidence which Bury felt in addressing his audience, however, was not caused by the difficulties inherent in a theme which had been discussed frequently by philosophers and historians but which seems to elude generally acceptable and accepted conclusions. Bury felt quite sure that he knew what the science of history was; the difficulty that troubled him was to do justice to a subject so vast, and of such importance and magnificence.

Bury saw history as a "powerful force for stripping the bandages of error from the eyes of men, for shaping public opinion and advancing the cause of intellectual and political liberty." In earlier times history had failed to fulfill these purposes because history had formed a part of literature or philosophy, or because the historian had aimed at immediate utility and had been concerned with the problems of the next week and the next year. Historians were now capable of higher and more lasting attainments because recently, as Bury said, "within three generations, three short generations, history began to forsake her old irresponsible ways and prepared to enter into her kingdom." The concepts and methods which had been introduced into the study of history in the nineteenth century permitted the establishment of an objective truth about the course of historical development. "History," according to Bury, "had become simply a science, no less and no more."

Today, sixty years later, all the questions Bury regarded as finally solved and decided seem open again. There are many who believe that the separation of history from literature was a loss rather than an advantage. We are wondering whether history is a science, and if so, to what extent; we would hardly claim that the historian is sure of the ways of the future and can guide others on the road to progress. Bury's statement about the promise contained in the pursuit of the science of history can be read only with a smile and perhaps with envy for the optimistic belief which, at the beginning of the twentieth century, historical scholars had in the importance and the usefulness of the work they were doing.

Bury's optimism—and his references to the three short generations which have passed since history entered into her kingdom makes this evident—was based on the revolutionary change which historical scholarship had undergone in the nineteenth century. We might not share the optimistic spirit that permeates Bury's speech, but it represents a striking indication of the feeling that with the nineteenth century a new era had opened for the study of history, that history had become something fundamentally different from what it had been in earlier times. We historians are proud to think of ourselves as belonging to a very old profession and to count Herodotus, Thucydides, and Tacitus among our members. But in less public moments I think that hardly any one of us claims to have come from such an exalted genealogical tree, not only because we can't do any longer what these historians did, but also—and I think this is a true statement—because we actually don't want to do any longer what these men did. We might not regard ourselves as "scientists" and we might consider the expression "science" as inappropriate for what we are doing; but we are not purely writers of history either. We are historical scholars. Our work forms part of that institutional complex into which the cultivation of scholarship and science has developed in modern times. This is the imprint history received in the nineteenth century.

Usually we connect the transformation of historical studies that took place in the nineteenth century with general intellectual movements arising in opposition to the ideas of enlightenment and natural law, with nationalism and romanticism, with the emphasis on the ideas of individuality and collective organism, and with the adoption of a new critical method necessitated by the application of these ideas and concepts to the writing of history. The crucial importance of the revolution of historicism for the development of historical thinking and historical work in the nineteenth century is undeniable. Nevertheless, it seems to me that the concentration of interest on the intellectual movements and trends that gave a new meaning to the study of history has somewhat concealed the institutional changes that accompanied the development of historical scholarship, and on which this development was based. An understanding of the institutional framework into which the study of history was fitted is of decisive importance. This is the topic with which I want to deal: to be precise, I want to make a few reflections on the history of the professor of history.

I must confess that before I made some investigations of the subject I had not been aware that the professor of history or chairs for history at the universities were a rather recent innovation, that professors of history did not exist in Europe before the nineteenth century. I am aware that in such a sweeping form this statement is misleading and that it needs some explanation and amplification. First of all, to say that there were no professors of history before the nineteenth century is not to say that no history was taught at the universities. Instruction in ecclesiastical history was given to theologians; there were special chairs for church history. Likewise, law students received instruction in legal history because it was believed that—I quote here from some of the justifications given for a historical approach in legal studies—"Law without history is blind" or "For the lawyer history is quite as necessary as the light of the sun for life." But although history was taught in the faculties of theology and law, and chairs for ecclesiastical and legal history can be found, history was regarded as an auxiliary science, not as a field which was to be studied for its own sake.

The place for history as an independent field of study would have been in the arts faculty, but there were no professors of history there. I might quote here from a letter which a professor at the University of Frankfort addressed to the Great Elector in 1650. He asked that "because the study of history is a very wide field and requires all of man's forces" he might be allowed to "lecture on history dissociated from all other fields." The point this letter illustrates is that, in general, history was taught in conjunction with other fields.

Humanist influences were responsible for the choice of the fields with which history was connected. The humanists had been concerned with history because of its value for instruction in rhetoric and ethics. Thus, at the universities the professor of eloquence was also the professor of history; the most frequent and regular combination, however, was that of moral philosophy and history. In this combination history was expected to achieve what since classical times was considered history's main purpose: to teach by examples. It scarcely needs to be added that, since history was considered to be subservient to rhetoric and moral philosophy, the historical writings and events with which professors dealt in their lectures were usually classical historians and ancient history.

Certainly there are instances which seem to contradict the sketch I have given of the role of history in the universities in the early modern period. The various uses for rhetoric and moral philosophy to which the writings of ancient historians could be put stimulated the establishment of some professor-ships of ancient history—for example, the Camden professor-ship in Oxford, and, in 1724, the Regius Professorships of Modern History in Oxford and Cambridge. The creation of these professorships seems to imply a recognition of history as an independent and autonomous field of study and instruction. But in reading the documents establishing these chairs it be-comes quite clear that the Regius Professors of Modern History were meant exclusively to serve the training of diplomats—to give the king "a constant supply of persons every way qualified for the management of such weighty affairs and negotiations as your Majesty's occasions may require." Nevertheless, the foun-dation of these Regius Professorships indicates that in the eighteenth century the view developed that history could fulfill a different and more extended function than it had in the past as an auxiliary to theology and law, to rhetoric and moral philo-sophy.

In the struggle over education that went on in the eighteenth century, instruction in history was one of the principal desi-derata of those who attacked the traditional classical curriculum and urged the teaching of practical and useful knowledge. D'Alembert stated in the *Encyclopédie* that it was shameful that "students leave school without knowing anything about the his-tory of their country, about geography, about chronology, about world history"; and Voltaire said about the results of his Jesuit training that "I learned neither whether Francis I had been made a prisoner nor where Padua is. I was uninformed about the country in which I was born, I knew neither the chief laws nor the interests of my fatherland. I learned Latin and stu-pidities." But the demand for more instruction in history did not lead to the recognition of history as an independent subject.

At some universities, such as Göttingen, which in 1737 was organized along modern lines, instruction in history was given in connection with politics, with investigations on the develop-ment of trade, with cameralism. However, as the remarks of D'Alembert and Voltaire indicate, geography was thought to be the proper field to be associated with history. The expansion of trade and commerce over the whole world, the discovery of old civilizations outside Europe, encounters with noble savages and their way of life—these experiences shook the religious concept of a universal history following the divine plans of a Christian God. Thus, a knowledge of the entire globe, based on the acquisition of geographical and historical facts, seemed the most appropriate subject of instruction for those who wanted to realize the promises of an enlightened age. After the men of the French Revolution had overcome their original rejection of history because they felt it was concerned with a past which had no meaning, they introduced into the schedule of colleges and lycées and universities instruction in history and geography. Although Napoleon theoretically acknowledged the usefulness of geographical and historical knowledge, he felt that, practically applied, it might lead to dangerous political criticisms. Nevertheless, at the Sorbonne, the chairs for history and geography which had been established in the revolutionary epoch remained. It was almost by chance that from these chairs there developed the first professorship at the Sorbonne devoted exclusively to history. For it was the need to create a position for the young François Guizot that led in 1812 to the transformation of the two chairs of history and modern geography and history and ancient geography into three chairs: one of geography, one of ancient history, and one of modern history.

Of course, it would be erroneous to ascribe the emergence of history as an independent field of university instruction to accidental circumstances and personal motives only. The weakening of the bonds between church and state in the revolutionary epoch, the spread of self-administration, the acceptance of the concept of general citizenship—all these factors forced the state into taking a more active role in the field of education, and made the universities the centers through which wider sectors of the population could be inspired with loyalty to the state and assimilated into the ruling group. Thus, by strengthening the inner coherence of the state, by moral conquests, the Prussian reformers hoped to compensate for territorial losses; and they regarded a reorganization of the educational system as an essential element in their task.

At the University of Berlin, founded to embody the new concepts of higher education, history was established as an independent field of study. The developments which led to the emancipation of history from other fields there are characteristic of the part history was expected to have in the new society. The distinctive feature of Humboldt's university reform was the creation of a philosophical faculty. This faculty replaced the traditional arts faculty but differed from it because it was placed on the same level as the professional schools of theology, law, and medicine, and thus was no longer merely a preparation for the "higher studies." It was even said that the philosophical faculty ought to be "the first and the mistress of all others." Instruction in the various fields of the philosophical faculty was supposed to reveal general insights into the nature of man. But this philosophical goal was to be reached by investigating an individual field according to its own inherent principles. Although the final aim of historical study and education remained the gaining of a philosophical insight, history became established as an independent area of instruction. We may here perhaps point to a feature of this development which has had lasting importance in forming the character of European, and particularly continental, historiography: history was separated from other fields but at the same time was conceived as an entity to which everything that had happened in the past belonged. The professor of history had as his domain the entire world of the past. Soon a chronological division took place; ancient and modern history were separated, then modern history was divided into medieval history and modern history. But in Europe in the nineteenth century, the area of competence of a professor of history did not become compartmentalized into particular geographical regions or special aspects of history.

The establishment of history as an autonomous field of academic instruction is only one of the institutional aspects in the development of historical scholarship in the nineteenth century. Another is the supervision and direction of research enterprises by the professor of history, again a novelty. Of course, historical research enterprises, pursued over decades, even centuries, and resulting in numerous publications, existed long before the nineteenth century. In 1607 Rosweyde sent out the prospectus for the *Acta Sanctorum,* zealously continued by the Bollandists until 1794. There were the manifold enterprises of

447

the Maurists, who could count Jean Mabillon, Edmond Martène, and Bernard de Montfaucon among their workers and could claim, with Martin Bouqet's *Recueil,* the position of predecessor to all national collections of medieval documents. And there were Ludovico Muratori and Thomas Rymer and Georg Friedrich von Martens to mention just a few of those associated with the research enterprises flourishing before the French Revolution. But those who worked in collecting and editing these materials had no connection with teaching or with universities. They were sometimes librarians of a prince or great lord; they were members of academies; almost all of them were members of religious orders—Jesuits, as were the Bollandists, or Benedictines, as were the Maurists. These enterprises were tied up with the ancien régime and disappeared with its collapse. Characteristic was the fate of the Bollandists. With the suppression of the Jesuit order in 1773, they escaped with some of their books to Belgium and indefatigably continued to publish from there until, in 1794, the armies of the convention flooded across Belgium and terminated work on the oldest and most famous of these collective historical research enterprises.

It was fitting that historical research enterprises were extinguished during a period when men believed they had overcome the past and were entering an entirely new era, the final age. But it was equally fitting and inevitable that the age of revolution was followed by the age of historical preoccupation. Attention was directed again to the work which had been accomplished in previous centuries. But the men and the organizations who had undertaken these researches no longer existed. The only agent large enough and strong enough to reassume the abandoned tasks of the previous centuries were the governments. This is expressed with remarkable directness in a memorandum which Guizot, as minister of education, addressed to Louis Philip in 1835: "In my opinion it is the government alone which can accomplish the great work of a general publication of all the important unpublished materials on the history of our fatherland. The government alone possesses the resources which such a large enterprise demands."

Guizot's path had been prepared. The Ecole des Chartes was established in 1822 to complete the work the Maurists had been forced to stop. The move to resume the research work of the ancien régime began in the early years of the restoration, and Guizot's policy of government aid for historical research only represents the culmination of this trend. Nevertheless, in giving his official support to the Société de l'histoire de France, which was to publish all the sources of French history, Guizot became a towering figure in guiding historical studies into new paths. As Augustin Thierry said of Guizot's achievements: "Through Guizot history became a national institution." A similar movement occurred in other countries. The *Monumenta* started as an enterprise financed by interested individuals, but soon became dependent on the support of the German governments and, of course, remained so. But the significant fact in the history of the professor of history was that when the governments looked for men who would direct these enterprises they naturally turned to those whom they employed for teaching history in the universities. One thinks of Leopold von Ranke or Theodor Mommsen, of William Stubbs or Pierre Claude François Daunou, one looks through the list of the collabborators and directors of the *Monumenta,* of the Society of French History, of the Rolls Series, and it becomes clear that the teaching of history and the directing of large research enterprises became wedded to each other. This union is a central and unique characteristic of historical studies in the nineteenth century.

If we look back upon the status of historiography before the nineteenth century we find three different channels of communication for the expression of historical interest. There was instruction in history at the universities, usually in a subordinated auxiliary form, there were the great research enterprises producing publications of source material, and there was historical literature composed by literary-minded statesmen like Guicciardini and Clarendon or by literary figures like Gibbon. With the rise of the professor of history two of these activities, teaching and research, were joined. Finally, the professor of history began to take on the responsibilities involved in the composition of historical books—or, at least, he began to set the standards which those who were writing history came to adopt. Authors who wrote historical works without academic connection became rare. And even those who did so—George Grote or Alexis de Tocqueville or Robert Davidsohn—were anxious to use the accepted critical methods. The impact of the professors of history on the writing of history was facilitated by the fact that in the nineteenth century some of the leading academic historians—for example, Ranke and Jules Michelet—were great writers. But a general acceptance of critical standards in writing history was also the result of the steadily increasing impetus gained by historical scholarship from the combination of research and teaching. Historical knowledge and study was necessary not only for teachers at high schools and lycées; archives, having become increasingly important, also had to be staffed with people trained in history, and positions in the research enterprises had to be filled. Since one research enterprise led to another one, the editorial tasks multiplied, and the presentation of the results demanded new periodicals of a specialized character. History became a going concern. The completion of one task created others. More and more historically trained people were needed.

It should be asked whether the emphasis I have placed on the institutional aspects of the development of nineteenth-century historical scholarship throws some light on the history of history.

To begin with a small point: nobody will deny or will want to minimize the crucial and decisive role of Ranke in the transformation of nineteenth-century histoiorgraphy. But the situation that existed when Ranke began to have a role in academic life was extremely favorable to his innovations: it promoted the identification of historical teaching with research training, and that, of course, represents Ranke's great contribution to the education of the professional historian.

It is more important, however, to realize that the increasing interest in historical scholarship in all European countries in the nineteenth century was due not only to the gradual diffusion of a historical spirit throughout Europe but also to political competition. History became a national institution in France, as well as in almost all European countries; governments supported historical institutes and research enterprises, and the status of historical scholarship formed part of a government's political reputation. This point of view justified the English government's subsidy for the publication of the Rolls Series. Political competition in historical enterprises is clearly evident in Austria and Bavaria. When Count Thun proposed to Emperor Francis Joseph in 1853 the foundation of an Austrian Institute for Historical Research, he explained that such an institution was needed "for political and intellectual reasons"; to strengthen the feeling of belonging together among the peoples of the Habsburg monarchy and to counter the influence of Prussia. Likewise, the Historical Commission at the Bavarian Academy served the purpose of providing Bavaria with a better image before the German public, as well as enhancing Bavaria's position vis-à-vis Austria and Prussia. The triumphal progress of history all over Europe in the nineteenth century was not purely an inevitable intellectual process: it was also the result of competitive policy.

There is one feature of nineteenth-century historiography, in particular, which might be better understood if it is seen in the light of the developments underlying the establishment of professorships of history. It is remarkable to what extent the writings and utterances of nineteenth-century historians abound in reflections and judgments of a moral character; for many of these historians world history was a world court. For Friedrich Christoph Schlosser and then for Jacob Burckhardt, "power was evil." For Johann Gustav Droysen, history belonged to those fields of knowledge which were meant to make men better, and history's best feature was its "ethical element." Lord Acton wrote that "It is the office of the historical science to maintain morality as the sole important criterion of men and things, and the only one on which honest minds can be made to agree." Admittedly, the nineteenth century was a moral age; nevertheless, the emphasis which many eminent historians of the nineteenth century placed on the connection between the teachings of history and moral doctrines had its roots in an age-old tradition of university instruction when history and moral philosophy were taught together.

In Burckhardt's case the influence of this tradition is very evident. He deplored the trend toward specialization and professionalization at the universities. Burckhardt's general historical lectures were meant to be, as he said, "propaedeutic," by which he meant to give the hearer no special knowledge in a particular field but general knowledge helpful in further studies and in life. Burckhardt was not interested in outlining the course of world history, but in providing reflections on world history which might aid and encourage people to form their philosophy of life.

Burckhardt, of course, was unique in his anxiety to keep traditions alive rather than to bow to the innovations of his century. For others who stressed the moral or ethical potential in history this view was tied up with the recently gained independence of historical study because the general insight which could be achieved alone justified the pursuit of a field of study. This issue is touched upon in a rather elusive passage of Bury's speech. He said, "It is remarkable that one of the most eminent English historians of the latter half of the last century whose own scientific work was a model for all students, should have measured out the domain of history with the compasses of political wisdom. That inconsistency is an illumination of the tenacity with which men cling to predilections that are incongruous with the whole meaning of their own lifetime." The historian to whom Bury referred was Stubbs. Although Stubbs was the first historian of the new critical school to be appointed to a Regius Professorship at Oxford, he emphasized in his inaugural lecture and in many of his statutory lectures the importance of history for the formation of ethical convictions and of a moral order of values. Thus, to the first generation of the new school of critical historians the relevance of their work to ethics was evident, even though the institutional connection between history and moral philosophy had been ended. To Bury's generation, history as a teacher of moral values or religious convictions no longer made sense. But in Bury's case, and in the view of many of his generation, this rejection of the moral ends of historical study was compensated for by the firm conviction that there was progress in world history, and that the historian was able to elucidate the laws of this progress and to help the forward march of mankind.

But what is our situation, for we believe neither in history as a means of teaching ethical values nor in the possibility of discovering laws to determine the process of world history?

Although we may not share the views of nineteenth-century historians on the purposes of historical study and what historical scholarship might achieve, we are still their heirs insofar as we are professors of history, and, as such, accept the framework established more than one hundred years ago—that is, recognition of the relationship between research and teaching, of the necessity for employing critical methods, and of the importance of maintaining professional standards. As remote as we seem to be from the assumptions and expectations of nineteenth-century historical scholarship, certain aspects of the history of the professor of history may still be relevant.

One is the view that history is indivisible and that everything that happened in the past belonged to the domain of the professor of history. History became an independent and autonomous field of study because it was recognized that special methods and procedures were necessary to study the past, but also because these methods and procedures were regarded as applicable to any aspect and period of the past. Before the nineteenth century history was chiefly an auxiliary science, and as an auxiliary to other fields of knowledge, historical study and research will always remain alive—now, perhaps, as an aid to political science, sociology, and area studies, rather than, as in the past, to moral philosophy, theology, or law. But if historians want their discipline to be more than an auxiliary science and to remain an autonomous and independent field of study, we should keep in mind that isolating our subjects is only one part of our work; the other is to seek for relationships, comparisons, and analogies.

A second aspect of the history of the professor of history is that history was expected to provide not only special and factual knowledge but also general insights about the nature of man. We might not feel that we can set our sights as high as that any longer. But, after all reservations have been made, we ought to remain aware that the man who acted and was acted upon in the past is the same man who acts in the present, and that the past is one way—and not the worst way—of acquiring the right and the criteria to judge the present. Our willingness to see the past as a whole, our willingness to take a stand, constitute our card of identity.

453

Publications of Felix Gilbert

Books

Johann Gustav Droysen und die Preussisch-Deutsche Frage, Beiheft 20 der Historischen Zeitschrift (Munich and Berlin, R. Oldenbourg, 1931), 148 pp.

Edited *Johann Gustav Droysen: Politische Schriften* (Munich and Berlin, R. Oldenbourg, 1933), 382 pp.

Edited *Hitler Directs His War* (New York, Oxford University Press, 1951), 187 pp.

Edited with Gordon A. Craig, *The Diplomats, 1919–1939* (Princeton, Princeton University Press, 1953), 700 pp.

To the Farewell Address: Ideas of Early American Foreign Policy (Princeton, Princeton University Press, 1961), 173 pp.

Niccolò Machiavelli e la vita culturale del suo tempo (Bologna, Il Mulino, 1964), 255 pp.

Machiavelli and Guicciardini: Politics and History in Sixteenth-Century Florence (Princeton, Princeton University Press, 1965), 349 pp.

History, with John Higham and Leonard Krieger (Englewood Cliffs, N.J., Prentice-Hall, 1965), 402 pp.

The End of the European Era, 1890 to the Present (New York, W. W. Norton, 1970), 426 pp.

Edited with Stephen A Graubard, *Historical Studies Today* (New York, W. W. Norton, 1972), 270 pp.

Edited, with an introductory essay, William Robertson, *The Progress of Society in Europe: A Historical Outline from the Subversion of the Roman Empire to the Beginning of the Sixteenth Century* (Chicago, University of Chicago Press, 1972), 185 pp.

Edited, with an introductory essay, *The Historical Essays of Otto Hintze* (New York, Oxford University Press, 1975), 493 pp.

Edited, with an introductory essay, *Bankiers, Künstler und Gelehrte: Unveröffentliche Briefe der Familie Mendelssohn aus dem 19. Jahrhundert* (Tübingen, Mohr (Siebeck), 1975), 329 pp.

Articles and Reviews

1933

"L'Histoire du despotisme éclairé: Allemagne," *Bulletin of the International Committee of Historical Sciences,* 5, III, 785–789.

Review of F. C. Church, *Italian Reformers,* in *Historische Zeitschrift,* 148, p. 187.

Publications of Felix Gilbert

1934
"Johann Gustav Droysen," *Pommersche Lebensbilder,* I, 141–154.
Review of H. Astholz, *Das Problem "Geschichte,"* in *Historische Zeitschrift,* 150, pp. 318–321.

1935
"Alcuni discorsi di uomini politici fiorentini e la politica di Clemente VII per la restaurazione medicea," *Archivio Storico Italiano,* 93, pp. 3–24.

1936
"Lorenz von Stein und die Revolution von 1848," *Mitteilungen des Österreichischen Instituts für Geschichtsforschung,* 50, pp. 369–387.
"The Germany of Contarini Fleming," *The Contemporary Review,* 149, pp. 74–80.

1937
"Machiavelli in an Unknown Contemporary Dialogue," *Journal of the Warburg Institute,* 1, pp. 163–166.

1939
"The Humanist Concept of the Prince and *The Prince* of Machiavelli," *Journal of Modern History,* 11, pp. 449–483.
"Machiavelli and Guicciardini," *Journal of the Warburg Institute,* 2, pp. 263–266.

1941
"Political Thought of the Renaissance and Reformation: A Report on Recent Scholarship," *The Huntington Library Quarterly,* 4, pp. 443–468.
Review of M. Werner, *Battle for the World,* in *Military Affairs,* 5, pp. 248–249.

1942
"An Unpublished Machiavelli Letter," *American Historical Review,* 47, pp. 288–291.
"Letters of Francis Kinloch to Thomas Boone, 1782–1788," *Journal of Southern History,* 8, pp. 87–105.
Review of J. D. Clarkson, ed., *War as a Social Institution,* in *Political Science Quarterly,* 57, pp. 435–437.
Review of C. Beuf, *Cesare Borgia,* in *Journal of Modern History,* 14, pp. 373–374.
Review of C. Van Doren, *Secret History of the American Revolution,* in *Military Affairs,* 6, pp. 116–118.

1943
"Machiavelli: The Renaissance of the Art of War," in Edward M. Earle, ed., *Makers of Modern Strategy: Military Thought from Machiavelli to Hitler* (Princeton, Princeton University Press, 1943), pp. 3–25.
"Jomini," with Crane Brinton and Gordon A. Craig, in Edward M. Earle, ed., *Makers of Modern Strategy: Military Thought from Machiavelli to Hitler* (Princeton, Princeton University Press, 1943), pp. 77–92.

1944
"The English Background of American Isolationism in the Eighteenth Century," *William and Mary Quarterly,* 3d ser., 1, pp. 138–160.
"Sir John Fortescue's 'Dominium Regale et Politicum,'" *Medievalia et Humanistica,* 2, pp. 88–97.
"Germany from the Early Middle Ages to the Nineteenth Century," *History of Germany,* Handbook of U.S. Military Government (original classification confidential).

Publications of Felix Gilbert

1946

Review of A. Taylor, *Renaissance Guides to Books*, in *American Historical Review*, 51, pp. 740–741.

1947

"Mitteleuropa—The Final Stage," *Journal of Central European Affairs*, 7, pp. 58–67.
"German Historiography during the Second World War: A Bibliographical Survey," *American Historical Review*, 53, pp. 50–58.
"Germany Revisited," *The World Today*, 3, pp. 424–431.
Review of L. Einstein, *Historical Change*, in *American Historical Review*, 52, pp. 353–354.
Review of G. G. Walsh, *Dante Alighieri*, in *American Historical Review*, 53, pp. 97–99.

1948

"Italy in Transition," *Saturday Review of Literature*, 21, pp. 19–35.
Review of *Documents on British Foreign Policy, 1919–1939, Second Series, Vol. I*, in *Political Science Quarterly*, 63, pp. 304–307.
Review of R. Lilge, *The Abuse of Learning*, in *Saturday Review of Literature*, 21, pp. 23–24.
Review of F. Guicciardini, *Le Cose Fiorentine dall'Anno 1375*, in *American Historical Review*, 53, pp. 318–321.
Review of G. Ritter, *Geschichte als Bildungsmacht*, in *American Historical Review*, 53, pp. 787–788.

1949

"Bernardo Rucellai and the Orti Oricellari: A Study on the Origin of Modern Political Thought," *Journal of the Warburg and Courtauld Institutes*, 12, pp. 10100131.
Review of G. Ritter, *Europa und die deutsche Frage*, in *American Historical Review*, 54, pp. 594–595.

1950

Review of F. Schevill, *The Medici*, in *American Historical Review*, 55, p. 965.
Review of R. Fischer, *Stalin and German Communism*, in *American Slavic and East European Review*, 9, pp. 60–62.

1951

"The 'New Diplomacy' of the Eighteenth Century," *World Politics*, 4, pp. 1–38.
"On Machiavelli's Idea of Virtù," *Renaissance News*, 4, pp. 53–55.
Review of G. C. Sellery, *The Renaissance*, in *American Historical Review*, 56, pp. 548–549,

1952

"L. C. Mackinney on Machiavelli," *Renaissance News*, 5, pp. 70–71.
Review of V. de Caprariis, *Francesco Guicciardini dalla Politica alla Storia*, in *American Historical Review*, 57, pp. 436–438.

1953

"The Composition and Structure of Machiavelli's *Discorsi*," *Journal of the History of Ideas*, 14, pp. 136–156.
"Ciano and His Ambassadors," in Felix Gilbert and Gordon A. Craig, eds., *The Diplomats, 1919–1939* (Princeton, Princeton University Press, 1953), pp. 512–536.
"Two British Ambassadors: Perth and Henderson," in Felix Gilbert and Gordon A. Craig, eds., *The Diplomats, 1919–1939* (Princeton, Princeton University Press, 1953), pp. 537–554.

Publications of Felix Gilbert

"A List of Desiderata," *Renaissance News*, 6, pp. 57–60.

"Countrymen of Caesar," *Saturday Review of Literature*, 36, pp. 16–17.

Review of H. Greiner, *Die Oberste Wehrmachtführung, 1939–1943*, in *American Historical Review*, 58, pp. 367–368.

1954

"The Concept of Nationalism in Machiavelli's Prince," *Studies in the Renaissance*, 1, pp. 38–48.

"Sulla Composizione dei 'Discorsi' del Machiavelli," *Rivista Storica Italiana*, 56, pp. 441–443.

Review of W. Goerlitz, *History of the German Staff*, in *United States Naval Institute Proceedings*, 80, pp. 1401–1403.

Review of Guicciardini, *Opere*, ed. V. de Caprariis, in *American Historical Review*, 59, p. 367.

1955

"Report on the Medici Correspondence," with Myron P. Gilmore, *Renaissance News*, 8, pp. 225–227.

Review of P. Renouvin, ed., *Histoire des Relations Internationales, Vol. II*, in *American Historical Review*, 60, pp. 338–339.

Review of M. A. Moriani, *Giovanni Guicciardini ed un Processo Politico in Firenze (1431)*, in *American Historical Review*, 61, p. 167.

1957

"Florentine Political Assumptions in the Period of Savonarola and Soderini," *Journal of the Warburg and Courtauld Institutes*, 20, pp. 187–214.

Review of R. v. Albertini, *Das florentinische Staatsbewustsein*, in *Journal of Modern History*, 29, pp. 260–162.

Review of H. Butterfield, *The Statecraft of Machiavelli*," in *Renaissance News*, 10, p. 157.

1958

"Guicciardini, Machiavelli, Valori on Lorenzo Magnifico," *Renaissance News*, 11, pp. 107–114.

Review of H. Rössler, *Europa im Zeitalter von Renaissance, Reformation und Gegenreformation*, in *American Historical Review*, 63, pp. 651–652.

Review of C. J. Friedrich, *Constitutional Reason of State*, in *American Historical Review*, 64, pp. 68–69.

1959

"Politics and Morality," *Yale Review*, 48, pp. 465–469.

Review of A. DeConde, *Entangling Alliance*, in *Pennsylvania Magazine of History and Biography*, 83, pp. 351–352.

Review of G. Sasso, *Niccolò Machiavelli*, in *Renaissance News*, 12, pp. 92–96.

Review of F. Chabod, *Machiavelli and the Renaissance*, in *American Historical Review*, 64, pp. 951–952.

1960

"Introduction" to Machiavelli's *History of Florence* (New York, Harper Torchbook, 1960), pp. ix–xvii.

"Cultural History and Its Problems," *Rapports du XIe Congrès International des Sciences Historiques* (Stockholm, Almquist-Wiksell, 1960), pp. 40–58.

Review of R. A. Graham, *Vatican Diplomacy*, in *Political Science Quarterly*, 75, pp. 426–429.

Publications of Felix Gilbert

1961

Review of R. Strauch, *Sir Neville Henderson*, in *Journal of Modern History*, 33, pp. 99–100.

1963

Review of C. C. Bailey, *War and Society in Renaissance Florence*, in *American Historical Review*, 68, pp. 1054–1056.

Review of R. Mandrou, *Introduction à la France Moderne*, in *Comparative Studies in Society and History*, 5, pp. 251–253.

1964

"The Eighteenth-Century Background," in W. H. Nelson, ed., *Theory and Practice in American Politics* (Rice University, Semicentennial Publications, 1964), pp. 1–12.

Review of G. Kisch, *Die Anfänge der Juristischen Fakultät der Universität Basel, 1459—1529*, in *Renaissance News*, 17, pp. 331–333.

Review of W. Thomas, *The History of Italy (1549)*, in *Journal of Modern History*, 36, p. 194.

Review of G. Sasso, ed., *Il Principe*, in *Journal of Modern History*, 36, p. 327.

1965

Review of G. Mattingly, *Catherine of Aragon, The Armada, Renaissance Diplomacy*, in *The Sunday Herald Tribune* (New York), April 18, pp. 12–13.

Review of F. Raab, *The English Face of Machiavelli*, in *American Historical Review*, 71, pp. 170–172.

Review of A. Gilbert, ed., *Machiavelli, The Chief Works*, in *Renaissance News*, 18, pp. 322–324.

1966

"The Present as Past," *Bryn Mawr Alumnae Bulletin*, 48, pp. 11–13.

Review of L. Gabel and others, *The Renaissance Reconsidered: A Symposium*, in *Journal of Modern History*, 38, pp. 67–68.

Review of G. Procacci, *Studi sulla Fortuna del Machiavelli*, in *American Historical Review*, 71, pp. 1380–1382.

Review of J. Herbst, *The German Historical School in American Scholarship*, in *History and Theory*, 5, pp. 217–219.

1967

"Christianesimo, Umanesimo e la Bolla 'Apostolici Regiminis' del 1513," *Rivista Storica Italiana*, 79, pp. 976–990.

"The Date of the Composition of Contarini's and Giannotti's Books on Venice," *Studies in the Renaissance*, 14, pp. 172–184.

"Political Power and Academic Responsibility: Reflections on Friedrich Meinecke's *Drei Generationen deutscher Gelenrtenpolitik,* "in Leonard Krieger and Fritz Stern, eds., *The Responsibility of Power: Historical Essays in Honor of Hajo Holborn* (New York, Doubleday, 1967), pp. 402–415.

"Cantimori at Princeton," *Belfagor,* 22, pp. 319–320.

"Machiavelli," *Encyclopedia of Philosophy,* 5, pp. 119–121.

Review of C. Bontems, *Le Prince dans la France des XVIe et XVIIe siècles*, in *American Historical Review*, 72, pp. 987–988.

1968

"The Venetian Constitution in Florentine Political Thought," in Nicolai Rubinstein, ed., *Florentine Studies* (London, Faber and Faber, 1968), pp. 463–500.

"The Renaissance Interest in History," in C. S. Singleton, ed., *Art, Science, and History in the Renaissance* (Baltimore, Johns Hopkins University Press, 1968), pp. 373–387.

"Ranke, Leopold von," *International Encyclopedia of the Social Sciences,* 13, pp. 323–325.

"Contarini on Savonarola: An Unknown Document of 1516," *Archiv für Reformationsgeschichte,* 59, pp. 145–150.

Review of B. Lane, *Architecture and Politics in Germany, 1918–1945,* in *Bryn Mawr Alumnae Bulletin,* 49, pp. 21–22.

Review of D. Queller, *Early Venetian Legislation on Ambassadors,* in *American Historical Review,* 74, pp. 141–142.

Review of R. Ridolfi, *The Life of Francesco Guicciardini,* in *American Historical Review,* 74, pp. 656–657.

1969

"Religion and Politics in the Thought of Gasparo Contarini," in Theodore K. Rabb and Jerrold E. Seigel, eds., *Action and Conviction in Early Modern Europe* (Princeton, Princeton University Press, 1969), pp. 90–116.

"Machiavelli e Venezia," *Lettere Italiane,* 21, pp. 389–398.

Review of C. G. Nauert, *Agrippa and the Crisis of Renaissance Thought,* in *Archiv für Reformationsgeschichte,* 60 (1969), pp. 131–132.

1970

"L'ambiente politico fiorentino tra il '400 e il '500," *Terzoprogramma,* I (1970), 7–15.

"Hajo Holborn: A Memoir," *Central European History,* 3, pp. 3–8.

"Machiavelli in Modern Historical Scholarship," *Italian Quarterly,* 14, pp. 9–26.

"Venetian Diplomacy Before Pavia: From Reality to Myth," in J. H. Elliott and H. G. Koenigsberger, eds., *The Diversity of History* (London, Routledge and Kegan Paul, 1970), pp. 79–116.

"Cesare Borgia,"*Dizionario Biografico degli Italiani,* 12, pp. 3–15.

"Introduction" to English translation of Friedrich Meinecke, *Cosmopolitanism and the National State* (Princeton, Princeton University Press, 1970), pp. 7–15.

Review of F. Ringer, *The Decline of the German Mandarins,* in *American Historical Review,* 75, pp. 1475–1477.

1971

"Biondo, Sabellico, and the Beginnings of Venetian Official Historiography," in J. G. Rowe and W. H. Stockdale, eds., *Florilegium Historiale* (Toronto, University of Toronto Press, 1971), pp. 276–293.

"Machiavelli," in R. Schwoebel, ed., *Renaissance Men and Ideas* (New York, St. Martins Press, 1971), pp. 53–65.

"Intellectual History: Its Aims and Methods," *Daedalus,* 100, pp. 80–97.

"Post Scriptum," *Daedalus,* 101, pp. 520–530.

1972

"Machiavelli's *Istorie Fiorentine:* An Essay in Interpretation," in Myron P. Gilmore, ed., *Studies on Machiavelli* (Florence, Sansoni, 1972), pp. 75–99.

"From Art History to the History of Civilization: Gombrich's Biography of Aby Warburg," *Journal of Modern History,* 44, pp. 381–391.

"The Culture Historian's Task," *Times Literary Supplement* (London), November 24, 1972, pp. 1411–1412.

"The Dynamics of Nazi Totalitarianism," *Social Research,* 39, pp. 191–203.

Review of R. Starn, *Donato Giannotti and His Epistolae,* in *Renaissance Quarterly,* 25, pp. 77–82.

Review of M. Mandelbaum, *History, Man and Reason,* in *American Historical Review,* 77, pp. 734–735.

Publications of Felix Gilbert

1973

"Venice in the Crisis of the League of Cambrai," in J. Hale, ed., *Renaissance Venice* (London, Faber and Faber, 1973), pp. 274–292.

"Machiavellism," *Dictionary of the History of Ideas,* 3, pp. 116–126.

"Revolution," *Dictionary of the History of Ideas,* 4, pp. 152–167.

"In the Interests of the Text," *Times Literary Supplement* (London), November 16, 1973, pp. 1385–1386.

1974

"Reflections on 'Higher education,'" *Daedalus, 103, pp. 12*–17.

"Italian Collections of Letters in the Second Part of the Sixteenth Century," *The Library Chronicle of the University of Pennsylvania,* 40, pp. 88–94.

"Le Istorie Fiorentine: Discussione," *Rivista Storica Italiana,* 86, pp. 720–722.

Review of F. Meinecke, *Historism,* in *History and Theory,* 13, pp. 59–64.

Review of *Mendelssohn Studien, Vol. I,* in *Lessing Yearbook,* 6, pp. 256–257.

1975

"Italy," in Orest Ranum, ed., *National Consciousness, History, and Political Culture in Early Modern Europe* (Baltimore, Johns Hopkins University Press, 1975), pp. 21–42.

"Georg Benjamin Mendelssohn und Karl Mendelssohn Bartholdy-Zwei Professoren aus dem neunzehnten Jahrhundert," *Mendelssohn Studien,* 2, pp. 183–201.

Review of D. Maffei, *IL Giovane Machiavelli banchiere con Berto Berti a Roma,* in *American Historical Review,* 80, pp. 1319–1320.

1976

"Corruption and Renewal," *Times Literary Supplement* (London), March 19, 1976, pp. 306–308.

"Bicentennial Reflections," *Foreign Affairs,* 54, pp. 635–644.

Review of E. Nolte, *Deutschland und der Kalte Krieg,* in *American Historical Review,* 81, pp. 618–620.

Notes

1. Johann Gustav Droysen

1. Letter to Theodor von Schön, March 9, 1850, in Johann Gustav Droysen, *Briefwechsel,* ed. Rudolf Hübner (Berlin and Leipzig, Deutsche Verlagsanstalt, 1929), I, 615; hereafter cited as *Briefwechsel.*

2. *Berliner Conversationsblatt für Poesie, Literatur und Kritik,* 52 (March 14, 1829).

3. *Des Aischylos Werke,* trans. Johann Gustav Droysen (Berlin, 1832), I, 169; hereafter cited as *Aischylos.*

4. *Aischylos,* I, 162, 180.

5. *Briefwechsel,* I, no. 14, pp. 33ff. The phrase "journal dealing with historical and political subjects" occurs in a letter to Ernst Moritz Arndt, no. 16, p. 37.

6. *Briefwechsel,* I, no. 16, pp. 37ff.

7. Hegel, *Vorlesungen über die Philosophie der Weltgeschichte,* in *Sämtliche Werke,* ed. Georg Lasson (Leipzig, Meiner, 1920), VIII, 926.

8. See Alexander Scharff, *Der Gedanke der preußischen Vorherrschaft in den Anfängen der deutschen Einheitsbewegung* (Bonn, A. Schroeder, 1929), p. 2.

9. See G. Droysen, "Johann Gustav Droysen und Felix Mendelssohn Bartholdy," *Deutsche Rundschau,* 111 (1902), 107–126.

10. See the statements of Abraham and Lea Mendelssohn Bartholdy on the July Revolution in Sebastian Hensel, *Die Familie Mendelssohn,* 18th ed. (Leipzig, Insel Verlag, 1924), I, 325, and Varnhagen von Ense, *Blätter aus der preussischen Geschichte* (Leipzig, 1869), V, 304.

11. On Börne at the Mendelssohns see Hensel, *Die Familie Mendelssohn,* I, 208. On Heine's relationship to Droysen see *Briefwechsel,* I, no. 2, p. 9.

12. Erich Rothacker, *Einleitung in die Geisteswissenschaften,* 2d ed. (Tübingen, Siebeck, 1930), p. 172, n. 1.

13. In an essay on Droysen reprinted in *Abhandlungen aus der neueren Geschichte* (Leipzig, 1876), Max Duncker gives great emphasis to this aspect of Droysen's background.

14. See Scharff, *Der Gedanke der preußischen Vorherrschaft,* pp. 13ff, and the literature Scharff cites there.

15. This is Friedrich Meinecke's view of Niebuhr's brochure. See *Weltbürgertum und Nationalstaat,* 7th ed. (Munich and Berlin, Oldenbourg, 1928), p. 217.

16. These are the same subjects that Ranke listed as topics of current public interest in a memorial he submitted to Christian Günther Bernstorff on November 1. See *Historische Zeitschrift,* 99 (1907), 56.

17. See Conrad Varrentrapp, "Rankes *Historisch-politische Zeitschrift* und das *Berliner Politische Wochenblatt,*" *Historische Zeitschrift,* 99 (1907). Otto Diether, *Leopold von Ranke als Politiker* (Leipzig, Duncker and Humblot, 1911), pp. 121ff, emphasizes the contrast between Friedrich Perthes and Ranke. Perthes's correspondence with Varnhagen is available in Wilhelm Dorow, *Krieg, Literatur und Theater* (Leipzig, 1845), pp. 145ff. In addition, see Clemens T. Perthes, *Friedrich Perthes' Leben,* 6th ed. (Hamburg and Gotha, 1872), p. 373, also pp. 356–358 on Perthes's views concerning Prussia and German unification.

18. See Hermann Oncken, "Zur inneren Entwicklung Rankes," *Bilder und Studien aus drei Jahrtausenden,* Gothein-Festgabe (Munich and Leipzig, Duncker and Humblot, 1923), esp. p. 210.

19. See Meinecke, *Weltbürgertum,* pp. 339ff.

20. Paul A. Pfizer, *Briefwechsel zweier Deutschen,* rev. ed. Georg Küntzel, vol. 144: *Deutsche Literaturdenkmale* (Berlin, B. Behr, 1911), p. 108.

21. Ibid., p. 164.

22. G. Droysen, *Johann Gustav Droysen* (Leipzig and Berlin, Teubner, 1910), p. 100, writes that the project of a political correspondence "was obviously inspired by Pfizer's book."

23. Meinecke, *Preußen und Deutschland im 19. und 20. Jahrhundert* (Munich and Berlin, Oldenbourg, 1918), p. 7.

24. "Germany's particularism cannot be allowed to be an eternal misfortune. It must lead to a higher, more perfect form." *Briefwechsel,* I, no. 16, pp. 37ff.

25. *Briefwechsel,* I, 39.

26. G. Droysen, *Johann Gustav Droysen,* p. 75.

27. *Aischylos,* II, 278.

28. Ibid., I, 163.

29. Ibid. "It was the Athenian accomplishment, I think, to have achieved a consciousness of freedom and put that consciousness into action."

30. Ibid., 175.

31. Ibid., II, 276.

32. Ibid., 277–278.

33. Ibid., 277.

34. Rothacker, *Einleitung in die Geisteswissenschaften,* p. 38, emphasizes classical philology as an independent major power in intellectual life.

35. Julius Kärst, "Studien zur Entwicklung und Bedeutung der universalgeschichtlichen Anschauung," *Historische Zeitschrift,* 106 (1911), 498–499.

36. See Friedrich Paulsen, *Geschichte des gelehrten Unterrichts,* 2d ed. (Leipzig, 1897), II, 208–209.

37. Friedrich A. Wolf, "Darstellung der Altertums-Wissenschaft," *Museum der Altertums-Wissenschaft,* ed. Friedrich A. Wolf and Philipp Carl Buttmann (Berlin, 1807), I, 124–125.

38. Ibid., p. 132.

39. From a letter of Erwin Rhode's, quoted by Wilhelm Kroll, *Geschichte der klassischen Philologie,* 2d ed. (Berlin and Leipzig, De Gruyter, 1919), p. 142.

40. August Böckh, *Staatshaushaltung der Athener* (Berlin, 1817), II, 158; Niebuhr, *Römische Geschichte* (Berlin, 1811), I, 13.

41. Böckh, *Staatshaushaltung,* I, 492; Niebuhr, *Römische Geschichte,* II, 402.

42. Böckh, *Enzyklopädie und Methodologie der Philologischen Wissenschaften,* ed. E. Bratuscheck (Leipzig, 1877), p. 56.

43. Böckh, *Enzyklopädie,* p. 12. See also Karl O. Müller, *Kleine deutsche Schriften,* ed. Eduard Müller (Breslau, 1847), I, 8, 15–16.

44. See Maximilian Hoffmann, *August Böckh* (Leipzig, Teubner, 1901), p. 35.

45. K. Otfried Müller, *Geschichten hellenischer Stämme und Städte* (Breslau, 1820), I, 8, 15. See August Baumeister in *Allgemeine Deutsche Biographie,* XXII, 664.

46. Böckh, *Enzyklopädie,* pp. 257 and 299.

47. Ibid., p. 257.

48. See Joachim Wach, *Das Verstehen: Grundzüge einer Geschichte der hermeneutischen Theorie im 19. Jahrhundert* (Tübingen, Mohr, 1926), I, 184.

49. Böckh writes in the *Enzyklopädie,* p. 6: "The ancient world is not comprehensible without the modern era as its complement."

50. On this point see Eduard Spranger, *Wilhelm von Humboldt und die Humanitätsidee,* 2d ed. (Berlin, Reuther, 1928), pp. 457–458.

51. Niebuhr, *Römische Geschichte,* I, 322, 418–419.

52. See Georg Küntzel, "Niebuhrs *Römische Geschichte* und ihr zeitgenössischer politischer Gehalt," in *Festschrift für F. C. Ebrard* (Frankfurt, Baer, 1920). In his introduction to the *Briefe Barthold Georg Niebuhrs,* ed. Dietrich Gerhard and William Norvin (Berlin, De Gruyter, 1926–29), I, lii, D. Gerhard refers to the "politically pedagogical motive" of Niebuhr's work. See Niebuhr's letter of November 9, 1811, to Perthes, *Briefe,* II, 229, for Niebuhr's own statement on the political allusions in his *Römische Geschichte.*

53. K. Otfried Müller, *Geschichten hellenischer Stämme und Städte: Die Dorier* (Breslau, 1824), III, 6.

54. Böckh, *Enzyklopädie,* 28.

55. Böckh, *Staatshaushaltung,* I, 56, 159, 221, 306. In other passages he expresses what might be considered a contrasting view when he emphasizes the unique premises of Athenian democracy (I, 162; II, 156–158).

56. Böckh, *Staatshaushaltung,* II, 159.

57. A summary of this lecture is available in G. Droysen, *Johann Gustav Droysen,* pp. 89–92. Unfortunately, the original on which G. Droysen based his summary could not be located. Franz Bopp's influence is evident in J. G. Droysen's remarks on linguistics here. Bopp and Carl Ritter were the nonclassicists who had the greatest influence on Droysen.

58. Ulrich von Wilamowitz-Moellendorf, *Einleitung in die Altertumswissenschaft,* ed. Alfred Gercke and Eduard Norden, vol. I, part I: *Geschichte der Philologie* (Leipzig and Berlin, Teubner, 1921), p. 69.

59. G. Droysen, *Johann Gustav Droysen,* p. 49, mentions among others *Logik und Metaphysik, Geschichte der Philosophie, Geschichte des Geistes, Vorlesungen über die Philosophie der Geschichte.*

60. *Briefwechsel,* I, 335.

61. Ibid., 38.

62. Ibid., 33.

63. Examples are the preface to the first volume of his *Geschichte des Hellenismus* and the structure of the first volume in his *Geschichte der Preußischen Politik.*

64. Hermann Heller, *Hegel und der nationale Machtstaatsgedanke in Deutschland* (Leipzig and Berlin, Teubner, 1921), pp. 176–182, discusses the effect Hegel's view of the state had on Droysen solely in terms of the idea of power politics, an idea Droysen accepted only after 1848.

65. Hegel, *Grundlinien der Philosophie des Rechts,* ed. G. Lasson, 2d ed. (Leipzig, 1921), p. 154 (Bourgeois society); p. 165 (Theory of Estates). On Hegel's theory of estates see Franz Rosenzweig, *Hegel und der Staat* (Munich and Berlin, Oldenbourg, 1920), II, 120ff.

66. Hegel, *Schriften zur Politik und Rechtsphilosophie,* ed. G. Lasson (Leipzig, 1913), p. 292.

67. See Ernst Troeltsch, *Der Historismus und seine Probleme* (Tübingen, Mohr and Siebeck, 1922), p. 254. This is true only of the later Hegel and does not mean, of course, that Hegel thought history was actually at its end but only that its further development would be a refinement and shaping of what had already been accomplished. On this idea see Julius Löwenstein, *Hegels Staatsidee: Ihr Doppelgesicht und ihr Einfluß im 19. Jahrhundert* (Berlin, Springer, 1927), pp. 50–52.

68. Rosenzweig, *Hegel und der Staat,* II, 161ff, denies that Prussia was the model Hegel used in developing his theory of the state, but Rosenzweig does admit that there is considerable correspondence between Hegel's theory and the institutions of the Prussian state. In any case, Hegel must have created the impression that he was idealizing the Prussian state, and he does in fact do so in his essay on the English Reform Bill.

69. See Troeltsch, *Der Historismus,* p. 254.

70. Ibid., p. 255.

71. *Briefwechsel,* I, 38.

72. Ibid., 44.

73. Otto Hintze, "Johann Gustav Droysen und der deutsche Staatsgedanke im 19. Jahrhundert," *Brodnitz' Zeitschrift für die gesamte Staatswissenschaft,* 88 (1930), 1–21, interprets Droysen's *Alexander* in this way; and Georg von Below, Eduard Fueter, Rothacker, and Meinecke are all in basic agreement with Hintze's interpretation.

74. In his introduction to the *Geschichte Alexanders des Grossen* he wrote: "Since you know I wrote my history of Alexander with the intention of going ahead to treat the period of the Diadochen and that of Hellenism."

75. See *Briefwechsel,* I, 24, and the preface of his dissertation, *De Lagidarum regno Ptolemaeo VI Philometore rege,* reprinted in J. G. Droysen, *Kleine Schriften zur Alten Geschichte* (Leipzig, 1894), p. 351; also G. Droysen, *Johann Gustav Droysen,* p. 101, and Meinecke, "Johann Gustav Droysen: Sein Briefwechsel und seine Geschichtsschreibung," *Historische Zeitschrift,* 141 (1929), 259.

76. Meinecke, *Historische Zeitschrift,* 141 (1929), 257. In pages 257–265 of this essay, Meinecke treats Droysen's concept of Hellenism in detail.

77. See Niebuhr, "Historischer Gewinn aus der armenischen Übersetzung der Chronik des Eusebius," *Abhandlungen der Berliner Akademie* (1820–21), p. 60.

78. Without Droysen's work, Jacob Burckhardt's formulation in *Griechische Kulturgeschichte,* ed. F. Stähelin, vol. VIII of the *Gesamtausgabe* (Berlin and Leipzig, 1930), p. 51, would have been impossible: The Greeks were "destined, in the course of time, to understand all peoples and to communicate their understanding to the world, to conquer the mighty lands and nations of the Orient, to make their own culture a world culture in which Asia and Rome would meet, to become the great catalyst of the ancient world."

79. See Richard Laqueur, *Hellenismus, Akademische Rede* (Giessen, Töpelmann, 1925).

80. This may have had something to do with his dissatisfaction with Berlin during his first semester there. See G. Droysen, *Johann Gustav Droysen,* pp. 50ff.

81. See Meinecke, *Historische Zeitschrift,* 141 (1929), 262. Laqueur, *Hellenismus,* p. 4, pointed out before Meinecke the importance of the Christian element in Droysen's concept of Hellenism.

82. I am not able to determine whether Droysen's concept of a religious dynamic in history drew any nourishment from the influence of theologians like Schleiermacher.

83. See Meinecke, *Historische Zeitschrift,* 141 (1929), 263.

84. Meinecke, *Historische Zeitschrift,* 141 (1929), 258.

85. Droysen uses this word in a letter to Moser dated November 10–29, 1831. See *Briefwechsel*, I, 47.

86. This is Meinecke's phrase, *Historische Zeitschrift*, 141, (1929), 263.

87. Dilthey proved this point in his *Jugendgeschichte Hegels*.

88. Berta Becker, *Johann Gustav Droysen's Geschichtsauffassung*, dissertation, Hamburg, 1928, pp. 25–41, presents a detailed analysis of Droysen's *Alexander*, with which I am not completely in accord.

89. Hegel, *Vorlesungen über die Philosophie der Weltgeschichte*, ed. George Lasson (Leipzig, Meiner, 1920), p. 652.

90. Hegel, *Vorlesungen*, pp. 529–530.

91. Hegel, *Vorlesungen*, p. 650.

92. See Droysen, *Alexander*, chap. 1, on Asia's struggle against Greece.

93. *Alexander*, p. 248, n. 53.

94. Hegel, *Vorlesungen*, p. 68.

95. *Alexander*, pp. 46, 64, 486.

96. *Alexander*, p. 205. See also Hegel, *Vorlesungen*, p. 76, and Ernst Simon, *Ranke und Hegel*, Supplement 15 of the *Historische Zeitschrift* (Munich and Berlin, 1928), p. 137.

97. Heinrich von Treitschke, *Deutsche Geschichte im 19. Jahrhundert* (Leipzig, 1927), III, 702.

98. *Alexander*, p. 13.

99. See Hegel, *Vorlesungen*, pp. 176, 551. See also Simon, *Ranke und Hegel*, pp. 160–161.

100. This is basically the view of *Alexander* that Hintze expresses in his essay "Johann Gustav Droysen und der deutsche Staatsgedanke im 19. Jahrhundert," p. 97. Droysen revised his *Geschichte Alexanders* heavily before issuing subsequent editions.

101. See, for example, *Alexander*, pp. 11–12.

102. Ibid., p. 41.

103. Ibid., p. 38.

104. Ibid., p. 13.

105. Ibid., p. 15.

106. Droysen used this phrase in his discussion of the "Chys, commentarius geographicus," *Berliner Jahrbücher für wissenschaftliche Kritik*, 1 (1833), 471. See *Alexander*, p. 422, for another comment on Napoleon.

107. *Alexander*, p. 538, contains a more emphatic affirmation of monarchy than Droysen had ever written up to this point.

108. *Schleiermachers Leben: In Briefen*, ed. W. Dilthey (Berlin, 1863), IV, 132, cited by Scharff, *Der Gedanke der preussischen Vorherrschaft*, p. 7.

2. Otto Hintze

The literature on Otto Hintze is not large. The article by Juergen Kocka in *Deutsche Historiker*, ed. H.-U. Wehler, III (Göttingen, Vandenhoeck and Ruprecht, 1972), pp. 41–64, although brief and condensed, provides an excellent analysis of Hintze's work and thought. Important contributions to our understanding of Hintze have been made by Gerhard Oestreich. He wrote the article on Hintze in the *Neue Deutsche Biographie* (vol. IX), with a list of Hintze's works and a complete bibliography; published a number of essays on particular aspects of Hintze's thought; and—most important—edited the recent, revised edition of the three volumes of Hintze's *Gesammelte Abhandlungen*, with extensive introductions. Even if one does not entirely agree with Oestreich, who finds in Hintze's development an increasing trend toward sociology, these introductions must form the point of departure for any study of Hintze's thought. Moreover, Oestreich also provides information about Hintze's personal life, about which we know very little.

The characterization of the young Hintze in Friedrich Meinecke's *Erlebtes* (Stuttgart, Koehler, 1964), is almost the only existing lively description of Hintze's personality. Single aspects of Hintze's thought have been discussed by Ludwig Dehio in his essay "Ranke and German Imperialism," in Dehio, *Germany and World Politics in the Twentieth Century* (New York, Knopf, 1960), pp. 38–71, in which he places Hintze's political views in the context of the political attitude of the German academic community, and by Theodor Schieder, who in his *Staat und Gesellschaft im Wandel unserer Zeit,* translated by C. A. M. Sym as *State and Society in Our Times* (London, T. Nelson, 1962), remarks on Hintze's definition of types. Some unpublished dissertations are mentioned in the bibliographies of Kocka and Oestreich.

The literature about Hintze in English is even more meager. His work is briefly discussed in Georg G. Iggers, *The German Conception of History* (Middletown, Conn., Wesleyan University Press, 1968), which also discusses the *Lamprecht Streit.* An article by Walter M. Simon, "Power and Responsibility: Otto Hintze's Place in German Historiography" in *The Responsibility of Power,* ed. Leonard Krieger and Fritz Stern (New York, Doubleday, 1967), pp. 199–219, analyzes Hintze's political views, but in isolating them from those of his contemporaries makes Hintze a more nationalistic figure than he was. Dehio's presentation of the same issue is more balanced. Dietrich Gerhard, "Otto Hintze: His Work and Significance in Historiography," *Central European History,* 3 (1970), 17–48, gives a good description of the content of Hintze's writings.

1. From Hintze's essay on "Gustav Schmoller," printed in *Gesammelte Abhandlungen* (Göttingen, Vandenhoeck and Ruprecht, 1962–67), III, 520. A bibliography of Otto Hintze's writings can be found in *Gesammelte Abhandlungen,* I, 563–579; it provides the place of printing of the articles discussed in this essay.

2. Ibid., III, 204–255, 313–418.

3. Ibid., p. 313.

4. See ibid., I, the essay "Wesen und Wandlung des modernen Staats," esp. pp. 470–496.

5. Ibid., p. 365.

6. Ibid., p. 379.

7. Ibid., p. 439.

8. Ibid., p. 469.

9. Ibid.

10. "Der Sinn des Krieges," in *Deutschland und der Weltkrieg,* ed. O. Hintze, F. Meinecke, H. Oncken, and H. Schumacher (Leipzig, S. Koehler, 1915). But see also in this volume Hintze's article "Deutschland und das Weltstaaten-system."

11. See *Gesammelte Abhandlungen,* I, 148.

12. Ibid., II, 381.

13. See ibid., p. 251.

14. See ibid., p. 380.

15. See Hintze, "Max Webers Soziologie," ibid., pp. 135–147.

16. See ibid., I, 470.

17. Ibid., pp. 470–471.

3. Friedrich Meinecke

1. Translated by J. E. Anderson (London, Routledge and Kegan Paul, 1972).

2. Translated by R. Kimber (Princeton, Princeton University Press, 1970).

3. Under the title *Machiavellism,* trans. Douglas Scott (New Haven, Yale University Press, 1957).

4. Changes in the evaluation of Meinecke's work are discussed by Hans Herzfeld,

"Friedrich-Meinecke-Renaissance im Ausland?" in *Festschrift fuer Hermann Heimpel,* vol. I (Göttingen, Vandenhoeck and Ruprecht, 1971), pp. 42–62; this article offers a useful bibliography of the literature on Meinecke. A brief summary of the debates about Meinecke since 1946 will be found in the "Postscript" of the book by Robert A. Pois, *Friedrich Meinecke and German Politics in the Twentieth Century* (Berkeley, University of California Press, 1972), pp. 148–156. For a complete recent bibliography see also Ernst Schulin, "Friedrich Meinecke," *Deutsche Historiker,* ed. H.-U. Wehler (Göttingen, Vandenhoeck and Ruprecht, 1971–72), I, 34–57.

5. After Meinecke's death, a collection and publication of Meinecke's writings was undertaken and, so far, eight volumes of his *Werke* have appeared (Stuttgart, S. F. Koehler, 1957–1969). His historical books, his writings on politics and historical theory, his autobiographical studies, and his correspondence have been published in single volumes in the framework of this collection. Each volume has an individual editor, who provides an introduction. These introductions are of fundamental importance for our knowledge of the facts of Meinecke's life and the genesis of his works, and I would like to express here my debt to Hans Herzfeld, C. Hinrichs, Walther Hofer, and Eberhard Kessel, who are the editors of the volumes most important for my essay. Nobody will expect me to always be in agreement with their interpretations.

6. See the volume *Autobiographische Schriften,* Meinecke's *Werke,* VIII, for Meinecke's own presentation of these relations.

7. Ibid., p. 306.

8. *Historische Zeitschrift,* 125 (1922), pp. 248–283. I discuss this article at greater length in my study "Political Power and Academic Responsibility," in *The Responsibility of Power,* ed. Leonard Krieger and Fritz Stern (New York, Doubleday, 1967), pp. 402–415.

9. See chapter 3 entitled "Statism Triumphant" in Pois, *Friedrich Meinecke.*

10. At the end of the introduction to *Idea of Reason of State.*

11. For the historical roots of this notion of freedom see Leonard Krieger, *The German Idea of Freedom* (Boston, Beacon Press, 1957).

12. See the volume *Zur Theorie und Philosophie der Geschichte,* Meinecke, *Werke,* IV.

13. I suppose that a terminological clarification is needed: "Geistesgeschichte" corresponds closely to what in the United States is called "history of ideas," whereas Meinecke's history of ideas (despite divergencies noted above) is derived from Ranke's notion of "idea" expressing the all-pervasive spirit of a time.

14. The best critical discussion of Meinecke's *Historism* can be found in E. Schulin, "Das Problem der Individualität: Eine kritische Betrachtung des Historismus-Werkes von Friedrich Meinecke," *Historische Zeitschrift,* 197 (1963), 102–133.

15. See "Die Idee der Staatsraeson in der neueren Geschichte," in Meinecke, *Werke,* I, xii.

4. The Humanist Concept of the Prince and *The Prince* of Machiavelli

1. In his edition of *Il principe* (Oxford, 1891), p. 232, L. A. Burd writes with reference to this sentence: "The following is the most important passage illustrating Machiavelli's purpose and method."

2. I quote from the English translation of *The Prince* by N. H. Thomson (Harvard Classics, vol. XXXVI). The latest critical edition of Machiavelli is *Tutte le opere storiche e letterarie di Niccolò Machiavelli,* ed. Guido Mazzoni and Mario Casella (Florence, G. Barbèra, 1929).

3. Burd, p. 282, states: "In the words 'molti si sono immaginati republiche' etc., it is

uncertain whether Machiavelli was thinking mainly of classical writings, and especially Plato, or of the political handbooks of the middle ages, such as Dante's *De monarchia,* and St. Thomas Aquinas's De regimine principum; probably he had both in view." But see P. Villari, *Niccolò Machiavelli e i suoi tempi* (Florence, 1881), II, 385: "E qui allude non tanto agli antichi, quanto agli scrittori del Medio Evo, come Egidio Colonna e Dante Alighieri, agli eruditi del secolo XV, come il Panormita, il Poggio, il Pontano ed altrimolti, i quali avevano sostenuto che il sovrano deve aver tutte le virtù, e ne avevano fatto un ritratto ideale di religione, di modestia, di giustizia e generosità." This passage is not in the English translation of Villari's book by Linda Villari (London, 1892). I am inclined to agree with Villari that Machiavelli was thinking mainly of the humanist literature of the quattrocento. This article is partly the outcome of investigations resulting from that assumption.

Subsequent to the acceptance of this article by the *Journal of Modern History,* two studies were published which deal with questions closely related to the subject of this study. The first is the article by D. Cantimori, "Rhetoric and Politics in Italian Humanism," *Journal of the Warburg Institute,* 1 (1937), 83–102, in which the question of Machiavelli's relation to humanism is discussed in a general way and some actual points of contact are established through an examination of the intellectual trends of the Orti Oricellari.

The other study is A. H. Gilbert, *Machiavelli's "Prince" and Its Forerunners: "The Prince" as a Typical Book de Regimine Principum* (Durham, N.C., Duke University Press, 1938). As this title seems to suggest that the subjects of A. H. Gilbert's book and of my article are very much alike, a few remarks on the differences seem necessary. The view that the connection between Machiavelli's *The Prince* and the mirror-of-princes literature needs investigation forms the background of both studies. A. H. Gilbert examines *The Prince* chapter by chapter, pointing out where passages of a similar kind or thoughts touching upon the same problems occur in the prince literature. He does not intend to prove that these works were sources for Machiavelli, but he believes that something can be learned from them about the general intellectual atmosphere in which *The Prince* was written. Moreover, it is Mr. Gilbert's main thesis that Machiavelli's *The Prince* is intended to fit into the regular pattern of the *de-regimine-principum* books, that it is "a typical book de regimine principum" and the "sole living representative" of this literary genre. There are two main ways in which I differ from A. H. Gilbert, which may explain the somewhat different results at which we arrive. Although I agree that Machiavelli tended to make his book conform to the usual pattern, I believe that this was an afterthought and had nothing to do with the original purpose and conception (see the last section of my article—written, of course, before A. H. Gilbert's book was published—where these questions are discussed at great length). The other point on which I differ from A. H. Gilbert is that I endeavor to establish direct links between Machiavelli and his literary predecessors. To this end, I find it necessary to distinguish between the mirror-of-princes literature in general and the specific form which humanism gave this literary genre, and to analyze, in considerable detail, the humanist ideas on princes and princeship.

After having indicated the differences between A. H. Gilbert's book and my own study, I wish to say that I consider the book very enlightening on the general background of Machiavelli's ideas. Since Machiavelli was the author not only of *The Prince* but also of the *Discorsi,* it would seem to me very useful if the material concerning the "good state" and republics could be brought together in a similar way. The investigation of the "intellectual milieu" of Machiavelli's works seems to me a much neglected but very promising path for achieving an understanding of his political realism. The fact that three different studies using this approach have appeared within such a short time may be considered proof of this contention.

4. The one recent contribution is the book by C. Curcio, *La politica italiana del'400* (Florence, Novissima Editrice, 1932). Besides this stimulating but brief survey, the only existing summaries, which are both incomplete and out of date, are those of G. Ferrari, *Corso sugli scrittori politici italiani* (Milan, 1862), and C. Cavalli, "La scienza politica in Italia," *Memorie del R. Instituto Veneto di scienza, lettere ed arti,* 11 (1862), 405ff. The only attempt comparable to the one here presented was made by F. von Bezold, "Republik und Monarchie in der italienischen Literatur des 15. Jahrhunderts," *Historische Zeitschrift,* 81 (1898), 433–468. I cite special studies in their appropriate place. General discussions of humanism will be found in V. Rossi, *Il quattrocento storia letteraria d'Italia* (Milan, Casa Editrice dottor Francesco Vallardi, 1933), and in G. Toffanin's most recent work, *Storia dell'umanesimo* (Naples, F. Perrella, 1935). A bibliography, giving the more recent Italian literature in the field of political thought, is contained in F. Battaglia, *Lineamenti di storia delle dottrine politiche* (Rome, Società Editrice del "Foro italiano," 1936), pp. 59–75.

5. L. K. Born's articles: "The Perfect Prince According to the Latin Panegyrists," *American Journal of Philology,* 55 (1934), p. 20; "The Specula Principis of the Carolingian Renaissance," *Revue belge de philologie et d'histoire,* 12 (1933), p. 583; "The Perfect Prince, a Study in Thirteenth and Fourteenth Century Ideals," *Speculum,* 3 (1928), p. 470, provide the first scientific analysis of the mirror-of-princes literature. A fairly complete bibliography of this literature, dating from the twelfth to the seventeenth centuries and classified according to countries will be found in L. K. Born's article, "Erasmus on Political Ethics," *Political Science Quarterly,* 43 (1928), 541. Born has collected the results of these studies in the introduction to his edition of Erasmus, *The Education of a Christian Prince* (New York, Columbia University Press, 1936). Some useful remarks concerning the general problems of the mirror-of-princes literature will be found in the introductory chapter of W. Kleineke, *Englische Fürstenspiegel vom Policraticus Johanns von Salisbury bis zum Basilikon Doron König Jacobs I* (Halle (Saale), M. Niemeyer, 1937).

6. See note 14, below, and Born's remarks in his article in *Revue belge,* 12, p. 583.

7. See Born in *Revue belge,* 12, p. 584.

8. Born's bibliography in his article in the *Political Science Quarterly,* 43, p. 541, gives the following quattrocento writings: "Leonardo Bruni, *De studiis et litteris,* for Battista de'Malatesti of Urbino (ca. 1444); Aeneas Sylvius Piccolomini, *Letter to Sigismund of Tirol* (1443) and *De liberorum educatione,* for Ladislaus of Hungary (1449); Francesco Filelfo, *De morali disciplina* and *Letter to Giovan Sforza* (ca. 1481); Baptista Saccus Platina, *Principis Diatyposis* (ca. 1481); Francesco Patrizi, *De regni et regis institutione* and *De institutione rei publicae* (ca. 1494); Joannus Jovianus Pontanus, *De principe liber* (ca. 1503); Bracciolini Poggio, *De officiis principis* (1504); Niccolò Machiavelli, *Il principe* (1513)." According to G. Gaida's introduction to Platina's *History of the Popes* in Muratori, *Rerum italicarum scriptores* (1913), III, part I, xiii, the date of Platina's book should be corrected to "between 1465 and 1468." Diomede Carafa, *De regis et boni principis officio* (ca. 1480), and Giuniano Majo, *De majestate* (ca. 1492), should be added to Born's list. The fact that the earlier writings are concerned mainly with the education of princes, while only the works dating from the latter part of the century deal with the nature of princeship, further underlines the developing interest in these problems in the course of the quattrocento.

9. Detailed accounts of Italian history during the trecento and quattrocento are contained in the *Cambridge Medieval History,* vol. VII, chaps. 1 and 2, and in J. Loserth, *Geschichte des späteren Mittelalters* (Munich and Berlin, R. Oldenbourg, 1903), pp. 306ff. The contrast between republican and monarchical Italy and the differences of type between the princes of the trecento and those of the quattrocento were first described in the first book of J. Burckhardt, *Civilisation of the Renaissance in Italy;* I quote Burck-

hardt from the recent German *Gesamtausgabe* (Berlin and Leipzig, Deutsche Verlagsanstalt, 1930), vol. V, which gives the unchanged original test.

10. See C. N. S. Woolf, *Bartolus of Sassoferrato* (Cambridge, Cambridge University Press, 1912), pp. 115, 121, 143.

11. It should, of course, be remembered that Florence was the center of humanism and that, because of that fact, republicanism was stronger and survived longer than would have been justified by the historical significance of the republican city-state within the Italian system. Nevertheless, the development characteristic for the whole of Italy, as outlined in the text, determined the change of emphasis in political thought.

12. See Burckhardt, p. 10.

13. See Bezold, "Republik," p. 449: "Die . . . Leistungen, die der Humanismus auf dem Gebiet der Staatslehre aufzuweisen hat, gehören zweifellos zu den schwächsten Seiten dieser . . . Literatur." This view is opposed in Curcio's book.

14. Certainly, the mirror-of-princes literature originated in antiquity, and the ancient world produced quite a number of treatises belonging to this category. See *Ueberwegs Grundriss der Geschichte der Philosophie,* I: *Die Philosophie des Altertums,* ed. K. Praechter (Berlin, E. S. Mittler und Sohn, 1926), p. 27. But they are not of great interest; only a few represent the type in a pure form, and none of them could claim the authority of a great name. The *Secretum secretorum,* doubtless of great influence on the medieval mirror of princes (see A. H. Gilbert, "Notes on the Influence of the *Secretum secretorum,*" *Speculum,* 3 [1928], 84–98) was omitted from the humanist translations of Aristotle's works. The two writings most frequently mentioned by the humanists—Isocrates's address to Nicocles and a treatise by Dion of Prusias—were regarded even by them as somewhat superficial and unimportant products. See F. Patricius, *De regno et regis institutione* (Paris, 1567), book I, chap. 4. Besides that, there were classical patterns for works on the "education of a prince" like Xenophon's *Cyropaedia* and the *Institutio Traiani,* ascribed to Plutarch. In general, see the chapter of "Ancient Theories of Statecraft" in L. K. Born's introduction to his edition of Erasmus, *The Education of a Christian Prince,* pp. 44–93.

15. In the century and a half between the golden age of the medieval mirror of princes and the humanist literature on the subject not a single essential new trait was introduced into the theoretical picture of the prince. Certainly interest in the problem did not completely die out during the "republican" period of humanism. The very fact that a proportion of humanists lived at princes' courts and depended on princes for their livelihood helped to keep interest in it alive (especially since Petrarch's letter to Francesco di Carrara and that of Salutati to Carlo of Durazzo provide examples of a friendly attitude toward princes on the part of leading humanists even in the early stages of the movement). The court humanists were often entrusted with the practical task of educating the prince's children. Thus the education of princes became a humanist topic. In this sphere Guarino (see G. Bertoni, *Guarino de Verona* [Geneva, L. S. Olschki, 1921]) and Vittorino da Feltre (see W. H. Woodward, *Vittorino da Feltre and other Humanist Educators* [Cambridge, Cambridge University Press, 1905]) were generally regarded as the most influential figures. See also W. H. Woodward, *Studies in Education During the Age of the Renaissance* (Cambridge, Cambridge University Press, 1924). The court humanists naturally also felt it incumbent upon them to come forward as defenders and champions of princeship. The question whether Caesar was a "tyrant" or a "true prince" produced the dividing-line between the "monarchist" and "republican" humanists, and discussion of this problem persisted throughout the fourteenth and fifteenth centuries. But the debate did not lead to a really thorough examination of the problem. The positive or negative attitude toward this problem is by no means a criterion of a medieval or modern outlook, as Burckhardt still assumed. See A. von Martin's preface to his edition of *Coluccio Salutati's Traktat "Vom Tyrannen"* (Berlin, Teubner, 1913), pp. 38ff; also E.

Walser, *Poggius Florentinus Leben und Werke* (Leipzig, Teubner, 1914), pp. 164–173; and, in general, F. Gundolf, *The Mantle of Caesar,* trans. J. W. Hartmann (New York, Vanguard Press, 1928), pp. 139ff.

16. For the medieval development see Born's article in *Speculum,* 3, pp. 502ff.

17. On the importance of Egidio's work see C. H. McIlwain, *The Growth of Political Thought in the West* (New York, Macmillan, 1932), pp. 338–343; for the wide popularity of Egidio's book see J. Roeder, *Das Fürstenbild in den mittelalterlichen Fürstenspiegeln auf französischem Boden,* dissertation, Münster, 1933, pp. 56ff; also Born in *Speculum,* 3, p. 488, n. 1, and, in general, R. W. and A. J. Carlyle, *A History of Mediaeval Political Theory in the West* (Edinburgh and London, W. Blackwood and Sons, 1928), V. I quote Egidio's book from the Rome edition of 1556.

18. That is, the maintenance of justice. The section on justice is in book III, sec. 2, as is also the distinction between *rex* and *tyrannus.*

19. The institution of councilors and their selection and use in book III, sec. 2, chaps. 17–20.

20. In a special section at the end of the book (book III, sec. 3), closely following Vegetius.

21. In the first part of the first book Egidio shows that a king should not covet worldly goods; the second and third parts treat of the virtues a king should possess. The classification of the virtues in the first four chapters of book I, sec. 2, clearly reveals the influence of Aristotle.

22. This is the theme of book II. The universal applicability of the rules there laid down is underlined by the constantly recurring phrase: "quod decet omnes cives et maxime reges et principes."

23. Egidio, p. 314: "Sciendum est regem et quemlibet principantem esse medium inter legem naturalem et positivam."

24. While the use of historical arguments is a general characteristic of this humanist literature, the exclusive referring to Roman history for this purpose is usually a sign of a definite political tendency. See H. Baron, "La rinascita dell'etica statale romana nell'umanesimo fiorentino del quattrocento," *Civiltà Moderna,* 7 (1935), 21.

25. I used an edition of 1608, printed in Frankfurt. On Platina see G. Gaida's introduction to Platina's *History of the Popes,* in Muratori, *Rerum italicarum scriptores* (1913), III, part I.

26. I used an edition of 1567, printed in Paris. On this book see G. Chiarelli's article, "*Il De regno* di Francesco Patrizi," *Rivista internazionale di filosofia del diritto,* 12 (1932), 716–738.

27. *De majestate* (Bibliothèque Nationale, Paris, Man. Ital. 1711).

28. Poggio Bracciolini (the younger), *De officiis principis liber* (Rome, 1504).

29. "De principe," in G. Pontano, *Opera omnia soluta oratione composita* (Venice, 1518), I.

30. "De optimo statu libellus," in Filippi Beroaldi, *Varia opuscula* (Basilea, 1515), pp. 123–133.

31. Egidio provides a relatively simple catalogue of the virtues: the cardinal virtues (*prudentia, justitia, fortitudo, temperantia*) are followed by eight minor virtues (*magnificentia, magnanimitas,* and so forth) and finally by the twelve passions. The exhaustive discussion of the virtues in Patricius, books V–VIII, comprising a complete statement of ancient psychology, on the other hand, contains some fifty virtues and vices. Platina again enumerates but a few, scarcely more than the main virtues—*prudentia, justitia, fides, fortitudo, modestia*—but including also *liberalitas* and *magnificentia.* On Pontano see below in this chapter.

32. This problem was originally raised in antiquity; then in Egidio, book I, sec. 3, chap. 3: "Quomodo decet reges et principes se habere ad odium et ad amorem." A very

interesting discussion of the subject will be found in Diomede Carafa, *De regis et boni principis officio* (Naples, 1668), p. 19, and in Pontano, p. 90. O. Tommasini, *La vita e gli scritti di Niccolò Machiavelli* (Rome, E. Loescher, 1911), II, 115, n. 2, characterizes it as a purely academic dispute.

33. See below in this chapter.

34. See Patricius, book III, chap. 1: "Sicut aliae sunt regis virtutes, aliae privatorum." Or Majo, chap. 18: "De lo peso che porta la Majestate"; here, the quiet life of the private individual is distinguished from that of the king "essendo sempre bisogno de arme e de compagni stare circumdato."

35. I refer to chaps. 15–19.

36. See Egidio, book II, sec. 2, chap. 13: "Sic ergo instruendi sunt pueri erga ludos, ut non omnino prohibeantur a ludis: sed ut moderate habeant ludos honestos et liberales"; also his attitude on wealth (book I, sec. 1, chap. 7) or to *magnificentia* (book I, sec. 2, chaps. 19–21).

37. See Patricius, pp. 105ff: "Nam mediocritas illa, quae in civili viro laudatur, nonnunquam in rege neutiquam satis esset, nec numerum perfectae laudis in eo impleret. Ea enim quae in viro privato liberalitas dicitur, in rege magnificentia sit oportet. Et frugalitas, quae modestiae temperantiaeque comes est, maximis laudibus effertur in civili viro: in rege autem minoris est laudis, et frigidior utique habetur." This passage is followed by the chapters on hunting, riding, games, and so on. For Majo's attitude see the two chapters on *magnificentia:* "*Prima magnificentia:* riding" and "*Seconda magnificentia:* hunting."

38. Pontano, p. 91: "Maxime autem opinionem tum subiectorum tum caeterorum hominum conciliabit ea quae hunc a quibusdam etiam non indoctis viris quamvis parum proprie majestas vocatur, sed non sit mihi de verbo controversia."

39. On Pontano's treatise see E. Gothein, "Die Renaissance in Süditalien," in his *Schriften zur Kulturgeschichte* (Munich and Leipzig, Duncker and Humblot, 1924), I, 197–203.

40. Pontano, p. 95. He says that if he had time, he would write a greatly needed special treatise on this subject.

41. Pontano, pp. 41ff.

42. See P. Funk's introduction to his translation of P. C. Decembrio, *Leben des Filippo Maria Visconti* (Jena, E. Diederichs, 1913), p. 29; also E. Satow, *Guide to Diplomatic Practice,* 3d ed. (London, Longmans, Green, 1932), p. 22, and, in general, Burckhardt, *Civilisation,* pp. 260, 262.

43. I quote from the original manuscript in the Bibliothèque Nationale, Paris, Man. Ital. 1711. On Majo see E. Percopo's article, "Nuovi documenti su gli scrittori e gli artisti dei tempi aragonesi," *Archivio storico per le provincie napoletane,* 19 (1894), 740. Further references to Majo in T. Persico, *Gli scrittori politici napoletani dal'400 al'700* (Naples, F. Perella, 1912), pp. 68–75, and G. Loiacano's article, "L'opera inedita 'de majestate' di Giuniano Majo e il concetto del principe," *Atti della R. Academia di scienze morali e politiche di Napoli,* 24 (1891), pp. 329ff. (This article gives excerpts from Majo's treatise.) Although I must regard Loiacano's estimation of this work as exaggerated, Persico's condemnation seems equally extreme.

44. As when he says that it was virtue alone that caused Ferrante to support Rhodes against the Turks (in chap. 7, "Benignita della majestate"). Similarly in chap. 11, "Amatore della verita," it is stated that it was only Ferrante's respect for his given word that caused him to reject an appeal from the people of Volterra, and therewith the possibility of making himself the master of Italy.

45. Chap. 17, "Pieta de re": "Hai tolta et extincta omne fattione mala et pernitione, tolta omne seditiosa partialita, omne discordia publica et omne guerra civile et intestina, non sono piu capo populi, ma uno capo . . . uno titulo, uno standardo socto una arma."

46. Instances in which the catalogue of the virtues was used for the discussion of wholly practical problems have already been cited, and similar traces of topical political impressions are clearly recognizable in many works of this type; see, for example, Prévité-Orton's introduction to his edition of Titus Livius Fruliviensis, *Opera hactenus inedita* (Cambridge, Cambridge University Press, 1932), pp. xxx–xxxv.

47. On Carafa see T. Persico, *Gli scrittori politici napoletani,* pp. 75–94, and Persico's biography, *Diomede Carafa, uomo di stato e scrittore del secolo XV* (Naples, 1899), in which, on pp. 147ff, he deals with Carafa's "doveri del principe." (I quote from a Latin translation of the Italian original, published in Naples in 1668, since only sections of the Italian original have been printed.)

48. On p. 17, Cicero; on p. 27, Caesar; on p. 81, Ovid.

49. As, for example, whether the prince should strive to be loved or feared, on p. 19: "Cum autem duae omnino regni tuendi rationes sint, amoris una, altera timoris."

50. For example, in his second chapter, on justice, like every humanist author he takes as his starting point the principle, "justitia omnis felicitatis humanae fundamentum"; but it immediately leads to a detailed discussion of the administration of justice (p. 38) and to making a whole series of observations on prison inspection (p. 43), safety of roads (p. 46), and the need for a special law for aliens (p. 49).

51. Carafa, p. 19: "Totius autem fere orbis reges populosque in gubernandi status sui deliberationibus commoda sua sequi et ea, tam generis quam affinitatis et amicitiae vinculis anteponere solere."

52. See Persico, *Carafa,* p. 148, n. 2.

53. Besides, it was written in Italian, not in Latin (see note 47, above).

54. See F. Meinecke, *Die Idee der Staatsräson in der neueren Geschichte* (Munich and Berlin, R. Oldenbourg, 1924), p. 52.

55. These writings contain references to the significance of monarchy and discuss whether monarchy should be given preference over the two other forms of government in the Aristotelian scheme, but the observations made on these topics are very superficial.

56. Meinecke's formulation, p. 348: "Demokratische Nivellierung des . . . Herrschers."

57. For these two lines of thought in the middle ages see Otto von Gierke, *Political Theories of the Middle Ages,* with introduction by F. W. Maitland (Cambridge, Cambridge University Press, 1900), p. 33: "So there was, on the one hand, a tendency to exalt the person of the Ruler," and p. 34: "None the less, however, the thought that Lordship is Office found emphatic utterance."

58. On Alberti, in general, see the latest study by G. Semprini, *L. B. Alberti* (Milan, Alpes, 1927).

59. Reprinted in L. B. Alberti, *Opere volgari,* ed. A. Bonucci (Florence, 1843), III, 7ff. The passages most important in the present context are on pp. 14–21 and 116–124.

60. Already Petrarch had drawn such "democratic" conclusions from the comparison between the prince and the father of a family (in the letter to Francesco Carrara).

61. On the comparison between state and family see Alberti, *Opere volgari,* pp. 122ff.

62. On the family as a working unit see ibid., p. 123.

63. Ibid., p. 18: "Forse non potendo il conditor delle leggi provvedere a tutte le cose particolari, diede ad alcuni, come al duttor dello esercito, al prefetto navale, così al principe, a minor magistrati qualche arbitrio."

64. Ibid., p. 20: "Il principe, cioè il sommo magistrato."

65. Ibid., p. 18: "Cosi seguita che il principato non concede arbitrio d'imponere nuova servitù alli altri, ma impone, a chi lo regge, necessità civile di conservare libertà e dignità alla patria, e quiete a'privati cittadini."

66. Ibid., p. 19: "Questa ragione di comandare, se tutti saranno modesti e ben sensati, pare a me sarà non altro che un esortarli, confermarli, sollecitarli."

67. See above, note 31.

68. See Gaida's biography of Platina, pp. xiii ff.

69. "Argumentum Marsilii Ficini in librum Platonis de regno, vel civilem," in Marsilii Ficini *Opera,* 2d ed. (Basle, 1576), II, 1294–1296. See also E. Gothein, "Platos Staatslehre in der Renaissance," *Sitzungsberichte der Heidelberger Akademie der Wissenschaften,* 3 (1912), 8–24.

70. "Eiusmodi vero gubernatorem atque curatorem saepius civilem vocat virum quam regem significans adeo humanum, ac si fieri possit, mitem esse debere, ut inter cives videatur esse concivis."

71. "Quod si quis longissimo quodam intervallo prudentia et justitia manifeste cunctos exuperet, hunc etiam si privatus vixerit, esse regem omnium a deo creatum absque controversia indicat." This Platonic view embodies his own opinions.

72. Alberti, *Opere volgari,* p. 21: "A me questo può persuadermi, ma alla moltitudine dubito; però che pare che all'imperio sia innato e additato farsi ubbidire imperando."

73. See E. Gothein, "Platos Staatslehre," although in this essay I carry the point further than Gothein.

74. Their importance was already stressed by Gemisthos Pletho, who can be regarded as the first Platonist of the Renaissance; his main work is entitled "Laws" (*Traité des lois,* ed. Alexander [Paris, 1858]). The significance which he attaches to the constitution is also clear from his political memoranda, published by A. Ellissen, *Analekten der mittel- und neugriechischen Literatur* (Leipzig, 1860), vol. IV, part II. Above all, see Ficino's commentary to Plato's *De re publica.*

75. Thus the idea of "mixed government," which plays such an important role in Guicciardini's and Giannotti's work, was regarded as Platonic (see, for example, George of Trebizond, *Comparationes phylosophorum Aristotelis et Platonis* [Venice, 1523], p. 136).

76. See Ficino in his *Vita Platonis;* Bessarion, *In calumniatorem Platonis libri IV,* printed in *Quellen und Forschungen der Görres-Gesellschaft,* XXII (Paderborn, 1927), p. 627; Gemisthos Pletho, *Traité des lois,* p. 30.

77. See especially the first two books of Christofero Landino, *Disputationes Camaldulenses.*

78. Highly characteristic in this respect is Bessarion's explanation of the meaning of the term *tyrannus* in antiquity: the ancients called thus "etiam eum, qui etsi optime imperat, sibi tamen omnia tribuit et in sua unius potestate rerum omnium arbitrium constituit, quem homines priscorum temporum vehementer detestabantur" (Bessarion, p. 583), and also "Legum latorem autem sine tyrannide in constituenda nova re publica et sanciendis legum praeceptis vix miti lustratione, qualis est in coloniam mittere, ad exterminandos malos mores agere posse . . . Neque enim fieri potest, ut homines, qui vel suo consilio non eligunt aguntque, quae meliora sunt, vel recte consulentibus non parent, aliter quam vi et summa quadam necessitate a pravis moribus discedere possint, quam melius longeque facilius unus princeps quam plures potest inferre" (p. 587). It is clear that Bessarion reproduces the views of Plato; but, on the other hand, the closeness of these ideas to Machiavelli's outlook is more than striking.

79. In the "Rappresentazione di San Giovanni e Paolo," Lorenzo de'Medici il Magnifico, *Opere,* ed. A. Simioni (Bari, Laterza, 1914), II, 111.

80. The supposition of such a connection is perhaps supported by Machiavelli's appeal to the founders of states in the sixth chapter of *The Prince;* they are Moses, Cyrus, and Romulus. Also, by the passage in chap. 26: "Nothing confers such honour on the reformer of a state as do the new laws and institutions which he devises . . . And in Italy material is not wanting for improvement in every form "in Italia non manca materia da introdurvi ogni forma"; I doubt whether the English translation gives fully the meaning of the Italian sentence.

81. See Tommasini, *Niccolò Machiavelli,* II, 89, and the edition of *The Prince* in the most recent critical edition of Machiavelli's works.

82. In spite of Tommasini's protest (II, 110) there appears to be no possible doubt concerning Machiavelli's imitation of Isocrates (which was first pointed out by Trianta-fillis, *Niccolò Machiavelli e gli scrittori greci* [Venice, 1875]). The argument that Machiavelli did not know Greek has to be invalidated by the fact that Latin translations of Isocrates existed; one by Erasmus was published in 1515 (1st ed., 1515; several other editions, 1516, and so on; see *Bibliotheca Erasmiana,* 2d ser. [Ghent, 1893]). There is no reason for assuming that the introduction to *The Prince,* which was composed later than the main work, was written before 1515. The assumption that Machiavelli derived his knowledge of Isocrates from Erasmus's translation would strengthen the supposition that Machiavelli was vitally interested in all new publications connected with the subject of princeship. Erasmus's translation of Isocrates was published in one volume with his *Institutio principis christiani;* it was also often bound together with Patricius's treatise.

83. See above, section II.

84. See above, section II.

85. I should like to point out that the passage quoted at the beginning, in which Machiavelli describes his realistic method, appears to me a direct paraphrase of certain sentences in Patricius. Patricius, *De regni et vegis institutione,* p. 71, writes: "Nos igitur de unius viri dominatu aut imperio dicturi in his libris si ratione ac via disserere volumus, ad ultimam sui generis formam ac speciem sermonem nostrum redigamus necesse est atque in optimo principe fingendo talem formemus qualis fortasse nemo unquam fuit. Non enim quaerendum a nobis est, quis eiusmodi fuerit sed videndum erit qualis debeat esse ille quem optimum regem aut principem esse statuimus." But this suggestion is, of course, hypothetical.

86. See Francesco Guicciardini's remark in his letter to Machiavelli, May 18, 1521: "ut plurimum estravagante di opinione della comune, e inventore di cose nuove ed insolite"; also Luigi Guicciardini's judgment: "oltre a questo volentieri tolsi il Machiavello per dipignere uno che con difficultà credessi le cose da credere non che quelle da ridersene." See F. Guicciardini, *Opere inedite,* IX (Florence, 1866), p. 267; and on the "dialogue" to which this statement refers see my article, "Machiavelli in an Unknown Contemporary Dialogue," *Journal of the Warburg Institute,* 1 (1937), p. 163.

87. Machiavelli, *Der Fürst,* Klassiker der Politik, VIII (Berlin, Reimar Hobbing, 1923). Meinecke's theory is opposed by F. Chabod in his article, "Sulla composizione de 'Il principe' di Niccolò Machiavelli," *Archivum Romanicum,* 11 (1927), 330–383. His arguments, however, do not appear to me convincing.

In the first place, he attempts to show that Meinecke interpreted Machiavelli's letter to Vettori in too literal a manner. This argument appears only permissible if Meinecke's "literal interpretation" had led to an improbable conclusion. Secondly, he suggests that chaps. 12 and 13 of *The Prince* do not, in fact, repeat problems that have already been discussed. Of course, these chapters are no mere "repetition"; but there can be no doubt that Machiavelli discusses in them questions which he has raised before and that the reader is at first surprised to note that he returns to them. In the third place, Chabod attempts to prove, independently from Meinecke, on the basis of a passage in chap. 13 alluding to the political situation in France, that *The Prince* was completed in December 1513. Even if this somewhat questionable method of arguing is accepted at its face value, it would prove no more than that the passage in question no longer applied to the situation in France during the summer of 1514 and that, therefore, *The Prince* must have been completed, at the very latest, during the spring of that year. All attempts to fix an earlier date for its completion on the basis of this passage are wholly artificial.

Machiavelli's original draft of *The Prince* does not exist. I do not understand, therefore, how the editors of *The Prince* in the recent critical edition of Machiavelli's works

(p. lxvii) can say that the state of the manuscripts conflicts with Meinecke's theory.

88. It has often been pointed out that chaps. 15–19 form a connected whole.

89. My conclusion can be summarized by stating that it combines the views of Meinecke and Tommasini. Like Meinecke, I distinguish between two main parts; but in advancing the claim that the second part was written in sections, I am led a step further and recognize subgroups, thus supporting Tommasini's division of *The Prince* into three distinct parts.

5. The Composition and Structure of Machiavelli's *Discorsi*

1. *The Discourses of Niccolò Machiavelli,* translated from the Italian with an introduction and notes by Leslie J. Walker, 2 vols. (New Haven, Yale University Press, 1950).

2. An important review is the one by J. H. Whitfield, *Italian Studies,* 4 (1951), 100–106.

3. The problem of the composition of the *Discorsi* formed the topic of a graduate seminar which I gave at Bryn Mawr College before the appearance of Walker's edition; but these investigations could never, or at least not so quickly, have led to definite results without Walker's edition.

4. From the prologue of Christopher Marlowe's *Jew of Malta;* Machiavelli is the speaker of this prologue.

5. For instance, see the statements of J. H. Whitfield, *Machiavelli* (Oxford, B. Blackwell, 1947), p. 106: "The *Discorsi,* whose composition extends over the years 1513 to 1519, represent the capital book of Machiavelli."

6. Whitfield, *Machiavelli,* p. 106. An exception, apart from Walker's introduction to his edition of the *Discorsi,* is the article by Friedrich Mehmel, "Machiavelli und die Antike," *Antike und Abendland,* 3 (Hamburg, 1948), 152–186. However, the discussion of *The Prince* in this article lacks knowledge of the recent English literature, which leads beyond the point which the author presents; and though the author indicates the importance of Machiavelli's relation to Livy for disentangling the structure of the *Discorsi,* he makes no real attempt to carry through this approach.

7. See note 5.

8. See Machiavelli's famous letter to Vettori, December 10, 1513.

9. *The Prince,* beginning of chap. 2: "Io lascerò indietro el ragionare delle republiche, perchè altra volta ne ragionai a lungo." I use Niccolò Machiavelli, *Tutte le opere storiche e letterarie,* a cura di Guido Mazzoni e Mario Casella (Florence, G. Barbèra, 1929), where this passage will be found on p. 5. English passages in the text are given according to Walker's translation.

10. *Discorsi,* II, chap. 11: "Come interverrebbe . . . a quel principe, che, confidatosi di Massimiliano imperadore, facesse qualche impresa" (*Opere,* p. 154).

11. See Table XIV, Discourses Indicating Dates, in Walker, II, 309–310.

12. For instance, the expression "ne' nostri tempi" includes any development which took place in Machiavelli's lifetime; an event which Machiavelli characterizes as having happened "pochi anni sono" occurred in 1495, and expressions like "prossimi tempi" and "freschissimo esemplo," which he uses interchangeably, refer to occurrences in quite different years, 1512, 1515, 1517; see Walker, II, 309–310.

13. "E, pochi giorni sono, il Papa ed i Fiorentini insieme non arebbono avuta difficultà in vincere Francesco Maria, nipote di papa Julio II, nella guerra di Urbino" (*Opere,* p. 152). Walker, I, 43, suggests that this remark refers to the recovery of Urbino by Leo X on September 17, 1517. Since the point of Machiavelli's statement is that a power that has money will be defeated by a power that has good soldiers, it would seem to me he must have thought of an event that showed the strength of the financially weak Fran-

cesco Maria, that is, his re-entry into Urbino; the campaign of Francesco Maria is also mentioned at another place (*Discorsi,* II, chap. 24). But for the purposes of the argument here, it makes no difference whether the event Machiavelli has in mind is the conquest of Urbino by Francesco Maria in February, or its recovery by Leo X in September. In our context, the important point is that the passage must have been written in 1517.

14. "Sopra che non si può dare il migliore esemplo che la città di Pistoia. Era divisa quella città, come è ancora, quindici anni sono, in Panciatichi e Cancellieri; ma allora era in sull'armi, ed oggi le ha posato" (*Opere,* p. 238).

15. See in particular the various references to the campaigns of Selim I in 1516 and 1517 and the chronological references listed by Walker, II, 309.

16. In general, see Walker, I, 42–44, and II, 133. There can be no doubt that the passage in *Discorsi,* II, chap. 24, that Ottavio Fregoso was able to hold Genoa without protection of a fortress against 10,000 men, does not refer to events of the year 1521, but to Fregoso's ability to remain in power when Francis I invaded Italy in 1515.

17. *Discorsi,* I, chap. 1; II, preface; III, chap. 1.

18. For instance, *Discorsi,* I, chap. 15: "E benchè questa parte più tosto, per avventura, si richiederebbe essere posta intra le cose estrinseche; nondimeno . . . mi è parso da connetterlo in questo luogo" (*Opere,* p. 83).

19. *Discorsi,* I, chap. 35 to I, chap. 40; II, chap. 20 to III, chap. 6; II, chap. 26 to III, chap. 6; II, chap. 29 to III, chap. 1.

20. The organization seems particularly loose in book III, formally devoted to the subject "how much the action of particular men contributed to the greatness of Rome and produced in that city so many beneficial results." Aside from Chapter 6 (On Conspiracies), chapters like 26 (How women have brought about the downfall of states), 27 (How unity may be restored to a Divided City, and how mistaken are those who hold that to retain possession of cities one must needs keep them divided), 29 (That the faults of Peoples are due to Princes), and 35 (What dangers are run by one who takes the Lead in advising some Course of Action; and how much greater are the Dangers incurred when the Course of Action is Unusual) have nothing to do with the main theme. Though the topic of the first book (internal affairs) is very comprehensive, chapters like 41 (A sudden transition from Humility to Pride or from Kindness to Cruelty without Appropriate Steps in between is both imprudent and futile), 43 (Those who fight for Glory's sake make Good and Faithful soldiers), 56 (Before Great Misfortunes befall a City or a Province they are preceded by Portents or foretold by Men), and 59 (What Confederations or other Kinds of League can be trusted most; those made with a Republic or those made with a Prince) hardly belong to this theme. The second book (external affairs) concerns everything that has to do with war.

21. The outstanding example is the treatment of military affairs, the chief topic in book II, but also discussed in various chapters of books I and III; the theme of mercenaries, for instance, appears at several different places. The Subject Index in Walker, II, 345–390, gives some insight into the treatment of the same topics at various places.

22. Whitfield, *Machiavelli,* p. 108, says that "out of Taine's discovery of an opposition between the *Prince* and the *Discorsi* arose a feeling in others of an indifference in Machiavelli to the matter he was analysing, an indifference which was interpreted as cynicism." Walker, I, 135, assumes the existence of a difference between the logical sequence of Machiavelli's ideas and the historical order adopted by him in the *Discorsi.*

23. On the various manuscripts in which the *Discorsi* are handed down to us, see Machiavelli, *Opere,* p. 54; the only material written by Machiavelli himself is a draft for the introduction. Two early manuscripts of single chapters are in existence, both in Florence—the one in the Biblioteca Nazionale, Msc. Palat. 1104 (not 1020 as erroneously stated in *Opere*), the other in the Archivio di Stato, R. Acquisto Rinuccini, X di

Balia, Responsive N. 119—but they are copies of a text of the entire manuscript and do not permit insight into the genesis of the *Discorsi.*

24. The exception is Walker, who uses this approach for a discussion of the genesis of the *Discorsi* in the introduction to his edition. The difference between Walker's approach and mine is that Walker lists the various Livy passages mentioned in a chapter of the *Discorsi* without making any distinction concerning their importance (see the Analytical Table of Contents, Walker, I, 165–198), while I try to differentiate between them and to establish the "main reference" around which the chapter is planned. The results of my analysis are shown in the table. The processes by which I arrive at this result are explained in notes 25–31. Note 25 lists those chapters of the *Discorsi* that mention only one Livy passage, and generally these statements are analogous to Walker's. Notes 26–31 show how I arrived at the establishment of a "main reference" in those chapters that mention two or more Livy passages, and naturally this analysis has no model in Walker. It should be easy for the reader to reconstruct my procedure and to examine its results on the basis of my table and notes 25–31. I want to add that, as I explain later on—quite in agreement with Walker, I, 61—the first eighteen chapters of the first book of the *Discorsi* are of a somewhat exceptional nature, and a re-examination will best begin with chapter 19 of the first book. Necessarily account is taken only of passages in Livy's first decade. Moreover, since Machiavelli frequently comments on entire stories from Livy, the references are often not to single Livy chapters, but to a series of chapters.

25. The following sixty-three chapters contain only one Livy reference:
Discorsi, I, chaps. 3, 5, 12, 14, 16, 19, 22, 25, 32, 33, 35, 36, 38, 40, 47, 50, 51, 53, 55, 56, 58, 60
Discorsi, II, chaps. 4, 7, 9, 13, 16, 19, 20, 21, 22, 25, 28, 31, 33
Discorsi, III, chaps. 2, 3, 4, 5, 10, 11, 13, 18, 19, 20, 25, 28, 29, 30, 31, 32, 34, 35, 38, 39, 40, 41, 42, 43, 44, 45, 46, 47

26. In the following eighteen chapters:
Discorsi, I, chaps. 7, 8, 11, 15, 31, 46, 57
Discorsi, II, chaps. 8, 18, 32
Discorsi, III, chaps. 12, 14, 15, 23, 24, 26, 37, 48
Example: *Discorsi,* III, chap. 26, where the riot in Ardea is the main reference, and not the outrage to Lucretia or Virginia.

27. These twenty-four chapters are:
Discorsi, I, chaps. 4, 13, 17, 20, 21, 23, 24, 29, 34, 41, 42, 43, 44, 45, 52, 54
Discorsi, II, chaps. 10, 11, 14, 15, 26, 30
Discorsi, III, chaps. 7, 27
Example: *Discoursi,* I, chaps. 23 and 24, are tied to the fight between the Horatii and Curiatii described in chap. 22.

28. These four chapters are *Discorsi,* I, chaps. 37, 39, 48, 49
Example: *Discorsi,* I, chap. 37, deals with "the scandals to which the Agrarian Laws gave rise in Rome"; the main reference is the Livy passage which describes the origin of the Agrarian Laws.

29. The main reference in *Discorsi,* III, chap. 36, follows from chap. 37.

30. I mean *Discorsi,* III, chaps. 8, 22, 49, which comment on two or more Livy passages from different books of Livy, and with regard to which I cannot find one reference to be more crucial than the other. I also have not been able to decide on a main reference in the following five cases: *Discorsi,* I, chaps. 9, 28; II, chaps. 23, 29; III, chap. 33, but in these cases the situation is somewhat different. The two Livy passages, to which these chapters refer, are taken from the same Livy book and are to be found in chapters which follow rather closely upon each other; moreover they deal with related subjects so that it would have been rather repetitive to form independent chapters.

31. To complete this analysis, I should mention those twenty-four chapters not dis-

cussed in notes 25–30. A few chapters (*Discorsi,* I, chap. 1; II, chaps. 1, 2, 3, 6; III, chap. 1) are so general that, though Livy is mentioned, they were not conceived as comments on Livy. A certain number of chapters contain no Livy references at all. Six of these chapters (*Discorsi,* I, chaps. 2, 6, 10; III, chaps. 6, 16, 17) are quite independent; others (*Discorsi,* I, chaps. 18, 26, 27, 30, 59; II, chaps. 5, 12, 17, 24, 27; III, chaps. 9, 21) continue a trend of thought from a previous chapter, though they have no connection with the Livy reference that started the discussion in the previous chapter.

32. There are four cases in which the same Livy reference is used in different books of the *Discorsi:* Livy, II, 4–5, in *Discorsi,* I, chap. 16 and III, chap. 3; Livy, II, 14–20, in *Discorsi,* I, chap. 58 and III, chap. 8; Livy, VII, 32, in *Discorsi,* I, chap. 60 and III, chap. 38; and Livy, VIII, 7–10, in *Discorsi,* II, chap. 16 and III, chap. 22. There are seven cases in which the same Livy passage forms the basis of discussion in two different chapters of the same book of the *Discorsi: Discorsi,* I, chaps. 8 and 58, 9 and 19, 16 and 25; *Discorsi,* II, chaps. 4 and 8, 16 and 22; *Discorsi,* III, chaps. 2 and 5, 22 and 34, discuss the same Livy passages. It should be noted, however, that the number of duplications would be still smaller if the first eighteen chapters of the first book of the *Discorsi,* which, as mentioned above, are somewhat exceptional, were not counted. Moreover, *Discorsi,* III, chap. 22, which appears twice on this list, is one of those chapters with no definite "main reference." As will be shown later (see note 38), all the duplications appear in chapters which do not form part of the fundamental pattern of the *Discorsi.* It is of no great help to bring the frequency of duplications into a statistical form: there are eleven duplications in the 142 chapters of the *Discorsi,* but if the exceptional eighteen chapters of the first book of the *Discorsi* and the fact that frequently a series of successive chapters is concerned with the same Livy passage are taken into account, the relation 84 to 7 might be more correct.

33. Formally, the sequence continues until the end of the first book of the *Discorsi,* since chapter 56 comments upon passages from Livy, V, and chapters 57–60 on passages from Livy, VI and VII; but the coverage of Livy, VI in just two chapters is so much less complete than the coverage of the previous Livy books in the preceding chapters of the *Discorsi* that it must be assumed that the sequence ends with chapter 56.

34. There can be no doubt with regard to *Discorsi,* I, chap. 35; in the previous chapter, Machiavelli had praised the wisdom of establishing the institution of dictatorship and explained that extraordinary powers given to one man, if clearly defined, are no danger to freedom. When he later comes to the Decemviri, he must have realized that their story seems contradictory to this previously expounded thesis, and so he inserts chapter 35 to remove this contradiction. Probably a case could also be made for chapter 31 being a later insert because of the somewhat conscious attempt in the first paragraph to justify the place of this chapter by relating it to the previous ones. But this is speculation.

35. As the table above shows, chapters 46, 47, and 48 should precede chapter 43 to make a perfect successive order.

36. Five of the duplications are concerned with the first 29 chapters of the third book of the *Discorsi.*

37. The three chapters with doubtful main references are *Discorsi,* III, chaps. 8, 22, 49; that is, the first two belong to the first twenty-nine chapters of the book, the last one is the concluding chapter of the book.

38. See above, notes 30–32. The two exceptions are the duplications in *Discorsi,* II; they are not very significant duplications. In the first case (chaps. 4 and 8), the chapters are close to each other and it could be questioned whether this is really a duplication or a continuation of the discussion of the same section; in the second case (chaps. 16 and 22), Machiavelli comments on a whole story, contained in several Livy chapters, then he comments on only the last chapter of that story. I listed these two cases as duplications, however, so that the reader would not feel that I gloss over difficulties.

39. This device is used thirteen times in these twenty-eight chapters (in chaps. 1, 2, 3, 4, 5, 8, 9, 16, 19, 20, 21, 22, 26); it is used only once in the rest of *Discorsi,* III (chap. 37), and only seventeen times in *Discorsi,* I and II (I, chaps. 2, 4, 6, 7, 16, 22, 25, 28, 47, 58; II, chaps. 1, 4, 11, 16, 19, 20, 31); seven of these seventeen instances belong to introductory or concluding sections, which, as we showed, do not belong to the general pattern of successive comments on Livy.

40. The rest has a number of chapters which have little or nothing to do with great men; for instance, chaps. 29, 32, 33, 35, 36, 40, 41, 43, 44, 48.

41. This is suggested by Bernardo di Giunta in his letter of dedication, which precedes the *Giunta edition of the Discorsi* (Florence, 1531); there he says he had heard that Machiavelli intended "di ridurre i lor capi a minor numero."

42. Beginning of chap. 9: "Ei parrà forse ad alcuno, che io sia troppo trascorso dentro nella istoria romana, non avendo fatto alcuna menzione ancora degli ordinatori di quella repubblica" (*Opere,* p. 72).

43. See Walker, II, 28–29.

44. Meinecke in his introduction to Machiavelli, *Der Fürst, Klassiker der Politik,* VIII (Berlin, Reimar Hobbing, 1923), p. 27.

45. *Discorsi,* I, chap. 9 (*Opere,* p. 73).

46. See above, note 9.

47. See the foreword of the Giunta edition, or Filippo de' Nerli, *Commentari de' Fatti Civili occorsi dentro la Città di Firenze* (edition of 1728), p. 138, or Jacopo Nardi, *Historie della Città di Firenze* (Lyon, 1582), p. 177 (in the seventh book).

48. Of course, this has been frequently observed, for instance in Walker, I, 56, without drawing any conclusion from this observation.

49. Nardi, *Historie,* p. 177 v: "Opera certo di nuovo argumento e non più tentata (che io sappi) da alcuna persona," or the foreword of the Giunta edition: Machiavelli "è stato il primo che dell'utilissimo campo historico ci ha insegnato mietere e riporre copiosissimo frutto, e che le attioni pubbliche e civili ha ridotte si fattamente a regola, che ogni tardo ingegnio può facilmente comprendere, come, e in quanti modi si fondino, e ordinino le Città, in che maniera prudentemente si governino, e a quelle s'acquisti, et mantengasi larghissimo imperio."

50. Nerli, *Commentari,* p. 138: "avendo convenuto assai tempo nell'orto de' Rucellai una certa scuola di giovani letterati, e d'elevato ingegno mentrechè visse Cosimo Rucellai, che morì molto giovane, ed era in grande aspettazione di letterato, infra quali praticava continuamente Niccolò Machiavelli (e io ero di Niccolò, e di tutti loro amicissimo, e molto spesso con loro conversavo), si esercitavano costoro assai, mediante le lettere, nelle lezioni dell'istorie, e sopra di esse, ed a loro instanza compose il Machiavello quel suo libro de' discorsi sopra Tito Livio, e anco il libro di que'trattati, e ragionamenti sopra la milizia."

51. Nardi, *Historie,* p. 177 v.

52. I believe this conclusion can be drawn from a reading of the letters written by Machiavelli during these years. See Machiavelli, *Lettere Familiari,* ed. Alvisi.

53. For these dates see Walker, II, 3; and, in general, see Chapter 9 in this volume.

54. It must also be mentioned that in the *Discorsi, The Prince* is mentioned as a completed treatise; see *Discorsi,* II, chap. 1; III, chaps. 19 and 42. In explanation of this fact, Luigi Russo, *Machiavelli* (Bari, Laterza, 1949), p. 39, assumes that Machiavelli put the *Discorsi* aside to work on *The Prince* after he had finished the first book of the *Discorsi;* but as the first book of the *Discorsi* contains references to events which occurred after 1514 (when *The Prince* was completed), such an easy explanation is not possible. Chabod, in his article "Sulla Composizione de 'Il Principe' di Niccolò Machiavelli," *Archivum Romanicum,* 11 (1927), 348, uses the argument that in the summer of 1514 Machiavelli must have had finished *The Prince* because he writes in a letter to Vettori that, having fallen in love again, he has "lasciato dunque i pensieri delle cose grandi e gravi;

non mi diletta più leggere le cose antiche, nè ragionare delle moderne." If this letter is considered as a serious argument for establishing the date of the composition of *The Prince,* it must also be taken as an argument against continuous composition of the *Discorsi* in the period between 1513 and 1519. These passages show that previous writers have been well aware of the difficulty of harmonizing the common opinion that the *Discorsi* were composed in the period from 1513 to 1519 with the facts, even if they did not initiate a thorough re-examination of the whole problem.

55. Letter to Francesco Vettori, December 10, 1513; I use the translation of A. H. Gilbert in Machiavelli, *The Prince and Other Works,* University Classics (Chicago, Packard and Co., 1941).

56. The treatise on the republics, which, as we have suggested, formed the basis of the first eighteen books of the *Discorsi,* might have belonged to the layer of general studies on the problems of government.

57. Most historical treatments of this period of Florentine history discuss this situation; the best treatment seems to me Antonio Anzilotti, *La crisi costituzionale della Repubblica Fiorentina* (Florence, B. Seeber, 1912).

58. Proemio of the first book of the *Discorsi:* "Ho deliberato entrare per una via, la quale, non essendo suta ancora da alcuno trita, se la mi arrecherà fastidio e difficultà, mi potrebbe ancora arrecare premio" (*Opere,* p. 56).

59. See, for instance, the passage quoted by Herbert Butterfield, *The Statecraft of Machiavelli* (London, G. Bell, 1940), p. 36, from Machiavelli's early memorandum on the "Method of dealing with the rebels of the Val di Chiana," and the other quotations on this and the next page.

60. For instance, *Discorsi,* I, chap. 17: "E benchè questo esempio di Roma sia da preporre a qualunque altro esempio, nondimeno voglio a questo proposito addurre innanzi popoli conosciuti ne' nostri tempi" (*Opere,* p. 86).

61. An interesting discussion of Machiavelli's "inductive method" will be found in Butterfield, *Statecraft,* particularly in the section on "The rise of the inductive method." Butterfield's views are disputed by Walker, I, 92–93. Certainly, Butterfield is right in cautioning against identification of Machiavelli's inductive method with induction in the modern sense of the term; we would hardly consider the facts reported by an ancient historian as empirical data. But if we abstract this difference in Machiavelli's and our own view of what empirical data are, we can say that he tries to arrive from the observation of facts to general rules; this approach seems to me more thoroughly used in the *Discorsi* than in *The Prince.*

62. See above, note 49.

63. Perhaps Machiavelli's relation to sixteenth-century commentaries on classical authors would deserve closer study and clearer definition.

64. See Chapter 4 in this volume.

65. See Leonardo Olschki, *Geschichte der neusprachlichen wissenschaftlichen Literatur Italiens,* II (Heidelberg, C. Winter, 1922), pp. 313–314; also F. Chabod's article on Machiavelli in the *Enciclopedia Italiana.*

66. See note 65 and particularly Toffanin, *Machiavelli e il Tacitismo* (Padua, A. Draghi, 1921).

67. This, of course, is a paraphrase of the famous sentence in the 15th chapter of *The Prince.*

6. Machiavelli's *Istorie Fiorentine:*
An Essay in Interpretation

1. See the Nota Introduttiva by Franco Gaeta to Niccolò Machiavelli, *Istorie Fiorentine, Opere,* VII (Milan, Feltrinelli, 1962), pp. 53–54.

2. See Luigi Russo, *Machiavelli* (Bari, Laterza, 1949), p. 59.

3. Roberto Ridolfi, *Vita di Niccolò Machiavelli* (Rome, A. Belardetti, 1954), p. 295.

4. See Eduard Fueter, *Geschichte der neueren Historiographie* (Munich and Berlin, R. Oldenbourg, 1925), pp. 67ff.

5. Luigi Malagoli, *Il Machiavelli e la Civiltà del Rinascimento* (Milan, Istituto per gli studi di politica internazionale, 1941), pp. 175ff.

6. J. H. Whitfield, *Machiavelli* (Oxford, B. Blackwell, 1947), pp. 159ff.

7. Gennaro Sasso, *Niccolò Machiavelli, Storia del suo pensiero politico* (Naples, Instituto Italiano per gli studi storici, 1958), pp. 494–496.

8. Published in Pasquale Villari, *Niccolò Machiavelli e i suoi tempi,* III (Florence, 1882), p. 121.

9. For example, Bartolommeo Fazio was employed by King Alfonso to write Alfonso's history and Giorgio Merula by Lodovico Moro; I am preparing a more detailed study on the subject of the public historiographer in the Renaissance.

10. For details see my article "Biondo, Sabellico and the Beginnings of Venetian Official Historiography" in *Florilegium Historiale: Essays Presented to Wallace K. Ferguson* (Toronto, University of Toronto Press, 1970), pp. 276–293.

11. "A scriver la historia dele cose nostre seguite da poi el fin dele Deche Sabellico," from the decree of Navagero's appointment published in *Nuovo Archivio Veneto,* n.s., 9 (1905), 332.

12. In the *proemio* of the *Istorie Fiorentine.* I shall use the Gaeta-Bertelli edition (Milan, Feltrinelli) throughout for Machiavelli's writings.

13. On this question see my article cited in note 10.

14. See Donald J. Wilcox, *The Development of Florentine Humanist Historiography in the Fifteenth Century* (Cambridge, Mass., Harvard University Press, 1969), p. 3. The lack of an official commission does not exclude the granting of advantages in gratitude for such work, although there is no proof of this either.

15. From ibid., p. 22.

16. Ibid., p. 204. Wilcox's book, although it may value this form of historiography somewhat too highly, is now the most complete discussion of humanist historiography. For a brief summary of its ideas see my *Machiavelli and Guicciardini* (Princeton, Princeton University Press, 1965), pp. 203–226.

17. See above, note 11, for the place of publication of the decree; the emphasis on selected events and on form of presentation is characteristic.

18. The phrase "vostro modello di storia" comes from a letter of Zanobi Buondelmonti to Machiavelli, September 6, 1520 (printed in Niccolò Machiavelli, *Lettere,* in *Opere,* VI, 394–395); the letter discusses Machiavelli's *Life of Castruccio,* which he had sent in manuscript form to his friends. Their criticisms are particularly concerned with style and form ("parole," "lingua," "horatione"). The result of their criticism is that: "Pare a tutti che voi vi dobbiate mettere con ogni diligentia a scrivere questa hystoria" (that is, *Florentine History*). It might be asked whether a biography can serve as model for the history of a city-state. But the remarks of Buondelmonti are so definite and the rhetorical character of Machiavelli's *Life of Castruccio* so obvious that it cannot be doubted that this is a trial run for the *Istorie Fiorentine.* This is also the opinion of most scholars. See, for instance, Ridolfi, *Machiavelli,* p. 272, and Franco Gaeta's introduction to the *Vita di Castruccio* in *Opere,* VII, 3–4. The one exception is J. H. Whitfield, "Machiavelli and Castruccio," *Italian Studies,* 8 (1953), 1–28; but Whitfield's interpretation seems to me not in consonance with the text he is interpreting.

19. A striking example is the quick transition from the dictatorship of the Duke of Athens in book II to the Revolt of the Ciompi in book III and then from there to the Rise of the Medici in book IV.

20. *Istorie Fiorentine,* I, chap. 8.

21. *Istorie Fiorentine,* VI, chap. 7.

22. *Istorie Fiorentine,* V, chap. 35.

23. Machiavelli stated in the *proemio* that it was an indication of the greatness of Florence that it grew despite inner dissensions; but this is a very artificial attempt to endow history with a glorifying character. About the *proemio,* see below.

24. *The Prince,* chap. 15.

25. *Proemio* of *Istorie Fiorentine,* p. 69.

26. See Franco Gaeta's introduction to the Feltrinelli edition of the *Istorie Fiorentine* for a brief statement, to which I add a few details.

27. Ridolfi, *Machiavelli,* pp. 264–267, 269–270.

28. Machiavelli, *Lettere,* p. 389.

29. See note 8, above. The documents that contain renewals of Machiavelli's appointment are lost, with the exception of those of 1525 and 1526. See Villari, *Niccolò Machiavelli e i suoi tempi,* III, 122 and Ridolfi, *Opuscoli* (Florence, Bibliopolis, 1942), p. 171.

30. I arrive at this date in the following way. Vettori, in his letter of March 8, 1525 to Machiavelli from Rome, indicated that he had seen the manuscript "insino alla morte di Lorenzo" (*Lettere,* p. 419)—that is, the entire existing version. Vettori had attended the presentation of the *Clizia* in Florence on January 13, 1525 and left Florence for Rome soon afterward (Ridolfi, *Machiavelli,* p. 316). At the beginning of January, Machiavelli was occupied with arranging the production of *Clizia,* so the manuscript of the *Istorie Fiorentine* must have been completed some time earlier. Ridolfi (p. 313) states that *Clizia* was written in great haste for the presentation on January 13 and this would make it likely that the *Istorie Fiorentine* was finished before Machiavelli embarked on *Clizia*—that is, November 1524 might be even more likely than the end of that year.

31. *Lettere,* p. 412, but see also p. 407.

32. See Ridolfi, *Machiavelli,* p. 297.

33. See the letter to Francesco del Nero of September 26, 1523, in which Machiavelli threatened to stop working on the *Istorie Fiorentine* if he did not receive his salary soon; throughout 1524 Machiavelli was entangled in his affair with the Barbera.

34. This results from the letter to Guicciardini of August 30, 1524 (*Lettere,* p. 417) in which Machiavelli alludes to his treatment of the Medici period. But the letter also suggests that a good part of the description of the Medici regime was finished by then ("mostrare dove io sono").

35. See *Lettere,* p. 421, and Ridolfi, *Opuscoli,* p. 171. The document published by Villari, III, 122, demonstrates that these payments were continued up to Machiavelli's death.

36. *Lettere,* p. 444.

37. *Lettere,* p. 444.

38. Such duties were included in the salary he received.

39. There are historical excerpts of years after 1492 among Machiavelli's papers but the handwriting makes it likely that they belong to an earlier period of his life; it has been suggested that Machiavelli already intended to write a historical work during his years in the Chancellery.

40. Published in the second volume of Niccolò Machiavelli, *Istorie Fiorentine, testo critico con introduzione e note,* ed. Plinio Carli (Florence, G. S. Sansoni, 1927).

41. Ridolfi, *Machiavelli,* p. 299: "Ma difficile, e a conti fatti senza molto costrutto, ci riesce oggi fissare cronologicamente i progressi dell'opera."

42. Eugenia Levi, "Due nuovi frammenti degli abbozzi autografi delle Istorie Fiorentine del Machiavelli," *Bibliofilia,* 69 (1967), 309–323.

43. Note that book I has no introductory chapter.

44. This is a brief summary of the results of Dottoressa Levi's article which provides detailed proof for these statements; what now follows is my own view of the matter.

45. The introductory chapters to books II and VI are exclusively connected with the first two chapters or even only the first chapter of these books. Also the introduction to book IV has bearing on the early parts of this book rather than on its bulk. The introductory chapters to books III and V are of such a general character that they have relevance for several books; this is directly stated by Machiavelli who wrote in the introductory chapter to book III: "Le quali cose per la lezione del precedente libro in parte si possono chiaramente cognoscere" (p. 213). Briefly, none of these introductory chapters points directly to the principal content of the following books as the introductory chapters of books VII and VIII do.

46. *Istorie Fiorentine*, p. 137.

47. See above, note 34.

48. "Io non posso scrivere questa Istoria da che Cosimo prese lo stato sino alla morte di Lorenzo come la scriverei se fossi libero da tutti i rispetti . . . E chi vorrà anco intendere questo, noti molto bene quello ch'io farò dire ai suoi avversari, perché quello che non vorrò dire io, come da me, lo farò dire ai suoi avversari." From a letter of Giannotti to Marcantonio Michiel, published in L. A. Ferrai, "Lettere inedite di Donato Giannotti," *Atti del R. Instituto Veneto di Scienze, Lettere ed Arti, Serie 6,* III (1884–1885), 1570. I have no doubts of the general veracity of Giannotti but the report is somewhat too detailed to permit belief that this is an exact reproduction of Machiavelli's words.

49. Strangely enough, it seems hardly ever to have been realized that much of the section regarding the Medici must have been written when Alessandro and Ippolito had not yet appeared in Florence, that is, when there was still a possibility that the Pope would render Florence free. On this issue see also the remarks in Franco Gaeta's introduction to the *Istorie Fiorentine*, p. 55.

50. *Istorie Fiorentine*, pp. 311–312.

51. *Istorie Fiorentine*, pp. 337–339, 482.

52. *Istorie Fiorentine*, pp. 487–488.

53. The contrast "vie publiche" and "modi privati" is described in the introduction to book VII (p. 452); that Cosimo used the reprehensible "modi privati" is frequently emphasized (pp. 308, 311, 313, 315–316, 456–461).

54. "Come le lettere vengono drieto alle armi, e che nelle provincie e nelle città prima i capitani e che i filosofi nascono" (introduction to book V, p. 325); for the Medici patronage of arts and letters see pp. 462 and 575.

55. *Istorie Fiorentine*, p. 211.

56. "Uomo veramente in ogni fortuna onorato" (p. 384).

57. *Istorie Fiorentine*, p. 303.

58. *Istorie Fiorentine*, pp. 323–324.

59. See my *Machiavelli and Guicciardini*, pp. 210 and 212–213; beginning with a survey of the existing situation is more characteristic of historians who describe a single event like Sallust than of historians writing the history of a city-state.

60. *Istorie Fiorentine*, pp. 89–90, 99–101, 117–119, 121–123.

61. *Istorie Fiorentine*, p. 124.

62. *Istorie Fiorentine*, p. 113.

63. *Istorie Fiorentine*, p. 101.

64. *Istorie Fiorentine*, p. 123.

65. *Istorie Fiorentine*, p. 102.

66. "E veramente, se alcuni tempi furono mai miserabili in Italia e in queste provincie corse da' barbari, furono quegli che da Arcadio e Onorio infino a lui erano corsi. *Istorie Fiorentine*, p. 81.

67. *Istorie Fiorentine*, p. 82.

68. "e tutto in terra." *Istorie Fiorentine*, p. 90.

69. *Istorie Fiorentine*, p. 90.

70. I think this can be said although in the time when Machiavelli wrote a foreigner was Pope for a short time.

71. *Istorie Fiorentine,* pp. 90 and 123.

72. *Istorie Fiorentine,* pp. 134–136.

73. The reference is placed into the future. Nevertheless, it refers to the account in a book in which domestic and foreign affairs ought still to have been separated and Machiavelli could know about his violation of this self-set rule only after he had written this book.

74. *Istorie Fiorentine,* p. 102.

75. It would have made no sense to call Rhodes "rimasa unico ostaculo alla potenzia de' Maumettisti" as long as Belgrade was in Christian hands. Belgrade was taken on April 29, 1521, and Suleiman's original intention was to undertake another campaign against Hungary the next summer. It became clear only in June 1522 that he had changed his mind. Then the Ottoman fleet began to assemble at Istanbul. The siege of Rhodes began in earnest at the beginning of August but until November it appeared that Rhodes would be able to resist successfully; the attacks of the Turks were repulsed and their commander, Mustafa Pasha, was even dismissed by the Sultan. The situation in Rhodes became hopeless only in December. The most appropriate time for Machiavelli to make his statement about Rhodes in the seventeenth chapter of the first book would be the late summer of 1522. For the data on the siege of Rhodes I am obliged to my colleague, Professor Kenneth Setton, who permitted me to read a manuscript in which he treats the siege and fall of Rhodes in 1522.

76. It is most regrettable that we have no documentary material about the renewal of Machiavelli's commission.

77. According to Ludwig von Pastor, *History of the Popes,* IX (St. Louis, Mo., B. Herder, 1950), pp. 184–185.

78. I say "easiest explanation" because other explanations are possible and the question of the dedication of the various books of the *Istorie Fiorentine* cannot be used in an indisputable manner. See Plinio Carli's introduction to his edition of the *Istorie Fiorentine,* I, p. lxi. Nevertheless, the uniformity of the dedications in the first five books is striking. It does not exist in the following books.

79. See the beginning of this essay.

80. *Istorie Fiorentine,* p. 325.

81. *Istorie Fiorentine,* p. 325.

82. Frank E. Manuel, *Shapes of Philosophical History* (Stanford, Stanford University Press, 1965), chap. 3.

83. Chapter 2 of the first book of the *Discorsi,* which follows Polybius, contains the most extensive discussion of the cyclical theory in Machiavelli's works. See also particularly the introduction to book V of the *Istorie Fiorentine.*

84. Explicitly stated in the dedication of *The Prince.*

85. *Istorie Fiorentine,* p. 180.

86. *Istorie Fiorentine,* p. 90.

87. *Istorie Fiorentine,* p. 485.

88. From Machiavelli's famous epigram on the death of Piero Soderini.

89. *Istorie Fiorentine,* pp. 455–456.

90. *Istorie Fiorentine,* p. 65.

91. *Istorie Fiorentine,* p. 81; see also above, note 66.

92. Last line of Machiavelli's *Primo Decennale.*

93. For this and the following see Ridolfi, *Machiavelli,* p. 319.

94. *Lettere,* p. 465.

95. The notions of "to redeem," "redemption," and "*redentore*" permeate the entire last chapter of *The Prince.*

96. See my *Machiavelli and Guicciardini;* but for the role of human psychology in humanist history see also Wilcox, *Development.*

97. Professor Marchand's article, in which he published two new fragments of Machiavelli's *Istorie Fiorentine* (*Bibliofilia,* 71 [1969]), appeared after my manuscript was completed. It does not, however, change my interpretation.

7. Machiavellism

Machiavelli's principal works—*The Prince,* the *Discorsi,* and the *Istorie Fiorentine*—were first printed in Rome in 1531, but before they were printed they circulated in manuscript copies, and throughout the sixteenth century handwritten copies remained as important for the spread of Machiavelli's ideas as printed editions. See Adolf Gerber, *Niccolò Machiavelli: Die Handschriften, Ausgaben und Übersetzungen seiner Werke im 16. und 17. Jahrhundert* (1913; Turin, Bottega d'Erasmo, 1962). Since the appearance of Gerber's book in 1913, additional handwritten copies of *The Prince* and the *Discorsi* have been discovered.

The classic work on the history of Machiavellism is Friedrich Meinecke, *Die Idee der Staatsräson* (Munich, Oldenbourg, 1924), translated by D. Scott as *Machiavellism* (New Haven, Yale University Press, 1957). The older work of Charles Benoist, *Le Machiavelisme,* 3 vols. (Paris, Plon, 1907–36) has now become obsolete, although its references to source materials remain valuable. Of a somewhat different character is the book by Giuliano Procacci, *Studi sulla Fortuna del Machiavelli* (Rome, Istituto Storico Italiano per l'Età Moderna e Contemporanea, 1965), which investigates the developments of Machiavelli scholarship rather than the history of the influence of Machiavelli's ideas.

On intellectual developments in the Middle Ages foreshadowing Machiavellism and the doctrine of reason of state see Gaines Post, *Studies in Medieval Legal Thought* (Princeton, Princeton University Press, 1964).

For developments from the later Middle Ages to the seventeenth century see Rodolfo de Mattei, *Dal premachiavellismo all'antimachiavellismo,* Biblioteca Storica Sansoni, n.s., XLVI (Florence, Sansoni, 1969), and the periodical *Il Pensiero Politico,* 1, no. 3 (Florence, 1969), an issue devoted to Machiavellism and anti-Machiavellism in the sixteenth century.

For eighteenth-century attitudes on Machiavelli and Machiavellism see Peter Gay, *The Enlightenment: An Interpretation,* I (New York, Knopf, 1966), and Chapter 13 in this volume.

For reason of state and for the change in views on Machiavelli in the nineteenth century see the article by Albert Elkan, "Die Entdeckung Machiavellis in Deutschland zu Beginn des 19. Jahrhunderts," *Historische Zeitschrift,* 119 (Munich and Berlin, 1919), 427–458. For more recent examples of the application of reason of state see Alfred Vagts, "Intelligentsia Versus Reason of State," *Political Science Quarterly,* 84 (1969), 80–105.

There are a number of studies on the influence of Machiavelli and Machiavellism in individual states. For Venice see William J. Bouwsma, *Venice and the Defense of Republican Liberty* (Berkeley, University of California Press, 1968). For France see the survey by Albert Cherel, *La pensée de Machiavel en France* (Paris, L'Artisan du livre, 1935); and, for the crucial second half of the sixteenth century, Vittorio de Caprariis, *Propaganda e pensiero politico in Francia durante le guerre di religione,* I, *1559–1572* (Naples, Edizioni scientifiche italiane, 1959) and Donald R. Kelley, *Foundations of Modern Historical Scholarship: Language, Law, and History in the French Renaissance* (New York, Columbia University Press, 1970). For England see Felix Raab, *The English Face Of Machiavelli* (London, Routledge and Kegan Paul, 1964).

For detailed investigations of Machiavelli's influence on individual writers see

George L. Mosse, *The Holy Pretence* (Oxford, B. Blackwell, 1957); Herbert Butterfield, *The Statecraft of Machiavelli* (London, G. Bell, 1940); and J. G. A. Pocock, "Machiavelli, Harrington, and the English Political Ideologies in the Eighteenth Century," *William and Mary Quarterly,* 3d ser., 22 (1965), 549–583.

For a recent bibliography see Richard C. Clark, "Machiavelli: Bibliographical Spectrum," *Review of National Literatures,* 1 (1970), 93–135.

8. The Venetian Constitution in Florentine Political Thought

1. The quotations from Burckhardt can be found in Part I, "The State as a Work of Art," in his *Civilization of the Renaissance in Italy.*

2. A previous study devoted to a part of this subject is Renzo Pecchioli, "Il 'mito' di Venezia e la crisi fiorentina intorno al 1500," *Studi Storici,* 3 (1962), 451–492. See also Gaeta's review of Pecchioli's article in *Bollettino dell'Istituto di Storia della Società e dello Stato Veneziano,* 4 (1962), 387–393.

3. See Hans Conrad Peyer, *Stadt und Stadtpatron im mittelalterlichen Italien* (Zürich, Europa Verlag, 1955).

4. On the "myth" of Venice see Gina Fasoli, "Nascita di un mito," *Studi storici in onore di Gioacchino Volpe* (Florence, Sansoni, 1958), I, 455–479, and Franco Gaeta, "Alcune considerazioni sul mito di Venezia," *Bibliothèque d'Humanisme et Renaissance,* 23 (1961), 38–75, with a detailed bibliography.

5. "de veoir tant de clochiers et de monasteres, et si grant maisonnement, et tout en l'eaue." *Mémoires,* book VII, chap. 18.

6. In general see Antonio Medin, *La Storia della Repubblica di Venezia nella Poesia* (Milan, Hoepli, 1904), and, for examples, see V. Rossi, "Jacopo d'Albizotto Guidi e il suo inedito poema su Venezia," *Nuovo Archivio Veneto,* 5 (1893), 397–451, and Sabellico, De Venetae urbis situ, in *Opera,* II (Basle, 1560), pp. 251–278, or the rather typical, but also rather envious description in Giovanni Ridolfi's report about his travels to Venice and Milan in 1480, Biblioteca Nazionale, Florence, Magl. II, IV, 195, fols. 209ff.

7. "Et illa hystoria est picta in aula civitatis Venetiarum. Ed est etiam picta in aula civitatis Senatorum." Bernardo Bembo, Commonplace Book, British Museum, Add. MSS. 41,068A, fol. 44; Bernardo Bembo's commonplace book is chiefly a collection of excerpts from other writers.

8. "Omnes principes Italiae sunt tiranni Duce Venetiarum excepto. Qui habent regimen temperatum. Verbi sunt Sancti Thome." Ibid., fol. 45. The relevant passage is to be found in *De regimine principum,* IV, chap. 8, that is, in the part written by Ptolemy of Lucca.

9. Petrarch, *Lettere senili,* book IV, no. 3: "urbs auri dives sed ditior fama, potens opibus sed virtute potentior, solidis fundata marmoribus sed solidiore etiam fundamento civilis concordie stabilita, salsis cincta fluctibus sed salsioribus tuta consiliis."

10. For a general statement of Venetian civic spirit by a Venetian patrician see Bernardo Giustiniani's funeral speech for Francesco Foscari in *Orazioni, Elogi e Vite . . . in lode di Dogi,* ed. G. A. Molina, I (Venice, 1795), pp. 21–67.

11. See G. B. Picotti, "Le Lettere di Lodovico Foscarini," *L'Ateneo Veneto,* 32 (1909), 21–49, esp. 43, and M. Foscarini, *Della Letteratura Veneziana* (Venice, 1854), pp. 245–248. These writers used the letters of Lodovico Foscarini, but they did not exhaust the material concerned with the search for a public historiographer in the codex containing Foscarini's correspondence (original in Vienna; a copy in Treviso, Biblioteca Communale, MS. 85).

12. *De republica veneta fragmenta,* ed. E. A. Ciconia (Venice, 1830). A manuscript of

this treatise in Venice, Biblioteca Marciana, no. 4576, Cl. Lat. XIV, cod. CCLV, shows variations, but they do not change the contents. The relevant passage runs: "Venetorum respublica optimatum administratione regitur. Ideoque aristocratiam greco vocabulo licet appellare quae inter regium popularemque principatum media est. Hec vero et tanto est melior quod, quoniam utrique laudabilium extremorum participat, ex omni genere laudabilis recte politice simul commixta est."

13. On Barbaro's relations with George of Trebizond see Percy Gothein, *Francesco Barbaro* (Berlin, Die Runde, 1932), pp. 147–151; Deno John Geneakopolos, *Greek Scholars in Venice* (Cambridge, Mass., Harvard University Press, 1962), esp. pp. 30–31; and Giorgio Castellani, "Giorgio da Trebisonda, maestro di eloquenza a Vicenza e a Vinegia," *Nuovo Archivio Veneto,* 11 (1896), 123–142. The following is based on Castellani's article, although I give fuller quotations from the correspondence between Barbaro and Trebizond.

14. "Leges quoque Platonis, ex quibus aperte intellexi, Majores vestros, qui Reipublicae vestrae fundamenta jecerunt, ex his certe libris omnia, quibus Respublica diu felix esse possit, collegisse. Non est enim credibile, casu ita omnia confluxisse, ut ad unguem praeceptis illius conveniant. Nullam, inquit ipse, beatam diu fore Rempublicam, nisi quae ita constituta sit, ut omnibus regendarum civitatum modis, Principis dico unius, Optimatum, Populique potestate gubernetur: quod nulli umquam sic exacte accidisse, quam vobis, perspicuum est." George of Trebizond to Barbaro, December 5, 1451, in *Francisci Barbari et aliorum ad ipsum Epistolae,* ed. M. A. Quirini (Brescia, 1743), no. 198, p. 290.

15. Barbaro to Trebizond, March 7, 1452, ibid., no. 199, pp. 292–295. Sections of this letter were published by Bessarion in his *In calumniatorem Platonis* (Aldus edition, 1516), fol. 87v. Bessarion wanted to demonstrate the unreliability of George of Trebizond who was now attacking Plato but, as Barbaro's letter showed, had once admired him. Bessarion was also incensed about George of Trebizond changing the dedication of his translation of Plato's *Laws,* but for this Barbaro's death seems a sufficient explanation.

16. The preface, which only elaborates the ideas expressed in the letter to Barbaro, is preserved in Vatican Codex Lat. 5220 but has never been published; for some quotations from the preface see M. A. Quirini, *Diatriba praeliminaris* (Brescia, 1741), p. 127.

17. "Legi Praefationem tuam in leges Platonis . . . opera tua feceris, ut sicut Athenienses Solone, Lacedaemonici Lycurgo, ita nos Veneti Platone, legum nostrarum conditore, gloriari possimus." Barbaro to Trebizond, January 13, 1452, *Epistolae,* no. 206, p. 300; a similar observation can be found in Barbaro's letter of March 7, 1452.

18. "quando presertim eiusmodi remuneratio talis esse potest que civitati nostre atque ipsi Georgio honori pariter usuique futura sit." Quoted by Castellani, "Giorgio da Trebisonda," p. 141.

19. George of Trebizond also stated this thesis in his *Comparationes Philosophorum Aristotelis et Platonis,* in a chapter of the second book entitled "Quod divinitus illud Platoni dictum est, optimam rem publicam non esse simplicem, quodque id solis Venetis contigit."

20. Plato, *Laws,* book III.

21. Aristotle, *Politics,* book II, chap. 3.

22. Aristotle, *Politics,* book IV, chaps. 9 and 10.

23. Aristotle, *Politics,* book IV, chap. 6.

24. Cicero's *De re publica,* with its emphasis on mixed constitution, was not known before the nineteenth century. The humanists were not concerned with the finer shadings of the classical views on constitutions, so that a modern interpretation of the classical theory—like that by Kurt von Fritz, *The Theory of the Mixed Constitution in Antiquity* (New York, Columbia University Press, 1954)—has little relevance to the ideas of the fifteenth century.

25. "apud Venetos, quorum Res Publica justitia, imperio, opulentia, et civium splendore, non modo in omni Italia, verum in universo quoque terrarum orbe praeclarissima habetur." *De Institutione Reipublicae Libri IX* (Strasburg, 1608), p. 71.

26. Ibid., pp. 24–25.

27. Poggio's laudation of Venice can be found in Poggius Bracciolini, *Opera omnia,* ed. Riccardo Fubini, II (Turin, Bottega d'Erasmo, 1966), pp. 919–937; see p. 925: "et aristocratiam, quam nostri optimatum appellant, et eam Cicero in libris de legibus optimam esse ait . . . Talem profecto nunquam nisi apud Venetos fuisse verissime affirmarim, apud quos soli optimates civitatem regunt, obtemperantes legibus intentique omnes ad publici status utilitatem, omni rei privatae cura post habita." Poggio's treatise is one of the best humanist summaries of all the elements of the Venetian myth—situation, government structure, public spirit; it describes as characteristic of an aristocracy that common good is placed above private interest and that the people are well treated but excluded from government. For a short account of the content of Poggio's piece see Ernst Walser, *Poggius Florentinus Leben und Werke* (Leipzig and Berlin, Teubner, 1914), pp. 291–292. Walser explains Poggio's reasons for writing this work and directs attention to the fact that a praise of Venice composed by Poggio's son Gianfrancesco (Biblioteca Marciana, no. 4370, Cl. Lat. XI, Cod. CXXXVIII) uses extensively his father's manuscript.

28. "Haec est Aristocratia illa, quam divinus Plato numquam statis laudatam credidit . . . his namque auspiciis Venetum imperium, quod late hodie terra marique patet, non solum est auctum, sed perpetua etiam ordinum concordia nullos saevientis fortunae reformidat impetus." *De Venetis magistratibus,* in *Opera,* II (Basle, 1560), p. 279.

29. *De aristocratia,* Biblioteca Marciana, no. 2753, Cl. Lat. VI, cod. VI. On Francesco Negri see Giovanni Mercati, *Ultimi contributi alla storia degli umanisti* (Vatican City, Biblioteca apostolica vaticana, 1939), pp. 24–109 and the appendix, esp. 40–58. On the basis of a version of Negri's manuscript in the Vatican Library, Cardinal Mercati showed that a connection existed between Negri's treatise and the book of the Count of Porcia, *De reipublicae venetae administratione* (Treviso, 1477), and suggests that Negri elaborated Porcia's book. It is true that the organization of the two works is very similar and some connection may have existed, but this relationship does not seem to me very significant. Porcia's book is poor and empty; Negri's manuscript, even if not very penetrating or profound, is full of substance.

30. *Negri, De aristocratia,* fol. iiv: "tertiam aristocraticam appellaverunt quam nos quidem optimam merito partem vocamus: optimam inquam: et quae optimo principe digna est et quae non minus optimam urbem optimam plebem optimumque reddit imperium," and Negri continues that this form of government exists only in Venice.

31. See Walser, *Poggius Florentinus,* pp. 290–291.

32. This episode of Florentine history has been treated in Guido Pampaloni, "Fermenti di riforme democratiche nella Firenze medicea del Quattrocento." *Archivio Storico Italiano,* 119 (1961), 11–62, who suggests that the plan was to create a Great Council. See also Nicolai Rubinstein, *The Government of Florence under the Medici (1434 to 1494)* (Oxford, Clarendon Press, 1966), pp. 146–147. The relevant source material has been published by Pampaloni, "Fermenti," pp. 240–281, and *Archivio Storico Italiano,* 120 (1962), 521–581.

33. *Archivio Storico Italiano,* 119, p. 246: "Civitates enim aut unus gubernat, aut pauci aut multitudo; et que ab uno aut paucis gubernantur non habere firmitudinem, sed cum a populo gubernantur, quia amore et benevolentia gubernantur."

34. Ibid., p. 261: 'Quod autem affertur novum eiusmodi est ut afferri videatur statum optimatium et imitationem quandam rei p. Venetorum. Cum autem videam, inquit, hanc rem p. nostram florentissimam esse factam populari administratione"; see also pp. 261–262, the speeches of Giovanni Pitti and Domenico Martilli. Because the expres-

sions "aristocrats" and "democrats" are rather vague, they seem appropriate English terms for characterizing the opposing Florentine groups. Aristocrats are in favor of a small strictly limited ruling group of wealthy and old families, democrats aim at a broadening of this ruling group; of course, nobody thought of including workers or men who were in an entirely dependent position.

35. *Cronica,* book XI, chap. 90.

36. See Hans Baron, *The Crisis of the Early Italian Renaissance,* rev. ed. (Princeton, Princeton University Press, 1966), p. 401.

37. "Similitudinem gubernandi publice et privatim vivendi et negotiandi." From an oration at the reception of a Venetian embassy, March 17, 1472, Archivio di Stato, Florence, Signori, Legazioni e Commissarie, Risposte Verbali d'Oratori, 2, fol. 42v. But see also ibid., fol. 45v, where, on the occasion of the reception of another Venetian embassy in 1474, exactly the same thought is expressed. The repetitive use of all such formulas weakens the thesis of the importance of republican ideology in the actual conduct of foreign policy as advanced by Baron, *Crisis,* pp. 387–403.

38. Gothein, *Francesco Barbaro,* pp. 100–104.

39. See Paul Oskar Kristeller, *Supplementum Ficinianum,* II (Florence, Olschki, 1937), p. 346.

40. For instance, see the report of the Florentine ambassadors Giovanbattista Ridolfi and Paolantonio Soderini from Venice, August 12, 1491, Archivio di Stato, Florence, Mediceo Avanti il Principato, filza XIX, fol. 619.

41. "Cum essem Florentiae proxima Quaresima, convenit me civis quidam mei studiosus ac nationi Venetae valde affectus. Is . . . policitus est mihi orationem quamdam Poggii in laudem Venetarum olim editam . . . Mitto itaque illam ad te, ut intelligas, quanti fecerit homo Florentinus rempublicam nostram. Et profecto idem fere universa Florentia de nostris sentit, cuius rei sum optimus testis." Pietro Delfino to Bernardino Monaco, April 27, 1487, in Martène et Durand, *Veterum Scriptorum et monumentorum . . . amplissima collectio,* III (Paris, 1724), p. 1146. On Delfino see Josef Schnitzer, *Peter Delfin, General des Camaldulenserordens, 1444–1525* (Munich, Reinhardt, 1926).

42. See Maria Pisani, *Un avventuriero del Quattrocento. La vita e le opere di Benedetto Dei* (Naples, Biblioteca della Rassegna, 1923), esp. pp. 102–104.

43. "Veneti appellantur Romani novelli." Bembo, Commonplace Book, fol. 44. See also B. Accolti, *De praestantia virorum sui aevi,* in Philippi Villani *Liber de civitatis Florentiae famosis civibus,* ed. G. C. Galletti (Florence, 1847), p. 119.

44. For instance, by Patrizi, *De institutione Reipublicae,* p. 116.

45. For instance, see Poggio, *Opera omnia,* II, 934.

46. See above, note 28.

47. *De rebus ac forma reipublicae venetae Gregorio Heymburg, Germanorum doctori praeclarissimo,* published in Valentinelli, *Biblioteca Manuscripta ad S. Marci Venetiarum,* III (Venice, 1868–73), pp. 231–264.

48. For these events see Nicolai Rubinstein, "Politics and Constitution in Florence at the End of the Fifteenth Century," *Italian Renaissance Studies,* ed. E. F. Jacob (London, Faber and Faber, 1960), pp. 148–83.

49. On Savonarola's politics see the two articles by Donald Weinstein, "Savonarola, Florence, and the Millenarian Tradition," *Church History,* 27 (1958), 3–17, and "Millenarianism in a Civic Setting: The Savonarola Movement in Florence," *Millenial Dreams in Action: Essays in Comparative Studies,* ed. Sylvia L. Thrupp (The Hague, Mouton, 1962), pp. 187–203.

50. The crucial sermon is the one of December 14, 1494, published in Savonarola, *Prediche Italiane ai Fiorentini,* ed. F. Cognasso, I (Perugia and Venice, La Nuova Italia, 1930), pp. 181–197.

51. Particularly in the sermon of December 16, ibid., pp. 215–226.

52. Ibid., esp. pp. 228–231.

53. Sermon of December 15, ibid., esp. p. 210.

54. The decisive recommendation of the Venetián government was made by Savonarola in his sermon of December 14, ibid., p. 195, but see also the sermon of December 21, ibid., esp. p. 293: "La reforma de' Veneziani sarebbe el vostro bisogno . . . e la esperienza lo demostra che non essendo però loro migliori degli altri non s'è udito nella città loro in tanto tempo che hanno retto le dissensioni e rivoluzioni che sono state qui in te, ne' tempi passati. Però ti bisogna, Firenze, levare via questo tuo modo vecchio . . . la volontà di Dio è che tu non ti regga più come tu hai fatto insino a quei ne'tempi passati."

55. Ibid., p. 195: "E così ancora credo sia bene per dare animo a ciascuno di portarsi virtuosamente, che gli artefici fussino in qualche modo beneficiati ed allettati a portarsi bene, per essere onorati."

56. "Il Consiglio grande è la tua salute; se tu tieni saldo el consiglio, non avete paura di uomo del mondo." Sermon of October 18, 1495, Savonarola, *Prediche,* II, 426, but see also the sermons of February 19, February 21, and March 9, 1496, ibid., III, part 1, pp. 76, 133; part 2, p. 478.

57. Sermon of October 11, 1495, ibid., II, 408.

58. "il reggimento tuo naturale è vivere populare." Sermon of February 24, 1496, ibid., III, part 1, p. 186.

59. See the sermon of October 18, 1495, ibid., II, 427.

60. "li predicatori susciteranno l'altre città e diranno a' popoli: andate a Firenze, andate a lei, che ell' ha el vero lume; pigliate da lei la forma del governo." Sermon of March 19, 1496, ibid., III, part 2, p. 196, but see also the sermons of April 4 and 10, 1496, ibid., pp. 486 and 580.

61. The developments discussed in this section are described at greater length and with documentary illustration in my book, *Machiavelli and Guicciardini: Politics and History in Sixteenth-Century Florence* (Princeton, Princeton University Press, 1965), pp. 49–78.

62. See Chapter 9 in this volume.

63. This characterization of the Venetian system of government comes from Rucellai's *De Bello Italico* (London, 1733), pp. 17–18: "Ea enim res Veneta est situ ipso urbis, ac legibus munita; ut admixta, particepsque earum artium, quae ad regnum, optimates, ceteramque bene institutam rempublicam pertinent; et ab intestina, externaque vi maxime tuta sit; et diurnitate imperii immota crescat ceterarum ruinis: quippe quae octingentos jam annos amplius senatori ordine, haud admissa plebe, unis moribus, neque fere mutatis legibus vivit."

64. The political literature of this period has been carefully treated by Rudolf von Albertini, *Das florentinische Staatsbewusstsein im Uebergang von der Republik zum Prinzipat* (Berne, Francke, 1955); see also the third chapter of my book on *Machiavelli and Guicciardini.* Notes will be limited to indicating the provenance of passages particularly relevant to our problem.

65. "[il governo viniziano] è el più bello ed el migliore governo non solo de' tempi nostri, ma ancora che forse avessi mai a' tempi antichi alcuna città, perché participa di tutte le spezie de'governi, di uno, di pochi e di molti." Francesco Guicciardini, *Dialogo e Discorsi del Reggimento di Firenze,* ed. R. Palmarocchi (Bari, Laterza, 1932), p. 138; this passage comes from the *Dialogo del Reggimento di Firenze.*

66. *Archivio Storico Italiano,* 1 (1842), 430.

67. Guicciardini, *Dialogo,* pp. 131, 147.

68. "se noi chiamassimo gentiluomini e' nostri, e questo nome appresso a noi non si dessi se non a chi è abile agli uffici, troveresti che el governo di Vinegia è populare

come el nostro e che el nostro non è manco governo di ottimati che sia el loro. Pagolantonio è stato due volte imbasciadore a Vinegia, e credo dirá el medesimo che dico io." Ibid., pp. 106–107.

69. For example, see previous note.

70. See Federico Chabod, *Machiavelli and the Renaissance* (London, Bowes and Bowes, 1958), pp. 81–82.

71. *Discorsi,* I, chap. 34; *Istorie fiorentine,* book I, chap. 28.

72. *Discorsi,* I, chap. 34.

73. *Discorsi,* I, chap. 49.

74. *Discorsi,* I, chap. 50.

75. See, for instance, *Discorsi,* I, chap. 36, Machiavelli's criticism of the Venetian prohibition against holding lower offices after having held offices of higher rank.

76. *Discorsi,* I, chap. 5.

77. *Istorie fiorentine,* book I, chap. 29.

78. *Discorsi,* III, chap. 31.

79. *Discorsi,* II, chap. 10.

80. *Discorsi,* I, chap. 6.

81. I mean the *Discursus florentinarum rerum post mortem junioris Laurentii Medices;* for the separation of the concept of mixed government from the idea of Venice in Machiavelli's thought see also Giorgio Cadoni, "Libertà, repubblica e governo misto in Machiavelli," *Rivista Internazionale di Filosofia del Diritto,* 39 (1962), 462–484.

82. On Giannotti see Roberto Ridolfi, "Sommario della vita di Donato Giannotti," in *Opuscoli* (Florence, Bibliopolis, 1942), pp. 55–164, and for some important additions to the factual account of Giannotti's life, Randolph Starn, "Additions to the Correspondence of Donato Giannotti: A List and Sampling of Fifty-Four Unpublished Letters," *Rinascimento,* 15 (1964), 101–122; Starn's article contains a bibliography. For an analysis of Giannotti's thought see Albertini, *Das florentinische Staatsbewusstsein,* pp. 108–166; p. 148, n. 3, gives a succinct, though somewhat oversimplified, statement on the role of Venice in Florentine sixteenth-century thought. For the factual course of events see Cecil Roth, *The Last Florentine Republic* (London, Methuen, 1925). I use the edition of Donato Giannotti, *Opere,* ed. G. Rosini (Pisa, 1819).

83. Ridolfi, "Sommario," p. 84; the source is *Lettere di Busini a Varchi,* ed. Milanesi (Florence, 1861), p. 30.

84. For a justification of the statements made in the text see my article "The Date of the Composition of Contarini's and Giannotti's Books on Venice," *Studies in the Renaissance,* 14 (1967), 172–184.

85. On this circle in Padua see V. Cian, *Un Decennio della vita di M. Pietro Bembo* (Turin, 1885).

86. See Albertini, *Das florentinische Staatsbewusstsein,* pp. 79–83.

87. Vergerio's treatise is a praise of the doge as example of a perfect prince, but the statement at the end of the book might have had some influence on Giannotti's plans: "Alterum librum excudet paulopost, in quo de legibus Venetis et Magistratibus copiosa disputatio futura est."

88. Giannotti, *Della Repubblica de' Veneziani,* p. 19.

89. Ibid., p. 76: "cose degne d'essere intese e considerate."

90. Ibid., p. 53. A valuable discussion of Giannotti's sources can be found in Giuseppe Sanesi, *La Vita e le Opere di Donato Giannotti* (Pistoia, 1899), pp. 91–102. Michiel was the possessor of a manuscript of the Dandalo chronicle, which he annotated on the basis of documentary material. (It is the *Cronica Andreae Dandoli Ducis,* Venice, Biblioteca Marciana, no. 3746, Cl. Lat. X, cod. CXXXX, and Michiel's annotations are published in the Muratori edition of Dandolo.)

91. Giannotti, *Della Repubblica de' Veneziani,* p. 21: "come l'uno sia collegato con l'altro, che dependenza abbia questo da quello."

92. Ibid., pp. 48–51.

93. Aristotle, *Politics,* book IV, chap. 11.

94. Giannotti, *Della Repubblica de' Veneziani,* p. 17.

95. Ibid., pp. 180–214.

96. It is strange that this relationship between Giovanni Borgherini and Niccolò Capponi seems never to have been noticed; it gave particular weight to the recommendation Borgherini wrote to Capponi on behalf of Giannotti in July 1527 (see Ridolfi, "Sommario," p. 82).

97. For Lorenzo Strozzi's political views, the life he wrote of his brother Filippo and Francesco Zeffi's "Vita di Lorenzo Strozzi" are of interest; see *Le Vite degli uomini illustri della Casa Strozzi,* ed. Pietro Stromboli (Florence, 1892). Machiavelli's *Arte della Guerra* was dedicated to Lorenzo Strozzi, and he remained a loyal friend of Giannotti also after 1530, as Giannotti's correspondence shows. On Lorenzo Strozzi's close relationship with the Borgherini see the letter of Ulisse da Fano to Lorenzo Strozzi, June 27, 1519, Archivio di Stato, Florence, Uguccione-Gherardi, CCXX, fol. 162. On Lorenzo Strozzi's close relationship with the branch of the Medici from which Lorenzino came see Strozzi's letter to Lorenzino's father, Pierfrancesco, in L. A. Ferrai, *Lorenzino de' Medici e la società cortigiana del Cinquecento* (Milan, 1891), p. 441. Lorenzo Strozzi was still Lorenzino's *procuratore* in 1531; see Archivio di Stato, Florence, *Archivio Mediceo avanti il Principato, Inventario,* III (Rome, 1957), p. 268 (hereafter cited as *M.a.P.*). Pierfrancesco Borgherini, the older brother of Giovanni Borgherini, was on friendly terms with Giovanni delle Bande Nere; see the letter, *M.a.P.,* filza CXXII, fol. 141.

About the doings of the two Medici boys, Lorenzino and Cosimo, in Venice in 1527, some information can be gained from the letters of Giovanfrancesco Zeffi, who was in charge of them; see *M.a.P.,* filza CXVIII. Giovanfrancesco Zeffi wrote on June 12 and July 7, 1527 two letters to Ruberto Bonsi in Florence describing the structure of the Venetian government; see Archivio di Stato, Florence, Carte Strozziane, seconda serie, XCV, fols. 222–227. They are not lost as Roth, *Last Florentine Republic,* p. 109, n. 41, assumes. Roth also confuses the author of these letters, Giovanfrancesco Zeffi, who was the companion of the two Medici boys, with Francesco Zeffi, the tutor of the children of Lorenzo Strozzi and author of Lorenzo Strozzi's life. In the first letter, Zeffi explains that "trovandomi in questa magnifica città, capo d'una republica la quale per li suoi buoni governi più centinaia di anni è stato non solo immobile ma sempre è in augumento proceduto." He believed that knowledge about Venice might be useful for the "reforma di una vera republica," which was going on in Florence. The description of Venice Zeffi gave is brief and uninteresting, but as an expression of the tendencies of the group to which Zeffi belonged, even if in a subordinate position, the existence of these letters is important. For other Florentines acquainted with Giannotti, and in Venice at the same time, see Michele Lupo Gentile, "Studi sulla storiografia fiorentina alla corte di Cosimo I de' Medici," *Annali della R. Scuola Normale Superiore di Pisa,* 19 (1906), particularly the essay on Segni. The anti-Medicean tendency emerges clearly in the material published by Gentile.

98. His speech congratulating Cardinal Giulio de' Medici in 1521 on restoring liberty to Florence was believed to have been lost, but it is in the Biblioteca Nazionale in Florence and deserves publication. Alessandro de' Pazzi broke with the Florentine republicans when the radicals gained the upper hand in Florence.

99. Giannotti, *Opere,* III, 27–47. For an analysis of this *Discorso sopra il fermare il governo di Firenze,* see Albertini, *Das florentinische Staatsbewusstsein,* pp. 113–115. How-

ever, I cannot agree with Albertini's view that this project was written in 1527; there seems to me no possible doubt that Roth, *Last Florentine Republic,* p. 109, n. 44, is right in placing this project in the year 1528. To the arguments adduced by Roth a strong further argument can be added. Giannotti speaks of "pratica nuovamente ordinata," and the law reorganizing the *practica* was issued on August 18, 1528.

100. In addition to Giannotti's project, there were two projects by Niccolò Guicciardini, published by Albertini, *Das florentinische Staatsbewusstsein,* pp. 377–399, and analyzed by him on pp. 117–121. Furthermore, a memorandum entitled 'Modo di riordinare la città di Firenze ed i suoi magistrati" can be found in Biblioteca Nazionale, Florence, Carte di Machiavelli, Cassetta 6, no. 80, which breaks off without ending. It is certainly not by Machiavelli. It shows strong Venetian influence and is close to, but exhibits differences from, Giannotti's style. In any case, this memorandum advocates a strong executive with fifteen *procuratori* at the top of a pyramid. Another constitutional project can be found in Carte Strozziane, seconda serie, XCV, fols. 82–87, which is more traditional. Its author maintains the Signoria, of which, however, only one-third would change every two months; abolishes the Gonfaloniere; and suggests a senate with life membership. There are also the two letters by Zeffi; see above, note 97. A "Parere" by Ceccotto Tosinghi in Carte Strozziane, seconda serie, XCV, fol. 22, does not seem to me to belong to this period; it might be from 1502 or 1512.

101. "poiche non possiamo ragionare de' fatti nostri, ragioneremo di quelli d'altri." Giannotti to Benedetto Varchi, June 10, 1538, in *Opere,* II, 200.

102. *Storia d'Italia,* book II, chap. 2.

103. "Lo che procede dall' esser questo governo popolare, mentre la plebe, la quale attende alle arti meccaniche, non può saper il modo del vero governo; e però rare repubbliche popolari si vede essere state diuturne." La Relazioni degli Ambasciatori Veneti, ed. E. Albéri, ser. 2, V (Florence, 1858), p. 411.

9. Bernardo Rucellai and the Orti Oricellari:
A Study on the Origin of
Modern Political Thought

1. Francesco Guicciardini, *Storie Fiorentine dal 1378 al 1509,* ed. Roberto Palmarocchi, Scrittori d'Italia (Bari, G. Laterza, 1931), esp. p. 283, a long characterization of Rucellai.

2. Guicciardini, *Storie Fiorentine,* p. 331: Bernardo Rucellai "scrisse una lettera alla signoria in sua giustificazione, repetendo tutti e' processi sua insino da Lorenzo, da Piero e dal frate, pe' quali si mostrava quanto sempre e' fussi stato caldo che la città stessi in libertà ed in quiete."

3. Signori Responsive, Lettere Esterne alla Signoria del 1508 da Gennaio a Dicembre, Archivio di Stato, Florence, fols. 55–56. The letter is mentioned in G. Pellegrini, *L'umanista Bernardo Rucellai e le sue opere storiche* (Leghorn, 1921), p. 20, but he does not reproduce any part of the contents, nor does he identify it with the one mentioned by Guicciardini.

4. "Non mi achade iustificarmi altrimente senon con processi del vivere mio che credo sia assai noto nel tempo che vixe Lorenzo de Medici che sempre mi sforzai che lui usassi bene la grandezza sua e su la morte non manco per me di redurre le cose al bene intanto che incorsi in grave pericolo e mio figliulo Cosimo ne fu facto rebelle e dipoi ne casi del frate fui el primo che persuade largamente la quiete e la pace. Queste cose possono essere note perche in verita sono cosi et se sono bastanti a iustificarmi contro alle suspitioni e alle gelosie che sono al presente me piacera."

5. The significant passages are quoted below, notes 47, 48.

6. For instance, see Luca Landucci, *Diario Fiorentino dal 1450 al 1516,* ed. Iodoco del Badia, (Florence, 1883) or the German translation, in two volumes, by Marie Herzfeld (Jena, E. Diedrichs, 1912–13), which has valuable annotations and an index; or the *Storia Fiorentina di Bartolommeo Cerretani.* I have used the copy preserved in Florence in the Biblioteca Marucelliana A.C.S. 20. Excerpts were published by Joseph Schnitzer, *Quellen und Forschungen zur Geschichte Savonarolas* (Munich, E. Stahl, 1904), III.

7. See Henri Jordan, *Topographie der Stadt Rom in Alterthum,* I (Berlin, 1878), p. 77.

8. Erasmus, *Opera omnia* (Leyden, 1703–06), IV, 363E, *Apophtegmata:* "Novi Venetiae Bernardum Ocricularium, civem Florentinum, cuius historias si legisses, dixisses alterum Sallustium, aut certe Sallustii temporibus scriptas."

9. On his influence on Florentine historiography see below, note 113.

10. For instance, see E. W. Nelson's article, "The Origins of Modern Balance-of-Power Politics," *Medievalia et Humanistica,* I (1943), 129.

11. On the literature on the Orti Oricellari see below, note 59.

12. I may here perhaps refer to my own bibliographical essay "Political Thought of the Rennaissance and Reformation," *Huntington Library Quarterly,* 4 (1941), 445–454.

13. For the following discussion of the shield of the Rucellai see the important article by Aby Warburg, "Francesco Sassettis letztwillige Verfuegung," most easily available in his *Gesammelte Schriften* (Leipzig, Teubner, 1932), I, esp. pp. 146–151, where the shield and the later-mentioned print are reproduced. On the correspondence between Ficino and Giovanni Rucellai see also Ernst Cassirer, *Individuum und Kosmos in der Philosophie der Renaissance* (Leipzig, Teubner, 1927), p. 81. On Giovanni Rucellai see Giuseppe Marcotti, *Un mercante fiorentino e la sua famiglia* (Florence, 1881), and H. P. Horne, "An Account of Rome in 1450," *Revue Archéologique,* 4th ser., X, 82–97.

14. The central importance of the problem is most brilliantly stated by Giovanni Gentile in his article, "Il concetto dell'uomo nel Rinascimento," now printed in his *Opere Complete* (Florence, Sansoni, 1940), XI, 49–113.

15. The only study of Rucellai's career of any value is the one by Pellegrini mentioned above. Pellegrini is exclusively interested in Rucellai as a historian, and more specifically in Rucellai's use of classical models; but in a short purely factual introduction to his study, he gives the highlights of Rucellai's career based on material from the archives. I shall refer to Pellegrini when the facts I mention are given by him, and I shall refer to the archives only when I add material which is not mentioned by Pellegrini or which deviates from him. Two older studies of Rucellai's life are A. M. Bandini, *Specimen Literaturae Florentinae Saeculi XV* (Florence, 1751), II, 76–83, and Luigi Passerini, *Genealogia e Storia della Famiglia Rucellai* (Florence, 1861), pp. 122–130; both are unreliable although they give some interesting references to documentary material.

16. Pellegrini, *L'umanista Bernardo Rucellai,* p. 3, and some further purely personal letters to his father-in-law, Piero, and his brothers-in-law, Lorenzo and Giuliano, in the Archivio di Stato, Florence, *Mediceo avanti il Principato* (hereafter cited as *M.a.P.*), filze 17, carte 422; filze 21, carte 165; filze 5, carte 641.

17. *M.a.P.,* filze 49, carte 90, October 19, 1486. This letter is also quoted by Roberto Palmarocchi, *La Politica Italiana di Lorenzo de' Medici* (Florence, Leo S. Olschki, 1933), p. 223.

18. Alfred von Reumont, *Lorenzo de' Medici il Magnifico* (Leipzig, 1883), II, 256.

19. Martin Wackernagel, *Der Lebensraum des Kuenstlers in der Florentinischen Renaissance* (Leipzig, E. A. Seeman, 1938), pp. 232–243, which describes Giovanni Rucellai's activities as art patron and compares him with Cosimo de' Medici.

20. Arnaldo della Torre, *Storia dell' Accademia Platonica di Firenze* (Florence, G. Carnesecchi e figli, 1902), p. 423.

21. Bartholomaeus Fontius, *Epistolarum Libri Tre,* ed. L. Juhasz (Budapest, Királyi Magyar Egyetemi Nyomda, 1931), book 2, no. 6, Fontius to B. Rucellai, March 1484.

22. Pellegrini, *L'umanista Bernardo Rucellai,* p. 5.

23. Torre, *Stora dell' Accademia Platonica,* p. 732; see also p. 824, Ficino's letter to B. Rucellai, and p. 614, B. Rucellai's negotiations with Ficino to pay the expenses of printing Ficino's Plato translation.

24. B. Rucellai became acquainted with Pontano when he was Florentine ambassador in Naples in 1486; see Pellegrini, *L'umanista Bernardo Rucellai,* p. 8. For Rucellai's letter on his literary discussion with Pontano see below, note 42.

25. Palmarocchi, *La Politica Italiana,* p. 114.

26. Pellegrini, *L'umanista Bernardo Rucellai,* pp. 6–9. On the political situation during these missions see the above quoted book by Roberto Palmarocchi and Palmarocchi's more recent biography, *Lorenzo de' Medici* (Turin, 1941).

27. Angelo Fabroni, *Laurentii Medices Magnifici Vita* (Pisa, 1784), II, 377–379, quotes Piero's letter to his father, May 10, 1490: "Di qui vi fu el conte dalla Mirandola, Messer Marsilio, M. Agnolo da Montepulciano, e per torre un cittadino, et non uscire di parente e letterato, togliemmo Bernardo Rucellai, che non so se habbiamo facto bene o male."

28. Guicciardini, *Storie Fiorentine,* p. 284; also further details on p. 329 of the manuscript of Cerretani's *Storia* in the Biblioteca Marucelliana.

29. See above, note 4.

30. Guicciardini, *Storie Fiorentine,* pp. 84–85, 90; these events are mentioned by most contemporary historians.

31. Pellegrini, *L'umanista Bernardo Rucellai,* pp. 13ff.

32. Guicciardini, *Storie Fiorentine,* p. 114, and Landucci, *Diario,* pp. 102, 107.

33. Guicciardini, *Storie Fiorentine,* pp. 133, 155.

34. Guicciardini, *Storie Fiorentine,* p. 167.

35. On the general policy of the Florentine aristocrats the best study is A. Anzilotti, *La Crisi Costituzionale della Repubblica Fiorentina* (Florence, B. Seeber, 1912), where, on p. 4, Rucellai is characterized as a typical representative of the aristocrats. The dissertation by H. Reinhard, "Lorenzo von Medic, Herzog von Urbino," Freiburg, 1935, gives a remarkably penetrating analysis of the Florentine political struggles in this time, especially pp. 17–18.

36. Guicciardini, *Storie Fiorentine,* pp. 206–209, 239–250; also Piero Parenti, quoted by M. Herzfeld in the German edition of Landucci's diary, II, 54–55.

37. Guicciardini, *Storie Fiorentine,* p. 284.

38. "Medicibus exactis, armisque turbata Republica, quum de ordinanda civitate, constituendoque imperio cives inter se dissiderent, quod alii paucorum potentiam sectarentur, pars conturbari miscerique omnia quo minus valerent ipsi, mallent, tum demum ambitione paucorum factum est ut civitas distructa seditionibus latiorem Reipublicae formam, ne dicam popularem, amplecteretur. Haec ego, qui post exactos Medices, legatus abfueram, quum in reditu meo offendissem, non destiti ea cogitare, ac monere, quae ad expoliendam rudem illam ut primam materiem pertinerent." Bernardus Oricellarius, *De Urbe Roma, sen Latinus Commentarius eiusdem in Pub. Victorem, ac Sext. Rufum De regionibus urbis,* printed in *Rerum Italicarum Scriptores ab anno aerae Christianae Millesimo ad Millesimum Sexcentesimum,* (Florence, 1770), II, 783.

39. Filippo Nerli, *Commentarii,* edition of 1728, p. 93; Guicciardini, *Storie Fiorentine,* pp. 272–273, and the literature mentioned above in note 35.

40. Sic ille nil miratur actus principum
　　　Nec sceptra regum suspicit
　　　Sed in virenti detinetur gramine
　　　Et se reservat posteris.
Poem by Pietro Crinito, *Ad Faustum: De sylva Oricellaria* in his *Commentarii De Honesta Disciplina* (Florence, 1504).

41. This can be deduced from the introduction to the book (parts of which were quoted above in note 38) and from the fact that Crinito, who died in 1505, mentions the work (see below, note 95); Pellegrini, *L'umanista Bernardo Rucellai,* p. 15, also quotes a passage from Crinitus's *De poetis Latinis,* in which Rucellai is said to be working on his book.

42. In an undated letter, written to R. Acciaiuoli, Rucellai mentions that he discussed the plan of a history of the invasion of Charles VIII with Pontano on a visit to Naples, *Sylloges Epistolarum a viris illustribus scriptarum,* ed. Petrus Burmannus (Leyden, 1727), II, 200–202; his only mission to Naples after the French invasion was the one of 1495. Because the exact date of the origin of this work has been much disputed, I shall list carefully all material bearing on this issue.

43. Lorenzo di Pierfrancesco de' Medici, who had been Rucellai's favorite among the Medici, had died in the same year as Piero (1503).

44. This event is discussed at great length by all the contemporary historians; in particular see Nerli, *Commentarii,* p. 99, and Guicciardini, *Storie Fiorentine,* pp. 325–332.

45. See Giovanni di Bernardo Rucellais letter to Lorenzo Strozzi, dated Avignon, May 13, 1506, published in Giovanni Rucellai, *Opere, per cura di Guido Mazzoni* (Bologna, 1887), pp. 243–244.

46. The data about Rucellai's visit to Marseilles come from his letter to Francesco da Diacceto, written in Marseilles, published in *Sylloges,* ed. Burmannus, II, 197–199. This letter includes a Latin description of Marseilles; Rucellai also asks Diacceto to give him his view about a part of his manuscript on the history of the French invasion, a report on the battle of the Taro, which he has sent to his son Palla.

47. "Come reitrovandomi a Marsilia ove mi pervenne alli orecchi che costi si dicono io esser andato secretamente al re di Romani fui constrecto per mia iustificatione a ritornare in Italia e a Milano dove alloggiai col signor Jacopo da Triulzi parendomi non potere errare essendo lui confidentissimo alla christianessima maesta de Re di Francia." Letter to the Signoria, mentioned above, note 3. On the political situation see Pasquale Villari, *Niccolò Machiavelli e i SuoiTempi,* book I, chap. 10, who discusses the question in detail because it was the issue that resulted in Machiavelli's mission to Germany.

48. "Mi fermai a Bologna fino che per la peste fui costrecto a partirmi." From his letter to the Signoria (see above, note 3), which was written in Venice on the last day of December 1508.

49. "Numquam tamen ab homine impetrare licuit ut mecum Latine loqueretur: subinde interpellabam, surdo loqueris, vir praeclare, vulgaris linguae vestratis tam sum ignarus quam Indicae. Verbum Latinum numquam quivi ab eo extundere." This is the continuation of the Erasmus passage quoted above, note 8. On the whole episode see Pierre de Nolhac, *Erasme en Italie* (Paris, 1888), pp. 47–48.

50. Fontius, *Epistolarum,* book 3, no. 5, writes to Bernardo Rucellai on June 1, 1509: "Non modo ad portum Neapolitanum commissum proelium, sed historiam totam Gallicam tuis in hortis biduo legi." After great praise of the work, he continues: "Quare te etiam atque etiam hortor, ad exitum perducas tantam historiam." This passage makes it entirely clear that the history, in the form in which we now have it, was already finished, because the battles of Naples and the Taro are in the latter half of the manuscript, and it should be noted that Fontius refers to the "historia tota." Fontius's admonition to continue means that he wants Rucellai to carry the story, which ends with the retreat of Charles VIII, up to the present time. An identical wish was expressed by Petrus Delfinus in 1511, and Schnitzer deduces from this that the book was not yet beyond its initial stages in 1511 (*Quellen und Forschungen zur Geschichte Savonarolas,* III, xxx). But the explanation is undoubtedly that these admonitions were meant to induce Rucellai to continue his work and to include the later French invasions. Schnitzer directs his criticisms at Leopold von Ranke, who, in *Zur Kritik neuerer Geschichtschreiber* (Berlin,

1824), places the book in 1500. On the basis of the material I have presented, it seems evident that the *terminus post quem* is 1495, that the *terminus ante quem* is 1509, and that large parts of the book received their final wording between 1506 and 1509.

51. Petrus Delfinus mentions, in a letter written to Paolo Giustiniano on September 24, 1511, that he has seen Rucellai recently in Florence. See Edmund Martène and Ursin Durand, *Veterum Sciptorum et Monumentorum . . . Amplissima Collectio* (Paris, 1724), III, 1173.

52. The details of these events are most comprehensively assembled from the rich source material in the German translation of Landucci's diary.

53. The two sons who were politically active at this time were Palla and Giovanni. Palla continued to play a great role in Florentine politics as leader of the aristocratic faction and partisan of the Medicis. In 1537, when Cosimo was elected duke (after the assassination of Alessandro), Palla voted against him; when told that the meeting hall was surrounded by soldiers of the Medici, he replied that he was seventy-two years old, and that no longer could much harm be done him. Giovanni (1475–1525), the famous poet, was a special favorite of Leo X, who died before he could carry out his intention to make Giovanni Cardinal. Bernardo had two other sons, Piero and Cosimo; both died young, but Cosimo left a son, Cosimino, the host of the Orti Oricellari in Machiavelli's time.

54. The most important positions were: August 1512, member of the committee to reform the constitution; September 1512, member of the Balìa, established by the Medici; November 1513, member of the Council of the Seventy. See Pellegrini, *L'umanista Bernardo Rucellai,* pp. 21–22.

55. Masi, *Ricordanze,* quoted in the German translation of Landucci's diary, II, 256–257.

56. Nerli, *Commentarii,* p. 125.

57. It may be appropriate at this point to tabulate Rucellai's literary works. The two main ones are *De Urbe Roma* (see above, note 38) and *De Bello Italico* (most easily available in the edition of 1733, Londini, typis Gulielmi Bowyer). There are three smaller works, all of them mainly stylistic exercises: *De Bello Pisano,* a Latin translation of Neri Capponi's *Commentarii* on the war against Pisa, although with some slight changes and additions; *Oratio de auxilio Tifernatibus adferendo;* and *Bellum Mediolanense,* which is a revision of the beginning of the 10th book of Bruni Aretino's *Florentine History.* Of these three works, the last has never been printed, while the two others can be found, together with his *De Bello Italico,* in the edition of 1733. Pellegrini, who discusses these minor works (*L'umanista Bernardo Rucellai,* pp. 23–36), proves that *De Bello Pisano* was written beforeLorenzo il Magnifico's death, and composition in Rucellai's early years is indicated for the two other minor works as well. It is necessary to regard as literary works two letter written in Latin, the one to Francesco Cattaneo da Diacceto, written from Marseilles (see above, note 46) and the one to R. Acciaiuoli, on his discussion with Pontano concerning the classical model to be imitated by a modern historian (see above, note 42). This letter is mentioned by Fontius in a letter to Rucellai, March 1512, *Epistolarum,* book 3, no. 2, but this is no proof that the letter might not have been written earlier.

There is a book called *Bernardi Oricellarii De Magistratibus Romanorum Veterum Commentarius,* ex libro manuscripto edidit H. E. I. Walchius (Leipzig, 1752). The editor states in the introduction that he received the manuscript in Florence, and Rucellai's authorship was derived from handwriting and style. At present, it is not possible to describe this manuscript in more detail; if it is still in existence, it may be in Jena, where Walchius was professor. It seems to me not impossible that this short work was in fact written by Rucellai because it fits exactly the plan of work outlined by Rucellai in his foreword to *De Urbe Roma* (see below, note 108). This would be quite interesting because a section on religion anticipated Machiavelli's view of religion as an institution useful mainly for political purposes. It is also reported in the short biography preceding the print of *De Urbe Roma* that he wrote a commentary on Livy: *Castigationes Decadum Livii.*

58. Hinc sat videbis alta Flora moenia

Et Faesulas bivertices . . .

(From Crinito's *De sylva Oricellaria,* mentioned above, note 40.) In the same poem there is also a long description of the plants in the garden. See also Machiavelli's *Arte Della Guerra,* which is placed in the Orti Oricellari, and which, at the beginning, gives some description of them. On the classical statues decorating the garden, which came in part from the Medici Palace, see Eugène Müntz, *Les Collections des Médicis au XV siècle* (Paris, 1888), p. 107. On the situation of the garden see L. Passerini, *Degli Orti Oricellari* in his *Curiosità storico-artistiche Fiorentine* (Florence, 1866), where it is proved that the gardens were not used before 1498.

59. The most authoritative scholarly treatment of the Orti Oricellari is that by Giuseppi Toffanin in his *Machiavelli e il "Tacitismo"* (Padua, Draghi, 1921), esp. chap. 1, "Venezia e Roma negli Orti Oricellari," which discusses the meetings in the second decade of the 16th century. They are placed in the same period in Toffanin's well-known *Il Cinquecento* (Milan, Vallardi, 1929), p. 396. This view, of course, is a reflection of the earlier views expressed in such well-known books as the Machiavelli biographies of Villari, *Niccolò Machiavelli,* and Oreste Tommasini, *La Vita e Gli Scritti di Niccolò Machiavelli* (Rome, 1883), and in the whole Machiavelli literature, or books like Henri Hauvette, *Un Exile Florentin a la Cour de France au XVI Siecle: Luigi Alamanni (1495–1556)* (Paris, 1903). There have been a few exceptions. Delio Cantimori, "Rhetoric and Politics in Italian Humanism," *Journal of the Warburg Institute,* I, 1937–38, p. 88, intimates, on the basis of Crinito, that the Rucellai garden meetings, which are "generally placed towards the second half of the second decade of the sixteenth century . . . must have begun much earlier." P. O. Kristeller in "Francesco da Diacceto and Florentine Platonism," *Miscellanea Giovanni Mercati,* IV, 15, states that "in the period prior to 1512" the Rucellai gardens were the center of a political *fronde* against Soderini. But even these two authors are by no means clear or definite about these earlier developments.

60. See above, note 40. Pietro Crinito, or Petrus Crinitus (1465–1505), humanist, disciple and editor of Politian; his true name was Riccio.

61. The most recent list of participants will be found in Kristeller, "Francesco da Diacceto," p. 15; but I think it is possible to get still more exact results, especially since Kristeller is not aware of the stages in the development of the meetings. The whole question is only a side-issue for him.

62. Jacopo Nardi (1478–1563), Florentine politician and historian, enemy of the Medici, who went into exile in 1530.

63. Filippo de' Nerli (1485–1556), Florentine aristocrat. For his *Commentarii de Fatti civili* I have used the edition of 1728.

64. Luigi Alamanni (1495–1556), Florentine democratic politician and poet; see Hauvette, *Un Exilé Florentin.*

65. Zanobi Buondelmonte, friend of Machiavelli's, to whom the *Discorsi* and the *Vita di Castruccio Castracani* are dedicated; he went into exile to France after 1522.

66. Antonio Brucioli (died 1556), went into exile after 1522, author of the *Dialoghi,* a book of moral philosophy, later translator of the Bible; see Cantimori, "Rhetoric and Politics."

67. Three Diacceti were participants in the meetings: Francesco Cattaneo da Diacceto (1466–1522), neo-Platonic philosopher, who was a follower of the Medici (see Kristeller, "Francesco da Diacceto"), and Francesco da Diacceto il Nero and Jacopo da Diacceto, who were both involved in the conspiracy of 1522. Jacopo was sentenced to death.

68. See previous note.

69. Nardi, *Storia di Firenze,* book 7, chap. 8.

70. Nerli, *Commentarii,* pp. 138–139.

71. Battista della Palla left Florence after 1522 and went to France; the French king sent him back as an agent to buy Italian works of art. Palla was in Florence when the revolution of 1527 began, participated in it, and was killed after its failure.

72. Nerli, *Commentarii,* p. 98.

73. Ibid., p. 107.

74. Crinito (see note 60), who must be regarded as belonging in this category, does not add any new names to the ones given by the others.

75. These names are taken from Brucioli's dialogue, "Del modo dello instruire i figliuoli," which is the fifth dialogue of the first book of Brucioli's *Dialogi* in the edition of 1537, and takes place in the Rucellai gardens. Strangely enough, Cantimori, in "Rhetoric and Politics," in which he is especially interested in Brucioli's relation to the Rucellai garden meetings, has overlooked this dialogue. The persons mentioned are: Giangiorgio Trissino (1478–1550), famous writer and philologist (see on him, for instance, Toffanin, *Il Cinquecento,* pp. 448–453); Giovanni Lascaris (1445–1535), famous Greek scholar; Francesco Guidetti, Florentine aristocrat.

76. Giambattista Gelli (1498–1563), one of the most famous writers of his time, author of *La Circe.* The Rucellai garden meetings are mentioned by him in his *Opere,* ed. A. Gelli (Florence, 1855), pp. 305, 310.

77. Gelli, *Opere,* p. 292.

78. Giovanni Canacci, contemporary of Bernardo Rucellai, Florentine aristocrat, one of Marsilio Ficino's intimate friends, opponent of Savonarola; on him see *Supplementum Ficinianum,* ed. P. O. Kristeller (Florence, 1937), I, 129.

79. Giovanni Corsi (1472–1547), influential Florentine politician and follower of the Medici, friend of Francesco Guicciardini and biographer of Ficino, as well as author of translations from Plutarch and editor of Pontano's *De Prudentia;* see P. O. Kristeller, "Un uomo di stato e umanista fiorentino: Giovanni Corsi, *"La Bibliofilia,* 38 (1936), 242–257.

80. Piero Martelli, Florentine aristocrat, disciple of Diacceto.

81. Francesco Vettori (1474–1539), the famous Florentine statesman, historian, friend of Machiavelli; see the biography by L. Passy, *Un ami de Machiavel: sa vie et ses oeuvres,* 2 vols. (Paris, 1914). He was a nephew of Rucellai.

82. The expression is "fanciullezza" and permits no interpretation except "childhood" (emphasis on small child).

83. It would be more correct to speak of second and third decade because the meetings ended only in 1522, with the conspiracy against the Cardinal de' Medici.

84. See above notes 21 and 50.

85. Bartholomaeus Fontius—or Bartolommeo della Fonte—or Fronzio—(1445–1513), humanist and epigrapher; see Fritz Saxl, "The Classical Inscription in Renaissance Art and Politics," *Journal of the Warburg Institute,* 4 (1940–41), 19–42.

86. Cosimo Pazzi (1466–1513), Bishop of Arezzo and, after 1508, Archbishop of Florence, son of Bianca de' Medici, Lorenzo il Magnifico's sister.

87. Bindaccio Ricasoli (ca. 1444–1524), Florentine aristocrat, close friend of Marsilio Ficino; see *Supplementum Ficinianum,* I, 124.

88. See the literature mentioned above in note 59, and Cantimori, "Rhetoric and Politics."

89. Pietro Crinito, *Commentarii De Honesta Disciplina,* book XI, chap. 12: "Itaque nuper in hortis Oricellariis inter alia complura quaesitum est de Sedigito vulcatio deque eius iudicio: quod ab eo factum est: de ingenio et ordine X comicorum qui apud latinos in pretio habiti sunt: item de poeticis vocabulis, ac veterum audacia in verbis inveniendis excogitandis atque componendis: cuiusmodi fuerunt M. Plautus, Gn. Nevius, P. Laberius."

90. Ibid., book V, chap. 14: "Egebatur nuper in hortis Oricellariis historia de Commodo Antonino imperatore qui inter alia scelera et flagitia (ut traditur) etiam mythriaca sacra homicidio pollent; quo loco dubitatum est a quibusdam non indictis viris qui aderant: quae nam sacra haec forent: aut cui potissimo numini dicata." See Fritz Saxl, "Pagan Sacrifice in the Italian Renaissance," *Journal of the Warburg Institute,* 2 (1939), on the significance and intellectual background of this issue, also on its political aspect, which emerges in Machiavelli's *Discorsi,* book II, chap. 2.

91. Crinito, *Commentarii De Honesta Disciplina,* book XI, chap. 12.

92. Ibid., book II, chap. 14. "In hortis Oricellariis cum nuper aliqot egregie docti Homines convenerunt: ubi de honestis litteris optimisque disciplinis saepe et copiose agitur; forte incidit mentio de veterum institutis: de regenda civitate; ac de Venetum clarissimo atque summo imperio."

93. See Kristeller, "Francesco da Diacceto," p. 20.

94. He had brought the manuscript from Naples to Florence before 1503; it was printed in 1508. See Kristeller, *Un Uomo di Stato e Umanista Fiorentino,* p. 247. The question of the relation of Giovanni Gioviano Pontano to this group deserves more study; see his praise of Lorenzo in *De Prudentia,* book 3, and his reflections on history in his dialogue "Actius," *Pontani Opera Omnia* (Venice, 1518–19).

95. Crinito, for instance, mentions Rucellai's work on Rome and Corsi's relation to Pontano, *Commentarii De Honesta Disciplina,* book IV, chap. 8; book IX, chap. 12.

96. Throughout his life, Francesco da Diacceto remained one of the most rigid custodians of Ficinian orthodoxy.

97. Fontius's main work was a painstaking collection of classical inscriptions (see above, note 85), and Crinito was mainly concerned with an exact philological explanation of the meaning of classical terms and statements.

98. "Mirum est quam horum temprum calamitosa conditio, quam nostra civitas alias florentissima, nunc aegra affectaque sit: quippe in qua cum optimus quisque, tum vel maxime nobilitas, praesertim bonis artibus imbuta, nunquam sit extra aleam invidiae; plerumque autem contumeliae iniuriaeque exposita. Quam Bernardus Oricellarius, vir priscae eruditionis ac gravitatis, veluti quandam impiam novercam abominatus, effugit." Francesco da Diacceto, *Opera Omnia* (Basel, 1564), p. 90. (Letter to Bindaccio Ricasoli dedicating to him Diacceto's *De amore.*)

99. See his letter of dedication to Bindaccio Ricasoli in his Ficino biography, in P. Villani, *Liber de civitatis Florentiae famosis civibus,* ed. G. C. Galletti (Florence, 1847), p. 189.

100. Crinito, *Commentarii De Honesta Disciplina,* book 16, cap. IX: "Nescio quo fato superiore anno evenerit; quo Francorum rex Carolus Italiam cum infecto exercitu et instructis copiis invasit: ut principes viri in literis atque in summis disciplinis clarissimi perierunt: hoc est Hermolaus Barbarus, Jo. Picus Mirandula et Angelo Politianus: qui omnes in ipso statim Francorum adventu et conatibus immaturo obitu ad superos converunt, sedenim literae ipsae ac studia bonarum artium simul cum Italiae libertate coeperunt paulatim extingui barbaris ingruentibus cum deesset hi homines qui illis suo patrocinio assiduisque studiis mirifice faverent: qualis inter alios vir summa sapientia et egregio animo Laurentius Medices . . . felicissime tunc ageretur cum literis atque literatis." "[Laurentius Medices] qui Florentinam rempublicam non minore tum consilio quam fortuna gubernabat."

101. Corsi, in the letter of dedication to Bindaccio Ricasoli in his Ficino biography (see above, note 99), p. 189: "appellataque tunc passim Florentinorum urbs ex conventu doctissimorum virorum Athenae alterae. Unde non immerito sane a quodam e docioribus ita scriptum: debere quidem literarum studia Florentinis plurimum, sed inter Florentinos Medicibus, inter veros Medices Laurentio: quocirca nostrorum temporum calamitas maxime miseranda; quandoquidem in nostra Civitate pro disciplinis ac bonis artibus inscitia et ignorantia, pro liberalitate avaritia, pro modestia et continentia am-

bitio et luxuria dominantur; atque adeo ut nihil omnino cum Repubblica, nihil cum legibus agatur, sed pro libidine cuncta, ita ut optimus quisque a plebe per ludibrium oppugnetur. Quam veluti saevissimam novercam detestatus nuper Bernardus Oricellarius, exsulandum sibi duxit potius quam diutius esse in ea urbe, unde una cum Medicibus omnium bonarum artium disciplinae atque optima majorum instituta exsularent."

102. Enrico Barfucci, *Lorenzo de' Medici e la Società Artistica del suo tempo* (Florence, Gonnelli, 1945), contains, particularly in its second chapter, a recent description of the humanist group around Lorenzo.

103. See the various judgments on Lorenzo, assembled by Joseph Schnitzer, *Savonarola* (Munich, Reinhardt, 1924), p. 52.

104. Guicciardini, *Storie Fiorentine,* pp. 73–82.

105. See Savonarola's sermon, *Sopra Haggeo,* and Joseph Schnitzer, *Savonarola* (Munich, 1924), pp. 206–208.

106. On this slanting of the truth see Platonicus, "Per la biografia di Marsilio Ficino," *Civiltà Moderna,* 36 (1938), 3–4.

107. See Schnitzer, *Quellen,* IV (the diaries of Piero Parenti), p. 299: September 1501 "Questo disordine faceva comendare e tempi di Lorenzo de Medici et molti appetivano si tornassi a similar stato et seminavano per il vulgo la buona stagione preterita, biasimando la presente"; in the same sense February 1504. The most striking statement of the transformation of Lorenzo il Magnifico from tyrant into ideal prince is in Francesco Guicciardini's *Storia d' Italia,* book I, chap. 15; "dopo la morte si convertì in memoria molto chiara."

108. Part of the dedication letter quoted above in note 38; he continues: "Quod ut facilius adsequi possem, nisus sum auctoritate exemplisque tum veterum, tum vero etiam Venetorum, quorum annales, ut non ignoras, iam pridem domi habemus perraros illos quidem, atque exscriptos de commentariis sanctioribus. Sed quum seditione civium nihil profecissem, non fuit consilium inter dissidentes, et, ut liberius loquar, infestos partibus homines frustra reliquam aetatem agere; sed ad honestum reversus otium, unde me post obitum Laurentii Medicis avunculi tui publica privataque discrimina averterant, statui ex Romanorum gestis, quaecumque obscuriora viderentur aperire proque viribus ante oculos ponere priscum illum in regenda Republica ordinem civitatis, ut si minus aetatis nostrae civibus, posteris salutem aut alienigenis conferre possemus. Nam etsi in tanta scriptorum copia qui ea posteris tradiderunt, elici posse sensus videatur; tamen evenit, ut saepe incidas in eum locum, unde ne explicare quidem, redigereque in ordinem ita, ut omnes eius partes constent, statum Reipublicae valeas: quod fieri cum promiscuo, militarique more vivendi maxime existimo; tum quod qui ex antiquis scripserunt, ut in tanto imperio, magna scriptorum copia minime obsolescere posse tam celebrem regendae civitatis rationem sunt arbitrati. Quod si quis cuncta quae a Graecis, Latinisque scriptoribus traduntur imitaturus observet, proponatque sibi ut in aedificando formulam, exemplar Romanae civitatis, profecto ingenue fateatur necesse est, qualem Rempublicam prisci habuerint, se satis percipere non potuisse. Haec nos, ut videmur, adsequuti, dum opitulandi nostrae civitati studio veterum monumenta prosequimur, opus ipsum adgrediemur si prius de situ Urbis . . . disseruerimus."

109. This motif became particularly strong in the following decades, when the Medici had returned to Florence. Then the writers of the aristocratic faction, Pazzi, Valori, Vettori, Francesco and Luigi Guicciardini, completed this idealizat ion of the Magnifico, trying to prove—against the emerging tendencies of Medicean absolutism—that Lorenzo had ruled as a *primus interpares* in an aristocratic regime. The process can be clearly observed in the changes of Francesco Guicciardini's Lorenzo il Magnifico picture—from the rather equivocal characterization in the *Storie Fiorentine* through the more friendly appraisal in the *Dialogo del Reggimento di Firenze* to the idealized picture in the *Storia d'Italia.* The concept of "balance of power," as containing the secret of

Lorenzo's success in foreign policy, was attributed to him at this time. It is also of importance that, in the early stage of the meetings, Venice *and* Rome were the examples to be imitated (see above, notes 108, 92); in later times Venice was monopolized by the aristocrats, Rome by the democrats. On this interesting but complicated development see the chapter: "Venezia e Roma negli Orti Oricellari," in Toffanin, *Machiavelli e il "Tacitismo."*

110. The subtitle of Toffanin, *Machiavelli e il "Tacitismo": La "politica storica" al tempo della Controriforma.*

111. See his letter to R. Acciaiuoli on his discussion with Pontano concerning the best classical pattern for the historian; mentioned above, note 42.

112. See above, note 57.

113. On Guicciardini's use of Rucellai's History see Roberto Ridolfi, *L'Archivio della Famiglia Guicciardini* (Florence, 1931), p. 72. Schnitzer, *Quellen,* III, xxx, indicates that the book was used by Cerretani for his historical works. Vettori was Rucellai's nephew and undoubtedly knew the book. Machiavelli's acquaintance with the book is likely, although excerpts found among his papers do not seem to be written in his hand. See Adolph Gerber, *Die Handschriften, Ausgaben und Uebersetzungen von Machiavelli's Werken* (Gotha, F. A. Perthes, 1912), p. 18. But as Delfinus wrote to Paolo Giustiniani, in Martène and Durand, *Veterum Scriptorum,* p. 1173: "Confert cum multis scripta sua."

114. See Frederick Antal, *Florentine Painting and Its Social Background* (London Kegan Paul, 1948), p. 106, and the literature given there.

115. Vittorio Rossi, *Il Quattrocento,* p. 337.

116. Cantimori, "Rhetoric and Politics," p. 83. I am in full agreement with the views which he expresses in this article on the political thought of Italian humanism. He seems to me to strike the right balance between an unjustified neglect of these writings as of no significance and the present trend in scholarly research of overevaluation, of assuming that because they had some significance and influence they were already the full blossoming of political realism.

117. *Ibid.,* p. 84.

118. See Emilie Herbst, *Der Zug Karl's VIII. nach Italien im Urteil der italienischen Zeitgenossen* (Berlin, W. Rothschild, 1911).

119. That is, of the Medici.

120. One of the historical "legends" which continues to appear in general histories—despite its rejection in more specialized treatments, like Ferdinand Schevill, *History of Florence* (New York, Harcourt, Brace and Company, 1936)—is that, in contrast to the aristocratic Albizzi, Cosimo was a protagonist of the popular forces.

121. The Rucellai are an interesting example of a family which, although originally opposed to the Medici, was not active enough politically to be exiled, and then was drawn into the ruling group. This gives an added point to the above-mentioned meaning of the Rucellai shield. The Strozzi were exiled, but, after the full establishment of the Medici rule, were permitted to return. The relationship between the two families remained rather complicated. It might be remarked that the system is very much like the system which existed in Rome in the last days of the republic, when the popular party was not based on "the people," but only on the opposition group in the Senate. Augustus's system then was tying all groups into his clientèle. See Lily Ross Taylor, *Party Politics in the Age of Caesar* (Berkeley, University of California Press, 1949).

122. This view is clearly stated by W. K. Ferguson, *The Renaissance,* Berkshire Studies in History (New York, H. Holt and Company, 1940), p. 75.

123. See the various papers on this problem, in particular those by Dana Durand and Hans Baron, assembled in the *Journal of the History of Ideas,* 4 (1943), 1–74; and, in general, W. K. Ferguson, *The Renaissance in Historical Thought* (Boston, Houghton, Miflin, Co., 1948).

124. Eugenio Garin, *Der Italienische Humanismus* (Bern, A. Francke, 1947) can be regarded as the best recent introduction to the problems and the literature of Italian humanism.

10. Religion and Politics in the Thought of Gasparo Contarini

1. In the section of Cannareggio, on the Fondamenta Contarini no. 3539, one sees the "bella facciata cinquecentesca del Pal. Contarini del Zaffo, fatto construire dal card. Gaspare Contarini" (*Venezia e Dintorni—Guida d'Italia del Touring Club Italiano*); the palace is now seat of the Centro Giovanni XXIII. The church of San Michele was built between 1469 and 1478.

2. *De magistratibus et republica Venetorum* (first published in Paris, 1543).

3. Franz Dittrich, *Regesten und Briefe des Kardinals Gasparo Contarini* (Braunsberg, 1885), and *Gasparo Contarini, eine Monographie* (Braunsberg, 1881), remain basic for all modern research, despite incompleteness of facts and the intellectual näiveté of the author. Bibliographies listing later literature may be found in Hanns Rueckert, *Die theologische Entwicklung Gasparo Contarinis,* Arbeiten zur Kirchengeschichte, VI (Bonn, 1926); Hermann Hackert, *Die Staatsschrift Gasparo Contarinis und die politischen Verhaeltnisse Venedigs im 16. Jahrhundert,* Heidelberger Abhandlungen zur mittleren und neueren Geschichte, LXIX (Heidelberg, C. Winter, 1940). See also the article on Contarini in the *Enciclopedia Cattolica* (Città del Vaticano, 1950). I shall refer to special studies relevant to the particular problem under investigation at the appropriate places.

4. See, for example, Zera S. Fink, *The Classical Republicans* (Evanston, Northwestern University Press, 1945), pp. 37–40.

5. See Hanns Rueckert, *Die Entwicklung Contarinis,* and, more recently, Hubert Jedin, "Gasparo Contarini e il contributo Veneziano alla Riforma Cattolica," in *La Civiltà Veneziana del Rinascimento,* Storia della Civiltà Veneziana, vol. IV, Centro di Cultura e Civiltà della Fondazione Giorgio Cini (Florence, Sansoni, 1958), pp. 105–124.

6. Indicative is the article "Gasparo Contarini" in the *Enciclopedia Italiana,* which concentrates on his activities as Cardinal, not mentioning his book on the Venetian republic.

7. There is a reason why in former years students have concerned themselves only with particular and partial aspects of Contarini's life and mind. A fuller understanding of Contarini has become possible only in recent years when a fortunate find brought to light a number of revealing personal letters written by Contarini during a critical period of his life. See note 13.

8. Sixteenth-century biographies of Contarini are those by Giovanni della Casa and Lodovico Beccadelli. Both authors knew Contarini well, Beccadelli having been Contarini's secretary. Casa's life of Contarini was published as an introduction to Contarini, *Opera* (Paris, 1571); Beccadelli's biography of Contarini can be found in his *Monumenti di Varia Letteratura* (Bologna, 1799), I, part 2. For a survey of early writings on Contarini see Dittrich, *Regesten,* pp. 1–7.

9. Pomponazzi's treatise *De reactione,* dated Bologna, July 13, 1515, was dedicated to Gasparo Contarini. The sentence about Contarini in this dedication runs as follows: "Verum cum te ab ineunte aetate fedissimam adulationem tam acriter detestari meminerim nihilque apud te antiquius aut sanctius aut magis venerandum esse cognoverim quam justitiam et veritatem ideo tuum judicium subire non dubitavi."

10. For a survey of the situation see Heinrich Kretschmayr, *Geschichte von Venedig* (Gotha, F. A. Perthes, 1920), II, 395–448.

11. Ludovico Muratori, *Rerum Italicarum Scriptores,* new ed. (Bologna, N. Zanichelli,

1934), XXII, 101 ("et prudentiae et virium miraculum") and 103–104 ("ut nunquam timere Deum desistamus"), from Caracciolo's "De Varietate Fortunae."

12. On the origin and development of the Venetian "myth" see Chapter 8 in this volume.

13. Giustiniani and Quirini, and their relation to Contarini, have been treated in a number of important articles by Hubert Jedin: "Ein Turmerlebnis des jungen Contarini," *Historisches Jahrbuch,* 70 (1951), 115–130; "Vincenzo Quirini und Pietro Bembo," *Miscellanea Giovanni Mercati* (Città del Vaticano, 1946), IV, 407–424; and, most important, "Contarini und Camaldoli," *Archivio Italiano per la Storia della Pietà,* 2 (1952), 53–117. In the last-mentioned article, Jedin published thirty letters of Contarini to Giustiniani and Quirini during the years 1511 to 1523; this important find has shed new light on Contarini's development. However, these letters must be read along with the letters of Giustiniani and Quirini to Contarini and other Venetian friends, published in *Annales Camaldulenses* (Venice, 1773), VIII, Appendix, 447–595. Important material on Giustiniani and Quirini is also in J. Schnitzer, *Peter Delfin, General des Camaldulenserordens* (Munich, 1926). After the completion of this essay the article by Innocenzo Cervelli, "Storiografia e problemi intorno alla vita religiosa e spirituale a Venezia nella prima metà del '500," *Studi Veneziani,* 1966 (Firenze, 1967), VIII, 447–476, was published. See pp. 455–466 for a perceptive analysis of Contarini's relations with Giustiniani and Quirini.

14. This is the point at which I differ from Jedin. Jedin starts from the assumption that Contarini had decided to become a monk and that he abandoned this plan only after, in a severe religious crisis, he had arrived at a "new" concept of the "justification through faith" which constituted an "innere Affinität" with Luther. Thus, according to Jedin, Contarini underwent a "conversion" that determined the course of his entire life and in relation to which all other issues and problems were of secondary importance, almost irrelevant. It must be fully acknowledged that Jedin's discovery of Contarini's correspondence with Giustiniani and Quirini is of fundamental importance for an understanding of Contarini's thought. And it is quite understandable that Jedin, who was interested chiefly in Contarini from the point of view of his contribution to church reform, tied the interpretation of his new material to the formula on "justification" to which Contarini agreed at the Diet of Ratisbon in 1541. Nevertheless, Jedin's assumption that Contarini intended to become a monk is erroneous. It cannot be reconciled with Contarini's repeated declaration that he was not suited to a monastic life. Although Contarini was certainly concerned with the problem of the salvation of his soul, this problem was integrated with the wider problem of the general relation between Christianity and secular activities. For this reason, I give an analysis of the correspondence of Contarini with Giustiniani and Quirini even though Jedin, in his above-mentioned articles, "Ein Turmerlebnis" and "Contarini und Camaldoli," has outlined the content of this exchange. Fine observations about the exchange between Contarini and Giustiniani can be found in the article by Heinz Mackensen, "Contarini's Theological Role at Ratisbon in 1541," *Archiv für Reformationsgeschichte,* 51 (1960), 36–56, but the author is too much influenced by Jedin's misleading point of departure. When I quote passages Mackensen cited, I have sometimes used his English rendering.

15. Contarini to Giustiniani, February 1, 1511: "Non dico però, aziò non ve inganate, de venir a farve compagnia: non è in mi sì boni pensieri" (Jedin, "Contarini und Camaldoli," p. 62). See also p. 65: "io, a chi non è dato una minima parte di core a fare quello fate vui."

16. Contarini to Giustiniani, November 1515: "[on becoming 'frate'] A me non solum [non] dilecta ma genera horrore un tal pensiero. Nè a me per niente pare che una tal perfectione di viver convenga a la infirmità et debellezza de l'animo mio." Ibid., p. 106.

Notes to Pages 251–253

17. See Contarini's letters to Quirini, December 26, 1511, ibid., pp. 72–76, and *Annales Camaldulenses,* pp. 539–543; this second letter, written in Latin, is much sharper than the letter in Italian printed by Jedin. Jedin suggests that the letter in Latin was not sent. In Giustiniani's letter to Contarini and Niccolò Tiepolo in *Annales Camaldulenses,* pp. 544–550, Giustiniani called Contarini and Tiepolo, because of their attempt to dissuade Quirini from entering the order, "anticristi, satanani, instrumenti del Diavolo."

18. Contarini to Quirini, June 13, 1514, in Jedin, "Contarini und Camaldoli," pp. 94–96.

19. "Il viver solitario non è natural a l'homo, el qual la natura ha fato animal sociabile, ma besogna che colui che vuol metersi a tal vita sia de una perfection excendente quasi la condition humana, tal che non cun li sensi ma solum cun lo intellecto viva." Ibid., p. 73.

20. "La vita de Religiosi, presertim de quelli Heremiti, era una vita de homeni perfectissimi, a la qual perfection . . . pochissimi pervengono." Ibid., p. 81.

21. "Ben sapeti melgio di me che, benchè la vita contemplativa sia più nobile de la activa, pur la vita activa, la qual versa ne l' adiuvar el proximo ne la vita spiritual, è più meritoria." Ibid., p. 69. This, of course, is a modification of a traditional formula.

22. "Et è venuto el tempo che, secundo lo antiquo mio desiderio, son per darme tuto a la Scritura Sacra." Ibid., p. 75.

23. "Ma non essendo nè via de solitudine, nè via de Religion certa, nè etiam la vita civil certa di perditione, ma in tute essendo modo di pervenir a salute et a perdition." Ibid., p. 70.

24. Contarini to Giustiniani, April 24, 1511: "Tamen, da l'altra parte vedendo quel che vui ditte di buon core, che, dapoi lassato tuto el mondo per amor di Christo, et dapoi fati una vita così austera, non restati però di temer che i peccati vostri commessi per il passato non siano di tal sorte che non siati per farze conveniente penitentia in questo avanzo di la vostra vita, in el qual pensier et in el qual timor ve vedo assai continuato." Ibid., p. 63.

25. "Non dormirò adonque io securo, benchè sia in mezo la città, benchè non satisfaci al debito che ho contracto, havendo io tal pagatore del mio debito? Veramente dormirò et vegierò così securo come se tuto el tempo di la vita mia fosse stado ne l'Heremo, con proposito di non mi lassar mai da tal apozo." From the same letter of April 24, 1511, ibid., p. 64.

26. Contarini to Giustiniani and Quirini, July 17, 1512: "Me son venuti in odio li studii, et quella sol cosa che a l'altra volta mi ralegrava, cioè la lection de la Scriptura Sacra, hora me dà grande molestia," ibid., p. 87.

27. Summary of Contarini's letter to Giustiniani, April 20, 1513, ibid., pp. 89–90. See esp.: "Hor cognosco che io son homo non solum separato dal vulgo, come io me credeva, immo, il più infimo del vulgo; et vivome in questa sorte di vita humile et bassa . . . In questo mezzo viverò in questa humilità, sempre sperando." See also p. 97: "[God] dispone le cose nostre humane et le actioni de' diversi homeni a diversi gradi, de li quali alguni sono altissimi, alguni mediocri et alguni bassi, le quali però tuti, quando che con animo humile sono aceptati, risultano et in bene di coloro che li aceptano et etiam in bene de l'universo."

28. Contarini to Giustiniani, June 28, 1515: "Io non so essere homo, ma, da uno certo fervore transportato, vorrei in un momento ascender sopra i cieli; nè molto dopoi cascho nel modo de' bruti animali, quasi disperando di consequire quello termine il quale me avevo io proposto ne l'animo . . . Nui qui semo in via, et nostro officio è non cercare di havere la nostra quiete de qui, nè vivendo potere pertingere a quella la quale aspeciamo." Ibid., p. 102. "La vita de l'huomo in terra è una continua militia." Ibid., p. 109.

29. "Le cause particulare." Ibid., p. 89.

30. See esp. the letter to Quirini, *Annales Camaldulenses,* pp. 539–543.

31. Friends and scholars mentioned in these letters are: Trifone Gabriele, Giovanni Baptista Egnazio, Alberto Carpi, Niccolò Dolfin, Baptista della Torre.

32. *Annales Camaldulenses,* pp. 467–496.

33. "Forse in quella celeste patria . . . bisognan dialettici argomenti, o filosofiche dispute, o matematiche discipline, o arte di medicina, forse o Greco, o Latino, o Tosco ivi si ragiona?" *Annales Camaldulenses,* p. 552. See also Giustiniani's letter on the erroneously reported death of Egnazio, ibid., pp. 589–594. For a more detailed discussion of Gustiniani's and Quirini's intellectual development, see my article, "Cristianesimo, umanesimo e la bolla 'Apostolici Regiminis' del 1513," *Rivista Storica Italiana,* 79 (1967), 976–990, esp. 983–986.

34. In the correspondence with Giustiniani, Contarini's views on this issue are reflected in a particular concern for the views of a recluse, living separate from the other Camaldolensians.

35. "Leggo etiam quel de Republica di Platone, el qual hora è stato impresso ne la sua lingua. Ricevo utilità et da le cose da quel excellente homo scripte et etiam da la lingua." Jedin, "Contarini und Camaldoli," p. 92.

36. Egnazio's work is mentioned ibid., p. 78. It was published, under the title *De exemplis Illustrium virorum Venetae civitatis atque aliarum gentium,* in 1554.

37. See Contarini's letters to Giustiniani of May 30 and June 9, 1515; in the latter see the joking remark: "Non più venetiano ma thoscano mi posso senza dubio chiamare." Ibid., p. 101.

38. See above, note 35.

39. "di quella moralità, la qual li philosophi hanno vista con el lume naturale, el qual è etiam dono grande di Dio, mi debba contentare." Ibid., p. 77.

40. For the date of the composition of Contarini's treatise on Venice see my article, "The Date of the Composition of Contarini's and Gianotti's Books on Venice," *Studies in the Renaissance,* 14 (1967), 172–184. I shall quote Contarini's works from their first edition in Contarini, *Opera* (Paris, 1571); I shall give the titles of the various works, but the page indications will refer to this volume, in which they were collected.

41. In *Compendium,* p. 170, Contarini refers to his writing against Pomponazzi; in *De elementis,* p. 8, to the *Compendium.*

42. *Compendium,* p. 95. See also Beccadelli's "Vita," *Monumenti,* pp. 41–46.

43. This is the view of Carlo Giacon, "L'Aristotelismo Avicennistico di Gaspare Contarini," *Atti del XII Congresso Internazionale di Filosofia* (Firenze, 1960), IX, 109–119, and my reading of Contarini is along the same lines. Rueckert, *Die Entwicklung Contarinis,* overestimates the influence of Aquinas because he limits himself to a consideration of Contarini's late theological works, in which Contarini consciously tried to relate his views to those of Aquinas; but the philosophical basis of Contarini's views is actually much broader. It might be mentioned that, just at the time when Contarini was studying at Padua, Avicenna's works were printed in Venice.

44. On Pomponazzi, in general, see John Herman Randall, *The School of Padua* (Padova, Editrice Antenore, 1961), pp. 69–115, and Paul Oskar Kristeller, *Eight Philosophers of the Italian Renaissance* (Stanford, Stanford University Press, 1964), pp. 72–90 (with bibliography). For a survey of the dispute aroused by Pomponazzi's thesis on the immortality of the soul see Etienne Gilson, "Autour de Pomponazzi," *Archives d'Histoire Doctrinale et Littéraire du Moyen Age,* 28 (1961).

45. "Hocque putamus esse vere philosophari, hancque philosophiam quae suum nescit defectum, perfectionem animi esse censemus. Illam vero quae putat lumen naturale sibi debere in omnibus sufficere, negatque scientiam eius inchoatam quia nequit pertingere ad perfectam: putamus nos esse philosophiam admodum periculosam et

quae instillare animo possit pestiferum et nocivum infidelitatis impietatisque venenum." *De immortalitate animae,* p. 231.

46. "lumen supernaturale non esse contrarium lumini naturali." Ibid., p. 229. See also p. 194.

47. "Non tamen quivis eius supremae scientiae erit auditor idoneus, neque mentis aciem poterit fingere in tam immensa luce: nisi prius caeteris scientiis fuerit imbutus atque pravis purgatur affectibus. Nam impuro purum tangere non licet, ut inquit Plato." *Compendium,* p. 99.

48. "Ea enim est natura intellectus humani, ut certos terminos in cognitione rerum non egrediatur." Ibid., p. 157.

49. "Formae materiales sint mortales. Formae vero immateriales sunt immortales et incorruptibiles." *De immortalitate animae,* p. 185.

50. "Nulla in rebus hisce, quae infra limam agitantur, substantia simplex est, sed omnis ex duabus partibus constat, quarum alteram dicimus formam, alteram vero materiam: forma actus, perfectio, ac propria uniuscuiusque rei natura est." *Compendium,* p. 169.

51. Ibid., p. 171.

52. "Omnibus vero in hoc officio anteferendi sunt illi, quibus nobili genere ortis paupertas ignominiae essere solet neque mercenarias artes exercere sine calumnia querunt." *De officio episcopi,* p. 430.

53. *Compendium,* p. 123.

54. "Omnem naturam, quatenus esse habet, bonam esse, neque omnino ab appetitu boni recedere posse: quamvis fortasse a potiori bono ad inferius retrocedat, fieri tamen nequit, ut omnino ab appetitu boni destituatur neve ipsa quodpiam bonum non sit . . . huic respondemus malum non esse in rebus veluti naturam, sed tamquam privationem quandam." Ibid., p. 127.

55. "Nulli namque dubium aut incompertum esse potest, quin contemplativae disciplinae factivis artibus atque activis sint praeferendae." Ibid., p. 98.

56. "Arcanum namque ipsius, cum verba ac capitationes deficiant, sacro silentio est venerandum." Ibid., p. 142.

57. "Quali sono più nobili e perfette: le scientie speculative over le virtù morali?" *Quattro Lettere di Monsig. Gasparo Contarino* (Florence, 1558).

58. "La virtù morale e la vita attiva è propria all'huomo, la contemplativa sopra l'huomo." Ibid., p. 38.

59. "priusquam absolutam obtineat, obtinere inchoatam." *De officio episcopi,* p. 410.

60. Ibid., p. 424.

61. Ibid., p. 411.

62. "multa namque plerumque ab amicis, veluti ex vivis libris decerpimus." Ibid., p. 420.

63. "Superiores vero vicissim amant inferiores et suae bonitatis ratione ac naturae. Appetitus vero huius primus motus ac praecipuus est amor, cuius objectum est bonum. Non enim est boni invidere, ac intra se bona sua continere sed effundere ac effluere. Nam intellectum quemcumque sequitur intellectualis appetitus, qui in ratione est et a philosophis voluntas nominatur." *Compendium,* p. 163.

64. See Hubert Jedin, "Das Bischofsideal der Katholischen Reformation," *Kirche des Glaubens: Kirche der Geschichte* (Freiburg, 1966), II, 84–86.

65. Printed in *Annales Camaldulenses* (Venice, 1773), IX, 613–719. For an early testimony of Contarini's interest in church reform see my article "Contarini on Savonarola: An Unknown Document of 1516," *Archiv für Reformationsgeschichte,* 59 (1968).

66. Hubert Jedin, *Geschichte des Konzils von Trient* (Freiburg, Herder, 1951), I, 103.

67. "Postremo, ut inquit Plato, praefectus civitatis talem in urbe institutionem facit, qualem prius in animi sui Republicae gesserat." *De officio episcopi,* p. 402.

68. "Reprehendet aliquis fortasse diligentiam hac in parte nostram quod potius civilem virum, quam Episcopum erudire videar. Cui responsum velim, morales ac civiles virtutes, quamvis non ita episcopi sint, ut aliis quoque non conveniant, quemadmodum nonnullae aliae, de quibus infra dicturi sumus non tamen ab episcopo putandum est alienas esse quin potius fundamenta sunt quaedam, quibus sublatis, caeterae quoque Episcopo peculiares et propriae ruant necesse est." Ibid., p. 406.

69. "Nulla enim capitalior pestis, nec quae facilius atheismo fenestram patefaciat quam haeresis est, quae fundamenta fidei cum tollat, etiam omnem Reipublicae statum subito evertit." Ibid., p. 425.

70. The one modern study devoted exclusively to Contarini's treatise on Venice is the book by Hackert (see note 3). The author provides a useful survey of Venetian political institutions at the beginning of the sixteenth century, but, since he does not recognize the consciously idealizing tendency of Contarini's treatise, he accuses Contarini of hypocrisy; in short, Hackert misses the point of Contarini's treatise. Cogent remarks on the idealizing character of Contarini's treatise can be found in Fink, *Classical Republicans,* pp. 39–40. It is interesting that the first French translation of Contarini's work, published in Lyon in 1557, bears the title: *La police et gouvernement de Venise, exemplaire pour le jourd'hui à toutes autres.*

71. "Verum aliud quiddam est in hac civitate, quod longe omnium praestantissimum censuerim ego; mecumque omnes qui civitatem non tantum moenia et domos esse putant, sed existimant civium conventum et ordinem potissimum hoc sibi nomem vendicare: reipublicae scilicet ratio et forma, ex qua beata vita hominibus contingit." *De Magistratibus et Republica Venetorum,* book I, in Contarini, *Opera,* p. 263.

72. "nulla tamen fuit, quae institutione ac legibus ad bene beateque vivendum idoneis, cum hac nostra conferri potest." Ibid.

73. See Chapter 8.

74. "respuit communis hominum sensus, officia bellica, quibus caedes ac mortalium detrimenta inprimis procurantur." *De magistratibus,* p. 264.

75. Contarini's role in the conclusion of the peace in Bologna in 1529 was usually regarded as his greatest political contribution.

76. He mentions, for example, Bernardo Giustiniani's *De origine urbis Venetiarum,* which is a much more realistic work. See below, note 77.

77. Bernardus Justinianus (Bernardo Giustiniani), *De Divi Marci Evangelistae Vita, translatione, et sepulturae loco,* was printed as an appendix to Giustiniani's *De origine* at Leyden in 1725. Bernardo Giustiniani was not a close relative of Tomaso Giustiniani.

78. "Quod agendum illa etiam res me non mediocriter commovebat, qui isse in oblivionem mihi sanctus videbatur. Ut plerique de nostris etiam (quod nefas dictu existimabam) dubitarent, an corpus illud sanctissimum, nunc etiam in templo sibi dicato situm perseveraret. Eam rem ex memoria pene omnium excidisse, non potui non aegre ferre." Ibid., p. 171.

79. "Ille enim Graecis, latinisque literis instructissimus variis amplisque magistratibus et legationibus a repub. ornatus, sic ab omnibus excipiebatur, ut numen quoddam in homine latere crederetur. Quare et procurator creatus, tanta bonitate humanitateque in omnes usus est, ut adhuc exemplum illius veluti oraculum, ab omnibus preferatur: scripsit ille summa diligentia et fide Venetas res pluribus libris, quos ut proposuerat ad suam usque aetatem absolvere non potuit. Scripsit etiam de divi Marci corpore Venetias translato libros duos." Joannes Baptista Egnatius, *De exemplis Illustrium Virorum Venetae civitatis atque aliarum gentium* (Venice, 1554), p. 70.

80. See above, note 37.

81. "Quam ob rem putavi ego exteris hominibus rem minime ingratam atque inutilem me facturum, si tam praeclarae Reipublicae institutionem literis mandarem, quum praesertim nullum his temporibus videam ex quamplurimis doctissimis viris, qui

multum ingenio, eruditione rerum omnium, ac eloquentia valent, hanc rem literis illustravisse." *De magistratibus,* p. 264.

82. *Calendar of State Papers,* ed. Rawdon Brown (London, 1869), III, 163. More and Contarini must have met again in London the same year when More, on behalf of the City of London, welcomed Charles V in whose suite Contarini had come to England. It is strange that no attention seems ever to have been given to the encounter between More and Contarini.

83. E. H. Harbison, *Christianity and History* (Princeton, Princeton University Press, 1964), p. 228.

84. See above, note 8.

85. Victor Trincarellus, in the dedication to Contarini of his edition of Themistius's *Opera omnia* (Aldus, 1533), emphasizes that Contarini was a combination of statesman and philosopher. "Oratio in laudem Gaspari Contareni" (never printed, in Biblioteca Correr, Venice, MS. Cic. 2903), though written after Contarini's appointment as Cardinal, praises chiefly his political efforts for peace and his patriotism, reflected in his book on Venice. In Joannes Pierius Valerianus Bellunensis's dialogue, *Contarenus seu de Literatorum infelicitate,* Contarini is a main speaker and appears chiefly as a humanist and diplomat of peace. Contarini is a speaker in Sperone Speroni's dialogue "Della vita attiva et contemplativa," *Dialoghi* (Venice, 1596), I, 184, but I cannot find that the views which Speroni puts in Contarini's mouth have much to do with his real opinions.

86. The most detailed report is that by Beccadelli: "Che Cardinale? Io son Consegliero della Signoria di Venetia." *Monumenti,* p. 21.

11. Venice in the Crisis of the League of Cambrai

1. For the following see Girolamo Priuli, *Diarii (Rerum Italicarum Scriptores,* ed. Muratori, vol. XXIV, part III), IV, 29–45, also 296–297.

2. Priuli, *Diarii,* p. 44: "Et il Principe et Padri Veneti volevano stare a chasa loro riposatamente et chomodamente et dormire sopra li sui consueti lecti et avere victoria, et questo he difficile et quasi impossibelle . . . Et veramente, se li Padri Venetti voranno mantenire et conservar statto in Ittallia, sarà necessario che li loro nobelli venetti, et dico deli primi, facino lo exercitio et mestiere del arme."

3. Marino Sanuto, *Diarii,* ed. R. Fulin (Venice, F. Visentini, 1879–1903), XIII, 139.

4. Sanuto, XVII, 102: "vidi il sol a hore 23 tutto rosso che pareva sangue per il fumo di tanti incendi."

5. See Sanuto, XVII, 94–323 from September to November 1513.

6. As examples see the speeches of the doge in Sanuto, IX, 117; XVI, 479, 489; XVII, 119, 245.

7. Sanuto, XIII, 246: "e confessa lui Principe fo di primi che disfè la lanziera a San Canzian in la soa casa per meter la tavola di la soa festa."

8. Sanuto, VIII, 119–120.

9. Archivio di Stato, Venice, *Senato Terra,* reg. 16, fol. 119v: "acio I priegano ei Signor Dio per el stado nostro." See also Sanuto, VIII, 112.

10. Archivio, *Maggior Consiglio, Deliberazioni*-25-Deda, June 12, 1513, fol. 102v.

11. *Senato Terra,* reg. 18, fol. 40v.

12. Sanuto, XIV, 420.

13. *Maggior Consiglio, Deliberazioni*-25-Deda.

14. The story of the legislation against luxury has been given, on the basis of the relevant documentary material, by G. Bistort, *Il Magistrato alle Pompe (Miscellanea di Storia Veneta,* ser. 3, vol. V; Venice, 1912), and the following report on the formation of the magistracy against luxury is dependent on Bistort.

15. Sanuto, XIV, 114–117, reproduced the main concepts of the decree, but the official text, which was accepted by the Senate (after a discussion mentioned by Sanuto, XIV, 200) and then published May 11, "supra scallis Rivoalti," was more complete. I use the official document in *Senato Terra,* reg. 18, May 8, 1512.

16. "un altra vituperosa e damnabile practica e consuetudine e introducta qual summamente offende la divina Maiesta cum dar mal exemplo a le pudiche verzene che stano ale feste driedo le zelosie a veder ballar che la prava zoventu balla certo inhonestissimo ballo de la bereta over del capello et alcuni altri balli francesi pieni di giesti lasciui e dannabili." For a description of these dances see Pompeo Molmenti, *Venice: The Golden Age* (London, J. Murray, 1907), II, chap. 13: "Private Entertainments, Balls and Banquets."

17. *Senato Terra,* reg. 17, fol. 77.

18. See the decree published in Sanuto, XVI, 151.

19. See the decree mentioned in note 17.

20. See Sanuto, XVI, 151.

21. *Senato Terra,* reg. 16, fol. 146.

22. Sanuto, IX, 245.

23. *Senato Terra,* reg. 17, fol. 30v.

24. *Senato Terra,* reg. 17, fol. 61. See also Sanuto, XV, 137–141.

25. *Senato Terra,* reg. 19, fol. 59v.

26. See Gino Luzzatto, *Storia economica di Venezia* (Venice, Centro Internazionale delle Arti, 1961), p. 248.

27. Sanuto, XVI, 643.

28. For the following see Luzzatto, *Storia economica,* pp. 236–262, and, in particular, Frederic C. Lane, *Venice and History* (Baltimore, Johns Hopkins University Press, 1966), pp. 69–86.

29. Archivio di Stato, Venice, *Consiglio dei Dieci, Miste* 1509–10, fol. 214, and many similar instructions.

30. *Senato Terra,* reg. 17, fol. 50v mentioned the "universal murmuratione" against the appointments by the *Signoria* and the *provveditori;* see also *Senato Terra,* reg. 19, fol. 137 for demands for annulment of appointments by the Collegio.

31. *Senato Terra,* reg. 16, foll. 21, 125v.

32. *Senato Terra,* reg. 16, foll. 157 ff.

33. There are many examples of this: see *Senato Terra,* reg. 16, foll. 26r and v, 81r and v, 82v, 140, 172, 178 for the years 1509 to 1510 alone.

34. Sanuto, X, 37–39.

35. *Senato Terra,* reg. 16, fol. 99.

36. *Senato Terra,* reg. 16, fol. 35v ("Resecar le superflue spese"); reg. 17, fol. 52v.

37. *Senato Terra,* reg. 19, foll. 78v and 79, December 30, 1515, and Sanuto, XXI, 425–426.

38. *Senato Terra,* reg. 16, fol. 120v.

39. *Senato Terra,* reg. 17, fol. 16v.

40. For some of these speeches see above, note 6.

41. For details see Gaetano Cozzi, "Law and Authority in Venice," in *Renaissance Venice,* ed. J. Hale (London, Faber and Faber, 1973).

42. *Senato Terra,* reg. 19, fol. 100v, and about the doge Loredan's son making use of this decree see Sanuto, XXII, 258.

43. Sanuto, XXI, 423–424.

44. *Senato Terra,* reg. 19, fol. 18, and Sanuto, XX, 15–19.

45. *Consiglio dei Dieci, Miste,* 1509–1510, fol. 210.

46. Sanuto, XVI, 489.

47. Sanuto, XVI, 490–491.

48. Priuli, *Diarii,* pp. 270, 282.

49. *Senato Terra,* reg. 16, fol. 113.

50. Sanuto, XVI, 476–477.

51. Hieronymus Borgia, *Historiae de bellis Italicis ab anno 1494 ad 1541,* Biblioteca Marciana, Venice, Cod. Lat. 3506, fol. 82r: "Neque veri Romani adversus Annibalem fortiores Venetis extitere."

52. For examples of heroic behavior see Sanuto, XII, 378; XVI, 473; XVII, 111, but a certain lack of enthusiasm can be noticed in Sanuto, VII, 254; XII, 570; XVII, 109, 111. The material advantages of this kind of military service are emphasized in Sanuto, XVI, 494. Sharp criticism of the doge and his sons is stated in Sanuto, XVII, 120, 208. An interesting criticism of the doge is to be found in the unpublished diary of Marcantonio Michiel, Biblioteca Correr, Venice, Cod. Cicogna 2848, fol. 89v. Michiel mentioned the speech of the doge in October 1513 and wrote about his effect: "Ne però alcuno so offerse de andar si perche haveano pocho in gratia el Principe per la mala for tuna sua, si etiam perche tantum li confortava con parole, ne però mandava uno di soi fioli o ne prestava danari."

53. Sanuto, XVI, 492, 536–538, 568, 576–577, 597, 626, 635; XVII, 160–162, and so on.

54. Priuli, *Diarii,* p. 279.

55. Sanuto, XI, 788; XIV, 639; XV, 329–330.

56. Priuli, *Diarii,* p. 94.

57. Sanuto, XII, 139, 303; XIII, 423; XVII, 13.

58. Sanuto, XVI, 206–207.

59. Sanuto, XII, 266, 375; XIV, 18.

60. See Chapter 10 in this volume.

61. See my article "Biondo, Sabellico, and the Beginnings of Venetian Official Historiography," *Florilegium Historiale,* ed. J. G. Rowe and W. H. Stockdale (Toronto, University of Toronto Press, 1971).

62. See William J. Bouwsma, *Venice and the Defense of Republican Liberty* (Berkeley, University of California Press, 1968) for a discussion of these issues in the later sixteenth century, although by then the Venice of the Renaissance had developed into the Venice of the Counter Reformation.

12. Venetian Diplomacy Before Pavia: From Reality to Myth

1. "Et quant aux Veniciens Ihon pourra tresbien leur remonstrer qu'ilz n'ont bein tenu ce qu'ilz ont promys et que sa Ma^té ne seroit tenu plus avant à l'observance du traicté, ains luy pourroit demander comme infractairs du traicté toutz les dommaiges, interes, qui s'ent sent ensuyz, et avec ce retourner aux premiers actions de tout ce qu'ilz ont usurpé de l'empire,—toutefois que sadite M^té pour le bien de la chrestienté entendoit pour le present supporter et excuser certe faulte." Report of Gattinara, published by Karl Brandi, "Berichte und Studien zur Geschichte Karls V.XVII. Nach Pavia," *Nachrichten von der Gesellschaft der Wissenschaften zu Goettingen,* Philologisch-Historische Klasse, Fachgruppe II: Mittlere und Neuere Geschichte, Neue Folge, II, 8.

2. Donald E. Queller, *Early Venetian Legislation on Ambassadors* (Geneva, Librairie Droz, 1966), pp. 56–58, rightly raises this question. Willy Andreas, *Staatskunst und Diplomatie der Venezianer* (Leipzig, Koehler und Amelang, 1943), provides a useful survey in his first essay entitled "Italien und die Anfänge der neuzeitlichen Diplomatie," but he is interested only in diplomatic representation abroad, not in the handling of foreign affairs by the government at home.

3. These papers form part of the diary of Marcantonio Michiel, which is preserved in two volumes in Venice, *Biblioteca Correr,* Cod. Cicogna, 2848 and 2551. While the first volume is original, the second volume, to which these papers belong, is a later copy of

sections of Michiel's diary; unfortunately, the codex is not paginated. A few excerpts concerned with Hungarian history were published in *Monumenta Spectantia Historiam Slavorum Meridionalium,* 6 (1875), 132–143; otherwise Michiel's diary has been neither published nor, as far as I can see, used.

4. Printed in DuMont, *Corps Universel Diplomatique* (Amsterdam, 1726), IV, part 1, pp. 182–183.

5. Printed in DuMont, *Corps Universel,* pp. 263–264; see also the brief abstract in "Libri Commemoriali" printed in Deputazione Veneta, *Monumenti Storici,* Serie Prima, Documenti (Venice, 1903), XI, 146.

6. The full text of this treaty is printed in Marino Sanuto, *Diarii,* ed. R. Fulin (Venice, F. Visentini, 1879–1903), XXXIV, 316–323, and for a summary in English see *Calendar of State Papers, Spanish,* ed. G. A. Bergenroth (London, 1866), II, 570–571, or see the summary in "Libri Commemoriali," pp. 171–173. For the negotiations on this treaty see Francesco Guicciardini, *Storia d'Italia,* book XV, chap. 2.

7. The best analysis of this treaty is in Guicciardini, book XV, chap. 3. The full text has never been published. See Stephan Ehses, "Die Politik des Papstes Clemens VII bis zur Schlacht von Pavia," *Historisches Jahrbuch,* 6 (1885), 561.

8. It is a different question whether there was a moral obligation for Clement VII to remain on the side of Charles V; this problem has been well argued by Ehses, "Politik des Papstes Clemens VII," p. 591; it may be added that, in the treaty of 1523, the emperor was willing to guarantee to the Cardinal of Medici and the Medici family their territorial possessions; this meant that the Cardinal of Medici implicitly was a member of the alliance.

9. Sanuto, XXXIII, 536, 539–540, 554, 634; XXXIV, 49, 105, 115, 240, 264–265, 292, 295, 301, 306, 309, 311, 314. The negotiations started in the autumn of 1522; for the instructions given to the Venetian negotiators see Archivio di Stato, Venice, *Senato. Secreta,* reg. 49; these documents show that a minority steadily opposed these arrangements, see fols. 154v, 161v, 162r. Guicciardini's report about these negotiations will be discussed below in this chapter.

10. Others of the same inclination were Leonardo Mocenigo, Girolamo da Pesaro, Francesco Bragadin, Luca Tron.

11. Sanuto, XXXIV, 309, also XXXIII, 634: Morosini had to defend himself against the reproach that he was *Francese;* he stressed that he had not sent his son to study in Paris.

12. Others on the French side were: Matteo Priuli, Andrea Trevisan, Sante Tron.

13. Guicciardini, book XV, chap. 2: "egli, collocato in quel grado, lasciata meramente la deliberazione al senato, non volle mai più nè con parole nè con opere dimostrarsi inclinato in parte alcuna."

14. Sanuto, XXXIV, 309.

15. Sanuto, XXXIV, 315: "quelli tien di Franza, come morti."

16. For a good exposition of the dangerous position of the Pope see Ehses, "Politik des Papstes Clemens VII," pp. 587–590, and on the precariousness of the Medicean position in Florence at this time see Chapter 8 in this volume.

17. See *Senato. Secreta,* reg. 50, fols. 107r–107v. Foscari's reports from Rome can be found in Archivio di Stato, Venice, *Capi del Consiglio dei Dieci, Lettere di Ambasciatori* (Rome, 1515–38), busta no. 22, but this collection has no reports written between July 23, 1524 and December 4, 1524; moreover, the letters from December 1524 are chiefly concerned with the attitude of the Duke of Ferrara and contain no material about the negotiations of the Pope with France.

18. *Senato. Secreta,* reg. 50, fols. 107r–107v, also a summary in the second volume of Michiel's diary.

19. Sanuto, XXXVII, 96.

20. My description of this discussion is based on the sources indicated in note 18.

21. The vote for the draft was 74 to 70; the vote against Bembo's motion 101 to 84. Briefly, the draft did not get an absolute majority of those present (185). On voting procedures in the Pregadi see Giuseppe Maranini, *La costituzione di Venezia* (Milan, La Nuova Italia, 1931), pp. 255ff.

22. For the meeting and the instruction see *Senato. Secreta,* reg. 50, fols. 107v–108v.

23. Both were candidates for the doganate when Gritti was elected; the amendment was also signed by Andrea Trevisan and Niccolò Bernardo.

24. *Senato. Secreta,* reg. 50, fol. 109v.

25. *Senato. Secreta,* reg. 50, fols. 109r–110v: the instruction included the formal document, empowering Foscari to conclude peace and make an alliance with the French king.

26. "Pare cosa nova, che un Imbas^{ré} presumesse tanto senza ordine del Senato, essendosi di qui pronto deliberare il contrario," from Michiel's diary; but see also Sanuto, XXXVII, 110.

27. See Ehses, "Politik des Papstes Clemens VII," pp. 595–597.

28. See the instruction to Foscari of October 29, *Senato. Secreta,* reg. 50, fol. 110r: "Nui sommaments laudamo, che sua Beat^{né} trovi forma de reservar loco honorificentissimo alla prefata Cesarea Ma^{tà} et procurar, che la intri in ditta pace."

29. "Donde superfluo e parlare di accordo dal quale l'una e l'altra parte tanto si discosti," Giberti to Cardinal Salviati, November 12, 1524, in *Négociations Diplomatiques de la France avec la Toscane,* ed. A. Desjardins (Paris, 1861), II, 788. See also *Delle Lettere di Principi,* ed. G. Ruscelli (Venice, 1581), pp. 140r–145v.

30. "Di la bona mente di questo stado," Sanuto, XXXVII, 171.

31. See Sanuto, XXXVII, 196, and the report on the meeting of November 15 in Michiel's diary.

32. For these two meetings, see chiefly Michiel's diary, but also Sanuto, XXXVII, 196, 202, and the drafts of the instructions, presented in Pregadi, *Senato. Secreta,* reg. 50, fols. 113r–115r.

33. "Vi dicemo cum Senatu, che ottenendo Francesi Pavia, laudamo che Sua Beat^{ne} continui la prattica cum il Re Christianissimo: ma non devenire a conclusione senza ordine nostro," *Senato. Secreta,* reg. 50, fol. 113v.

34. According to Sanuto, XXXVII, 196, the *Savi della terra ferma* (Marcantonio Contarini, Zaccaria Bembo, Domenico Venier, Giovanni Francesco Badoer) also were unenthusiastic about the draft, and this may have influenced its rejection.

35. For Mocenigo's speech see Michiel's diary.

36. The same story is reported by the ambassador of Federigo Gonzaga from Rome on November 28: "A questi di intesi, ch'el re christianissimo proponeva Ferrara al papa vincta a sue spese se l'voleva farsi Francese, e questo lo diceva Alberto." This report was published by Ludwig von Pastor, *History of the Popes,* IX (St. Louis, B. Herder, 1950), 495. On the influence of Alberto Pio da Carpi in Rome see Pastor, *History of the Popes,* IX, 268ff. The enmity between the Pios and the Estes, and particularly between Alberto Pio and the Duke of Ferrara, is a well-known historical fact. Because of his pro-French attitude, Alberto Pio lost Carpi, which was given by Charles V to the Duke of Ferrara in 1527.

37. See Michiel's diary for Mocenigo's speech, and for the other speeches described.

38. "la natura de Francesi essere arrogantissima e molto superba."

39. An allusion that the Spanish rule over Milan was somewhat disguised; it was exerted by means of the Sforza Duke, with Girolamo Morone as principal adviser.

40. "Savii Progenitori nostri, li quali in niun tempo, in ruina, calamità, per niuna occasione non vollero mai rompere la fede ad alcun Prencipe non pure Christiano ma infedele oltroche ponevano lo stato loro in manifesto pericolo."

41. "questo però è un operar così violento e contra natura che non può havere in se stesso poco o nulla firmezza o fondamento."

42. "materia di tanta importanza di fare una pace nuova, e romper una Tregua vecchia ed una confederazione tanto solennemente giurata."

43. "il tutto remettemo al sapientissimo iudicio della Beat.ne Sua." See *Senato. Secreta,* reg. 50, fol. 115.

44. "Ond'io non credo . . . che Sua Maesta sene voglia rimuovere, anzi pensa farlo con piu apparecchio." From a report, Giberti's from Parma on November 25, 1524, published in *Negociations,* ed. Desjardins, p. 739; Giberti's reports from the French camp show that he was highly impressed by the French king, for instance, ibid., p. 787.

45. For these negotiations, see Ehses, "Politik des Papstes Clement VII," pp. 598–601, and Pastor, *History of the Popes,* IX, 263–271. There are some differences between the facts given in these books and those facts which arise from the Venetian material. For instance, the Venetian materials do not indicate that the Pope planned to give Milan to the second son of Francis I. On the other hand, only the Venetian materials seem to mention the idea of making Francesco Sforza a cardinal for abandoning his claims to Milan. In our context these details are of no great significance, but I ought to mention that I see little justification for Ehses's view that Lannoy was willing to let the French have Milan; my interpretation of the relevant documents would be that he was playing for time because all his envisaged concessions were very much hedged in, and Lannoy's reports to Charles V from November and December 1524, published in Leon E. Halkin and Georges Dansaert, *Charles de Lannoy, Vice-Roi de Naples* (Paris, Desclée de Brouwer, 1934), pp. 246–254, seem to me to confirm this interpretation.

46. Printed in Sanuto, XXXVII, 232–235.

47. The note speaks of the "vane voci et grandissime bravate" of the French and emphasized in contrast "la consueta et da voi ben cognosciuta realità" of the Spaniards: "gli francesi se vadino adiutando con voci et parole, poichè le cesarei procurano de adiutarsi con effetti." According to the report in Michiel's diary, the ambassadors gave exact account of the military strength of their troops. Until the alliance with France became public, the demands of the Spanish and Milanese ambassadors continued to be pressed, and the Venetians took recourse to delaying tactics, even to what seems to have been a diplomatic illness of the doge. Despite their continued demands, the ambassadors seem to have had little illusions about a possible success and the audiences with them became acrimonious and sharp words were exchanged. See Sanuto, XXXVII, 252 (*alta parola*), 260, 273, 282, 299, 300, 302, 303; but see also Michiel's diary on a meeting with the ambassadors on December 2.

48. For the following see *Senato. Secreta,* reg. 50, fols. 116v–117r, and Michiel's diary.

49. "Ma quello, che nui da singular satisfactione è la resolutione divinitus fatta per Sua San.tà a questo effetto di pace, di fav quella divisione delli dui stati de Napoli, et Milano: fra questi dui Re, excogitata da lei, stabiliendola, et firmandola con la confederatione"; this is a "salutifera opera."

50. "aspettare il benefitio che sole portare il tempo" and "chi corre a furia nelle deliberationi delli stati, corre più presto al pentirsi," from Michiel's diary.

51. "potendo sempre con il contropeso dell'altro diffendersi, non volendo in alcuno tempo Li Cesarei che il Re di Francia sia il Signor della Italia, nè il Re Christianesimo che l'Imperatore sia Monarca del Mondo," like all the quotations from speeches from Michiel's diary.

52. Sanuto, XXXVII, 283, December 5, 1524, referring to an answer to a letter from Rome of November 30, and see *Senato. Secreta,* reg. 50, fols. 118r–119v for the instruction sent to Foscari. The meeting in the Pregadi of December 5 is also reported in Michiel.

53. "siamo contenti concorrere cum sua Beat.ne alla conclusione della ditta pace, et

accordo secreto fra lei, il christianissimo Re, et la Signoria nostra, et usarete della faculta vi habbiamo data cum senatu a di XXIX ottobre," *Senato. Secreta,* reg. 50, fol. 118r; the vote was: pro, 125; contro, 21; undecided, 24.

54. For the text see Aimé Louis Champollion-Figeac, *Captivité du Roi Francois I* (Paris, 1847), p. lxxviii, no. 5, or the abstract in *Calendar of State Papers, Spanish,* II, 684, and, in general, Ehses, "Politik des Papstes Clement VII," p. 602; the treaty renewed the alliance between Venice and France concluded in 1513. Venice was not obligated, however, to assist France in the present war for the conquest of Milan. This treaty was secret. It was followed by the public treaty between Clement VII and Francis I of January 5, 1525, published in Sanuto, XXXVII, 418–420, which was joined by Venice, and which Charles V, Archduke Ferdinand, and the English king were asked to join; this treaty implied the cession of Milan to France. See also the digest in the "Libri Commemoriali," vol. XI, under 1524, December 12.

55. There was a further meeting of December 9—see *Senato. Secreta,* reg. 50, fols. 119v–120r—but it discussed only the best way to decline further military cooperation with the Spaniards.

56. For this and the following see Sanuto, XXXVII, 296, under December 7, and *Senato. Secreta,* reg. 50, pp. 119r–119v.

57. Moro's speech is given at length in Michiel. It is directed primarily against the Pope, who had made no real attempt to conclude peace among the Christian princes, but, under the pretence of making peace, had pursued an anti-Spanish policy. Venice had committed a grave mistake in accepting the guidance of the Pope in its policy.

58. Clearly these four were Luca Tron, Paolo Capello, Andrea Trevisan, and Leonardo Mocenigo.

59. "per esser homo nassuto in città libera, dirà liberamente il sentimento suo, e per mal governo questo stado è tra l'ancadine e il martello." Sanuto, XXXVII, 296.

60. In addition to his report on Gabriele Moro's speech in Sanuto, XXXVII, 296, see p. 196, and see Michiel's diary, which describes Paolo Capello as speaking "con grande collera."

61. For the similarity between the Venetian and the Florentine outlook on foreign affairs see my article, "Florentine Political Assumptions in the Period of Savonarola and Soderini," *Journal of the Warburg and Courtauld Institutes,* 20 (1957), particularly 196–202.

62. Zaccaria Bembo, who played such a role in 1524, was on the *terra ferma* as *provveditore* in 1523.

63. It would go far beyond the scope of this essay to investigate whether the attitude of the individuals was influenced by economic interest or other personal reasons, but I hope that this study suggests the possibility and the importance of such investigations.

64. See Nicolai Rubinstein, *The Government of Florence under the Medici (1434–1494)* (Oxford, Clarendon Press, 1966), p. 227.

65. See my article mentioned in note 61.

66. Of course, debates in the Pregadi had a strictly hierarchical aspect; those in the higher rank—the *savi*—talked before the others, and if a *savio* had opposed a proposal, the proposal had to be defended by a person of the same rank, that is, also a *savio*. It would seem that, because there was great difference in the Collegio about the course to follow, so many *savi* became involved in the debate that it never went below this rank. For the organization of debates and voting in the Pregadi see Maranini, *Costituzione di Venezia,* pp. 246ff, 255ff.

67. See Giuseppe Vedovato. *Note sul Diritto Diplomatico della Repubblica Fiorentina* (Florence, Sansoni, 1946).

68. Gaetano Cozzi, "Cultura Politica e Religione nella Pubblica Storiografia Veneziana del'500," *Bollettino dell'Istituto di Storia della Società e dello Stato Veneziano,* 5/6 (1963–64), 267–290.

69. Francesco Guicciardini, *Storia d'Italia,* book XV, chap. 2.

70. For the history of Venetian public historiography see the article by Gaetano Cozzi mentioned in note 68.

71. Aloysii Contarini, "Delineatio Historiae, quae res gestas Venetorum complectitur, nulla diligentia contexta, iterum atque iterum expolienda et debitis coloribus exornanda, in quatuordecim libros distincta," Venice, *Biblioteca Marciana,* classe lat. x, cod. 285 (3,180); the most relevant passages are on fols. 24–25.

72. Cozzi, "Cultura," pp. 250ff, discusses the relations between Agostino Valier and Alvise Contarini. Valier dedicated a book which outlined the "perfect historian" (*Ricordi per Sciver le Historie della Repubblica di Venezia di Questi Tempi*) to Alvise Contarini, and he wrote a kind of outline of Venetian history, entitled *Dell'Utilita che si puo ritrarre dalle cose operate di Veneziani Liori XIV,* published for the first time, Padua, 1787. This might be considered a collection of examples, teaching the usefulness of following a moral and Christian course. On p. 275, where Valier touches upon the negotiations before Pavia, he speaks of "molte consulte, pretendendo alcuni che si dovesse anteporre l'amicitia del Re di Francia," but his description of events is brief, superficial, and confusing. Cozzi, "Cultura," p. 253, emphasizes the influence of Valier on Alvise Contarini, but he states that in Contarini's book the moral principles are somewhat more subdued. I must say that my view would be that Contarini had a much stronger political sense than Valier; the difference between the two seems to be greater than Cozzi assumes.

73. For Paolo Paruta's *Historia Venetiana* and for Andrea Morosini's *Historia Veneta* I used the editions in *Istorici delle Cose Veneziane i quali hanno scritto per pubblico Decreto* (Venice, 1718–22); Paruta is printed in vols. III and IV, Morosini in vols. V–VII.

74. Paruta's description of the diplomatic negotiations between 1523 and 1525 can be found in *Istorici,* III, 360–389.

75. Marc Antonio Trevisan, doge, 1553–1554.

76. Sanuto, XXXVII, 85.

77. *Istorici,* III, 379. The speeches of Corner and Trevisan on pp. 379–389.

78. *Istorici,* p. 385.

79. *Istorici,* V, 106: "ii qui in rebus publicis, imperiisque regendis floruere consilia nonnumquam temporum rationibus accomodando patriam e summis periculis eripuere." For Trevisan's speech see pp. 104–107.

80. *Istorici,* p. 107: "nemo sane ignorat qua fide integritate constantia sanctissimi illi viri, qui nobis florentissimam istam Rempublicam, atque imperium veluti per manus tradidere, societates folderaque coluerunt"; p. 108: "omnia prius expeviri antequam . . . pacta infringeretis." For Mocenigo's speech see pp. 107–109.

81. I might mention that, as far as I can see, Morosini is the only writer who reports about the suggestion of the Pope to make Francesco Sforza a cardinal; see *Istorici,* p. 115. Cozzi's characterization of Morosini's historiography in Cozzi, "Cultura," pp. 288–289, seems to me questionable because he is unaware of Morosini's careful use of sources. On Morosini's *Historia Veneta* see also William J. Bouwsma, *Venice and the Defense of Republican Liberty* (Berkeley, University of California Press, 1968), pp. 557–561.

82. *Istorici,* V, 110.

83. Paolo Paruta, *Della Perfettione della Vita Politica* (Venice, 1599), on pp. 212–219, deals with the significance of historical writing and discusses also in particular the question of the composition and the use of speeches by historians. Paruta regards speeches as inserts; he warns against speeches whose contents are entirely speculative and philosophical. Speeches ought to remain somewhat connected with events and ought to set forth in a general and abstract form what can be learned from the events described in the historical narrative. These theoretical views are rather close to Paruta's practice in his *Historia Venetiana.* For a description of Paruta's views on history in his

Della Perfettione see also Bouwsma, *Venice,* pp. 219–223, although Bouwsma's analysis seems to me to read into this work notions which it does not contain.

84. Alvise Contarini, on fol. 20 of his "Delineatio," states that criticisms of Venice by historians have their origin in that they "invidiam adducunt et ut prudentiores aliis esse videantur calumniis opprimunt." It is rather amusing, however, how belief in Venetian wisdom and righteousness has continued into modern treatments of this episode. Heinrich Kretschmayr, *Geschichte von Venedig* (Gotha, F. A. Perthes, 1934), III, 12, combines Guicciardini, Sanuto, and Paruta into a mixture that has no relation to fact. But recent Italian historians as well, considerably more steeped in the sources, continue the myth: Roberto Cessi, *Storia della Repubblica di Venezia* (Milan, G. Principato, 1946), II, 83, and Cozzi, "Cultura," p. 289, propound the thesis that Venice really did not break the treaty with Charles V because it did not promise assistance to Francis I in the current war. But this thesis is untenable; as the speeches in the Pregadi or, later, Andrea Morosini show, the Venetians themselves did not claim that the treaty with Francis I was compatible with their alliance with Charles V.

85. For the origin of the Venetian myth see Chapter 8 in this volume. The Venetian myth, of course, emerged long before the sixteenth century, when it was "codified."

13. The "New Diplomacy" of the Eighteenth Century

1. On this question see Egon Ranshofen-Wertheimer, "Geneva and the Evolution of a New Diplomacy," *World Organization: A Balance Sheet of the First Great Experiment* (Washington, American Council on Public Affairs, 1942), pp. 14–29.

2. In an article by G. J. A. Ducher; see note 106. Ducher's political and literary activity has been described and analyzed by F. L. Nussbaum, *Commercial Policy in the French Revolution* (Washington, American Historical Association, 1923). Any reader of Nussbaum's book could discover the term there, but since the book was written before the postwar interest in the concept of a "new diplomacy," the author made no special mention of Ducher's part in the history of the use of this concept.

3. In the following, the terms "radicals" and *philosophes* are used rather loosely for all those writers who were concerned with plans of political and social reform in the eighteenth century. Since I am interested in working out certain basic ideas which they all had in common, such rather general and indiscriminate use of these terms seems justified. For the same reason, no special attention is given differences and nuances in the ideas of the various writers, though I am quite aware that, from identical basic premises, they frequently arrived at very different recommendations about practical measures and details.

4. See such standard works as Henri Sée, *Les Idées politiques en France au XVIIIe siècle* (Paris, Hachette, 1920); Kingsley Martin, *French Liberal Thought in the Eighteenth Century* (Boston, Little, Brown, 1929), which has only a rather brief and spotty chapter on "Peace, Fraternity and Nationalism"; J. Salwyn Schapiro, *Condorcet and the Rise of Liberalism* (New York, Harcourt, Brace, 1934); or the brief treatment of these issues in George Weulersse, *Le Mouvement Physiocratique en France de 1756 à 1770,* 2 vols. (Paris, F. Alcan, 1910). A number of special studies have touched upon the problems with which this essay is concerned; two recent ones are Edmond Silberner, *La Guerre dans la Pensée Economique du XVIe au XVIIIe siècle,* Etudes sur l'histoire des théories économiques, VII (Paris, Librairie du Recueil Sirey, 1939), and Elizabeth V. Souleyman, *The Vision of World Peace in Seventeenth and Eighteenth Century France* (New York, G. P. Putnam's Sons, 1941). I am obligated to these two studies in various ways, and their bibliographies make a detailed bibliographical apparatus superfluous, but their approach is different from mine. They follow the development of the ideas on peace and war

through the centuries, while I attempt to place these ideas into the system of eighteenth-century thought.

5. Le Trosne, *De l'Ordre Social* (Paris, 1777), p. 367: "En effet, le système de l'Europe a pris une consistence qui semble devoir en maintenir la durée et conserver à peu près chaque puissance dans l'état où elle se trouve"; also the remarks by Diderot on the new situation in Europe in "Fragments Politiques," *Oeuvres Complètes* (Paris, 1875), IV, 41–42, or by Mably in his "Droit Public," *Collection Complète des Oeuvres,* ed. Guillaume Arnoux (Paris, 1794–95), VII, 128.

6. Although the Abbé de Saint-Pierre wrote his project for an eternal peace prior to Utrecht, its publication at the time of the conclusion of the Peace certainly strengthened its influence; see Joseph Drouet, *L'Abbé de Saint-Pierre, L'homme et l'oeuvre* (Paris, Champion, 1912), pp. 107ff.

7. Turgot, "Plan d'un ouvrage sur la géographie politique," *Oeuvres,* ed. G. Schelle (Paris, F. Alcan, 1913), I, esp. 262–263: "Réflexions générales sur la manière dont les nations, d'abord isolées, ont porté leurs regards autour d'elles . . . qu'il s'est formé plusieurs de ces mondes dans toute l'étendue du globe, indépendants les uns des autres et inconnus réciproquement; qu'en s'étendant sans cesse autour d'eux, ils se sont rencontrés et confondus, jusqu'à ce qu'enfin la connaissance de tout l'univers, dont la politique saura combiner toutes les parties, ne formera plus qu'un seul monde politique, dont les limites sont confondues avec celle du monde physique." See also Turgot's speech in the Sorbonne of December 11, 1750, ibid., pp. 214ff.

8. Sedaine, *Le philosophe sans le savoir,* crit. ed. by Th. E. Olivier, University of Illinois Studies, IV (Urbana, University of Illinois Press, 1913), pp. 105–106: "Ce n'est pas un peuple, ce n'est pas une seule nation qu'il sert; il les sert toutes, et en est servi; c'est l'homme de l'univers . . . La guerre s'allume; tout s'embrace; l'"Europe est divisée; mais ce Négociant Anglois, Hollandois, Russe ou Chinois, n'en est pas moins l'ami de mon coeur; nous sommes sur la superficie de la terre autant de fils de soie qui lient ensemble les nations et les ramènent à la paix par la nécessité du commerce."

9. For instance, Le Mercier de la Rivière, *L'ordre naturel et essentiel des sociétés politiques,* 1767, publié avec une notice par Edgard Depitre, Collection des Economistes et des Réformateurs Sociaux de la France (Paris, 1910), pp. 251, 349, 354; Le Trosne, *De l'Ordre Social,* pp. 355, 393; Gaillard, *Mélanges* (Paris, 1806), p. 66.

10. See Georges Lefebvre, "La Révolution Française et la Rationalisme," *Annales Historiques de la Révolution Française,* 18 (1946), 18ff.

11. See Dietrich Gerhard, "Kontinentalpolitik und Kolonialpolitik im Frankreich des Ausgehenden Ancien Regime," *Historische Zeitschrift,* 147 (1932), 21–31.

12. Le Trosne, *De l'Ordre Social,* pp. 430–431: "O France! O ma patrie! Violà le rôle qu'il te convient de remplir en Europe . . . Il ne faudroit pour opérer cette révolution si heureuse, que l'exemple d'une grande nation"

13. D'Argenson, *Considérations sur le gouvernement ancien et présent de la France* (Amsterdam, 1765), p. 18: "Tel est cependant le véritable objet de la science qu'on appelle Politique, perfectionner le dedans d'un Etat de tous les degrés de perfection dont il est susceptible . . . Les flatteurs persuadent aux Princes que le dedans ne doit servir qu'aux affaires du dehors; le devoir leur dit le contraire." Also Le Trosne, *De l'Ordre Social,* p. 420; Le Mercier, *L'ordre naturel,* p. 252; Rousseau, *Political Writings,* ed. C. E. Vaughan (Cambridge, The University Press, 1915), I, 381–382.

14. D'Argenson, *Considérations,* pp. 19–20: "A-t-on toujours exactement calculé, combien il a coûtoit à l'abondance des anciennes Provinces pour en acquérir une nouvelle? . . . Violà pourtant les grand objets qu'on attribue ordinairement à la Politique; violà l'éclat des Règnes et le sujet des monuments Historiques: fâcheux préjugés! reste de Barbarie! vestiges de l'ancien chaos."

15. Condillac, *Le Commerce et le Gouvernement* (Amsterdam, 1776), pp. 407–408:

"cette gloire que les peuples, dans leur stupidité, attachent aux conquêtes, et que les historiens, plus stupides encore, aiment à célébrer jusqu'au point d'ennuyer le lecteur; quel sera leur avantage?" Or Le Trosne, *De l'Ordre Social,* pp. 377, 387–389; Mirabeau, *L'Ami des Hommes ou Traité de la Population,* pt. 3 (Avignon, 1756), pp. 399–400; and, of course, the third chapter of Voltaire's *Candide.*

16. Condorcet, "Discours de réception à l'Académie Française," *Oeuvres* (Paris, ed. O'Connor and Arago, 1847–49), I, 396: "cette fureur des conquêtes si longtemps décorée du nom d'héroisme."

17. Mirabeau, *L'Ami,* p. 404: "Idée favorite des gazettes et des caffés politiques"; or Le Mercier, *L'ordre naturel,* p. 244; Le Trosne, *De l'Ordre Social,* p. 394; Mirabeau, *L'Ami,* p. 116; and the particularly detailed, somewhat later analysis of William Godwin, *Enquiry Concerning Political Justice,* facsimile ed. by F. E. L. Priestley (Toronto, University of Toronto Press, 1946), pp. 155–157.

18. Mably, "Principes des Négociations," *Oeuvres,* V, 66: "réduisant toute la science de la politique à ne savoir qu'un mot, elle flattoit également l'ignorance et la paresse des ministres, des ambassadeurs et de leurs commis."

19. Gaillard, *Mélanges,* I, 79: "Le système de l'équilibre est un système de résistance, par conséquent d'agitation, de choc et d'explosion."

20. Rousseau, *Political Writings,* I, 369; also Le Trosne, *De l'Ordre Social,* p. 374.

21. Raynal, *Histoire Philosophique et Politique des Etablissements et du Commerce des Européens dans les deux Indes* (Geneva, 1781), VI, 284: "trahisons préparées."

22. D'Argenson, *Considérations,* p. 327: "Les ligues défensives qu'ils contractent sont toujours offensives au fond."

23. Le Trosne, *De l'Ordre Social,* p. 395: "Cet art obscur qui s'enveloppe dans les plis et les replis de la dissimulation, qui craint de se laisser entrevoir, et croit ne pouvoir réussir qu'à l'ombre du mystère." Also p. 421; or Mably, *Oeuvres,* V, 182.

24. This is an extract of Diderot's "Principes de Politique des Souverains," as given in J. Oestreicher, *La Pensée Politique et Economique de Diderot* (Vincennes, Impr. Rosay, 1936), p. 70: "Ne former des alliances que pour semer des haines.—Allumer et faire durer la guerre entre mes voisins.—Point des ministres au loin, mais des espions.— . . . Etre neutre, ou profiter de l'embarras des autres pour arranger ses affaires, c'est la même chose." The whole will be found in Diderot, *Oeuvres Complètes* (Paris, 1875–77), II, 461ff.

25. Mably, "Entretiens de Phocion," *Oeuvres,* X, 172: "Mon cher Aristias, poursuivit Phocion, j'ai tâché de ramener à des principes fixes et certains cette science qu'on nomme politique, et dont les sophistes nous avoient donné une idée bien fausse. Ils la regardent comme l'esclave ou l'instrument de nos passions; de-là l'incertitude et l'instabilité de ses maximes; de-là ses erreurs, et les révolutions qui en sont le fruit. Pour moi, je fais de la politique le ministre de notre raison, et j'en vois résulter le bonheur des sociétés." Also D'Argenson, *Considérations,* p. 20; or Rousseau, *Political Writings,* pp. 510–511.

26. Diderot, art. "Paix" in "Encyclopédie," *Oeuvres,* XVI, 188: "Les passions aveugles des princes les portent à étendre les bornes de leurs états."

27. Characterized as "anecdote connue" in the debates of May 16, 1790, of the Assemblée Nationale, *Archives Parlementaires de 1787 à 1860,* première série, ed. by Maridal et Laurent (Paris, 1883), XV, 188.

28. Mably, *Oeuvres,* V, 17.

29. For instance, Mably, *Oeuvres,* V, 19–20: "Chaque état tient de ses lois, de ses moeurs et de sa position topographique, une manière d'être qui lui est propre et qui décide seule de ses intérêts."

30. For instance, Mirabeau, *L'Ami,* p. 427: "le seul arbitre des ses desseins." Or Mably, *Oeuvres,* V, 17: "Maîtresse de la fortune."

31. Mirabeau, *L'Ami,* p. 84: "malheureux principe renfermé dans ce proverbe: Nul ne perd que l'autre ne gagne, principe barbare autant que faux; et moi je dis, soit dans le physique, soit dans le moral: Nul ne perd qu'un autre ne perde." Or Le Trosne, *De l'Ordre Social,* p. 393.

32. For instance, Condorcet, "Eloge de Franklin," *Oeuvres,* III, 420: "Sa politique était celle d'un homme qui croit au pouvoir de la raison et à la réalité de la vertue." Or Mably, *Oeuvres,* XIII, 139; Turgot, "Plan d'un ouvrage," III, 683–686.

33. For instance, Le Mercier, *L'ordre naturel,* p. 252, or Mirabeau, *L'Ami,* pp. 82ff.

34. For instance, Condorcet, *Oeuvres,* IX, 93: "Vieille Politique"; Le Mercier, *L'ordre naturel,* p. 244: "fausse politique."

35. Baudeau, *Première Introduction à la Philosophie Economique, 1767,* ed. A. Dubois (Paris, P. Geuthner, 1910), p. 99: "L'opposition des intérêts fait l'essence de la politique usurpatrice. L'unité d'intérêt fait l'essence de la politique économique. Les relations de l'une sont de guerre, d'empêchement, de destruction. Les relations de l'autre sont de société, de combinaisons des travaux, de partage amical et paisible des fruits de ces travaux."

36. For this and the following see Le Trosne, *De l'Ordre Social,* pp. 417–429; Le Mercier, *L'ordre naturel,* pp. 243–253; Baudeau, *Première Introduction,* pp. 97–99.

37. Mirabeau, *L'Ami,* p. 31: "Oh! quand les deux arlequins se rencontrent, c'est à qui surpassera son compétiteur en grimaces, et voilà la politique des prétendus hommes d'Etat qui ont voulu bannir de leur science l'équité."

38. See Heinz Holldack, "Der Physiokratismus und die absolute Monarchie," *Historische Zeitschrift,* 145 (1931–32), 517–549.

39. See Condorcet, "Lettres d'un Bourgeois de New Haven à un citoyen de Virginie," *Oeuvres,* IX, 41–42, 45–46; and, in general, Schapiro, *Condorcet,* pp. 145–147.

40. Condorcet, "Lettres d'un Bourgeois," p. 45: "Les traités d'alliance me paraissent si dangereux et si peu utiles, que je vois qu'il vaut mieux y renoncer en temps de paix . . . Ce n'est qu'un moyen donné aux chefs des nations de les précipiter dans des guerres dont ils profitent pour couvrir leurs fautes, ou pour porter à la liberté des atteintes sourdes, et aux quelles la nécessité sert alors de prétexte." It is likely that Condorcet's distrust of entangling alliances was somewhat influenced by the unpopularity of the Austrian Alliance in France.

41. This analysis of Rousseau's views is based on his "Extrait du Projet de Paix Perpétuelle de M. l'Abbé de Saint-Pierre"; see Rousseau, *Political Writings,* I, 364–396. It should be kept in mind that Rousseau had some reservations about the project of the Abbé; see Georges Lassudrie-Duchêne, *Jean-Jacques Rousseau et le Droit des Gens* (Paris, H. Jouve, 1906).

42. Bentham's "Principles of International Law," written 1786–1789, published in his *Works,* ed. John Bowring (Edinburgh, 1843), II, 535ff, can be considered as a summation of the reformist program.

43. See, for instance, Le Mercier, *L'ordre naturel,* p. 250, or Le Trosne, *De l'Ordre Social,* p. 353.

44. Le Trosne, *De l'Ordre Social,* p. 421: "Sa politique sera aussi franche et aussi ouverte que sa conduite avec ses sujets"; also p. 419. Against secret diplomacy in general, Mably, *Oeuvres,* VII, 89ff, and Bentham, "Principles," pp. 554–560.

45. Le Trosne, *De l'Ordre Social,* pp. 428–429: "Il ne cherchera point à se faire des alliés; sa politique fraternelle le rendra nécessairement l'ami de toutes les nations . . . Et que pourroient lui servir des alliances?"

46. Ibid., p. 426: "Aucune nation n'aura chez lui de privilège ni de faveur par le commerce, et les Négocians domiciliés chez lui n'en auront pas davantage. Son code, à cet egard, sera aussi simple et aussi court que ses principes . . . On entrera chez lui, on en

sortira de même: on traversera son territoire sans y rencontrer ni tarif, ni préposés, ni barrières." Mably, *Oeuvres,* V, 194–195: "Jamais elles n'auroient parlé, dans leur traités de commerce, que des conventions générales propres à assurer la liberté des mers et de la navigation."

47. Rousseau, "Considérations sur le Gouvernement de Pologne," *Political Writings,* II, 510: "Ne vous ruinez pas en ambassadeurs et ministres dans d'autre cours."

48. For instance, concerning Venice see Mably, *Oeuvres,* V, 34, or Voltaire's article in the *Dictionnaire Philosophique:* "Venise, et par occasion, de la liberté." Concerning the Netherlands see Diderot, "Voyage de Hollande," *Oeuvres,* XVII, 390–391.

49. John de Witt (the real author was Pierre de la Court), *Political Maxims of the State of Holland* (London, 1743), pp. 214–215.

50. The admiration for Walpole and Fleury as ministers of peace is interesting in Gaillard, *Mélanges,* I, 63, or in Raynal, *Histoire Philosophique,* V, 202.

51. On the "quixotic policy of d'Argenson" see Walter L. Dorn, *Competition for Empire* (New York, Harper and Brothers, 1940), pp. 159ff.

52. See Samuel Flagg Bemis, *The Diplomacy of the American Revolution* (New York, D. Appleton-Century Co., 1935), pp. 26ff.

53. See Heinz Holldack, "Die Neutralitätspolitik Leopolds von Toskana," *Historische Vierteljahrsschrift,* 30 (1935–36), 732–756.

54. *Journals of the Continental Congress,* ed. W. C. Ford (Washington, Government Printing Office, 1906), V, 425; hereafter cited as *Journals.*

55. See Edmund Cody Burnett, *The Continental Congress* (New York, Macmillan, 1941), pp. 170–171.

56. See Arthur M. Schlesinger, *The Colonial Merchants and the American Revolution, 1763–1776* (New York, Columbia University Press, 1918), esp. chap. 15.

57. See Burnett, *Continental Congress,* p. 141; although some "feared to burn the bridges behind them without having made sure of European aid," see John C. Miller, *Origins of the American Revolution* (Boston, Little, Brown, 1943), p. 483.

58. Letter to Secretary Livingston, Paris, February 5, 1783, *The Works of John Adams,* ed. Charles Francis Adams (Boston, 1850–56), VIII, 35.

59. These terms are quite cursorily picked from the relevant volumes of Baron Jean Dumont, *Corps Universel Diplomatique de Droit des Gens* (Amsterdam, 1726–31).

60. See the "notes of debates," published in *Journals,* III, 471ff.

61. To Priestley, July 7, 1715: "We have not yet applied to any foreign power for assistance, nor offered our commerce for their friendship," in *Letters of Members of the Continental Congress,* ed. E. C. Burnett (Washington, The Carnegie Institution of Washington, 1921–36), I, 156; hereafter cited as *Letters.* See also Franklin to Dumas, December 19, 1775, in *Revolutionary Diplomatic Correspondence of the United States,* ed. Francis Wharton (Washington, 1889), II, 65.

62. Bonvouloir's report of December 28, 1775: "qu'ils ignoraient si, en cas que cela en vint aux propositions, la France se contenterait d'avoir chez eux pendant un temps limité un commerce exclusif pour l'indemniser des frais que lui occasionnerait leur cause," in Henri Doniol, *Histoire de la Participation de la France à l'Etablissement des Etats-Unis d'Amérique* (Paris, 1886), I, 290.

63. Deane's "Memoir on the Commerce of America": "The importance of improving the present for possessing this single branch of commerce of the United Colonies is very great, but to have a preference of the whole, is an offer which may not ever be made again," in *Deane Papers,* New-York Historical Society, *Collections,* XIX (New York, 1887), I, 184.

64. Thomas Paine speaks in *Common Sense* of "alliance." *Complete Writings,* ed. P. S. Foner (New York, The Citadel Press, 1945), I, 20. John Adams writes in "Novanglus":

"The colonies were considered formerly . . . as allies rather than subjects" and, also in "Novanglus," characterizes the bond existing between England and the American colonies as "a treaty of commerce, by which distinct states have been cemented together in perpetual league and amity." *Works,* IV, 110, 114. Of course, this is the chief idea in Franklin's "Vindication" of the summer of 1775. *Writings,* ed. A. H. Smyth (New York, Macmillan, 1905–07), IV, 412–419. Interesting also is the frequent use of the expression "commercial alliance," in, for instance, *Letters,* I, 368, or Peter Force, *American Archives, 4th series* (Washington, 1844), V, 1209.

65. Cato's "Letter to the People of Pennsylvania," March 1776, in Force, *American Archives,* V, 542–543.

66. R. H. Lee to Landon Carter, June 2, 1776: "Supplies of Military Stores and Soldiers, clothing, Ships of War to cover our Trade and open our Ports, which would be an external assistance altogether, could never endanger our freedom by putting it in the Power of our Ally to Master us," in *Letters,* I, 469. Or see, in the letter by Cato mentioned in the previous note, p. 544: "Nor let it be said that the wished-for assistance is not that of armies, but of fleets for trade, and commercial protection."

67. The draft treaty will be called "model treaty," but it should not be confused with the famous model treaty of 1784.

68. *Journals,* V, 575ff, 696, 709–710, 718, 768ff, 813ff, 827. In general see Bemis, *Diplomacy,* pp. 45–48, and Burnett, *Continental Congress,* pp. 206–210, though my interpretation of the facts differs somewhat from that given in these two studies.

69. The following analysis omits John Adams's claim to have advocated as early as the fall of 1775, in a speech on a motion by Samuel Chase for sending ambassadors to France, that "we should make no treaties of alliance with any European power; that we should consent to none but treaties of commerce; that we should separate ourselves, as far as possible, from all European politics and wars." Letter to Benjamin Rush, September 30, 1805, *Works,* I, 200. This claim was repeated in his Letters, published in the *Boston Patriot* in 1809, and in his Autobiography, *Works,* IX, 243, and II, 505. This would have made Adams an advocate of a complete system of isolationist foreign policy as early as 1775. G. Chinard, *Honest John Adams* (Boston, Little, Brown, 1933), p. 88, writes that "it is very doubtful that this principle appeared so clearly at the time to the mind of Adams, and unfortunately all traces of the deliberations of Congress on the matter seem to have disappeared." A confirmation of the existence of Chase's motion can be found, however, in Adams's letter to Chase of July 9, 1775: "Your motion last fall for sending ambassadors to France with conditional instructions, was murdered; terminating in a committee of secret correspondence, which came to nothing," in *Works,* IX, 421. The casual manner in which Adams mentions the outcome of Chase's motion confirms rather than invalidates Chinard's suggestion that, in his later years, Adams deceived himself about what happened to Chase's motion; he would hardly have needed to remind Chase of what happened to this motion if a long and important debate had taken place, as he later maintained. Moreover, such detailed suggestions about the future system of foreign policy would have been entirely inappropriate in the fall of 1775, when independence still seemed far off. Such views do not even correspond with Adams's ideas at that time. As the following discussion shows, he then still had great hopes for a complete change of the foreign policy of all powers, to be achieved by a "reformation" of the commercial system. His views hardened into a rigid isolationism only during his stay in Europe. Adams's efforts in his later years to appear as the originator and inventor of all the important ideas determining the course of American policy have done great injustice to himself; he now strikes us as a rather doctrinaire and arid thinker, while actually, he had a great gift for absorbing experience and learning from it, and he underwent an interesting development in his thinking—a development which probably was representative of a whole generation.

70. John Adams, *Works,* II, 488–489; characterized as "notes for speeches," dated March 1, 1776, but in *Letters,* I, 371, no. 6, it is suggested that they are personal memoranda because no discussion of the subject indicated took place on March 1 and 4. Just at this time, however, Deane received his instructions for his mission to France; a connection between Adams's notes and this event seems possible.

71. John Adams to W. Cushing, June 9, 1776, *Letters,* I, 478.

72. John Adams to J. Winthrop, June 23, 1776, *Letters,* I, 502.

73. This passage comes from Adams's Autobiography, *Works,* II, 516; since this statement is confirmed by external evidence, I have used it here, though in general Adams's Autobiography must be considered a most questionable historical source.

74. The "Plan of Treaties" is in *Journals,* V, 768–779; the "instructions," ibid., pp. 813–817. Of the thirty articles of the "Plan of Treaties," eighteen are concerned with the rules of trade, navigation, and so forth. The remaining twelve articles (1–5, 7–9, 11–14) are of a somewhat different character. Some of them (1 and 2) deal with the most basic principles of commerce, one (14) with the French *droit d'aubaine,* others (3, 4, 5, and 7) with special problems arising out of the independence of the United States (fishery in Newfoundland, conveying of American ships, protection against Barbary States), and still others with the consequences of France's participation in the war (8, 9, 11, 12, and 13). Because these twelve articles refer to specific issues arising out of the relations between France and the United States, only the remaining eighteen articles can have had direct models in previous treaties. Of these eighteen articles, twelve are derived from the Treaty of 1713 (Article 15 of the "Plan of Treaties" corresponds to Article 25 of the Treaty of 1713, 16 to 26, 17 to 27, 18 to 28, 19 to 35, 20 to 36, 25 to 15, 26 to 17, 27 to 18–20, 28 to 21, 29 to 22–23, 30 to 24–25); four are derived from the Treaty of 1686 (Article 10 of the "Plan of Treaties" corresponds to Article 5 of the Treaty of 1686, 21 to 7, 22 to 6, 24 to 15); the remaining two (6 and 23) seem to have been taken from other treaties. (I have found a pattern for Article 6 in the treaty between England and the Netherlands of July 21, 1667.) In general, see the statement of Bemis, *Diplomacy,* p. 46, that "the general principles of the model 'Plan of 1776' were picked by the committee out of eighteenth-century practice, as reflected in the treaty of Utrecht and generally in the treaties of the small-navy powers." But the treaties of the small-navy powers can have played only a very subordinate role, if any role at all. Aside from the tendency toward commercial toleration, the choice of the model seems to have been determined by the aim of placing American merchants into the same position as English merchants.

75. Articles 26 and 27, corresponding to Articles 17–20 of the Treaty of Utrecht.

76. Articles 1 and 2, and the instructions concerning these articles.

77. Articles 4, 5, 7, 9, 11, 12, 13; see above, note 74.

78. *Journals,* V, 814–815.

79. Ibid., p. 817.

80. Ibid., p. 815.

81. In emphasizing this point, I deviate from the prevailing view on the approach of the colonists to foreign affairs. This does not mean that I am not obligated to studies examining the origin of American isolationism. For instance, the material assembled in a study such as J. Fred Rippy and Angie Debo, *The Historical Background of the American Policy of Isolation,* Smith College Studies in History, IX, nos. 3 and 4 (Northampton, Mass., Department of History of Smith College, 1924) has been invaluable. Nor is it my intention to deny the existence of an isolationist outlook in the United States at the end of the eighteenth century; see my "The English Background of American Isolationism in the Eighteenth Century," *William and Mary Quarterly,* 3d ser., 1 (1944), 138–160. But I maintain that the isolationist features of early American foreign policy have been overemphasized, and that, in the early years of American independence, iso-

lationist and internationalist elements are by no means clearly separated, and the course which American foreign policy would take was by no means fixed. These contradictory trends could go hand in hand because both placed decisive importance on commerce.

82. *Journals,* V, 769.

83. Ibid., p. 813.

84. In modern terms, the original suggestion of the model treaty would be called a reciprocity clause. See Gottfried von Haberler, *The Theory of International Trade* (London, W. Hodge, 1936), pp. 361ff. While the most-favored-nation clause had come into use in the seventeenth century, the reciprocity clause was not usual (among European states, I found it in the *Pacte de Famille* between France and Spain of 1761, where its aim seems to have been to create a solid bloc against the outside world). Because, in modern times, reciprocity is attached to persons and not to goods, reciprocity and most-favored-nation clauses are not mutually exclusive, but can exist side by side in the same treaty. This was not the view of the Americans. That the Americans considered a reciprocity clause and most-favored-nation clause as alternatives, and that they considered reciprocity more difficult to obtain than most-favored-nation treatment, is proof they regarded the articles in which they suggested reciprocity as of extreme significance. They must have expected thereby to secure complete equality for the merchants of different nations, a real emancipation of trade from all shackles of customs, tariffs, and so forth.

85. John Adams to Secretary Jay, August 10, 1785, *Works,* VIII, 298.

86. John Adams to Secretary Jay, September 23, 1787, ibid., 454.

87. John Adams to Franklin, August 17, 1780, *Revolutionary Diplomatic Correspondence,* IV, 35.

88. John Adams to Secretary Jay, August 10, 1785, *Works,* VIII, 299.

89. It is superfluous to give any detailed proof of the acquaintance of the leading American statesmen with the thoughts of the *philosophes;* for it is obvious. It may be mentioned, however, that in 1782 John Adams had a meeting with Mably, in which they discussed "open diplomacy." See *Works,* III, 350. The study of Michael Kraus, *The Atlantic Civilization: Eighteenth-Century Origins* (Ithaca, Cornell University Press, 1949) is chiefly concerned with a problem diametrically opposite to the one discussed in this essay, "the impact of the New World upon the Old," but the work bears upon our subject in pointing out the intimate intellectual connection between the two worlds.

90. An early reflection of this appears in John Adams's letter to Jay, April 13, 1785, on the "supposition that we are independent of France, in point of moral and political obligation" (*Works,* VII, 235).

91. This is the famous statement of principle regarding the American attitude toward armed neutrality, June 12, 1783, *Revolutionary Diplomatic Correspondence,* VI, 482.

92. See Jefferson's letter to William Short, January 23, 1804, *American Historical Review,* 33 (1927–28), 832–835: "I have ever considered diplomacy as the pest of the world, as the workshop in which nearly all the wars of Europe are manufactured. On coming into the administration I dismissed one half of our missions and was nearly ripe to do so by the other half. The public opinion called for it, and would now be gratified by it: and as we wish not to mix in the politics of Europe, but in her commerce only, Consuls would do all the business we ought to have there, quite as well as ministers." And, for Jefferson's practice, see his Memorandum made to a Committee of the Senate on the subject of diplomatic nominations, January 4, 1792, *Writings,* ed. by P. L. Ford (New York, 1892), I, 170–173.

93. This and the following quotation are from a statement of the commissioners entrusted with negotiations of a commerce treaty with Prussia, March 14, 1785, *Diplomatic Correspondence of the United States from 1783 to 1789* (Washington, 1832), I, 555.

94. Outlined in the "Plan of 1784" and carried into practice in the commercial treaty

with Prussia; see S. F. Bemis, *A Diplomatic History of the United States* (New York, H. Holt, 1936), pp. 66ff.

95. Speech of Pétion de Villeneuve, May 17, 1790, *Archives Parlementaires de 1787 à 1860, première série,* ed. L. Mavidal et Laurent (Paris, 1883), XV, 541: "C'est à cette marche ténébreuse de l'administration, à ces opérations clandestines du ministère que nous devons attribuer ces déprédations, ces iniquités et cette foule de maux enfin qui désolent le royaume"; and p. 540: "Le secret, dit-on, est l'âme de la politique. . . . Et moi, je soutiens que ce mystère dont on fait tant de cas, auquel on attache de si précieux avantages, ne sait, au fond, qu'à cacher les passions, les fautes et les erreurs de ceux qui gouvernent."

96. Speech of Rewbell, May 18, 1790, ibid., p. 564: "Les traités d'alliance ne sont autre chose que le droit de lever des impôts et de ruiner le Trésor de l'Etat . . . une grande nation ne doit avoir d'alliés que la providence, sa force et la justice."

97. Speech of Cazalès, May 21, 1790, ibid., p. 640: "Je ne réponds pas sérieusement à ceux qui ont dit que la France doit s'isoler du système politique de l'Europe."

98. Speech of Mirabeau, May 20, 1790, ibid., p. 621: "Je me suis demandé d'abord à moi-même si nous devions renoncer à faire des traités, et cette question se réduit à savoir si, dans l'état actuel de notre commerce, et de celui de l'Europe, nous devons abandonner au hasard l'influence des autres puissances sur nous, et notre réaction sur l'Europe . . . Le temps viendra sans doute où nous n'aurons que des amis et point d'alliés, où la liberté du commerce sera universelle, où l'Europe ne sera qu'une seule famille."

99. "Un grand peuple, un peuple libre et juste est allié naturel de tous les peuples, et ne doit point avoir d'alliances particulières qui le lient au sort, aux intérêts, aux passions de tel ou tel peuple," as quoted in Frédéric Masson, *Le Département des Affaires Étrangères pendant la Révolution, 1787–1804* (Paris, 1877), p. 151. The memorandum was written in 1791; Dumouriez became foreign minister in March 1792.

100. Gouverneur Morris, *A Diary of the French Revolution,* ed. Beatrix Cary Davenport (Boston, Houghton Mifflin, 1939), II, 439.

101. See Jean Belin, *La Logique d'une idée-force, L'Idée sociale et la Révolution Française (1789–1792)* (Paris, Hermann et cie, 1939), pp. 186–187: "Dumouriez écrit, par exemple, à un agent français à Berlin: 'Comme le système politique que j'ai adopté en entrant dans le ministère est franc, loyal et constitutionnel, M. Bays communiquera cette instruction toute entière à M. Hertzberg, comme un hommage!'"

102. Talleyrand, "Mémoire sur les rapports actuels de la France avec les autres Etats de l'Europe," November 25, 1792, published in G. Pallain, *Le Ministère de Talleyrand sous le Directoire (Correspondence Diplomatique de Talleyrand* [Paris, 1891]), pp. xlii–lvi.

103. Ibid., p. xlix: "La France formera entre elle et tous ces peuples des traités solennels de fraternité où les intérêts de la défense commune soient établis et déterminés d'une manière immuable, et où de nouvelles sources de commerce et d'industrie soient ouvertes avec libéralité aux besoins et à l'activité de l'espèce humaine."

104. Ibid., p. 1: "Elle doit se lier à eux, non par des traités permanents d'alliance et de fraternité, mais par des conventions passagères sur les intérêts politiques et commerciaux qui naîtront des circonstances."

105. See Raymond Guyot, *Le Directoire et la paix de l'Europe* (Paris, F. Alcan, 1911); in particular, chap. 6, "Le Grand Dessein du Directoire," pp. 187–195, and the last section on the contrast between "la politique des frontières naturelles" and "la politique impériale, au sens romain du mot" (p. 902).

106. On Ducher's relationship to the French Foreign Ministry see Masson, *Le Départment,* pp. 240ff; for an exhaustive analysis of his political views and influence see F. L. Nussbaum, *Commercial Policy,* which has the subtitle "A Study of the Career of G. J. A. Ducher," and contains a list of Ducher's articles in the *Moniteur,* pp. 322–328.

Nussbaum's study shows Ducher's importance in the development of a protectionist policy in the French Revolution, which may seem to place him in contrast to the trends in diplomacy discussed here. But he is connected with these trends in his emphasis on the necessity of a commercial diplomacy in contrast to traditional power politics. Perhaps for propagandistic reasons, he presents in later years the protectionist policy as a temporary weapon, through which England's "commercial monarchy" over the globe could be broken, and through which France could achieve "freedom of the seas, for herself, and for all other peoples, neutral and enemy," pp. 295–298. This aspect of Ducher's views is particularly significant in our context and is exclusively emphasized here.

107. Article, "Attribution de la régie des Douanes extérieures au ministre des affaires étrangères," *Moniteur,* May 7, 1793: "Il n'est pas de la dignité ni des intérêts du peuple Français de conclure avec aucune puissance étrangère aucun traité particulier d'alliance ni de commerce . . . La République Française existe par elle-même; elle n'a besoin d'aucune garantie, sa force naturelle la met au-dessus du secour d'un allié, quel qu'il soit . . . Hors des atteintes des intrigues de tous les cabinets de l'Europe, elle ne sera jamais en guerre que pour elle-même; gardant une neutralité absolue dans toute guerre entre les rois, elle sera dans un autre hémisphère; libre, paisible, amie de tous les peuples, sans être liée par aucun de ces traités insidieux dont l'ensemble est contradictoire, dont les clauses de secours offensif et défensif, et les conditions commerciales sont, à volonté, des prétextes de rupture et de guerre, où les rois regrettent peu le sang du peuple, s'il doit augmenter leur autorité."

108. Article, "Diplomatie Commerciale," *Moniteur,* December 5, 1793: "La République Française se déshonorerait en naissant, si elle n'abjurait pas toute politique autre que celle du courage, toute autre diplomatie que celle du commerce, le lien naturel des peuples, la base la plus solide de leur prospérité, le plus puissant moyen pour maintenir ou recourvrer leur liberté politique."

109. Article, "De la Paix et des Traites de commerce," *Moniteur,* September 20, 1795: "Il y aurait pusillanimité et déraison à rentrer dans nos anciennes limites commerciales. Les traités actuels de commerce sont le territoire de l'Angleterre; un traité général fondé sur l'egalité et l'indépendance des Nations sera une vraie conquête pour chacune d'elles sur l'insulaire ennemi de la paix et des manufactures des continentaux . . . Vous qui avez conspiré contre la liberté du peuple, français, voulez-vous sincèrement la paix du continent de l'Europe: unissez-vous à lui par un traité de commerce qui rende à chaque Nation égalité et indépendance. Qu'il n'y ait plus de distinction de nation; s'il y en a une plus favorisée, il y a jalousie, haine, cause de guerre."

110. His article in *Moniteur,* June 9, 1793, is called "Nouvelle Diplomatie"; "new diplomacy" means a "Diplomatie Régenerée" (title of article in *Moniteur,* October 24, 1794) and is identical with a "Diplomatie Commerciale" (title of article in *Moniteur,* December 5, 1793); it is the opposite of the "vieille diplomatie" (title of article in *Moniteur,* October 3, 1793: "Déroute de la vieille diplomatie").

111. Though Wilson's interest was strengthened by British attempts to secure fuller parliamentary and popular control of foreign affairs. See Hajo Holborn, *The Political Collapse of Europe* (New York, Knopf, 1951), p. 105.

14. Ciano and His Ambassadors

1. Galeazzo Ciano, *1937–1938 Diario* (Bologna, Cappelli, 1948), p. 40.

2. Ibid., p. 55.

3. On the authenticity of Ciano's diary and on the value of its various editions see Mario Toscano, "Fonti documentarie e memorialistiche per la storia diplomatica della seconda guerra mondiale," *Rivista Storica Italiana,* 60 (1948), 106–108.

4. Roberto Cantalupo, *Fu la Spagna: Ambasciata presso Franco Febbraio–Aprile 1937* (Verona, A. Mondadori, 1948), p. 42.

5. See Raffaele Guariglia, *Ricordi 1922–1946* (Naples, Edizioni scientifiche italiane, 1949), pp. 212.

6. Ibid., pp. 213, 328.

7. Grigore Gafencu, *The Last Days of Europe* (London, F. Muller, 1947), p. 136.

8. For instance, Ciano, *1937–1938 Diario,* pp. 34, 125.

9. Ramon Serrano Suñer, *Entre Hendaya y Gibralter* (Mexico, Epesa Méxicana, 1947), p. 325.

10. It should perhaps be noted that, while Ciano's noble title was not of Fascist creation, its origins were very recent. His father had been made Count as a reward for his naval exploits in the war.

11. Giuseppe Bottai, *Vent'Anni e un Giorno* (Milan, Garzanti, 1949).

12. Ciano, *1937–1938 Diario,* p. 221, also p. 124.

13. Serrano Suñer, *Entre Hendaya y Gibraltar,* p. 316.

14. Mario Donosti, *Mussolini e l'Europa* (Rome, Edizioni Leonardo, 1945), p. 15.

15. For a list of the Italian diplomatic corps as of January 23, 1939 and the officials of the Italian Foreign Office as of October 12, 1938, see *Documenti Italiani,* 8th ser., XII, 633–645.

16. Cantalupo, *Fu la Spagna,* pp. 67–68.

17. On the role of the Gabinetto, see—in addition to Cantalupo—Emanuele Grazzi, *Il Principio della Fine* (Rome, Faro, 1945), pp. 8–11, and in general, Donosti, *Mussolini e l'Europa,* pp. 12–20. See also the introduction to *Documenti Italiani,* 8th ser., XII, ix–x.

18. Grazzi, *Il Principio della Fine,* p. 10.

19. He has written very revealing memoirs: Filippo Anfuso, *Roma Berlino Salò (1936–1945)* (Milan, Garzanti, 1950). He remained loyal to Mussolini till the end.

20. Mario Toscano, *L'Italia e gli Accordi Tedesco-Sovietici dell' Agosto 1939* (Florence, Sansoni, 1952), p. 38.

21. Ciano, *1937–1938 Diario,* pp. 75–76, or *Diario* (Milan, Rizzoli, 1946), I, 17.

22. Cantalupo, *Fu la Spagna,* p. 67.

23. Guariglia, *Ricordi,* pp. 357–358; Grazzi, *Il Principio della Fine,* p. 123.

24. Guariglia, *Ricordi,* p. 357; Grazzi, *Il Principio della Fine,* p. 18; Dino Alfieri, *Due Dittatori di fronte* (Milan, Rizzoli, 1948), p. 23.

25. Grazzi, *Il Principio della Fine,* p. 104.

26. Anfuso, *Roma Berlino Salò,* pp. 20–26.

27. See note 41 below.

28. For the following see Cantalupo, *Fu la Spagna,* pp. 62–67, 75–78, 244–250.

29. For the text see Galeazzo Ciano, *L'Europa verso la Catastrofe* (Milan, A. Mondadori, 1947), pp. 120–121.

30. Guariglia, *Ricordi,* p. 193.

31. As an example see Grandi's report on his interview with Neville Chamberlain and Anthony Eden in February 1938, shortly before Eden's dismissal, in Ciano, *L'Europa verso la Catastrofe,* pp. 249–278. For further examples of the approved *tono fascista* see *Documenti Italiani,* 8th ser., XII, 82–83, 120–125, 157–158, 507, 610.

32. Guariglia, *Ricordi,* p. 743.

33. Ibid., pp. 355–357, where Guariglia's original draft and Ciano's revised text are both printed.

34. Grazzi, *Il Principio della Fine,* pp. 12–13.

35. "The brazen and extensive use made of material thus acquired" is discussed by Namier in his review of "Ciano's Early Diary," in L. B. Namier, *Europe in Decay* (London, Macmillan, 1950), pp. 112–115, where most of the facts mentioned above are

discussed. The article by Mario Toscano, "Problemi Particolari della Storia della Seconda Guerra Mondiale," *Rivista di Studi Politici Internazionali,* 17 (1950), 388–398,
deals with the interesting question of the influence which these interceptions had on the
course of Italian foreign policy.

36. Ciano, *L'Europa verso la Catastrofe,* p. 286, 338: "contrario allo nostro stile diplomatico per il suo carattere di Patto collecttivo."

37. Ciano, *Diario,* I, 34, 52, 61.

38. See the report about a conversation with Mussolini in Cantalupo, *Fu la Spagna,*
p. 42.

39. Ciano, *Diario,* I, 12; Ciano, *L'Europa verso la Catastrofe,* p. 375.

40. Ciano, *1937–1938 Diario,* p. 44; *Diario,* I, 99.

41. Ciano, *1937–1938 Diario,* pp. 118, 140, 150, 165, 170, 267; *Diario,* I, 24, 34,
35, 55, 64; *L'Europa verso la Catastrofe,* pp. 305–316, 409–412.

42. Ciano, *L'Europa verso la Catastrofe,* p. 311.

43. For a discussion of the situation at the end of the Abyssinian War see Maxwell H.
H. Macartney and Paul Cremona, *Italy's Foreign and Colonial Policy, 1914–1937*
(London, Oxford University Press, 1938), chap. 15, and Donosti, *Mussolini e l'Europa,*
p. 42. For the historical roots of the contrast between a rational and emotional-aggressive
Italian foreign policy see Federico Chabod, *Storia della Politica Estera Italiana dal 1870
al 1896,* vol. I, *Le premesse* (Bari, G. Laterza, 1951).

44. For the text see Royal Institute of International Affairs, *Documents on International Affairs, 1937* (London, 1939), pp. 87–89.

45. For the text see *Documents on International Affairs, 1938,* pp. 141–156.

46. For a summary of the British complaints see the "Extracts from Foreign Office
Memorandum on Anglo-Italian Relations," in *British Documents,* 3d ser., III, 812–815.

47. Ibid., 478; IV, chap. 4.

48. Ciano, *Diario,* I, 20; see also the somewhat reticent tone of Mussolini's and
Ciano's telegrams at the end of the visit, in *British Documents,* 3d ser., III, 540.

49. The basic work on the relations between Italy and Germany remains Elizabeth
Wiskemann, *The Rome-Berlin Axis* (New York, Oxford University Press, 1949), but
material which has come out since its publication must now be taken into account.
Mario Toscano, *Le Origini del Patto d'Acciaio* (Florence, Sansoni, 1948) is based on the
Italian Foreign Office documents and gives an admirable presentation of the details of
the diplomatic negotiations. The most recent survey is given by M. Magistrati, "Berlino
1939: da Praga al Patto d'Acciaio," *Rivista di Studi Politici Internazionali,* 19 (1952),
597–652.

50. Ciano, *Diario,* I, 55–58.

51. Ciano, *1937–1938 Diario,* pp. 114, 263.

52. See Ciano's instructions to Grandi in Ciano, *L'Europa verso la Catastrofe,* pp.
245–246.

53. Toscano, *Patto D'Acciaio,* pp. 30–35.

54. The bellicose speeches which Mussolini made in September are explained as a
means to maintain contact with Hitler so that Hitler would accept Mussolini's media-
tion.

55. The most recent treatment is in Toscano, *L'Italia e gli Accordi Tedesco-Sovietici.*
Ciano's reports are in *L'Europa verso la Catastrofe,* pp. 449–459, and in *Diario,* I,
140–141. Magistrati, Ciano's brother-in-law, who was a member of the Italian embassy
in Berlin and present in Salzburg, has written two articles "Salisburgo 1939," and "Le
Settimane Decisive," *Rivista di Studi Politici Internazionali,* 16 (1949), 479–509, and 17
(1950), 187–232, while Attolico's views are given in Leonardo Simoni, *Berlino Ambasciata d' Italia 1939–1943* (Rome, Migliaresi, 1946), pp. 11–18. Important information
is also contained in Donosti, *Mussolini e l'Europa,* pp. 198–201.

56. See, for instance, *Documenti Italiani,* 8th ser., XII, 263–264, 291, 378–381, 559–562.

57. Ciano, *Diario,* I, 146.

58. This point had been made by Ciano to Ribbentrop in Milan and had again been stressed in the so-called *Memoriale Cavallero* of May 30. See Toscano, *Patto d'Acciaio,* pp. 186–191.

59. See note 20 above.

60. Simoni, *Berlino Ambasciata d'Italia,* p. 17.

61. Ciano, *1937–1938 Diario,* p. 134; *Diario,* I, 57, 60, 62.

62. Ciano, *1937–1938 Diario,* p. 269.

63. This differs from the interpretation given by Toscano, *Patto d'Acciaio,* pp. 33–34.

64. Ciano, *Diario,* I, 104.

65. Such expressions are collected by Namier, *Europe in Decay,* pp. 108–110.

66. See Ciano's remark to Serrano Suñer, *Entre Hendaya y Gibraltar,* p. 317.

67. See *The Diplomats, 1919–1939,* ed. Gordon A. Craig and Felix Gilbert (Princeton, Princeton University Press, 1953), pp. 214–215.

68. Ciano, *1937–1938 Diario,* p. 52.

69. Anfuso, *Roma Berlino Salò,* pp. 392, 451.

70. Quotations from his letter to Serrano Suñer about Ciano's death, in Serrano Suñer, *Entre Hendaya y Gibraltar,* p. 323.

71. Rudolf Rahn, *Ruheloses Leben* (Düsseldorf, Diederichs, 1949), p. 251.

16. The Historian as Guardian of National Consciousness: Italy between Guicciardini and Muratori

1. Benedetto Croce, "La Crisi Italiana del Cinquecento e il legame del Rinascimento col Risorgimento," *La Critica,* 37 (1939), 401–411. I used the English translation of this article, published in *The Late Italian Renaissance 1525–1630,* ed. Eric Cochrane (New York, Harper Torchbooks, 1970), pp. 23–42. The quoted passages can be found on pp. 34, 36, 38.

2. For a summary of discussions of this problem, see Alessandro Passerin d'Entrèves, "Riflessioni sulla Storia d'Italia," *Dante Politico e altri Saggi* (Turin, Einaudi, 1955), esp. pp. 20–25.

3. For a refutation of the view that Machiavelli abandoned such hopes in the last years of his life see Chapter 6 in this volume.

4. I prefer these terms to the concept of civic humanism. The influence which humanism exerted on political thought was not limited to republics, and the same humanist could in one work praise republics and in another, monarchies.

5. P. S. Allen, *Opus Epistolarum Erasmi* (Oxford, Clarendon Press, 1906–58), II, 491.

6. Clearly, one of the reasons for the condemnation of Erasmus was the stimulus which his work had given to Luther and the Reformers. But the limited number of classical heroes treated in Marino's collection of "portraits in poems" is striking. In the 1667 edition of Marino's *La Galeria,* the Negromanti will be found on pp. 138–142.

7. For the facts given in the following description of papal Rome see L. Pastor, *History of the Popes* (St. Louis, Mo., B. Herder, 1912–14), esp. vols. XIX, XXI, XXII.

8. Torquato Tasso, *Opere,* ed. Bruno Maier (Milan, Rizzoli, 1964), II, no. 1389, p. 112; Tasso's numerous poems celebrating Rome's restoration by Sixtus V are characteristic of a new attitude toward antiquity.

9. Fritz Saxl, *Antike Götter in der Spätrenaissance,* Studien der Bibliothek Warburg, VIII (Berlin, Teubner, 1927), has directed attention to the anticlassical trend in the period of the Counter Reformation; see esp. pp. 26–33. Since then, these tendencies

have been frequently mentioned in general works on the period, but we still need a systematic study of this phenomenon.

10. Rodolfo de Mattei, *Dal Premachiavellismo all' Antimachiavellismo* (Florence, Sansoni, 1969), is the most recent comprehensive survey of the discussions that Machiavelli's ideas provoked in the Italian political literature of the cinquecento and seicento.

11. The concept "Counter Reformation" is a very dubious one. Here and in the following it is used in a purely chronological sense, designating the period between 1560 and 1625.

12. Scipione Ammirato, *Discursus in Cornelium Tacitum* (Helenapoli, Schönwetti, 1609), p. 325; Ammirato calls Machiavelli "autor discursum."

13. Giovanni Botero, *The Reason of State (Ragione di Stato)*, trans. P. J. Waley and D. P. Waley (London, Routledge and Kegan Paul, 1956), p. 50.

14. Ibid., p. 51.

15. Traiano Boccalini, *Ragguagli di Parnaso* (Bari, G. Laterza, 1948), III (a cura di Luigi Firpo), 152.

16. For instance, Ammirato, *Discursus.*

17. "Est vulgus otiosa bestia, quae verum a falso non discernit." Ammirato, *Discursus,* p. 353.

18. "Gregge di pecore." Boccalini, *Ragguagli,* I, 232.

19. Botero, *Reason of State,* p. 50.

20. The classical historical treatment of the development of this idea in sixteenth-century Italy is Friedrich Meinecke, *Die Idee der Staatsräson in der neueren Geschichte* (Munich and Berlin, R. Oldenbourg, 1924).

21. One of the most delightful discussions of the idea of "balance of power" will be found in Boccalini, *Ragguagli,* III, 34–44; the chapter is entitled "Pesa de'stati di tutti i principi e monarchie d'Europe fatta da Lorenzo de' Medici."

22. Boccalini, *Ragguagli,* II, 289–292. On p. 290: "legge utile agli stati, ma in tutto contraria alla legge d'Iddio e degli uomini."

23. See Felix Gilbert, "Machiavelli e Venezia," *Lettere Italiane,* 21 (1969), 389–398.

24. "i senatori veneziani per ultimo scopo del viver loro aveano la pace, ove il senato romano solo ebbe la guerra . . . a lei solo bastava di posseder tanto imperio, che dalle armi degl'inimici stranieri assicurasse la libertà veneziana, e che ella non amava la grandezza dello Stato per ambizion di comandare, ma per gloria di non servire." Boccalini, *Ragguagli,* I, 292.

25. "i principi non si sogliano muover se non per propri interessi." This is the beginning of Francesco Contarini's report after his mission to Mantua, October 31, 1588. The following quotations come from the reports on Savoy by Simon Contarini, dated August 3, 1601, and from the reports on Tuscany by Francesco Contarini, dated June 1589. All these reports were edited by Eugenio Albèri in vol. V of the second series of the *Relazioni degli Ambasciatori Veneziani* (Florence, 1839–63).

26. On this genre see Luigi Firpo, *Lo Stato ideale della Controriforma* (Bari, Laterza, 1957). See also Paul F. Grendler, *Critics of the Italian World* (Madison, University of Wisconsin Press, 1969), which contains a very comprehensive bibliography, though the writers with whom Grendler deals precede the period with which we are concerned.

27. Of the rich and detailed literature on Campanella, the chapter "Giordano Bruno and Tommaso Campanella" in Frances A. Yates, *Giordano Bruno and the Hermetic Tradition* (London, Routledge and Kegan Paul, 1964) is particularly relevant for us.

28. Alessandro Visconti, *L'Italia nell'Epoca della Controriforma* (Verona, Mondadori, 1958), is the best-known general survey of the period. For an outstanding analysis of social developments see Giuliano Procacci, *History of the Italian People,* trans. Anthony Paul (New York, Harper and Row, 1970).

29. See Grendler, *Critics of the Italian World,* chap. 3, entitled "La Misera Italia."

30. For the facts see Vittorio di Tocco, *Ideali d'Indipendenza in Italia durante la Preponderanza Spagnuola* (Messina, Principato, 1926), though the exclusive concentration on expressions of national feeling gives a somewhat distorted picture of the general character of political thought.

31. "prencipi del nostro sangue, nati ed allevata con i costumi nostri d'Italia." Alessandro Tassoni, *Prose Politiche e Morali,* ed. G. Rossi (Bari, Laterza, 1930), p. 353.

32. "la plebe, vile di nascimento e di spirito, ha morto il senso a qualsivoglia pungente stimolo di valore e di onore." Tassoni, *Prose,* p. 343. See also notes 17 and 18 above.

33. J. H. Elliott, "Revolts in the Spanish Monarchy," *Preconditions of Revolution in Early Modern Europe,* ed. Jack P. Greene (Baltimore, Johns Hopkins University Press, 1970), provides an up-to-date statement of the events in southern Italy. "A Note on Further Reading," pp. 129–130, lists the relevant literature.

34. For events in Naples, Rosario Villari, *La Rivolta Antispagnola a Napoli* (Bari, Laterza, 1967) is of fundamental importance. But see also the relevant articles in the *New Cambridge Modern History* (Cambridge, Cambridge University Press, 1970), IV.

35. For events in Milan see Ugo Petronio, *Il Senato di Milano* (Rome, Giuffrè, 1972).

36. See the two articles by Samuel Berner, "Florentine Society in the Late Sixteenth and Early Seventeenth Centuries," *Studies in the Renaissance,* 18 (1971), 203–246, and "Florentine Political Thought in the Late Cinquecento," *Pensiero Politico,* 3 (1970), 177–199. In a subsequent article, "The Florentine Patriciate in the Transition from Republic to Principato," *Studies in Medieval and Renaissance History,* 9 (1972), 3–15, Berner emphasizes that the Florentine patriciate continued commercial activities throughout the sixteenth century.

37. The most recent work on Venice in this period is William J. Bouwsma, *Venice and the Defense of Republican Liberty* (Berkeley, University of California Press, 1968), though my interpretation of this period in Venetian history is very different from his.

38. The following quotations come from Sarpi's "Considerazioni sopra le Censure della Santità di Papa Paolo V," easily available in Paolo Sarpi, *Opere,* ed. G. Cozzi and L. Cozzi (Milan and Naples, R. Ricciardi, 1969).

39. See Carlo M. Cippola, "The Economic Decline of Italy," *Crisis and Change in Venetian Economy,* ed. Brian Pullan (London, Methuen, 1968); this is the revised and translated version of an article which appeared first in *Economic History Review,* 2d ser., 5 (1952).

40. For the establishment of academies in general see Visconti, *L'Italia,* pp. 567–570, and in particular, Stillman Drake, "The Academia dei Lincei," *Galileo Studies* (Ann Arbor, University of Michigan Press, 1970).

41. Like Angeli di Costanzo, who, in his *Istoria del Regno di Napoli,* (Aquila, 1582), I, p. xliii, stated: "Ho voluto scriverla in lingua comune Italiana, a tal che possa essere letta e intesa da tutti"; it does not matter that it will not come "a notizia di nazioni esterne."

42. "mostrare alle nazioni forestieri, che di questa materia se ne sa tanto in Italia, e particolarmente in Roma, quanto possa mai averne imaginato la diligenza oltramontana." From our point of view, the fact that this foreword was written in compliance with ecclesiastical requests is irrelevant.

43. See Donald Kelley, *Foundations of Modern Historical Scholarship, Language, Law and History in the French Renaissance* (New York, Columbia University Press, 1970).

44. See particularly the programmatic statements at the beginning of the first book of Caroli Sigonii, *Historiarum De Regno Italiae Libri Quindecim . . .* (Venice, 1574; Frankfurt, 1591).

45. "primi magnifica aedificia a fundamentis erexere quibus posteri quippe deinde superstruere potuerunt." Ludovico Muratori, "Vita Caroli Sigonii," *Raccolta delle Opere Minori* (Naples, 1757–64), XVIII, 16.

46. "Nam aut nimium superbientis, aut delicati, dicam etiam ingrati animi est, Italiam tantummodo victricem ac triumphantem velle nosse, victam vero atque ab exteris Nationibus subactam aversari. Eadem est in utroque verum statu mater nostra, atque illius non minus felicem, quam adversam fortunam cognoscere ad filios potissimum spectat."

17. From Political to Social History: Lorenz von Stein and the Revolution of 1848

1. Ernst Grünfeld takes note of this fact in his *Lorenz von Stein und die Gesellschaftslehre* (Jena, G. Fischer, 1910), p. ii. Eduard Fueter, for example, does not even mention Stein in his *Geschichte der neueren Historiographie* (Munich, Oldenbourg, 1911). See, too, Gottfried Salomon's introduction to Stein's *Geschichte der sozialen Bewegung in Frankreich* (Munich, Drei Masken Verlag, 1921), p. v.

2. See the compilation of literature on Stein in H. Nitzschke, *Die Geschichtsphilosophie Lorenz von Steins,* Supplement 26 of the *Historische Zeitschrift* (1932), pp. 144–145.

3. Nitzschke, *Geschichtsphilosophie.* That I have some objections to Nitzschke's work does not detract from its basic importance. Nitzschke uses the expression "biography of Stein's intellectual development" on page 119.

4. According to Nitzschke, the first period (1835–1840) stood under the influence of Hegel and the Historical school. The second period (1841–1851) shows the predominant influence of French social science. In the third period (1852–1868) Stein was working toward a reconciliation between idealism and positivism.

5. Günther Ipsen, "Soziologie des deutschen Volkstums," *Archiv für angewandte Soziologie,* 4 (1932), 145. Grünfeld, *Lorenz von Stein,* pp. 9 and 29 also emphasizes the importance of social theory for Stein. Moritz Ritter, *Die Entwicklung der deutschen Geschichtswissenschaft* (Munich, Oldenbourg, 1919), p. 349, emphasizes the significance of the changes that Stein made in his *Geschichte der sozialen Bewegung.*

6. For example, "Class Struggles in France" and "The Eighteenth Brumaire of Louis Bonaparte."

7. See the bibliographical survey in Charles Seignobos, "La Révolution de 1848" in vol. VI of Ernest Lavisse, *Histoire de la France contemporaine* (Paris, Hachette, 1921), p. 2.

8. Alexis de Tocqueville, *Souvenirs,* publiés par le Comte de Tocqueville (Paris, 1893), translated as *The Recollections of Alexis Tocqueville* (New York, Meridian, 1959).

9. Alphonse de Lamartine, *Histoire de la révolution de 1848,* 2 vols. (Paris, 1848). Louis Blanc, *Histoire de la révolution de 1848,* 2 vols. (Paris, 1860), a collection of previously published studies.

10. This also explains, in my view, why the intellectual repercussions of the year 1848 were so important, indeed, more important than the political significance of the year's events would seem to justify. It explains, too, why the year 1848 must stand as the dividing point between the idealistic and positivistic halves of the nineteenth century.

11. Tocqueville, *The Recollections,* pp. 68–69.

12. See Nitzschke, *Geschichtsphilosophie,* pp. 119ff.

13. Stein, *Sozialismus,* 2d ed., p. 193, also p. 195.

14. Stein, *Sozialismus,* 2d ed., pp. 187–195, on the incipient development of the principle of égalité in France.

15. Lorenz von Stein's first book on French affairs was his *Der Sozialismus und Communismus des heutigen Frankreich* (Leipzig, 1842). A second enlarged edition in two volumes, completed in September 1847, appeared early in 1848, also in Leipzig. In the later half of the same year, 1848, appeared a supplement, entitled *Dis Sozialis-*

tischen und communistischen Bewegungen seit der dritten französischen Revolution; this volume was written in the late summer of 1848. Two years later, Stein treated this subject in a much broader framework, under the title: *Geschichte der sozialen Bewegung in Frankreich von 1789 bis auf unsere Tage* (Leipzig, 1850), 3 vols. We shall quote the second edition of *Der Sozialismus und Communismus des heutigen Frankreich* as "Sozialismus," *Die Sozialistischen und communistischen Bewegungen seit der dritten französischen Revolution* as "Supplement," and the *Geschichte der sozialen Bewegung in Frankreich* as "Geschichte," using the edition mentioned in note 1. The differences between these three works reflect the development in Stein's thought which the revolution of 1848 brought about, and with which this study is concerned.

16. *Supplement,* p. 14 and see also pp. 17–19.

17. *Supplement,* p. 14. See also *Geschichte,* III, 221, on the inability of pure democracy to govern a state and a people. In *Sozialismus,* 2d ed., p. 71, where Stein emphasizes the importance of the "science of government," we find his first preliminary thoughts on separation of constitution and administration. See Nitzschke, *Geschichtsphilosophie,* p. 134, on Robert von Mohl's influence on Stein concerning this question.

18. *Supplement,* p. 26. *Geschichte,* I, contains more on this subject in a section in the Preface entitled "Soziale Reform."

19. *Sozialismus,* 2d ed., p. 62. See also p. 59.

20. *Geschichte,* I, xxxii.

21. This point is of considerable importance for the interesting and much discussed question of the relationship between Marx and Stein. If the tendency of this discussion at present is to assume that Marx was influenced by Stein in the early 1840s, my views here rather exclude this possibility, if not in certain details, then at least as far as fundamental issues are concerned. For my argument is that Stein's revised thinking took clear form only after 1848 and that he came to accept an economic theory of history only them. On the other hand, of course, the possibility exists that Stein could have been influenced by the *Communist Manifesto.* However, we have no documentation whatsoever to support such a case, and my argument above would seem to preclude this possibility. Indeed, the entire discussion of this question to date seems to me to suffer from an inadequate understanding of Stein's development.

22. From Friedrich Gundolf, *Shakespeare und der deutsche Geist* (Berlin, Boudi, 1920).

23. See Ernst Troeltsch, *Der Historismus und seine Probleme* (Tübingen, Mohr and Siebeck, 1922), p. 254, and Julius Löwenstein, *Hegels Staatsidee: Ihr Doppelgesicht und ihr Einfluss im 19. Jahrhundert* (Berlin, Springer, 1927), pp. 50–52.

24. Stein, *Die Munizipalverfassung Frankreichs* (Leipzig, 1842), p. 8.

25. *Sozialismus,* 2d ed., p. 196.

26. *Sozialismus,* 2d ed., p. 197.

27. *Geschichte,* I, vii. The entire introduction is relevant here.

28. *Geschichte,* I, p. v–vi. There are suggestions of this view in *Sozialismus,* 2d ed., pp. vi and xiii, as well.

29. See, for example, *Geschichte,* I, cxxv.

30. *Geschichte,* I, lxxvi.

31. *Geschichte,* I, lxxxviii. See also p. xcvi, where Stein contrasts "revolutionary" and "philosophical" constitutions, and his comment on Sieyes: "Where a constitution is possible only in theory, no constitution is possible at all yet."

32. *Geschichte,* I, xxxii. See also p. lxxx.

33. *Geschichte,* I, lxxx.

34. On this point see *Geschichte,* I, xxii and xlii. See also Stein, *Gesellschaftslehre* (Stuttgart, 1856), pp. 454ff; Nitzschke, *Geschichtsphilosophie,* p. 75.

35. *Geschichte,* I, xcvi.

36. This is Ritter's view, too. See his *Die Entwicklung der deutschen Geschichtswissenschaft,* p. 349.

37. Nitzschke, *Geschichtsphilosophie,* p. 135; also Grünfeld, *Lorenz von Stein und die Gesellschaftslehre,* p. 47. As Salomon wrote in his introduction to Stein's *Geschichte der sozialen Bewegung in Frankreich,* p. 42, Marx is reported to have said of Stein that "he was a realist who went about wearing a wide cloak of idealism."

38. *Sozialismus,* 2d ed., p. 196.

Index

541

Index

Francis I, king of France, 210, 295–307, 315, 317, 445

Francis Joseph, Austrian emperor, 356, 451

Franco, Francisco, 359–361

Franklin, Benjamin, 336–339

Frederick I, king of Prussia, 46

Federick II the Great, king of Prussia, 42, 46, 78, 165, 168, 169

Frederick William I, Great Elector of Brandenburg, 444

French Invasion of 1494, 104, 105, 153, 191, 216, 222, 225, 227, 238, 242, 309

French Revolution of 1789, 20, 27, 47, 81, 82, 158, 168, 172, 173, 324, 413, 414, 446, 448

Freud, Sigmund, 429

Friedrich, Carl Joachim, 77

Gabriele, Trifone, 205, 255

Gafencu, Grigore, 353

Galilei, Galileo, 387, 406

Gans, Eduard, 20, 22

Gattinara, Mercurino, 295

Gelli, Giovan Battista, 231, 232

Gentili, Alberico, 166

Gentillet, Innocence, 159

Germany, 18–31, 35–37, 41, 42, 44, 53, 54, 56, 63, 67–69, 72–79, 85, 271, 272, 310, 360, 363, 365–375, 425, 430, 432, 434. See also Emperor; Weimar Republic; William II

Ghirlandaio, Domenico, 381, 427

Giannotti, Donato, 142, 143, 204–214, 239, 245

Giberti, Matteo, 302, 307, 317

Giovanna, queen of Naples, 147

Giovanni delle Bande Nere, 211

Giustiniani, Bernardo, 265, 266

Giustiniani, Tomaso, 249–256, 261, 262, 290

Gobineau, Josef Arthur Count, 424

Goes, Hugo van der, 426

Goethe, 83, 85, 163, 168

Gombrich, Ernest H., 423, 424, 427, 431, 433, 437

Gonzaga, House of, 399

Gramsci, Antonio, 175, 404

Grandi, Dino, 352, 354, 356, 363

Grazzi, Emanuele, 357, 359

Great Britain, 335–338, 341, 342, 344, 367–371. See also England

Greece, Greek, 24, 26–28, 31, 32, 34–36, 205, 255, 363, 365, 366, 435

Grimani, Antonio, 289, 314

Grimani family, 289

Gritti, Andrea, 287, 289, 298, 303, 309, 314, 316

Grote, George, 449

Guariglia, Raffaele, 356, 363

Guicciardini, Francesco, 140, 151, 201, 202, 213, 215–217, 235, 239, 240, 243, 245, 296, 298, 314–316, 319, 320, 389, 407, 449

Guidetti, Francesco, 231

Guiraudet, Charles Philippe Toussaint, 172

Guise, House of, 159, 166

Guizot, François, 446, 448, 449

Gundolf, Friedrich, 417

Habsburg, House of, 305, 306, 310, 312, 319, 329, 388. See also Charles V; Ferdinand; Francis Joseph; Leopold; Maximilian I; Philip II

Halifax, Edward Viscount, 368

Haller, Karl Ludwig von, 70

Hannibal, 288

Harbison, E. Harris, 266

Harrington, James, 167

Hegel, Hegelian, Hegelianism, 19, 29–31, 33–35, 44, 70, 71, 163, 417

Heimburg, Gregory of, 191

Heine, Heinrich, 20

Hellenism, 32–36

Henry VIII, king of England, 297

Herder, Johann Gottfried, 85

Herodotus, 443

Hintze, Hedwig, 40, 41, 47

Hintze, Otto, 39–65, 74, 83, 84

Historiography, 35, 63, 68, 82, 85, 137, 179, 230, 244, 291, 314, 316, 317, 319, 320, 327, 447, 456. See also Benedictines; Bollandists; Maurists

Historism, 76, 82, 436

History, 19, 24, 25, 28, 29, 33, 35, 37, 42–44, 57, 58, 61, 63–65, 72–74, 78–83, 85, 86, 103, 105, 131, 137–139, 148, 149, 152, 319–321, 407, 414, 417–421, 425, 430, 431, 433, 434, 443, 444, 447, 452, 453. See also Comparative history; Historiography; Historism; Intellectual history; Progress; Prussian Historical School;

Index

Index

Negri, Francesco, 186
Nerli, Filippo de', 128, 230, 231
Netherlands, 334, 347, 426, 427
Neville, Henry, 167
Niebuhr, Barthold Georg, 21, 26, 27, 70
Nietzsche, Friedrich, 175, 176, 424
Norden, Eduard, 431
Novalis (Friedrich von Hardenberg), 70

Oppenheim family, 437
Oppenheimer, Franz, 57, 60
Ovid, 379, 381

Paine, Thomas, 339
Palla, Battista, 140, 230, 231
Panofsky, Erwin, 431
Papacy, Pope, 94, 145, 150, 156, 160, 183, 210, 219, 227, 228, 404. *See also* Adrian VI; Alexander VI; Clement VII; Julius II; Leo X; Pius V; Sixtus V
Papinius Statius, 379
Parenti, Piero, 236
Paris Peace Conference, 76, 342, 356
Parliamentarism, parliamentary, 53, 54, 56, 59, 75, 76, 364, 375
Paruta, Paolo, 171, 296, 316–320
Patrizi, Francesco, 99, 186
Pavia, Battle of, 210
Pazzi, Alessandro, 202, 204, 211
Pazzi, Cosimo, 232
Pazzi family, 141
Perthes, Friedrich, 22
Pesaro, Girolamo, 300, 301, 306–308, 311, 319
Petrarch, Francesco, 183, 218, 226, 390
Pfizer, Paul A., 22, 24, 31
Philip II, king of Spain, 401
Philosophy of history, 29, 65
Physiocrats, 324, 330, 331, 334
Pico della Mirandola, 384
Pisani family, 279
Pius V, Pope, 390
Platina (Bartolommeo Sacchi), 99, 107
Plato, 107–109, 184–186, 205, 234, 241, 255–257
Plotinus, 256
Poggio Bracciolini, 99, 137, 186, 187, 189, 242
Pole, Reginald, 158
Politian, Agnolo, 379–386
Pollaiuolo, 220
Polybios, 126
Pomponazzi, Pietro, 248, 255, 257, 258

Pontano, Giovanni Gioviano, 99, 100, 102, 220, 232, 233
Power, 103, 169, 170, 403
Power politics, 31, 77, 79, 80, 170, 264, 327, 330, 335, 342–347, 367
Pragmatism, 61, 62, 84
Praxiteles, 260
Priuli, Girolamo, 269–273, 278, 279, 285, 287, 289
Progress, 43, 44, 54, 72, 74, 442, 452
Protestantismus, Protestant, 17, 30, 32, 34, 68, 402
Prussia, Prussian, 17, 18, 20–25, 30, 31, 36, 37, 40, 41, 46–49, 52, 54, 56, 68, 69, 73, 74, 168, 446, 451. *See also* Brandenburg; Frederick I; Frederick II the Great; Hohenzollern
Prussian Historical School, 40–42
Psychology, 43–45, 64, 71, 85, 431–436
Public historiographer, 40, 53

Quattrocento, 93, 101–103
Quirini, Girolamo, 289
Quirini, Vincenzo, 249–256, 261, 262, 290

Radicalism, 345, 346
Rahn, Rudolf, 376
Ranke, Leopold von, 21, 22, 42–45, 48, 60–62, 70, 71, 82, 173, 449, 450
Rational, reason, 62, 257, 260, 261, 330, 429, 430, 432, 435, 437, 438
Raumer, Friedrich von, 36
Realism, realistic, 92, 93, 96, 100, 101, 103–105, 108, 110, 111, 114, 131, 182, 206, 207, 245, 246, 417, 426, 427, 432
Reason, *see* Rational
Reason of State, 57, 58, 77, 80, 169–171, 318, 320, 321, 329, 376, 393–395
Reformation, 248, 425, 430
Reimer, Karl, 21
Reitzenstein, Richard, 431
Religion, religious, 31, 32, 85, 277, 278, 435
Renaissance, 156, 175, 179, 204, 217, 274, 296, 309, 310, 312, 313, 381, 386, 387–392, 396, 402, 405–408, 424–429, 436–438
Representative, 58, 59, 63
Republicanism, Republics, 94, 95, 105, 127, 130, 167, 183, 186–188, 193, 203, 216, 233, 240, 241, 263, 264, 267, 333, 408

Index

Stein, Lorenz von, 411–421
Stendhal (Henri Beyle), 162
Stojadinovic, Milan, 364–366
Strozzi, Filippo, 225, 226
Strozzi, Lorenzo, 210
Strozzi family, 216, 222, 225, 226
Stubbs, William, 449, 452
Suleiman II, Sultan, 147
Suñer, Serranu, 354, 355
Suriano, Antonio, 214

Tacitus, 392, 443
Talleyrand-Périgord, Charles Maurice de, 346, 347
Tasso, Torquato, 387, 391, 397, 405, 406
Tassoni, Alessandro, 398, 399
Testi, Fulvio, 398, 399
Themistios, 256
Theodoric, king of the Goths, 145, 150
Thierry, Augustin, 449
Thode, Henry, 424, 425
Thomas of Aquinas, 256, 257
Thucydides, 155, 443
Thun-Hohenstein, Leo Graf, 451
Titian, 283
Tocqueville, Alexis de, 47, 412, 413, 416, 449
Torre, Marcantonio della, 254
Totalitarianism, 176, 365
Trajan, 391
Trebizond, George of, 184, 185
Treitschke, Heinrich von, 40, 41
Trent, Council of, 404
Trevisan, Andrea, 304, 311
Trevisan, Domenico, 289, 298, 304, 317–319
Trissino, Gian Giorgio, 231
Trivulzio, Giangiacomo, 227
Troeltsch, Ernst, 57, 60, 83, 84
Tron, Antonio, 289
Tron, Luca, 301, 304, 306, 308
Turgot, Ann Robert Jacques, 325, 334
Tuscany, 395, 401. See also Cosimo I; Leopold

Uccello, 220
United States, 43, 57, 63, 340, 342, 343, 348. See also America; Continental Congress
Usener, Hermann, 432, 433
Utopia, 396, 397
Utrecht, Peace of, 325, 337
Uzzano, Niccolò, 142

Valerius Maximus, 255
Vansittart, Sir Robert, 363
Varnhagen von Ense, Karl August, 20, 22
Vasari, Giorgio, 402
Venice, 95, 126, 136, 142, 144, 145, 165, 179–214, 220, 227, 233, 236, 237, 247–249, 252, 253, 255, 256, 262–267, 269–291, 295–321, 334, 388, 394, 395, 402, 404
Venier, Domenico, 300, 304
Venier, Marcantonio, 298
Vergennes, Charles Gravier Comte de, 334
Vergerio, Pier Paolo, 184
Vergerio, Pietro Paolo (the Younger), 205
Verrocchio, 220
Vespucci, Simonetta, 382
Vettori, Francesco, 112, 129, 231, 232, 234, 243, 245
Villani, Giovanni, 188
Vischer, Friedrich Theodor, 432
Visconti, House of, 95, 180
Vitetti, Leonardo, 357
Volney, Constantin François, Comte de, 345
Volpi, Giuseppe, 354
Voltaire, François-Marie Arouet, 85, 165, 445

Walker, Leslie J., 115, 116
Wallenstein, Albrecht von, 166
Warburg, Aby, 423–439
Warburg family, 436
Wars, see Abyssinian War; First World War; Second World War; Seven Years War; Spanish Civil War; Spanish Succession
Weber, Max, 58, 62, 434
Weimar Republic, 39, 41, 79
William II, emperor, 39, 70, 73
Williams, T. Harry, 174
Wilson, Woodrow, 174, 323, 348
Witt, Jan de, 334
Wolf, Friedrich August, 26
World history, 24, 25, 35, 36, 42, 324
World power, 53, 55, 56

Yugoslavia, 364–366

Zen, Luca, 289
Zogu, king of Albania, 366